W9-AWJ-750

METROPOLIS IN CRISIS

METROPOLIS

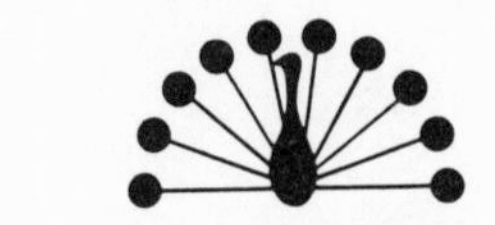

F. E. PEACOCK PUBLISHERS, INC.
ITASCA, ILLINOIS

IN CRISIS

SOCIAL AND POLITICAL PERSPECTIVES

EDITED BY

JEFFREY K. HADDEN
Case Western Reserve University

LOUIS H. MASOTTI
Case Western Reserve University

CALVIN J. LARSON
Purdue University

Library of Congress
Catalogue Card Number 67-28510
Second Printing 1968

PREFACE

During the past few years there has been an enormous amount of attention devoted to American cities. There are many reasons for this growing concern, the most notable of which is that man is becoming more and more an urban dweller. The proportion of persons in the United States who reside in cities has increased with each decennial census. The first census of this nation in 1790 enumerated only about 5 percent of the population as living in cities. The census enumeration for 1960 showed that just under 70 percent of the population was living in cities.

Not only are increasing numbers residing in cities, but there is also a trend toward residence in *larger* cities. In 1960 approximately 63 percent of the nation's population resided in 212 Standard Metropolitan Statistical Areas. In 1940 the proportion in urban centers corresponding to these SMSA's was only about 40 percent of the total population.

Estimates of when the ratio of rural to urban residence will stabilize are more a matter of speculation than scientific prediction, but there is no indication that the trend of increasing proportions living in cities will cease in the immediate future. Various estimates indicate that this nation will have between 55 and 60 million new urban residents between 1960 and 1980. This is more urban residents than currently reside in the 18 largest SMSA's, or the central cities of the 182 largest SMSA's. In just two decades, the population increase of urban America will be roughly the equivalent of 30 cities the size of the Cleveland metropolitan area.

Impressive as these figures are, they represent only a backdrop to the emerging urban dilemma. On the one hand are the hope and possibility of exceeding the highest expectations of the founders of this nation in terms of freedom, economic prosperity, and moral strength. On the other hand looms the emerging shadow of crisis which has grown out of our inability to move swiftly enough to meet the challenges of social and economic justice as well as our inability to implement our technological know-how to solve such problems as urban blight, housing, crime, pollution, and transportation. In short, our nation is in the midst of a revolution of hope and at the same time in the throes of a crisis of doubt and uncertainty as to whether our enormous scientific and technological know-how can create a truly great society.

Cities are more than just a *context* within which the dilemma is raging. In creating the city, man has created a "way of life" which permeates not only his physical style of life, but his social institutions and his values—indeed, the very meaning he ascribes to life. While there have been cities for many centuries, the experience of urban life for more than a very small proportion of the earth's population is still a new phenomenon. We are only beginning to experience and understand the consequences and implications of high-density living and complex social organizations.

From the highest levels of government to the blighted ghettos of our central cities, the concept *crisis* has become commonplace in our discussion of the urban condition. One can hardly read a daily metropolitan newspaper without spotting some event which constitutes an indicator of the deepening crisis. Book titles such as *A City Destroying Itself, Sick Cities, The Withering Away of the City* and *Crisis in Our Cities* further reflect the growing sense of the seriousness of metropolitan problems.

Yet at the same time, the word crisis is one that defies a clear meaning. We live in an age in which one can examine almost any institution or structured interaction on our planet and conclude that the state of affairs is one of deep and entangling crisis. As we are completing the editing of this volume, the world is confronted with political crises in Southeast Asia and the Middle East. We describe the struggle of emerging nations to achieve economic and industrial development as a crisis. Similarly, the rapid rate of population increase on this planet is viewed by many as a grave crisis. On the domestic scene, we speak of race relations, crime, education, and the dissemination of psychedelic drugs as crisis phenomena.

The widespread use of the concept crisis calls for a sober appraisal of the very term and the reasons why we use it so freely. Do we truly live in an Age of Crisis, or does the concept reflect an impatience of a world, which has been able to make astonishing technological progress, to put an end to all problems? In one sense, man has always lived in crisis, but never before have the expectations and the resources to eliminate problems been so abundant. The end of war, poverty, and injustice appear for the first time to be within man's grasp. Perhaps we cry crisis because the pace at which we are moving toward the accomplishment of these lofty goals is slow when compared with human expectations.

Yet, to suggest that we call a moratorium on the concept crisis conveys a rather naive assumption that if we ignore problems they will go away. Human progress is always a double-edged sword, and if the prospects for the next century are greater than they have been in any previous age, so are the problems and dangers. Man has not yet put an end to war, and the possibility of unleashing nuclear holocaust constitutes a problem and responsibility that human beings have never had to confront before. Man has not eliminated poverty and the problems involved in doing so appear to be quite serious. If man fails to achieve this goal, the consequences are almost certain to be grave. The poor are increasingly concentrated in urban areas where their expectations for a better life are rising. Failure to eliminate poverty must inevitably result in continued social unrest or the creation of a garrison caste society which is strongly at variance with the major ideological thrusts of Western civilization.

And so it goes with many of the social problems which we label with the concept crisis. Failure to meet the many social challenges which twentieth century man confronts may well result in consequences which we view as detrimental to the human condition. Thus, the term crisis is perhaps an appropriate word, for it conveys something of the seriousness of the many problems we face. At the same time, it should be recognized that excessive use or misuse of a concept may result in a weakening of its impact. The word crisis calls for a response and if it becomes commonplace it may no longer convey a sense of urgency.

Our use of the word crisis in the title of this volume is not without some misgivings. But if crisis is an appropriate word to use at all, it seems to us appropriate to apply it to the city. The city is not only the locus in which many human crises are occurring, but the very process of urbanization and man's response to this process constitute the fundamental background which has produced crisis.

It should also be recognized that the concept crisis is at least in part a value-laden term. In part, crises are crises because we perceive them as such. The values we affirm and where we stand to look at a problem have a great deal to do with the way we perceive it. Lincoln Steffens, who wrote the *Shame of the Cities* near the turn of the century, viewed the corrupt political machines of the cities with great alarm. Today, political scientists and sociologists are inclined to take quite a different view: machines filled a gap in political organization which had not emerged and without which the development of cities might have been much slower and more painful. Thus, it may very well be that a half-century from now scholars may view processes which alarm us today, such as political fragmentation, conflict, and violence, as the very means by which progress was achieved. However, we are concerned with these problems today because our future depends on how we respond to these problems, and there is evidence to suggest that our response is not always geared to the needs of the future.

That the editors of this volume view the city in crisis cannot be divorced from the fact that two of us live in a metropolitan area which is perhaps in deeper trouble than any other city in America. It would take a lengthy essay to simply list the problems of Cleveland. The following is an abbreviated list of some of the problems which have developed in Cleveland during the past year while we have been assembling materials for this volume:

- The summer of 1966 saw Cleveland hit with the worst race riot of the summer, and one of the worst in the nation's history. A Grand Jury dismissed the disturbances as the work of communists and other outside agitators. Others responded with more understanding, but the promises made in the heat of the summer have been slow in being fulfilled. The major changes can be summarized as follows: (1) there are fewer merchants in the ghetto due to cancellations of insurance and a phenomenal rise in armed robberies; (2) there is greater frustration among Negroes and the emergence of some organization among militants; and (3) the city has beefed up its police force in anticipation of more trouble. A militant black nationalist astrologer predicted massive violence on May 9th of this year. The date passed relatively uneventfully, but few informed sources believe that the summer of 1967 will pass without more eruptions of violence.
- Cleveland has undertaken the largest urban renewal program in the nation, but its record of accomplishment is among the poorest in the country. An estimated $26 million of real estate has been removed from the tax rolls, and the city still owns most of the land parcels in the renewal areas. Two skyscrapers, one already a year overdue on completion, stand alone as symbols of progress in the Erieview Renewal Project. In January of 1967, the Department of Housing and Urban Development cut off Cleveland's urban renewal funds, the first such action by the Federal government.

- The city direly lacks financial resources to meet the needs of the city. In the fall of 1966 the city council passed a ½ of 1 percent city income tax against the mandate of the voters. A subsequent referendum upheld the council's decision, but it now seems fairly clear that most of the money will be needed to cover increases in the salaries of city employees and an expansion of the police force.
- Public and private reports on the needs of the city have been blatantly ignored by City Hall, and the mayor has repeatedly rejected assistance from the private sector.
- In February the Moody Bond Survey reduced the city's credit rating which will result in higher interest rates on municipal bonds.
- In May the Federal government cut off several million dollars worth of construction funds in Cleveland because of the failure of the construction industry to comply with Federal policies for assuring equal job opportunities for minority groups.
- Also in May a Federally financed study announced that only four cities in the nation ranked above Cleveland in the amount of pollution in the air, and Cleveland industry continues to contribute more than its share of pollution to Lake Erie, already the most polluted body of water in the world.
- Finally, in May, the home of a Negro in a predominantly white eastern suburb was bombed for the second time in less than a year. Earlier in the year, a Negro minister's home in a west side suburb was hit by an arsonist. The suburbs of Cleveland remain almost lily white, except for a few enclaves near the edge of the ghetto on the city's southeast side. More than 95% of the Negroes in the metropolitan area reside in the central city.

As we pointed out above, this is a very abbreviated list of the indicators of crisis in our own city. Yet in the midst of all these problems, the mayor continues to plead for an "accentuation of the positive" and the "cosmos" (ethnic groups as they are referred to in Cleveland) largely agree with the mayor that Cleveland is "The Best Location in the Nation."

But Cleveland does not stand alone in its failure to meet its problems with constructive programs. *If* Cleveland is the worst situation in the nation, there are many other cities that are not far behind. The public storm over city problems has not been created by the failures of a single city. While some cities have made much greater progress than others, there probably is no city in America that is not plagued with a host of unsolved problems. Similarly, while not all cities have the same problems with the same degree of intensity, the similarity of problems from one city to the next is considerable.

The problems of metropolis, as we shall see in this volume, cannot be reduced to incompetent administrators and apathetic citizens. To be sure, these factors can and do complicate the situation in many cities, but the essence of urban problems has its origins in what social scientists refer to as structural variables. By this we mean the very way in which cities are organized and have developed socially, politically, and economically. As we have noted, there are many books and articles on the urban crisis, but very substantial proportions of these materials do not go beyond elaborating the problems. The table of contents from Mitchell Gordon's *Sick Cities* is fairly typical in its coverage of problems:

- Traffic Jam: The Concrete Spread
- Beware of the Air
- Water: Filthier and Farther
- No Place for Fun
- Help, Police!
- Fire!
- School Bells—and Burdens
- Libraries and a Couple of Nuisances: Noise and Birds
- The City Dump
- The Public Purse
- Too Many Governments
- City Limits
- Urban Blight and Civic Foresight[1]

To be sure, an awareness and sensitivity to problems are important and necessary prerequisites to action. But beyond awareness must come an *understanding* of the problems and how they got to be problems. Unless we are able to understand and analyze the social processes which have produced urban problems, we are likely to set out on action programs which have only limited possibilities for success, or perhaps more likely, we will simply join the ranks of the frustrated who feel too totally helpless to do anything about urban problems.

The editors of this volume, two sociologists and a political scientist, are committed to the proposition that our disciplines have something to contribute to an understanding of metropolitan problems. Furthermore, we have discovered that a large majority of the students who enroll in our courses in urban sociology and metropolitan government do so out of a desire to understand something about the nature of the urban environment they inhabit or will inhabit. Yet, we have also discovered that students have a difficult time seeing the relevance of the traditional theoretical and empirical research interests of our disciplines. *Gemeinschaft* and *gesellschaft,* social area analysis, and concentric zones may provide some intellectual satisfaction for the theoretically minded, but to most students these concepts seem esoteric and far removed from the "real" problems of the city. Actually, it is understandable that students with little, if any, background in sociology or political science would find our traditional theoretical approaches too abstract and too remote from the issues which have motivated them to enroll in our courses.

In collecting material for this volume, we have attempted to ask ourselves the question, "What are the most basic issues which one must know something about in order to understand the nature of the urban crisis?" Our own answer to this question is relatively complex in detail, yet fairly simple in terms of basic issues. First of all, we feel that the student of the city ought to have a general understanding of the origins, processes, and consequences of urbanization. Secondly, it is important to understand how ideology affects the nature of social organization. Finally, the student of the city should understand something about the nature of political process. Man is a political animal, and unless one grasps this, he can neither understand nor become effectively involved in the city.

The outline of this reader basically corresponds to these three basic issues. Part I, "The Challenge of Metropolis," is a brief introduction to the problems and prospects of urban life. Part II traces the historical development of cities and elaborates the process and consequences of urbanization. Part III deals with ideology—the way man thinks and feels about the city. Man is unique in his ability to give meaning to his environment, and we shall see that the meaning which he has ascribed to urban life has significantly affected the very nature of the city. To the extent that man has a philosophy or ideology of urban life, it is negative. He tends to view the problems of metropolis as inherent in the monster itself, rather than in the way he has built and organized the city. Having developed historical, sociological, and ideological perspectives for viewing the city, we turn in Part IV to an elaboration of the dimensions of the urban crisis. Here we look at specific urban problems: race, housing, poverty, education, crime, transportation, air pollution, and finance. Obviously, we have not been able to deal with all of these problems in depth, but we have tried to select readings which focus on some of the more critical issues.

Finally, in Part V, we examine the ability of the urban community to organize itself to meet the urban crisis. We look at the problems created by the fragmentation of political power, both within the central city and among the communities of the metropolitan area, and the potential of overcoming these obstacles through more effective leadership, reorganization of the governmental structure, and an infusion of financial aid from the nation and the states.

---

[1]Mitchell Gordon, *Sick Cities* (Baltimore: Penguin Books, 1963).

CONTENTS

PART I

The Challenge of Metropolis: An Introduction

INTRODUCTION

In the midst of great concern for cities is an ideology that basically rejects the crisis view of cities. This ideology takes a variety of forms which are not necessarily independent of one another, but nevertheless analytically distinguishable. The first, and dominant, view is that high-density living is not really a necessary condition for modern man. The suburban way of life is one which unites the best of urban and rural living. While the city, as a market place, may be a necessity for a highly industrialized society, it brings with it a whole host of characteristics which are deplorable and to be avoided, if possible. Cities are not only impersonal and anonymous, they are the inevitable breeders of crime, dirt, noise, suspicion, and fear. Suburbia, this view holds, is a viable alternative which provides quiet and spacious living where one can develop strong personal ties with neighbors as well as participate in local government and civic affairs.

There can be little doubt but that this is the predominant ideology of millions of Americans who inhabit the politically independent communities which encircle the decaying central cities. Their views are shared by millions more who inhabit the central city but dream of the day when they can join the migration to their own ranch-style home surrounded by green acres at the fringe of the metropolis.

Perhaps suburbia is the best of all possible worlds, but in this volume we want to raise some questions which may challenge the assumptions of this ideology. We want to at least pose the proposition for consideration that the suburban style of life is self-indulgent, apathetic, and a retreat from the realities and responsibilities of our complex social order. Furthermore, we would like to suggest that the utopia we think we are creating today may turn out to have advantages of neither rural nor urban living and disadvantages of both.

Another view of urban life which rejects the crisis thesis is essentially a free enterprise doctrine. This view holds that the "invisible hand" of the private market will determine the structure of the physical environment which is best. Cities are as cities are, and we ought not to intervene in the "natural" evolutionary process. This view does not hold in disdain the *inadequacies* of the interventionary role of government in urban redevelopment, but rather the fact that the government has intervened at all. If the central core of the city has anything to offer, the private sector will assume responsibility for its redevelopment and rehabilitation, and if not, we should not grieve over its demise.

A third view does not deny the critical nature of many urban problems, but holds that the crisis is not as bad as many have made it out to be. Furthermore, this point of view holds that the crisis becomes almost trivial when compared with the problems cities faced near the turn of the century.

This point of view has some compelling arguments which cannot be easily dismissed. It is not easy to compare cities today with cities near the turn of the century and come up with empirical indicators which permit one to conclude which was better or worse. Nevertheless, comparisons lend some credence to the view that the urban condition of today is not as bad as it was at earlier points in history. There can be little doubt but that the *proportion* of urban dwellers who live in dire poverty is less today. Similarly, general housing conditions and the standard of living have improved rather remarkably during this century. But proportions and total numbers are not the same. In 1900 there were approximately 75 million Americans and only 40 percent lived in urban areas. Today the population of the United States is almost 200 million and the percentage living in urban environments is in excess of 70 percent. While the living conditions of the tenements may have been worse at the turn of the century, the absolute number of Americans who live in inadequate housing with inadequate financial means must certainly be larger.

Housing conditions and poverty levels constitute only a limited framework for comparing American cities at different points in time. City governments are almost unquestionably more honest than they were near the turn of the century. In spite of glaring inadequacies, the judicial system operates more fairly for a greater proportion of the people. And so one could add many more arguments for the case that today's cities are in better shape than they have ever been.

But perhaps an even more important comparison of cities over time is along the line of the persistence of problems. The slums of today may not be as bad as the filth- and rot-infested slums of fifty or a hundred years ago, but they do persist. And the same is largely true for every other urban problem we face. The general technological and economic level of our nation has changed very dramatically in this century. The important question is whether the *relative* level of our urban problems has improved or become worse. The answer to this question is not obvious. We only know that the problems persist and that there is considerable reason to believe that some of them will worsen in the years ahead.

If the past provides a reminder of the unfinished business of creating an inhabitable environment, an examination of the present provides a perspective which in large part makes the past irrelevant. A large number of social scientists today tell us that poverty is a senseless waste that can be eliminated, and these prognostications have become assimilated into rising hopes and expectations. Thus, in a century of rising expectations, we must compare our cities with what might be and what is possible.

There are other reasons which mitigate against placing too much stock in comparing our cities today with the cities of the past. We live in an age of exploding population. Cities today are much larger than they were a half-century ago, and we know that the cities of tomorrow are going to be even larger. Machiavelli, Durkheim, and Marx were perceptive of the implications of large concentrations of people in a confined area. Whether our motives are humanitarian or utilitarian, the aspirations and unfulfilled expectations of people in highly concentrated areas must be contended with. As expectations rise and concentrations of human populations increase, the time left for response diminishes. There is no question but that this nation *has* responded to these rising expectations. The fruits of the labor and civil rights movements bear testimony to this. The question is whether the response has kept pace with the increasing population, technological capabilities, and human hope. Today we see more clearly the needs of the future and the consequences of not fulfilling these needs, and hence the necessity for response becomes more urgent.

The editors of this volume believe that the problems of the city are real, that they are serious, and that they are not going to go away if we ignore them or pretend that they don't exist. This position, however, is not to be equated with "alarmist" or "prophet of doom" views. We do not believe that urban problems are insurmountable. There is a great deal that can be done and a considerable amount of energy and resources that is currently being directed toward the pursuit of solutions. Our concern is simply that the resources and commitment may not be emerging fast enough to assure a favorable outcome. Furthermore, we believe that the more people understand about the nature and implications of urban problems, the greater the prospects are for constructive solutions. It is the goal of this book to make a modest contribution toward the understanding of urban problems.

The purpose of the first part of this volume is simply to introduce the challenge of the city and the broad scope of concern. While clearly not all people are concerned with urban problems, concern does traverse every level of our society. Our first selection is a cry of despair from the Negro ghetto. In the foreword to his autobiography, *Manchild in the Promised Land,* Claude Brown communicates the hope and the disappointment of the Negro in urban America. Southern Negroes poured into the cities of the North with the expectation of a promised land, but it didn't turn out that way. To be sure, the Negro's experience with the city has some unique features, but it also bears remarkable similarities to that of the millions of ethnic groups who crossed the Atlantic only to find that the opportunities and hopes were not to be realized in their generation.

The next selection moves from the streets of Harlem to 1600 Pennsylvania Avenue and the highest office in our nation. While the language is not the same, the content bears a good deal of similarity to the first selection by Brown. President Johnson reflects a sober realization of the failure of our society to meet the challenge of metropolis as well as an expression of hope and determination to find solutions.

The selection by Senator Abraham Ribicoff discusses the findings of the Senate Subcommittee on Executive Reorganization's hearings on urban problems. These were the hearings where the figure of $1 trillion for the rebuilding of American cities caught the attention of the popular press. Senator Ribicoff does not feel that it is realistic to think in terms of investing this amount of federal funds. Rather, he suggests that the Federal Government " . . . can determine the key pressure points and . . . apply leverage . . . so that private investment will multiply the original force of public investment."

In the next selection, Bernard Weissbourd asks the question: Are cities obsolete? Weissbourd's article is a penetrating analysis of the interrelatedness of the many problems which face our cities: blight, transportation, finance, migration patterns, population growth, and the role of government in shaping the city. He is cautiously optimistic that cities can avoid obsolescence if we will act creatively. "It is possible to shape the character of our urban environment. The population explosion provides the opportunity and federal subsidies provide a means."

It is important to note that optimism is not "Pollyanna-ish" in any of these selections. The future of our cities is clouded with grave doubt and uncertainty. There are few who would dare to predict what the cities of the 21st Century will be like as environments for human habitation. However, it does seem fairly clear that we have the technological skills and financial resources to make of the city what we will. Thus social questions become much more important. Are our social structures adequate to control and plan the destiny of our cities? But perhaps the most overriding question of all is simply: Do we really care about our cities?

1. Foreword: Manchild in the Promised Land

CLAUDE BROWN

I want to talk about the first Northern urban generation of Negroes. I want to talk about the experiences of a misplaced generation, of a misplaced people in an extremely complex, confused society. This is a story of their searching, their dreams, their sorrows, their small and futile rebellions, and their endless battle to establish their own place in America's greatest metropolis—and in America itself.

The characters are sons and daughters of former Southern sharecroppers. These were the poorest people of the South, who poured into New York City during the decade following the Great Depression. These migrants were told that unlimited opportunities for prosperity existed in New York and that there was no "color problem" there. They were told that Negroes lived in houses with bathrooms, electricity, running water, and indoor toilets. To them, this was the "promised land" that Mammy had been singing about in the cotton fields for many years.

Going to New York was good-bye to the cotton fields, good-bye to "Massa Charlie," good-bye to the chain gang, and, most of all, good-bye to those sunup-to-sundown working hours. One no longer had to wait to get to heaven to lay his burden down; burdens could be laid down in New York.

So, they came, from all parts of the South, like all the black chillun o' God following the sound of Gabriel's horn on that long-overdue Judgment Day. The Georgians came as soon as they were able to pick train fare off the peach trees. They came from South Carolina where the cotton stalks were bare. The North Carolinians came with tobacco tar beneath their fingernails.

They felt as the Pilgrims must have felt when they were coming to America. But these descendants of Ham must have been twice as happy as the Pilgrims, because they had been catching twice the hell. Even while planning the trip, they sang spirituals as "Jesus Take My Hand" and "I'm On My Way" and chanted, "Hallelujah, I'm on my way to the promised land!"

It seems that Cousin Willie, in his lying haste, had neglected to tell the folks down home about one of the most important aspects of the promised land: it was a slum ghetto. There was a tremendous difference in the way life was lived up North There were too many people full of hate and bitterness crowded into a dirty, stinky, uncared-for closet-size section of a great city.

Before the soreness of the cotton fields had left Mama's back, her knees were getting sore from scrubbing "Goldberg's" floor. Nevertheless, she was better off; she had gone from the fire into the frying pan.

The children of these disillusioned colored pioneers inherited the total lot of their parents—the disappointments, the anger. To add to their misery, they had little hope of deliverance. For where does one run to when he's already in the promised land?

2. Message on the Cities

PRESIDENT LYNDON BAINES JOHNSON

Throughout man's history, the city has been at the center of civilization. It is at the center of our own society.

Over 70 percent of our population—135 million Americans—live in urban areas. A half century from now 320 million of our 400 million Americans will live in such areas. And our largest cities will receive the greatest impact of growth.

Numbers alone do not make this an urban nation. Finance and culture, commerce and government make their home in the city and draw their vitality from it. Within the borders of our urban centers can be found the most impressive achievements of man's skill and the highest expressions of man's spirit, as well as the worst examples of degradation and cruelty and misery to be found in modern America.

SOURCE: Message to the Congress of the United States on Housing and Urban Development (March 5, 1965), *Congressional Quarterly,* pp. 349-350.

The city is not an assembly of shops and buildings. It is not a collection of goods and services. It is a community for the enrichment of the life of man. It is a place for the satisfaction of man's most urgent needs and his highest aspirations. It is an instrument for the advance of civilization. Our task is to put the highest concerns of our people at the center of urban growth and activity. It is to create and preserve the sense of community with others which gives us significance and security, a sense of belonging and of sharing in the common life.

Aristotle said: "Men come together in cities in order to live. They remain together in order to live the good life."

The modern city can be the most ruthless enemy of the good life, or it can be its servant. The choice is up to this generation of Americans. For this is truly the time of decision for the American city.

In our time, two giant and dangerous forces are converging on our cities: the forces of growth and of decay.

Between today and the year 2000, more than 80 percent of our population increase will occur in urban areas. During the next 15 years, 30 million people will be added to our cities—equivalent to the combined population of New York, Chicago, Los Angeles, Philadelphia, Detroit and Baltimore. Each year, in the coming generation, we will add the equivalent of 15 cities of 200,000 each.

Already the old cities are tending to combine into huge clusters. The strip of land from southern New Hampshire to northern Virginia contains 21 percent of America's population in 1.8 percent of its areas. Along the West Coast, the Great Lakes, and the Gulf of Mexico, other urban giants are merging and growing.

Our new city dwellers will need homes and schools and public services. By 1975 we will need over two million new homes a year. We will need schools for 10 million additional children, welfare and health facilities for 5 million more people over the age of sixty, transportation facilities for the daily movement of 200 million people and more than 80 million automobiles.

In the remainder of this century—in less than 40 years—urban population will double, city land will double and we will have to build in our cities as much as all that we have built since the first colonist arrived on these shores. It is as if we had 40 years to rebuild the entire urban United States.

Yet these new overwhelming pressures are being visited upon cities already in distress. We have over nine million homes, most of them in cities, which are run down or deteriorating; over four million do not have running water or even plumbing. Many of our central cities are in need of major surgery to overcome decay. New suburban sprawl reaches out into the countryside, as the process of urbanization consumes a million acres a year. The old, the poor, the discriminated against are increasingly concentrated in central city ghettos; while others move to the suburbs leaving the central city to battle against immense odds.

Physical decay, from obsolescent schools to polluted water and air, helps breed social decay. It casts a pall of ugliness and despair on the spirits of the people. And this is reflected in rising crime rates, school dropouts, delinquency and social disorganization.

Our cities are making a valiant effort to combat the mounting dangers to the good life. Between 1954 and 1963 per capita municipal tax revenues increased by 43 percent, and local government indebtedness increased by 119 percent. City officials with inadequate resources, limited authority, too few trained people, and often with too little public support, have, in many cases, waged a heroic battle to improve the life of the people they serve.

But we must do far more as a nation if we are to deal effectively with one of the most critical domestic problems of the United States.

Let us be clear about the core of this problem. The problem is people and the quality of the lives they lead. We want to build not just housing units, but neighborhoods; not just to construct schools, but to educate children; not just to raise income but to create beauty and end the poisoning of our environment. We must extend the range of choices available to all our people so that all, and not just the fortunate, can have access to decent homes and schools, to recreation and to culture. We must work to overcome the forces which divide our people and erode the vitality which comes from the partnership of those with diverse incomes and interests and backgrounds.

The problems of the city are problems of housing and education. They involve increasing employment and ending poverty. They call for beauty and nature, recreation and an end to racial discrimination. They are, in large measure, the problems of American society itself. They call for a generosity of vision, a breadth of approach, a magnitude of effort which we have not yet brought to bear on the American city.

Whatever the scale of its programs, the Federal Government will only be able to do a small part of what is required. The vast bulk of resources and energy, of talent and toil, will have to come from state and local governments, private interests and individual citizens. But the Federal Government does have a responsibility. It must help to meet the most urgent national needs; in housing, in education, in health and many other areas. It must also be sure that its efforts serve as a catalyst and as a lever to help and guide state and local governments toward meeting their problems.

We must also recognize that this message, and the program it proposes, does not fully meet the problems of the city. In part, this is because many other programs, such as those for education and health, are dealt with separately. But it is also because we do not have all the answers. In the last few years there has been an enormous growth of interest and knowledge and intellectual ferment. We need more thought and wisdom and knowledge as we painfully struggle to identify the ills, the dangers and the cures for the American city. We need to reshape, at every level of government, our approach to problems which are often different than we thought and larger than we had imagined . . .

We begin with the awareness that the city, possessed of its own inexorable vitality, has ignored the classic jurisdictions of municipalities and counties and states. That organic unit we call the city spreads across the countryside, enveloping towns, building vast new suburbs, destroying trees and streams. Access to suburbs has changed the character of the central city. The jobs and income of suburbanites may depend upon the opportunities for work and learning offered by the central city. Polluted air and water do not respect the jurisdictions of mayors and city councils, or even of governors. Wealthy suburbs often form an enclave whereby the well-to-do and the talented can escape from the problems of their neighbors, thus impoverishing the ability of the city to deal with its problems.

The interest and needs of many of the communities which make up the modern city often seem to be in conflict. But they all have an overriding interest in improving the quality of life of their people. And they have an overriding interest in enriching the quality of American civilization. These interests will only be served by looking at the metropolitan area as a whole, and planning and working for its development.

3. The Competent City: An Action Program for Urban America

SENATOR ABRAHAM RIBICOFF

Mr. President, I introduce for appropriate reference a number of bills dealing with urban affairs, which I shall discuss this afternoon.

The Subcommittee on Executive Reorganization of the Government Operations Committee held 6 weeks of hearings last year on the Federal role in urban affairs. We heard the testimony of 75 witnesses —Federal and local government officials, representatives of industry, labor, finance, universities, foundations, private organizations, and the ranks of the citizens themselves.

Our inquiry was wide ranging. We proceeded from the premise that the appropriate organization of the Federal Government's efforts—and therefore the direction of our national efforts—to solve the continuing problems of American cities should be determined by examining the nature of the problems themselves.

Our witnesses described urban America. We examined both sides of the urban coin. On one side we found the highest standard of living known to man, a strong and growing economy, high wages, and record employment.

The other side of the urban coin is etched with the acid of despair. There is an urban America seething with discontent, erupting in violence, rotting at the core of its cities, bound with the chains of problems too long unsolved and too massive to be ignored.

Witnesses recited a long series of statistics, calculated to demonstrate the magnitude of the crisis—but so familiar that we have become immune to their significance.

We heard from witnesses, too, who live with—and are—the statistics. They described the hopelessness that comes from cycle after cycle of frustration and despair—from dangling on the cliff between unemployment and underempolyment. Their children attend schools described by educators as custodial—not educational—institutions. And they spend a far greater proportion of their meager incomes than the rest of us on the basic necessities—food, shelter, and clothing.

Sixteen million poor live in our metropolitan areas—10 million in the central cities of America. Another 26 million live in the shadowland of deprivation—with incomes above the minimum poverty level, but below what most authorities define as "adequate" means.

But it would be a tragic mistake to regard our poor and near-poor

SOURCE: *Congressional Record* (January 23, 1967), pp. S709-S710.

as basically different from the rest of us—with different hopes and different dreams. Like all Americans, they want a decent job and a home in a decent environment. The urban poor want to participate in the American free enterprise system. This system has worked for most Americans—now we must make it work for all.

The crisis in the American city is a crisis of doubt—doubt that the promise of America can be kept. It is the danger that exists when a legitimate hope is frustrated and aspirations destroyed. For when men cannot accomplish their goals in acceptable ways, they resort to shortcuts—and far too often, violence is the shortcut chosen.

Violence is self-defeating. It cannot result in true progress. But one of the tragic lessons of last summer's riots was that violence—the last alternative—often accomplished short-term results where reasoned approaches and orderly protest failed. Riots seemed to produce results—from sprinklers on fire hydrants to increased job opportunities.

Law and order must be maintained. But punishment alone is no answer. Orderly cities cannot be based on the passive order of a citizenry bowed into submission. They must be built on the order of a democracy working together for the common good.

Trucks, tanks, troops, and guns can restrain violence. But only citizens can maintain democracy—citizens with the self-respect that comes from participation in the society and the recognition of the rewards of initiative. Citizens denied the chance to achieve self-respect—economic, social, and moral—are denied fundamental justice.

How, then, shall we attain this justice? Not by talk. We have talked a great deal about the problems of our cities. To solve them, we have too often resorted to rhetoric—our most abundant resource.

Nor will we attain our objectives by continuing on our present course. The temptation to do so is great. We are at war in southeast Asia. We have committed the lives of our men and the material of our industry to the defense of a nation thousands of miles away. And when foreign battle threatens, domestic efforts slow. We are tempted, then, to trust to good luck and fortune to muddle through—to keep on doing what we have done, but a little slower and a little less.

I submit that to take that road is to dissipate our resources. It assumes that our domestic programs are fully relevant to the problems of today, that they are properly organized for an effective attack on these problems, and that—if our foreign commitments were reduced—we would achieve automatic success in our cities.

That simply is not the case. For our current approach to solving social problems is programmatic—not systematic—in nature. For 35 years we have acted as if each individual problem in our society—large or small—could be solved by passing a new program. In view of the progress we have made in this Nation, it often is difficult to understand the need for a new approach at the Federal level.

Consider, for example, that since 1935 our gross national product has climbed 843 percent; per capita disposable income—inconstant dollars—has increased 125 percent; unemployment has been reduced by seven times to a current rate of 3.7 percent. Examine the profits of corporations, which reached a new level of $48.2 billion in 1966—an increase of 1,612 percent since the bleak days of 1935.

Our people are both better educated and better employed. As late as 1940, the median education level in America was between the eighth and ninth grade. Today, it is close to a full high school education—a jump from 8.4 years of learning to 11.8 years.

Back in 1930, only 14.2 percent of our labor force was employed in managerial and professional capacities—while 19.8 percent were unskilled laborers. By 1965, the proportion of managerial and professional people in the labor force had risen to nearly 40 percent—and our unskilled labor force had dropped to 11.3 percent.

For more than three decades, and through the administrations of five Presidents, we have educated the young, cured the sick, protected the aged, and promoted industrial growth. And there can be no question that our efforts were crowned with a success beyond the highest dreams of those who worked in the New Deal to found a new concept of government. Yet even the programs of the Great Society represent the end—not the beginning—of an era.

Our society has changed—and so our task has changed. We have moved from a nation staggering in the depths of a great depression to a nation of great affluence—from a society in which the bond between man and neighbor was forged of crying need and common desperation—to a society capable of living in large measure apart from the tragedy of our inner cities.

But we cannot continue to move ahead—to eliminate the slums of America today and build the competent city tomorrow—unless we change our tools and our techniques. For these are the most massive and complex domestic goals this Nation has ever set.

The hearings before the Subcommittee on Executive Reorganization demonstrated the magnitude of the task ahead. It is enormous—as large as life itself—for we are speaking of the future life of an urban nation.

The cost of the task has been estimated as $1 trillion—but that number can cause as much fear as concern. Let us examine that awe-inspiring figure.

One of the best analyses was included in *Capital Requirements for Urban Development and Renewal* by John W. Dykman and

Reginald R. Isaacs. The authors estimate the capital requirements to accomplish the rehabilitation of America's cities at nearly one thousand billion dollars over a 12-year period. They define rehabilitation as:

> The total of all public and private actions which must be taken to provide for the continuous sound maintenance and development of urban areas.

Under their assumption, there would be—

> safety and comfort in housing, highways, and public places, and availability of full utilities and community facilities, including police, fire and health protection. . . . All slums would be cleared and all existing structures would be replaced, renovated or repaired, and all new structures maintained in standard condition.

It is self-evident that the job is too big to be accomplished by government alone. Dykman and Isaacs believe the ratio of private to public investment should be 7 to 1. In testimony before the subcommittee, David Rockefeller, president of the Chase Manhattan Bank, stated that five private dollars should be involved to every one governmental dollar.

So let us not think of a trillion dollars of Federal money. Let us rather approach the subject systematically—as a question of assembling capital investment—something we have done in this Nation time and again. In times of war—in the assault on space—in the construction of a supersonic transport—even when we decided to lay rails across the continent, we have taken public actions to generate response by the private sector. So we must take public actions today to aid the cities where most Americans live.

There is no gimmick—no slogan—no simple mechanism called "Comsat" or anything else—that will automatically generate private investment in the rebuilding of our cities. Rather, there is a need for commitment—a commitment of time, money and talent—a commitment sufficient to shape the future. We must make that commitment and take constructive and selective actions to carry it out.

Imagine, for a moment, that all the problems of the cities were contained in a large, heavy, and irregularly shaped rock. We want to move that rock—to get our cities and their problems off dead center. One strategy would be to strike the rock with a massive force. We could commit $1 trillion of new Federal money to solving the problems. That would be both unrealistic and inefficient. Another strategy would be to try and move the rock by throwing many smaller stones at it—by continuing our present programs. That would only chip away at the surface. Obviously, there is a more effective way. We can determine the key pressure points and then move the rock by applying leverage in the right places. We must apply leverage at the pressure points in our cities, so that private investment will multiply the original force of public investment.

Rebuilding our cities is a task of great magnitude—a difficult task which challenges our sense of responsibility as citizens. Assembling capital to build mechanical devices—whether they are trains or spacecraft—is far less complex and formidable a job than assembling the resources necessary to rebuild people's lives.

Since we are dealing with people, since we must understand the forces at work in the city and our society, then we must look at the people, not the houses—at the individual, not the group—at what a man wants, not what someone else tells him he needs.

An age symbolized by the computer and the megalopolis carries with it the threat of a nation of anonymous individuals—a lonely crowd of people without personal identities. Our policies must reflect the conviction that the larger our society becomes, the more we are dutybound to pay attention to its smaller units—the individual and the neighborhood.

The need is for Federal programs flexible enough to allow for local decisions and local control by the citizens who participate in them. We must measure our successes not in terms of conformity, but in terms of concrete impact on the life of the individual.

I have described the Great Society as the successful end of the New Deal, and the beginning of a new era. Fundamentally, the New Deal was a major innovation in the organization of the Federal Government—an innovation in scope and scale. Agencies and departments were reorganized and created to deal with the monumental problems of the depression.

Those problems are in large part solved. Now we have another set of problems, equally challenging. Yet our Federal agencies continue to administer programs in the time-honored traditions of the 1930's.

As the problems of the 1930's forced the Federal Government to reorganize, so the problems of the second half of the 20th century demand that the Government be modernized again.

It was Franklin Delano Roosevelt who said:

> The principal object of every Government all over the world seems to have been to impose the ideas of the last generation on the present one. That is all wrong.

We should heed this call to change today.

And so I propose a five-point program to improve life in our cities—a program that offers no single solution, because there is none—a program to provide:

First. Guaranteed job opportunities for all;

Second. A home in a decent environment;

Third. Maximum encouragement for private investment in rebuilding our cities;

Fourth. Involvement of the individual and an emphasis on neighborhood development; and

Fifth. Reorganization in the executive branch to meet the challenges of today with the techniques of the present—not the methods of yesterday.

4. Are Cities Obsolete?

BERNARD WEISSBOURD

From 55,000,000 to 60,000,000 more people will be living in metropolitan areas in 1980 than were living there in 1960. How will we manage? Already our cities are decaying faster than they can be rebuilt. Parking is a universal problem. The tax base of the city is eroding as industry moves to the suburbs. A significant part of the white population is also moving to the suburbs, while the cores of our cities are filling with Negroes as the migration from the South steadily rises. The cost to the cities of trying to adjust the migrants to a new kind of existence imposes additional burdens upon the city's tax base.

Taxes are also rising in the suburbs to pay for the high cost of municipal services spread out over areas of low population density. Open space is being consumed at a terrifying rate, so that suburbs once in open country are now surrounded. Travel time to the city has multiplied as the expressways get clogged during rush hours.

Some experts do not find these problems of city decay and suburban sprawl unduly alarming. They maintain that the continuing dispersal that present trends indicate for the future is inevitable, and not necessarily undesirable. I believe the opposite.

Suburban sprawl and urban decay have not come about solely because people have made a free choice in a free enterprise market.

SOURCE: *Saturday Review* (December 19, 1964), pp. 12-15, 66; also published by the Center for Democratic Institutions under the title "Segregation, Subsidies, and Megalopolis."

That choice has been influenced by federal housing subsidies, which, purporting to be neutral, have in fact subsidized low-density middle-income living in the suburbs and have thereby financed the flight of white population from the city. Another factor affecting this dispersal has been our segregation practices within the city.

The lack of public discussion about the influence of housing segregation and federal housing subsidies upon urban growth patterns has been a barrier to understanding the problems of the city and suburbs and has created a feeling of hopelessness about the future of America's cities. It is my purpose here to show that it is possible to deal constructively with the problems of the metropolitan region if these important factors are not ignored.

Compared to the time span of Western civilization the modern urban complex, sometimes called megalopolis, is a new, young phenomenon. Some people are confident that a new technology of communication and transportation will solve many of the most intractable problems of the metropolitan region and that, in time, the region of the future will emerge. One author envisions "continuous low-density urban belts stretching from Maine to Virginia, from Toronto and Pittsburgh to Milwaukee, and from Amsterdam to Frankfort and Mannheim. . . . However, there seems to be no reason why, properly organized and interlaced with greenbelts, freeways, natural reservations, and sites of historic interest, and accented vertically by occasional high-rise elements, these low-density urban regions of tomorrow should not be more livable and effective in satisfying the totality of human values than the transitional urban forms of today."

While no businessman whose offices must be located in the central business district, and no dweller in the city slums, can accept the decline of the city with equanimity, it is quite likely that if we do nothing to alter present trends the low-density urban region will be the pattern of the future. The New York metropolitan region, for example, has grown outward along major transportation arteries. Its axis of growth extended five miles in 1900, twenty-five miles in 1960, and may become fifty miles by 1985.

Acceptance of low-density regional growth implies, of course, a curtailment of mass transportation, for mass transportation works well only in highly concentrated areas where trip origins and destinations are clustered rather than widely dispersed. Conversely, the automobile, which functions so efficiently for decentralized traffic, becomes highly inefficient under conditions of intense demand. Suburban sprawl will thus bring about a further decline in mass transportation, as increasing reliance on the automobile brings further congestion to central business districts.

Each new expressway not only undercuts the market for mass transportation but accelerates the movement of industry away from the central cities. The truck and the car have given the manufacturer new opportunities to select sites in outlying areas. The movement of industry from central city locations to outlying suburban locations has created a new phenomenon—out-commuting.

Nor have the results of the federal programs for slum clearance, urban renewal, and public housing so far given any reason to expect that the trend toward city decline and low-density regional settlement will be reversed. Slums in the cities are growing faster than we can clear them. We should not expect urban renewal to work so long as there is no place for persons evacuated from the slums to live. People displaced by urban renewal and by the new expressways have created new slums.

Moreover, no one is satisfied with public housing. By rejecting all those whose incomes exceeded the prescribed limits, public housing has developed a concentration of those members of society who are not able to support themselves. Coupled with the fact that most cities have followed a deliberate program of segregation in public housing, the result has been to create in many places an environment lacking in all the positive attributes of urban life. The second generation of many public housing occupants is now coming to maturity and it is already clear that many of them will never become viable, self-supporting members of society.

Urban renewal programs aimed at aiding the central business district show greater promise of long-range success, probably because there is considerable strength in the central business district to begin with. New office buildings in the central areas of each of the metropolitan regions demonstrate that financial and commercial institutions, public utilities, newspapers and magazines, and government, together with the lawyers, accountants, stockbrokers, and others involved in serving these institutions, require a centralized location. Thus, although a sizable number of people and industries has moved out of the central city, there has been far less movement of office activities to outlying areas than speculative reports would lead us to believe.

The movement of white population to suburban areas and the concentration of Negro population in the central city will be intensified during the next fifteen years if present trends continue. Since the end of World War II the Negro population has been increasing even faster than the white population. Philip Hauser points out that the decline of the non-white death rate together with the increase in their birth rate has resulted in a rate of growth for non-whites 60 per cent higher than for whites. This great national rise is dwarfed by an even more explosive increase of non-whites in metropolitan areas. By 1990 about 2,500,000 Negroes are expected to be living in the Chicago metropolitan area, about 1,500,000 more than in 1960. The migration to the cities of rural Negroes and Southern whites and Puerto Ricans has already imposed heavy tax burdens on the city. In 1959, for example, New York City spent $50,000,000 for remedial programs for its Puerto Rican newcomers, more than it spent on all its parks, libraries, zoos, and museums in that year. In its 1959-60 budget New York City assigned 23 per cent to public hospitalization, health, and welfare and 20 per cent to education. The great growth rate of the Negro population in New York, through continued migration as well as natural increase during the next fifteen years, will tend to increase even further the city's costs for welfare, health, and education.

The picture that emerges from these forecasts is far from salutary. Low-density regional settlements in which industry and the white populations spread out over the countryside without adequate mass transportation contrast with the concentrated Negro occupancy of the center city, whose tax base has diminished by the flight of industry and whose expenses have increased for the care of its immigrants. Moreover, a growing number of the center-city population will be commuting to jobs in the suburbs while many of the suburban whites will continue to travel to jobs in a still strong central business district.

The waste of human resources and money in this increased commuting, the inability of the automobile and the expressways to handle the traffic, the changing character of the city largely occupied by a financial and business community and a segregated Negro population, the financing of public services for a migrant population in the face of disappearing industry and lost taxes, the interdependence of the financial and commercial life of the suburbs and the city—these are all reasons for not allowing present trends to continue.

But are there alternatives? As we have noted, there are many who doubt whether the trends are reversible. I believe the pattern can be changed, but first it is necessary to say something about the federal housing subsidies, because they are both one of the causes of the current suburban growth and one of the possible tools for creating a different picture for the future.

It is important to understand that dispersal of the urban population in the United States has not come about solely as a result of a free and open market. Government inducements to buy in the suburbs have been substantial and have brought about a remarkable increase in home ownership since the war. In 1957, of the total mortgage debt of $107 billion on one- to four-family non-farm homes, $47.2 billion was FHA-insured or V.A.-guaranteed. Of the balance, so-called conventional loans, a substantial portion was held by savings and loan associations. The funds involved in the federal encouragement of home ownership are thus enormous compared to the amounts involved for rental housing in the city.

The success of the federal housing program in suburbia results from the availability of mortgage funds that have not had to measure up to the usual free-market considerations of risk and competitive yield of other investments. Guarantees and insurance by the United States provide money for suburban home ownership at interest rates lower than the market over longer periods of time.

A subsidy is also involved in the activities of federal and state savings and loan associations. Because law restricts the investments of these associations largely to home mortgages, the flow of capital has been directed artificially to suburbia, and money has been made available for houses at rates lower than those that would have been available if the home owner had had to compete for the funds with other sources of investment of comparable risk. To the extent that deposits in savings and loan associations are insured by the federal government under the Federal Home Loan Bank System, capital is attracted that *must* be invested in home mortgages. The federal insurance, therefore, constitutes an indirect subsidy.

Another heavily subsidized federal housing program—public housing—has also contributed to the condition of our cities. Public housing has been the prisoner of its opponents, who have largely determined its character. Locating public housing projects in the inner city has contributed to keeping lower-income people in the city and has strengthened the patterns of segregation, except in a few cases where careful planning has been able to achieve successfully integrated projects. One arm of the federal housing program has financed housing for middle-income families in the suburbs. The question may well be asked: "Why should not the opposite program have been adopted?"

Other federal subsidies have also had their influence. The disproportionate amount of the federal budget allotted to agriculture has helped bring about the mechanization of the farm and speeded up the migration of both Negro and white farm labor to the city. Similarly, the federal defense highway program has represented an enormous subsidy to the automobile at the expense of mass transportation. Whether these subsidies have been beneficial or detrimental is not pertinent here; what they indicate is that the condition of our metropolitan regions is not the result of "natural" forces alone. The federal government has played a major role in contributing to the shape and character of urban America.

The forces at work in the city and region are cumulative. They all move together toward making the city a more desirable or less desirable place to live. The federal subsidies that have encouraged highway construction instead of mass commuter transportation and thus drawn industry out of the city have reduced the city's tax base. A lower tax base means less money for education and for the adjustment of rural migrants to urban life. Poor schools and changing neighborhoods encourage middle-class white families to move to the suburbs. Higher welfare costs increase the tax rate and thus encourage industry to relocate in outlying areas. All these factors are interrelated. If they can be altered, it might be possible to reverse the cycle of urban decay and deterioration and move the forces of the market place toward renewal and reconstruction.

A total program that recognizes the interdependence of city and suburbs is needed. The creation of new communities on the outskirts of suburbia is a necessary element in the restoration of the inner city. The vitality of the city is, in turn, important for all the inhabitants of the region. A total program must be able to differentiate between which of the forces at work in the region must be shaped by government action in a private enterprise system and which do not lend themselves to it.

We cannot, for example, prevent those industries that do not require a central location from moving to less expensive land in outlying areas. However, through a regional open-space plan, we can limit the areas in which these industries may choose to locate. We cannot prevent middle-class white families from leaving the cities because their children are not being educated in accordance with middle-class standards. But we can induce middle-class families to live within the city if we can create areas large enough to establish a genuine community with good schools. We can find the land for these communities by clearing industrial as well as residential slum property, provided that we undertake to relieve the city of part of its tax burden or change the methods by which it collects taxes.

"New towns" are already being created in areas beyond suburbia to accommodate an exploding population, but these "new towns" may become exclusive suburbs, which in time will be engulfed by suburban sprawl.

I am suggesting a different kind of "new town" program. We should attempt to create "new towns" pursuant to regional open space and transportation plans. These towns will also accommodate industrial workers and industries displaced by an intensified residential and industrial slum clearance program in the core areas of our major cities. At the same time, on the land within the cities made available by slum clearance, new communities can be established for middle-income families.

This program would make both the central city and the "new towns" more heterogeneous in social composition, reduce travel distances to work and thus diminish the urban transportation problem, and, finally, bring suburban sprawl under control through regional planning of open spaces and mass transportation.

Present segregation practices are a serious obstacle to this kind of program; at the same time they provide an additional reason why a program designed to create heterogeneous communities both within the city and beyond the suburbs has become imperative. Not only is the Negro population of our cities increasing in numbers but housing for Negroes is becoming increasingly segregated. The question of segregation is always present when the character and location of public housing and urban renewal projects are being determined. An unwillingness to face up to it has paralyzed city planning. It is necessary to deal with the question not only for the sake of civil rights for Negroes but in order to free city planning from some unspoken assumptions that underlie almost everything that happens about housing in our cities.

Juvenile delinquency and adult crime, school drop-outs and unemployment, the spread of slums and the cost of welfare are all related to segregation in the cores of our cities. The social and economic costs of these problem areas both to the Negro and to the community as a whole are enormous.

The Negro ghettos will not dissolve of themselves. The middle-class Negro family has had great difficulty in finding suitable housing outside of the segregated lower-income neighborhoods; only very recently has housing for these and higher-income Negroes begun to open up. A policy of nondiscrimination in rentals or sales can help, but the ghettos are still so large that only a major plan to induce a substantial part of the Negro working population to live in outlying "new towns" can bring about a more uniform and just distribution of these people among the population as a whole.

We should not underestimate the difficulties of creating interracial communities. Experience shows, however, that it is possible to create interracial housing in stable communities where the housing is sufficiently subsidized. The existence of heterogeneous communities in outlying areas will make it more possible for the Negro to relate to the urban culture. Schools in a smaller community, for example, can be so located that even if there are neighborhoods within the community that are predominantly white or predominantly Negro all of the children can attend the same schools. So many industrial workers are Negro that any problem for creating outlying "new towns" for industry and industrial workers must aim for heterogeneity. As for the cities, where Negroes are already established, a program to bring back middle-income white families must encompass the creation of interracial middle-income neighborhoods. If America is not prepared to accept interracial communities, there is little hope for arresting the decline of the city.

Only a slight extension of the tools already in hand is needed to foster the development of middle-income communities within the city and of "new towns" on the outskirts of suburbia. The Housing Community Development Act of 1964 (which was not enacted into law) proposed for the first time that the Federal Housing Administration insure mortgages for the purchase of land leading to the development of new communities. The Administration thus proposed to finance "new town" developments, although the result may well have been that under such a program the "new towns" would have become exclusive suburbs like many "new towns" now being built with private financing.

Assume, however, that FHA and V.A. financing were abandoned except in urban renewal areas in the city and in "new town" developments. In addition, assume that a regional open space and transportation plan were required before this financing is made available. Assume, further, that the regulations governing savings and loan associations were amended to allow them to allocate a substantial portion of their funds to financing mortgages for multiple dwellings, and to limit financing of either homes or multiple dwellings to established suburban areas, to the cities, or to "new towns" in regions where an open space and transportation plan exists. Moreover, suppose that the V.A. and FHA regulations prohibiting discrimination because of race were also applied to savings and loan associations. Suppose, in addition, that the FHA programs for middle-income housing were made available in the "new towns," so that the goal of an economically heterogeneous community would be vigorously pursued. Suppose, finally, that each "new town" were required to provide some minimum of public housing and housing for the elderly in order to be eligible for federal financing.

These federal tools, almost all of them readily adaptable, would be powerful inducements for the creation of heterogeneous "new towns" in which individuals and industry displaced from the city, together with some of the 80,000,000 new people to be housed between now and 1980, could be accommodated. Moreover, federal incentives could be geared to the creation of "new towns" of higher density so that effective mass transportation between them and the center city could be developed.

Assume that the federal urban renewal programs for clearing residential slums and renewing central business districts were extended to permit the clearance of industrial slums. And assume that the federal government was prepared to finance the construction of industrial facilities in "new town" industrial parks. Can there be any doubt that such a program would have enormous impact in hastening the creation of "new town" developments and in clearing land within the city for the construction of middle-income communities?

It should be clear by now that I am proposing regional planning only in a most restricted sense. It is not necessary for public agencies to provide comprehensive master plans for each region, leaving no room for diversity created by private choices. Some planning, however, is necessary, particularly by the agencies responsible for water, sewer, and transportation because they must be able to project the future needs for public services of an ever-expanding population. In many places these agencies plan independently of each other, and the federal agencies that subsidize housing do no planning at all. What each region now needs is a plan covering all of the agencies already involved in the expenditure of public funds, stating where and when the public will spend its money for water systems, sanitary and storm sewers, highways, and rapid mass transportation, and in what areas subsidies will be available for housing. Regional growth can thus be controlled, with private enterprise left to develop variety within the over-all framework of the plan.

An essential part of the program I am describing is the clearance of industrial slums at the cores of most of America's cities. One of the major obstacles to this has been the reluctance of cities to lose industry for fear of further jeopardizing their real estate tax base. But industry is moving to the suburbs anyway, and the real estate tax structure of the city will have to be revised in any event. Real estate taxes in most places have already reached the limits of economic feasibility. Assessments against property are still the major means by which cities collect taxes, and they have fallen behind in their share of the total tax dollar.

A case can be made that the wealth produced by the cities has been drained out by federal taxes and redistributed first to agriculture, second to suburbia, and third to the cities. At the same time the welfare costs of the cities have increased their tax rates, so that what the federal government has contributed in the form of urban renewal has been taken away by the costs of municipal services. The cities must revise the methods by which they raise revenues, and a greater share of the cost of health, welfare, and education must be allocated to the federal government. The migration to the cities of rural Negroes, Southern whites, and Puerto Ricans is a national problem; the federal government should bear the tax burdens this has created.

Before state as well as federal power becomes available to solve the problems of real estate tax revision and regional planning, the now rural-dominated state legislatures must develop greater sympathy than they have exhibited for the problems of the city and region. The recent decisions of the United States Supreme Court on reapportionment give some hope that city and suburb may soon have more influence upon state legislatures in their dealings with urban problems.

Obviously, each city or each region has unique problems that require more specific solutions than have been suggested here. Nevertheless, these proposals are not offered just as a panacea. We should bring suburban sprawl under control so that we can get better transportation, water and sewer control, and more open space, but a regional plan will not necessarily produce a beautiful region. There is still much to learn about "new town" development, about the creation of communities in which the citizens can govern themselves and in which life is pleasant and interesting. Similarly, the restoration of middle-income families to the city does not automatically solve the financial problems of the city, nor will troubles in race relations disappear even if all communities are racially heterogeneous. We should not try to control too much. At best, we can give direction to economic and social forces already at work and seek to provide better communities in which people can create a variety of environments appropriate to their way of life.

It is possible to shape the character of our urban environment. The population explosion provides the opportunity and existing federal subsidies provide a means. If we deal realistically with segregation and with the sources of city revenues, we can create a more livable community. Public thinking and discussion can clarify what we value about urban life. If we know what kind of urban environment we want, the power and the tools to create it are at our disposal.

PART II

From Mudhuts to Megalopolis: The Historical Development of the Urban Area

INTRODUCTION

In light of his gregariousness, it is somewhat surprising to realize that man did not become an urban dweller until quite recently in his history. While physically modern man has been in existence some 40,000 years, the first cities were not in evidence until roughly five to six thousand years ago. Even after their inception, cities grew slowly in number, size, and influence. It was not until the nineteenth century, and the advent of large-scale industrialization, that the process of urbanization began to assume major proportions.

For the greater part of his existence, man has lived in small, rural, communal settlements. The question many have sought to illuminate is why man was initially led to make the drastic switch from a rural to an urban way of life. Why and how did cities come into being? Were the first cities accidentally or deliberately created? What prerequisites were necessary for city building? Did cities originate in one kind of geographical setting rather than another? Why did some cities grow rapidly and become more important than others? Why did still other cities grow into prominence only to decline or even wither away? The two articles in section A reflect a concern with questions such as these.

It is generally accepted today, at least in the occidental section of the world, that the first cities emerged in the Middle East. The best archeological evidence points specifically to lower Mesopotamia and the valleys of the Tigris and Euphrates rivers as the site of the initial cities. Slightly later, cities also appeared in the Nile River Valley.

Some scholars have put forth an environmental challenge and response thesis to account for the emergence of cities in lower Mesopotamia and the Nile Valley. It is hypothesized that cities grew in the river valleys rather than on the more fertile hilly flanks area of the Fertile Crescent because the harnessing of the rivers represented a greater challenge to man's ingenuity and promised a greater economic reward.

The challenge and response theory leaves much to conjecture. In order to respond to a challenge as great as the control of a river, men must be prepared intellectually and socially. Men must not only possess the requisite knowledge for such an undertaking, but also they must have available the organized manpower to carry it out. It is assuming a great deal to imply that a single challenge could provoke both into existence in just the correct proportions to solve a desired problem. However, as archeological evidence is difficult to come by, it is doubtful that problems such as this will ever be capable of satisfactory resolution. Despite this fact, the thesis at least provides plenty of food for thought.

In the first paper, Robert M. Adams presents the archeological record for the early Mesopotamian cities. Adams eschews single-factor theories in favor of the view that the world's first cities evolved in this area because of the interaction of a number of factors. Nevertheless, he places emphasis on the social factor and suggests that the maturation of complex social organization antedated the use of agricultural techniques. He finds that the evidence indicates that the practice of irrigation "must have helped induce the growth of cities," but that irrigation systems came after cities had been established. In Adams' view, the first evidence of Mesopotamian cities was the rise of temples. It seems to him that new patterns of religious thought provided the necessary impetus for the creation of the Mesopotamian city.

In the second paper, Gideon Sjoberg discusses the origin of cities and also endeavors to identify the evolutionary stages through which cities passed prior to the current stage of urbanization. Three stages or types of societies are identified and placed on an evolutionary continuum. These are the folk society, the preindustrial society, and the industrial society.

The folk society is a small, homogeneous enclave with little division of labor among its members except that based on age and sex. The search for food dominates the life activities of its inhabitants. The preindustrial society is characterized by the presence of domesticated plants and animals, specialization of labor, and writing. In Sjoberg's scheme, cities emerged in the context of the preindustrial society. The industrial society is described as possessing, above all, mass literacy, a fluid class system, and technology permitting the use of inanimate sources of energy.

As does Adams, Sjoberg stresses the importance of social organization and the development of technology in the origin of cities. He does not concern himself with which came first or which is most important. Further, it should be noted that Sjoberg does not postulate a unilinear theory of evolution in which cities develop through successive phases of a determined cycle. Instead, he describes a progressive pattern which may or may not be relevant to any particular society or city.

The three articles in section B deal with the process of urbanization—its historical pattern, its current trend in different parts of the world, and its consequences.

The first selection by Philip M. Hauser sketches the broad picture of the process and consequences of urbanization. Hauser sees urbanization emerging out of four interrelated processes: (1) population growth; (2) control of environment; (3) technological achievement; and (4) development of complex social organization. These four factors represent an irreducible set of processes from which urbanization can be theoretically deduced. Hauser's article is an excellent elaboration of these processes.[1] While these processes may appear at first to be overly simple, a careful consideration will reveal that the interrelationships of this matrix are enormously complex and profound in their implications. Man has spent most of his existence as a nomad, drifting across the face of the earth as the sands drift across the desert. Permanent settlements were not possible until he developed some minimal control over his *environment*. The ability to control environment is intricately related to the development of *technology*. It was only with the development of simple agricultural technology (the domestication of plants and animals and the emergence of simple tools) that man was able to develop a surplus of food which permitted, indeed necessitated, more or less permanent settlement patterns. This surplus, in turn, was to release some of man's time from the task of seeking out subsistence, which in turn made it possible for the development of a more sophisticated technology. Large human *populations* did not emerge until very recently because there have never been large numbers of human beings. As Hauser points out, the paleolithic age (a period of some 600,000 years) produced no more than five to ten million people, less than currently inhabit the metropolitan New York area. The *rate* of population growth since the beginning of the neolithic age has increased roughly a thousandfold, and much of that acceleration has been in the past few centuries. In short, the potential inhabitants of cities simply didn't exist until very recently. But the sheer existence of human populations is insufficient. Large agglomerations of human settlement in a relatively dense area require the development of *complex social organization*. This organization must embrace not only a hinterland from which dense settlements may acquire food, but also working relationships among those who are living in close proximity. In the absence of some organizational principles which define what is possible, desirable, and essential, human beings in close proximity would be in a constant state of war. In a small settlement of people, these working relationships may be worked out rather easily, but as human settlements increase in size, the task becomes much more complex.

To be sure, social organization in the twentieth century has become enormously complex. Nevertheless, our ability to organize to utilize our technological development and to meet the needs of large populations remains in many ways rather crude. To use a medical analogy, we have developed the anatomy of complex organization, but the physiology which is sensitive to the needs of the organism and efficient in the performance of tasks is not fully developed. We are all more or less aware of the problems of bigness. It has become a common part of our culture to knock waste in the federal government, impersonal universities, and inefficient and insensitive city halls. But to the extent that we attempt to destroy these organizational aspects of our society, we are inhibiting the development of a physiology which is sensitive and efficient. In Part V we examine the problems and processes of organizing a city to accomplish its goals.

The processes of urbanization have produced consequences which are far-reaching in their implication. As man has become an urban dweller, the very nature of his life has changed dramatically. The chart listing social processes illustrates the impact of this change.

	Simple Agrarian Society	*Complex Urban Society*
1. Socialization	Centralized in the family	Decentralized in many social institutions
2. Division of Labor	Minimal	Extensive
3. Social Control	Informal	Formal, legal
4. Values	Homogeneous	Heterogeneous
5. Thought Processes	Adherence to tradition	Rational, pragmatic
6. Interaction Patterns	Personal, integrated, persistent through time	Impersonal, functional, transitory, segmentalized
7. Family Organization	Extended kinship	Nuclear

Hauser's article is an excellent analysis of the process and consequences of these changes and should be studied carefully.

In the second paper, Kingsley Davis traces the pattern of world urbanization from the past to the present. The impact of industrialization on urbanization is given particular consideration. For example, he points out that with rapid industrialization in the period from 1801 to 1900, Britain made the transition from a rural to an urbanized society.

Davis defines urbanization as "the proportion of the total population concentrated in urban settlements, or . . . a rise in this proportion." As he indicates, it is common to make the mistake of thinking of urbanization as simply the growth of cities. However, since a society is composed of both rural and urban populations, "the 'proportion urban' is a function of both of them." Consequently, there can be city growth without urbanization "provided that the rural population grows at an equal or a greater rate." Davis illustrates the use of the definition by accounting for the seemingly anomalous finding that while cities in underdeveloped countries are growing more rapidly than cities ever have, their rate of urbanization is only slightly above that experienced by the industrial nations during their periods of rapid expansion. The fact is that the underdeveloped countries have been undergoing a general population explosion in rural as well as urban areas. Thus, the rate of urbanization appears to belie the general impression that cities in underdeveloped nations are burgeoning in population.

The final selection by Jean Gottmann provides a picture of an emerging trend in the urbanization process—the Megalopolis. A Megalopolis is essentially a combination of overlapping metropolitan areas. It is a highly dense, far-ranging population concentration. Gottmann identified that portion of the northeastern seaboard extending from the southeastern tip of New Hampshire to Washington, D. C., as a Megalopolis. He points out that the residents of this broad area have sufficient interaction and are sufficiently interdependent economically to warrant overall administration and the coordination of area-wide facilities.

---

[1]These four processes, which sociologists refer to as the "ecological complex," have been elaborated elsewhere. See, for example, Otis Dudley Duncan, "Human Ecology and Population Studies," in Philip M. Hauser and Otis Dudley Duncan (eds.), *The Study of Population: An Inventory and Appraisal* (Chicago: University of Chicago Press, 1959); and Otis Dudley Duncan and Leo F. Shnore, "Cultural, Behavioral, and Ecological Perspectives in the Study of Social Organization," *American Journal of Sociology,* 65 (1959), pp. 132-146.

A. THE EMERGENCE OF CITIES

5. The Origin of Cities

ROBERT M. ADAMS

The rise of cities, the second great "revolution" in human culture, was pre-eminently a social process, an expression more of changes in man's interaction with his fellows than in his interaction with his environment. For this reason it marks not only a turning but also a branching point in the history of the human species.

Earlier steps are closely identified with an increasing breadth or intensity in the exploitation of the environment. Their distinguishing features are new tools and techniques and the discovery of new and more dependable resources for subsistence. Even in so advanced an achievement as the invention of agriculture, much of the variation from region to region was simply a reflection of local differences in subsistence potential.

In contrast the urban revolution was a decisive cultural and social change that was less directly linked to changes in the exploitation of the environment. To be sure, it rested ultimately on food surpluses obtained by agricultural producers above their own requirements and somehow made available to city dwellers engaged in other activities. But its essential element was a whole series of new institutions and the vastly greater size and complexity of the social unit, rather than basic innovations in subsistence. In short, the different forms that early urban societies assumed are essentially the products of differently interacting political and economic—human—forces. And the interpretive skills required to understand them are correspondingly rooted

---

more in the social sciences and humanities than in the natural sciences.

Even the term urban needs qualification. Many of the qualities we think of as civilized have been attained by societies that failed to organize cities. At least some Egyptologists believe that civilization advanced for almost 2,000 years under the Pharaohs before true cities appeared in Egypt. The period was marked by the development of monumental public works, a formal state superstructure, written records and the beginnings of exact science. In the New World, too, scholars are still searching the jungles around Maya temple centers in Guatemala and Yucatán for recognizably urban agglomerations of dwellings. For all its temple architecture and high art, and the intellectual achievement represented by its hieroglyphic writing and accurate long-count calendar, classic Maya civilization apparently was not based on the city.

These facts do not detract from the fundamental importance of the urban revolution, but underline its complex character. Every high civilization other than possibly the Mayan did ultimately produce cities. And in most civilizations urbanization began early.

There is little doubt that this was the case for the oldest civilization and the earliest cities: those of ancient Mesopotamia. The story of their development, which we will sketch here, is still a very tentative one. In large part the uncertainties are due to the state of the archeological record, which is as yet both scanty and unrepresentative. The archeologist's preoccupation with early temple-furnishings and architecture, for example, has probably exaggerated their importance, and has certainly given us little information about contemporary secular life in neighboring precincts of the same towns.

Eventually written records help overcome these deficiencies. However, 500 or more years elapsed between the onset of the first trends toward urbanism and the earliest known examples of cuneiform script. And then for the succeeding 700 or 800 years the available texts are laconic, few in number and poorly understood. To a degree, they can be supplemented by cautious inferences drawn from later documents. But the earliest chapters rest primarily on archeological data.

* * *

. . . by 5500 B.C., or even earlier, it appears that the village-farming community had fully matured in southwestern Asia. As a way of life it then stabilized internally for 1,500 years or more, although it continued to spread downward from the hills and piedmont where it had first crystallized in the great river valleys.

Then came a sharp increase in tempo. In the next 1,000 years some of the small agricultural communities on the alluvial plain between the Tigris and Euphrates rivers not only increased greatly in size, but changed decisively in structure. They culminated in the Sumerian city-state with tens of thousands of inhabitants, elaborate religious, political and military establishments, stratified social classes, advanced technology and widely extended trading contracts. . . . The river-valley agriculture on which the early Mesopotamian cities were established differed considerably from that of the uplands where domestication had begun. Wheat and barley remained the staple crops, but they were supplemented by dates. The date palm yielded not only prodigious and dependable supplies of fruit but also wood. Marshes and estuaries teemed with fish, and their reeds provided another building material. There was almost no stone, however; before the establishment of trade with surrounding areas, hard-fired clay served for such necessary agricultural tools as sickles.

The domestic animals—sheep, goats, donkeys, cattle and pigs by the time of the first textual evidence—may have differed little from those known earlier in the foothills and northern plains. But they were harder to keep, particularly the cattle and the donkeys which were needed as draft animals for plowing. During the hot summers all vegetation withered except for narrow strips along the watercourses. Fodder had to be cultivated and distributed, and pastureland was at a premium. These problems of management may help explain why the herds rapidly became a responsibility of people associated with the temples. And control of the herds in turn may have provided the stimulus that led temple officials frequently to assume broader control over the economy and agriculture.

Most important, agriculture in the alluvium depended on irrigation, which had not been necessary in the uplands. For a long time the farmers made do with small-scale systems, involving breaches in the natural embankments of the streams and uncontrolled local flooding. The beginnings of large-scale canal networks seem clearly later than the advent of fully established cities.

In short, the immediately pre-urban society of southern Mesopotamia consisted of small communities scattered along natural watercourses. Flocks had to forage widely, but cultivation was confined to narrow enclaves of irrigated plots along swamp margins and stream banks. In general the swamps and rivers provided an important part of the raw materials and diet.

Where in this pattern were the inducements, perhaps even preconditions, for urbanization that explain the precocity of the Mesopotamian achievement? First, there was the productivity of irrigation agriculture. In spite of chronic water shortage during the earlier part of the growing season and periodic floods around the time of the harvest, in spite of a debilitating summer climate and the ever present danger of salinity in flooded or overirrigated fields, farming yielded a clear and dependable surplus of food.

Second, the very practice of irrigation must have helped induce the growth of cities. It is sometimes maintained that the inducement lay in a need for centralized control over the building and maintaining of elaborate irrigation systems, but this does not seem to have been the case. As we have seen, such systems came after the cities themselves. However, by engendering inequalities in access to productive land, irrigation contributed to the formation of a stratified society. And by furnishing a reason for border disputes between neighboring communities, it surely promoted a warlike atmosphere that drew people together in offensive and defensive concentrations.

Finally, the complexity of subsistence pursuits on the flood plains may have indirectly aided the movement toward cities. Institutions were needed to mediate between herdsman and cultivator; between fisherman and sailor; between plowmaker and plowman. Whether through a system of rationing, palace largesse or a market that would be recognizable to us, the city provided a logical and necessary setting for storage, exchange and redistribution. Not surprisingly, one of the recurrent themes in early myths is a rather didactic demonstration that the welfare of the city goddess is founded upon the harmonious interdependence of the shepherd and the farmer.

In any case the gathering forces for urbanization first become evident around 4000 B.C. Which of them furnished the initial impetus is impossible to say, if indeed any single factor was responsible. We do not even know as yet whether the onset of the process was signaled by a growth in the size of settlements. And of course mere increase in size would not necessarily imply technological or economic advance beyond the level of the village-farming community. In our own time we have seen primitive agricultural peoples, such as the Yoruba of western Nigeria, who maintained sizable cities that were in fact little more than overgrown village-farming settlements. They were largely self-sustaining because most of the productive inhabitants were full-time farmers.

The evidence suggests that at the beginning the same was true of Mesopotamian urbanization: immediate economic change was not its central characteristic. As we shall see shortly, the first clear-cut trend to appear in the archeological record is the rise of temples. Conceivably new patterns of thought and social organization crystallizing within the temples served as the primary force in bringing people together and setting the process in motion.

Whatever the initial stimulus to growth and reorganization, the process itself clearly involved the interaction of many different factors. Certainly the institutions of the city evolved in different directions and at different rates, rather than as a smoothly emerging totality. Considering the present fragmentary state of knowledge, it is more reasonable here to follow some of these trends individually rather than to speculate from the shreds (or, rather, sherds!) and patches of data about how the complete organizational pattern developed.

Four archeological periods can be distinguished in the tentative chronology of the rise of the Mesopotamian city-state. The earliest is the Ubaid, named for the first site where remains of this period were uncovered. . . .

At little more than a guess, it may have lasted for a century or two past 4000 B.C., giving way to the relatively brief Warka period. Following this the first written records appeared during the Protoliterate period, which spanned the remainder of the fourth millennium. The final part of our story is the Early Dynastic period, which saw the full flowering of independent city-states between about 3000 and 2500 B.C.

Of all the currents that run through the whole interval, we know most about religious institutions. Small shrines existed in the early villages of the northern plains and were included in the cultural inventory of the earliest known agriculturalists in the alluvium. Before the end of the Ubaid period the free-standing shrine had lost its original fluidity of plan and adopted architectural features that afterward permanently characterized Mesopotamian temples. The development continued into the Early Dynastic period, when we see a complex of workshops and storehouses surrounding a greatly enlarged but rigidly traditional arrangement of cult chambers. No known contemporary structures were remotely comparable in size or complexity to these establishments until almost the end of the Protoliterate period.

At some point specialized priests appeared, probably the first persons released from direct subsistence labor. Their ritual activities are depicted in Protoliterate seals and stone carvings. If not immediately, then quite early, the priests also assumed the role of economic administrators, as attested by ration or wage lists found in temple premises among the earliest known examples of writing. The priestly hierarchies continued to supervise a multitude of economic as well as ritual activities into (and beyond) the Early Dynastic period, although by then more explicitly political forms of organization had perhaps become dominant. For a long time, however, temples seem to have been the largest and most complex institutions that existed in the communities growing up around them.

The beginnings of dynastic political regimes are much harder to trace. Monumental palaces, rivaling the temples in size, appear in the Early Dynastic period, but not earlier. The term for "king" has not yet been found in Protoliterate texts. Even so-called royal tombs apparently began only in the Early Dynastic period.

Lacking contemporary historical or archeological evidence, we must seek the origins of dynastic institutions primarily in later written versions of traditional myths. Thorkild Jacobsen of the University of Chicago has argued persuasively that Sumerian myths describing the world of the gods reflect political institutions as they existed in human society just prior to the rise of dynastic authority. If so, they show that political authority in the Protoliterate period rested in an assembly of the adult male members of the community. Convoked only to meet sporadic external threat, the assembly's task was merely to select a short-term war leader.

Eventually, as the myths themselves suggest, successful war leaders were retained even in times of peace. Herein lies the apparent origin of kingship. At times springing up outside the priestly corporations, at times coming from them, new leaders emerged who were preoccupied with, and committed to, both defensive and offensive warfare against neighboring city-states.

The traditional concerns of the temples were not immediately affected by the new political leadership. Palace officials acquired great landed estates of their own, but the palace itself was occupied chiefly with such novel activities as raising and supplying its army, maintaining a large retinue of servants and entertainers and constructing a defensive wall around the city.

These undertakings took a heavy toll of the resources of the young city-states, perhaps too heavy to exact by the old "democratic" processes. Hence it is not surprising that as permanent, hereditary royal authority became established, the position of the assembly declined. In the famous epic of Gilgamesh, an Early Dynastic king of Uruk, the story opens with the protests of the citizenry over their forced labor on the city walls. Another episode shows Gilgamesh manipulating the assembly, obviously no longer depending on its approval for his power. Rooted in war, the institution of kingship intensified a pattern of predatory expansionism and shifting military rivalries. The early Mesopotamian king could trace his origin to the need for military leadership. But the increasingly militaristic flavor of the Early Dynastic period also can be traced at least in part to the interests and activities of kings and their retinues as they proceeded to consolidate their power.

As society shifted its central focus from temple to palace it also separated into classes. Archeologically, the process can best be followed through the increasing differentiation in grave offerings in successively later cemeteries. Graves of the Ubaid period, at the time when monumental temples were first appearing, hold little more than a variable number of pottery vessels. Those in the cemetery at Ur, dating from the latter part of the Early Dynastic period, show a great disparity in the wealth they contain. A small proportion, the royal tombs (not all of whose principal occupants may have belonged to royal families), are richly furnished with beautifully wrought weapons, ornaments and utensils of gold and lapis lazuli. A larger number contain a few copper vessels or an occasional bead of precious metal, but the majority have only pottery vessels or even nothing at all. Both texts and archeological evidence indicate that copper and bronze agricultural tools were beyond the reach of the ordinary peasant until after the Early Dynastic period, while graves of the well-to-do show "conspicuous consumption" of copper in the form of superfluous stands for pottery vessels even from the beginning of the period.

Early Dynastic texts likewise record social and economic stratification. Records from the main archive of the Baba Temple in Girsu, for example, show substantial differences in the allotments from that temple's lands to its parishioners. Other texts describe the sale of houseplots or fields, often to form great estates held by palace officials and worked by communities of dependent clients who may originally have owned the land. Still others record the sale of slaves, and the rations allotted to slaves producing textiles under the supervision of temple officials. As a group, however, slaves constituted only a small minority of the population until long after the Early Dynastic period.

Turning to the development of technology, we find a major creative burst in early Protoliterate times, involving very rapid stylistic and technical advance in the manufacture of seals, statuary and ornate vessels of carved stone, cast copper or precious metals. But the number of craft specialists apparently was very small, and the bulk of their products seems to have been intended only for cult purposes. In contrast the Early Dynastic period saw a great increase in production of nonagricultural commodities, and almost certainly a corresponding increase in the proportion of the population that was freed from the tasks of primary subsistence to pursue their craft on a full-time basis. Both stylistically and technologically, however, this expansion was rooted in the accomplishments of the previous period and produced few innovations of its own.

Production was largely stimulated by three new classes of demand. First, the burgeoning military establishment of the palace required armaments, including not only metal weapons and armor but also more elaborate equipment such as chariots. Second, a considerable volume of luxury goods was commissioned for the palace retinue. And third, a moderate private demand for these goods seems to have developed also. The mass production of pottery, the prevalence of such articles as cylinder seals and metal utensils, the existence of a few vendors' stalls and the hoards of objects in some of the more substantial houses all imply at least a small middle class. Most of these commodities, it is clear, were fabricated in the major Mesopotamian towns from raw materials brought from considerable distance. Copper, for example, came from Oman and the Anatolian plateau, more than 1,000 miles from the Sumerian cities. The need for imports stimulated the manufacture of such articles as textiles, which could be offered in exchange, and also motivated the expansion of territorial control by conquest.

Some authorities have considered that technological advance, which they usually equate with the development of metallurgy, was a major stimulant or even a precondition of urban growth. Yet, in southern Mesopotamia at least, the major quantitative expansion of metallurgy, and of specialized crafts in general, came only after dynastic city-states were well advanced. While the spread of technology probably contributed further to the development of militarism and social stratification, it was less a cause than a consequence of city growth. The same situation is found in New World civilizations. Particularly in aboriginal Middle America the technological level remained very nearly static before and after the urban period.

Finally we come to the general forms of the developing cities, perhaps the most obscure aspects of the whole process of urbanization. Unhappily even Early Dynastic accounts do not oblige us with extensive descriptions of the towns where they were written, nor even with useful estimates of population. Contemporary maps also are unknown; if they were made, they still elude us. References to towns in the myths and epics are at best vague and allegorical. Ultimately archeological studies can supply most of these deficiencies, but at present we have little to go on.

The farming villages of the pre-urban era covered at most a few acres. Whether the villages scattered over the alluvial plain in Ubaid times were much different from the earlier ones in the north is unclear; certainly most were no larger, but the superficial appearance of one largely unexcavated site indicates that they may have been more densely built up and more formally laid out along a regular grid of streets or lanes. By the end of the Ubaid period the temples had begun to expand; a continuation of this trend is about all that the remains of Warka and early Protoliterate periods can tell us thus far. Substantial growth seems to have begun toward the end of the Protoliterate period and to have continued through several centuries of the Early Dynastic. During this time the first battlemented ring-walls were built around at least the larger towns.

A few Early Dynastic sites have been excavated sufficiently to give a fairly full picture of their general layout. Radiating out from the massive public buildings of these cities, toward the outer gates, were streets, unpaved and dusty but straight and wide enough for the passage of solid-wheeled carts or chariots. Along the streets lay the residences of the well-to-do citizenry, usually arranged around spacious courts and sometimes provided with latrines draining into sewage conduits below the streets. The houses of the city's poorer inhabitants were located behind or between the large multiroomed dwellings. They were approached by tortuous, narrow alleys, were more haphazard in plan, were less well built and very much smaller. Mercantile activities were probably concentrated along the quays of the adjoining river or at the city gates. The marketplace or bazaar devoted to private commerce had not yet appeared.

Around every important urban center rose the massive fortifications that guarded the city against nomadic raids and the usually more formidable campaigns of neighboring rulers. Outside the walls clustered sheepfolds and irrigated tracts interspersed with subsidiary villages ultimately disappearing into the desert. And in the desert dwelt only the nomad, an object of mixed fear and scorn to the sophisticated court poet. By the latter part of the Early Dynastic period several of the important capitals of lower Mesopotamia included more than 250 acres within their fortifications. The city of Uruk extended over 1,100 acres and contained possibly 50,000 people.

For these later cities there are written records from which the make-up of the population can be estimated. The overwhelming majority of the able-bodied adults still were engaged in primary agricultural production on their own holdings, on allotments of land received from the temples or as dependent retainers on large estates. But many who were engaged in subsistence agriculture also had other roles. One temple archive, for example, records that 90 herdsmen, 80 soldier-laborers, 100 fishermen, 125 sailors, pilots and oarsmen, 25 scribes, 20 or 25 craftsmen (carpenters, smiths, potters, leatherworkers, stonecutters, and mat- or basket-weavers) and probably 250 to 300 slaves were numbered among its parish of around 1,200 persons. In addition to providing for its own subsistence and engaging in a variety of specialized pursuits, most of this group was expected to serve in the army in time of crisis.

Earlier figures can only be guessed at from such data as the size of temple establishments and the quantity of craft-produced articles. Toward the end of the Protoliterate period probably less than a fifth of the labor force was substantially occupied with economic activities outside of subsistence pursuits; in Ubaid times a likely figure is 5 percent.

It is not easy to say at what stage in the whole progression the word "city" becomes applicable. By any standard Uruk and its contemporaries were cities. Yet they still lacked some of the urban characteristics of later eras. In particular, the development of municipal politics, of a self-conscious corporate body with at least partially autonomous, secular institutions for its own administration, was not consummated until classical times.

Many of the currents we have traced must have flowed repeatedly in urban civilizations. But not necessarily all of them. The growth of the Mesopotamian city was closely related to the rising tempo of warfare. For their own protection people must have tended to congregate under powerful rulers and behind strong fortifications; moreover, they may have been consciously and forcibly drawn together by the elite in the towns in order to centralize political and economic controls. On the other hand, both in aboriginal Central America and in the Indus Valley (in what is now Pakistan) great population centers grew up without comprehensive systems of fortification, and with relatively little emphasis on weapons or on warlike motifs in art.

There is not one origin of cities, but as many as there are independent cultural traditions with an urban way of life. Southern Mesopotamia merely provides the earliest example of a process that, with refinements introduced by the industrial revolution and the rise of national states, is still going on today.

6. The Origin and Evolution of Cities

GIDEON SJOBERG

Men began to live in cities some 5,500 years ago. . . . however, the proportion of the human population concentrated in cities did not begin to increase significantly until about 100 years ago. These facts raise two questions that this article proposes to answer. First, what factors brought about the origin of cities? Second, through what evolutionary stages did cities pass before the modern epoch of urbanization? The answers to these questions are intimately related to three major levels of human organization, each of which is characterized by its own technological, economic, social and political patterns. The least complex of the three—the "folk society"—is preurban and even preliterate; it consists typically of small numbers of people, gathered in self-sufficient homogeneous groups, with their energies wholly (or almost wholly) absorbed by the quest for food. Under such conditions there is little or no surplus of food; consequently the folk society permits little or no specialization of labor or distinction of class.

Although some folk societies still exist today, similar human groups began the slow process of evolving into more complex societies millenniums ago, through settlement in villages and through advances in technology and organizational structure. This gave rise to the second level of organization: civilized preindustrial, or "feudal," society. Here there is a surplus of food because of the selective cultivation of grains—high in yield, rich in biological energy and suited to long-term storage—and often also because of the practice of animal husbandry. The food surplus permits both the specialization of labor and the kind of class structure that can, for instance, provide the leadership and command the manpower to develop and maintain extensive irrigation systems (which in turn make possible further increases in the food supply). Most preindustrial societies possess metallurgy, the plow and the wheel—devices, or the means of creating devices, that multiply both the production and the distribution of agricultural surpluses.

Two other elements of prime importance characterize the civilized preindustrial stage of organization. One is writing: not only the simple keeping of accounts but also the recording of historical events, law, literature and religious beliefs. Literacy, however, is usually confined to a leisured elite. The other element is that this stage of organization has only a few sources of energy other than the muscles of men and livestock; the later preindustrial societies harnessed the force of the

---

wind to sail the seas and grind grain and also made use of water power.

It was in the context of this second type of society that the world's first cities developed. Although preindustrial cities still survive, the modern industrial city is associated with a third level of complexity in human organization, a level characterized by mass literacy, a fluid class system and, most important, the tremendous technological breakthrough to new sources of inanimate energy that produced and still sustains the industrial revolution. Viewed against the background of this three-tiered structure, the first emergence of cities at the level of civilized preindustrial society can be more easily understood.

Two factors in addition to technological advance beyond the folk-society level were needed for cities to emerge. One was a special type of social organization by means of which the agricultural surplus produced by technological advance could be collected, stored and distributed. The same apparatus could also organize the labor force needed for large-scale construction, such as public buildings, city walls and irrigation systems. A social organization of this kind requires a variety of full-time specialists directed by a ruling elite. The latter, although few in number, must command sufficient political power—reinforced by an ideology, usually religious in character—to ensure that the peasantry periodically relinquishes a substantial part of the agricultural yield in order to support the city dwellers. The second factor required was a favorable environment, providing not only fertile soil for the peasants but also a water supply adequate for both agriculture and urban consumption. Such conditions exist in geologically mature mid-latitude river valleys, and it was in such broad alluvial regions that the world's earliest cities arose.

What is a city? It is a community of substantial size and population density that shelters a variety of nonagricultural specialists, including a literate elite. I emphasize the role of literacy as an ingredient of urban life for good reasons. Even though writing systems took centuries to evolve, their presence or absence serves as a convenient means for distinguishing between genuinely urban communities and others that in spite of their large size and dense population must be considered quasi-urban or nonurban. This is because once a community achieves or otherwise acquires the technological advance we call writing, a major transformation in the social order occurs; with a written tradition rather than an oral one it is possible to create more complex administrative and legal systems and more rigorous systems of thought. Writing is indispensable to the development of mathematics, astronomy and the other sciences; its existence thus implies the emergence of a number of significant specializations within the social order.

As far as is known, the world's first cities took shape around 3500 B.C. in the Fertile Crescent, the eastern segment of which includes Mesopotamia: the valleys of the Tigris and the Euphrates. Not only were the soil and water supply there suitable; the region was a crossroads that facilitated repeated contacts among peoples of divergent cultures for thousands of years. The resulting mixture of alien and indigenous crafts and skills must have made its own contribution to the evolution of the first true cities out of the village settlements in lower Mesopotamia. These were primarily in Sumer but also to some extent in Akkad, a little to the north. Some—such as Eridu, Erech, Lagash and Kish—are more familiar to archaeologists than to others; Ur, a later city, is more widely known.

These early cities were much alike; for one thing, they had a similar technological base. Wheat and barley were the cereal crops, bronze was the metal, oxen pulled plows and there were wheeled vehicles. Moreover, the city's leader was both king and high priest; the peasants' tribute to the city god was stored in the temple granaries. Luxury goods recovered from royal tombs and temples attest the existence of skilled artisans, and the importation of precious metals and gems from well beyond the borders of Mesopotamia bespeaks a class of merchant-traders. Population sizes can only be guessed in the face of such unknowns as the average number of residents per household and the extent of each city's zone of influence. The excavator of Ur, Sir Leonard Woolley, estimates that soon after 2000 B.C. the city proper housed 34,000 people; in my opinion, however, it seems unlikely that, at least in the earlier periods, even the larger of these cities contained more than 5,000 to 10,000 people, including part-time farmers on the cities' outskirts.

The valley of the Nile, not too far from Mesopotamia, was also a region of early urbanization. To judge from Egyptian writings of a later time, there may have been urban communities in the Nile delta by 3100 B.C. Whether the Egyptian concept of city living had "diffused" from Mesopotamia or was independently invented (and perhaps even earlier than in Mesopotamia) is a matter of scholarly debate; in any case the initial stages of Egyptian urban life may yet be discovered deep in the silt of the delta, where scientific excavation is only now being undertaken.

Urban communities—diffused or independently invented—spread widely during the third and second millenniums B.C. By about 2500 B.C. the cities of Mohenjo-Daro and Harappa were flourishing in the valley of the Indus River in what is now Pakistan. Within another

1,000 years at the most the middle reaches of the Yellow River in China supported urban settlements. A capital city of the Shang Dynasty (about 1500 B.C.) was uncovered near Anyang before World War II; current archaeological investigations by the Chinese may well prove that city life was actually established in ancient China several centuries earlier.

The probability that the first cities of Egypt were later than those of Sumer and the certainty that those of the Indus and Yellow rivers are later lends weight to the argument that the concept of urban living diffused to these areas from Mesopotamia. Be this as it may, none will deny that in each case the indigenous population contributed uniquely to the development of the cities in its own area.

In contrast to the situation in the Old World, it appears certain that diffusion played an insignificant role or none at all in the creation of the pre-Columbian cities of the New World. The peoples of Mesoamerica—notably the Maya, the Zapotecs, the Mixtecs and the Aztecs—evidently developed urban communities on a major scale, the exact extent of which is only now being revealed by current investigations. Until quite recently, for example, many New World archaeologists doubted that the Maya had ever possessed cities; it was the fashion to characterize their impressive ruins as ceremonial centers visited periodically by the members of a scattered rural population. It is now clear, however, that many such centers were genuine cities. At the Maya site of Tikal in Guatemala some 3,000 structures have been located in an area of 6.2 square miles; only 10 percent of them are major ceremonial buildings. Extrapolating on the basis of test excavations of more than 100 of these lesser structures, about two-thirds of them appear to have been dwellings. If only half the present-day average household figure for the region (5.6 members) is applied to Tikal, its population would have been more than 5,000. At another major Maya site—Dzibilchaltun in Yucatán—a survey of less than half of the total area has revealed more than 8,500 structures. Teotihuacán, the largest urban site in the region of modern Mexico City, may have had a population of 100,000 during the first millennium A.D.

Although only a few examples of writing have been identified at Teotihuacán, it is reasonable to assume that writing was known; there were literate peoples elsewhere in Mesoamerica at the time. By the same token, the achievements of the Maya in such realms as mathematics and astronomy would have forced the conclusion that they were an urban people even in the absence of supporting archaeological evidence. Their invention of the concept of zero (evidently earlier than the Hindus' parallel feat) and their remarkably precise calculation of the length of the solar year would surely have been impossible if their literate elite had been scattered about the countryside in villages rather than concentrated in urban centers where a cross-fertilization of ideas could take place.

Mesoamerica was by no means the only area of large, dense communities in the New World; they also existed in the Andean region. A culture such as the Inca, however, cannot be classified as truly urban. In spite of—perhaps because of—their possession of a mnemonic means of keeping inventories (an assemblage of knotted cords called a quipu) the Incas lacked any conventionalized set of graphic symbols for representing speech or any concepts other than numbers and certain broad classes of items. As a result they were denied such key structural elements of an urban community as a literate elite and a written heritage of law, religion and history. Although the Incas could claim major military, architectural and engineering triumphs and apparently were on the verge of achieving a civilized order, they were still quasi-urban at the time of the European conquest, much like the Dahomey, Ashanti and Yoruba peoples of Africa.

The New World teaches us two lessons. In Mesoamerica cities were created without animal husbandry, the wheel and an extensive alluvial setting. One reason for this is maize, a superior grain crop that produced a substantial food surplus with relatively little effort and thus compensated for the limited tools and nonriverine environment. In the Andean region imposing feats of engineering and an extensive division of labor were not enough, in the absence of writing, to give rise to a truly urban society.

In spite of considerable cultural diversity among the inhabitants of the Near East, the Orient and the New World, the early cities in all these regions had a number of organizational forms in common. The dominant pattern was theocracy—the king and the high priest were one. The elite had their chief residences in the city; moreover, they and their retainers and servants congregated mainly in the city's center. This center was the prestige area, where the most imposing religious and government buildings were located. Such a concentration had dual value: in an era when communications and transport were rudimentary, propinquity enhanced interaction among the elite; at the same time it gave the ruling class maximum protection from external attack.

At a greater distance from this urban nucleus were the shops and dwellings of artisans—masons, carpenters, smiths, jewelers, potters—many of whom served the elite. The division of labor into crafts, apparent in the earliest cities, became more complex with the passage of time. Artisan groups, some of which even in early times may have belonged to specific ethnic minorities, tended to establish themselves in special quarters or streets. Such has been characteristic of preindustrial cities in all cultural settings, from the earliest times to the present day. The poorest urbanites lived on the outskirts of the city, as did part-time or full-time farmers; their scattered dwellings finally blended into open countryside.

From its inception the city, as a residence of specialists, has been a continuing source of innovation. Indeed, the very emergence of cities greatly accelerated social and cultural change; to borrow a term from the late British archaeologist V. Gordon Childe, we can properly regard the "urban revolution" as being equal in significance to the agricultural revolution that preceded it and the industrial revolution that followed it. The city acted as a promoter of change in several ways. Many of the early cities arose on major transportation routes; new ideas and inventions flowed into them quite naturally. The mere fact that a large number of specialists were concentrated in a small area encouraged innovation, not only in technology but also in religious, philosophical and scientific thought. At the same time cities could be strong bulwarks of tradition. Some—for example Jerusalem and Benares—have become sacred in the eyes of the populace; in spite of repeated destruction Jerusalem has retained this status for more than two millenniums. . . .

The course of urban evolution can be correctly interpreted only in relation to the parallel evolution of technology and social organization (especially political organization); these are not just prerequisites to urban life but the basis for its development. As centers of innovation cities provided a fertile setting for continued technological advances; these gains made possible the further expansion of cities. Advanced technology in turn depended on the increasingly complex division of labor, particularly in the political sphere. As an example, the early urban communities of Sumer were mere city-states with restricted hinterlands, but eventually trade and commerce extended over a much broader area, enabling these cities to draw on the human and material resources of a far wider and more diverse region and even bringing about the birth of new cities. The early empires of the Iron Age—for instance the Achaemenid Empire of Persia, established early in the sixth century B.C., and the Han Empire of China, established in the third century B.C.—far surpassed in scope any of the Bronze Age. And as empires became larger the size and grandeur of their cities increased. In fact, as Childe has observed, urbanization spread more rapidly during the first five centuries of the Iron Age than it had in all 15 centuries of the Bronze Age.

In the sixth and fifth centuries B.C. the Persians expanded their empire into western Turkestan and created a number of cities, often by building on existing villages. In this expansion Toprakkala, Merv and Marakanda (part of which was later the site of Samarkand) moved toward urban status. So too in India, at the close of the fourth century B.C., the Mauryas in the north spread their empire to the previously nonurban south and into Ceylon, giving impetus to the birth of cities such as Ajanta and Kanchi. Under the Ch'in and Han dynasties, between the third century B.C. and the third century A.D., city life took hold in most of what was then China and beyond, particularly to the south and west. The "Great Silk Road" extending from China to Turkestan became studded with such oasis cities as Suchow, Khotan and Kashgar; Nanking and Canton seem to have attained urban status at this time, as did the settlement that was eventually to become Peking.

At the other end of the Eurasian land mass the Phoenicians began toward the end of the second millennium B.C. to spread westward and to revive or establish urban life along the northern coast of Africa and in Spain. These coastal traders had by then developed a considerable knowledge of shipbuilding; this, combined with their far-reaching commercial ties and power of arms, made the Phoenicians lords of the Mediterranean for a time. Some centuries later the Greeks followed a rather similar course. Their city-states—actually in a sense small empires—created or rebuilt numerous urban outposts along the Mediterranean shore from Asia Minor to Spain and France, and eastward to the most distant coast of the Black Sea. The empire that did the most to diffuse city life into the previously nonurban regions of the West—France, Britain, the Low Countries, Germany west of the Rhine, central and even eastern Europe—was of course Rome.

Empires are effective disseminators of urban forms because they have to build cities with which to maintain military supremacy in conquered regions. The city strongholds, in turn, require an administrative apparatus in order to tap the resources of the conquered area and encourage the commerce needed both to support the military garrison and to enhance the wealth of the homeland. Even when a new city began as a purely commercial outpost, as was the case under the Phoenicians, some military and administrative support was necessary if it was to survive and function effectively in alien territory.

There is a significant relation between the rise and fall of empires and the rise and fall of cities; in a real sense history is the study of urban graveyards. The capitals of many former empires are today little more than ghostly outlines that only hint at a glorious past. Such was the fate of Babylon and Nineveh, Susa in Persia, Seleucia in Mesopotamia and Vijayanagar in India. Yet there are exceptions.

Some cities have managed to survive over long periods of time by attaching themselves first to one empire and then to another. Athens, for example, did not decline after the collapse of Greek power; it was able to attach itself to the Roman Empire, which subsidized Athens as a center of learning. Once Rome fell, however, both the population and the prestige of Athens dwindled steadily; it was little more than a town until the rise of modern Greece in the 19th century. On the other hand, nearby Byzantium, a city-state of minor importance under Roman rule, not only became the capital of the Eastern Roman Empire and its successor, the Ottoman Empire, but as Istanbul remains a major city to this day.

In the light of the recurrent rise and decline of cities in so many areas of the world, one may ask just how urban life has been able to persist and why the skills of technology and social organization required for city-building were not lost. The answer is that the knowledge was maintained within the framework of empires—by means of written records and oral transmission by various specialists. Moreover, all empires have added to their store of skills relating to urban development as a result of diffusion—including the migration of specialists—from other civilized areas. At the same time various civilized or uncivilized subjects within empires have either been purposely educated by their conquerors or have otherwise gained access to the body of urban lore. The result on occasion is that the subjects challenge the power of the dominant ruling group.

The rise and fall of the Roman Empire provides a highly instructive case study that illuminates several relations between the life-span of cities and the formation and decline of empires. The Romans themselves took many elements of their civilization from the Etruscans, the Greeks and other civilized peoples who came under their sway. After Rome's northward expansion in western Europe and the proliferation of Roman cities in regions inhabited by so-called "barbarians"—in this instance preliterate, or "noncivilized," peoples—the Roman leaders were simply unable to staff all the bureaucratic posts with their own citizens. Some of the preliterates had to be trained to occupy such posts both in their own homelands and in the cities on the frontier. This process made it possible for the Romans to exploit the wealth of conquered regions and may have pacified the subjugated groups for a time, but in the long run it engendered serious conflicts. Eventually the Ostrogoths, Vandals, Burgundians and others—having been partially urbanized, having developed a literate elite of their own and having acquired many Roman technological and administrative skills—turned against the imperial power structure and engineered the collapse of Rome and its empire. Nor is this a unique case in history; analogies can be perceived in the modern independence movements of such European colonies as those in Africa.

With the breakup of the Roman Empire, not only did the city of Rome (which at its largest may have had more than 300,000 inhabitants) decline markedly but many borderland cities disappeared or shrank to small towns or villages. The decline was dramatic, but it is too often assumed that after the fall of Rome cities totally disappeared from western Europe. The historian E. Ewig has recently shown that many cities continued to function, particularly in Italy and southern France. Here, as in all civilized societies, the surviving cities were the chief residences and centers of activity for the political and religious elite who commanded the positions of power and privilege that persisted during the so-called Dark Ages.

In spite of Rome's decline many of the techniques and concepts associated with literate traditions in such fields as medicine and astronomy were kept alive; this was done both in the smaller surviving urban communities of Europe and in the eastern regions that had been ruled by the Romans—notably in the cities of the succeeding Eastern Roman Empire. Some of the technology and learning associated with Rome also became the basis for city life in the Arab empires that arose later in the Near East, North Africa, Spain and even central Asia. Indeed, the Byzantine and Arab empires—which had such major intellectual centers as Constantinople, Antioch, Damascus, Cairo and Baghdad—advanced beyond the knowledge inherited from antiquity. The Arabs, for example, took from the Hindus the concept of zero and the decimal system of numerals; by utilizing these concepts in both theory and practice they achieved significant advances over the knowledge that had evolved in the West. Eventually much of the new learning was passed on to Europe, where it helped to build the foundations for the industrial revolution.

In time Europe reestablished extensive commercial contact with the Byzantine and Arab empires; the interchange that followed played a significant role in the resurgence of urban life in southern Europe. The revitalization of trade was closely associated with the formation of several prosperous Italian city-states in the 10th and 11th centuries A.D. Venice and other cities eventually were transformed into small-scale empires whose colonies were scattered over the Mediterranean region—a hinterland from which the home cities were able to extract not only many of their necessities but also luxury items. By A.D. 1000 Venice had forged commercial links with Constantinople and other cities of the Eastern Roman Empire, partly as a result of the activities of the Greek colony in Venice. The Venetians were able to draw both on the knowledge of these resident Greeks and on the practical experience of sea captains and other specialists among them. Such examples make it clear that the Italian city-states were not merely local creations, but rather products of a multiplicity of cultural forces.

Beginning at the turn of the 11th century A.D. many European cities managed to win a kind of independence from the rulers of the various principalities and petty kingdoms that surrounded them. Particularly in northern Italy urban communities came to enjoy considerable political autonomy. This provided an even more favorable atmosphere for commerce and encouraged the growth of such urban institutions as craft guilds. The European pattern is quite different from that in most of Asia (for instance in India and China), where the city was never able to attain a measure of autonomy within the broader political structure. At the same time the extent of self-rule enjoyed by the medieval European cities can be exaggerated and often is; by the close of the Middle Ages urban self-rule was already beginning to be lost. It is therefore evident that the political autonomy of medieval cities was only indirectly related to the eventual evolution of the industrial city.

It was the industrial revolution that brought about truly far-reaching changes in city life. In some nations today, . . . the vast majority of the inhabitants are city dwellers; nearly 80 percent of the people in the United Kingdom live in cities, as do nearly 70 percent of the people of the U.S. Contrast this with the preindustrial civilized world, in which only a small, socially dominant minority lived in cities. The industrial revolution has also led to fundamental changes in the city's social geography and social organization; the industrial city is marked by a greater fluidity in the class system, the appearance of mass education and mass communications and the shift of some of the elite from the center of the city to its suburban outskirts.

Although there are still insufficient data on the rise of the industrial city—an event that took place sometime between 1750 and 1850—and although scholars disagree over certain steps in the process, the major forces at work in the two or three centuries before the industrial city emerged can be perceived clearly enough. Viewed in the light of Europe's preindustrial urban era, two factors are evident: the expansion of European power into other continents and the development of a technology based on inanimate rather than animate sources of energy. The extension of European trade and exploration (which was to culminate in European colonialism) not only induced the growth of cities in Asia, in parts of nonurban Africa and in the Americas but also helped to raise the standard of living of Europeans themselves and made possible the support of more specialists. Notable among the last was a new occupational group—the scientists. The expansion abroad had helped to shatter the former world view of European scholars; they were now forced to cope with divergent ideas and customs. The discoveries reported by the far-ranging European explorers thus gave added impetus to the advance of science.

The knowledge gained through the application of the scientific method is the one factor above all others that made the modern city possible. This active experimental approach has enabled man to control the forces of nature to an extent undreamed of in the preindustrial era. It is true that in the course of several millenniums the literate elite of the preindustrial cities added significantly to man's store of knowledge in such fields as medicine, astronomy and mathematics, but these scholars generally scorned mundane activities and avoided contact with those whose work was on the practical level. This meant that the scholars' theories were rarely tested and applied in the everyday realm. Moreover, in accordance with prevailing religious thought, man was not to tamper with the natural order or to seek to control it, in either its physical or its social aspect. For example, medical scholars in Greek and Roman cities did not dissect human cadavers; not until the 16th century in Europe did a physician—Andreas Vesalius of Brussels—actually use findings obtained from dissection to revise ancient medical theories.

In the field of engineering, as late as the 17th century most advances were made by artisans who worked more or less on a trial-and-error basis. With the development of the experimental method, however, the learning of the elite became linked with the practical knowledge of the artisan, the barber-surgeon and the like; the result was a dramatic upsurge of knowledge and a fundamental revision of method that has been termed the scientific revolution. Such was the basis of the industrial revolution and the industrial city.

That the first industrial cities appeared in England is hardly fortuitous; England's social structure lacked the rigidity that characterized most of Europe and the rest of the civilized world. The Puritan tradition in England—an ethical system that supports utilitarianism and empiricism—did much to alter earlier views concerning man's place in nature. In England scholars could communicate with artisans more readily than elsewhere in Europe.

The advent of industrialism brought vast improvements in agricultural implements, farming techniques and food preservation, as well as in transportation and communication. Improved water supplies and more effective methods of sewage disposal allowed more people to congregate in cities. Perhaps the key invention was the steam engine, which provided a new and much more bountiful source of energy.

Before that time, except for power from wind and water, man had no energy resources other than human and animal muscle. Now the factory system, with its mass production of goods and mechanization of activity, began to take hold. With it emerged a new kind of occupational structure: a structure that depends on highly specialized knowledge and that functions effectively only when the activities of the component occupations are synchronized. This process of industrialization has not only continued unabated to the present day but has actually accelerated with the rise of self-controlling machines.

The evolution of the industrial city was not an unmixed blessing. Historians have argued through many volumes the question of whether the new working class, including many migrants from the countryside, lost or gained economically and socially as the factory system destroyed older social patterns. Today, as industrialization moves inexorably across the globe, it continues to create social problems. Many surviving traditional cities evince in various ways the conflict between their preindustrial past and their industrial future. Nonetheless, the trend is clear: barring nuclear war, the industrial city will become the dominant urban form throughout the world, replacing forever the preindustrial city that was man's first urban creation.

B. THE PROCESS OF URBANIZATON AND ITS CONSEQUENCES

7. Urbanization: An Overview

PHILIP M. HAUSER

THE BASES OF URBANIZATION

The origin of the urban agglomeration as a form of human settlement is not precisely known. There is, however, a literature on the origin and development of cities, based in part on legend, myth, and speculation, in part on archaeology, and in part on the known origins of cities that have emerged during the period of recorded history. It seems clear that the emergence and development of the city was necessarily a function of four factors: (1) the size of the total population; (2) the control of natural environment; (3) technological development; and (4) developments in social organization.[1]

Population size is necessarily a factor in urban development because to permit any agglomeration of human beings there must be some minimum number to sustain group life; and to achieve large urban aggregations relatively large total populations are required. Similarly, the environment must be amenable to control in the sense that it meets at least minimal requirements for aggregative living. Thus, although earliest cities apparently were located in river valleys and alluvial plains, the ingenuity of man has permitted the use of a wide variety of natural environments for urban development. In any case, the natural environment, by means of relatively primitive technology, provided the necessities for survival—food, shelter, protective clothing, and, of course, an adequate water supply.

SOURCE: *The Study of Urbanization*, Philip M. Hauser and Leo F. Schnore (eds.) (New York: John Wiley & Sons, Inc., 1965), pp. 1-47.

Permanent human settlement had to await technological innovation—the inventions of the neolithic revolution. It was only with the achievement of domesticated plants and animals that it became possible for man to lead a relatively settled existence. Apart from these requirements, however, other techniques were involved and certainly played a major role in determining the size that the agglomeration could reach. Foremost among these was the development of agricultural technology to a point where a surplus was possible, that is, a food supply in excess of the requirements of the cultivators themselves. The emergence of the crafts and their proliferation was necessarily a function of the size of the surplus, permitting some persons to engage, at least part time, in activities other than agricultural. With improved technology, including the wheel, the road, irrigation, cultivation, stock breeding, and improvements in fishing, the surplus became large enough to support a sizable number of persons freed from the production of food. Certain it is that developments of this type were associated with the first units of settlement ten times and more the size of any known neolithic villages, as revealed in the archaeological finds in Egypt, Mesopotamia, and the Indus Basin.[2]

The development of relatively large agglomerations of population required more, however, than an increasingly efficient technology. Relatively large aggregations of population required more complex social organization, including improved communication, and social and political mechanisms permitting some form of exchange among the emergent specialists, agricultural and nonagricultural. Chief among the social organizational requirements was a working arrangement between the population agglomeration and the hinterland, its source of food and raw materials. In the history of cities there is evidence of great variation in forms of organization by means of which integration and coordination of activities was achieved between city and hinterland and within the city. The rise and fall of empires, as recorded in ancient history, may be read in large measure as a chronicle of developments in social organization by means of which the ancient cities acquired a hinterland. The Roman Legion may be interpreted as a form of social organization enabling the city to achieve effective working arrangements with a hinterland.[3] The same function centuries later was performed by emergence of the market mechanism, including money as an instrumentality of exchange.

It was not until the nineteenth century that mankind had achieved both the level of technological development and social organization that permitted the relatively widespread appearance of very large cities. On the technological side the developments included techniques that greatly increased productivity in agriculture as well as in nonagricultural commodities. A critical factor in increased productivity was, of course, the utilization of nonhuman energy in production—the emergence of the machine, powered first by water or wind, then by steam, and now by mineral fuels or electricity derived therefrom, with atomic energy in prospect.[4] Technological advance proceeded at an exponential rate under the impetus of the "scientific revolution."

Social organizational developments paralleled the technological. Strong central governments evolved, bringing relative peace and tranquility to increasingly large areas and permitting the development of local, regional, national, and international markets. Increasing division of labor and specialization were accompanied by various forms of formal and informal organization providing essential integration and coordination. New social institutions evolved or were invented to meet the needs of the increasingly complex and interdependent social and economic orders. A full account of the emergence of the large city in the context of its antecedents is yet to be achieved, if indeed it ever can be documented. But the available literature certainly provides a basis for at least pointing to the major factors associated with the emergence of the city and of relatively highly urbanized nations.[5]

In a neo-evolutionary approach, Gras has outlined with broad strokes the relationship between economic development and settlement or habitation patterns in his account of economic history.[6] He has fused historical ways of making a living with technological developments, on the one hand, and with developments in human settlement on the other. Gras writes the history of Western civilization in terms of this joint classification. He delineates five stages or periods: (1) the collectional economy; (2) the cultural-nomadic economy; (3) the settled village economy; (4) the town economy; and (5) the metropolitan economy.

The settled village economy was possible only with the development of agriculture as the dominant way of making a living. The town economy was a function of increased agricultural productivity, the proliferation of the crafts, more efficient transport, and the development of trade. The metropolitan economy was a product of the combination of technological and organizational changes associated with industrialization and the emergence of the metropolitan complex with the large city as a nucleus for an interdependent hinterland. Although Gras's five-stage scheme of urban development is open to serious question, a general neo-evolutionary interpretation of urban development has not been attempted since Gras, indicating, perhaps, a serious gap in the literature.

Economic history as seen by Gras is, in effect, an analysis of the pattern of human habitation considered as a dependent variable. Lampard approaches the problem in the same way in his treatment of urban-industrial development, following the stages, if not the language, of Geddes.[7] The antecedents of the preindustrial city may be seen in his description of cities in Europe and America toward the end of the sixteenth century: "Urban centers were court cities, cathedral cities, fortress cities, markets, ports, country towns, and mere villages. Many, of course, were composites of several types." The preindustrial European city was "limited (dominated) by the needs and capacities of the rural hinterland and a highly stratified society." The preindustrial European city was "essentially a loose-knit system of food economies centering on a few relatively large mercantile-administrative capitals, with a growing inter-regional commerce but no marked territorial division of labor."

The industrial city was the product of acceleration in agricultural productivity and industrial technology during the eighteenth century. It was "a major outlet for capital accumulated in commercialized agricultural production." Its development was facilitated by the emergence of coal and steam as sources of power and particularly by the centripetal force of the steam engine. Factories and population piled up in the industrial city as is documented in the history of English industrial cities such as Manchester and Birmingham. This history was paralleled during the first half of the nineteenth century in France, the Low Countries, and northeastern United States. Major ingredients in the very rapid development of industrial cities in Europe and the United States included the utilization of new fuels as sources of nonhuman energy, new materials, mechanical aids, improved transport and communication, and a closer integration of productive and managerial processes.

The twentieth century "metropolitan city" was the product of the extensive application of science to industry, the diffusion of electric power and the advent of the automobile. The metropolitan city, as compared with the industrial city, was the product of the accelerating technological revolution that permeated virtually all phases of life. Whereas the steam engine and the belt and the pulley had set centripetal forces into motion creating dense population around factory plants, the combination of electric power, the automobile, and the telephone set centrifugal forces in motion which simultaneously diffused population and industry widely over the landscape and permitted larger agglomerations of both. The metropolitan city is a nucleus or core of a metropolitan area which has become a basic economic and social unit not only in regional and national economies but also in the world economy. It is a highly complex and interdependent unit binding centralization with decentralization and specialization and differentiation of function with integration and coordinating mechanisms. . . .

* * *

HISTORICAL PERSPECTIVE

Despite limited data it is possible to reconstruct, generally, the growth of world and urban population. Such a reconstruction provides significant perspectives prerequisite to an understanding of contemporary urbanization and its consequences.

Among the more significant of the great changes that have characterized the modern era are the increases in the size and concentration of world population. Man in all the millennia of his existence on this planet had produced a population of only 500 million persons by mid-seventeenth century. By 1962, however, world population exceeded three billion. Within the three centuries of the modern era, world population had increased by an amount five times that generated throughout man's previous habitation of the globe.[14] Similarly, although man has inhabited this planet for perhaps two million years, permanent human settlement was not achieved until relatively recently—in the neolithic age some 10,000 years ago. Moreover, although only 2.4 per cent of the world's peoples lived in places of 20,000 or more as recently as 1800, this proportion increased ninefold during the following century and a half.[15]

Although the first census of all of mankind has yet to be taken, it is possible, at least in approximation, to reproduce the population history of the world. It is not known exactly when *Homo sapiens,* the present version of man, first appeared, but he was much in evidence in Europe 25,000–30,000 years ago. It has been estimated that for the some 600,000 years of the paleolithic age world population growth approximated 0.02 per thousand per year.[16] By the end of the neolithic period, world population has been estimated at ten million and may have been as little as five million. At the beginning of the Christian era, the population of the globe probably numbered between 200 and 300 million. It increased to about 500 million by the beginning of the modern era (1650). By that time the rate of world population growth had increased to about four-tenths of 1 per cent per year. At the present time it approximates 2 per cent per year. Ignoring population prior to the paleolithic period, it may be stated that in the course of man's development since, his rate of population growth has risen from about 2 per cent per millennium to 2 per cent per year—a thousandfold increase.

The rate of world population increase is still accelerating. It took all the millennia of man's existence on this planet prior to 1850 to produce a population of about one billion persons simultaneously alive. To produce a figure of two billion simultaneously alive required only an additional seventy-five years, for this number was achieved by about 1925. To reach a total of three billion persons required only an additional thirty-seven years—by 1962. In accordance with the trend, a fourth billion would be attained in about fifteen years and a fifth billion in less than an additional ten years.

Over most of the millennia of his existence man was a nomad. As has been indicated, it was not until the neolithic age that man was able to achieve permanent settlement.[17] The neolithic village was limited by its technology and culture to a population restricted to a few hundred persons at most and was "permanent" in a relative sense. By reason of limited agricultural techniques, villages had to be shifted every twenty years or so to achieve even minimal returns from the land. It took at least 1500 years, from 5000 to 3500 B.C., for the city to develop from the neolithic peasant village, the first of which appeared in Mesopotamia and Egypt in about the middle of the fourth millennium B.C. Cities as large as 100,000 or more probably did not exist prior to the Greek or Roman period. Although it is possible that a city of a million was achieved in ancient China and in eighteenth-century Japan,[18] cities of a million or more were largely the product of eighteenth- and nineteenth-century developments.

Data on the urban population of the world as a whole are available with reasonable accuracy only since 1800.[19] Of the approximately 900 million persons on the globe in 1800, it is estimated that 1.7 per cent lived in cities of 100,000 and over; 2.4 per cent in cities of 20,000 and over; and 3 per cent in urban places of 5000 or more inhabitants.

Accelerating world population growth was accompanied by even more rapid increase in urban population since at least the beginning of the nineteenth century. Between 1800 and 1950, world population increased over two and a half times. Population in places of 5000 and over, however, increased twenty-six times; population in places of 20,000 and over twenty-three times; and population in places of 100,000 and over more than twenty times. In consequence, by mid-twentieth century almost one-third (30 per cent) of the world's people lived in urban places having 5000 and over. About 21 per cent were in places of 20,000 and over, and 13 per cent in places of 100,000 and over. Even by 1950, however, only 4 per cent of the world's people lived in places of a million or more inhabitants.

In the United States both total population growth and urban concentration far exceeded the world rates. During the three centuries of the modern era the population of the United States increased from perhaps a million Indians and a few shiploads of Europeans to about 180 million persons as reported in the eighteenth decennial census in 1960.[20] When the first census of the United States was taken in 1790, 95 per cent of the population lived in rural places of fewer than 2500 persons. There were only twenty-four urban places in the nation, only two of which had populations in excess of 25,000. By 1960, however, there were about 5400 urban places containing 70 per cent of the entire population. For the first sixty years of the present century the population of the United States increased from about 75 million to 180 million. The increase in urban population over the same period absorbed 92 per cent of the total increase of the nation. In the last decade of that period, 1950–1960, increase in the urban population accounted for more than 100 per cent of the total population growth of the country. That is, for the first time in the history of the nation, rural population actually declined during the intercensal decade. The extent to which the population of the country is becoming concentrated is even more dramatically indicated by growth of metropolitan and large metropolitan area populations. Over the first sixty years of the century, the increase in metropolitan population absorbed 85 per cent of the total growth of the nation. Although the increase in population of metropolitan areas between 1950 and 1960 (using 1960 boundaries) absorbed about the same proportion of total national growth during the decade, the increase in population classified as metropolitan (boundaries as in 1950 and 1960, respectively) absorbed 97 per cent of the total growth of the nation during the decade.

In 1900 there were only five metropolitan areas having a million or more persons in the United States. They contained about 16 per cent of the total population. By 1960 there were twenty-four such places in which over a third of the nation's population resided (34 per cent). Over the first sixty years of the century, the increase in large metropolitan area population absorbed 48 per cent of total national growth. In the decade between 1950 and 1960, population increase in large metropolitan areas accounted for 60 per cent of total national growth. Over the first sixty years of the century, then, total population increased about two and a half times, urban population increased almost fourfold, metropolitan area population increased more than fourfold, and large metropolitan area population increased fivefold.

During this same period the United States changed from a predominantly rural to a predominantly urban nation. At the turn of the century, about two-fifths of the population was urban. It was not until 1920 that more than half of the inhabitants were urban (51.2 per cent). In 1960, 70 per cent of the population was urban. It will not be until the end of this decade, 1970, that the United States will have completed its first half century as an urban nation—which is why there is still evidence that it is in transition from a preindustrial and preurban order to "urbanism as a way of life."[21]

"URBANIZATION" AND "URBAN"

The degree of urbanization of a nation for statistical purposes is generally defined as the proportion of the population resident in urban places. This demographic conception of urbanization, however, is transcended by many other uses of the term in which urbanization is recognized as a social process which has brought about great transformations in man's way of life. For purposes of convenience, especially in statistical studies, "urban" and "urbanization" are usually considered merely in a demographic sense, as agglomerations of a given size or as the proportion of a total population living in places of a given size. In the consideration of the city or the urban place either as a dependent or an independent variable, however, much more than the demographic definition is necessarily involved.

Urbanization as a process of population concentration has been systematically treated by Hope Tisdale Eldridge.[22] It involves two elements: (1) "the multiplication of points of concentration"; and (2) "the increase in the size of individual concentrations." As a result the proportion of the population living in urban places increases.

Although urban population is widely understood to include the population resident in cities, the definition of urban is, nevertheless, a complex matter. Population classified as "urban" varies greatly country by country. The delineation of areas as "urban" or "rural" is often related to administrative, political, historical, or cultural considerations as well as demographic criteria. As the United Nations *Demographic Yearbook* has indicated, definitions of "urban" fall into three major types: "(1) Classification of minor civil divisions on a chosen criterion which may include: (*a*) type of local government, (*b*) number of inhabitants, (*c*) proportion of population engaged in agriculture; (2) classification of administrative centers of minor rural divisions as urban and the remainder of the division as rural; and (3) classification of certain size localities (agglomerations) as urban, irrespective of administrative boundaries."[23] Even for census purposes, then, the definition of urban involves a multidimensional approach and the setting of arbitrary cutting points in differentiating "urban" from "rural."

In the United States "urban" is defined as a place having 2500 or more persons. The definition was restricted to "incorporated places" prior to the 1950 Census, but includes unincorporated as well as incorporated places since. Moreover, in the United States four different designations are used in the reporting of agglomerations of population. In addition to "urban" places, data are presented for "urbanized areas," for "Standard Metropolitan Statistical Areas," and for "Standard Consolidated Areas." The urbanized area, in brief, includes a central city plus all contiguous territory in which people live at densities of about 2000 per square mile, ignoring political boundaries. The "Standard Metropolitan Statistical Area" includes a city (or cities) of 50,000 or more, the county in which it (or they) is located, and such adjoining counties as by various social and economic criteria depend on the central city (or cities). The "Standard Consolidated Areas" are contiguous Standard Metropolitan Statistical Areas. Only two were delineated in the 1960 Census, one for "New York-Northeastern New Jersey" and the other for "Chicago-Northwestern Indiana."[24]

Increasing attention is being given to still another form of agglomeration—the coalescence of metropolitan areas more comprehensive than those represented by the complexes recognizd by the United States government as Standard Consolidated Areas. The term "megalopolis" refers to the coalescence of a series of metropolitan areas, as represented, for example, on the Atlantic seaboard of the United States from Boston to Washington, D. C.[25]

An effort has been made to delineate the metropolitan areas of the world on a comparable basis. The Institute of International Studies[26] at the University of California has applied uniform criteria to areas containing more than 100,000 inhabitants and delimited boundaries for some 720 areas of a total of 1046 metropolitan areas in the world. Limited population figures are presented for these areas for the last census before 1954 and population estimates are given for about 1955.

By reason of the complexity of the problem, the United Nations Population Commission has recommended that, in addition to "urban-rural" statistics as defined by individual countries, data be presented by size of locality or identifiable agglomeration. This makes possible improved international comparability even though the cutting point for "urban" population may remain an arbitrary matter. In practice, many comparative international studies use populations in places of 20,000 or more as "urban" because the data are generally available on that basis and because an agglomeration of this size is not likely to retain rural characteristics.

Manifestations and Consequences of Urbanization

Although the consideration of urbanism and urbanization as a dependent variable is of major interest in the social sciences, even greater interest, perhaps, is to be found in the consideration of the city as an independent variable. That the city makes a difference in the way of life was perceived by the ancients and recorded in the earliest historical records.[27] In the nineteenth century Maine, Tönnies, and Durkheim, and in the twentieth century Sumner, Goldenweiser, Redfield, and Wirth grappled with various aspects of the difference that aggregative living makes.

THE SIZE-DENSITY MODEL

A relatively simple size-density model provides a basis for treating the city as an independent variable in a broad and comprehensive way. The theoretical basis for the development and consideration of the model is given by Durkheim. He has stated:

> Social life rests on a substratum whose size as well as its form is determined. This substratum is constituted by the mass of individuals who make up society, the way in which they are distributed on the soil, and the nature and configuration of all sorts of things that affect collective relationships. The social substratum differs according to whether the population is large or small and more or less dense, whether it is concentrated in cities or dispersed over the countryside, how cities and houses are constructed, whether the area occupied by the society is more or less extensive, and according to the kind of boundaries that delimit it.[29]

Let us consider the implications of variation in size and density of population, confining our attention to a fixed land area. For purposes of convenience, consider a circle with a radius of 10 miles. Such a circle would have a total area of approximately 314 square miles. The size of the total population in such a circle under different density conditions is shown in the Table.[30] The population densities shown are not unrealistic ones. The population density of 1 may be taken as an approximation of the density of the United States prior to European occupancy. Actually, the Indian population was approximately one-third as dense as this, but 1 is a convenient figure with which to work. The density of 50 is approximately that of the United States in 1960, and approximately the population density of the world as a whole. The density of 8000 in round numbers is not too far from the density of the average central city in metropolitan areas of the United States in 1960. The density figure 17,000 is approximately that of Chicago, the figure of 25,000 approximately the density of New York, and the figure of 75,000 approximately the density of Manhattan Island.

Assumed Population Density (persons per square mile)	*Area with Approximate Density Assumed*	*Number of Persons in Circle of 10-Mile Radius*
1	U. S. in 1500	314
50	World in 1960	15,700
8,000	Average central city in metropolitan area in U. S.	2,512,000
17,000	Chicago	5,338,000
25,000	New York	7,850,000
75,000	Manhattan	23,550,000

In aboriginal America a person moving within the ten-mile circle could potentially make only 313 different contacts with other human beings. In contrast, the density of the United States as a whole today would make possible 15,699 contacts in the same land area. The density of the average central city in the United States would permit over 2.5 million contacts, the density of Chicago over 5.3 million contacts, the density of New York City over 7.8 million contacts, and the density of Manhattan over 23.5 million contacts in the same land area. The potential number of contacts, when considered as a measure of potential human interaction, provides, in a simplistic way to be sure, a basis for understanding the difference that city living makes.

Since Durkheim, in his consideration of the structure of the social order, spoke of "social morphology," the multiplier effect on potential human interaction of increased population density in a fixed land area can appropriately be described as an index of the social-morphological revolution. The size-density model presented may be taken as a quantification of the social-morphological revolution and provides at least one theoretical basis for considering the city as an independent variable. More specifically, it may be stated as an hypothesis that the increase in potential human interaction produced by aggregative living has produced in the social realm a major transformation the equivalent of genetic mutation in the biological realm. Discussion of the consequences of the social-morphological revolution or social mutation is the subject matter of most of the remainder of this chapter...

* * *

THE CITY AS AN ECONOMIC MECHANISM

The city owes its origin to the economic advances represented by the domestication of plants and animals and the proliferation of the crafts. Once permanent human settlement was attained, however, aggregative living exerted profound influences on economic activity.

The characteristics of the city as an economic mechanism were clearly discernible in the development of the ancient Oriental urban cultures. Ever larger agglomerations of population made possible both a greater division of labor and a greater number of nonagricultural specialists. A relatively complex division of labor and specialization resulted in increased productivity permitting even greater surplus. In the matrix of ancient urban areas, a number of key economic elements became significant, including "work," "property," "economic power," "luxury," "poverty," and new forms of economic administration such as gang slavery, the ancient state system of cultivation, and an elaboration of the right to private property.[41]

Self-interest as a key economic motivation—incentive not only to secure means of subsistence but also to get as much as possible of the surplus—was manifest. Self-interest was bolstered by increasing size and density of population which tended to devalue personal and familial relationships founded on close interpersonal interaction and sentiment. Increased size and density of population produced more and more minute division of labor, specialization, and the shifting of economic relationships from "status" to "contract."

The proliferation of the crafts and increasing numbers of artisans led to an important element in the preindustrial city's economic organization—its guild system.[42] This in turn influenced the physical pattern of the city, for the guilds—craft, service, and merchant—tended to become localized into "quarters" along specific streets. Increased division of labor and specialization necessitated heightened exchange activities and generated merchants in ever larger numbers. The proliferation of specialists led also to specialization in the provision of services—the barber, the sweeper, the scavenger, and the like. Money, credit, the price system, financial institutions, all were consequences of increased division of labor and specialization. They may be regarded as mechanisms for the integration and coordination of economic activity necessitated by the increasing size and density of the population clumping. The urban economy increased the status position of the trader and manufacturer over that of the landlord and led also, in time and with organization, to a greatly increased economic power position for workers.

Increased division of labor and specialization also acclerated technological advance. It was easier to devise a machine to do a relatively simple part of a job than to produce an entire product. Technological advance, implying ever-increasing use of nonhuman energy, produced the industrial plant and the "factory system." Workers became increasingly "operatives" rather than artisans and employees rather than self-employed.

Broadened markets, partly a function of the emergence of central governments with increased jurisdiction over broader expanses of territory, encouraged "mass production." The industrial city provided increasing evidence of economies of scale, permitted external economies, operated to minimize frictions of space and communication, and led to more complex forms of economic organization. The joint stock company and corporate organization involving limited liability developed. Capital was amassed, management became professionalized and separated from ownership. Gigantic industrial combines evolved including "integrated" economic empires. To cope with large management, labor unions were organized. "Big labor" evolved to deal with "big management."

With the emergence of the industrial city and the expansion of trade, the market mechanism was increasingly relied upon to order the economy—to allocate resources and to regulate the production of goods and services. This was achieved largely through the play of competition and the operation of the price mechanism. Increasing size and density of population and increasing complexity in economic organization, with ever-increasing interdependence and vulnerability, brought to the fore various problems such as abuses of labor, inequitable distribution of wealth, extreme fluctuations in the level of economic activity, increasing levels of unemployment, monopolistic practices, adulteration of products, and large-scale fraud. Despite Adam Smith's injunction that each man acting in his own interest would as "if guided by an invisible hand" act in the interests of the larger society, government increasingly intervened into the operation of the economy. Intervention took many forms including the establishment of various regulatory agencies, provision for more equitable distribution of income (for example, income tax), encouragement of labor organization, and the creation of various forms of social security such as unemployment compensation, old-age pensions, and medical care.

Increasing government intervention tended to provide greater protection for the weak and enormously to expand the services of government. Thus the public sector of the economy was greatly expanded, including the local governmental sector, in the provision of greatly expanded services for education, health, welfare, recreation, protection, transportation, and so on. This development was largely the result of greater population size and density which generated new collective needs. Because these needs were not met through the market mechanism, they became increasingly the province of government. Urbanization together with industrialization, then, by creating greater interdependence and new forms of vulnerability (for example, unemployment, industrial accident, sweat shops, contagious disease, water and air pollution), stimulated the expansion of government functions and personnel. The most extreme form of interventionism, of course, became manifest in the Soviet Union and in the Communist Bloc, in general.

In summary then, the increased size and density of population agglomerations profoundly affected the ways in which man makes a living. They generated the highly complex form of economic organization that characterizes contemporary life. Needless to say, in the process, productivity tremendously increased, producing unprecedented levels of living for mass populations. As an inevitable consequence of the increased division of labor and specialization, an ever more interdependent society has necessarily evolved new forms of coordination and integration, including increasing government interventionism. The city, itself a product of economic advance, also became a major force in economic development—the emergence of our contemporary form of complex economic organization.[43] . . .

THE CITY AND HUMAN BEHAVIOR

In a small, sparsely settled population, the potential of human interaction is much below that in a large, high-density population. This is illustrated in the size-density model shown earlier. In the small community, not only are potential and actual contacts fewer, but because they are fewer, they tend also to be quite different in character. In consequence, many students have tried to show the way in which the city influences human behavior. The classical treatment of the effect of size and density and, also, heterogeneity of population on behavior is that of Louis Wirth.[44] He stated: "On the basis of the three variables, number, density of settlement, and degree of heterogeneity, of the urban population, it appears possible to explain the characteristics of urban life and to account for the differences between cities of various sizes and types."

According to this hypothesis the small community is characterized by "primary-group" contacts.[45] They tend to be face-to-face, intimate contacts of persons who meet and interact with one another in virtually all spheres of activity. In such a setting personal relations tend to be based on relatively full knowledge of the other person—on sentiment and emotion. In contrast, according to this hypothesis, in the large, high-density population situation, contacts tend to be "secondary" rather than primary, segmental rather than integral, utilitarian rather than sentimental. Moreover, in the large-size, high-density situation, populations are apt to be more heterogeneous—to include peoples of greater range and diversity in background, attitudes, and behavior. The person is subjected, therefore, to a greater variety of ways of thought and action.

The combination of heterogeneous and secondary contacts, it is held, tends greatly to modify human behavior. Thus, thought and action tend to become increasingly rational as opposed to traditional, and interpersonal relations become based on utility rather than sentiment. With increased size, density, and heterogeneity of population, the constraints of tradition—the influence of the folkways and mores—diminish. In ever larger spheres of thought and action, behavior is determined by a willful decision taken by the person, rather than automatically determined by the norms of the group. The sphere of personal decision-making is greatly extended, including areas of activity previously determined by tradition, such as kind and degree of education, occupation or profession, residential location, choice of mate, size of family, political affiliation, religiosity or even religion.

It follows, then, that increased size and density of population, especially if accompanied by heterogeneity, diminishes the power of informal social controls. Informal social control, effected largely through the play of folkways and the mores, gives way to increased formal control, the control of law, police, courts, jails, regulations, and orders. The breakdown in informal social controls is largely responsible for increased personal disorganization as manifest in juvenile delinquency, crime, prostitution, alcoholism, drug addiction, suicide, mental disease, social unrest, and political instability. Formal controls have by no means proved as efficacious as the informal in regulating human behavior.

The effect of the city on the way of life may be observed in the adjustment problems of the in-migrant.[46] The city as a recipient of migrants has played and continues to play a prominent role in the modification of thought and behavior in subjecting people with traditional and rural backgrounds to the conditions of urban living. Most of the severe physical, social, and economic problems of the city are disproportionately manifest among newcomers and are symptomatic of the difficulties of adjustment to urban life. In-migrant populations provide an opportunity for observing the impact of urbanization on the human being. In the accommodation of the rural newcomer to the city, such transformation in thought and behavior as may be effected may be traced.

In the United States, for example, the newest newcomers to urban and metropolitan areas are the Negro, the Puerto Rican, the Mexican, and the American Indian. They are now faced with accommodation to the urban milieu as were earlier immigrant groups. Each of the newcomer groups to the urban and metropolitan areas of the United States followed essentially a similar pattern with respect to location in space, the economy, and society.[47] Each of the in-migrant strains found its port of entry or areas of first settlement in the inner, older, blighted zones of the city. The longer the period of settlement, the farther out was the median location point of the newcomer group and the more dispersed was its residential pattern. The shorter the period of settlement, the closer to the center of the city was its median location and the more concentrated or segregated was its residential pattern. Similarly, the shorter the period of settlement, the lower was the occupational level and income of the newcomers. The longer the period of settlement, the higher the educational and occupational level and income. Finally, with respect to social status, a common pattern was also visible. Each of the newcomer groups was in turn greeted with hostility, suspicion, distrust, prejudice, and discriminatory practices. With the passage of time each of the newcomer groups climbed the social as well as the economic ladder to achieve access to the broader social and cultural life of the community and increased general acceptability.

The patterns by which immigrant groups became "Americanized" indicate in general the processes by which the newest newcomers—the Negro and the Puerto Rican—will make the transition from traditional behavior in their rural areas of origin to urbanism as a way of life. The process of acculturation will be similar in many respects to the process by which immigrants before them settled in American cities and metropolitan areas. This is not to say that there will not also be differences arising from their greater visibility and differences in cultural background.[48]

Such transformations in thought and behavior as are induced by increased size and density of population are, of course, greatly augmented by the increased heterogeneity of the population. Since increasing size and density of human agglomerations increase the probabilities of greater heterogeneity, the city may in a fundamental sense be regarded as the source of a whole range of problems arising from intergroup differences, whether based on language, culture, religion, or race. The problem of intergroup relations is essentially an urban problem, or at least reaches its most critical manifestations in the urban area.

The hypotheses considered have been a major factor in leading to the distinction between "folk" and "urban" societies.[49] Although the above-described impact of urbanism (size, density, and heterogeneity of population) on the way of life has been widely accepted, it remains an hypothesis yet to be subjected to the test of empirical research. Similarly, the extension of the hypothesis into the differentiation of "folk" and "urban" societies is largely an ideal-type construct which empirical investigation, as yet inadequate, suggests is inapplicable to the developing areas and of questionable usefulness in the economically advanced countries.

It may be that to the extent that size, density, and heterogeneity of population have changed behavior in urban places they represent necessary, rather than sufficient, conditions for such a transformation. It is clear that much behavior in urban places, both in the economically advanced and underdeveloped areas, is still traditional rather than rational, and in other respects resembles folk rather than urban characteristics. The work of Oscar Lewis, Edward M. Bruner, Douglas S. Butterworth, Theodore Caplow, William L. Kolb, O. D. Duncan and Albert Reiss, Herbert J. Gans and the Detroit Area Study at the University of Michigan indicates preurban societies that do not conform to the folk pattern or city populations that do not manifest the attitudes or behavior hypothesized as a consequent of size, density, and heterogeneity.[51] Moreover, a striking example of high urban density without the concomitants hypothesized by Wirth is afforded by Hoselitz's reference to a density of about 840,000 per square mile in a section of a ward in Bombay.[52]

The explanation for this may lie in the difference between *potential* human interaction in the city, as portrayed in the size-density model, and that *actually* achieved. That is, in large population clumpings of high density, which are essentially an agglutination of separate and distinct noninteracting communities, human behavior may still be largely the product of the primary group. In the city, although heterogeneity is present, confinement of contacts to one's own cultural group is also possible in varying degrees to almost complete isolation. In fact, large population size may actually facilitate isolation and insularity. This is evident in the history of immigration to the United States. Some immigrants have chosen to continue to live in enclaves even within metropolitan areas and thus continue traditional behavior and attitudes even with prolonged exposure to urban living. Others, in contrast, have elected to leave their enclaves, avail themselves of diversity of contacts and social world, and adopt "urbanism as a way of life."

Similarly, the patterns of accommodation and acculturation of immigrants or in-migrants may vary with differences in the cultural background of the newcomers, differences in the societies of destination, and variations in the degree to which the potential interaction possible is actually realized. . . .

THE CITY AND SOCIAL ORGANIZATION

Social organization has necessarily been greatly modified by reason of the increasing size and density of human agglomerations. Increased division of labor and specialization, in creating a much more complex and interdependent society, affected social as well as economic organization. It is held that the basis for social cohesion was altered in that a society became dependent or "organic" rather than "mechanical" solidarity.[53] That is, cohesion is effected organically in the urban setting through interdependence and the mechanisms of coordination and integration, rather than achieved mechanically through the operation of a homogeneous culture. In the large-size, high-density society, organization may be increasingly based on "contract" rather than "status." Relationships among persons or groups are made explicit in terms of reciprocal obligations and duties, on the one hand, and rights or powers on the other. Needless to say, utility rather than sentiment enters into the definition of the relationships.

As a microcosm of the social whole, the family is a convenient unit through which to trace many of the influences of the city on social institutions. The family in most societies is regarded as the primary social unit. The colonial family in early America, predominantly resident in rural areas, was the keystone of social organization. For example, it was a basic and largely self-sufficient economic unit; it had primary responsibility for the socialization and education of the young; it was a focal point for religious training and practices; it provided for the security and protection of its members; and it was the center for their affectional and recreational life.[54]

The family in contemporary urban United States, however, has certainly been transformed. Compared with the colonial family the urban family today is smaller; it is more often childless and has few children, if fertile. The urban family, collectively and individually, is much more mobile; it is not rooted to the soil or even to a home in the manner of its rural counterpart. It possesses comparatively little economic or social unity; it is more frequently broken by separation or divorce and, as William F. Ogburn demonstrated some time ago, has long since lost or shared many of its various historic functions with new, specialized urban institutions.[55] Examples of these new institutions include, on the one hand, the clothing store, the grocery, and the restaurant, and on the other, the school, the library, and social security system.

Accompanying these changes in the family have been redefinitions in the roles of its members—in the relationships of spouses and in parent-child and sibling interrelationships. Especially important in this regard is the changed role of the woman in the family and in society at large, a phenomenon certainly not unrelated to the changed conditions of urban life.

Finally, in respect of the family, it may be noted that in the urban milieu the "nuclear" family, the two-generation family, tends to replace the "extended," the three or more generation family as the model household unit.[56] This, however, does not necessarily mean that the larger family unit disappears as a system of interaction and as an important element of social organization. More study is needed on the role of the extended family in an urban area even when it no longer occupies a single household.[57]

In the city, social institutions tend to be "enacted" rather than "crescive," that is, spontaneous.[58] In the mass society social institutions are frequently invented, are the product of administrative edict or legislation, rather than the result of slow development representing the crystallization of patterns of thought and action as a product of group life. New institutions arise in great number partly as the result of the breakdown of traditional ones that do not meet the requirements of urban living, and partly through the need to invent new institutions by reason of unprecedented situations and problems for which tradition has no answers. Examples of the multiplication of new institutions in response to new and unprecedented needs is represented by the proliferation of such institutions associated with urban living as the police and fire departments, the welfare agency, and public housing.

In the city, "bureaucracy" becomes a ubiquitous form of organization. It is a rational-formal-legal organization which is an inevitable and indispensable concomitant of populations of large size and density and high levels of interaction. It is a form of complex organization involving (1) the distribution in a fixed way of regular activities, (2) the distribution in a fixed way of authority in accordance with rules, (3) the methodical provision for fulfillment of duties and execution of rights, and (4) the selection of personnel on the basis of qualifications rather than of birth or status.[59] Bureaucracy in this sense is found not only in government but also in business enterprise, in labor unions, in religious organizations, in educational institutions, in fraternal organizations—in brief, in all aspects of the mass society in which collective activity is required on a continuing basis. Bureaucracy is necessarily impersonal and requires the subordination of the individual to the organization. It produces "organization man,"[60] despite the fact that it also produces greater individual freedom. City life makes man relatively free from the constraints of tradition and opens wide avenues of choice in many realms, even while it may require conformity in some facets of existence as exemplified in "organization man." This is more an apparent than a real contradiction—for conformity in an organization touches only a single segment of the total human experience. Though conformity in some realms is stifling and may incite rebellion, it is nonetheless a necessary aspect of life in a mass society.

The development of the city has altered and produced forms of social stratification, both on a power and a prestige basis. The surplus making cities possible was at first controlled by the king and the priest or, as in Egypt, the two fused into one.[61] The military, an adjunct of the top administration, was closely associated with the elite and enjoyed the distinction of being part of the upper class. Workers, merchants, peasants, craftsmen, or slaves were subordinate and lower classes.

The rise of the commercial city greatly increased the importance of the merchants, who became an ever more powerful group. With the increasing size and power of the city, merchants displaced landlords not only in the power structure of the cities but increasingly in the power structure of larger entities, including nations as a whole. With the ascendancy of the industrial city, the industrialist, the financier, and the manager achieved positions of power arising from wealth and strategic location in the economy. Older sources of social stratification also persisted and the "upper" social strata, in varying degrees, included persons whose position was based on status, that is, birth or "social" honor, as well as on economic power.[62] The development of intellectual traditions, bolstered by the scientific revolution, provided high status to persons in intellectual and professional pursuits.

Contemporary Western society, therefore, tends to be stratified on three axes, power as achieved through wealth, status as achieved through birth, and prestige as achieved largely through intellectual and professional pursuits. The tremendous increase in mass levels of living, however, and the emergence of a large middle class which increasingly becomes a predominant proportion of the population tends, of course, to undermine existing systems of social stratification.

THE CITY GOVERNMENT[63]

We have noted that government in its earliest form in the city performed primarily the function of distributing the agricultural surplus which made aggregative living possible. Early government also embodied defense and police functions and, in collaboration with the religious hierarchy, played some role in respect to the welfare and spiritual life of the people.

The increasing size and density of population, the increasing interdependence of the social order, the breakdown of traditional social controls, and the inability of inherited social institutions to cope with the new problems of urban life have led inexorably to the manifold expansion of government functions and powers. This process is by no means yet completed. A few concrete examples may serve to clarify this point. There is certainly some relationship between the inability of the family as an inherited social institution to cope with the security problems posed by urban health hazards, industrial accidents, and unemployment and the development of government programs throughout the Western world such as the various public health services, workmen's compensation laws, and unemployment insurance benefits. Similarly, the creation of government agencies to regulate public utilities, stock exchanges, and the manufacture and distribution of food and drugs; and the provision by government of various services such as transportation, recreation, education, public housing, urban renewal, sewerage, water, solid waste disposal, and fire and police protection are additional examples of the expanded functions of government necessitated by increasing urbanization and industrialization.

The complex of technological, economic, and social changes which have been both antecedent to, and consequent upon, increasing urbanization not only profoundly affected the role of government but also political ideology. Significant changes in such ideology, dependent upon increasing size and density of population, are apparent in the history of the Western world. For example, the Constitution of the United States, which established the framework of the federal government, and, in the main, the constitutions of the individual states, which in turn created the local governments, were drawn in a preindustrial, rural setting. The political thought that dominated the minds of Americans in the critical period during which the federal government and many of the state and local governments were established was composed of many strains reflecting the transition of the political order from a feudal-autocratic to a liberal-democratic state. The great alterations which have occurred in the original governmental system established by the founding fathers, and which are still in process in the United States, may be interpreted as a consequence of the changes which have occurred in the size, distribution, and composition of the population.

At the risk of oversimplification it may be said that foremost in the concept of the role of government in the American political heritage, the product of a preurban world, is emphasis on the tenet that "that government is best which governs least." This doctrine, coupled with the liberal tradition in economic thinking, that each man acting in his own interest automatically acts in the interest of the larger whole, constitutes fundamentally the inherited framework of principles on the basis of which the founding fathers laid out American government. Yet, despite the dominance of these principles in the political philosophy of the United States, the record, reflecting the power of forces of social change, shows that the functions of American government on all levels have tremendously expanded and multiplied in the course of history; and that the expansion has been continuous without regard to the complexion of the political party in power.

Similar changes in the role of government, and ideology in respect to it, are evident in the history of the West, in general.[64] The issue of "big" versus "little" government is by no means yet resolved and constitutes a major source of cleavage in the world political scene as evident in the postures of the "communist" nations, on the one hand, and the "capitalist" nations, on the other. Moreover, there is, of course, considerable variation in practice both among capitalist and communist nations on the extent to which government actually regulates or operates economic and social affairs.[65]

Increasing size and density of population have also brought about great changes in the nature of representative government. Representative government in the Western world was, in general, an adaptation of the "democracy" of the Greek city-state. It is one thing, however, for a representative to speak for a small, homogeneous, rural, agricultural constituency, and quite another thing to "represent" a large heterogeneous population with diverse and often conflicting interests. The contemporary representative must determine for himself just whom he represents in his votes on specific issues, and he is almost mercilessly subjected to conflicting pressures and influences. The emergence of the public opinion poll may be regarded as an invention in the urban setting for the measurement of "the will" of the people. It may play an increasingly important role in representative government in the years to come.

Increasing urbanization has generated some of the foremost political issues of the time. First, the very role of government itself has become a major political issue. It constitutes undoubtedly the major point of cleavage between "conservatives" and "liberals" throughout the world. Then, too, specific issues, especially those involving increasing provision of welfare and security measures and increasing regulation of economic and social affairs, arise from conditions of urban living.

The complex and often technical character of urban problems has changed the requirements of "governing." In the urban setting, governmental problems grow increasingly technical and require professional attention. The "expert" has emerged as a new and powerful element in government, and "public administration" has become a profession. With the proliferation of government functions, government has become increasingly "bureaucratized," and because of its conspicuous role in mass society, government bureaucracy is frequently misinterpreted as the only form of bureaucracy in the contemporary order. Government bureaucracy, like other forms of bureaucracy, has become an indispensable tool in the functioning of the mass society.

Urban growth accompanied by increasing regional, national, and international interdependence has exerted new forces affecting the interrelations of central, regional, and local governments. In greatly decentralized systems such as in the United States, there has been a growing tendency to increase direct central-municipal governmental relationships. In greatly centralized systems such as in Latin America, there has been a tendency, however, for municipalities to seek greater autonomy.[66] It may be that increasing urbanization may produce convergence in present centralized and decentralized systems, respectively, in the interrelationship of central and local governments. Robson states that "the general tendency seems to be for the higher authorities to exercise, or at least to acquire, increasing powers of control over the great city."[67]

Accelerating urban growth has also placed great strains on local governmental structures throughout the world. The emergence of the twentieth-century metropolis has made obsolete many inherited forms of municipal government. The metropolitan area characterized by governmental fragmentation is experiencing increasing strain and conflict of various types.[68]

The combined trends of population concentration into metropolitan areas and decentralization within them have greatly altered intrametropolitan-area relationships. Population and community changes, along with economic and technological changes, have jurisdictionally separated place of residence and political responsibility, on the one hand, and place of work and economic responsibility, on the other. Moreover, they have also sometimes jurisdictionally separated both place of work and place of residence from place of shopping, place of recreation, or place of schooling. In consequence, great disparities have arisen among local jurisdictions within metropolitan areas between the need for urban services and the utilization of such services, and ability adequately to plan for, administer, and finance them.[69] The common explanation for these afflictions is to be found in the outmoded assumption, valid in the premetropolitan world, that the area of local governmental jurisdiction was simultaneously the area of residence, work, consumer expenditure, schooling, religious observance, and living in general. The differentiation of function and urbanism as a way of life exacerbate the frictions produced by the disparity between twentieth-century clumpings of people and economic activities and inherited local governmental structure.

One specific and serious source of difficulty arises from the pattern of intrametropolitan-area population distribution described above. The tendency for higher socioeconomic elements of the population to move outward in many Western cities has left central cities with increasingly larger proportions of population with relatively low socioeconomic status. Thus, central cities find they are confronted with a shrinking tax base even as their problems—physical, human, and governmental—become more severe, and even though they continue to provide indispensable services to the entire metropolitan complex.

Moreover, in many metropolitan areas throughout the world, municipal governments without suburban jurisdiction face acute problems in respect to the control of outlying land uses that affect the welfare and destiny of the central city.[70] Basic deficiencies of present metropolitan governmental organization are becoming ever more apparent, and proposals for changes in local governmental structure may be expected to increase.[71] This is manifested in increasing movements toward consolidation of local governments, in the creation of metropolitan-area agencies to perform specific functions, in the creation of metropolitan-area planning agencies and in the creation in Canada of the Toronto metropolitan governmental structure, which may serve as a prototype for other metropolitan areas.

Finally, rapid urbanization may create strains in the relative political power position of urban and rural population groupings. In some countries, as in the United States, urban populations may be underrepresented in government by reason of the failure of those political institutions to reflect the rapidly changing urban-rural population composition.[72] In other areas, as in parts of Asia and Latin America, rapidly growing urban centers, especially the capital cities, may exert disproportionate control over the entire nation by reason of their strategic location in the economy and government.[73]

Urbanization, then, has profoundly affected government as one form of social organization. It has greatly increased government interventionism, challenged traditional ideologies with respect to the role of government, modified the nature of representative government, introduced new substantive political issues, changed the character of public administration, altered central, regional, and local intergovernmental relationships, and made obsolete many local governmental structures. Rapid urbanization has also increasingly affected the political power position of urban and rural population groupings, respectively.

Finally, the impact of urbanization on the role of government is by no means restricted to national boundaries. Worldwide urbanization has produced increasing international interdependence which in turn is modifying the traditional concepts of "sovereignty" and "nationalism." The role of individual nations as members of the United Nations, and its specialized agencies, has certainly profoundly altered inherited concepts of both. The ever-shrinking world and manifestations of international order may also be viewed as constituting, in some measure, a consequence of world urbanization.

THE CITY AND POPULATION GROWTH

Increases in urban population are affected through three sources —natural increase, net migration, and reclassification. Natural increase is the excess of births over deaths. Net migration is the excess of in-migration over out-migration. Reclassification is the allocation of populations of places previously defined as "rural" to "urban" at that point at which the criterion for becoming "urban" is achieved. That is, in the statistics relating to rural-urban population, an appreciable proportion of the increase in urban population from census to census is the result of reclassification of population from rural to urban.

Adequate data are not available to trace the growth of the cities in terms of each of these components over long periods of time. It is probably true that the early neolithic village grew primarily as a result of natural increase up to the relatively low population ceiling imposed by its limited technology and social organization. The evidence indicates that the neolithic village, when it attained its population limit, generated another village through a process of fission.[74] That is, some considerable part of the original village migrated as a group to a favorable site for a new village.

As advancing technology and social organization permitted larger population agglomerations, in-migration must have increased in importance as a source of urban population growth. Certain it is that with the emergence of the large industrial and commercial city, the conditions of life producing relatively high mortality and relatively low fertility, in part as a result of selective male in-migration, must have made natural increase a relatively minor factor in urban growth. In contemporary developing nations, available data indicate that net migration is a very important source and, perhaps, for most nations the most important source of urban growth.[75] Under contemporary conditions, net migration, although consisting largely of rural to urban movement, includes for some nations relatively important components of net immigration, that is, migration from abroad. In six of ten Latin American countries for which estimates are available, for example, migration accounted for more than half of total urban growth over periods ranging roughly from 1930 to 1950 (Venezuela, Colombia, the Dominican Republic, Nicaragua, Paraguay, and El Salvador). In three additional countries, migration accounted for more than 40 per cent of total urban growth (Brazil, Chile, and Mexico).

In the history of the economically advanced countries, urban-rural differences in fertility and mortality have apparently been the rule, at least since the emergence of the industrial city.[76] Early industrial cities tended to have relatively high mortality induced by conditions of congestion, poor environmental sanitation and personal hygiene, and abysmally poor working conditions. In the United States the recorded mortality of urban population was much higher than that of the rural population throughout the nineteenth century.[77] Despite the limitations of the data, this urban-rural differential was probably real, for even in nineteenth-century America poor living conditions, lack of sanitation, and the high incidence of infectious diseases generated relatively high death rates.

In contrast with mortality, fertility apparently was lower in urban than in rural areas in the early city.[78] Selective migration brought disproportionately large numbers of men into the cities, contributing to low urban fertility. Infectious and debilitating diseases contributing to high mortality also played some role in restricting the birth rate. In the United States differences in urban and rural fertility have been evident throughout the history of the nation.

The unsatisfactory character of the data does not permit accurate evaluation of the roles of net migration and natural increase, respectively, to urban growth over the years. In the United States vital statistics do not permit satisfactory allocation of urban and rural births and deaths. It is possible, however, to evaluate the respective roles of natural increase and net migration in the recent growth of metropolitan areas in the United States. Between 1950 and 1960, the Bureau of the Census has estimated that of the total increase of 23.2 million persons in "metropolitan state economic areas," 15.1 million was the result of natural increase and 8.1 million the result of net migration.[79] It is to be borne in mind, however, that between 1950 and 1960 the birth rate of the United States was still relatively high as a result of the postwar boom in marriages and babies. In contrast, the increase of 4.7 million in "non-metropolitan state economic areas" was made up of the natural increase of 10.2 million persons and a net out-migration of 5.5 million persons.

In contemporary underdeveloped areas, fertility in both rural and urban communities is generally high with indications that there is no uniformity in such differentials that can be measured. Robinson found in his analyses of selected non-Western countries that urban fertility was below rural in about half the cases, whereas in the remaining countries there was no apparent difference or urban fertility appeared to be higher than rural.[80] Moreover, he demonstrates that the apparent urban-rural differences in fertility as measured by fertility ratios (a ratio of children under five to women of childbearing age as reported in a census) are mainly the result of differences in infant mortality.

In underdeveloped areas in Asia and the Far East, evidence indicates that the death rates of the population in general, and particularly of infants, appears to be higher in cities than in rural areas, but the evidence is neither clear nor consistent. In the five countries in Latin America for which mortality data are reasonably good, infant mortality is lower in urban than in the rural areas. It is difficult to draw a firm conclusion about urban-rural differences in general mortality in the developing regions.[81]

The experience of the economically advanced nations does permit some firm conclusions with respect to the impact of their urbanization on fertility and mortality trends. With respect to mortality it is clear that in the Western nations a combination of factors, including improved environmental sanitation, personal hygiene and modern medicine, including the antibiotics and the insecticides, is operating to effect convergence in urban and rural mortality rates at low levels.

It is also clear in the experience of the West that great declines in fertility were first evident in urban areas.[82] With the emergence of urbanism as a way of life, rational decision-making was extended to size of family, and fertility was deliberately controlled by urban populations. Within urban areas, family planning originated among the elite, better-educated, and higher-income groups, and then diffused to the remainder of the population. This process is by no means yet completed. The poor and uneducated even in urban areas are not yet controlling their fertility. Although it is true that birth rates have gone up in urban even more than in rural areas with fluctuations in fertility, the general pattern of lower urban than rural fertility is ubiquitous and persistent. It is also clear in the more economically advanced nations that family planning has spread from urban to rural areas and that rural fertility is now also experiencing a great decline. There is some evidence, at least in the United States, of convergence in urban and rural fertility, although the data are far from adequate and conclusive.

The emergence of the city was, in some measure, a function of rapid population growth to which it in turn also contributed. In the West, the city in due course has become the point of origin and diffusion of fertility control. The city in the advanced areas increasingly holds forth the prospect of deliberate control of population growth. Up to the present time, however, the city in the underdeveloped areas has given little evidence of playing a similar role. But the concerted efforts under way on an ever greater scale to induce fertility control may eventually achieve their objective. It may be anticipated that major successes in regulation of family size will first occur in the urban rather than the rural population in the developing areas.

Urbanization in Advanced and Developing Nations

The foregoing consideration of the consequences of urbanization necessarily is based primarily on the observed and hypothesized experience of the economically advanced nations. Although there are many similarities with respect to urbanization in the advanced nations and the present developing areas, there are also important differences.[83] The differences merit attention for at least two reasons. First, they demonstrate that it may be hazardous to assume that all of the patterns of urbanization observed in the past in the advanced areas will necessarily apply in the future to the developing regions; second, critical examination of the process and impact of urbanization in the developing areas may provide a basis for testing the generalizations and the hypotheses in respect of urbanization derived from the experience of the West. Urbanization in the developing regions of the world provides an opportunity for significant research which not only may help to explain the process and its consequences in specific underdeveloped regions but also may shed light on the antecedents and consequences of urbanization in the West.

Among the differences between urbanization in the advanced areas and in the developing regions are: (1) differences in the world political situation at the present time as compared with that prevalent when the advanced nations first experienced rapid urbanization; (2) differences in the forces making for urbanization; (3) differences in the ratio of population to resources and levels of living; (4) differences in basic outlook and value systems.

THE WORLD POLITICAL SITUATION

There can be little doubt that the differences in the world political situation today, as contrasted with that in the eighteenth and nineteenth centuries, are influencing the course of urbanization in the developing regions. The world since the Second World War is characterized by an unprecedented degree of international organization. The presence of the United Nations, its international agencies and various forms of regional organization, is providing the developing areas with stimulation and assistance in economic growth and urbanization. The international organizations have contributed materially to the "revolution of rising expectations" which has led virtually all peoples on the face of the earth to aspire to higher levels of living and political independence if not yet achieved. A number of the international organizations have specific programs designed to deal with problems of urbanization as well as economic development in general.[84] Moreover, technical assistance is also being provided bilaterally by governments and various private organizations. Such technical assistance through bilateral arrangements is stimulated by the polarization of world politics. As a result of these influences it seems reasonable to anticipate that the pace of urbanization may be accelerated for the underdeveloped areas and that both the antecedents and the consequences of urbanization may differ from those observed in the past.

FORCES OF URBANIZATION

Several other forces also are operating to effect differences in urbanization among the present developing nations from that observed in the past in the economically advanced areas. For one thing, partly as a result of the changed world political framework, it may be anticipated that central planning will play a much more prominent role in urbanization than it previously did. In the present advanced nations industrialization, urbanization, and economic development in general are largely the product of market forces through which differentiation of function, spatial arrangement, resource allocation, and economic growth were largely achieved. It may be argued that rapid industrialization and urbanization and attendant higher levels of living were experienced by the economically advanced nations despite the fact that the interplay of factors most conducive to efficient and balanced development and orderly urbanization were far from fully understood. In increasing the mix of government interventionism and central planning in the urbanization of the present developing areas, it is possible that many of the problems of Western urbanization may be avoided or ameliorated. But it is also possible that new and equally difficult types of problems will be encountered. In the developing nations there is a great need for a full understanding of the forces making for economic growth and urbanization to provide a sound basis for policy and action. That is, there is greater need for knowledge among the underdeveloped areas today than there ever was in the early stages of urbanization in the present advanced nations. In the absence of such knowledge there is danger of effecting serious diseconomies in planning urbanization. Certainly, what little is known of the experience of countries which have employed central planning indicates that it is by no means free of serious economic, social, and political problems.[85] In any case, although planning was definitely a factor in development in many parts of the West, the increased use of central planning in the developing areas is also likely to contribute to different patterns of urbanization than that observed in the West.

Differences in the urbanization of the present developing areas may arise also from their colonial heritage. In many of the countries in Asia, Latin America, and Africa, cities are more the product of colonial experience—that is, the result of exogenous factors—than indigenous economic development. Many of the underdeveloped nations have but one major city, "the primate city," which dominates the urban situation. The "great city" is often five to ten times as large as the next largest city, and the urban population in general does not portray the same "system" as observed in Western development.

The primate city generally owes its origin and growth largely to its function as an *entrepôt* between the colony and the imperial country. It owed its growth and development to its role in an imperial system rather than to indigenous national economic growth. With the disruption of empire many of the cities in the economically underdeveloped areas experienced some loss of basic economic function. To the extent that this has occurred, such cities must await further national economic growth adequately to support their present size. As a result, many of the underdeveloped countries may have larger urban populations than is justified by their degree of industrialization and economic development by the standards observed in the development of cities in the West.

The position that underdeveloped areas are in this sense "overurbanized" has been challenged, among others by N. V. Sovani.[86] He also marshals data which tend to refute the contention that rural "push" is a major factor in urban growth in developing areas. It is clear, nevertheless, that urbanization in the developing areas has not been associated with dramatic increases in levels of living as in the West, where the city was a consequent of, and antecedent to, increased productivity.

Another force making for differences in urbanization between the present advanced and economically developing areas is found in the fact that the developing regions now have available to them twentieth-century technology. In the developing regions, the entire complex of twentieth-century technology, including electric power, the automobile, and the telephone, is available for effecting and influencing urban growth. In consequence, developing cities today, by diffusion from the West simultaneously, rather than sequentially, can experience the centrifugal and centripetal forces, respectively, generated by changing technology. Both general and specific forms of spatial arrangements of plant and population, therefore, may vary considerably from that observed in the past. A technological factor that may impede urban development in present developing areas is to be found in their relatively primitive state of agricultural technology. Agricultural technology in the West at the beginning of its rapid industrial development was in a more advanced state than in the underdeveloped areas today, and improving agricultural technology along with more plentiful land undoubtedly contributed to industrialization in the West by providing increased income and, therefore, savings for industrial investment.[87]

The accelerated growth of many of the cities in the underdeveloped areas since the end of the Second World War may also be regarded, in part, as the result of their colonial heritage. Disorganization occasioned by the war and postwar developments generated social unrest and political instability which have contributed to large refugee populations flooding the cities. Accelerating urban growth in many of the underdeveloped areas therefore is not so much the product of economic development and the pull of population into cities from rural areas but rather is the result of the push of population from troubled and insecure rural areas. The push is further augmented by accelerating total population growth, discussed further below.

POPULATION AND RESOURCES

The third factor which may account for differences in urbanization in the developing areas from that observed in the past is to be found in differences in the ratio of population to resources. In most of the developing areas today the ratio of population to resources is much higher than that which prevailed at the beginning of the industrialization and urbanization of the West. Population was relatively sparse in relation to resources at the outset of Western industrialization and urbanization. Moreover, as the demographic revolution advanced with increased industrialization and urbanization in the West, such surplus populations as were generated were free to migrate to the vast unexploited and relatively uninhabited continents of the Western Hemisphere and Oceania. In contrast, many of the developing areas today are already characterized by a very high ratio of population to land and other resources. Moreover, they are experiencing a more rapid decline in mortality than was ever experienced in the Western world and consequently more rapid rates of population increase.[88] Much of urban growth in the developing areas today is in fact the result of the push of population from the already overpopulated rural countryside. Moreover, in the contemporary world there are no uninhabited lands to which overpopulated nations may send their surplus peoples. The problem of effecting economic exchange between urban and rural populations is therefore more difficult and poses serious political as well as economic problems.[89]

BASIC OUTLOOK

Finally, a fourth factor which may differentially affect patterns of urbanization is to be found in the differences between the West and the developing areas in basic outlook and value system. The differences in outlook and values are exemplified in the differences between the "Protestant ethic," on one hand, and Hindu, Buddhist, and Islamic traditions on the other. Some scholars have taken the position that a prerequisite to Western economic development producing urbanization was the value system of the West as exemplified in the Protestant ethic.[90] This outlook has been characterized as rational rather than traditional and as involving a willingness and ability to defer immediate gratifications for more desirable later ones. It places emphasis on achievement and success as distinguished from status and prestige, the cosmopolitan as distinguished from the parochial, and the material as distinguished from the spiritual. It embraces interrelationships that are impersonal and utilitarian as distinguished from personal and sentimental. It is a moot question, however, whether the Western outlook so characterized is an antecedent or consequent of urbanization or something of both. It is also a moot question as to whether this outlook or elements of it really are essential ingredients of economic development and urbanization.[91] Conceivably, the differences between outlook in the advanced and developing areas may produce different types of urbanization. It is also conceivable that much of what has been written on the subject is a product of generalizations based solely on Western experience and is therefore subject to the limitations of historicism.

SOME DIFFERENCES IN CONSEQUENCES

Perhaps, by reason of the types of differences indicated, both the processes and consequences of urbanization in the developing areas may differ from those in the advanced areas of the world. For example, the physical patterning of the large city in the underdeveloped areas tends to differ appreciably from that of cities in the economically advanced nations. Although many of the cities in the developing areas have central cores resembling the structure of Western cities (as part of the colonial heritage), such cores are usually surrounded by vast populations living in "native quarters." Thus cities in the underdeveloped areas tend to have a dual form of structure. There is some tendency for lower-income groups to live toward the central area with higher-income groups living toward the periphery within their Westernized cores. But surrounding the entire central core are the native quarters containing the poorest and newest in-migrants. Thus the large city in the developing area may portray a pattern of population distribution within its central core of a type similar to that found in the United States; but it may also resemble the structure of the medieval and ancient city in that the poorest and newest in-migrants are likely to be found on the periphery of the total agglomeration.[92] Similarly, the differences in levels of living between cities in the developed and developing areas may be traced to the differences between them in the forces making for urbanization. Kuznets has demonstrated that the levels of living in the economically advanced areas were higher at their point of take-off in economic development than is prevalent in the underdeveloped regions today.[93] This situation, coupled with the fact that urban growth in the developing areas may be more the result of the push of population from the impoverished countryside than the pull of population to urban areas by reason of greater economic opportunity and productivity,[94] may help to account for the relatively low level of living found in urban places in the underdeveloped nations.

Similarly, the differences in economic organization and the extent to which urbanism as a way of life prevails may be traced to differences in forces making for urbanization in the developed as contrasted with the developing areas. In the developing areas, large population agglomerations are largely the product of agglutination, that is, the compressing into physical proximity of what remain essentially discrete population groupings. Under such circumstances, large population size does not necessarily lead to greatly increased division of labor, specialization, and its concomitants leading to increased productivity per capita and more complex economic organization. Similarly, the agglutinated character of the population agglomeration in developing areas may account for the absence of more manifestations of urbanism as a way of life. Although the cities in the developing areas have large size, high density, and often heterogeneous populations, they do not portray the consequences of urbanization in the transformation of human nature, social organization, and government as observed in the West. The explanation for this phenomenon may lie in Durkheim's consideration of "moral density," that is, in the absence of interaction and intercommunication between the diverse elements of the urban population.[95] . . .

---

[1]Otis Dudley Duncan, "Human Ecology and Population Studies," in Philip M. Hauser and Otis Dudley Duncan (Eds.), *The Study of Population: An Inventory and Appraisal* (Chicago: University of Chicago Press, 1959), pp. 681ff.

[2]Ralph Turner, *The Great Cultural Traditions,* Vol. I, *The Ancient Cities* (New York: McGraw-Hill, 1941), pp. 126ff.

[3]*Ibid.,* Vol. II, *The Classical Empires,* pp. 856ff.

[4]Fred Cottrell, *Energy and Society* (New York: McGraw-Hill, 1955).

[5]For example, Ralph Turner, *op. cit.,* Vols. I, II; V. Gordon Childe, *Man Makes Himself* (London: Watts, 1941), Chaps. 5–6; *What Happened in History* (London: Penguin Books, 1946), Chaps. 3–4; Robert J. Braidwood and Gordon R. Willey (Eds.), *Courses Toward Urban Life* (Chicago: Aldine, 1962); N. S. B. Gras, *An Introduction to Economic History* (New York: Harper, 1922); Lewis Mumford, *The City in History* (New York: Harcourt, Brace & World, 1961).

[6]N. S. B. Gras, *op. cit.*

[7]Eric E. Lampard, "The History of Cities in the Economically Advanced Areas," *Economic Development and Cultural Change,* 3 (January 1955), pp. 103–104.

[14]United Nations, *Determinants and Consequences of Population Trends* (New York: United Nations, 1953), Chap. 2.

[15]Kingsley Davis, "The Origin and Growth of Urbanization in the World," *American Journal of Sociology* (special issue on "World Urbanism" edited by Philip M. Hauser), 60 (March 1955), p. 433.

[16]J. Fletcher Wellemeyer (in consultation with Frank Lorimer), "Appendix," *Population Bulletin,* 18 (February 1962), p. 19.

[17]Ralph Turner, *op. cit.,* Vol. I, pp. 51ff.

[18]Gideon Sjoberg, *The Pre-Industrial City* (Glencoe, Ill.: Free Press, 1960), pp. 80–81.

[19]Kingsley Davis, *op. ct.,* pp. 429–437.

[20]Statistics related to the United States are drawn from publications of the U. S. Bureau of the Census unless otherwise indicated. The historical data are drawn largely from: U. S. Bureau of the Census, *Historical Statistics of the United States, Colonial Times to 1957* (Washington, D. C.: U. S. Government Printing Office, 1960); and U. S. Bureau of the Census, *Statistical Abstract of the United States,* issued annually. Other data are drawn mainly from decennial census volumes. To save space and repetition, specific references to the census publications are not given.

[21]Louis Wirth, *Community Life and Social Policy* (Chicago: University of Chicago Press, 1956), pp. 110–132.

[22]Hope Tisdale Eldridge, "The Process of Urbanization," in J. J. Spengler and O. D. Duncan (Eds.), *Demographic Analysis* (Glencoe, Ill.: Free Press, 1956), pp. 338–343.

[23]United Nations, *Demographic Yearbook* (New York: United Nations, 1955), p. 16.

[24]U. S. Bureau of the Census, *U. S. Census of Population: 1960,* Vol. I, *Characteristics of the Population,* Part A, "Number of Inhabitants" (Washington: U. S. Government Printing Office), pp. XIV–XXVII.

[25]Jean Gottmann, *Virginia at Mid-Century* (New York: Holt, 1955), pp. 41, 174, 472–479; also, *Megalopolis–The Urbanized Northeastern Seaboard of the United States* (New York: Twentieth Century Fund, 1961).

[26]International Urban Research, *The World's Metropolitan Areas* (Berkeley: University of California Press, 1959), pp. 6–33.

[27]Joyce O. Hertzler, *The Social Thought of the Ancient Civilizations* (New York: McGraw-Hill, 1936), pp. 298ff., 350.

[29]Emile Durkheim, *L'annee Sociologique,* Vol. II, 1897–1898.

[30]Adapted from Amos H. Hawley, *Human Ecology* (New York: Ronald Press, 1950), pp. 100ff.

[41]Ralph Turner, *op. cit,* Vol. I, pp. 277ff.

[42]Gideon Sjoberg, *op. cit.,* pp. 187ff.

[43]N. S. B. Gras, *op. cit.;* Edgar M. Hoover and Raymond Vernon, *Anatomy of a Metropolis* (Cambridge: Harvard University Press, 1959).

[44]Louis Wirth, *op. cit.,* pp. 117ff.

[45]Charles Horton Cooley, *Social Organization* (New York: Scribner, 1925), Chap. 3; Louis Wirth, *op. cit.,* pp. 118ff.

[46]For example, Bureau of Social Affairs, United Nations, "Urbanization and Crime and Delinquency in Asia and the Far East," in Philip M. Hauser (Ed.), *Urbanization in Asia and the Far East* (Calcutta: UNESCO, 1957), Chap. 9; Philip M. Hauser (Ed.), *Urbanization in Latin America* (Paris: UNESCO, 1961), especially "Migration and Urbanization—The Barriadas of Lima: An Example of Integration into Urban Life," Chap. 6; Andrew Pearse, "Some Characteristics of Urbanization in the City of Rio de Janeiro," Chap. 7; Gino Germani, "Inquiry into the Social Effects of Urbanization in a Working Class Sector of Greater Buenos Aires," Chap. 8; J. R. B. Lopes, "Aspects of the Adjustment of Rural Migrants to Urban-Industrial Conditions in Sao Paulo, Brazil," Chap. 9; H. Rotando, "Psychological and Mental Health Problems of Urbanization Based on Case Studies in Peru," Chap. 10; UNESCO, *The Social Implications of Industrialization and Urbanization—Five Studies in Asia* (Calcutta: UNESCO, 1956); UNESCO, *Social Implications of Industrialization and Urbanization in Africa South of the Sahara* (Paris: UNESCO, 1956).

[47]Philip M. Hauser, *Population Perspectives* (New Brunswick, N. J.: Rutgers University Press, 1960), pp. 120ff.; Oscar Handlin, *The Uprooted* (Boston: Little, Brown, 1951), and *The Newcomers* (Cambridge: Harvard University Press, 1959); Otis Dudley Duncan and Beverly Duncan, *The Negro Population of Chicago* (Chicago: University of Chicago Press, 1957).

[48]Philip M. Hauser, *op. cit.,* pp. 149ff.

[49]Robert Redfield, "The Folk Society," *American Journal of Sociology, 52* (January 1947), pp. 293–308; Louis Wirth, *op. cit.,* pp. 110–132.

[51]Oscar Lewis, *Life in a Mexican Village: Tepotzlan Restudied* (Urbana: University of Illinois Press, 1951); Edward M. Bruner, "Urbanization and Culture Change: Indonesia" (paper read at the 58th Annual Meeting of the American Anthropological Association, Mexico City, December 28, 1959); Douglas S. Butterworth, "A Study of the Urbanization Process Among Mixtec Migrants from Tilantongo in Mexico City," *America Indigena,* 22 (July 1962), pp. 257–274; Theodore Caplow, "The Social Ecology of Guatemala City," *Social Forces,* 28 (December 1949), pp. 113–135; William L. Kolb, "The Social Structure and Function of Cities," *Economic Development and Cultural Change,* 3 (October 1954), pp. 30–46; O. D. Duncan and Albert J. Reiss, Jr., *Social Characteristics of Urban and Rural Communities, 1950* (New York: Wiley, 1956); Herbert J. Gans, *The Urban Villagers: Group and Class in the Life of Italian-Americans* (Glencoe, Ill.: Free Press, 1962); *A Social*

Profile of Detroit, 1955 (Ann Arbor: Department of Sociology and Survey Research Center, University of Michigan, 1956).

[52]Bert F. Hoselitz, "A Survey of the Literature on Urbanization in India," in Roy Turner (Ed.), *India's Urban Future* (Berkeley: University of California Press, 1962), p. 427.

[53]Emile Durkheim, *On the Division of Labor in Society,* trans. by George Simpson (New York: Macmillan, 1933), Book I, Chaps. 2 and 3.

[54]William F. Ogburn (with the assistance of Clark Tibbitts), "The Family and Its Functions," Report of the President's Research Committee on Social Trends, *Recent Social Trends* (New York: McGraw-Hill, 1933), Vol. I, pp. 661–708.

[55]*Ibid.,* pp., 662ff.

[56]Arthur W. Calhoun, *A Social History of the American Family* (Cleveland: Clark, 1919), Vol. III, pp. 169ff.; William J. Goode, *World Revolution and Family Patterns* (New York: Free Press of Glencoe, 1963), pp. 128–129.

[57]*A Social Profile of Detroit, 1955, op. cit.;* Herbert J. Gans, *op. cit.,* Chap. 3.

[58]William Graham Sumner, *Folkways* (Boston: Ginn, 1907), p. 54.

[59]*From Max Weber: Essays in Sociology,* trans. and ed. by H. H. Gerth and C. Wright Mills (New York: Oxford University Press, 1946), pp. 196ff.

[60]William H. Whyte, *The Organization Man* (New York: Doubleday, 1957).

[61]Ralph Turner, *op. cit.,* Vol. I, p. 182.

[62]Max Weber, *op. cit.,* pp. 180ff.

[63]Adapted from Philip M. Hauser, *On the Impact of Population and Community Changes on Local Government,* Seventh Annual Wherrett Lecture on Local Government (Pittsburgh: Institute of Local Government, University of Pittsburgh, 1961), pp. 19ff. A major treatment of problems of government in great cities in the world is given in William A. Robson (Ed.), *Great Cities of the World, Their Government, Politics and Planning,* 2nd ed. (New York: Macmillan, 1957).

[64]Karl Polanyi, *The Great Transformation* (New York: Farrar and Rinehart, 1944); Gunnar Myrdal, *Beyond the Welfare State* (New Haven: Yale University Press, 1960).

[65]In general, political science and comparative government textbooks and treatises have treated this problem only tangentially. For a discussion bearing directly on this point, see D. W. Brogan and Douglas V. Verney, *Political Patterns in Today's World* (New York: Harcourt, Brace & World, 1963), Chaps. 4 and 9. Also useful: Taylor Cole, *European Political Systems* (New York: Knopf, 1959), Chaps. 5 and 6.

[66]Morton Grodzins, "The Federal System," *Goals for Americans* (President's Commission on National Goals), 1960, pp. 265–284. Wallace S. Sayre, "Cities and the State" and "State-City Government Relations," *Final Report* (New York State-New York City Fiscal Relations Committee, November 1956), pp. 55–65, 281–288. J. Medina Echavarria and Philip M. Hauser, "Rapporteurs' Report," in Philip M. Hauser (Ed.), *Urbanization in Latin America* (Paris: UNESCO, 1961), pp. 70ff.

[67]William A. Robson, *op. cit.,* p. 79.

[68]*Ibid.,* pp. 55–71.

[69]*Ibid.,* pp. 83–87; C. E. Merriam, A. Lepawsky, and S. Parratt, *The Government of Metropolitan Chicago* (Chicago: University of Chicago Press, 1933); Victor Jones, *Metropolitan Government* (Chicago: University of Chicago Press, 1942); Douglas Price, *The Metropolis and Its Problems* (Syracuse: Syracuse University Press, 1960); Paul Studenski, *The Government of Metropolitan Areas in the United States* (New York: National Municipal League, 1930).

[70]J. Medina Echavarria and Philip M. Hauser, *op. cit.,* p. 60; Bureau of Social Affairs, United Nations, "Some Policy Implications of Urbanization," *op. cit.,* pp. 319ff.

[71]William A. Robson, *op. cit.,* pp. 98–105.

[72]*Ibid.,* p. 78; Paul T. David and Ralph Eisenberg, *Devaluation of the Urban and Suburban Vote* (Charlottesville: University of Virginia Press, 1961), p. 9; Andrew Hacker, *Congressional Districting* (Washington, D. C.: The Brookings Institution, 1963), p. 84; Gordon Baker, *Rural vs. Urban Political Power* (New York:

Doubleday, 1955); The Commission on Intergovernmental Relations, *A Report to the President for Transmittal to Congress* (June 1955), pp. 40, 102–103.

[73]Bureau of Social Affairs, United Nations, *op. cit.,* p. 305.

[74]V. Gordon Childe, "The Urban Revolution," *Town Planning Review,* 21 (April 1950), p. 5.

[75]Population Branch, United Nations, "Demographic Aspects of Urbanization in Latin America," in Philip M. Hauser (Ed.), *Urbanization in Latin America* (Paris: UNESCO, 1961), p. 110.

[76]John Graunt, *Natural and Political Observations . . . Made Upon the Bills of Mortality* (American edition: Baltimore: Johns Hopkins Press, 1939), pp. 41–42; Frank Lorimer, "The Development of Demography," in Philip M. Hauser and Otis Dudley Duncan (Eds.), *The Study of Population* (Chicago: University of Chicago Press, 1959), pp. 155ff.

[77]Conrad Taeuber and Irene B. Taeuber, *The Changing Population of the United States* (New York: Wiley, 1958), pp. 269ff.

[78]John Graunt, *op. cit.,* pp. 52ff.; Louis I. Dublin, Alfred J. Lotka, and Mortimer Spiegelman, *Length of Life* (New York: Ronald Press, 1949), Chap. 4.

[79]U. S. Bureau of the Census, "Components of Population Change, 1950 to 1960, for Counties, Standard Metropolitan Statistical Areas, State Economic Areas and Economic Subregions," *Current Population Reports,* Series P23-7 (November 1962), p. 85.

[80]Warren G. Robinson, "Urbanization and Fertility: The Non-Western Experience," *The Milbank Memorial Fund Quarterly,* 41 (July 1963), pp. 291–308.

[81]Population Branch, United Nations, "Demographic Aspects of Urbanization in the ECAFE Region," in Philip M. Hauser (Ed.), *Urbanization in Asia and the Far East* (Calcutta: UNESCO, 1957), pp. 116ff., 111ff.; "Demographic Aspects of Urbanization in Latin America," in Philip M. Hauser (Ed.), *Urbanization in Latin America* (Paris: UNESCO, 1961), pp. 102ff., 106–107.

[82]United Nations, *Determinants and Consequences of Population Trends* (New York: United Nations, 1953), pp. 78ff.

[83]Adapted and elaborated from Philip M. Hauser, "World and Asian Urbanization in Relation to Economic Development and Social Change," in Philip M. Hauser (Ed.), *Urbanization in Asia and the Far East* (Calcutta: UNESCO, 1957), pp. 86ff.

[84]They include the United Nations, UNESCO, ILO, and WHO. The seminars on urbanization in Latin America, Asia, and the Far East and other activities have been cooperative enterprises by these agencies.

[85]United Nations, *Processes and Problems of Industrialization in Underdeveloped Countries* (New York: United Nations, 1955), pp. 71ff.; ECAFE, "Economic Development Policies in Relation to Types, Scale and Location of Industries, as a Factor Likely to Influence Urbanization Trends in ECAFE Countries, Joint UN/UNESCO Seminar on Urbanization in the ECAFE Region," in Philip M. Hauser (Ed.), *Urbanization in Asia and the Far East* (Calcutta: UNESCO, 1957), pp. 163–178.

[86]N. V. Sovani, "The Analysis of 'Over-Urbanization,'" *Economic Development and Cultural Change,* 12 (January 1964), pp. 113–122.

[87]Simon Kuznets, "Quantitative Aspects of the Economic Growth of Nations–II, Industrial Distribution of National Product and Labor Force," *Economic Development and Cultural Change,* Supp. to Vol. 5 (July 1957), pp. 52ff.

[88]Harold Dorn, "World Population Growth," in Philip M. Hauser (Ed.), *The Population Dilemma* (Englewood Cliffs, N. J.: Prentice-Hall, 1963), pp. 8ff.

[89]Nathan Keyfitz, *loc. cit.*

[90]Max Weber, *The Protestant Ethic and the Spirit of Capitalism* (London: Allen and Unwin, 1930).

[91]Philip M. Hauser, "World and Asian Urbanization . . . ," *op. cit.,* pp. 91–92.

[92]Richard W. Redick, "A Demographic and Ecological Study of Rangoon, Burma: 1953" (unpublished Ph.D. dissertation, Department of Sociology, University of

Chicago, 1961); Paul Cressey, "The Ecological Organization of Rangoon, Burma," *Sociology and Social Research,* 40 (January 1956), pp. 166–169.

[93]Simon Kuznets, *Six Lectures on Economic Growth* (Glencoe, Ill.: Free Press, 1959), pp. 23–28.

[94]Philip M. Hauser, "Summary Report of the General Rapporteur," *Urbanization in Asia and the Far East, op. cit.,* pp. 6–10; J. Medina Echavarria and Philip M. Hauser, "Rapporteurs' Report, *Urbanization in Latin America, op. cit.,* pp. 55–56.

[95]Emile Durkheim, *op. cit.,* Book II, Chap. 2.

8. The Urbanization of the Human Population

KINGSLEY DAVIS

Urbanized societies, in which a majority of the people live crowded together in towns and cities, represent a new and fundamental step in man's social evolution. Although cities themselves first appeared some 5,500 years ago, they were small and surrounded by an overwhelming majority of rural people; moreover, they relapsed easily to village or small-town status. The urbanized societies of today, in contrast, not only have urban agglomerations of a size never before attained but also have a high proportion of their population concentrated in such agglomerations. In 1960, for example, nearly 52 million Americans lived in only 16 urbanized areas. Together these areas covered less land than one of the smaller counties (Cochise) of Arizona. According to one definition used by the U.S. Bureau of the Census, 96 million people—53 percent of the nation's population—were concentrated in 213 urbanized areas that together occupied only .7 percent of the nation's land. Another definition used by the bureau puts the urban population at about 70 percent. The large and dense agglomerations comprising the urban population involve a degree of human contact and of social complexity never before known. They exceed in size the communities of any other large animal; they suggest the behavior of communal insects rather than of mammals.

Neither the recency nor the speed of this evolutionary development is widely appreciated. Before 1850 no society could be described as predominantly urbanized, and by 1900 only one—Great Britain—could be so regarded. Today, only 65 years later, all industrial nations

---

SOURCE: Reprinted with permission.

are highly urbanized, and in the world as a whole the process of urbanization is accelerating rapidly.

Some years ago my associates and I at Columbia University undertook to document the progress of urbanization by compiling data on the world's cities and the proportion of human beings living in them; in recent years the work has been continued in our center—International Population and Urban Research—at the University of California at Berkeley. The data obtained in these investigations are reflected . . . in terms of one index of urbanization: the proportion of the population living in cities of 100,000 or larger. Statistics of this kind are only approximations of reality, but they are accurate enough to demonstrate how urbanization has accelerated. Between 1850 and 1950 the index changed at a much higher rate than from 1800 to 1850, but the rate of change from 1950 to 1960 was twice that of the preceding 50 years! If the pace of increase that obtained between 1950 and 1960 were to remain the same, by 1990 the fraction of the world's people living in cities of 100,000 or larger would be more than half. Using another index of urbanization—the proportion of the world's population living in urban places of all sizes—we found that by 1960 the figure had already reached 33 percent.

Clearly the world as a whole is not fully urbanized, but it soon will be. This change in human life is so recent that even the most urbanized countries still exhibit the rural origins of their institutions. Its full implications for man's organic and social evolution can only be surmised.

In discussing the trend—and its implications insofar as they can be perceived—I shall use the term "urbanization" in a particular way. It refers here to the proportion of the total population concentrated in urban settlements, or else to a rise in this proportion. A common mistake is to think of urbanization as simply the growth of cities. Since the total population is composed of both the urban population and the rural, however, the "proportion urban" is a function of both of them. Accordingly cities can grow without any urbanization, provided that the rural population grows at an equal or a greater rate.

Historically urbanization and the growth of cities have occurred together, which accounts for the confusion. As the reader will soon see, it is necessary to distinguish the two trends. In the most advanced countries today, for example, urban populations are still growing, but their proportion of the total population is tending to remain stable or to diminish. In other words, the process of urbanization—the switch from a spread-out pattern of human settlement to one of concentration in urban centers—is a change that has a beginning and an end, but the growth of cities has no inherent limit. Such growth could continue even after everyone was living in cities, through sheer excess of births over deaths.

The difference between a rural village and an urban community is of course one of degree; a precise operational distinction is somewhat arbitrary, and it varies from one nation to another. Since data are available for communities of various sizes, a dividing line can be chosen at will. One convenient index of urbanization, for example, is the proportion of people living in places of 100,000 or more. In the following analysis I shall depend on two indexes: the one just mentioned and the proportion of population classed as "urban" in the official statistics of each country. In practice the two indexes are highly correlated; therefore either one can be used as an index of urbanization.

Actually the hardest problem is not that of determining the "floor" of the urban category but of ascertaining the boundary of places that are clearly urban by any definition. How far east is the boundary of Los Angeles? Where along the Hooghly River does Calcutta leave off and the countryside begin? In the past the population of cities and towns has usually been given as the number of people living within the political boundaries. Thus the population of New York is frequently given as around eight million, this being the population of the city proper. The error in such a figure was not large before World War I, but since then, particularly in the advanced countries, urban populations have been spilling over the narrow political boundaries at a tremendous rate. In 1960 the New York–Northeastern New Jersey urbanized area, as delineated by the Bureau of the Census, had more than 14 million people. That delineation showed it to be the largest city in the world and nearly twice as large as New York City proper.

As a result of the outward spread of urbanites, counts made on the basis of political boundaries alone underestimate the city populations and exaggerate the rural. For this reason our office delineated the metropolitan areas of as many countries as possible for dates around 1950. These areas included the central, or political, cities and the zones around them that are receiving the spillover.

This reassessment raised the estimated proportion of the world's population in cities of 100,000 or larger from 15.1 percent to 16.7 percent. As of 1960 we have used wherever possible the "urban agglomeration" data now furnished to the United Nations by many countries. The U.S., for example, provides data for "urbanized areas," meaning cities of 50,000 or larger and the built-up agglomerations around them.

* * *

It is curious that thousands of years elapsed between the first appearance of small cities and the emergence of urbanized societies in the 19th century. It is also curious that the region where urbanized societies arose—northwestern Europe—was not the one that had given rise to the major cities of the past; on the contrary, it was a region where urbanization had been at an extremely low ebb. Indeed, the societies of northwestern Europe in medieval times were so rural that it is hard for modern minds to comprehend them. Perhaps it was the nonurban character of these societies that erased the parasitic nature of towns and eventually provided a new basis for a revolutionary degree of urbanization.

At any rate, two seemingly adverse conditions may have presaged the age to come: one the low productivity of medieval agriculture in both per-acre and per-man terms, the other the feudal social system. The first meant that towns could not prosper on the basis of local agriculture alone but had to trade and to manufacture something to trade. The second meant that they could not gain political dominance over their hinterlands and thus become warring city-states. Hence they specialized in commerce and manufacture and evolved local institutions suited to this role. Craftsmen were housed in the towns, because there the merchants could regulate quality and cost. Competition among towns stimulated specialization and technological innovation. The need for literacy, accounting skills and geographical knowledge caused the towns to invest in secular education.

Although the medieval towns remained small and never embraced more than a minor fraction of each region's population, the close connection between industry and commerce that they fostered, together with their emphasis on technique, set the stage for the ultimate breakthrough in urbanization. This breakthrough came only with the enormous growth in productivity caused by the use of inanimate energy and machinery. How difficult it was to achieve the transition is agonizingly apparent from statistics showing that even with the conquest of the New World the growth of urbanization during three postmedieval centuries in Europe was barely perceptible. I have assembled population estimates at two or more dates for 33 towns and cities in the 16th century, 46 in the 17th and 61 in the 18th. The average rate of growth during the three centuries was less than .6 percent per year. Estimates of the growth of Europe's population as a whole between 1650 and 1800 work out to slightly more than .4 percent. The advantage of the towns was evidently very slight. Taking only the cities of 100,000 or more inhabitants, one finds that in 1600 their combined population was 1.6 percent of the estimated population of Europe; in 1700, 1.9 percent, and in 1800, 2.2 percent. On the eve of the industrial revolution Europe was still an overwhelmingly agrarian region.

With industrialization, however, the transformation was striking. By 1801 nearly a tenth of the people of England and Wales were living in cities of 100,000 or larger. This proportion doubled in 40 years and doubled again in another 60 years. By 1900 Britain was an urbanized society. In general, the later each country became industrialized, the faster was its urbanization. The change from a population with 10 percent of its members in cities of 100,000 or larger to one in which 30 percent lived in such cities took about 79 years in England and Wales, 66 in the U.S., 48 in Germany, 36 in Japan and 26 in Australia. The close association between economic development and urbanization has persisted.

* * *

Clearly modern urbanization is best understood in terms of its connection with economic growth, and its implications are best perceived in its latest manifestations in advanced countries. What becomes apparent as one examines the trend in these countries is that urbanization is a finite process, a cycle through which nations go in their transition from agrarian to industrial society. The intensive urbanization of most of the advanced countries began within the past 100 years; in the underdeveloped countries it got under way more recently. In some of the advanced countries its end is now in sight. The fact that it will end, however, does not mean that either economic development or the growth of cities will necessarily end.

* * *

The end of urbanization cannot be unraveled without going into the ways in which economic development governs urbanization. Here the first question is: Where do the urbanites come from? The possible answers are few: The proportion of people in cities can rise because rural settlements grow larger and are reclassified as towns or cities; because the excess of births over deaths is greater in the city than in the country; or because people move from the country to the city.

The first factor has usually had only slight influence. The second has apparently never been the case. Indeed, a chief obstacle to the growth of cities in the past has been their excessive mortality. London's water in the middle of the 19th century came mainly from wells and rivers that drained cesspools, graveyards and tidal areas. The city was regularly ravaged by cholera. Tables for 1841 show an expectation of life of about 36 years for London and 26 for Liverpool and Manchester, as compared to 41 for England and Wales as a whole. After 1850, mainly as a result of sanitary measures and some improvement in nutrition and housing, city health improved, but as late as the period 1901–1910 the death rate of the urban counties in England and Wales, as modified to make the age structure comparable, was 33 percent higher than the death rate of the rural counties. As Bernard Benjamin, a chief statistician of the British General Register Office, has remarked: "Living in the town involved not only a higher risk of epidemic and crowd diseases . . . but also a higher risk of degenerative disease—the harder wear and tear of factory employment and urban discomfort." By 1950, however, virtually the entire differential had been wiped out.

As for birth rates, during rapid urbanization in the past they were notably lower in cities than in rural areas. In fact, the gap tended to widen somewhat as urbanization proceeded in the latter half of the 19th century and the first quarter of the 20th. In 1800 urban women in the U.S. had 36 percent fewer children than rural women did; in 1840, 38 percent and in 1930, 41 percent. Thereafter the difference diminished.

With mortality in the cities higher and birth rates lower, and with reclassification a minor factor, the only real source for the growth in the proportion of people in urban areas during the industrial transition was rural-urban migration. This source had to be plentiful enough not only to overcome the substantial disadvantage of the cities in natural increase but also, above that, to furnish a big margin of growth in their populations. If, for example, the cities had a death rate a third higher and a birth rate a third lower than the rural rates (as was typical in the latter half of the 19th century), they would require each year perhaps 40 to 45 migrants from elsewhere per 1,000 of their population to maintain a growth rate of 3 percent per year. Such a rate of migration could easily be maintained as long as the rural portion of the population was large, but when this condition ceased to obtain, the maintenance of the same urban rate meant an increasing drain on the countryside.

Why did the rural-urban migration occur? The reason was that the rise in technological enhancement of human productivity, together with certain constant factors, rewarded urban concentration. One of the constant factors was that agriculture uses land as its prime instrument of production and hence spreads out people who are engaged in it, whereas manufacturing, commerce and services use land only as a site. Moreover, the demand for agricultural products is less elastic than the demand for services and manufactures. As productivity grows, services and manufactures can absorb more manpower by paying higher wages. Since nonagricultural activities can use land simply as a site, they can locate near one another (in towns and cities) and thus minimize the friction of space inevitably involved in the division of labor. At the same time, as agricultural technology is improved, capital costs in farming rise and manpower becomes not only less needed but also economically more burdensome. A substantial portion of the agricultural population is therefore sufficiently disadvantaged, in relative terms, to be attracted by higher wages in other sectors.

In this light one sees why a large flow of people from farms to cities was generated in every country that passed through the industrial revolution. One also sees why, with an even higher proportion of people already in cities and with the inability of city people to replace themselves by reproduction, the drain eventually became so heavy that in many nations the rural population began to decline in absolute as well as relative terms. In Sweden it declined after 1920, in England and Wales after 1861, in Belgium after 1910.

Realizing that urbanization is transitional and finite, one comes on another fact—a fact that throws light on the circumstances in which urbanization comes to an end. A basic feature of the transition is the profound switch from agricultural to nonagricultural employment. This change is associated with urbanization but not identical with it. The difference emerges particularly in the later stages. Then the availability of automobiles, radios, motion pictures and electricity, as well as the reduction of the workweek and the workday, mitigate the disadvantages of living in the country. Concurrently the expanding size of cities makes them more difficult to live in. The population classed as "rural" is accordingly enlarged, both from cities and from true farms.

For these reasons the "rural" population in some industrial countries never did fall in absolute size. In all the industrial countries, however, the population dependent on agriculture—which the reader will recognize as a more functional definition of the nonurban population than mere rural residence—decreased in absolute as well as relative terms. In the U.S., for example, the net migration from farms totaled more than 27 million between 1920 and 1959 and thus averaged approximately 700,000 a year. As a result the farm population declined from 32.5 million in 1916 to 20.5 million in 1960, in spite of the large excess of births in farm families. In 1964, by a stricter American definition classifying as "farm families" only those families actually earning their living from agriculture, the farm population was down to 12.9 million. This number represented 6.8 percent of the nation's population; the comparable figure for 1880 was 44 percent. In Great Britain the number of males occupied in agriculture was at its peak, 1.8 million, in 1851; by 1961 it had fallen to .5 million.

In the later stages of the cycle, then, urbanization in the industrial countries tends to cease. Hence the connection between economic development and the growth of cities also ceases. The change is explained by two circumstances. First, there is no longer enough farm population to furnish a significant migration to the cities. (What can 12.9 million American farmers contribute to the growth of the 100 million people already in urbanized areas?) Second, the rural nonfarm population, nourished by refugees from the expanding cities, begins to increase as fast as the city population. The effort of census bureaus to count fringe residents as urban simply pushes the definition of "urban" away from the notion of dense settlement and in the direction of the term "nonfarm." As the urban population becomes more "rural," which is to say less densely settled, the advanced industrial peoples are for a time able to enjoy the amenities of urban life without the excessive crowding of the past.

Here, however, one again encounters the fact that a cessation of urbanization does not necessarily mean a cessation of city growth. An example is provided by New Zealand. Between 1945 and 1961 the proportion of New Zealand's population classed as urban—that is, the ratio between urban and rural residents—changed hardly at all (from 61.3 percent to 63.6 percent) but the urban population increased by 50 percent. In Japan between 1940 and 1950 urbanization actually decreased slightly, but the urban population increased by 13 percent.

The point to be kept in mind is that once urbanization ceases, city growth becomes a function of general population growth. Enough farm-to-city migration may still occur to redress the difference in natural increase. The reproductive rate of urbanites tends, however, to increase when they live at lower densities, and the reproductive rate of "urbanized" farmers tends to decrease; hence little migration is required to make the urban increase equal the national increase.

I now turn to the currently underdeveloped countries. With the advanced nations having slackened their rate of urbanization, it is the others—representing three-fourths of humanity—that are mainly responsible for the rapid urbanization now characterizing the world as a whole. In fact, between 1950 and 1960 the proportion of the population in cities of 100,000 or more rose about a third faster in the underdeveloped regions than in the developed ones. Among the underdeveloped regions the pace was slow in eastern and southern Europe, but in the rest of the underdeveloped world the proportion in cities rose twice as fast as it did in the industrialized countries, even though the latter countries in many cases broadened their definitions of urban places to include more suburban and fringe residents.

Because of the characteristic pattern of urbanization, the current rates of urbanization in underdeveloped countries could be expected to exceed those now existing in countries far advanced in the cycle. On discovering that this is the case one is tempted to say that the underdeveloped regions are now in the typical stage of urbanization associated with early economic development. This notion, however, is erroneous. In their urbanization the underdeveloped countries are definitely not repeating past history. Indeed, the best grasp of their present situation comes from analyzing how their course differs from the previous pattern of development.

The first thing to note is that today's underdeveloped countries are urbanizing not only more rapidly than the industrial nations are now but also more rapidly than the industrial nations did in the heyday of their urban growth. The difference, however, is not large. In 40 underdeveloped countries for which we have data in recent decades, the average gain in the proportion of the population urban was 20 percent per decade; in 16 industrial countries, during the decades of their most rapid urbanization (mainly in the 19th century), the average gain per decade was 15 percent.

This finding that urbanization is proceeding only a little faster in underdeveloped countries than it did historically in the advanced nations may be questioned by the reader. It seemingly belies the widespread impression that cities throughout the nonindustrial parts of the world are bursting with people. There is, however, no contradiction. One must recall the basic distinction between a change in the proportion of the population urban, which is a ratio, and the absolute growth of cities. The popular impression is correct: the cities in underdeveloped areas are growing at a disconcerting rate. They are far outstripping the city boom of the industrializing era in the 19th century. If they continue their recent rate of growth, they will double their population every 15 years.

In 34 underdeveloped countries for which we have data relating to the 1940's and 1950's, the average annual gain in the urban population was 4.5 percent. The figure is remarkably similar for the various regions: 4.7 percent in seven countries of Africa, 4.7 percent in 15 countries of Asia and 4.3 percent in 12 countries of Latin America. In contrast, in nine European countries during their period of fastest urban population growth (mostly in the latter half of the 19th century) the average gain per year was 2.1 percent. Even the frontier industrial countries—the U.S., Australia–New Zealand, Canada and Argentina —which received huge numbers of immigrants, had a smaller population growth in towns and cities: 4.2 percent per year. In Japan and the U.S.S.R. the rate was respectively 5.4 and 4.3 percent per year, but their economic growth began only recently.

How is it possible that the contrast in growth between today's underdeveloped countries and yesterday's industrializing countries is sharper with respect to the absolute urban population than with respect to the urban share of the total population? The answer lies in another profound difference between the two sets of countries—a difference in total population growth, rural as well as urban. Contemporary underdeveloped populations have been growing since 1940 more than twice as fast as industrialized populations, and their increase far exceeds the growth of the latter at the peak of their expansion. The only rivals in an earlier day were the frontier nations, which had the help of great streams of immigrants. Today the underdeveloped nations—already densely settled, tragically impoverished and with gloomy economic prospects—are multiplying their people by sheer biological increase at a rate that is unprecedented. It is this population boom that is overwhelmingly responsible for the rapid inflation of city populations in such countries. Contrary to popular opinion both inside and outside those countries, the main factor is not rural-urban migration.

This point can be demonstrated easily by a calculation that has the effect of eliminating the influence of general population growth on urban growth. The calculation involves assuming that the total population of a given country remained constant over a period of time but that the percentage urban changed as it did historically. In this manner one obtains the growth of the absolute urban population that would have occurred if rural-urban migration were the only factor affecting it. As an example, Costa Rica had in 1927 a total population of 471,500, of which 88,600, or 18.8 percent, was urban. By 1963 the country's total population was 1,325,200 and the urban population was 456,600, or 34.5 percent. If the total population had remained at 471,500 but the percentage urban had still risen from 18.8 to 34.5, the absolute urban population in 1963 would have been only 162,700. That is the growth that would have occurred in the urban population if rural-urban migration had been the only factor. In actuality the urban population rose to 456,600. In other words, only 20 percent of the rapid growth of Costa Rica's towns and cities was attributable to urbanization per se; 44 percent was attributable solely to the country's general population increase, the remainder to the joint operation of both factors. Similarly, in Mexico between 1940 and 1960, 50 percent of the urban population increase was attributable to national multiplication alone and only 22 percent to urbanization alone.

The past performance of the advanced countries presents a sharp contrast. In Switzerland between 1850 and 1888, when the proportion urban resembled that in Costa Rica recently, general population growth alone accounted for only 19 percent of the increase of town and city people, and rural-urban migration alone accounted for 69 percent. In France between 1846 and 1911 only 21 percent of the growth in the absolute urban population was due to general growth alone.

The conclusion to which this contrast points is that one anxiety of governments in the underdeveloped nations is misplaced. Impressed by the mushrooming in their cities of shantytowns filled with ragged peasants, they attribute the fantastically fast city growth to rural-urban migration. Actually this migration now does little more than make up for the small difference in the birth rate between city and countryside. In the history of the industrial nations, as we have seen, the sizable difference between urban and rural birth rates and death rates required that cities, if they were to grow, had to have an enormous influx of people from farms and villages. Today in the underdeveloped countries the towns and cities have only a slight disadvantage in fertility, and their old disadvantage in mortality not only has been wiped out but also in many cases has been reversed. During the 19th century the urbanizing nations were learning how to keep crowded populations in cities from dying like flies. Now the lesson has been learned, and it is being applied to cities even in countries just emerging from tribalism. In fact, a disproportionate share of public health funds goes into cities. As a result throughout the nonindustrial world people in cities are multiplying as never before, and rural-urban migration is playing a much lesser role.

The trends just described have an important implication for the rural population. Given the explosive overall population growth in underdeveloped countries, it follows that if the rural population is not to pile up on the land and reach an economically absurd density, a high rate of rural-urban migration must be maintained. Indeed, the exodus from rural areas should be higher than in the past. But this high rate of internal movement is not taking place, and there is some doubt that it could conceivably do so.

To elaborate I shall return to my earlier point that in the evolution of industrialized countries the rural citizenry often declined in absolute as well as relative terms. The rural population of France—26.8 million in 1846—was down to 20.8 million by 1926 and 17.2 million by 1962, notwithstanding a gain in the nation's total population during this period. Sweden's rural population dropped from 4.3 million in 1910 to 3.5 million in 1960. Since the category "rural" includes an increasing portion of urbanites living in fringe areas, the historical drop was more drastic and consistent specifically in the farm population. In the U.S., although the "rural" population never quite ceased to grow, the farm contingent began its long descent shortly after the turn of the century; today it is less than two-fifths of what it was in 1910.

This transformation is not occurring in contemporary underdeveloped countries. In spite of the enormous growth of their cities, their rural populations—and their more narrowly defined agricultural populations—are growing at a rate that in many cases exceeds the rise of even the urban population during the evolution of the now advanced countries. The poor countries thus confront a grave dilemma. If they do not substantially step up the exodus from rural areas, these areas will be swamped with underemployed farmers. If they do step up the exodus, the cities will grow at a disastrous rate.

The rapid growth of cities in the advanced countries, painful though it was, had the effect of solving a problem—the problem of the rural population. The growth of cities enabled agricultural holdings to be consolidated, allowed increased capitalization and in general resulted in greater efficiency. Now, however, the underdeveloped countries are experiencing an even more rapid urban growth—and are suffering from urban problems—but urbanization is not solving their rural ills.

A case in point is Venezuela. Its capital, Caracas, jumped from a population of 359,000 in 1941 to 1,507,000 in 1963; other Venezuelan towns and cities equaled or exceeded this growth. Is this rapid rise denuding the countryside of people? No, the Venezuelan farm population increased in the decade 1951–1961 by 11 percent. The only thing that declined was the amount of cultivated land. As a result the agricultural population density became worse. In 1950 there were some 64 males engaged in agriculture per square mile of cultivated land; in 1961 there were 78. (Compare this with 4.8 males occupied in agriculture per square mile of cultivated land in Canada, 6.8 in the U.S. and 15.6 in Argentina.) With each male occupied in agriculture there are of course dependents. Approximately 225 persons in Venezuela are trying to live from each square mile of cultivated land. Most of the growth of cities in Venezuela is attributable to overall population growth. If the general population had not grown at all, and internal migration had been large enough to produce the actual shift in the proportion in cities, the increase in urban population would have been only 28 percent of what it was and the rural population would have been reduced by 57 percent.

The story of Venezuela is being repeated virtually everywhere in the underdeveloped world. It is not only Caracas that has thousands of squatters living in self-constructed junk houses on land that does not belong to them. By whatever name they are called, the squatters are to be found in all major cities in the poorer countries. They live in broad gullies beneath the main plain in San Salvador and on the hillsides of Rio de Janeiro and Bogotá. They tend to occupy with implacable determination parks, school grounds and vacant lots. Amman, the capital of Jordan, grew from 12,000 in 1958 to 247,000 in 1961. A good part of it is slums, and urban amenities are lacking most of the time for most of the people. Greater Baghdad now has an estimated 850,000 people; its slums, like those in many other underdeveloped countries, are in two zones—the central part of the city and the outlying areas. Here are the *sarifa* areas, characterized by self-built reed huts; these areas account for about 45 percent of the housing in the entire city and are devoid of amenities, including even latrines. In addition to such urban problems, all the countries struggling for higher living levels find their rural population growing too and piling up on already crowded land.

I have characterized urbanization as a transformation that, unlike economic development, is finally accomplished and comes to an end. At the 1950–1960 rate the term "urbanized world" will be applicable well before the end of the century. One should scarcely expect, however, that mankind will complete its urbanization without major complications. One sign of trouble ahead turns on the distinction I made at the start between urbanization and city growth per se. Around the globe today city growth is disproportionate to urbanization. The discrepancy is paradoxical in the industrial nations and worse than paradoxical in the nonindustrial.

It is in this respect that the nonindustrial nations, which still make up the great majority of nations, are far from repeating past history. In the 19th and early 20th centuries the growth of cities arose from and contributed to economic advancement. Cities took surplus manpower from the countryside and put it to work producing goods and services that in turn helped to modernize agriculture. But today in underdeveloped countries, as in present-day advanced nations, city growth has become increasingly unhinged from economic development and hence from rural-urban migration. It derives in greater degree from overall population growth, and this growth in nonindustrial lands has become unprecedented because of modern health techniques combined with high birth rates.

The speed of world population growth is twice what it was before 1940, and the swiftest increase has shifted from the advanced to the backward nations. In the latter countries, consequently, it is virtually impossible to create city services fast enough to take care of the huge, never ending cohorts of babies and peasants swelling the urban masses. It is even harder to expand agricultural land and capital fast enough to accommodate the enormous natural increase on farms. The problem is not urbanization, not rural-urban migration, but human multiplication. It is a problem that is new in both its scale and its setting, and runaway city growth is only one of its painful expressions.

As long as the human population expands, cities will expand too, regardless of whether urbanization increases or declines. This means that some individual cities will reach a size that will make 19th-century metropolises look like small towns. If the New York urbanized area should continue to grow only as fast as the nation's population (according to medium projections of the latter by the Bureau of the Census), it would reach 21 million by 1985 and 30 million by 2010. I have calculated that if India's population should grow as the UN projections indicate it will, the largest city in India in the year 2000 will have between 36 and 66 million inhabitants.

What is the implication of such giant agglomerations for human density? In 1950 the New York–Northeastern New Jersey urbanized area had an average density of 9,810 persons per square mile. With 30 million people in the year 2010, the density would be 24,000 per square mile. Although this level is exceeded now in parts of New York City (which averages about 25,000 per square mile) and many other cities, it is a high density to be spread over such a big area; it would cover, remember, the surburban areas to which people moved to escape high density. Actually, however, the density of the New York urbanized region is dropping, not increasing, as the population grows. The reason is that the territory covered by the urban agglomerations is growing faster than the population: it grew by 51 percent from 1950 to 1960, whereas the population rose by 15 percent.

If, then, one projects the rise in population and the rise in territory for the New York urbanized region, one finds the density problem solved. It is not solved for long, though, because New York is not the only city in the region that is expanding. So are Philadelphia, Trenton, Hartford, New Haven and so on. By 1960 a huge stretch of territory about 600 miles long and 30 to 100 miles wide along the Eastern seaboard contained some 37 million people. . . . Since the whole area is becoming one big polynucleated city, its population cannot long expand without a rise in density. Thus persistent human multiplication promises to frustrate the ceaseless search for space—for ample residential lots, wide-open suburban school grounds, sprawling shopping centers, one-floor factories, broad freeways.

How people feel about giant agglomerations is best indicated by their headlong effort to escape them. The bigger the city, the higher the cost of space; yet, the more the level of living rises, the more people are willing to pay for low-density living. Nevertheless, as urbanized areas expand and collide, it seems probable that life in low-density surroundings will become too dear for the great majority.

One can of course imagine that cities may cease to grow and may even shrink in size while the population in general continues to multiply. Even this dream, however, would not permanently solve the problem of space. It would eventually obliterate the distinction between urban and rural, but at the expense of the rural.

It seems plain that the only way to stop urban crowding and to solve most of the urban problems besetting both the developed and the underdeveloped nations is to reduce the overall rate of population growth. Policies designed to do this have as yet little intelligence and power behind them. Urban planners continue to treat population growth as something to be planned for, not something to be itself planned. Any talk about applying brakes to city growth is therefore purely speculative, overshadowed as it is by the reality of uncontrolled population increase.

9. Megalopolis: Main Street of the Nation

JEAN GOTTMANN

The Northeastern seaboard of the United States is today the site of a remarkable development—an almost continuous stretch of urban and suburban areas from southern New Hampshire to northern Virginia and from the Atlantic shore to the Appalachian foothills. The processes of urbanization, rooted deep in the American past, have worked steadily here, endowing the region with unique ways of life and of land use. No other section of the United States has such a large concentration of population, with such a high average density, spread over such a large area. And no other section has a comparable role within the nation or a comparable importance in the world. Here has been developed a kind of supremacy, in politics, in economics, and possibly even in cultural activities, seldom before attained by an area of this size.

SOURCE: *Megalopolis: The Urbanized Northeastern Seaboard of the United States* (New York: Twentieth Century Fund, 1961) (Cambridge: The M.I.T. Press, 1965), pp. 3-16.

A Very Special Region: Megalopolis

This region has indeed a "personality" of its own, which for some three centuries past has been changing and evolving, constantly creating new problems for its inhabitants and exerting a deep influence on the general organization of society. The modern trends in its development and its present degree of crowding provide both examples and warnings for other less urbanized areas in America and abroad and call for a profound revision of many old concepts, such as the usually accepted distinctions between city and country. As a result new meanings must be given to some old terms, and some new terms must be created.

Great, then, is the importance and significance of this section of the United States and of the processes now at work within it. And yet it is difficult to single this area out from surrounding areas, for its limits cut across established historical divisions, such as New England and the Middle Atlantic states, and across political entities, since it includes some states entirely and others only partially. A special name is needed, therefore, to identify this special geographical area.

This particular type of region is new, but it is the result of age-old processes, such as the growth of cities, the division of labor within a civilized society, the development of world resources. The name applied to it should, therefore, be new as a place name but old as a symbol of the long tradition of human aspirations and endeavor underlying the situations and problems now found here. Hence the choice of the term *Megalopolis*, used in this study.

Some two thousand years before the First European settlers landed on the shores of the James River, Massachusetts Bay, and Manhattan Island, a group of ancient people, planning a new city-state in the Peloponnesus in Greece, called it *Megalopolis*, for they dreamed of a great future for it and hoped it would become the largest of the Greek cities. Their hopes did not materialize. Megalopolis still appears on modern maps of the Peloponnesus but it is just a small town nestling in a small river basin. Through the centuries the word *Megalopolis* has been used in many senses by various people, and it has even found its way into Webster's dictionary, which defines it as "a very large city." Its use, however, has not become so common that it could not be applied in a new sense, as a geographical place name for the unique cluster of metropolitan areas of the Northeastern seaboard of the United States. There, if anywhere in our times, the dream of those ancient Greeks has come true.

An Urbanized Area with a Nebulous Structure

As one follows the main highways or railroads between Boston and Washington, D.C., one hardly loses sight of built-up areas, tightly woven residential communities, or powerful concentrations of manufacturing plants. Flying this same route one discovers, on the other hand, that behind the ribbons of densely occupied land along the principal arteries of traffic, and in between the clusters of suburbs around the old urban centers, there still remain large areas covered with woods and brush alternating with some carefully cultivated patches of farmland. These green spaces, however, when inspected at closer range, appear stuffed with a loose but immense scattering of buildings, most of them residential but some of industrial character. That is, many of these sections that look rural actually function largely as suburbs in the orbit of some city's downtown. Even the farms, which occupy the larger tilled patches, are seldom worked by people whose only occupation and income are properly agricultural. And yet these farm areas produce large quantities of farm goods!

Thus the old distinctions between rural and urban do not apply here any more. Even a quick look at the vast area of Megalopolis reveals a revolution in land use. Most of the people living in the so-called rural areas, and still classified as "rural population" by recent censuses, have very little, if anything, to do with agriculture. In terms of their interests and work they are what used to be classified as "city folks," but their way of life and the landscapes around their residences do not fit the old meaning of urban.

In this area, then, we must abandon the idea of the city as a tightly settled and organized unit in which people, activities, and riches are crowded into a very small area clearly separated from its nonurban surroundings. Every city in this region spreads out far and wide around its original nucleus; it grows amidst an irregularly colloidal mixture of rural and suburban landscapes; it melts on broad fronts with other mixtures, of somewhat similar though different texture, belonging to the suburban neighborhoods of other cities. Such coalescence can be observed, for example, along the main lines of traffic that link New York City and Philadelphia. Here there are many communities that might be classified as belonging to more than one orbit. It is hard to say whether they are suburbs, or "satellites," of Philadelphia or New York, Newark, New Brunswick, or Trenton. The latter three cities themselves have been reduced to the role of suburbs of New York City in many respects, although Trenton belongs also to the orbit of Philadelphia.

The "standard metropolitan areas,"[1] first used by the U. S. Bureau of the Census in 1950, have clarified this confused situation somewhat but not entirely. For example, the New York–Northeastern New Jersey standard metropolitan area cuts across political boundaries to reveal the relationships of this vast region to the core city of New

York. And yet the mechanical application of the term "standard metropolitan area" has resulted in the establishment of separate areas for Trenton, which is closely tied to both Philadelphia and New York, and for Bridgeport, which is for many practical purposes part of the New York area. Similar problems can be found in other parts of Megalopolis.[2]

Thus an almost continuous system of deeply interwoven urban and suburban areas, with a total population of about 37 million people in 1960, has been erected along the Northeastern Atlantic seaboard. It straddles state boundaries, stretches across wide estuaries and bays, and encompasses many regional differences. In fact, the landscapes of Megalopolis offer such variety that the average observer may well doubt the unity of the region. And it may seem to him that the main urban nuclei of the seaboard are little related to one another. Six of its great cities would be great individual metropolises in their own right if they were located elsewhere. This region indeed reminds one of Aristotle's saying that cities such as Babylon had "the compass of a nation rather than a city."

Megalopolis—Main Street and Crossroads of the Nation

There are many other large metropolitan areas and even clusters of them in various parts of the United States, but none of them is yet comparable to Megalopolis in size of population, density of population, or density of activities, be these expressed in terms of transportation, communications, banking operations, or political conferences. Megalopolis provides the whole of America with so many essential services, of the sort a community used to obtain in its "downtown" section, that it may well deserve the nickname of "Main Street of the nation." And for three centuries it has performed this role, though the transcontinental march of settlement has developed along east-west axes perpendicular to this section of the Atlantic seaboard.

In recent times Megalopolis has had concentrated within it more of the Main Street type of functions than ever, and it does not yet seem prepared to relinquish any of them. Witness, for example, the impact of the Federal government in Washington, D. C., as it tightens up over many aspects of national life; the continued crowding of financial and managerial operations into Manhattan; New York's dominance of the national market for mass communication media, which resists all attempts at erosion; and the pre-eminent influence of the universities and cultural centers of Megalopolis on American thinking and policy-making. Megalopolis is also the country's chief façade toward the rest of the world. From it, as from the Main Street of a city, local people leave for distant travel, and to it arriving strangers come. For immigrants it has always served as the chief debarkation wharf. And just as passing visitors often see little of a city except a few blocks of its Main Street, so most foreign visitors see only a part of Megalopolis on their sojourns in the United States.

Just as a Main Street lives for and prospers because of the functions of the whole city, rather than because of any purely local advantages of its own, so is Megalopolis related to the whole United States and its rich resources. In general, Megalopolis itself was blessed only moderately by nature. It has no vast expanse of rich soils (there are some good soils but more poor ones), no special climatic advantages (its cyclonic climate is far from ideal), and no great mineral deposits (though there are some). In these respects it cannot compare with the generous natural potential of the Middle West or Texas or California. But it does excel in locational advantages—deep harbors of a drowned shoreline, on which its principal cities were early established, and a connecting-link relationship between the rich heart of the continent and the rest of the world. By hard work man has made the most of these locational resources, the most outstanding ones in an otherwise average natural endowment. As a result, early in its history Megalopolis became a dynamic hub of international relations, and it has maintained and constantly expanded that role to the present day. It is now the most active crossroads on earth, for people, ideas, and goods, extending its influence far beyond the national borders, and only as such a crossroads could it have achieved its present economic pre-eminence.

Megalopolis as a Laboratory of Urban Growth

Modern technology and social evolution provide increasing opportunity in urban pursuits on the one hand, and on the other steadily improving means of producing more agricultural goods with less manpower. The forces at work in our time, coupled with the growth in population, are, therefore, bound to channel a rising flow of people toward urban-type occupations and ways of life. As this tide reaches more and more cities they will burst out of old bounds to expand and scatter all over the landscape, taking new forms like those already observable throughout Megalopolis. This region serves thus as a laboratory in which we may study the new evolution reshaping both the meaning of our traditional vocabulary and the whole material structure of our way of life.

Tomorrow's society will be different from that in which we grew up, largely because it will be more urbanized. Nonagricultural ways of life will be followed by more and more people and will occupy much more space than they ever did, and such changes cannot develop without also deeply modifying agricultural life and production. So great are the consequences of the general evolution heralded by the present rise and complexity of Megalopolis that an analysis of this region's problems often gives one the feeling of looking at the dawn of a new stage in human civilization. The author has visited and studied various other regions of the world but has not experienced such a feeling anywhere else. Indeed, the area may be considered the cradle of a new order in the organization of inhabited space. This new order, however, is still far from orderly; here in its cradle it is all in flux and trouble, which does not facilitate the analyst's work. Nevertheless, a study of Megalopolis may shed some light on processes that are of great importance and interest.

* * *

New *patterns of intense living* that have become normal in Megalopolis affect not only land use. They also exert a strong influence on the economic and social foundations of society. . . . The density of activities and of movement of all kinds is certainly the most extraordinary feature of Megalopolis, more characteristic even than the density of population and of skyscrapers. It has become a means of maintaining economic growth and stabilizing society; but how far can it go without destroying itself? For example, the growth of Megalopolis owes much to the automobile, but highway traffic jams are beginning to strangle city activities and to take the pleasure and efficiency out of driving a car. At the same time cars contribute to the ruination of other means of transportation, made more necessary than ever by the massive tidal currents of people and goods. The self-defeating effect of dense concentrations may be observed also in other fields than transportation. Many industries, for example, are now aiming at decentralization. The intense living of Megalopolis makes a great deal of waste inescapable, waste of space and time as well as of materials. For a long time such waste may have seemed justifiable, for, paradoxically, the crowding that caused it brought higher economic yields. Now this crowding seems at times to defeat its own aims. Why and how does such intense living grow and threaten itself? Answers to these queries build up a general picture of a dynamic and prosperous society, obviously responsible for maintaining the growth of large-scale urbanization but responsible also for the problems the process creates and for finding the badly needed solutions.

It is easier to accept responsibility for solutions than to provide them. The many millions of people who find themselves *neighbors in*

Megalopolis, even though they live in different states and hundreds of miles from one another, are barely becoming aware of the imperatives of such a "neighborhood." . . . Responsible public opinion is becoming conscious of the problems involved, and the struggle to find solutions has started. It is especially difficult because no one problem can be tackled without affecting the others. Transportation, land use, water supply, cultural activities, use and development of resources, government and politics—all are interrelated.

Today it is essential that solutions be found to save this area from decay and to reassure the nation and the world about the kind of life modern urbanization trends presage for the future. Megalopolis has been built and often reshaped by its people. These people are now wealthier, better educated, and better endowed with technological means than ever. They ought to be able to find ways of avoiding decline of the area.

For the Better or for the Worse?

The preceding paragraph may seem to imply an unwarranted optimism about society's ability to control itself. True, history records a long list of brilliant civilizations that have sunk under the pressure of internal decay and external jealousy. We remember their names: Babylon, Corinth, Sparta, Athens, Rome, and many others. In the shadowy vistas of ancient times they vanished into the distance like shipwrecked ships loaded with ambition and precious cargo. Can such a fate be looming in the offing for Megalopolis? Modern urban sprawl is viewed by many as a threat to progress and general welfare. What is happening in Megalopolis today has been described as a pathological phenomenon, a sickness, a cancer. Such views are held by distinguished and respectable citizens of the area. One may well be alarmed by their invectives, all the more so as one does not have to go far away from Megalopolis to hear expressions of distrust and jealousy inspired by the amazing concentration of wealth and power in the great seaboard cities. Are people both in and out of this extraordinary region united in condemning it?

Urban growth in general has been discussed and condemned on moral grounds for a long time. Such debate is expectable and desirable, but on the whole history has shown the condemnation to be unjust, as can be seen by a brief review of some of the consequences of crowding.

Contrasts between rich and poor, for example, are especially striking in the crowded communities of cities. These may exist in rural areas too, but there they are diluted by scattering and veiled in greenery. The growth of urban pursuits (industries, trade, services) sharpens the contrasts by condensing them into a smaller area. Rich and poor live within short distances of one another and mix together in the streets in a way that often arouses righteous indignation. It seems brutally amoral to witness destitution neighboring on elegant sophistication, poverty mixing with prosperity. And yet, alas, a growing city's environment can hardly escape offering such sights. For many centuries there was an enormous difference between the advancement possible in trade and industry on the one hand and in farming on the other (though modern farm mechanization and subsidies to agriculture have substantially increased the profit possibilities of farming), and so to rise economically within the span of one lifetime has traditionally been easier in cities than in rural areas. The affluence of those who have so risen draws to the city large groups of humbler people, who come there to profit by the local abundance of money and the volume of spending and to serve the wealthier. In contrast to the more conservative "open" country, the "closed-in" city offers a more dynamic environment, socially and economically.

In cities, too, other vicious aspects of economic growth and social life have always been more evident than in the country. As urban development was accelerated by the Industrial Revolution, some of these vicious aspects became increasingly obvious. Slums and mobs grew worse than ever, making the urban landscape ethically and aesthetically shocking to those who cared about the people. From his sojourns in an industrializing western Europe, and especially from Paris during the French Revolution, Thomas Jefferson brought back impressions that reinforced his normal Virginian opposition to great cities and the development of manufacturers or large-scale commerce. As slums and mobs became more general in European cities in the first half of the nineteenth century there arose more awareness about the classes of society and social injustice. There was more discussion of these matters, and the early Socialist doctrines were largely inspired by them. Then came the teachings of such philosophers as Fourier and Proudhon in France and Engels and Karl Marx in Germany, opposing great urban concentration as much as great concentration of capital. Engels' writings on the slums and working conditions in the then fast-developing British cities, such as Manchester, are well known. Because urban conditions of living and working were largely at the root of nineteenth-century Socialist doctrines, Karl Marx stressed that his theories applied much more to the industrialized countries of western Europe, which had accumulated large amounts of capital, than to the rural, little-urbanized countries to the east. Twentieth-century events have proved him wrong on this score, however, for communism has conquered the mainly rural countries, and the forms of socialism that developed in the more urban and capitalistic countries of the West have turned away from Marxism.

Crowding of population within a small area creates shortages of various resources, and most of the crowded people are bound to suffer in some ways because of the shortages. To alleviate them, to make crowding more bearable and the population happier, ways and means of constantly better distribution must be found. Otherwise no lasting growth can develop, and the whole enterprise will soon be doomed. From the struggle against such shortages have come some of mankind's most important advances. In the arid areas of the Middle East, for example, early civilization arose when people first congregated around the main springs and permanent rivers. As the settlement grew, the supply of both water and irrigable land became scarce. To insure survival of the people a proper distribution system had to be achieved, and rules and regulations had to be set up and accepted. Thus organized society, ruled by law, was born. Because authorities were needed to enforce law, political power arose, and people organized themselves to avoid more oppression than was necessary. Everywhere, the more crowded people have become in cities the more they have craved both security and freedom. Modern political life and its concepts of liberty, self-government, and democracy are the products of urban growth, the inheritance of cities in process of growth and development—places such as Jerusalem, Athens, Rome, Bruges, Florence, Paris, London, to mention only those that have been most studied by historians. And the same places, or similar urban centers, have contributed most of our scientific and technological developments, either because people there were struggling to solve pressing problems or because urban societies make possible a leisurely enough elite, some of whose members can devote themselves to disinterested research and a search for a better understanding of the universe.

Thus urban crowding and the slums and mobs characteristic of it may be considered growing pains in the endless process of civilization.

In the same way, the picture of Megalopolis is not as dark as the outspoken pessimists and frequent protests would seem to paint it. Crowded within its limits is an extremely distinguished population. It *on the average*, the richest, best educated, best housed, and best serviced group of similar size (i.e., in the 25-to-40-million-people range) in the world. The area is still a focus of attraction for successful or adventurous people from all over America and beyond. It is true that many of its sections have seen pretty rural landscapes replaced by ugly industrial agglomerations or drab and monstrous residential developments; it is true that in many parts of Megalopolis the air is not clean any more, the noise is disturbing day and night, the water is not as pure as one would wish, and transportation at times becomes a nightmare. Many of these problems reflect the revolutionary change that has taken place as cities have burst out of their narrow bounds to scatter over the "open" countryside. In some ways this suburban sprawl may have alleviated a crowding that had threatened to become unbearable, for residential densities of population per square mile have decreased. But new problems have arisen because of the new densities of activities and of traffic in the central cities and because the formerly rural areas or small towns have been unprepared to cope with the new demands made upon their resources. New programs are needed to conserve the natural beauty of the landscape and to assure the health, prosperity, and freedom of the people. In spite of these problems, however, available statistics demonstrate that in Megalopolis the population is on the average healthier, the consumption of goods higher, and the opportunity for advancement greater than in any other region of comparable extent.

Thus the type of urban growth experienced here generates many contrasts, paradoxes, and apparently contradictory trends. It calls for debate and naturally excites passionate opinions for and against it. Are its results for the better or for the worse? It is not for our generation to moralize on the matter, but to strive to make the outcome be for the better, whatever obstacles may be in the way. Megalopolis stands indeed at the threshold of a new way of life, and upon solution of its problems will rest civilization's ability to survive. In the search for such solutions there will be found no easy keys to success, no "gimmicks" or "open-sesames." Solutions must be thought out, ironed out, and constantly revised in the light of all the knowledge that can be acquired by all concerned. It is the author's hope that this report, a systematic and sometimes critical analysis of the past and present of Megalopolis, will contribute to the gathering of such knowledge and to its distribution. At the same time, it will tell the story of an extraordinary region as its people have made it.

---

[1]The U.S. Bureau of the Census defined a standard metropolitan area as "a county or group of contiguous counties which contains at least one city of 50,000 inhabitants or more. In addition to the county, or counties, containing such a city, or cities, contiguous counties are included in a standard metropolitan area if according to certain criteria they are essentially metropolitan in character and socially and economically integrated with the central city." In New England, "towns and cities, rather than counties, are the units used in defining standard metropolitan areas."

[2]For the 1960 Census the term "standard metropolitan area" was changed to "standard metropolitan statistical area." The definition was modified and a somewhat different set of criteria used which resulted in breaking down several of the formerly recognized larger metropolitan areas into smaller such units. The results thus achieved may be more precise in some respects but in the case of Megalopolis they may cause

some confusion. The New York-Northeastern New Jersey standard metropolitan area of 1950 has been replaced by four standard metropolitan statistical areas: one for New York in New York State and three in New Jersey, those of Paterson-Clifton-Passaic, Jersey City, and Newark. The stricter definition of metropolitan integration of adjoining counties now excludes Somerset and Middlesex counties, formerly classified as metropolitan. As a result the percentage of the population of New Jersey residing in metropolitan areas fell from 89.9 in 1950 to 78.9 in 1960—a statistical trend surprising to those who know how much more metropolitan—or should we say Megalopolitan—the whole of New Jersey grew through the 1950's. To compensate for such an impression and for the separation between New York City and Northeastern New Jersey, a new term has been created and defined: "Standard Consolidated Areas," of which there were two (recognized for 1960) in the country: the New York–Northeastern New Jersey area (which included Somerset and Middlesex counties in New Jersey), and the Chicago–Northwestern Indiana area. The recognition of these broader areas was intended to stress "the special importance of even more inclusive metropolitan statistics" (see Executive Office of the President, Bureau of the Budget, *Standard Metropolitan Statistical Areas,* U. S. Government Printing Office, Washington, D. C., 1961). The metropolitan area of Philadelphia remained unchanged in both its Pennsylvania and New Jersey parts.

PART III

Ideological Perspectives: The Anti-Urban Bias

INTRODUCTION

One of the most unique features of man is his capacity to give meaning to his behavior and environment which he in turn passes on to succeeding generations. The meanings which man gives to life are commonly referred to as value orientations or ideologies. By value orientation or ideology we mean an underlying set of assumptions which are taken for granted about the nature of reality: an internalized conception of the good, the true, and the beautiful. Of course, not all people share exactly the same values, and as we saw in Section II one of the consequences of urbanization has been the bringing together of peoples with different value orientations. Today we are probably more acutely aware of diversity in ideology than we have ever been before. Urbanization and technological innovations in the mass media have placed us all in closer contact with those who hold ideologies different from our own. Yet, in spite of diversity, there is a great deal that almost all members of our pluralistic society hold in common, and it is this common core of shared values which holds society together. Without some considerable consensus of values, which gets translated into normative prescriptions for behavior, no society could exist.

While most shared values tend to integrate society, it does not follow that all values perform this positive function. Values may also inhibit our ability to see things clearly or as they really are. As a result, we often fail to perceive real problems as such. Similarly, we may treat symptoms rather than getting at the heart of a social or personal problem.

The kind of ideological perspective which man brings to any problem will significantly affect how he attempts to deal with the problem.

One of the central themes of this volume is that our value orientations have seriously gotten in the way of our seeing clearly the nature of the urban crisis. The readings in this section have been selected to illustrate how one underlying ideology, anti-urbanism, has inhibited man's ability to cope with urban problems.

The argument, in essence, is that part of our failure to tackle urban problems realistically grows out of the fact that we have been and continue to be influenced by a long history of anti-urban sentiment. In short, most men don't really like the city. God created the countryside in all its beauty and man created the city with all its wickedness. This ideology seems ironic when we consider that the city has been the locus of nearly all of man's technological, cultural, and ideological innovations. To be sure, one finds an intensification of all aspects of human existence in the city: beauty and ugliness; good and bad; absurdity and sublimity. But for all the magnanimous accomplishments of urban life, man has tended only to see the failures of the city. Furthermore, he has tended to believe that there is something inherently wrong with urban life itself rather than examining the possibility that the problems of urban life grow out of his own failure to fully realize the potential of the city.

The emergence of this anti-urban sentiment is enormously complex, and at the same time relatively simple. For those who have studied history, it is clear how very slowly fundamental ideologies change. For example, in a very real sense, the entire history of American democracy has been a gradual realization of the *implications* of the Declaration of Independence. The problems of race and poverty in this nation today dramatize the fact that the American Revolution is incomplete. And if we look into history, it is abundantly clear that the Declaration of Independence did not emerge in a vacuum, but rather represented a milestone in Western Civilization which in many respects traverses most of human history.

In the same sense that one must look at a broad sweep of human history in order to understand the American experiment in democracy, so one must paint with broad strokes to understand man's negative sentiment toward the city. As we saw in Section II, *homo sapiens* have spent only a relatively short period of their existence as urban dwellers. Cities did not emerge until a few thousand years ago. At the turn of this century only about five percent of the world's population resided in cities of one hundred thousand or greater. It was not until 1920 that the majority of residents of this nation became urban dwellers and that represented nearly a hundred percent growth in urban residence over the previous half-century.

The process of urbanization has been painful. Most urban dwellers during the early part of the industrial revolution suffered all the disadvantages of urban life without experiencing many of its benefits. High density living was typified by poor shelter and poor sanitation, and the industrial revolution created almost inhuman working conditions. As recently as the late 19th century there were epidemics of deadly diseases (i.e., smallpox and typhus) in New York City. In brief, early urban living was not very pleasant except for an elite few. Why should man feel kindly toward the city?

But to grasp the full roots of anti-urban sentiment, it is necessary to go back much further than the industrial revolution. Early cities were made possible by forms of complex social organization that were unprecedented in human history. Professor Philip Hauser has commented that "The rise and fall of empires, as recorded in ancient history, may be read in large measure as a chronicle of the development of social organization by means of which the ancient cities acquired a hinterland. The Roman Legion may be interpreted as a form of social organization enabling the city to achieve effective working arrangements with a hinterland."[1] These working arrangements often contributed little to the benefit of the hinterlands. The rural areas were in large part the conquered victims of an exploiting city–state and there were few reciprocal benefits. Thus, disdain for cities almost certainly emerged as early as cities themselves.

The definitive work on anti-urbanism is yet to be written, and while not all scholars share this interpretation of history,[2] the evidence seems to us to be compelling. The most dominant theme in man's ideology about the city is disgust and distrust. To say that anti-urbanism has been and continues to be the dominant ideology of human culture is not to say that this has been a monolithic value orientation. There have been notable exceptions throughout history. Furthermore, a systematic analysis of commentary on cities would probably show an increasing amount of positive sentiment toward cities. But even today, most of the concern for cities does not grow out of a positive attitude toward them, but rather out of a concern that the problems of the city are getting out of hand.

In 1958 the editors of *Fortune* published a collection of articles entitled *The Exploding Metropolis*. The first sentence of the introduction by William H. Whyte, Jr., states "This is a book by people who like cities." Whyte goes on to say:

> Everybody, it would seem, is for the rebuilding of our cities . . . But this is not the same thing as *liking* cities. It is the contention of this book that most of the rebuilding under way and in prospect is being designed by people who don't like cities. They do not merely dislike the noise and the dirt and the congestion. They dislike the city's

variety and concentration, its tension, its hustle and bustle. The new redevelopment projects will be physically in the city, but in spirit they deny it—and the values that since the beginning of civilization have always been at the heart of the great cities.[3]

The editors of this volume feel that little has happened in the past decade which would call for any significant revision of Whyte's comments. Perhaps it is too much to expect a nation which has inherited deep anti-urban roots to suddenly start liking the city. But it does seem appropriate that we begin to understand the implications and consequences of the values which we hold. The readings in this section are designed to illustrate various aspects of anti-urbanism and the consequences of this sentiment for the shape of contemporary urban America.

The first brief selection is taken from the introductory remarks of Senator Joseph S. Clark in a statement before the Senate Subcommittee on Executive Reorganization in August, 1966. Clark sees the anti-urban bias as fundamental to our inability to cope constructively with the problems of the metropolis. He calls for the Subcommittee to cut through the nostalgic myth of rural utopia and address itself to "the crying needs of urban life."

The second selection, "Urbanism and American Democracy," by Francis E. Rourke traces the manifestations of anti-urban sentiment in American political history. While Jefferson's denunciations of urban life are probably the most frequently quoted of all public figures in American history, Rourke finds that Jefferson is far from alone in his disparaging comments on urban living. "More surprising," Rourke writes, " . . . is the fact that there was no dissent from his adverse judgment regarding cities. . . . " Rourke finds, however, that much of the anti-urban thought was implicit rather than explicit in the literature of agrarian revolt. Nevertheless, anti-urban sentiment remains a formidable aspect of American political life well into the present century. In the 1920's Al Smith is seen not only as a Catholic, but as a symbol of the sinister machine politics of the big city.

Rourke finds this historic distrust of the city lacking in empirical evidence. To the contrary, he feels that " . . . there is an impressive amount of evidence which points to the conclusion that it is with urban America that the flowering of democracy in this country can be most clearly identified." Nevertheless, he concludes that, "The force of tradition being what it is, Americans may, in the future as in the past, continue to look for the meaning of their democratic experience in the prairies rather than on the pavements."

Morton and Lucia White provide yet another perspective on the history of anti-urban sentiment in this nation. In a summary of their stimulating book, *The Intellectual Versus the City,* they argue that while American intellectuals today express concern for the future of the city, this providence has not been predominant in the intellectual history of this nation. American intellectuals, they argue, have expressed a good deal more ambivalence and animosity toward the city than appreciation and hope. They appropriately point out that while "much of what they said was the product of doctrinaire ideology, of blindness, ignorance, and prejudice, . . . it is also true that they were responding to urban situations which were really objectively bad." This selection gives the reader some of the flavor of the intellectuals' reluctant struggle to come to grips with a changing environment.

The next selection by Robert C. Wood views suburbia as an ideological retreat to the "republic in miniature" of early American history. Two sections of Wood's book, *Suburbia: Its People and Their Politics,* are reproduced here. The first traces the historical roots of the "republic in miniature" ideology. The second part picks up on the emergence of the suburb as a reincarnation of the nostalgic image of the past. Wood's analysis of the organizational, political, and economic consequences of suburbia strongly supports our central theme that America's values about urban life are one of the principal obstacles standing in the way of a constructive approach to urban problems.

Thus far, all of our readings have dealt with the ideological aspects of urban life in America. We indicated above, however, that the roots of distrust for urban life are much older than the history of this nation. In a passage from *Urban Behavior* by E. Gordon Ericksen we find a concise accounting of more than two thousand years of thought about urban life. While Ericksen's style is curt, his conclusions are impressive. Beginning with ancient religious writings of the Middle East, Persia, India, and Japan, and moving to the dominant political philosophers of the Enlightenment, Ericksen finds a persistence of admiration of agrarian life and a concomitant distrust of the city.

We have seen that at least part of man's repugnance toward the city has grown out of objective reality. Yet at the same time, man has been slow to acknowledge that cities have been the breeding grounds of the greatest human accomplishments. Today the problems of urban living are intensified by man's inability to think creatively about the city. Man's distaste for urban living is rapidly creating a type of environment which is neither urban nor rural; an environment which if continued unchecked over the next few decades will have the advantages of neither urban nor rural living and the disadvantages of both.

It would seem that if man is to avoid this misfortune, he must begin to see the possibilities as well as the liabilities of the city. In short, he needs to develop positive value orientations toward the city which will challenge the negative ideologies which have dominated his thinking throughout most of history.

In 1965 a young theologian, Harvey Cox, published a little book entitled *The Secular City* which is almost certain to be viewed by historians as a giant step in the direction of a creative urban philosophy. Rather than repudiating the rise of urbanization and secularization, Cox is exulted by the possibilities which these two developments represent.

His analysis pivots on four themes which may be interpreted as the consequences of urbanization and secularization: *anonymity, mobility, pragmatism,* and *profanity*. Each of these developments has been viewed by many intellectuals with a good deal of consternation and despondency, but Cox sees them as forces of liberation. With urbanization and secularization man has become free from the bondage of traditional moral sanctions and ideologies which have focused his attention upon supernatural concerns. Secular man is free to make of the world what he will.

Cox sees no reason to lament *anonymity* and impersonal relationships. True, the high density of the city makes personal relationships with everyone that one encounters impossible, but at the same time, one has a wider range of alternatives from which to choose and establish deeper and more personal relationships. But this, in turn, demands some discipline of selectivity.

Mobility, to be sure, disrupts tradition, but Cox sees this also as a liberating and humanizing force. The traditions which have been disrupted are those which have held man in bondage. Cox describes mobility as the "weapon of the underdog" and notes that most of us are better off today because our ancestors were mobile. Endless movement, of course, can have drawbacks; it can become a mechanism of shiftlessness and an unwillingness to assume responsibility for oneself and one's society. But on balance, Cox views mobility as a contributing factor to human emancipation.

Urban-secular man is *pragmatic,* i.e., he is preoccupied with the question "Will it work?" Cox rejects the existentialist's lamenting that our society has become without meaning and purpose. To the contrary, Cox argues, "Our culture does *not* lack purpose; it lacks only the particular purpose the existentialists have grown used to." Again, pragmatism, as anonymity and mobility, is a double-edged sword. It can become a closed world-view of the Orwellian variety which tolerates nothing that does not fit into the very narrow purposes of a monolithic state. But Cox seems not to be too concerned about this since it is urban-secular society which has given birth to tolerance and pluralism.

Finally, Cox defines *profanity* as " . . . the disappearance of any supramundane reality defining [man's] life." Secular man " . . . views the world not in terms of some other world but in terms of itself. He feels that any meaning to be found in this world originates in this world itself." To be profane is to be profoundly concerned with questions of ethics and meaning.

In short, Cox has taken some of the most central developments of modern urban life which have been sources of deep concern for other scholars and concluded that these are the very developments in modern urban civilization which have given life deeper meaning and greater possibilities than man has ever had in all of history.

Cox's discussion of the relationship of urbanization and the demise of traditional religion seems to us to be a profound and penetrating analysis of the most significant developments in contemporary Western culture. As a theologian he brings unique insight and interpretations to the process of urbanization which sociologists have more or less understood for at least a half-century. Some may feel that Cox is overly optimistic about man's ability to use this new freedom and responsibility in a creative way. Perhaps so, but it seems to us that it is hard to quarrel with the proposition that Cox has made an enormously important and imaginative contribution toward the development of a creative ideology of urbanization.

The reading selection reproduced here has been edited from three different chapters of *The Secular City*. Since we are primarily interested in his sociological insight, most of his theological interpretation has been edited from the adaptation. We are especially grateful to Professor Cox for granting us permission to reproduce the materials.

---

[1]Hauser, Philip, "Urbanization: An Overview" from P. Hauser, and Leo F. Schnore (eds.), *The Study of Urbanization* (New York: John Wiley & Sons, Inc., 1965), p. 2.

[2]For example, see: Glaab, Charles N., and Brown, A. Theodore, *A History of Urban America* (New York: The Macmillan Company, 1967).

[3]Whyte, William H., Jr., "Introduction," from Fortune Editors, *The Exploding Metropolis* (Garden City, New York: Doubleday and Company, Inc., 1958), p. vii.

10. Cities in Crisis: An Ideological Problem

SENATOR JOSEPH S. CLARK

America's cities are in a state of crisis today, beset by a host of financial, political and environmental problems. But the chief problem, in my view, is none of these. It is psychological.

Our basic trouble is that we, as a nation, have gone off to live in the wicked city and we're still ashamed to write home and admit that we like it.

This is not to say we do not have our urban financial, environmental and political problems. We do, in shocking degree. But each of these maladies is related to a fundamental American bias against urban life, as somehow less pure, virtuous and enobling than life on the farm.

The nostalgia for the mode of life epitomized in *Tom Sawyer* and Grant Wood's famous painting, "American Gothic," is probably unquenchable. I suspect it will be with us forever. I cannot imagine a 21st Century version of "American Gothic" showing a man with a brief case standing in front of a high rise apartment. Neither brief cases nor high rises fit in with our romantic image. Yet the irresistible drift to the cities began at least as early as World War I. Most of the popular songs of my youth—I was born in 1901—were nostalgic yearnings of the city dweller for a return to the cows and chickens back in the country. Some members of this Subcommittee are perhaps old enough to remember the final lines of the smash hit of 1915:

> "That's why I wish again
> that I was in Michigan
> down on the farm."

But the die was cast for the big city. Right after the November 4,

---

SOURCE: Hearings before Subcommittee on Executive Reorganization (August 15, 1966), pp. 12-13.

1919, armistice, "How're you goin' to keep them down on the farm after they've seen Paree," swept the country. The jig was up for Reuben. He had moved to the city.

There is an increasing realization that when we talk about the quality of American life, what we are talking about is life as it is lived in the metropolitan area. In a nation already predominantly urban, and becoming more so with every passing census, it could not long remain otherwise. But the grip of the past is still firm in conservative circles, particularly legislatures. We are still torn between our romantic dreams of rural utopia, and the crying needs of urban life.

I hope that this Subcommittee, through these extremely useful and necessary hearings, will be able to find a way to cut through the nostalgic myth and lay bare the urgent reality. I have no easy solutions to offer, and I suspect that there are none. But if I am right in my assertion that the basic problem is psychological, perhaps—as in psychiatry—self revelation can show the way to the cure.

11. The Intellectual Versus the American City

MORTON AND LUCIA WHITE

Although the city has become one of the most absorbing and most intensively studied social problems in America today, and although it is now fashionable for intellectuals to express an almost tender concern for its future, to hope that its decay can be arrested, and to offer plans for its revitalization, this has not always been the attitude of our greatest American thinkers.[1] For a variety of reasons they have expressed different degrees of hostility toward urban life in America, hostility which may be partly responsible for a feeling on the part of today's city planner and urban reformer that he has no mythology or mystique on which he can rest or depend. We have no tradition of romantic attachment to the city in our highbrow literature, nothing that remotely resembles the Greek philosopher's attachment to the *polis* or the French writer's affection for Paris. And this fits very well with the frequently defended thesis that the American writer has been more than usually alienated from the society in which he lives, that he is typically in revolt against it. Throughout the nineteenth century our

SOURCE: "The Intellectual Versus the American City," *Daedalus,* 90 (Winter, 1961). The central thesis of this article is further developed and documented in the Whites' book, *The Intellectual Versus the City: From Jefferson to Frank Lloyd Wright* (Harvard University and M.I.T. Press, Cambridge, Mass., 1962).

society was becoming more and more urbanized, but the literary tendency to denigrate the American city hardly declined in proportion. If anything, it increased in intensity.

Faced with this fact about the history of American thought, the contemporary student of the city can take one of two opposing attitudes. He, at his peril, can turn his back on the tradition of Jefferson, Emerson, Thoreau, Hawthorne, Melville, Poe, Henry Adams, Henry James, Louis Sullivan, Frank Lloyd Wright, and John Dewey. In this case he will treat some of the American city's profoundest critics as irresponsible literary men or as idle metaphysicians who fled the city rather than face its problems. Or he can regard this critical tradition as a repository of deep, though troubling, wisdom, one which raises basic questions for any urban reformer, and some of whose premonitions and fears have been more than justified by the passage of time. There is no doubt that the second is the wiser course. He who would improve the American city can only profit by an awareness of what some of our greatest minds have said, felt, and thought about one of the most conspicuous and most troubling features of our national life.

One cannot deny, of course, that there were pro-urban literary voices like Whitman's, or that there were urban sociologists like Robert Park who tried to speak up for the city. But they are voices in "the city wilderness," never comparing in volume with the anti-urban roar in the national literary pantheon. The urbanist must face the fact that the anti-urbanist does not live only in the Kentucky hills, in the Rockies, in the Ozarks, in the Cracker country, or the bayous. He lives in the mind and heart of America as conceived by the intellectual historian. The intellect, whose home is the city, according to some sociologists, has been the American city's sharpest critic. Everyone knows that Jefferson once hoped to discourage the development of the city in America, but he was only the first of a long and varied list of critics of the city.

Jefferson despised the manners and principles of the urban "mob" as he knew it in Europe and he hoped to keep it from crossing the Atlantic intact. He certainly did not think of the city as "The Hope of Democracy," as some Progressive theorists did at the turn of the twentieth century. He adopted a conciliatory tone about the city in his old age when he said in 1816 that we could not possibly depend on England for manufactures, as he had originally thought, and therefore we *needed* cities. But this does not show any *love* for the city. The country and its yeomen Jefferson loved all his life; in his old age he grudgingly accepted the manufacturing city as a necessity.

The same War of 1812 which led Jefferson to reassess his views was followed by a great expansion of the American city. It inaugurated a major phase of urban civilization between the Revolution and the Civil War. By 1860 the urban population was eleven times what it had been in 1820. The early decades of the nineteenth century saw the decline of Jefferson's empiricism among American intellectuals, and the emergence of philosophical transcendentalism, but a distaste for the city persisted among American writers.

The growth of the city in the North produced an even sharper reaction in Ralph Waldo Emerson than the European city had produced in Jefferson. Emerson's first philosophical work, *Nature,* appeared in 1836, in the middle of that interval which witnessed an eleven-fold increase in our urban population. Its very title was a protest against what he thought was happening. Partly under the influence of English romanticism, Emerson and some of his friends took to deprecating manufacture, art, and civilization, and so it was not long before they took to criticizing the city, the greatest of artifacts. The distaste for the city as an artificial creation was associated in Emerson's mind, as it was in the case of many romantic thinkers, with doubts about the value of science as an avenue to truth. And yet Emerson agreed with the scientifically minded Jefferson about the nasty manners and principles of the city. Whereas Jefferson was given to arguing the defects of the city in common-sense political terms, Emerson sought to buttress his feelings by a metaphysical theory. Hence we may label his period as the metaphysical period of anti-urbanism. To be is to be natural for Emerson. In the wilderness he said he found "something more dear and connate than in streets or villages." The life of the city was "artificial and curtailed"; it destroyed solitude, poetry, and philosophy.

One will find passages in which Emerson extolled the application of science and the virtues of civilization, the need for sociability to educate a man's sympathies, and the advantages of specialization that allow each man to develop his own talents. This suggests a more friendly view of the industrial urban society which was emerging in his own lifetime. But he always harped on the human failings of State Street and commercialism. At times Emerson could celebrate the artifice of pure technology, but he persistently attacked the debasement of moral standards by those who pursued nothing but wealth in the cities as he knew them. One is reminded of Thorstein Veblen's praise of urban industry even as he attacked its financial captains, for it was Veblen who saw the modern industrial city as the *locus classicus* of conspicuous waste.

Thoreau went even farther than Emerson in his distaste for civilization and the city, for Thoreau also attacked the village and the farm. *Walden* is a bible of anti-urbanism, in which Thoreau celebrates the life of the isolated individual, living in Nature and free of *all* social attachments. No wonder that Thoreau refused to visit the Saturday Club, which provided one of the few values of Boston in Emerson's eyes: intellectual conversation. And when Thoreau refused, Perry Miller reminds us, he put his refusal in no uncertain terms: "The only room in Boston which I visit with alacrity is the Gentlemen's Room at the Fitchburg Depot, where I wait for cars, sometimes for two hours, in order to get out of town."[2] No wonder Henry James said that Thoreau "was essentially a sylvan personage."[3]

If Jefferson attacked the city on political grounds, and if Emerson and Thoreau may be represented as criticizing it from the point of view of transcendental metaphysics, what shall we say of Poe, Hawthorne and Melville, all of whom may be added to our list of pre-Civil War critics of the city? They were far from political theorists or metaphysicians but all of them saw the city as the scene of sin and crime. Speaking of them, Harry Levin says: "For our dreamers, America was a garden, an agrarian Eden, which was losing its innocence by becoming citified. Melville had located his City of Woe in London or Liverpool; Poe had tracked down imaginary crimes in the streets of an imagined Paris; and Hawthorne had exposed sins most luridly among the ruins of Rome."[4] As in Jefferson's case, the urban models of extreme crime and sinfulness were not located in the United States by most of our pre-Civil War anti-urbanists, but they saw dark omens in the streets of American cities which made them fear that they might become like Paris, London, Liverpool or Rome.

The observant de Tocqueville expressed his worry about the American city in 1835, one year before Emerson's essay *Nature* appeared. He said that the fact that America as yet had no dominating metropolis was one of those circumstances which tended to maintain a democratic republic in the United States and to counteract that great danger to which all democracies are subject—the tyranny of the majority. But de Tocqueville thought that the "lower ranks" which inhabited Philadelphia (pop. 161,000) and New York (pop. 202,000) in the 1830's "constitute a rabble even more formidable than the populace of European towns. They consist of freed blacks . . . who are condemned by the laws and by public opinion to a hereditary state of misery and degradation. They also contain a multitude of Europeans who have been driven to the shore of the New World by their misfortunes or their misconduct; and they bring to the United States all our greatest vices, without any of those interests which counteract their baneful influence. As inhabitants of a country where they have no civil rights, they are ready to turn all the passions which agitate the community to their own advantage; thus, within the last few months, serious riots have broken out in Philadelphia and New York."[5] So seriously did de Tocqueville treat this matter that he said: "I look upon the size of certain American cities, and especially on the nature of their population, as a real danger which threatens the future security of the democratic republics of the New World; and I venture to predict that they will perish from this circumstance, unless the government succeeds in creating an armed force which, while it remains under the control of the majority of the nation, will be independent of the town population and able to repress its excesses."[6]

If this could be the conclusion of the most astute foreign observer ever to visit our shores, it is not surprising that some of our great literary figures might have developed less than an admiring view of our urban culture between the Revolution and the Civil War. Optimistic empiricists like Jefferson, optimistic transcendentalists like Emerson, pessimistic believers in original sin like Hawthorne and Melville, all forgot their philosophical differences when they looked upon the American city, even before it developed into the industrial jungle it was to become between the Civil War and the end of the nineteenth century . . . .

Among the most influential and most fastidious observers of this development were Henry Adams and the younger Henry James. Both were men of literary genius, both were members of cultivated families with wealth in their backgrounds, and for both of them the American city provided a profound spiritual problem. Because Henry Adams and Henry James lived in the age of the city's supremacy, they did not speak of it, as Jefferson had, as a remote future phenomenon or as something existing in Europe alone. And, unlike Thoreau, they did not feel as though they had only the American city and the American wilderness to choose between. Adams and James were both refined, civilized, indeed urban men whose animadversions on the American city are made more significant precisely because they were not opposed to cities in principle. They demonstrate what a hard time the American city had at the hands of nineteenth-century intellectuals. For here at last were two *city* types who also found the American city sadly wanting. Their reaction to the American city is more esthetic, more literary, more psychological than that of their predecessors Jefferson and Emerson.

The two most important documents for an understanding of the views of Adams and James are the former's *Education* and the latter's *The American Scene*. It is significant that the great problem of the *Education of Henry Adams* was to steer a course between the poles of town and country, between the Boston and Quincy of his childhood. "Town," Adams tells us, "was restraint, law, unity. Country, only seven miles away, was liberty, diversity, outlawry, the endless delight of mere sense impressions given by nature for nothing, and breathed by boys without knowing it."[8] Adams also tells us that he spent his life trying to choose between the ways of life they represented, without ever making up his mind. And yet, in a sense, he did make up his mind, or the social forces of America made it up for him. He could not go back to the Quincy house of his grandfather Adams. And, being no Thoreau, he had to live in the American city if he was to live anywhere in America. But what was *the* American city in his mature years? Surely not Boston, but New York. And when Henry Adams looked at the New York of 1868, he tells us in a book which he wrote in 1905 that he felt swept aside by the forces pushing the country in a new direction. "His world," he lamented, "was dead. Not a Polish Jew fresh from Warsaw or Cracow—not a furtive Yaccob or Ysaac still reeking of the Ghetto, snarling a weird Yiddish to the officers of the customs—but had a keener instinct, and intenser energy, and a freer hand than he—American of Americans, with Heaven knew how many Puritans and Patriots behind him, and an education that had cost a civil war."[9] Adams felt like the dispossessed Indian and the buffalo in America after 1865, for it was a banker's, and neither a buffalo's nor a Bostonian's world. To Henry Adams, New York symbolized the spiritual confusion of America at the end of the nineteenth century.

Henry James, as one might expect, also complained about his birthplace, New York, after a period of flirtation with it. James attacked it most explicitly in *The American Scene,* published in 1907 as the report of an expatriate revisiting the country of his birth. He, too, spoke of the city's chaos, and even the New York skyline insulted his very expressively complex sensibilities. He complained of the lack of history and of the lack of time for history in a way that reminds one of his early critical work on Nathaniel Hawthorne. The buildings, he said, "never speak to you, in the manner of the builded majesties of the world . . . towers, or temples, or fortresses or palaces with the authority of things of permanence or even of things of long duration."[10] History had given way to commerce: "The great city is projected into its future as practically, a huge continuous fifty-floored conspiracy against the very idea of the ancient graces."[11] The city lacked order, structure, dignity, history. James speaks of it as "a heaped industrial battlefield" and as a scene of "the universal will to move—to move, move, move, as an end in itself, an appetite at any price."[12] He missed what he called "organic social relations,"[13] and he felt some pleasurable relief when he visited Philadelphia, because it didn't "bristle," and because "it went back."[14] In this spirit he warned: "Let not the unwary . . . visit Ellis Island"[15] as Henry Adams might have warned in *his* snobbish way. James was upset by what he called "that loud primary stage of alienism which New York most offers to sight."[16] And he dreamed "of the luxury of some such close and sweet and *whole* national consciousness as that of the Switzer and the Scot."[17] His final head-shaking conclusion was "that there was no escape from the ubiquitous alien into the future or even into the present; there was no escape but into the past."[18]

* * *

Although we are primarily concerned with recording the theme of *anti*-urbanism in American writing and thinking, it would be absurd to argue that *every* great writer or thinker in the American pantheon was hostile to urban life. The fact is that at the end of the nineteenth century there emerged a tendency to view the American city in a more friendly manner. By contrast to his brother Henry, William James had very little desire to escape from the American city into the past. His philosophy was one of hope, of optimism, of possibility—indeed, a little bit too much so—and it was this that allowed him to view the urbanization of America in a way that might encourage Americans to do something about urban problems. Unlike Henry, he did not adore the great cities of Western Europe. For ten days after his arrival in Florence in 1875 he "was so disgusted with the swarming and reeking blackness of the streets and the age of everything, that enjoyment took place under protest."[20] As for London, during his visit of 1889 he wrote his sister that he was "thoroughly sated" with it, and "never cared to see its yellow-brownness and stale spaciousness again."[21]

William James loved the country but his love of nature was tempered by a fondness for sociability, and therefore he was unable to subscribe either to Thoreau's primitivism or to the ultracivilized sentiments of his brother. With Emerson he looked to the future, but unlike Emerson he did not think that the future excluded the possibility of a decent life in the cities of America . . . .

William James, like Walt Whitman, saw virtue and promise in the American city. Both William James and Whitman not only accept the city as an inescapable part of America, but they *enjoy* it, as Jefferson most certainly did not. The year of William James's discovery of what he called "the new New York" was 1907, when he delivered his most famous set of lectures, entitled *Pragmatism,* at Columbia. James thought his philosophy would mediate between the views of those whom he called "tenderfoot Bostonians" and those he labeled "Rocky Mountain toughs" in philosophy. It is not too fanciful to suppose that James identified the great future city, along with his pragmatic philosophy, as a blend of, a compromise between, the insipidity of Boston and the craggy brutality of the Rockies. A livable city on earth, one is tempted to say, is the social counterpart of James's pragmatism, and therefore he is one of the first great American writers to associate himself with the effort to accept what is good and to root out what is bad in the American city. He does not escape to the country with Emerson and Thoreau, or to the past with his brother and Henry Adams. He revives the wisdom of the older Jefferson after a century of transcendentalism, Brook-farming and expatriation, and adds to it a love of the city. In doing so he becomes the herald of a pragmatic phase in urban thinking.

But this pragmatic phase, in which the city was joyfully described by Frederic C. Howe in 1905 as "The Hope of Democracy," did not last very long. Indeed, Howe's book contained within itself the classical argument for the central city's impending destruction. "The open fields about the city are inviting occupancy," Howe said, "and there the homes of the future will surely be. The city proper will not remain the permanent home of the people. Population must be dispersed. The great cities of Australia are spread out into the suburbs in a splendid way. For miles about are broad roads, with small houses, gardens, and an opportunity for touch with the freer, sweeter life which the country offers."[25] Howe calls the city the hope of democracy, but he is, it would appear, a suburban booster rather than a city-lover. He shares the basic inability of greater American intellectuals to go all out in their admiration for the modern American city.

A more striking illustration of the same thing may be found in the writings of John Dewey, the disciple of William James, who sympathized with so much of James's interest in the American city. In his earlier writing Dewey expressed a typically progressive interest in the city. This was part of the political liberalism of the period, with its interest in urban planning, social work, socialism, the single tax, and muck-raking. The city was not regarded as a perfect form of life, but it was seen as having promise. And, to the extent to which it showed promise, it became the concern of all sorts of people who could criticize it in a constructive spirit quite different from that which dominated the work of militant anti-urbanists from Jefferson to Henry James. For a variety of reasons Chicago became the most conspicuous locale of this new way of looking at the city. It was the home of a great university, which had opened its doors in the 'nineties and which became a center of urban sociology and, it might be said, of urban philosophy. One can understand, therefore, why William James looked to Dewey and other Chicago intellectuals as his friends, and why they regarded him as their spiritual leader. For Chicago at the turn of the century was the home of James's pupil, Robert Park, his worshipper, Jane Addams, and his disciple, John Dewey.

As early as 1899 Dewey was urging that the congregation of men into cities was one of the most conspicuous features of the modern world and that no theory of education could possibly disregard the fact of urbanization. Indeed, *the* problem of education, as Dewey saw it in his *School and Society,* was how to adjust the child to life in the city. The earlier kind of rural environment, in which he had been raised as a boy in Vermont, had its virtues, he admitted. It encouraged habits of personal orderliness, industry, and responsibility; it led to a firsthand acquaintance with nature. But, Dewey said in 1899, "it was useless to bemoan the departure of the good old days . . . if we expect merely by bemoaning and by exhortation to bring them back."[26] The problem, as Dewey saw it, was that of retaining some advantages of the older mode of life while training the child to cope with the new urban world. The school, therefore, was to be a miniature urban community, a microcosmic duplication of macrocosmic Chicago, much as Hull House was in Jane Addams' eyes. The essence of society, said Dewey—and in this he was joined by Robert Park and other sociologists—was communication—and therefore the school was to encourage and develop this peculiarly social phenomenon, this salient feature of the urban age. Dewey's progressivism in educational theory was defined by his broad conception of communication, his idea that it takes place while children are building blocks, dancing, and cooking, as well as on the more formal level of asserting propositions.

Soon, however, a new and more critical attitude toward the city began to enter Dewey's writing. In *The Public and Its Problems* (1927) he concluded that steam and electricity, the very forces that had created modern society, that had provided it with the means of transportation and communication that made urban concentration possible, were creating a situation in which communication at its most human level was being destroyed. The very forces which brought Bangkok and Chicago closer to each other and which brought people from isolated farms to urban centers had diminished the possibility of "face-to-face" relationships. The primary group, in the phrase of the sociologist, Charles Horton Cooley, was disappearing rapidly. And while Dewey did not use our current jargon, he said, in effect, that modern society was becoming a lonely crowd of organization men.

Dewey warned: "Unless local communal life can be restored, the public cannot adequately resolve its most urgent problem: to find and identify itself."[27] But the local communal unit of which Dewey spoke now was not the enormous city as it was coming to be known in the twentieth century. It was more like the University Elementary School at the University of Chicago, or Hull House. "Democracy must begin at home," Dewey said, "and its home is the neighborly community."[28] As a result, a curious reversal takes place in Dewey's thinking. Instead of taking the city as the model *for* the progressive school, he almost speaks as though the urban community should be modeled *on* the progressive school. Jefferson wrote at the end of his life: "As Cato concluded every speech with the words, 'Carthago delenda est,' so do I every opinion with the injunction, 'Divide the counties into wards.' " At the end of his life Dewey seemed to conclude every speech with the words, "Divide the cities into settlement houses."

It is ironic to find the most influential philosopher of the urban age in America reverting to the localism of Jefferson, but no more ironic than the anti-urbanism of Louis Sullivan and Frank Lloyd Wright, our most distinctive architects. For functionalism, like pragmatism, is one of a complex of American ideas that could not exist in a non-urban society, and yet its greatest spokesmen seem to hate the American city. Sullivan's *Autobiography* records his distaste for Boston in his childhood, and in his *Kindergarten Chats* he fulminates against New York and Chicago. "Lieber Meister," as Wright called Sullivan, bequeathed this hostility to his disciple, and the disciple, as everyone knows, added his own powerful spice to the brew of anti-urbanism. John Dewey may have reverted to Jefferson's localism, but Wright was a little more partial to Emerson. Not only are there copious references to Emerson in Wright's books, but he adds as a red-printed appendix to *The Living City* a long excerpt from Emerson's essay, "Farming," which concludes with a typically transcendental warning: "Cities force growth and make men talkative and entertaining, but they make them artificial." And so the great American architect of the twentieth century went back spiritually to Concord, while the great American philosopher retreated to Monticello.

One moral of this tale is that city-loving urban reformers will not find much boosting or sentimental admiration of city life in the writings of those who have been canonized in our national literature and philosophy. A brief flurry of pro-urban sentiment in the late nineteenth and early twentieth century under the encouraging eye of Walt Whitman and William James was swiftly buried by the exploding megalopolis, but after it our most sensitive and gifted intellectuals went on criticizing the American city. Readers who may feel that this story is based on an excessively narrow selection of writers and thinkers should remember that other readers will find in these pages the names of our greatest political thinker, our greatest essayist, our greatest philosopher, our greatest theorist of education, our greatest novelist, our greatest autobiographer, and our greatest architect, all of them throwing up their hands about the most distinctive and most pressing features of our national life. If *their* views should not be typical of the nation's view on this topic, that in itself would be a fact that is worth recording and pondering. Moreover, it is impossible to produce a list of *pro*-urban American thinkers who remotely approach this collection in distinction and intellectual influence.

In spite of the anti-urbanism of our literary and philosophical tradition, the city planner would make a grave mistake if he were to dismiss that tradition, if he were to treat it as a point of view from which nothing could be learned, if he were to forget it and disregard it. Those who must live in today's American city or who like to live in it can profit by taking seriously the urban criticism of our great writers, for it was deep and many-sided. It was not only esthetic but also moral in character. Henry James spoke most persuasively for those who saw the city as a scene of chaos as it presented itself to "the painter's eye." It lacked order, structure, history, and dignity in 1907, and God knows that these virtues have not been miraculously supplied in the age of urban sprawl and suburban slums. But the city, as Robert Park said, is a state of mind as well as an esthetic object, and the profoundest critics of the American city have found other faults with it.

When Jefferson warned of the dangers of what he called the city mob, when Emerson complained of the city's artificiality and conventionalism, when John Dewey lamented the decline of neighborliness, all of them thought of the city as a place in which certain basic human values were being subverted, values which are cherishable today as they were in the eighteenth century of Jefferson, the nineteenth century of Emerson, and the twentieth century of Dewey. And what are these values? Jefferson's worry about the mobs of the city arose from doubt about the American city's capacity to educate its inhabitants in a way that would preserve and extend the democratic process. And when Emerson worried about the growth of artificiality and conventionalism in the city, he was thinking, as were his contemporaries, Kierkegaard and John Stuart Mill, about the increase in conformity, about the decline of individuality which was proportional to the increase of urbanization in America. Dewey's main concern was with the improvement of human communication within the city; and by communication he did not mean the exchange of information alone. He valued the capacity to share feelings and experiences, the capacity to discuss with, to learn from and intelligently persuade others, and to *live* with them in the profoundest sense.

Who can deny in 1960, then, that the great problem of the American city is to demonstrate at least three things: first, that it can solve the problem of education for the millions of people who are entering its gates, that it can absorb the Puerto Rican, as it has other immigrant groups, into the democratic process; second, that it can foster individuality, the capacity and the right of the human being to develop into a rounded personality who is concerned with more than merely commercial values; and third, that it can be more than a vast prison of unconnected cells in which people of different occupations, color, class, or creed fail to understand one another on the basic human issues of social life, let alone agree with one another.

The moral message of the intellectual critic of the city today is not fundamentally different from what it was in the age of Jefferson, Emerson, and Dewey. For today's serious thinker must also build upon a respect for the fundamental values of education, individuality, and easy communication among men. But, unlike his predecessors, he cannot deceive himself about the *place* in which those values must be realized today. The wilderness, the isolated farm, the plantation, the self-contained New England town, the detached neighborhood are things of the past. All the world's a city now and there is no escaping urbanization, not even in outer space.

---

[1]The theme of this essay is being developed more fully in a larger work. Much of the research and writing has been done under the auspices of the Twentieth Century Fund's Study of Megalopolis, directed by Jean Gottmann, and of the Joint Center for Urban Studies of the Massachusetts Institute of Technology and Harvard University.

[2]Perry Miller (editor), *Consciousness in Concord* (Boston, 1958), p. 46.

[3]Henry James, *Hawthorne* (New York, 1880), p. 80.

[4]Harry Levin, *The Power of Blackness* (New York, 1958), p. 234.

[5]Alexis de Tocqueville, *Democracy in America* (New York, 1945), Vol. I, p. 289, note.

[6]*Ibid.*

[8]Henry Adams, *The Education of Henry Adams* (Boston, 1918), pp. 7-8.

[9]*Ibid.*, p. 238.

[10]Henry James, *The American Scene* (reprint, New York, 1946), p. 77.

[11]*Ibid.*, p. 92.

[12]*Ibid.*, p. 84.

[13]*Ibid.*, p. 279.

[14]*Ibid.*, pp. 275, 280.

[15]*Ibid.*, p. 85.

[16]*Ibid.*, p. 86.

[17]*Ibid.*

[18]*Ibid.*, p. 115.

[20]Ralph Barton Perry, *The Thought and Character of William James* (Boston, 1935), Vol. I. p. 351.

[21]*Ibid.*, p. 412.

[25]Frederic C. Howe, *The City: The Hope of Democracy* (New York, 1905), p. 204.

[26]John Dewey, *School and Society* (Chicago, 1899), p. 9.

[27]Dewey, *The Public and Its Problems* (reprint edn., Chicago, 1946), p. 216.

[28]*Ibid.*, p. 213.

12. Urbanism and American Democracy

FRANCIS E. ROURKE

"The United States," writes Richard Hofstadter in his *Age of Reform,* "was born in the country and has moved to the city. From the beginning its political values and ideas were of necessity shaped by country life." Few could disagree with this appraisal. At the time of the first census in 1790, more than nine out of ten Americans lived in rural territory, and as late as 1860 the proportion of the population living outside of cities remained well over 75 per cent. Thus, from the Revolution to the Civil War, agrarian dominance was a major fact of life in American politics. This was a time when rural ascendancy rested on the solid basis of numerical superiority rather than upon the legislative malapportionment and gerrymandering that have since served to shore up agrarian power against the steady erosion of population in rural areas.

What was most striking about this early system of domination by agrarian interests was the uncontested philosophical justification it received at the hands of Jefferson and those who followed in his wake. No such fervent ideological support was to crown the power of either of the other major groups who were in time to lay claim to supremacy in American politics—the business elite which came into prominence in the period following the Civil War, or the popular coalition which has sustained the broad outlines of the welfare state since the presidency of Franklin Roosevelt. In the days of agrarian supremacy, political power and political ideology were linked together in a neat pattern of harmony, while since that time they have often been poles apart.

Easily the most familiar protagonist of this system of agrarian democracy was Thomas Jefferson. As Griswold points out: "No one believed so implicitly as he in a causal connection between the occupation of farming and the political system of democracy, and no one, before or since his time, has given that belief a greater impetus among his countrymen."[2] Of course the doctrine of agrarian superiority which Jefferson espoused—"those who labor in the earth are the chosen people of God"—is a very old theme in Western thought. It was widely prevalent in both Greek and Roman culture, from Hesiod to Horace, and this classical view was adopted and advanced in subsequent European literature, drawing on Christian as well as pagan

SOURCE: Reprinted from *Ethics,* 74 (July, 1964), pp. 255-268, by Francis E. Rourke by permission of the University of Chicago Press.

sources to support the comparison it drew between the virtue and vitality of the countryside and the vices and decay of urban society.

Much of this pastoral tradition stresses the physical, economic, and moral advantages of agricultural life; but throughout it there also runs the persistent theme that farming makes for better citizens as well as healthier, nobler, and more affluent men. Western intellectual history provided ample precedent for Jefferson's view that the farmer was not only the mainstay of the economy and the pillar of civil rectitude, but the backbone of the state as well: "The proportion which the aggregate of the other classes of citizens bears in any State to that of its husbandmen, is the proportion of its unsound to its healthy parts."

With the steady advance of urbanization in American society, the passages in Jefferson which retain the most telling impact today are those in which he takes specific note of what he considers to be the ill effects of cities upon the healthy functioning of a democratic society. For it was Jefferson who set the style for the treatment the city was to receive in subsequent political thought. Few statements in American political doctrine are as celebrated as his assertion that "the mobs of great cities add just so much to the support of pure government as sores do to the strength of the human body." But the view he put forward in a letter to Benjamin Rush was even more extreme. There he argued that a recent outbreak of yellow fever in coastal cities, however unfortunate its consequences in terms of human suffering, might at least have the advantage of discouraging the establishment of large urban centers in this country. For such cities, Jefferson declared, are more "pestilential" than yellow fever "to the morals, the health and the liberties of man."[3]

It has been suggested—most recently by Morton and Lucia White in their study of attitudes toward the city in American intellectual history—that Jefferson recanted these antiurban sentiments after he became president.[4] If so, this retraction was a grudging one, based largely on Jefferson's belated recognition during the Napoleonic Wars that the political independence of this country might ultimately be lost if it remained completely dependent upon the industrial cities of Europe for manufactured goods. Nor was it a permanent conversion, since Jefferson returned to his agrarian outlook in the later years of his life. Certainly there is little in Jefferson's career to support the Whites' description of him as "a great intellectual defender" of the American city.

But it is interesting to note that for a time at least the harsh realities of international politics forced Jefferson to accept some measure of urbanization, even though he regarded this development as altogether undesirable for a democratic society from a purely domestic point of view. For the individual as opposed to the state, Jefferson never lost his conviction that the highest degree of political independence rested upon the economic security provided by ownership of a small farm. But as has often been true in American history, when the requirements of foreign policy required a modification of domestic political doctrine, this modification was quickly forthcoming. The needs of national security soon overcame even Jefferson's antipathy for cities. As he himself put it in a letter to DuPont: "What is practicable must often control what is pure theory."

Jefferson's views on the negative impact of urbanization were not disputed by any of the more influential of his contemporaries. James Madison, for example, faithfully echoed the same sentiment in his own writings. "The life of the husbandman is pre-eminently suited to the comfort and happiness of the individual," he wrote. "The extremes both of want and of waste have other abodes. 'Tis not the country that peoples either the Bridewells or the Bedlams. These mansions of wretchedness are tenanted from the distresses and vices of overgrown cities."

More surprising, perhaps, than the support Jefferson received from a fellow Virginian planter like Madison was the fact that there was no dissent from his adverse judgment regarding cities on the part of leading Federalists of the day. For in principle at least these Federalists were committed to a course of economic development, the encouragement of manufacturing and commerce, which would inevitably promote the growth of urban centers. Alexander Hamilton nowhere attempted to refute the Jeffersonian point of view, however much his "report on manufactures" may have contributed to urbanization, and John Adams affirmed his belief that "agriculture is the most essential interest of America."[5]

Later on, Federalists like Chancellor Kent were even to use Jefferson's attacks on cities to buttress their own aristocratic stand against eliminating suffrage restrictions. In New York, for example, the proposal to extend the franchise stirred prolonged and bitter controversy at the state constitutional convention in 1821, and on that occasion leading Federalist spokesmen sounded warnings against the city that were thoroughly Jeffersonian in tenor:

> Elisha Williams, the young Van Buren's brilliant adversary in the courts of Columbia County and chief figure in the haughty Columbia Junto, explicitly dared the Democratic delegates to confront the reasoning of their great god Jefferson on the moral influence of cities. Would Jefferson's disciples spread "the contents of those [urban] sores through the whole political body" and so expose the yeoman interest to the will of "the ring streaked and speckled population of

our large towns and cities, comprising people of every kindred and tongue?" "These cities," Williams warned, "are filled with men too rich, or too poor to fraternize with the yeomen of the country." With Kent, he placed the democratic menace in the city and the future.[6]

Not the least of the paradoxical aspects of Jefferson's impact on American politics is thus the fact that his prejudice against cities ultimately became a weapon in the hands of his bitterest political opponents.

THE JEFFERSONIAN HERITAGE

Since Jefferson's antiurban views were in accord with traditional political doctrine and were expressed at a time when the overwhelming majority of all Americans lived outside of cities, these sentiments certainly did not expose him to any substantial political risk. Quite to the contrary, Jefferson's agrarian posture may be said to have served him quite well from the point of view of political advantage. Much more remarkable was the way in which this Jeffersonian attitude was to persist down through American history even into the day when the great majority of Americans had come to live in an urban environment. While Jefferson's agrarian point of view was neither risky nor original, it proved to be an extraordinarily durable part of the American political tradition.

When the Jacksonian Democrats came to power, their political base rested on the support of the labor vote in the eastern cities as well as the farmers of the West. Antagonism toward the "money power" provided the bond of unity between these two divergent groups. And yet, Jefferson's dislike of cities continued to weave its spell over large sections of the Jacksonian movement, in part perhaps because the hated banking interests were themselves located in the cities. In his study of the Jackson era, Schlesinger points out that Jackson's followers were far from happy over the dependence of their party upon the votes it received in urban areas:

> The situation in New York, where the country regularly voted Whig and the city Democratic, very much worried the *Democratic Review,* a fairly pious organ of Jeffersonianism. "As a general rule," the *Review* observed in some perplexity, "we are free to confess that we prefer the suffrages of the country to those of the city. . . . The farmer is naturally a Democrat—the citizen may be so, but it is in spite of many obstacles."[7]

Other Jacksonian Democrats attempted to relieve their anxiety over the party's urban support by arguing that great cities need not necessarily be as "great sores" on the American body politic as Jefferson had originally believed.

In the decades immediately preceding the Civil War the Jeffersonian antagonism toward the city was clearly discernible in the arguments put forward by the southern apologists for slavery. This was one of the few occasions in which the proslavery argument had occasion to lean upon Jefferson's support, since Calhoun, Fitzhugh, and the other writers prominent in defense of the southern cause generally found it necessary to spend much of their time refuting Jeffersonian heresies, including the notion of the inherent equality of all mankind as expounded in the Declaration of Independence. But the defense of slavery was based in large measure on the proposition that the condition of the slave on a southern plantation was often a good deal better than the life of the wage earner in northern and European cities. And in this connection southern criticism of the odious characteristics of industrial cities bore a close resemblance to Jefferson's strictures against an urban civilization. "Large cities," wrote George Fitzhugh, "are great curses, because they impoverish a world to enrich a neighborhood."[8]

Since the Civil War hostility toward the city has also found repeated expression in the various movements of political protest which have agitated rural America, from the Grangers in the 1870's to the Farmers' Holiday Association in more recent times. Much of this antiurban sentiment is implicit rather than explicit in the literature of agrarian revolt. It is reflected in the fulsome praise lavished upon the occupation of husbandry, in dogmatic assertions regarding the indispensable role which agriculture plays in the national economy, or in persistent tirades against banking and other urban commercial interests disliked by farmers. But it is praise of agriculture which is at the center of attention rather than overt attacks on the city.

William Jennings Bryan perhaps symbolized more strikingly than any other figure the spirit of agrarian protest in American politics, and Bryan's preference for the country over the city was never left in doubt. It received its most vivid expressed in his Cross of Gold speech at the 1896 Democratic national convention: "The great cities rest upon our broad and fertile prairies," said Bryan in his fervent peroration. "Burn down your cities, and leave our farms, and your cities will spring up again as if by magic; but destroy our farms and the grass will grow in the streets of every city in the country." But as a presidential candidate bidding for support in urban as well as rural constituencies, Bryan could ill afford to reject the city altogether. In setting forth to begin the presidential campaign of 1896 in New York City, he spoke of his trip as one he was taking into the "enemy's country," but this was an area, he hastened to add, "we hope to be our country before this campaign is over."[9] Politicians like Bryan with ambitions which depended for their fulfilment upon urban as well as farm support were compelled to avoid the cruder kinds of assault upon the city in which a purely rural politician could indulge. Some of the lesser Populists were under no such inhibitions.

In its manifestations in the early part of this century, the antagonism toward cities was reinforced by two interdependent developments which exercised a major influence upon the course of American politics, the nativist movement and the drive for national prohibition. Early nativist sentiment was, as John Higham has shown in his *Strangers in the Land,* largely an urban rather than a rural phenomenon. The hostility toward immigrants was initially strongest in the areas where native Americans most frequently rubbed elbows with newcomers from other countries—in the great cities of the East. By the turn of the century, however, the antagonism toward the foreign-born had come to be centered in rural areas, where it blended with and helped to harden the historic agrarian prejudice against the city. The "foreign" character of American cities became one of their major liabilities in rural America—the region most aroused by the wave of nativist sentiment which swept the country in the years following World War I. Speaking of the role of the Ku Klux Klan during this period, Higham writes: "Significantly, the Klan's home was not in the great cities. Its strength came chiefly from the towns, from the villages, and from the ordinarily tranquil countryside."

The prohibition movement was also predominantly rural in its origins, and like nativism served to sharpen hostility toward cities. The city saloon was in fact the bête noire of the temperance crusade, and the attack upon it was an effort at political as well as moral reform, since the saloon was regarded as the headquarters of, and the sustaining force behind, the system of boss rule in cities. "At the door of the saloon was laid the blame for political corruption. It was represented as the *sine qua non* of such political machines as Tammany Hall and the Cox Machine of Cincinnati, 'none of which could continue in existence for a day but for the liquor traffic.' "[10] The nativist movement likewise had the purification of city politics as a central goal in its efforts to restrict the influx of immigrants, since the support of the foreign-born was widely looked upon as a major prop upon which the power of the urban political machine rested.

The fusion between the traditional agrarian dislike of cities, nativism, and the prohibition movement came to white heat in the 1920's at both the Democratic national convention in 1924 and during the presidential campaign of 1928. In each case it was the presidential candidacy of Al Smith which triggered this reaction, since Smith was simultaneously a product of the Tammany political machine in New York City, a descendant of urban Catholic immigrants, and a "wet." It would be difficult to conceive of a less prepossessing set of qualifications from the standpoint of rural America, and the campaign against Smith became at times a crusade against the city and all that it had traditionally symbolized in American politics. Witness the viewpoint of even a liberal Republican like William Allen White: "I make no claim . . . that Smith is a Tammany plug-ugly. . . . But the Tammany system goes on today, as it went on 100 years ago, and, indeed, as it will go on in our American cities unless Governor Smith and the sinister forces behind him are overthrown. Tammany is indeed Tammany, and Smith is its Major Prophet."[11]

Walter Lippmann, himself a Smith supporter, explained the resistance to his candidate in these terms: "Quite apart even from the severe opposition of the prohibitionists, the objection to Tammany, the sectional objection to New York, there is an opposition to Smith which is as authentic, and, it seems to me, as poignant as his support. It is inspired by the feeling that the clamorous life of the city should not be acknowledged as the American ideal. . . . The cities exist, but they are still felt to be alien, and in this uncertainty as to what the cities might yield up, men turn to the old scenes from which the leaders they have always trusted have come."[12] And in the wake of Smith's defeat, interpretations of the 1928 election echoed the same theme. An editorial in one midwestern newspaper proclaimed that "America is not yet dominated by its great cities. Control of its destinies still remains in the smaller communities and rural regions, with their traditional conservatism and solid virtues. . . . Main Street is still the principal thoroughfare of the nation."[13]

While the agrarian prejudice against cities has thus been a continuous theme in American politics since pre-Revolutionary days, the precise nature of the danger which urbanism represents to the rural mind has varied considerably over time. During some periods it has been the propertied classes in cities—the merchants, the shippers, and the bankers—whose activities helped mold rural resentment of cities. On other occasions, and particularly in recent times, it has been the submerged proletariat which has been looked upon as the chief source of danger from urban areas—the industrial hirelings, the newly arrived immigrants, the trade union members, and, in today's metropolitan city, the non-white population.

At different times, the city has thus been regarded as a center of entrenched plutocracy and as a hotbed of radical doctrines subversive of the free-enterprise system, and it has been attacked with equal vehemence by opponents of both capitalism and socialism. Perhaps there is some reconciliation of this seeming contradiction in the fact that the farmer has, depending upon his economic circumstances, tended to regard himself both as a member of the "toiling masses" and as an entrepreneur, and these varying conceptions of the agricultural role in the economy are actually embodied in two distinct national farm organizations, the Farmer's Union and the Farm Bureau Federation.

The tendency of the city to become an odious symbol in the dialogue of American politics found its most eloquent expression in the work of Josiah Strong. Strong argued that American civilization in the closing years of the nineteenth century was confronted by a variety of perils, including immigration, Romanism, intemperance, and socialism. But it was the city which Strong identified as the focal point of all these evils. In the city, he contended, "the dangerous elements of our civilization are each multiplied and all concentered." With Strong as with other writers, the rejection of the city was—quite apart from considerations of religious and ethnic prejudice—a negative response to the industrialization which had spawned large urban centers. For it was industrialism which was regarded as the source of the worst features of urban life, especially the great extremes in wealth—"the rich are richer and the poor are poorer in the city than elsewhere"—which appeared to be so characteristic of an urban economy.[14]

The Impact of Agrarian Thought

There is a sense in which the recurrent note of antagonism toward the city in American political thought may be regarded as but another illustration of the lack of congruence between political doctrine and the actual course of political events. For even as the city was being treated with such persistent disdain in the formal literature of political philosophy during the nineteenth and early twentieth centuries, the general population was simultaneously voting with its feet for urban life—moving into the city in ever increasing numbers in response to economic and other incentives. The trend toward urbanization was certainly not reversed by the hostility shown the city in the American political tradition. Indeed much of this antagonism may rather be viewed as a peevish reaction against a development that could not be prevented.

And yet it cannot be assumed that the rural assault upon the city was altogether without practical effect. For while its influence cannot be precisely measured, the argument for agrarian superiority has certainly played a useful role in providing an ideological underpinning for the prevailing pattern of underrepresentation of the urban population that has characterized the legislative process in this country at both the state and national levels of government for better than half a century. The identification of farming with democracy may not have prevented the movement of population from rural areas, but it could and did provide rural politicians with a convenient line of defense against the impact of this loss of population might otherwise have had upon their own power.

The extent of this urban underrepresentation has been underscored in numerous studies of state legislative apportionment in the United States. To be sure, this inequity has slowly been modified in recent years as a result of the exodus of population from city to suburb that has occurred since World War II. In many parts of the country today it is the suburbs rather than the cities which are most grossly discriminated against in terms of legislative apportionment.The movement of population thus tended to bring the representation of urban centers in state legislatures into much closer accord with their proportionate share of the population even before the decision of the Supreme Court in *Baker* v. *Carr,* which provided cities with a judicial remedy against the traditional pattern of discrimination to which they have been subject. However, a statistical analysis of state legislative representation published in 1961 was still able to conclude that "as of 1960, the average value of the vote in the big city was less than half the average value of the vote in the open country, so far as electing members of the state legislature is concerned."[15]

In the debates which have taken place across the country over the reapportionment problem, the Jeffersonian theme of urban inferiority has often been sounded by groups interested in preserving the disproportionate influence of rural areas in state legislatures. One of the oddities of this system of underrepresentation is the fact that it has very often been given impressive support by urban residents themselves. This was the case in Michigan in 1953, where urban as well as rural residents voted in favor of continuing a system of legislative apportionment highly disadvantageous to the cities. Of course the city is far from unified from a political point of view, and there are, in fact, important urban groups which have long had a vested interest in urban underrepresentation. Many of the salient economic interests centered in cities—business concerns and public utilities, for example, have strong grounds for preferring a system of legislative representation which discriminates against cities simply because the pressure for regulatory legislation adverse to their interests may reasonably be expected to originate in urban rather than rural constituencies. In many parts of the country these business interests have been as much the beneficiary of the prevailing practice of underrepresenting cities in state legislatures as the farmers themselves.

However, it is by no means inconceivable that there is an element of honest conviction as well as self-interest in the apparent willingness of urban dwellers to resign themselves to a system of legislative representation in which they are discriminated against politically. In some cases this tolerance may simply reflect the sentimental tie of many urban residents with the rural milieu in which they were raised and which they left in order to seek their fortune in the city. Hofstadter suggests that such an ambivalent orientation was characteristic of earlier periods of American history: "Throughout the nineteenth century hundreds upon hundreds of thousands of farm-born youths . . . sang the praises of agriculture but eschewed farming as a vocation and sought their careers in the towns and cities."[16]

The most confirmed of all supporters of agrarian dominance may thus be the city resident with ancestral roots in the country, just as some of the most ardent support today for the policy of preserving wilderness areas in their primitive simplicity may come from eastern urbanites, transplanted from their native habitat in the West to the alien pavements of New York. And in point of fact the agrarian vision of the city as an infamous creation has always received considerable support from the romantic fascination with nature that has been an enduring tradition in American life. The fact that the city has been so aesthetically unappealing to urban nature lovers has not been the least of the political disadvantages under which it has labored.

Reforming the City

At its root, the Jeffersonian point of view was characterized by a fundamental antipathy toward cities. If it had been possible, some of the more fervent agrarians would unquestionably have prevented the development of cities altogether, so destructive to democracy did they regard the city as a political force. And in point of fact a great deal of energy was actually expended on efforts to keep people on the farm, or to launch "back-to-the-farm" movements when periods of temporary urban distress gave such proposals hope for success. From Jefferson to Bryan, the note of overt hostility toward cities in agrarian thought is clear and unmistakable.

However, in the decades following the Civil War, a critique of the city began to emerge which was quite different in character from this Jeffersonian point of view. The source of this new criticism was the movement for urban reform which sprang up in the latter part of the nineteenth century and has remained a salient force in municipal politics down to the present time. As a group, the reformers were highly critical of the political development of cities as it was taking place in the Gilded Age. Indeed, if the movement had a text, it was Bryce's celebrated dictum in the *American Commonwealth* that the "government of cities is the one conspicuous failure of the United States." But the reformer's orientation was one of redemption rather than antagonism; the cities were to be saved, to be lifted up, and, hopefully, even to become showcases of American democracy.

The rise of the reform movement was in direct response to the widespread corruption and mismanagement which characterized municipal government in the post–Civil War period. All of Jefferson's worst forebodings regarding the evil effects which cities would eventually have upon American democracy seemed amply justified by the exposures of the Tweed Ring in New York and the other scandals which plagued municipal governments in the nineteenth and early part of the twentieth centuries. As a matter of fact it would have been much easier for Jefferson to obtain evidence to support his condemnation of cities in the decades following the Civil War than it was during his own life time, when American cities were on the whole comparatively well governed.

The typical urban reformer did not, however, share Jefferson's pessimism regarding the city. From the reformer's point of view, there was no necessary reason why cities should have fallen to so low an estate. Frederic Howe, for example, saw cities as having great potential for improving American life. "Here life is full and eager," he wrote. "Here the industrial issues, that are fast becoming dominant in political life, will first be worked out. In the city democracy is organizing. It is becoming conscious of its powers. And as time goes on, these powers will be exercised to an increasing extent for the amelioration of those conditions that modern industrial life has created."[17] The reform creed was thus resolutely optimistic in its conviction that cities could be saved, and energetic in its pursuit of the means by which this salvation could be secured.

Within the reform movement there was widespread disagreement as to why cities had fallen upon such evil days. Some placed responsibility for municipal misgovernment upon the rapid growth of cities in the United States, and the great temptation to dishonesty that was generated by the need to develop a complex system of public works and services in urban areas within a very short space of time. Others traced the ills of urban life to the swelling tide of immigration from abroad in the decades following the Civil War and the ease with which the foreign-born population allowed itself to be exploited by corrupt political machines. And there was a strong tendency to explain the problems of cities as stemming from the failure to develop either forms of government suitable for urban areas, or a tradition of administrative expertise in the handling of municipal affairs.

But there was also a deep conviction that the corruption of urban politics reflected a very fundamental malaise in American life, the growth of a commercial spirit and a weakening in the moral fiber of the population that was endemic in society and the economy as well as government. "The boss is not a political, he is an American institution," wrote Lincoln Steffens, and this point of view was widely shared. What was needed from the reformer's perspective was a moral regeneration of American life—a "great awakening" which would cleanse and purify not only local but national politics as well, since the movement for urban reform was only part of a much larger reform effort directed at uplifting the tone of public life in every sector of the nation's business, including the practices of private institutions where they impinged on the public interest. Symbolic of this evangelical zeal for moral improvement was the fact that a number of Protestant clergymen associated themselves with the movement for municipal reform and took a prominent part in its activities. Like abolition before it, urban reform was a moral crusade.

Moreover, in its heyday, the boss system represented an effort to govern the city through the methods of politics alone. As a result, early efforts at reform tended to place almost exclusive emphasis upon the importance of competent administration to the successful functioning of city government. In reaction against the more discreditable features of machine politics, efforts were made to "depoliticize" city government and to augment the role of the impartial expert through civil service reform, the city manager plan, and other devices. Subject as it was to simultaneous influence by doctrines of moralism and scientific management, the movement for urban reform thus sought to make city government as clean as the church and as efficient as business.

At no time did reformers lose hope that substantial improvement could be effected in the government of American cities. A great deal of this optimism was based on their knowledge of the successful operation of European cities and their conviction that American municipalities could profitably be modeled after their European counterparts. *Century Magazine* stated its belief that "we can hope for no municipal reform which shall be radical and lasting till we change our leadership to the European models." "In a score of different directions," wrote Josiah Quincy while serving as mayor of Boston, "the interests of the average citizen are better and more fully cared for, his wants more fully met, in the great city of Europe than in that of America." While recognizing the difficulty of transplanting institutions from one country to another, Richard T. Ely nevertheless argued that "what is good for Berlin is likely to be good for New York, and what answers the needs of Paris will be likely to supply a want in Chicago."[18] But there was often some discomfort attached to unfavorable comparisons of American cities with Continental cities which were political subdivisions of regimes Americans looked upon as reactionary or despotic. English cities were, therefore, the object of more unqualified admiration.

Certainly there was no doubt in the reform mind regarding the urgency of doing something to elevate urban politics, lest the corrupt city eventually corrupt the nation. Elihu Root, for example, warned his Republican colleagues that the malodorous GOP organization in Philadelphia was a source of infection in their party that could not be localized. "It is my profound conviction," he declared, "that a determined effort is necessary to save national parties from the demoralization inevitably consequent upon municipal spoliation, and, as a Republican, zealous for the welfare and reputation of my party, I advocate the foundation of a non-partisan civil movement." Unless the reform of urban politics is successful, Josiah Strong asserted, "the boss will certainly rule the city when the city rules the nation," and Strong quoted Wendell Phillips as prophesying that "the time will come when our cities will strain our institutions as slavery never did."[19]

As noted earlier, the reform perspective differed sharply from the traditional agrarian outlook inasmuch as it sought to face and solve the problems presented by the city rather than turning away in a hostile rejection of the trend toward urbanization. But it should also be remembered that much of the reform argument for the city was essentially apologetic or defensive in tone. It was conceded that the city had fallen to a very low estate politically, and the claim was simply made that the spirit and practice of urban government could—with effort—be improved. Moreover, many of the reformers were gifted publicists, and their exposures of graft and corruption in urban government, while motivated by the desire to eliminate these conditions, had also the effect of reinforcing the rural image of the city as an iniquitous environment in which the ideals of American democracy were being betrayed. In essence the reform defense of cities was based on their potentialities, not their achievements.

URBANISM AND AMERICAN DEMOCRACY

Insofar as its political reputation is concerned, the city was thus only slightly better served by reformers sympathetic to it than it was by the agrarians who looked upon it as the invariable source of political corruption. And even today, the city has still to find its philosophical protagonist, at least in the area of political thought. This is true in spite of the fact that there is an impressive amount of evidence which points to the conclusion that it is with urban America that the flowering of democracy in this country can be most clearly identified. The place of the city in the American experience has in fact been much more honorific than its position in American thought.

From a historical perspective, Arthur Schlesinger points out that it was the cities of the East which led the way in the movement for national independence which culminated in the American revolution. "Throughout the decade of controversy the seaports set the pace of resistance, supplying most of the militant leaders, conducting turbulent demonstrations at every crisis, and mobilizing farmer support when possible." In a similar vein he underlines the prominent role played by the cities in the struggle to strengthen democracy once it had been established in this country: "The first great victory for freedom of press was won by a Philadelphia lawyer defending a New York editor. . . . Faced by interstate trade restrictions, stay laws and growing social turmoil, the urban business and creditor classes feared for their future welfare and the sanctity of property rights. The framing and ratification of the Constitution represented in considerable degree their triumph over the debtor groups and small farmers of the interior."[20]

Recent research in the general area of political behavior has also tended to refute the assumption that there is any necessary antipathy between the growth of cities and the vitality of the democratic process. In terms of some of the more obvious yardsticks that might be used to measure commitment to the norms of democracy, the urban citizen very often shows up much better than his rural counterpart. This is true, for example, with respect to two of the central attributes of democratic citizenship, an acceptance of the right of minorities to dissent from majority opinion, and an interest in the affairs of government as evidenced by participation in elections.

In a landmark study of civil liberties in the United States published in 1954, Samuel Stouffer found that rural residents were uniformly less tolerant of deviant minorities than urbanites. This rural attitude was partially explainable in terms of the operation of factors other than place of residence, especially the lower level of education which prevails in the countryside, but there nevertheless remained a residue of intolerance that was clearly associated with living in the country. As Stouffer put it:

> Rural people in every region are less likely to be tolerant of nonconformists than city people, even when we compare urban and rural people with the same amount of schooling. There is something about life in a small community that makes it less hospitable to divergent opinions than is the case in our urban centers. In the anonymity of city life it is much easier for deviant behavior to flourish than in the goldfish bowl of a small community. In the large community there are sometimes so many goldfish that nobody bothers to look at them. In the small town a lone exotic specimen can be viewed with careful, critical, and occasionally devastating attention.[21]

In support of his findings, Stouffer also cites earlier studies of the degree of tolerance which prevails in various sectors of the community, including a Gallup poll conducted in 1940 which showed rural residents as being much less willing than urban dwellers to see a Catholic elected President, and a Roper study in 1947 which revealed that urbanites were far more tolerant than their rural brethren of that most unpopular minority in recent times—members of the Communist party.

Of course the fact that city people generally exhibit so much more tolerance of nonconformity than rural residents must simultaneously be weighed against the fact that cities have been quite receptive to the appeal of totalitarian ideologies, or at least have been the areas from which Communist and Fascist political groups have traditionally recruited most of their active members in this country. If the greatest threat to civil liberties is judged to come from the small ideological groups dedicated to their destruction, then the city may well be looked upon as a greater source of peril to minority rights than the country. But if the chief danger to civil liberties is rather seen as a weakening of commitment on the part of the mass of citizens to their preservation, then it is from rural America that the right to dissent has been chiefly endangered in modern times.

As far as political participation is concerned, Robert E. Lane concluded after a comprehensive survey of the literature of political behavior that residents of large cities have a much better record in this respect than citizens living in rural areas. He finds that residents of larger cities "participate in elections more than those in smaller cities" and that inhabitants of smaller cities are "more likely to vote than residents of rural areas." According to Lane, this difference in turnout mainly reflects the heightened degree of political tension in the more densely populated parts of the country. The group conflict engendered by class and ethnic rivalries in urban centers has the effect of stimulating political activity. But a variety of other factors also plays a role here, including the greater exposure of the urban citizen to stimuli from the mass media, which helps to sharpen political awareness and a sense of civic obligation in cities.

The extent to which citizens participate in politics is also related to their sense of political efficacy—the degree to which they believe such activity will have meaningful results. In this respect also Lane finds that urban citizens show up much better than rural residents: "those living in metropolitan centers have, in general, a higher sense of political efficacy than those in rural or small town areas. Perhaps because of the greater politicalization of the urbanites, their exposure to more political news and comment, their more salient class and ethnic cleavages, and their higher educational level, they are led to make politics a more significant part of their lives."[22]

It also has been suggested that urbanization has promoted the development of a two-party system in the United States, thus invigorating political discussion and activity in all parts of the country. The growth of urban population is, for example, sometimes credited with the fact that presidential elections are now closely contested in virtually all the states. However, the actual impact of urbanization upon party competition in this country is far from clear. While some studies of state politics show a correlation between the extent of urbanization and the strength of party competition, other investigations indicate that there may well be a negative relationship between the two phenomena. Certainly, there is no disputing the fact that many of the big cities in this country have become one-party enclaves.

But if such empirical evidence as exists does not always support the conclusion that democracy is inevitably strengthened by the advent of urbanization, it certainly stands in flat contradiction to the conventional agrarian assumption that rural areas are necessarily the backbone of a democratic society. Whether this evidence will seriously undermine the Jeffersonian mystique remains, however, to be seen. The force of tradition being what it is. Americans may, in the future as in the past, continue to look for the meaning of their democratic experience in the prairies rather than on the pavements. This tendency is as pronounced in the twentieth as it was in the nineteenth century: "Somewhere in our agricultural past there lie the roots of Americanism. What we are in body and spirit is not to be discovered growing embryonically in any early city; its beginnings are to be found on the homestead or in the village, and only there."[23]

---

[1]This study was undertaken under a grant from the Rockefeller Foundation, for which the author wishes to make grateful acknowledgment.

[2]A. Whitney Griswold, *Farming and Democracy* (New York, 1948), p. 19. See also Richard Hofstadter, *The Age of Reform* (New York, 1960), pp. 23–36, and Henry Nash Smith, *Virgin Land* (New York, 1959) pp. 138–50.

[3]The quotations from Jefferson are from the *Writings of Thomas Jefferson* (Washington, D.C., 1903), II, 229–30, and X, 173.

[4]Morton and Lucia White, *The Intellectual versus the City* (Cambridge, Mass., 1962), pp. 17–19.

[5]Madison's comment is found in *The Writings of James Madison,* ed. Gaillard Hunt (New York, 1906), VI, 96–98, while the statement by Adams appears in *The Works of John Adams* (Boston, 1852), VII, 47.

[6]See Marvin Meyers, *The Jacksonian Persuasion* (New York, 1960), p. 240.

[7]Arthur M. Schlesinger, Jr., *The Age of Jackson* (Boston, 1946), p. 310, n. 11.

[8]George Fitzhugh, *Sociology for the South* (Richmond, Va., 1854), p. 139. However, there were southern writers who recognized that their region was greatly weakened by its failure to develop the commercial civilization associated with cities (see H. R. Helper, *The Impending Crisis of the South* [1860], esp. pp. 331–59). And Fitzhugh himself explicitly rejected the Jeffersonian prejudice in favor of an exclusively agricultural society. "Farming is the recreation of great men, the proper pursuit of dull men," he stated. "Let the ambitious South cultivate, not spurn the mechanic arts" (*op. cit.,* pp. 156, 160).

[9]See Paul W. Glad, *The Trumpet Soundeth* (Lincoln, Neb., 1960), p. 112. When the returns from the election of 1896 were in, they showed the core of Bryan's electoral strength as lying in the rural Midwest and mountain regions. However, there were some states, notably in New England, where Bryan received more support in urban than he did in rural areas (see William Diamond, "Urban and Rural Voting in 1896," *American Historical Review,* XLVI (January, 1941), 281–305.

[10]Peter Odegard, *Pressure Politics: The Story of the Anti-Saloon League* (New York, 1928), p. 44.

[11]As quoted in Edmund A. Moore, *A Catholic Runs for President* (New York, 1956), p. 133.

[12]Walter Lippmann, *Men of Destiny* (New York, 1927), p. 8.

[13]Quoted in Roy V. Peel and Thomas C. Donnelly, *The 1928 Campaign: An Analysis* (New York, 1931), p. 121.

[14]See Josiah Strong, *Our Country* (New York, 1885), pp. 133, 130.

[15]Paul T. David and Ralph Eisenberg, *Devaluation of the Urban and Suburban Vote* (Charlottesville, Va., 1961), p. 10.

[16]Richard Hofstadter, *Age of Reform* (New York, 1960), pp. 31–32.

[17]Frederic C. Howe, *The City: The Hope of Democracy* (New York, 1[illegible] pp. 7–8.

[18]"An Object Lesson in Municipal Government," *Century Magazine,* XXXIX (March, 1890), 792; Josiah Quincy, "The Development of American Cities," *Arena,* XVII (March, 1897), p. 529; and Richard T. Ely, "Model Towns," *Christian Union,* November 27, 1890.

[19]See Robert Treat Paine, "The Elimination of National Party Designations from Municipal Ballots," in *Proceedings* of the Fifteenth Annual Meeting of the National Municipal League, 1909, p. 292; and Josiah Strong, *The Twentieth Century City* (New York, 1898), pp. 101–2.

[20]Arthur M. Schlesinger, *Paths to the Present* (New York, 1949), pp. 213, 214, 215.

[21]*Communism, Conformity, and Civil Liberties* (New York, 1955), p. 130.

[22]Robert E. Lane, *Political Life* (Glencoe, Ill., 1959), pp. 265, 151–52.

[23]Harry J. Carman and Rexford G. Tugwell, "The Significance of American Agricultural History," *Agricultural History,* XII (April, 1938), 100.

13. Suburbia as an Ideological Retreat

ROBERT C. WOOD

. . . Suburbia, defined as an ideology, a faith in communities of limited size and a belief in the conditions of intimacy, is quite real. The dominance of the old values explains more about the people and the politics of the suburbs than any other interpretation. Fundamentally, it explains the nature of the American metropolis. It indicates why our large urban complexes are built as they are, why their inhabitants live the way they do, and why public programs are carried out the way they are. If these values were not dominant it would be quite possible to conceive of a single gigantic metropolitan region under one government and socially conscious of itself as one community. The new social ethic, the rise of the large organization, would lead us to expect this development as a natural one. The automobile, the subway, the telephone, the power line certainly make it technically possible; they even push us in this direction.

But the American metropolis is not constructed in such a way; it sets its face directly against modernity. Those who wish to rebuild the American city, who protest the shapeless urban sprawl, who find some value in the organizational skills of modern society must recognize the potency of the ideology. Until these beliefs have been accommodated reform will not come in the metropolitan areas nor will men buckle down to the task of directing, in a manner consonant with freedom, the great political and social organizations on which the nation's strength depends. A theory of community and a theory of local government are at odds with the prerequisites of contemporary life and, so far, theory has been the crucial force that preserves the suburb. There is no economic reason for its existence and there is no technological basis for its support. There is only the stubborn conviction of the majority of suburbanites that it ought to exist, even though it plays havoc with both the life and government of our urban age.

The American Miniature

If a belief in small government and small society helps explain why the modern suburb exists in an age of bigness, the suburban renaissance should not be surprising. The conviction that provincial life is best has been with us for a long time and it has endured in the

---

SOURCE: *Suburbia: Its People and Their Politics* by Robert C. Wood. Reprinted by permission of the publisher, Houghton Mifflin Company, 1958, 18-28, 66-87.

face of greater attacks than the ones contemporary America presents. We show our instinctive commitment to the ideology by the fact that we rarely examine its assumptions critically. We show our conscious allegiance by the oratorical homage we pay to the ideal of small neighborhoods, single homes, and political jurisdictions of limited size.

It is difficult to overestimate the vigor and pervasiveness of the belief. Three centuries stand behind the heritage—a full two hundred years of spectacular success and one hundred years of abject failure. The first period endowed the American cult of localism with its basic articles of faith: an assertion that local communities should maintain their own identity and manage their own affairs, and a justification for that assertion by the claim that the small society is the natural home of democracy. The last hundred years added endurance and stubbornness to the ideal by the very adversity which the reality of the urban world inflicted upon it. But whether made confident by success or contentious by disaster, the creed has remained to shape the American metropolis and make it what it is today.

Not the least of the reasons for the strength of the ideology is in its natural partiality to the American habitat. Grassroots life existed in fact in the United States long before the justification for its existence was ever articulated. The first settlements on the new continent were by necessity small and relatively isolated, and the characteristics usually associated with small town life developed spontaneously. Colonial conditions led to a similarity of interests, and a sharing of customs, aims and ambitions. Some degree of economic interdependence and equality, a constant recognition of a vast, unexplored land beyond the frontier outposts, close daily contact, bred early a conscious sense of community identity.

Under these social circumstances, nothing was more natural than the independence in fact, if not in legal theory, of local political institutions. Technically speaking, the first New England towns relied on grants of power from the Massachusetts Bay Company and later from the colonial legislature. Early settlements in the other colonies used the medieval corporation as the model for their authority. But in actual fact, colonial towns exercised independently the essential powers of police and taxation, and were, from the beginning, self-governing. They were independent because there was no other alternative; local authority stemmed from "the exercise of English common sense combined with the circumstance of the place."

Not only were the towns possessed with self-conscious identity, but by any standard of seventeenth century life, their political institutions seemed democratic. Small groups of people, barely sustaining themselves economically and faced with constant dangers, congregated without forethought to discuss common affairs. They elected their own officials, and these officials knew they were accountable to the citizens. In Lane Lancaster's words:

> The original government of the New England town was that of a pure democracy. We may well admit that it was inquisitive and gossipy, that it gave too liberal rein to the crank, the bore, the windbag and the troublemaker, that it put a premium upon talk, and that it was tolerant of somnolent administration. But in spite of these defects, it had the sovereign merit of bringing the rulers and the ruled together, it made easy the ventilation of grievances, it encouraged an intelligent and disinterested attitude toward public questions, and it fostered at its best a keen sense of the reality of the community.

This state of affairs usually contrasted sharply with contemporary conditions in the Old World, though the forms of local social organization and government appeared similar and scholars later sought to trace the principle of local autonomy back to the rights accorded English boroughs and before them to Teutonic and ecclesiastical sources. Yet no European locality, however consciously a community, exhibited the autonomy and democracy of its American counterpart.

Even in England the parish of the seventeenth century, that mixture of church and secular authority, could not parallel the colonial experience. Theoretically, all members of the parish had their say in civic management, but actually only the "most substantial" exercised authority. Nor was the second unit of English local organization, the manor, a truer expression of the local will. In this jurisdiction the eminent landlord of the area presided aristocratically as justice of the peace and principal officer of the countryside. At the county level, no pretense of local autonomy or democracy was maintained: the lord lieutenant, the high sheriff, and the justice of the peace were appointed by the king from among the county gentry. While the American localities moved toward increasing autonomy, comparable English governments remained oligarchies, organs of "local obligation," "thoroughly undemocratic and thoroughly responsible."

From the middle of the seventeenth century to well into the nineteenth, local communities in America ran their own affairs, by and large, and ran them by a popular political process. Along the entire Atlantic seaboard, counties, cities, towns and villages tackled energetically the problems of land disposition, the regulation of commerce, public health, law enforcement, fire protection, building control, and education. The manageable size of even the largest colonial city and its relative isolation allowed the town fathers to behave both decisively and responsibly; the New England selectmen might seem to have "the broad finality of dictatorship in local matters," but "the spirit of their service resembles the humblest agent . . . thoroughly and publicly checked."

Even the Revolution and the subsequent establishment of state authority by the Constitution did not seriously affect these prerogatives. Although the states were granted legal control over public activities below the national level, their authority existed mainly in the law books. The exercise of government, in fact, depended on the town and county. It was the local unit which, almost to the Civil War, collected the taxes, established the schools, cared for the poor, maintained the roads—in short, which exercised the responsibility for prime community endeavors. Practice and habit kept local democracy strong, even when legal independence was denied.

Of course, neither perfect autonomy nor pure democracy, even of the character sanctioned by the times, was ever completely realized. So far as political institutions were concerned, the structures which were later to define suburbia were sometimes hobbled at the very start. In the case of Charlestown, for example, the colonial government interfered so continually and so closely in local affairs that genuine self-government never developed and the legacy of legislative dominance continues in South Carolina to this day. For the larger cities, the medieval corporation was everywhere an imperfect model and never provided all the powers needed properly to direct municipal growth.

So far as popular control was concerned, both formally and informally, there were limitations on democracy. Almost immediately after settlement the ministry and the merchants exercised disproportionate influence, and property restrictions limited participation. In New England there was a distinction between the freeman and the inhabitant in the early town meeting, and in other colonies the voting electorate was even more narrowly defined. There was also, throughout the colonies, class conflict—accusations that social position rather than numbers was decisive in the management of town affairs. A tendency toward tight political dominance by a few, a forerunner of city machines, could be discerned in Boston, New York, Philadelphia, and Charlestown by 1700, and editors and ministers could thunder against cliques and individual misuse of public authority generations before the Constitution.

These aberrations were real enough, and not to be discounted in painting an accurate picture of colonial life in the United States. The fact remains, however, that the predominant tendency was toward autonomy and democracy, and in sufficient measure so that when men came to rationalize these institutions the characteristics they recognized were distinctively these two. The schoolboy's conception of the American miniature republic is right, by and large, when applied to our early history.

When the abstractions about localism began to appear, then, there was historical precedent and a tradition of actual practice on which to rest the case. And the eloquence and distinction of the men who chose to advance its cause added luster to the theory. Jefferson before the Revolution, Tocqueville afterward—what better advocates could be imagined to hand on the faith to coming generations?

It was Jefferson who first proclaimed the superiority of the New England town and urged the rest of the nation to follow this example. "Those wards," he wrote, "called townships in New England, are vital principles of their governments, and have proved themselves the wisest inventions ever devised by the wit of man for the perfect exercise of self-government. Each ward would be a small republic within itself and every man in the State would thus become an active member of the common government, transacting in person a great portion of its rights and duties, subordinate indeed, yet important and entirely within his competence."

No contemporary disputed Jefferson's opinion. The founding fathers found the local governments in being when they met to organize the nation. In drafting the new state constitutions, sometimes the legal authorities of the large municipalities were revised. The new doctrine of the separation of powers was occasionally extended downward, apparently stimulated as much by a desire to carry logic to its ultimate conclusion as to correct deficiencies. But the new Congress showed its approval of the basic pattern of local government in the Northwest Ordinance of 1789, when it established the township as the basic unit in the new territory and decreed its universality.

Forty years later Tocqueville found the image flourishing. He was in error when he asserted that American political authority originated in the township and that municipal independence was a natural consequence of the sovereignty of the people. But in actual practice, he was close to the truth—close enough, at any rate, so that his generalizations sounded right to his generation and to ours. His unbounded enthusiasm reinforced and extended Jefferson's early claims. To Tocqueville, the careful deference paid to local autonomy within the federal system was the secret of American political success. On the one hand, it permitted a centralized government of sufficient power to face world problems. On the other, it required decentralized administration, which precluded usurpation.

But even more important than institutional checks and balances, this pattern of government set benign influences to work upon the people and their social life. The dissemination of power, Tocqueville was certain, created a town spirit which civilized all who felt its touch, stimulating affection rather than ambition and reason in place of emotion. To him, "the township, at the center of the ordinary relations of life, serves as a field for the desire of public esteem, the want of exciting interest, and the taste for authority and popularity; and the passions which commonly embroil society change their character, when they find a vent so near the domestic hearth and family circle." Thus "provincial" institutions became the best protection against despotism or the license of mob, for otherwise, "How can a populace, unaccustomed to freedom in small concerns, learn to use it temperately in great affairs?" In short, vigorous small governments enhanced the influence of small communities, and small communities, by their very nature, brought out the best in man, the qualities of reason and good will on which a Lockian commonwealth was based.

So the image crystallized. Small communities apparently experienced the sense of self-identity, the compactness, the self-sufficiency necessary to produce interdependence and equality and the sharing of common values and objectives. Given these circumstances, their governments should be independent, positive and aggressive, asserting their claim to all the powers and prerogatives they could possibly exercise, with a minimum of supervision and restraint.

Small towns deserved their autonomy because they were the natural home of democracy. Only in small governments could each man participate effectively, not in selfish pursuit of his own interests but with the capacity to understand the problems his community faced and thus further the common good. Independent local governments had legitimate claims to power because they were closest to home. And in the early days of the nation, the concept of home, of distinct social groupings, discrete social systems, was real and tangible. Small town life was the American way because there was, beyond the seaports, literally no other method to organize communal existence.

In this way the miniature republic was established, beginning as institution and rationalized brilliantly as a theory of how government and society actually did operate and should operate in America. Because initially it worked, and worked well, and because it was sanctioned by illustrious native philosophers and distinguished foreign observers, it has been, like all beliefs so established, a powerful force. Since its logic was simple, consisting of only two parts, easily grasped and instinctively felt by every man, its force expanded exponentially. With no other better way at hand for organizing government, the prospects for serious criticism of its propositions diminished, also exponentially. With the passing of the years, the conditions under which the working principles of autonomy and direct democracy were first established became obscure and hardly recognized; only the principles themselves remained in view. In this way, the image became a legacy, and like all legacies, was accepted as something precious and therefore useful for each generation.

When men receive legacies under new conditions of society, they are more prone to try to adjust their circumstances so that the bequest may be applied than to abandon their inheritance. This has been done in many areas of American government and social life; our founding fathers were so successful that they have often inhibited our own search for success. It was true with a vengeance in the case of Jefferson's miniature republic. When alternatives for the organization of local government and local communities arose, we could not see them. For a hundred years, we strove to make the facts fit the beliefs, never pausing to consider the possibility that the legacy itself was no longer precious. . . .

CRISIS IN AUTONOMY

The nostalgic image found a new frame then, in suburbia, and its popularity justified suburban independence. Faith in the ideology discouraged the creation of new political institutions to serve the entire metropolitan area and provided an appealing rationale for the preservation of local town halls and county court houses. It served to crystallize the new region into hundreds of small communities, each more or less conscious of its own identity.

But was suburbia a legitimate recipient of the legacy? Did it offer a genuine renaissance or only a pale counterfeit of the real article? The suburb, after all, was not an early New England town, a southern market center, or a western trading village. The United States was no longer rural, but urban and industrial, and destined to become more so. The pattern of large-scale organization, the values of togetherness, the political philosophy of positive government, all penetrated suburbia, made it something more and less than a replica of earlier times. There was an economic interdependence of the region as a whole, a new pattern of social intercourse throughout the area, and these developments had both direct and subtle influences on the reinvigorated jurisdictions. In the short run at least, the immediate answer to the question as to whether or not the suburb was the carrier of the grassroots faith depended upon the success of the local governments in maintaining their autonomy. If they went under and were absorbed by the metropolis, then no amount of imagery could re-establish the small community in its essential form.

In the beginning, this issue of genuineness and the critical role of suburban independence was scarcely recognized. The new environment was overlooked, and men took at face value the revival of the small-scale jurisdictions surrounding the large cities and the apparent renaissance of independent, healthy community life after one hundred years of somnolence. The issue in municipal reform throughout the last half of the nineteenth century had been so much the question of size—how to reduce urban congestion or manage it in accordance with historic values—and the solutions had been so tentative that its seemingly automatic resolution was accepted with delight, and with little critical examination.

For those who had emphasized the necessity of breaking up the mammoth city to guarantee a satisfactory local government, the suburb was an intimation of dreams about to come true. More pleasing still, their aspirations were turning into reality quite naturally, without the tremendous political and educational efforts that Geddes and Howard thought necessary. Writing at the turn of the century, Adna Weber could view the development of suburban towns even then as "the most encouraging feature of the whole situation." "The rise of the suburbs," he wrote, "is what furnishes the solid basis of a hope that the evils of city life, so far as they result from overcrowding, may be in large part removed . . . It will realize the wish and prediction of Kingsley, 'a complete interpenetration of city and country, a complete fusion of their different modes of life and a combination of the advantages of both, such as no country in the world has ever seen.' " And twenty-five years later, Harlan Douglass could speak of the suburban evangel, and after a biting indictment of the city, look to a new motivation for life in the satellite town of open land and cottage home. He could confidently predict, "A crowded world must be either suburban or savage." For the first planners, the trend was nothing awesome, but a movement devoutly prayed for and constantly encouraged.

Even the more pragmatic municipal reformers, those who believed they had solved the problem of size by political and administrative adjustments, never claimed that their program of reform was superior to the genuine article. Proportional representation, nonpartisanship, the short ballot, the small council had been offered as substitutes in a large city for the direct self-government possible in smaller places. Certainly these experts felt that the suburbs could profit by employing a city manager and business methods of organization and administration, but they did not believe that the suburban trend was contradicting their own efforts. Instead it appeared to reduce the size of their job, for now they could concentrate on the central cities of the metropolitan areas, secure in the knowledge that the surrounding towns could take care of themselves.

Of course, a nagging doubt as to what was happening to the metropolitan region as a whole tugged at the National Municipal League's conscience, and metropolitan problems were discussed spasmodically at annual meetings from 1917 to 1925. But the League did not publish its first report on the government of metropolitan areas until 1930, and although the study was hailed as "the first comprehensive survey of its kind," it arrived at no specific recommendations. Indeed, its conclusions were regarded as "so general in their scope that it is virtually impossible to disagree with them—a sure sign that they have little value." The perfection of the structural and procedural mechanisms of reform continued to hold the center of the stage, and though there were hints that suburbia might cause trouble, they received low priority on the agenda.

So the trend intensified, and far from vanishing, the number of governmental units within each metropolitan area multiplied at an astonishing rate. In 1900, the New York region had 127 minor civil divisions, by 1920, 204; in Cook County (Chicago) there were 55 in 1890 and 109 in 1920; around Pittsburgh, 107 units existed in 1920 where thirty years earlier only 91 were formally incorporated. For the seventeen largest cities, incorporations of new governments around the fringe of the city went on and on—most rapidly at the turn of the century, but steadily for the next fifty years. Between 1952 and 1957 alone, 170 new municipalities came into being in metropolitan areas and 519 new special districts were created. By 1957, there were over 3000 governments that could be said to possess more or less general municipal powers, and there was, of course, that awesome figure of 15,658 legally distinguishable local units. Village, hamlet, school district, city, county, town, they were each one equipped with the legal prerogatives of government, each claiming to speak for a separate constituency. They jostled one another in the crowded confines of the metropolitan backyard, jealous of their authority and suspicious of their neighbors.

These units were democratic, at least in the sense that their citizens popularly determined the course of their own affairs, and certainly they were independent. They squabbled incessantly over jurisdictional problems: the intersection of streets at town boundaries, the acquisition of water supply, the disposal of sewage, the health nuisances which one government visited upon another. They maintained their own schools, their own police forces, their own fire departments. They had the capacity to govern and legal and political weapons to preserve themselves. They were autonomous, then, in the sense of independence, but as the governments multiplied, observers took a second reading on the word "autonomous." Were suburban governments presiding over distinct and meaningful small communities, or had the foundations on which their political autonomy depended been swept away by the onrush of the growing metropolis?

The issue first came into the open by the drab route of public finance. Here, the intrusion of metropolitan life took concrete and specific form, for as municipal budgets and tax rates climbed and climbed, the suspicion grew that the new-found suburban grassroots splendor might be only Indian summer. Previously men had always assumed that the economic, social and political conditions of small town life went hand in hand; that legal and financial self-sufficiency existed naturally together. Yet in suburbia and the metropolitan region at large, established governing bodies, faithful to the requirements for independence and democracy, suddenly lacked the resources to govern. The communities flourished, their inhabitants were employed, and there was a rising standard of living, but there were not sufficient public revenues for communal purposes. Even the cities of the 1880's with their bosses, their treasuries pilfered by dishonest contractors, their incredible extravagances, had not known bankruptcy. Taxable wealth was always available to provide a surplus, whether to be squandered or preserved. But now the neat fit between supply and demand disappeared. The property tax, divided among so many jurisdictions, did not suffice; the sum of the parts did not equal the whole. The multiplication of jurisdictions brought to the entire region, in good times as well as bad, municipal poverty, and the principle of genuine autonomy for local governments, in the sense of the financial as well as legal capacity to manage their own affairs, went by the boards.

What had occurred, of course, as the suburban trend developed, was an uneven distribution of tax resources and service needs throughout the new metropolitan areas. The divergent pattern of residential and industrial dispersion, unnoticed in the first blush of enthusiasm, played havoc with the development of financially secure governments. These were not the balanced communities that Howard had envisioned; they were only slices of the metropolitan complex. Surrounded by political boundaries, some communities residential, some industrial, some mixed in the pattern of their land uses, suburbs and central cities alike faced unequal demands and commanded widely disparate resources.

The central cities felt the pinch first. With the middle class steadily abandoning their downtown residences, commercial districts, industrial sections, governmental centers, and slums became the major land uses of the metropolitan core. A two-way squeeze took place: in the daytime commuters poured into the city, shooting the working population up 30 to 50 per cent above its permanent number, requiring services in transport, streets, water, police and fire protection on a level artificially pegged for the crowds between nine and five. But taxable resources steadily declined, and as residential areas deteriorated, the slums took up 20 per cent of the nonbusiness area, siphoning off 45 per cent of total municipal expenditures but contributing only 6 per cent of the revenue. As a further complication, as the city became more and more the educational or civic center of the region, the amount of tax-exempt property increased steadily. With service demands at least as high as when most of the urban population lived within its limits, and with the tax base declining relatively or absolutely, most large American cities ran out of money. By 1930, tax rates were rising everywhere, and municipal borrowing was moving ever closer to established debt limits.

Boston provided the extreme example. In 1930 its assessed valuation of taxable property was $1,972,000,000; in 1939, $1,524,000,000; in 1947, $1,558,000,000; in 1951, $1,570,000,000—four hundred million less than the value twenty years earlier. Faulty assessment practices and other deficiencies of the property tax as such accounted for some of the difficulty. But during that same period, the value of tax-exempt real estate increased by 216 million dollars, an increase from 19 to 40 per cent of total real property value. Despite a policy of postponing capital improvements until schools, parks, hospitals and equipment were at the point of abandonment, expenditures rose from 80 million in 1937 to 95 million in 1947 to 132 million in 1951. As a consequence, Boston's assessment on commercial and industrial property rose to the unheard-of rates of 100 per cent of true value and the tax rate reached $86 per $1000, a point at which the business community could complain with some justice that an increase much "beyond the present level could well spell disaster."

But the runaway tax rates of the central city—Boston, New York, or Chicago—were not the only sign of incipient urban bankruptcy. Some suburbs were in trouble too. There were windfalls for a few but scarcity for many others. While exclusive towns could finance twice-a-week garbage collections, skating rinks, recreational centers, and miles of parkway, others scraped the bottom of the municipal treasury to keep the schools open and the streets repaired.

By 1930, tax rates among metropolitan suburbs in New York varied from $2.21 to $4.73; in Detroit from $1.89 to $2.54; in Cleveland from $.93 to $2.19; and in Boston from $1.92 to $4.88. The inherent inadequacies of the property tax as an adequate source of revenue were compounded as rich suburbs sealed themselves off from the central city and their neighbors and industrial and low-income cities struggled to provide the bare necessities. With staggering new demands for urban services, approaching the 21 billion mark by 1953, the disparity between needs and resources seemed to reach the breaking point. If autonomy depended on financial independence, most of the local governments in the United States, in the opinion of many observers, were going under.

Nor was financial adversity the only difficulty which the American miniature found in its new environment. As suburbs ringed the central city, obvious conditions of interdependence appeared. When sixteen thousand separate jurisdictions carried out local functions in a land area comprising less than 7 per cent of the country, the determination of local governments to maintain separate services was not just expensive, it was frequently absurd. Separate water systems, separate sewer lines, separate street and highway programs, individual police and fire departments—these affronted common sense and, more significantly, the scientific principles of administrative management. How could efficiency and economy be assured when no central authority planned for the provision of transit facilities and utilities? Who would provide an "articulated highway system adequate for metropolitan transit?" What was to be done with the obviously common problems of harbor and stream pollution, of storage and distribution of water, of control of contagious diseases, integration of police work, and coordination of fire fighting systems? The maze of local governments, each presenting a full array of public services, confounded logic. In this new governmental congestion, autonomy obviously did not guarantee efficiency although, surely, efficiency was supposed to be a major justification of autonomy.

From the organizational as well as the financial point of view then, the failure of the city to expand concurrently with the growing urban area seemed disastrous. The "crazy quilt hodge podge of local governmental agencies" could appear to H. G. Wells as far back as 1910, "like fifteenth century houses which have been continuously occupied by a succession of enterprising but short-sighted and close-fisted owners, and which have now been, with the very slightest use of lath and plaster partitions and geyser hot-water apparatus, converted into modern residential flats." To Victor Jones, thirty years later, the problem of metropolitan government remained much the same: "The need for servicing a large population scattered under the jurisdiction of many units of local government, most of which are crippled by limited powers over a restricted area, by inadequate tax resources and by such consequences of premature subdivision as heavy indebtedness and extensive tax areas." And Betty Tableman, writing in 1951, insisted indignantly that "no governmental unit is an island. Sins of omission and commission of any one municipality affect not only its own citizens but all persons living in the metropolitan area." Criminals were escaping because no police jurisdiction had effective control; fires raged while unused equipment lay idle across artificial boundaries; sewage dumped in a river by one government contaminated the neighboring jurisdiction's lake; master highway plans could not be completed on an area-wide basis. The urban center was no longer, in Luther Gulick's words, "floating around in a great and green rural hinterland." Rather, "it is now elbow to elbow with other paved urban centers."

Suburbia was not, then, to slip smoothly into the modern world, as its first supporters had fondly imagined. It was causing trouble, real trouble, for the metropolis of which it was a part. The first tenet of its political ideology—independence for each locality—no longer had an economic or social base, and the justification for autonomy apparently collapsed. A collection of small governments, without financial self-sufficiency and some spatial isolation from each other, made for ineffective political structures, and the principle of autonomy no longer went hand in hand with its companion doctrine—democracy—to justify these small-scale reconstructions of an earlier culture. The two doctrines were turned against each other, and the close democracy a suburb promised almost guaranteed ineffective government for the region as a whole. The threat to American localism was not from Washington or the state capitals; the creed was doing itself in and its greatest virtue had been subverted into its greatest vice.

Suburbia Besieged

The realization that suburbs could not, realistically, be independent entities set loose again the theory of cultural lag. The conviction grew that suburban political institutions were, after all, only relics, "holdouts" against the rush of metropolitan culture, soon to disappear. From 1930 to the present day most experts in metropolitan reform have agreed that something has to give, and gradually they have crystallized their doctrine to the point of proposing the abolition or drastic curtailment of the last artifact of the ideology, suburban political independence.

At first, metropolitan reformers offered no quarter; they mounted a frontal assault on suburbia. Looking at the financial and service plight of the metropolitan area, they were appalled at the callousness with which the suburbanite viewed his neighbors in the city, the indifference he showed to the problems of the region as a whole, and the waste and confusion he tolerated in public affairs. If it were a question of faithfully preserving the legacy or meeting the demands of urbanity, the early metropolitan reformer sided with his own generation. Financial self-sufficiency for the region as a whole, orderly, responsible consideration of regional priorities, autonomy in the true sense of the word, was of first importance. If the social and political worlds on which the miniature republic rested had split apart, then the suburban renaissance must be illusory. There was no alternative but a return to the program of mechanistic reform, to force the American people to face the fact that the small community could not be re-created in an industrial society. Approximate grassroots political philosophy as closely as possible, these reformers reasoned, but give primary emphasis to attaining regional self-sufficiency.

The attack came in two waves: a blunt denial that the suburbs were in fact true representatives of the republic in miniature, and a subsequent drive to merge the outlying municipalities with the central city, abolishing their independent governments outright. H. G. Wells announced the broad strategy that later arguments were to utilize. He flatly rejected the suburb's claim to small town status in the Anglo-Saxon tradition. "These local government areas of today represent for the most part what were once distinctly organized and individualized communities, complete minor economic systems, and they preserve a tradition of what was once administrative convenience and economy. Today, I submit, they do not represent communities at all, and they become more wasteful and more inconvenient with every change in economic necessity . . . Probably you find the thinnest sham of a community . . . where a clerk or a working man will shift his sticks from one borough to another and move on to a third without ever discovering what he has done." Lewis Mumford scorned, as pitiful mockeries of what they might have been, the phony communities with "neither the intellectual penetration to analyze their condition nor the courage and imagination to transform it. The suburb was a pharisaic way of passing by on the other side; leaving the civic organism itself in the gutter."

These men recognized only the metropolitan community as genuine, and turned their efforts toward removing the suburban roadblocks that cluttered the road to progress. Disposing of suburbia as illusion, the metropolitan pioneers proposed that the central city annex all the territory that surrounded it. The simplest solution was the best: let Elmwood extend its boundaries until it was Greater Elmwood; and for a time it seemed that this formula might work.

Until 1918, America's largest cities managed to annex sizable territory without substantial difficulty. The ten largest at least doubled their area and some increased from three- to tenfold. In 1891, New York completed the greatest single extension of territory, adding over 250 square miles to the city; Boston doubled its size in 1914; Baltimore added 60 square miles in 1918; and St. Louis gained 43 square miles in 1876. For cities of more than 100,000 residents, 605 square miles were annexed between 1890 and 1900, 413 in 1900–1910, and 628 and 521 square miles respectively in the next two decades. In Virginia and Texas, "automatic" annexation procedures were established by the legislature, and in every urban state special legal provisions were made for the extension of municipal boundaries.

But annexation did not keep pace with metropolitan growth, and just at the time when the metropolitan problem became critical, annexation petered out. Despite a few sizable territorial additions to Detroit and Los Angeles, and a spurt of small acquisitions after the Second World War, political opposition to the absorption of outlying towns increased. Completely surrounded by the territory of the central city, enclaves in Los Angeles, Boston, Cincinnati, Cleveland, Detroit, and Pittsburgh clung to their separate governmental identities and they were joined by towns and villages on the fringe. By 1933 R. D. McKenzie could write that "annexation is no longer practicable as a means of coordinating with the central city the vast areas into which the automobile and the paved highways have poured urban population." Ten years later Victor Jones could echo, "Annexations in the past half-century have contributed little toward a solution of the problem of metropolitan government . . . The large American cities have never been able to keep pace, by means of annexation or consolidation, with the accumulation of population on the margin of the city." Cool expert logic was no match for emotional loyalties to the old image, and the frontal attack collapsed, even in the rapidly growing new cities of the West.

But scarcely had the suburbs silenced the cries for "one community —one government" and frustrated the building of Greater Elmwood when a more stealthy invasion was upon them. The second wave of metropolitan reformers were less openly hostile; they did not propose to abolish the suburbs, but only to compromise them. The new experts were quite willing to permit suburbia to continue its independent existence; they would settle for something less than maximum efficiency and financial stability. All the suburbs had to do was to relinquish those functions and programs which were most obviously metropolitan in character to a regional government in which they would have representation. The new breed of reformer did not ask the suburb to pass from the scene, but only to face the reality of modern life.

Partly, the change in plans was dictated by tactical considerations, since annexation was obviously not working. But in good measure, the members of this movement were—and are—sincere. They had genuine doubts about the kind of political process that would result in a single metropolitan government many times larger than any municipality that had ever existed before. Some of them suspected the earlier reform principles of "automatic" democracy, and almost all of them were afraid of the vastness of the enterprise which annexation would involve. Moreover, they were not ready to dismiss suburbia outright; they detected at least vestiges of small town life in the new communities. They valued these remnants, for the new reformers were members of the faith themselves. They believed in the ancient image.

So, in the 1940's and 1950's, a whole series of proposals blossomed forth, designed not to abolish suburbia but to tame it. The modified objective was to preserve legal autonomy wherever possible, to make only grudging concessions to urban growth. From scholars' studies and administrators' desks came an increasing flow of recommendations, analyses, and evaluations. In place of annexation, why not isolate only a few of the most critical metropolitan functions and vest them in, say, the county, that established agent of the state? Or if the county was too small to encompass the new urban complex, why not a multi-purpose special district, which operated not just bridges, tunnels, and airports, but every program that was truly metropolitan in nature? Or if this plan found popular disfavor, then what about consolidating functions one by one? Establish a single parkway authority, or water commission, or sanitary district, or transit agency, under the state or by agreement with the municipalities. Sooner or later, they would likely as not come together, and a genuine metropolitan government might be on its way. At least, create a regional planning commission to plot a sensible and systematic land-use map as a guide for zoning development among all the cities and towns, or pool tax resources to make sure that the basic metropolitan needs of water and sewerage are provided for. The proposals began as early as the limitations of annexation became obvious, and painstakingly, in each metropolitan region, research studies were authorized, experts hired and set to work, bills drafted to be presented to state legislatures.

Finding "solutions" to the metropolitan problem took on the aspects of an academic crusade. Survey tumbled after survey, following the injunction of the National Municipal League that "there can be no single answer to the problem of metropolitan organization, applicable to all conditions and times." In thirty years, in twenty-six states, 88 separate projects, studies, commission reports, surveys and programs came forth, all designed to bring order out of chaos, restore efficiency, rationalize the "ineffective arrangement of multiple jurisdictions" while preserving suburbia itself. Schemes for intermunicipal cooperation, for exchanges of services, consolidation of city and county, separation of city and county, special authorities, federations, mergers, solutions with "no structural changes," solutions with "structural changes," from Birmingham to Boston and New York to Los Angeles, all came off the drawing board, all seeking to make the suburbs reasonable, to find a new type of local government.

Far and away the most popular plan recommended was a federal structure for the metropolitan area. By 1950, half a dozen schemes for federation in different metropolitan areas had been put forward, and in 1952, Toronto broke the logjam and established a "genuine" federated government. The theory of these federal plans was simple: the twin principles of autonomy and democracy could be reconciled by a new method of representation. Keep the suburbs, but create a new limited government with the authority to carry out obvious metropolitan programs in planning, land-use control, water use, sewerage, and transportation. Give the suburbs membership in the governing body of the metropolitan organization. Establish two tiers of local government, divide up functions or aspects of functions, allocate them variously to the two levels, and thereby secure regional cooperation while preserving suburban democracy. Surely this was a workable compromise, and citizens in Boston, Miami, Atlanta, St. Louis, and Cleveland pricked up their ears.

But as a rule, the suburbs were unimpressed, and even though signs of limited breakthroughs were apparent after the Toronto story became widespread, suburbia hesitated. The federated scheme seemed a vast improvement over previous programs, but two implications became steadily more apparent. The first concerned the allocation of authority: how does one decide what is a metropolitan problem and what is a suburban problem? Theoretically, there were more or less objective administrative standards that could be applied, but the closer the suburb looked at the model of federalism, the more it became apparent that as one gave up functions, the significance of legal autonomy diminished rapidly. Just as suburban legal authority interfered with metropolitan self-sufficiency, so even limited metropolitan authority decreased genuine suburban autonomy. What meaning did independence have, if all the suburban citizen could decide was where to place traffic lights and street signs and how much to spend for the library? If highways, planning, police, water, and recreational services were removed from his control, what value did local government possess? And how were the boundary lines between local and metropolitan affairs to be maintained? Every previous federal model envisioned a judicial body to arbitrate the inevitable disputes between the levels of government. Where was the supreme court of the metropolis, except at the state level, to resolve the issue of authority with all the subtle niceties by which the legal profession justifies its existence?

A second difficulty seemed even more serious. What happened to grassroots democracy itself when the regional functions moved upstairs? By definition, the process of local representation in the "Greater Government" was an indirect one, with town officials representing their constituencies in the larger councils. But the justification for suburbia was based precisely on the fact that its political process was the closest approximation of direct popular participation. Abandon control over the important functions of local government and the direct method of accountability that kept the bureaucracy in check and what was left of the Town Meeting?

Instinctively, rather than by rational rebuttal, most suburbanites interpreted the plans for federation for what they were: not compromise but seduction. Even if they could not explain the inconsistencies in the scholar's logic, they recognized the end product: a reduction in the real significance of their legal autonomy, and a belittling of the political process they possessed. Metropolitan reform was depriving the suburbs of their options in deciding public policy and, although the region and perhaps some suburbs themselves experienced financial adversity and administrative chaos, the ancient legacy was what counted. Sadly viewing the metropolitan scene in 1950, Thomas Reed, consultant to civic groups and city fathers on the grand design of the metropolis for over a quarter of a century, concluded, "Many better and wiser city planners and political scientists than myself have poured out millions of words, by tongue, pen and typewriter, on the same theme, but frankness requires me to say that so far we have accomplished little more than the world's record for words used in proportion to cures effected."

Suburbia Triumphant

Annexation, consolidation, merger, country-city separation—suburbia considered all of them and concluded usually that it wanted none of them. It preferred legal autonomy and small town politics above all, and it continued to expand. The New York region by 1954 boasted 1071 separate jurisdictions; Chicago, 960; Philadelphia, 702; St. Louis, 420; until, all in all, 14 per cent of all local governments in the United States were in the metropolitan areas. Against all appeals that this multiplicity fostered political irresponsibility and defeated "both the theory of popular control and the government's ability to provide services," the suburbs were adamant. They knew that what reform actually entailed was a reunion, at least in part, with the central city and its corrupt politics, its slums, immigrants, criminals, and the vicious elements from which they had only recently escaped. The reformers had demonstrated the expense of maintaining this isolation, but to most suburbanites, the figures merely proved that the price of liberty was always high.

In only one way did the suburbs adjust to modernity. When obvious breakdowns appeared in basic public utilities, metropolitan-wide institutions were permitted, so long as they were not governments. Public corporations, authorities, special districts are popular with suburbanites; they were self-supporting and businesslike in form. They were allowed to assume the money-making activities of local government—the building and operation of bridges, tunnels, terminals, and airports—and because they were run by state-appointed commissioners, aloof from the undignified ordeal of vote-getting, they were acceptable. By that curious *non sequitur* so appealing to Americans—that the authorities had "taken government out of politics"—the suburbs reasoned they had nothing to fear. These institutions could not be threats because they were not governments.

Thus the only way in which big organizations entered local government was by masquerade. The metropolitan agencies now at work are in the form of *ad hoc* special districts, in highways, sanitation, airports, mosquito control, water, garbage collection, hospitals, almost every conceivable local activity. The New York Port Authority, the Boston Metropolitan District Commission, the transit authorities, the Golden Gate Bridge and Highway District, these have been the novelties permitted. No period in American history saw more inventions in forms of pseudo government than the decades between 1920 and 1950, when the baffling array of "nonpolitical" boards, commissions, and agencies sprang up across the country.

They were, of course, pseudo governments. Victor Jones was quite right when he wrote that their lack of direct accountability and numerical addition to the local governments already in existence "confuses the citizens and voters and makes it difficult to secure responsible local government in large urban communities." But the suburbs were satisfied; if the small town could not carry out a local function, then it was better to remove the program from government entirely. Grassroots democracy or big business—no other vehicle is trustworthy in the United States.

There was stubborn resistance, however, to all proposals for genuine government. The answer could be found in the words of Arthur E. Morgan about Great Neck, Long Island, in the twenties: "All the people in that area moved in about the same time. They were young married couples with one or two children . . . the men have a volunteer fire department and have recently built a beautiful fire house which is equipped for recreational purposes as well . . . The women very often do the shopping cooperatively. If anyone is ill, everyone will do her bit to help . . . The church is a community church. The minister is young and has done much for all ages. A social is held once a month for the married couples. There are frequent dances for the young people. It seems that something is going on every week." Or it could come in the forthright declaration of the resident of Tarrytown that "I would feel that I had surrendered some of my manhood if I gave to the politicians in White Plains the legal right to control in the slightest degree the education of my children."

However presented, the suburban choice in the twentieth century had been to retain the form of government most closely resembling Jefferson's legacy—a choice, moreover, made in defiance of the compelling values of the modern world: large-scale organization, efficiency, economy and rationalization. Fortuitously supported by two decades of prosperity, the suburbanite has been able to brush aside the specter of municipal bankruptcy, ignore the obviously illusory nature of his legal autonomy, and retain his independent community. The nation's wealth for the moment supports his idol, and the Great Society, at least in the political sense, is excluded from his hearth and home.

This overwhelming victory implies, of course, some serious weaknesses in the doctrines of metropolitan reform. One tactical error seems clear immediately: for all their energy and ingenuity, for all their battle cries of annexation, merger and federation, the reformers have mounted only a limited offensive. They have challenged the feasibility of small government and small communities in the twentieth century, but they have never seriously questioned the desirability of small government whenever it can possibly be sustained. In the end, the reformers have offered only an alternative program for better metropolitan financial and administrative management; they have never promised a better brand of politics.

This reluctance to launch a full-scale attack on the ideology as well as the practicality of small government diminishes the prospects for reform's success. It allows the suburb the heroic role of defender of democracy, even though it remains the villain in the melodrama of metropolitan development. Thus the suburb possesses an almost impenetrable line of defense, for what citizen, faced with a choice of an ineffective government democratically controlled or an effective government less democratically controlled, will not wrap himself in high moral principle and choose the first?

By refusing to challenge the grassroots faith itself, reformers are forced back to a single argument: that the suburban claim to the status of a small community is necessarily counterfeit. Yet, even here, taking their stand as hard-bitten realists, they are on weak ground. They assume that the loss of financial self-sufficiency among suburban governments and the end of social isolation means inevitably the collapse of small town life and consciousness. On this assumption reformers conclude that the suburban commitment to the colonial legacy must be, of necessity, illusionary. And, on this assumption, they have constructed the best alternative structure they can devise in the belief that some day suburbanites will realize that their allegiance is nostalgia, a commitment to a shadow world which existed only in the past.

But it is a serious mistake to believe that an ideology simply reflects the social and political organization in a particular period of history, lingering for a while, but ultimately giving way to an expression of a new reality. When they are powerful enough, ideologies may shape —as well as mirror—the world about them. This fact metropolitan reformers are discovering today, for it is not the simple memory of the heritage which thwarts their efforts. It is the power of that heritage as a very real expression of the aspirations and values of the present generation which blocks the progress of reform.

In the final analysis, Wells and Mumford, as the early discoverers of the organization man, never challenged the suburban evangel to any real effect for a good reason: the more closely suburbs are studied, the more genuine their claim to provinciality appears. In many essential qualities many suburbs seem like the American small towns of the past, much more impervious to modern life than is commonly supposed.

14. Some Historical Perspectives on the Anti-Urban Bias

E. GORDON ERICKSEN

Ancient Times

The Old Testament places agriculture and husbandry on a high level. In Genesis, Jehovah did not approve of the attempt by Noah's descendants to "build a city and a tower whose top may reach unto heaven." We have a similar negative attitude manifested toward the city in the story of Sodom and Gomorrah. In fact, the general attitude expressed in the Old Testament seems more sympathetic with the pastoral life than the agricultural, and especially more than with the urban life. Cities are described as places of sin and depravity; as places of refuge for criminals. Here the streets are morally dangerous; wisdom and folly live side by side. As centers for the accumulation of wealth and luxury they are the places that must be constantly guarded by God in order that they may not perish.

When we consider the ancient Persian literature, in particular that of the Zoroastrian religion, we find that men who pursued occupations of an urban character held generally the lowest status. Engaging in agriculture was like performing a ceremonial to sacred beings. Lowest in rank were the urban tradesmen, artisans, market dealers, and tax-gatherers. Only the professional men of the city ranked alongside the cultivators, who in turn were placed beneath the men of great knowledge, those learned in religion, kings and judges.[10]

In the Hindu world of India, agriculture was regarded as being more noble than any of the other modes of subsistence, with the exception of learning and receiving alms. The principal occupations and attitudes may be classified as learning, mechanical arts, working for wages, traffic, contentment with little, soliciting alms, receiving interest on money, and cattle-raising. Agriculture was definitely superior to commerce. Only the lower castes engaged in such urban occupations as trade and money-lending, modes of life considered by the higher castes as a "mixture of truth and falsehood," a "dog's mode of life." From the meager literature of the ancient Hindus and Zoroastrians, we learn how cultivators were ranked below the classes of priests and rulers but above the occupational groups of traders, artisans, business men, and the class of nonagricultural labor generally.

Ancient Japanese and Chinese records rank urban life as the least

SOURCE: Reprinted with permission of The Macmillan Company from *Urban Behavior,* pp. 68-75, by E. Gordon Ericksen. Copyright 1954 by The Macmillan Company.

desirable. The Japanese claimed that emperors from the urban world were rarely the best. In China, as a rule, the emperors were in the first place "expert farmers" who were required to demonstrate ability in tilling the soil. The people considered the best emperors to be the best husbandmen, since the promotion and improvement of agriculture comprised the most important function of government.

In ancient Greece the farmer class was viewed favorably as being the very foundation of the social order. Farmers were considered stable, law-abiding, hard-working, vigorous, healthy, moral, patriotic, religious, and brave. Farm life was regarded as the best school for physical training, for the development of the best soldiers, and for producing honest, industrious citizens. But there was one inconsistency. While Plato, Aristotle, Xenophon, and other Greek writers praised the farmer class, they also rated it below the classes of full-fledged urban citizens. Everyone praised the farmer, but no one wanted to become one or place him on an equal level with urban citizens.

However, a clear picture of Greek life is obscure owing to the prevailing serfdom, and the fine remarks made about farmers were directed toward free farmers and not to the slaves working in agriculture. In Plato's *Republic*, where a picture is painted of what an ideal state should be, Plato framed his republic in an agricultural setting. He had the farmers training in farming and not in governing, since the latter was the job of the philosophers. In his *Laws*, agriculture was the primary business of the state and all citizens were to be landowners. Commerce, trade, money-lending, and similar occupations were excluded as being unnecessary and undesirable. Agriculture was considered more necessary than urban occupations.

Plato felt that in the primeval world, long before cities came into being, the blessed state and way of life existed, of which "the best ordered of existing states is a copy."[11] He wrote:

> In the first place, the desolation of these primitive men would create in them a feeling of affection and good-will towards one another; and, secondly, they would have no occasion to quarrel about their subsistence, for they would have pasture in abundance, except just at first, and in some particular cases; and from their pasture-land they would obtain the greater part of their food in a primitive age, having plenty of milk and flesh; moreover they would procure other food by the chase, not to be despised either in quantity or quality. They would also have abundance of clothing, and bedding, and dwellings, and utensils either capable of standing on the fire or not; for the plastic and weaving arts do not require any use of iron; and God has given these two arts to man in order to provide him with all such things, that,

> when reduced to the last extremity, the human race may still grow and increase. Hence in those days mankind were not very poor; nor was poverty a cause of difference among them; and rich they could not have been, having neither gold nor silver:—such at that time was their condition. And the community which has neither poverty nor riches will always have the noblest principles; in it there is no insolence or injustice, nor, again, are there any contentions or envyings. And therefore they were good, and also because they were what is called simple-minded; and when they were told about good and evil, they in their simplicity believed what they heard to be very truth and practiced it. No one had the wit to suspect another of a falsehood, as men do now; but what they heard about Gods and men they believed to be true, and lived accordingly; and therefore they were in all respects such as we have described them. . . . Would not many generations living on in a simple manner, although ruder, perhaps, and more ignorant of the arts generally, and in particular of those of land or naval warfare, and likewise of other arts, termed in cities legal practices and party conflicts, and including all conceivable ways of hurting one another in word and deed;—although inferior to those who lived before the deluge, or to the men of our day and in these respects, would they not, I say, be simpler and more manly, and also more temperate and altogether more just? . . .[12]

Aristotle preferred the agriculturists, but unlike Plato he excluded the agricultural class from citizenship in his ideal city-state. The reason for this is not so much the inferiority of farmers as their lack of training for highly responsible governmental functions and their lack of leisure time for carrying out the functions of citizens. He felt that the best government is that which is composed of highly trained, selected experts who give all their time to government, a requirement which could not be met by the farm population. Nevertheless, Aristotle stressed the superiority of the farming class over the city rabble. Next in superiority to the agriculturists were the pastoral people who lived by their flocks. To Aristotle, they were the best trained of any for war, and were robust in body and able to camp out.

Rome reflected the stability of agricultural life, since it was a parasite city, depending upon the surrounding agriculturists. Consequently, the writers of ancient Rome had high praise for the class of free farmers and the effects of agricultural work upon the mind and body and the social order. Such writers as Virgil, Horace, Seneca, and Tacitus noted how the city depended upon the country, and how the destitute always came to the city for free grain. Seneca stated in his *Epilogue* that the strongest soldiers came from the rough country, while the lazy ones came from the city. The very foundation of Rome and its expansion during the early period was due to the Roman farmers, who were also the Roman soldiers. Consequently what was won by the Roman farmer-soldier was quickly consolidated by the power of the plow of the Roman farmer-soldier-colonist.

MEDIEVAL PERIOD

From the year 400 A.D. to approximately 1400 A.D. there was only a meager amount of reflection on city versus country life. Cities, during these Dark Ages, were mainly frontier outposts rather than cultural centers. Only since the thirteenth and fourteenth centuries in Europe do we begin to find any statements about rural-urban life.

In Arabia from the fifth to the twelfth century, however, we find great progress in science, art, and literature following Arab victories over many countries. The most important observation on rural-urban sociology was made by Ibn-Khaldun (1332–1406), a celebrated historian and philosopher, who made a detailed and surprisingly accurate description of the social life of the Arab. This distinguished historian urged that history should not simply consider rulers, dynasties, and wars, but also racial factors, climatic forces, the laws of association, and the stages of associative life. Although he evolved a spiral theory of social evolution, beginning with the crudest primitive life and ending with the most civilized urban life, he claimed that nomadic rural people were braver and more moral, and that their family life was stronger than that of city dwellers. The city, he claimed, had to be replenished constantly by the stronger country people.[13] His convictions and observations may be summarized under six points: (1) Nomadic and rural people are more healthy, brave, sound, resourceful, moral, self-reliant, less degenerate than urban people; (2) family life is cleaner and family relationships are stronger in the rural districts than in the cities; (3) mutual aid and sociality are developed more in the desert and country than in the city; (4) the position of women and older people is better, and they are more respected and valued in the country than in the city; (5) the city population is incessantly replenished by the migration of country people, and these migrants are recruited chiefly from the more wealthy rural families; and (6) the city leads to degeneration of people and the consequent decay of the entire society, since urbanism means unhealthy environment, luxury, vice, indulgences, and other debilitating conditions. There are, without doubt, many people today who support Khaldun's claim that with the development of science, commerce, and art in the cities, comes the inevitable decay of all society.

European Thinkers Before the Nineteenth Century

As we proceed to the sixteenth and seventeenth centuries, the theories about rural-urban life become more and more developed. A new interest in city life arises, as is indicated in the writings of Rousseau, Thomas More, and Machiavelli. Before their time Saint Thomas Aquinas (1225–1274) had proclaimed the city as a self-sufficient, natural state for man, and the country as unnatural, which was a somewhat exceptional attitude to take in his era. Contrary to Aristotle of ancient Greece, he visualized the city with many houses neatly divided into many streets, with each home being the location for a certain occupational group whose totality makes the city self-sufficient. He claimed that peasants lived outside of the city not because they disliked it, but that because of their poverty, lack of ability, and inferiority, they could not make the move. He agreed with Aristotle, at least in regarding the city-state as the best and highest form of socio-political organization.

Sir Thomas More (1478–1535) in his *Utopia*,[14] took a more moderate position than that of Thomas Aquinas by describing a plan whereby everyone could find his greatest pleasure in giving to others. He believed that the strongest league of peoples or nations is not that which is united chiefly by treaties or covenants, but that which is knit together by love and a benevolent attitude. More conceived of agriculture and country life as being the most suitable setting for this genuine Christian brotherhood. He did figure cities into his scheme, though, and required that every urban community be a garden city, that every house possess a garden plot. Agriculture was an occupation which was obligatory upon all persons of his ideal society for a period of two years, regardless of whether they were born in the city or country.

Niccolo Machiavelli (1469–1527), an Italian, differed from Sir Thomas More in many ways by declaring that people should be considered as they are, and not according to false teachings about them. He advocated either an autocratic or democratic form of government, depending upon the conditions of the time and place. His "relentless empiricism" gave direction to the trend of social thinking which resulted in inductive researches in the field of social analysis and social control. On the subject of city life, however, he agrees with More, for he points to the city as a breeder of tumult, disorder, luxury, and vice. He proclaimed that class struggle very often and very successfully originates in cities. The city to Machiavelli was generally the source of social disorganization and demoralization. He did not take the extreme position of Rousseau who later asserted that city life meant an inevitable and unavoidable social decay.[15]

Jean Jacques Rousseau (1712–1778) held a negative view toward the city. He was a romanticist who claimed that man is naturally good and that a simple society such as agricultural life is best for man. This romantic view is developed in his *Discourse about Science and Arts* and his *Social Contract*. He felt that the happiest and most virtuous life is the simple life of primitive people where there are no cities, sciences, arts, or complex civilizations. Social decay is the consequence of the growth of cities, with their commerce, industries, luxury, effeminacy, and injustice.

Baron de Montesquieu (1689–1755) was neutral regarding rural-urban life.[16] His feelings can be summed up in four statements: (1) agriculture is a basic industry and should be encouraged; (2) commerce and urbanism follow after agriculture and ruralism in importance; (3) the arts and sciences, as well as commerce, function positively to refine the mores, thus extend peace, labor, efficiency, orderliness, sagacity, and regularity. But Montesquieu pointed out how the arts and sciences of city life can lead to the corruption of the mores, increasing inequality and disorder, thus establishing an all too formal justice and a weakening of sincerity and hospitality. He claimed (4) that in the main, population decrease is due to a lack of a free farm population and a farmer proprietorial class. To increase population fertility Montesquieu believed a society must have a landed class whose living conditions are satisfactory.

David Hume (1711–1776) took a somewhat indefinite view, so far as is shown by the remarks in his various essays.[17] Under some conditions agriculture is better than industrial life, he claimed, yet under other circumstances the reverse is true. Agriculture is not the only productive class. He observed that enormous cities are destructive to society since they give rise to vice and disorder, starve the nearby provinces, and raise prices. On the other hand, he looked favorably on the development of manufacturing, industry, arts, commerce, luxury (when it was not vicious), and other processes of life in the city.

Adam Smith (1723–1790), like Hume, did not regard the farmer as the only productive person. He claimed that the classes of manufacturers, artisans, merchants, and professionals were also productive, but remarked that the city had its origin and grew out of rural production. In the final analysis, Smith believed, a condition of cooperation exists between country and city, and there is no one-sided development of either at the expense of the other.[18]

[10]The Zend-Avesta and Pahlavi texts, which compose the principal texts of the Zoroastrian religion, were written after the beginning of our era. However, their content is old and goes back several centuries before our era and may be relied upon as excellent sources for early Persian thought. See F. Max Muller's *The Sacred Books of the East (SBE)* for early Persian, Indian, and Chinese thought.

[11]Plato, *Laws,* trans. B. Jowett, Vol. II, *The Dialogues of Plato* (New York: Random House, Inc., 1937), p. 484.

[12]*Ibid.,* pp. 454-455.

[13]Ibn-Khaldun, "Prolegomenes historiques," *Notices et extraits des manuscripts de la Bibliotheque Imperial,* XIX and XX (Paris, 1862).

[14]George Simpson (ed.), *The Utopia of Sir Thomas More,* Bohn's Classical Libraries (London: Bell and Sons, 1910).

[15]N. Machiavelli, *The Florentine History,* Tudor translations (London, 1905), pp. 130-177; "Discorsi sopra la prima deca di Tito Livio," *Opere Complete di N. Machiavelli* (Florence, 1943), pp. 279 ff.; *The Prince,* Tudor translations (London, 1905), pp. 293-294.

[16]Baron de Montesquieu, *The Spirit of Laws,* trans. Thomas Nugent (Cincinnati, 1873), Vol. I, xxxi.

[17]David Hume, *Essays, Moral, Political, and Literary* (London, 1870).

[18]Adam Smith, *An Inquiry into the Nature and Causes of the Wealth of Nations,* ed. by Edwin Cannan (London, 1920), Vol. II, Bk. IV, Chap. ix; Vol. I, Bk. II, Chap. iii.

15. In Praise of the Secular City

HARVEY COX

The rise of urban civilization and the collapse of traditional religion are the two main hallmarks of our era and are closely related movements. Urbanization constitutes a massive change in the way men live together, and became possible in its contemporary form only with the scientific and technological advances which sprang from the wreckage of religious world-views. Secularization, an equally epochal movement, marks a change in the way men grasp and understand their life together, and it occurred only when the cosmopolitan confrontations of city living exposed the relativity of the myths and traditions men once thought were unquestionable. The ways men live their common life affects mightily the ways they understand the meaning of that life, and vice versa. . . . Societies and the symbols by which those societies live influence each other. In our day the secular metropolis stands as both the pattern of our life together and the symbol of our view of the

SOURCE: Reprinted with permission of The Macmillan Company from *The Secular City,* pp. 1-14, 38-84, by Harvey Cox.

world. If the Greeks perceived the cosmos as an immensely expanded polis, and medieval man saw it as the feudal manor enlarged to infinity, we experience the universe as the city of man. It is a field of human exploration and endeavor from which the gods have fled. The world has become man's task and man's responsibility. Contemporary man has become the cosmopolitan. The world has become his city and his city has reached out to include the world. The name for the process by which this has come about is *secularization.*

What is secularization? The Dutch theologian C. A. van Peursen says it is the deliverance of man "first from religious and then from metaphysical control over his reason and his language."[1] It is the loosing of the world from religious and quasi-religious understandings of itself, the dispelling of all closed world-views, the breaking of all supernatural myths and sacred symbols. It represents what another observer has called the "defatalization of history," the discovery by man that he has been left with the world on his hands, that he can no longer blame fortune or the furies for what he does with it. Secularization is man turning his attention away from worlds beyond and toward this world and this time.

* * *

The forces of secularization have no serious interest in persecuting religion. Secularization simply bypasses and undercuts religion and goes on to other things. It has relativized religious world-views and thus rendered them innocuous. Religion has been privatized. It has been accepted as the peculiar prerogative and point of view of a particular person or group. Secularization has accomplished what fire and chain could not: It has convinced the believer that he *could* be wrong, and persuaded the devotee that there are more important things than dying for the faith. The gods of traditional religions live on as private fetishes or the patrons of congenial groups, but they play no role whatever in the public life of the secular metropolis. . . . Pluralism and tolerance are the children of secularization. They represent a society's unwillingness to enforce any particular world-view on its citizens. Movements within the Roman Catholic Church culminating in the Second Vatican Council indicate its growing readiness to be open to truth from all sides. Pluralism is breaking out where once a closed system stood.

The age of the secular city, the epoch whose ethos is quickly spreading into every corner of the globe, *is* an age of "no religion at all." It no longer looks to religious rules and rituals for its morality or its meanings. For some religion provides a hobby, for others a mark of national or ethnic identification, for still others an esthetic delight.

For fewer and fewer does it provide an inclusive and commanding system of personal and cosmic values and explanations.

* * *

It will do no good to cling to our religious and metaphysical versions of Christianity in the hope that one day religion or metaphysics will once again be back. They are disappearing forever and that means we can now let go and immerse ourselves in the new world of the secular city. The first step in such an immersion is learning something about its peculiar characteristics. But before we do we must ask more precisely about the other key term we have used in describing the ethos of our time, *urbanization*.

If secularization designates the content of man's coming of age, urbanization describes the context in which it is occurring. It is the "shape" of the new society which supports its peculiar cultural style. In trying to define the term *urbanization*, however, we are confronted with the fact that social scientists themselves are not entirely agreed about what it means. It is clear, however, that urbanization is not just a quantitative term. It does not refer to population size or density, to geographic extent or to a particular form of government. Admittedly some of the character of modern urban life would not be possible without giant populations concentrated on enormous contiguous land masses. But urbanization is not something that refers only to the city. As Vidich and Bensman have shown in *Small Town in Mass Society*,[3] high mobility, economic concentration, and mass communications have drawn even rural villages into the web of urbanization.

Urbanization means a structure of common life in which diversity and the disintegration of tradition are paramount. It means a type of impersonality in which functional relationships multiply. It means that a degree of tolerance and anonymity replace traditional moral sanctions and long-term acquaintanceships. The urban center is the place of human control, of rational planning, of bureaucratic organization—and the urban center is not just in Washington, London, New York, and Peking. It is everywhere. The technological metropolis provides the indispensable social setting for a world of "no religion at all," for what we have called a secular style. . . .

For purposes of convenience we shall divide the *manière d'être* of the secular city into its *shape* (the social component) and its *style* (the cultural aspect). . . .

The Shape of the Secular City

What comes to mind when we think of the *shape* of technopolis? We visualize contours. We envisage networks of radial and circumferential thoroughfares, grids of disparate but interlocking land-use regions, a profile carved out by the city's natural topography—a mountain range, a lakefront, a river. We also see buildings, short and squat, tall and erect. Terminals, stations, offices, residences jostle each other for space. These are the physical shapes of the city.

But what about the social shape of the secular metropolis, its human silhouette, the institutional basis for its culture? The shape of the secular city, along with its style, comprises its *manière d'être*. Its shape is its social system as distinguished from its cultural system. The distinction is of course merely analytic. In reality shape and style merge, but for purposes of discussion, . . . we shall focus on the shape of the secular city and on its style . . . [separately].

Let two images drawn from the physical setting of technopolis suggest the elements of its social shape on which we wish to concentrate. The first is the *switchboard*, the key to communication in the city, linking human beings to one another through modern electronic magic. The next is the highway *cloverleaf*, the image of simultaneous mobility in many different directions. These symbols suggest both possibility and problems. They illustrate two characteristic components of the social shape of the modern metropolis: *anonymity* and *mobility*. But why focus on them?

Not only are anonymity and mobility central. They are also the two features of the urban social system most frequently singled out for attack by both religious and nonreligious critics. How often has one heard that urban man's existence has been depleted and despoiled by the cruel anonymity and ceaseless mobility of the city? How frequently is urban man depicted by his detractors as faceless and depersonalized, rushing to and fro with no time to cultivate deeper relationships or lasting values? It is in part because anonymity and mobility have been made into antiurban epithets that we need to examine them and to point out the positive side. We shall do this first by showing how both anonymity and mobility contribute to the sustenance of human life in the city rather than detracting from it, why they are indispensable modes of existence in the urban setting. . . .

ANONYMITY

Every college sophomore knows that modern man is a faceless cipher. The stock in trade of too many humanities courses and religious emphasis weeks is the featureless "mass man," reduced to a number or a series of holes in an IBM card, wandering through T. S. Eliot's Waste Land starved for a name. "Loss of identity" and "disappearance of selfhood" have come to play an ever larger role in the popular pastime of flagellating urban culture. Where does this fear of anonymity originate?

Regardless of how cheapened and trite such criticisms have become in our time, they do stem from an impressive intellectual ancestry. Søren Kierkegaard fulminated brilliantly against certain elements of mass society and urban life in *The Present Age* (1846). José Ortega y Gasset, the Spanish philosopher, exemplifies the aristocratic repugnance for the erasing of class lines and the anonymous character of modern society in his *Revolt of the Masses* (1932). Rainer Maria Rilke's book *Notebooks of Malte Lauridi Brigge* (English translation 1930) displays a metaphysical horror for the impersonality of life and for the loss of the mystery of things which he found in the city. Above all, the refusal of Franz Kafka to endow the main characters of two of his late novels with any name has sometimes been interpreted as a protest against urban and bureaucratic anonymity.

Must the modern writer be antiurban?

The truth is that, for a genuine literary artist, the city is the setting but not the real target of his onslaught. Many nineteenth- and early-twentieth-century writers did not see that urban anonymity has its distinct benefits as well as its horrors. A writer who becomes *essentially* antiurban forfeits his claim to greatness, for what is often left unsaid by the morbid critics of anonymity is, first, that without it, life in a modern city could not be human, and second, that anonymity represents for many people a liberating even more than a threatening phenomenon. It serves for large numbers of people as the possibility of freedom in contrast to the bondage of the law and convention. Let us look first at how the anonymity of city living helps preserve the privacy which is essential to human life. . . .

The Man at the Giant Switchboard. Technopolitan man sits at a vast and immensely complicated switchboard. He is *homo symbolicus,* man the communicator, and the metropolis is a massive network of communications. A whole world of possibilities for communication lies within his reach. The contemporary urban region represents an ingenious device for vastly enlarging the range of human communication and widening the scope of individual choice. Urbanization thus contributes to the freedom of man. This is perfectly evident when we think for example of cinema theaters and restaurants. Residents of a city of 10,000 may be limited to one or two theaters, while people who live in a city of a million can choose among perhaps fifty films on a given night. The same principle holds for restaurants, schools, and even in some measure for job opportunities or prospective marriage partners. Urban man is free to choose from a wider range of alternatives. Thus his manhood as *homo symbolicus* is enhanced.

But freedom always demands discipline. The mere availability of such a wide spectrum of possibilities requires an adjustment of urban man's behavior. He must exercise choice more frequently, and choice always means exclusion. He doesn't just "go to the movies" on a free evening, as his more rural counterpart might; he must choose one from among the fifty films now showing. This means a conscious decision *not* to see the other forty-nine.

In the area of personal relationships this selectivity becomes more demanding. Urban man has a wider variety of "contacts" than his rural counterpart; he can choose only a limited number for friends. He must have more or less impersonal relationships with most of the people with whom he comes in contact precisely in order to choose certain friendships to nourish and cultivate. This selectivity can best be symbolized perhaps by the unplugged telephone or the unlisted number. A person does not request an unlisted number to cut down on the depth of his relationships. Quite the opposite; he does so to guard and deepen the worthwhile relationships he has against being dissolved in the deluge of messages that would come if one were open on principle and on an equal basis to anyone who tried to get through, including the increasing army of telephone salesmen who violate one's privacy so arrogantly. Those we want to know have our number; others do not. We are free to use the switchboard without being victimized by its infinite possibilities.

Urban man must distinguish carefully between his private life and his public relationships. Since he depends on such a complex net of services to maintain himself in existence in a modern city, the majority of his transactions will have to be public and will be what sociologists call functional or secondary. In most of his relationships he will be dealing with people he cannot afford to be interested in as individuals but must deal with in terms of the services they render to him and he to them. This is essential in urban life. Supermarket checkers or gas-meter readers who became enmeshed in the lives of the people they were serving would be a menace. They would soon cause a total breakdown in the essential systems of which they are integral parts. Urban life demands that we treat most of the people we meet as persons—not as things, but not as intimates either. This in turn produces the kind of "immunization" against personal encounters which Louis Wirth explains this way:

> Characteristically, urbanites meet one another in highly segmental roles. They are, to be sure, dependent upon more people for the satisfactions of their life-needs than are rural people and thus are associated with a greater number of organized groups, but they are less dependent upon particular persons, and their dependence upon others

is confined to a highly fractionalized aspect of the other's round of activity. This is essentially what is meant by saying that the city is characterized by secondary rather than primary contacts. The contacts of the city may indeed be face to face, but they are nevertheless impersonal, superficial, transitory, and segmental. The reserve, the indifference, and the blasé outlook which urbanites manifest in their relationships may thus be regarded as devices for immunizing themselves against the personal claims and expectations of others.[1]

This immunization results in a way of life which often appears cold and even heartless to those unfamiliar with the dynamics of urban living. Here both writers and sociologists have missed the point. Cultural romantics such as Rilke and Ortega recoiled in distaste at what they took to be the cruelty of the city. In sociology a similar criticism was also voiced. Relationships in the city, it was complained, tended to be divested of their really human substance and made mechanical and lifeless.

One of the most influential sociological critics of the shape of urban life was a German scholar named Ferdinand Tönnies (1855–1936), whose work has continued to exert a considerable influence on modern sociology and cultural analysis. In 1887 Tönnies published a book in which he contrasted the coherent, organic togetherness of *Gemeinschaft* (community) with the more rational, planned, and partial nexus of the *Gesellschaft* (society). Kaspar Naegele summarizes Tönnies' distinction:

> Relations of the *Gemeinschaft* type are more inclusive; persons confront each other as ends, they cohere more durably. . . . In *Gesellschaft* their mutual regard is circumscribed by a sense of specific, if not formal obligation. . . . A transaction can occur without any other encounters, leaving both parties virtually anonymous.[2]

Tönnies is talking about what some sociologists describe as "primary" versus "secondary" relationships, or "organic" versus "functional" relationships. Having lived both as a villager and as an urbanite I know just what these terms mean. During my boyhood, my parents never referred to "the milkman," "the insurance agent," "the junk collector." These people were, respectively, Paul Weaver, Joe Villanova, and Roxy Barazano. All of our family's market transactions took place within a web of wider and more inclusive friendship and kinship ties with the same people. They were never anonymous. In fact, the occasional salesman or repairman whom we did not know was always viewed with dark suspicion until we could make sure where he came from, who his parents were, and whether his family was "any good." Trips to the grocery store, gasoline station, or post office were inevitably social visits, never merely functional contacts.

Now, as an urbanite, my transactions are of a very different sort. If I need to have the transmission on my car repaired, buy a television antenna, or cash a check, I find myself in functional relationships with mechanics, salesmen, and bank clerks whom I never see in any other capacity. These "contacts" are in no sense "mean, nasty or brutish," though they do tend to be short, at least not any longer than the time required to make the transaction and to exchange a brief pleasantry. Some of these human contacts occur with considerable frequency, so that I come to know the mannerisms and maybe even the names of some of the people. But the relationships are unifaceted and "segmental." I meet these people in no other context. To me they remain essentially just as anonymous as I do to them. Indeed, in the case of the transmission repairman, I hope I never see him again—not because he is in any way unpleasant, but because my only possible reason for seeing him again would be a new and costly breakdown in my car's gear box. The important point here is that my relationships with bank clerks and garagemen are no less human or authentic merely because we both prefer to keep them anonymous. . . .

Urban anonymity need not be heartless. Village sociability can mask a murderous hostility. Loneliness is undoubtedly a serious problem in the city, but it cannot be met by dragooning urban people into relationships which decimate their privacy and reduce their capacity to live responsibly with increasing numbers of neighbors. . . .

The small-town dweller, on the other hand, lives within a restricted web of relationships and senses a larger world he may be missing. Since the people he knows also know one another, he gossips more and yearns to hear gossip. His private life is public and vice versa. While urban man is unplugging his telephone, town man (or his wife) may be listening in on the party line or its modern equivalent, gossiping at the kaffee-klatsch.

Urban man, in contrast, wants to maintain a clear distinction between private and public. Otherwise public life would overwhelm and dehumanize him. His life represents a point touched by dozens of systems and hundreds of people. His capacity to know some of them better necessitates his minimizing the depth of his relationships to many others. Listening to the postman gossip becomes for urban man an act of sheer graciousness, since he probably has no interest in the people the postman wants to talk about. Unlike my parents, who suspected all strangers, he tends to be wary not of the functionaries he doesn't know but of those he does. . . .

MOBILITY

Every tendency in modern society points to accelerated mobility. Technology closes the saddlemaker's shop and opens electronic labs. Industrialization not only lures people off the farms and into the cities; it also invades the farms, transforming them into food factories and steadily diminishing the number of hands required to do the work. The modern city is a mass movement. It has been described by one writer as a kind of staging area where people pause in their complex movements from one place to another. Not only do we migrate between cities in search of improvement, but we migrate within cities to find more convenient or congenial surroundings. Commutation represents a small daily migration. We commute not only to work but also to play, to shop, to socialize. Everybody is going places, but what is happening to us as a people along the way?

Many view the high mobility of modern life in the most negative possible light. A whole literature of protest has grown up, much of it religious in nature, which bewails the alleged shallowness and lostness of modern urban man. Countless sermons deplore the "rush-rush of modern living" and the diminution of spiritual values supposed to accompany the loss of more sedentary cultural patterns. On a more serious level, themes of rootlessness and alienation constantly appear in contemporary literature. Indeed, the greatest novelists of our century have chosen to create heroes who wander far from home in the midst of strangers and foreigners. Thomas Mann's *Joseph in Egypt,* James Joyce's *Ulysses,* and Franz Kafka's *The Castle* come to mind immediately. Albert Camus and André Gide dealt with similar themes. Time and again there returns the image of man as a harried and homeless wanderer, frequently with absorbing artistic power. The question is, however: Must man necessarily be impoverished by mobility? Can he travel without getting lost? Can he move without meandering? . . .

The Man in the Cloverleaf. Technopolitan man is on the go. In addition to the giant switchboard, he can be pictured as a driver in a cloverleaf intersection. Other images of the city include the airport control tower, high-speed elevators, and perpetually moving escalators in department stores and offices. The modern metropolis is a system of roads—thruways, subways, airways—linking the city to others and parts of the city to each other. It is also a system of vertical facilitators, snatching people from the street to the penthouse, from the janitor's basement to the executive suite and back again. Urban man is certainly in motion, and we can expect the pace and scope of mobility to increase as time goes on.

Analysts sometimes distinguish between two types of mobility—geographic and occupational. Sometimes status mobility, class mobility, and other forms of "social" mobility are added. But since these are so closely related to job and residence mobility, we shall restrict ourselves here to discussing the problems and possibilities of movement to new jobs and homes.

There are many critics of residential and occupational mobility. They use different rhetoric but quite frequently paint verbal landscapes of home and vocation which are laden with religious sentiments. For many people these images have a real appeal. To be born and reared in the same clapboard house where one may even grow old and die does have a certain cozy attractiveness. To work at the same job in the same place through all one's adult years might also provide elements of comfort. But those who bewail the passing of the era in which this stable, idyllic condition was supposed to have obtained forget one important fact: only a tiny minority of people ever really enjoyed such pastoral permanence. The majority of people in pre-mobile societies lived and worked in ways we would not want to return to. Most of us today would vigorously object to living in the house or doing the job our great-grandfathers did. The fact is that most people's great-grandparents were dirt-poor and lived in hovels. Most of us are much better off today because our forebears *were* mobile. Mobility is always the weapon of the underdog. The desire to combat mobility, to encourage residential and occupational *im*mobility, is a romantic distortion which springs from a reactionary mentality.

Mobility is closely linked to social change; so guardians of the status quo have always opposed mobility. They are perfectly consistent in doing so. They sense that changes in one area of life—job or residence—will lead to other kinds of change; and they are against change. The conservatives in the polis of Athens were right in their fierce opposition to constructing a port at Piraeus. They knew that mixed with the exotic products of foreign shores there would come strange people with exotic ideas which would shake their security. Virulent opposition to the building of railroads was voiced by the lords of the English establishment in the early nineteenth century, not just because railroads were loud or dirty, but because even lowly villagers would now travel to other towns. There they could not be kept from coming under strange influences since they would wander about without the normal social controls. Worst of all, it was argued, they would meet people who had never heard of their local squires. They would see their own towns in perspective and might lose all respect for traditional authority.

The World War I song "How Ya Gonna' Keep 'Em Down on the Farm Now that They've Seen Paree?" illustrates the relationship between mobility, urbanization, and social change. Those who have been drawn into the tradition-demolishing orbit of urban life are never quite the same again. They will always know that things *could* be different; they will never again accept the farm as given; and this is the seedbed of revolution.

In our own country the emergence of the Negro Freedom Movement provides a particularly good example of the link between mobility and social change. Many observers believe that the movement of large numbers of Negroes out of rural areas in the South and into urban industrial centers, plus the experience of thousands of young Negroes in the military service, supplied the indispensable social exposure which has resulted in the civil rights revolution. Negroes discovered that things did not have to be the way they were. Those who acted against oppression were young, and they were geographically and occupationally mobile. Their battles, unlike those of the Civil War which took place at heretofore unknown villages—Bull Run and Gettysburg—now took place in urban centers such as Birmingham, and spread to the provinces. Mobility had unlocked the cage.

Geographic mobility always points to social or occupational mobility. Even in the storybooks, the son leaves the family homestead "to seek his fortune." Mobility in one area signifies mobility in another. People on the move spatially are usually on the move intellectually, financially, or psychologically. All of this naturally threatens those who already occupy the positions of power and influence in the society. It is the people on the bottom who have everything to gain and nothing to lose from a mobile society. Consequently it is not difficult to discover class prejudice behind religious objections to mobility. Since romanticism and reaction often stroll hand in hand, it is equally easy to spot an aristocratic or conservative ideology in those pleas for occupational stability and home-sweet-home inertness that are often fused with religious appeals. Mobility threatens the top dog and the status quo.

An advanced industrial society strangles without mobility. People must be ready to move. New jobs appear in different places. Technology renders skilled operators obsolescent; even if they are retrained, their newly acquired skill may become equally obsolescent before they know it. Promotion in most firms and increasingly in educational institutions involves moving from place to place. Travel and vacationing expose people to numberless new vistas of experience. Those tendencies in our society which tend to retard or discourage mobility almost always arise from people who are trying to prevent other people from enlarging their share of the power or the rewards of the society. But impairing mobility inevitably damages the whole society. Thus housing and employment patterns which reduce the mobility of Negroes, for example, function like sand in the gear box of the economy, and the whole society suffers. . . .

Mobility is not the menace religious romantics paint it. It has its pitfalls. Endless movement from place to place can betray the same kind of unwillingness to take responsibility for decisions which can be seen in switching wives. But by and large the mobile man is less tempted than the immobile man to demote Yahweh into a baal. He will usually not idolatrize any town or nation. He will not be as likely to see the present economic and political structure as the unambiguous expression of how things always have been and always should be. He will be more open to change, movement, newness. There is no reason why Christians should deplore the accelerating mobility of the modern metropolis. The Bible does not call man to renounce mobility, but to "go to a place that I will show unto you." Perhaps the mobile man can even hear with less static a Message about a Man who was born during a journey, spent his first years in exile, was expelled from his own home town, and declared that he had no place to lay his head. High mobility is no assurance of salvation, but neither is it an obstacle to faith. . . .

The Style of the Secular City

Technopolis, like the civilization it displaces, has its own characteristic style. The word *style* here refers to the way a society projects its own self-image, how it organizes the values and meanings by which it lives. The secular-urban style springs in part from the societal shape provided by the anonymity and mobility we have just discussed. But it is not merely a product of these factors. The style has a life of its own which in turn influences and alters the shape on which it is based. Style and shape affect each other. Both comprise that configurational whole which we have called the *manière d'être* of the secular city.

Two motifs in particular characterize the style of the secular city. We call them *pragmatism* and *profanity*. We use these words at some risk of confusion, since for many people pragmatism refers to a particular movement in American philosophy and profanity simply means obscene language. Both these usages are derivative, however, and our intention here is to call to mind their original meanings.

By *pragmatism* we mean secular man's concern with the question

"Will it work?" Secular man does not occupy himself much with mysteries. He is little interested in anything that seems resistant to the application of human energy and intelligence. He judges ideas, as the dictionary suggests in its definition of pragmatism, by the "results they will achieve in practice." The world is viewed not as a unified metaphysical system but as a series of problems and projects.

By *profanity* we refer to secular man's wholly terrestrial horizon, the disappearance of any supramundane reality defining his life. *Profane* means literally "outside the temple"—thus "having to do with this world." By calling him profane, we do not suggest that secular man is sacrilegious, but that he is unreligious. He views the world not in terms of some other world but in terms of itself. He feels that any meaning to be found in this world originates in this world itself. Profane man is simply *this*-worldly.

To make even clearer what we mean by pragmatism and profanity, two characteristically twentieth-century men have been introduced as personifications of these elements of the secular style. The late American President John F. Kennedy embodies the spirit of the pragmatic; Albert Camus, the late French novelist and playwright, illustrates what we mean by this-worldly profanity.

* * *

If secular man is no longer interested in the ultimate mystery of life but in the "pragmatic" solution of particular problems, how can anyone talk to him meaningfully about God? If he discards suprahistorical meanings and looks in his "profanity" to human history itself as the source of purpose and value, how can he comprehend any religious claim at all? Should not theologians first divest modern man of his pragmatism and his profanity, teach him once again to ask and to wonder, and *then* come to him with the Truth from Beyond?

No. Any effort to desecularize and deurbanize modern man, to rid him of his pragmatism and his profanity, is seriously mistaken. It wrongly presupposes that a man must first become "religious" before he can hear the Gospel. It was Dietrich Bonhoeffer who firmly rejected this erroneous assumption and pointed out that it bore a striking parallel to the long-discarded idea that one had to be circumcised a Jew before becoming a Christian. Bonhoeffer insisted that we must find a nonreligious interpretation of the Gospel for secular man. He was right. . . . Pragmatism and profanity, like anonymity and mobility, are not obstacles but avenues of access to modern man. His very pragmatism and profanity enable urban man to discern certain elements of the Gospel which were hidden from his more religious forebears. Let us now examine each of these elements in turn.

JOHN F. KENNEDY AND PRAGMATISM

Urban-secular man is pragmatic. In the dictionary sense of the word, this means he concerns himself with "practical or material affairs" and is interested in the "actual working out of an idea in experience." He devotes himself to tackling specific problems and is interested in what will work to get something done. He has little interest in what have been termed "borderline questions" or metaphysical considerations. Because religion has concerned itself so largely precisely with these things, he does not ask "religious" questions.

The preceding paragraph could very well serve as a thumbnail sketch of the political style of John F. Kennedy. Once at a dinner party, a guest seated next to Walt W. Rostow, at that time planning director for the State Department, asked him what President Kennedy was "really like." After some hesitation Rostow replied, "Well, I would use one word to characterize him. He is a pragmatist." Though cryptic, Rostow's answer was actually exceedingly apt. Mr. Kennedy represented just that no-nonsense practicality and interest in workable solutions that is best characterized by the word *pragmatism*.

From Europe comes a similar judgment about the late President. Writing on the mastery of technological civilization, World Council of Churches staff member Harry O. Morton reminds us quite rightly that such mastery "requires the competence to isolate a problem, to exclude from view enough of the important but not immediately relevant data in order that one may study the problem by itself, and thus find for it a workable solution."[1] Morton concedes that all such solutions are only partial and temporary, that if they work they will in fact present us with a whole new series of problems, and this is just what we expect to happen. Most interesting for our purposes, Morton uses John F. Kennedy to illustrate this method. He describes the Kennedy government as one which "springs from this approach rather than from a systematically developed ideology." Morton was especially impressed with Kennedy's flair for bringing together teams of experts "to study special problems and to work out an immediate coherent policy in a limited field."

To say that technopolitan man is pragmatic means that he is a kind of modern ascetic. He disciplines himself to give up certain things. He approaches problems by isolating them from irrelevant considerations, by bringing to bear the knowledge of different specialists, and by getting ready to grapple with a new series of problems when these have been provisionally solved. Life for him is a set of problems, not an unfathomable mystery. He brackets off the things that cannot be dealt with and deals with those that can. He wastes little time thinking about "ultimate" or "religious" questions. And he can live with highly provisional solutions.

He sees the world not so much as an awesome enigma, evoking a sense of hushed reverence, as a series of complex and interrelated projects requiring the application of competence. He does not ask religious questions because he fully believes he can handle this world without them.

Technopolitan man's understanding of truth is therefore pragmatic.

* * *

. . . Pragmatism as a style and a method should never be allowed to degenerate into pragmatism as a new ontology. The danger of functional thinking is that it narrows into "operationalism." This hazard arises when, having isolated some particular aspect of a phenomenon for special attention, we then forget that there *are* other aspects. It results from taking a helpfully restricted view of something and then deciding there is nothing more to it—the age-old temptation to forget that there are an infinite number of ways to look at the same blackbird.

The same aberration must be guarded against in a society, like ours, which judges everything in terms of "usefulness." The secular man asks most frequently of the stranger he meets *not* who he *is* but what he *does*. Or, to be more accurate, when he asks who someone *is* the answer he expects is a description of what that person *does*. Thus the question of meaning is identified with the question of purpose, human serviceability.

There is nothing intrinsically wrong with seeing meaning and value in terms of human purpose. The existentialist claim that our culture is meaningless or purposeless is simply wrong. Our culture does *not* lack purpose; it lacks only the particular purpose the existentialists had grown used to. Our culture *is* a teleological, or purpose-oriented, culture, and man is the fashioner of purposes. We size things up by asking what they are *for*, and to say of something or of someone that he is useless is about the worst thing we can say.

But usefulness, like pragmatism, must not degenerate into a new closed world-view. To write off artistic beauty, poetry, or even whole groups of people because they appear useless constitutes a terrible threat. Hitler wanted to gas Jews, invalids, and mentally retarded people because they could not make a contribution to the New Order of the Third Reich. People whose outlook is influenced by technological utopianism (for instance some of the scientific and business elites in the U.S.A. and the U.S.S.R.) tend to denigrate abstract art and music as worthless because to them they serve no useful function. Students and young adults with compulsive career orientations shun any hobby, recreation, or pastime which does not make a direct contribution to their professional development. So there are dangers here, but the dangers do not lie in the subsuming of worth and meaning under purpose. They lie rather in the catastrophic *narrowing* of the idea of usefulness and thus of worth to the purposes and programs one's own group considers important. The peril lies in an unwillingness to widen and deepen the purview of significant human purposes to include those outside the orbit of one's group or nation.

Thus neither Nazis nor technological utopians are really secular or pragmatic. They represent groups which are still to some extent bogged down in the metaphysical and religious stages of human development. For Hitler it was sometimes "God" and sometimes the *Zeitgeist* which had called him to fulfill Germany's destiny. The meaning of history was to be consummated in a Thousand-Year Reich. For the orthodox Communist there is an inner logic in history which is not dependent on man, a meaning to which man must adjust his personal projects or suffer the consequences. So long as it preserves elements of this fatalism, communism will continue to be a kind of godless "religion." Likewise, for the American business careerist, success is a residual religious vocation. It is *the* meaning, not *a* meaning, of life—and he cannot tolerate suggestions that there may be highly divergent patterns of life within which people find significance in ways totally different from his. Hence, for example, the bureaucrat's fear and resentment of the beatnik.

The rejection of meanings which do not contribute to those of one's own group is the opposite of secularization. It is a remnant of the metaphysical period when "*the* meaning of history" seemed discernible. It is a leftover of tribal and town culture in which radical inclusiveness had still not emerged. Augustine's God or Adam Smith's invisible hand or Karl Marx' dialectic as *the* pattern moving behind and within all the events of history entails for the devotee a necessary intolerance of other views and purposes.

On the other hand, when history is seen to be man's responsibility, the justification for inquisition is called into question. If men rather than metaphysical phantoms bear the meaning of historic life, then purposes other than those of one's own clan can be appreciated rather than repudiated. Separate world-views present the occasion not for mutual destruction but for fashioning a societal framework within which such variance can be encouraged and nourished. Ideally the secular city is such a society. It provides a setting in which a hodgepodge of human purposes and projects can thrive because each recognizes itself as provisional and relative. Authentic secularity demands that no world-view, no tradition, no ideology be allowed to become *the* officially enforced world-view beside which no others are tolerated. This in turn requires pluralistic social and political institutions.

We should not be dismayed by the fact that fewer and fewer people are pressing what we have normally called "religious" questions. The fact that urban-secular man is incurably and irreversibly pragmatic, that he is less and less concerned with religious questions, is in no sense a disaster. It means that he is shedding the lifeless cuticles of the mythical and ontological periods and stepping into the functional age. He is leaving behind the styles of the tribe and the town and is becoming a technopolitan man. As such he may now be in a position to hear certain notes in the biblical message that he missed before. He may be ready, in some respects, to "do the truth" in a way his superstitious and religious forerunners were not.

ALBERT CAMUS AND PROFANITY

When the Nobel Prize committee named Albert Camus recipient of the award for literature in 1957, they cited him correctly as one who "illuminates the problems of the human conscience in our time." Camus addressed himself to the most salient issue of the modern consciousness: how to live with direction and integrity in a world without God. For Camus, however, the absence of God was not simply a lamentable fact; it was a necessary reality. Hopes and values which reach beyond this world he rejected as a betrayal of this world and therefore of one's fellow man. Unlike Voltaire, who said, "If God did not exist, we should have to invent Him," Camus would say, aligning himself with Bakunin, "If God *did* exist, we should have to abolish Him."

For Camus there was an unavoidable contradiction between the existence of God and human responsibility. He had to be an atheist. But every atheist must be a particular kind of atheist: He must disbelieve in some particular God. Camus was plainly a classical "Christian atheist." He found the God of orthodox Christian theology irreconcilable with human freedom and justice. Therefore he had to reject him. Yet he did not do so in a mood either of vindictiveness or of despair, and this is what propelled Camus far beyond the anguished existentialism of many of his contemporaries. Though he began with a declaration that the world was absurd, he refused any forlorn or crestfallen response to such a reality. Instead, he celebrated the joy of what he called "the invincible summer" within, the sheer beatitude of human reciprocity.

Camus did not allow his atheism to deteriorate into a fanatic antitheism, which would have been a new religion. He soon lost the stridency of his early novel *The Stranger*, and modulated his tone. He was more interested in this world, its hopes and its pains, than he was in the nonexistence of some other world. In this sense he was like Kennedy who, though he was a Roman Catholic, did not allow his belief in some other world to divert him from a passionate concern for this one. Both Kennedy and Camus were secular men; both focused on the issues which torment men within the terrestrial horizon. For Kennedy these were problems of politics, for Camus they were the issues of ethics and meaning. . . .

We have found technopolitan man to be pragmatic and profane. But in taking him seriously in his pragmatism and profanity, we have found that he stands at these very points closer to the biblical view of man than did his religious and metaphysical predecessors of preurban culture. Still, it might be suggested that there is something ironic in our having called upon John F. Kennedy and Albert Camus as personifications of the buoyant reasonableness and calm sense of assurance which characterizes the best in our epoch. Not only are there other, darker currents in our time, but both these men have become for some people symbols of blind fate and human futility. Both were dashed into oblivion by eruptions of irrationality. The careers of both were terminated just as they had begun to flower, one by an assassin's bullet and the other in an automobile crash. Do not their meaningless early deaths conjure up the dark irrational fears of our world and call into question the notions of adulthood and reasoning responsibility they championed?

I think not. Though Kennedy was an artist in the application of reason to politics, and his alleged assassin seems a character from the pages of a Dostoyevski novel, it is still the spirit of Kennedy which triumphs, not that of his murderer. In the same way for Camus, not even the terror of wars and concentration camps could cause him to change the judgment with which he ends *The Plague*—"there are more things to admire in men than to despise."

---

[1]Professor van Peursen's remark is quoted from a mimeographed report assembled by Professor Charles West on a conference held at the Ecumenical Institute of Bossey, Switzerland, September 1959.

[3]Arthur J. Vidich and Joseph Bensman, *Small Town in Mass Society* (Garden City, New York: Anchor, 1958).

[1]Louis Wirth, "Urbanism as a Way of Life" in Paul Hitt and Albert J. Reiss, Jr. (eds.), *Cities and Society* (Glencoe, Ill.: The Free Press, 1958), p. 541

[2]Kaspar D. Naegele, "The Institutionalization of Action," in Talcott Parsons, *et al.* (eds.), *Theories of Society* (Glencoe, Ill.: The Free Press, 1961), p. 184.

[1]Harry O. Morton, "The Mastery of Technological Civilization," *The Student World,* LVI (First Quarter 1963), p. 46.

PART IV

Dimensions of the Crisis

INTRODUCTION

The selection in Part II focused on the processes which have changed man's dominant mode of existence from a simple rural-agrarian society to a complex urban-industrial order. Also we have seen some of the consequences of this fundamental reorganization of human life. But man does not simply respond to his environment in a vacuum. He is uniquely a culture-creating being who ascribes meaning to his environment, which in turn structures the very nature of that environment. In Part III we saw how man's images and ideologies about the city have affected the shape and nature of his urban milieu.

The crisis of metropolis did not emerge suddenly, but rather is a logical and predictable consequence of the forces of urbanization and human ideology. In Part IV we move to an examination of some of the problems of contemporary urban life. Obviously, a comprehensive examination of urban problems would be impossible in a single volume. What we have attempted to do in this section of the book is to single out some of the problems that are generally recognized as the most critical, and in turn select readings which illumine the nature and implications of the problem.

In the first selection in this book we saw a succinct portrait of the American Negro's hope and frustration in the city. Interestingly enough, while Claude Brown's *Manchild in the Promised Land* has been a best seller, the Negro response has been cool. As one reviewer commented, "He doesn't tell us anything that we have not all felt and experienced." The articles in this section elaborate the condition of the Negro in the metropolis.

Schnore and Sharp briefly summarize the population statistics on the rise of the "New Majority" in the central city. The data dramatically indicate the rapidity with which Negroes have migrated to large urban centers and the corresponding swiftness of the movement of whites to the suburbs. By 1960 Negroes had already become a majority of the population in Washington, D.C., and during the next three decades they are almost certain to become the majority in the central cities of most major metropolitan areas. The implications of these dramatic population shifts constitute one of the most significant developments in the history of this nation.

Willhelm and Powell present a blunt picture of the position of the Negro in American social structure. They argue that technology and automation have fundamentally shifted the position of the Negro from exploitation to uselessness. The fact that the majority of Negroes are uneducated and unskilled places them in the unfortunate position of being unneeded. "He [the Negro] is not so much oppressed as unwanted; not so much unwanted as unnecessary; not so much abused as ignored." Willhelm and Powell's position is one that is not often heard in discussing the racial situation in this nation, but it is a provocative argument with wide-reaching implications. Perhaps the most fundamental question raised here is: "What are the responsibilities of an affluent society in integrating and assimilating a culturally and economically disadvantaged minority into the mainstream of life?"

Another question which is implicit in the Willhelm and Powell article is: "What are the implications and consequences of ignoring a large minority group?" This latter question is dealt with in the article by Robert Blauner, "Whitewash Over Watts." Blauner's critical review of the McCone Commission report on the Watts riots of 1965 suggests that the consequences of neglect and failure to understand are quite serious. The urban violence which has erupted in ghettos since the Watts riot further suggests that the cry from the ghetto cannot be ignored.

"A decent home and a suitable living environment for every American family," has been the "official" national goal since Congress passed the Housing Act of 1949. Yet housing remains one of the most basic problems in urban America. Urban renewal is a complex process riddled with many ambiguities. On the one hand, urban renewal as an *ideology* (or theory) is an expression of America's deepest aspirations to create a truly great society. As a *program*, however, urban renewal has fallen far short of its lofty goals. In the opening sentence of his penetrating analysis of urban renewal, Scott Greer comments, "At the cost of more than three billion dollars the Urban Renewal Agency has succeeded in materially reducing the supply of low-cost housing in America."[1] This indictment reflects only one aspect of the failures of urban renewal. Yet it would be a mistake to dismiss urban renewal as a total failure, and urban renewal constitutes only one of several issues involved in housing. The selection by Nathan Glazer discusses several of these issues including the quality of existing housing, the effects of crowding, the nature of public housing policies, and the various criticisms which have been leveled at public housing programs.

Dwight Macdonald reviews data on the extent of poverty in the United States. He carefully describes the limitations of poverty statistics and finds that there is considerable disagreement as to the extent and meaning of poverty in America. However, "The point is," he says, "that all recent studies agree that American poverty is still a mass phenomenon."

Esther Peterson follows Macdonald's essay with an examination of the spending patterns of the poor. It is her point that the poor pay more not only because of deliberate discrimination, but because of the nature of the distribution systems which serve low-income neighborhoods. Low-income people are more likely to have to buy their food and clothing in the small neighborhood stores that have to have a large profit to break even.

The next section contains two statements on the equality of education in the United States. James S. Coleman reviews the findings of the Commissioner of Education's study of the Equality of Educational Opportunity. Among the central findings of the study that Coleman summarizes are the following: (1) minority children have a serious educational deficiency at the start of school, which is obviously not a result of school; (2) they have an even more serious deficiency at the end of school, which obviously is in part a result of school; and (3) the sources of inequality of educational opportunity appear to lie first in the home itself and the cultural influences immediately surrounding the home, then in the schools' ineffectiveness to free achievement from the impact of the home, and in the schools' cultural homogeneity which perpetuates the social influences of the home and its environs.

Henry H. Hill surveys the trends of school desegregation in the North and the South. "Surely and not too slowly," he states, "the big city systems of the North are becoming more and more segregated, with more Negroes attending all-Negro schools and fewer Negroes attending white schools." He contends that school desegregation is occurring more in the South than in the big Northern and Western cities. It is important to see the relationship between this article and the conclusions of Schnore and Sharp. Desegregation in Northern urban areas has become increasingly difficult because fewer and fewer whites are residing in the central cities.

In the next section, James Q. Wilson astutely analyzes the deficiencies of crime statistics in America and points out how the public and the mass media often draw incorrect inferences from these statistics. When most people think of crime, they think of crimes against the person (murder, rape, aggravated assault), yet these crimes constitute only a tiny fraction of the crime statistics. There is considerable evidence to suggest that the incidence of personal crimes has remained relatively constant, if it has not declined in recent years. It is crimes against property (burglary, larceny, and theft), which make up the bulk of crime in the United States, that have been on the upswing.

The second selection on crime is a summary of the conclusions and recommendations of the President's Commission on Crime. This is an excellent statement on the nature of the crime problem and an assessment of the programs that are necessary to bring about a significant reduction in crime.

Moving large numbers of people and goods in an expanding and decentralizing metropolis is the problem to which Lyle Fitch directs himself in "The Transportation Problem." To anyone familiar with city life, it should come as no surprise that Mr. Fitch concludes that the facilities for swift, convenient, and comfortable travel are not presently available for the urban traveler. The reasons offered in this analysis are institutional—administrative fragmentation, road versus rail conflicts, archaic financing—and conceptual—too little attention to the kinds of cities we are creating through unplanned growth, and the integrated modes of transportation needed to service people who live in them.

Those who live in the central cities of large metropolitan areas cannot help but be aware of the discomfort, annoyance, and health hazards of air pollution. In two feature articles from the *New York Times*, Gladwin Hill discusses this mounting problem. In the first selection he points out that it is not technology, but politics that prevents a significant reduction in poisonous gases that are making our cities increasingly uninhabitable. In the second selection he discusses some of the programs that have been initiated in recent years. While estimates of the cost necessary to clean our air vary considerably, none of the estimates exceeds the cost which we currently pay in property damage. In another selection by Mitchell Gordon, the question of the relationship between air pollution and health is raised. In the strictest sense of scientific proof, the deleterious consequences of air pollution to health remain open to some doubt. Nevertheless, the mounting evidence is sufficient to indicate a probable causal relationship. Thus, cost becomes a relatively insignificant consideration and the determination to organize to win the battle against air pollution becomes paramount.

The final selection in this part of the volume deals with another critical urban problem: finance. This is a summary of a round table discussion which assembled some of the nation's leading finance experts at Claremont Men's College. The author of the summary statement concludes that "none of us would dream of suggesting that local tax reform will cure all the ills of our cities. But most of us see a *clear, close,* and *causal*[2] connection between what is wrong with our cities today and what is wrong with their tax systems." The participants in the conference also tended to see the tax system as encouraging the persistence of slums and urban sprawl, thus multiplying the cost of municipal services. Included in the suggestions for tax reform are the following: (1) more equitable assessment, (2) taxation of site value instead of property value, and (3) higher assessments against property owners whose property values will be increased by improved services rather than against all owners of the community.

---

[1]Scott Greer, *Urban Renewal and American Cities* (Indianapolis: The Bobbs-Merrill Company, Inc., 1965).

[2]Emphasis added.

A. RACE

16. The Changing Color of Our Big Cities

LEO F. SCHNORE AND HARRY SHARP

It is no exaggeration to call the growth of nonwhite population in our major cities one of the truly outstanding social trends of the twentieth century. In 1900, when 43 percent of the white population was living in urban communities, only 22.7 percent of the nonwhite population lived in cities. At our most recent census in 1960, 69.5 percent of all whites and 72.4 percent of all nonwhite were urban dwellers, making the nonwhites more urbanized than the rest of the American population.

The concentration of nonwhites in very large cities is even more dramatic. The central cities of our twelve largest metropolitan areas contained 13.2 percent of the United States population in 1960. At the same time, these cities held over 31 percent of American Negroes. (These cities are New York, Los Angeles-Long Beach, Chicago, Philadelphia, Detroit, San Francisco-Oakland, Boston, Pittsburgh, St. Louis, Washington, Cleveland, and Baltimore. In the California cities there are substantial numbers of persons of Chinese and Japanese ancestry, who are also treated as "nonwhites" in census statistics; but the nonwhite population in most cities is almost entirely Negro.)

Actually the rapid influx of nonwhites is not confined to a handful of very large places. Every one of the fifty largest cities in the continental United States—each containing at least 250,000 inhabitants in 1960—showed increases in their proportions of nonwhites between 1950 and 1960, our two most recent censuses. This trend was evident in all sections of the country, North and South, East and West. In some cases (e.g., Minneapolis, St. Paul, and El Paso), the increases

SOURCE: Reprinted from *TRANS-ACTION* Magazine, Washington University, St. Louis, Mo., 1 (January, 1964), pp. 12-14.

are modest, with a difference of only one or two percentage points. In other instances, however, the changes are substantial; for example, Newark changed from 17.2 to 34.4 percent nonwhite, and Washington's proportion of nonwhites rose from 35.4 to 54.8 in 1960.

There were regional differences, however, in the experience of metropolitan areas. Fully 70 percent of the 212 Standard Metropolitan Statistical Areas currently recognized showed increasing proportions of nonwhites between 1950 and 1960, but this figure conceals an important difference between the South and the rest of the country. Outside the South, nine out of every ten metropolitan areas showed nonwhite increases over the decade. In the South itself, the trend was radically different, for only 35 percent of the southern metropolitan areas (27 out of 77) experienced relative gains in numbers of nonwhites. *In other words, six out of every ten southern metropolitan areas had lower proportions of nonwhites in 1960 than in 1950.* In general, it was only the larger southern metropolitan areas that gained large numbers of nonwhites.

Dark Core

The twelve largest metropolitan areas listed earlier now contain almost a third of the American Negro population. The proportion of whites in the United States who lived in the twelve central areas has fallen slightly but steadily since 1930, while the proportion of nonwhites has consistently increased, doubling in the thirty-year interval. Between 1950 and 1960 these central cities lost over two million whites while gaining 1.8 million nonwhites. In addition, although the white population has become progressively more concentrated in the suburban "rings" around these cities, the relative number of nonwhites in these rings (only 3 percent in 1930) has grown by just two percentage points in thirty years.

The collective pattern described above is generally reproduced in each of the twelve areas taken individually. *The total population increased rather slowly in the depression decade of 1930-1940, then grew faster over the last two decades, with the nonwhite populations growing at rates from two to four times greater than those of the white populations.*

In fact, the only central area of the twelve which did not experience an absolute loss in number of whites between 1950 and 1960 was Los Angeles-Long Beach; and in this case the rate of growth of whites fell off during the last decade while that for nonwhites continued to rise at an extremely rapid rate. As a result of these trends, eight of the twelve central cities have considerably fewer whites within their borders now than they did thirty years ago. New York, San Francisco-Oakland, and Washington have approximately the same number as in 1930. Only the Los Angeles-Long Beach area can show a noticeable *absolute* increase in the number of whites in 1960 as compared to 1930 and a substantial proportion of its central growth must be attributed to annexations.

WHITES LEAVE WASHINGTON

Thus the *relative* number of whites in every one of the twelve large central cities has decreased drastically over the last thirty years. This trend started slowly in the 'thirties, gained momentum in the 'forties, and became most pronounced during the 'fifties. The experience of one central city—Washington, D.C.—touches on the dramatic. In 1930 almost three-quarters of the inhabitants living in the city of Washington were white; currently, more than one-half of the residents of this city are nonwhite.

In contrast to the sharp drop in the proportion of whites in the central cities, the most common pattern in the suburban rings is one of near stability in racial composition. Thus despite the rapid absolute growth of the ring area, and despite the fact that the nonwhite *rate* of growth in the ring often is higher than that of the whites, the proportion of whites in eight of the twelve suburban rings changed by less than three percentage points between 1930 and 1960. In Washington, D.C., and in Baltimore, the relative number of whites in the ring actually *increased* substantially during these thirty years.

WHITE RINGS

Since 1930 the nonwhite population has expanded rapidly in every one of the large central cities; correspondingly, the central city white population has remained relatively stable or has substantially declined. This process of racial turn-over reached a peak of intensity between 1950 and 1960. The population decline of our largest cities would have been much more pronounced if increased numbers of nonwhites had not partially compensated for the loss of the white population. As we have noted, the flow to the rings was even greater over the last ten years than it was earlier.

But this "decentralization" movement involves a distinct color line. While the cities are becoming more and more nonwhite, the rings maintain an amazingly high and constant proportion of white residents; without exception, from 93 to 99 percent of the population in the rings of our twelve largest metropolitan communities are white and this situation is basically unchanged since 1930.

Continuation of the trends documented here would certainly have tremendous implications for the future of the metropolitan community in the United States.

- What are the reasons for these massive shifts?
- How far will the population redistribution by race continue?
- Will our largest metropolitan areas eventually consist of white rings surrounding nonwhite cities?

Why the Population Shifts

One reason why the central city is losing its white population is that whites in the city are older and have higher death rates. More importantly, under-developed city land for the building of new homes is in very short supply. Those dwellings that are available often are not as attractive to young white families as comparably priced homes in the suburbs. Finally, for a number of whites, fears of various kinds—threats of possible physical violence, hazards of declining property values, concern over the color composition of schools—begin to operate when nonwhites become neighbors.

The ring population is increasing at a tremendous rate not only because of movements into them but also because suburban areas have a high proportion of young couples who are producing children at a very rapid pace. They are "baby farms" in an almost literal sense. Additional factors which have contributed to the accumulation of population in the ring include the greater ability of American families to pay the higher costs of transportation; the decentralization of industrial and commercial enterprises; and the construction of vast suburban housing tracts and massive expressways which lead into the heart of the city.

Nonwhites are increasing in the larger cities because of the higher birth rates of central city nonwhites and because of the "pull" of a more favorable political-economic climate. The big cities have jobs to which nonwhites can aspire, even though they may not pay well.

Why have nonwhites clustered near the center of the city and avoided the outer city and the ring? Part of the explanation is certainly the low economic status of the nonwhite and his inability to afford a new home in a more expensive neighborhood. *Most observers would agree, however, that the major factors in residential clustering by race are restrictive selling practices which ultimately create separate housing markets for whites and nonwhites.*

Forecast for Chicago

In any case, the trend is one of long standing and is not likely to be reversed in the near future. A series of population projections by two University of Chicago sociologists, Donald J. Bogue and D. P. Dandekar, is instructive. The city of Chicago lost almost 400,000 white residents between 1950 and 1960 and gained 328,000 nonwhites in exchange. Part of this was due to "natural increase" on the part of nonwhites, for births exceeded deaths by almost 171,000. (The other 157,000 new nonwhites were migrants.) Nonwhite fertility was higher than that of the white population; in fact it increased 17 per cent between 1950 and 1960, while white fertility went up by only 9 percent. The projections by Bogue and Dandekar assumed that the volume of Negro in-migration will remain about the same as in recent decades, but that Negro fertility will decline.

On this basis, the population of Chicago in 1990 would consist of 1,941,000 whites and 1,777,000 nonwhites, or a bare majority of whites. This compares with the 76.4 percent white population counted in the 1960 census. If the exact trends of the 1950-60 decade were to be extrapolated into the future, however, Chicago nonwhites would achieve a majority as early as 1975.

We can anticipate that the rest of the twentieth century will be marked by a continuation of the established trend toward concentration of the American Negro in large cities and a continuation of the accompanying social upheavals that have captured the attention of the nation in recent years.

17. Who Needs the Negro?

SIDNEY M. WILLHELM AND EDWIN H. POWELL

A discontented, restless generation of American Negroes, anxious to abandon a history of enslavement for equal participation in our society, has abruptly ended centuries of seeming lethargy. But is their demand for "Freedom NOW" a genuine Negro revolt? Is there actually a civil rights struggle? Is the fundamental conflict between black and white?

The tendency to look upon the racial crisis as a struggle for equality between Negro and white is too narrow in scope. The crisis is caused not so much by the transition from slavery to equality as by a change

SOURCE: Reprinted from *TRANS-ACTION* Magazine, Washington University, St. Louis, Mo., 1 (September/October, 1964), pp. 3-6.

from an economics of exploitation to an economics of uselessness. With the onset of automation the Negro is moving out of his historical state of oppression into uselessness. Increasingly, he is not so much economically exploited as he is irrelevant. And the Negro's economic anxiety is an anxiety that will spread to others in our society as automation proceeds.

The tremendous historical change for the Negro is taking place in these terms: he is not needed. He is not so much oppressed as unwanted; not so much unwanted as unnecessary; not so much abused as ignored. The dominant whites no longer need to exploit him. If he disappeared tomorrow he would hardly be missed. As automation proceeds, it is easier and easier to disregard him.

After Them the Tempest

The Negro movement is merely the advance turbulence of a general tempest. At the moment that the Negro passes a major milestone in his struggle for full citizenship our society shifts from an industrial to an automated economy. He is like the breathless runner in the nightmare who, no matter how he strains, can only see his goal recede farther in the distance. Even if he won his demands for civil rights he could not keep up with the spreading effects of the introduction of total machine production. The "Negro Problem" therefore is not only one of civil rights but is also one of economic and human rights: How are we to re-arrange our social life in response to the rapid alterations in economic production?

On the face of it the idea of a "Negro Revolution" is absurd. The Negro is not challenging basic American values. He wants to join the white man's system, not upset it; he wants to come into the house, not bomb it. Rather than being engaged in a revolution to overthrow an oppressive system, the Negro is being disengaged by the system.

Negro Removal

The Negro flees the South—one region to another. He abandons the country for the city. And the white's response? He flees the Negro, abandoning the city to him. The usual explanation is that the Negro leaves his rural birthplace because the city needs his labor, especially after the cutting off of European immigration. But if this is so, why is the Negro's unemployment rate in urban centers so high?

Basically, 20,000,000 Negroes are unwanted. Our values inhibit genocide—so we discard them by establishing new forms of "Indian reservations" called "Negro ghettos." We even make them somewhat economically self-sufficient through an "Indian hand-out." One out of every four Negroes in Chicago, for example, receives some form of public welfare assistance. Is it an exaggeration to suggest that the deteriorated city has now become the junk heap upon which the economically worthless are thrown?

Urban renewal is often offered as a remedy, a medication which can help check the spreading blight of slum neighborhoods and slum lives. But what in fact has urban renewal brought about? Isn't the Negro simply being shuttled around—turned over to the onward rush of economic interests as the Indian was? Reservation lands were once thought worthless—so they were given to the Indian; when this turned out to be wrong economically, they were taken away again. So with Negro slums as they become less profitable than middle-class urban renewal. The Negroes—and the slums—are being moved from one part of the city to another, while their old neighborhoods are converted into bulldozer wastelands ("Hiroshima flats" as one famous project has been nicknamed) until more prosperous tenants finally arrive. Presumably the bulldozers can then move to the "new" Negro neighborhoods, by then probably sufficiently blighted to require a new urban renewal project. One writer comments: "Planners endeavor to improve city life by property improvement: to upgrade property values rather than human values." "Urban Renewal" becomes "Negro Removal."

- *Migration.* In 1940, 59 percent of the Negro population lived in the South while only 22 percent lived in the North. By 1960, the share of the Negro population living in the South dropped to 40 percent while that in the North had grown to 34 percent. The border states remained constant at around 25 percent. Between 1950 and 1960 the twelve largest United States cities lost over 2 million "Anglos" and gained nearly 2 million Negro residents.
- *Urban Renewal. Fourteen years after the adoption of urban renewal by our federal government, only a handful of racially integrated new neighborhoods exist although many old integrated neighborhoods have been razed.* "There is, if anything, more rigid housing segregation today in our cities than there was a decade ago," declares one writer. And of the people relocated by urban renewal 72 percent are non-white and of these most are Negroes—another source claims 80 percent of the families are Negroes. Moreover, one-half of the land cleared through urban renewal goes to autos as highways and parking lots, so that at most one-fourth of the land area is used for housing. *Urban renewal thus provides fewer housing units than it supplants.*
- *Employment.* In the late 1940's, the non-white unemployment rate was about 60 percent larger than that for whites—in 1948,

the unemployment rate for non-whites was 5.2 percent and for whites, 3.2 percent. By 1954, the non-white rate of unemployment was twice that of whites—8.9 percent for non-whites compared to 4.5 percent for whites. In 1962, it was almost 2½ times greater—11 percent against 4.5 percent. This disproportionate growth in Negro unemployment took place in spite of a narrowing difference in education. Further, three out of four non-farm Negro male workers are in unskilled or semiskilled occupations compared to one out of three for Anglos.

These items seem separate. But for the Negro they come together and spell out: *unwanted.*

For the Negro knows what is happening to him. He knows that the main problem is unemployment—and that he is being removed from economic participation in white society. He recognizes that urban renewal is Negro removal. He sees that he embarrasses even white liberals—that he contaminates what many whites consider to be conducive to pleasant urban life. He is aware of the attempt to wall him off, out of sight and out of mind. And he also knows that he cannot let this happen to him.

Arise and Conform

In one shameful sense the Negro demands *are* revolutionary. The Negro is so disadvantaged economically and socially that any real attempt to bridge the gap nationally (not to single out the South) would involve a tremendous, even "revolutionary" re-allocation of financial resources—particularly in light of the cry "Now!"

But there is no real revolution. Our basic institutions are being appealed to, not overturned. Except for a loud minority, what Negroes even actually demand the massive remedy—to which they are certainly entitled? "Freedom NOW!" is an inspirational myth. How little most Negroes demand in comparison with what many whites already have!

- In 1960, the median money wage was $3,058 for Negroes compared to $5,425 for whites: 71 percent of Negro families earned less than $5,000 while only 39 percent of the white families had incomes below $5,000.
- The relative gap between Negro and white family income has been increasing since the mid-fifties, indicating that Negro family income has not kept pace with whites. Since 1952 the Negro level has been faltering.
- Of 280,000 new houses constructed in Chicago between 1950-1960 less than ½ of 1 percent were occupied by Negroes.

- Only ½ of 1 percent of people with an income below $5,000 per year have received FHA assistance.
- A Negro boy has about half the chance to complete high school as a white boy; one third as much to complete college or become a professional man; one seventh as much of earning $10,000 a year; twice as much chance of becoming unemployed. His average life expectancy is seven years shorter.
- The average Negro with four years of college will earn less in his lifetime than the average white who never went beyond the eighth grade. The figures differ little between North and South.

Quest for Identity

As the Negro becomes an outcast he seeks to reorient himself through the civil rights struggle. The civil rights movement is a *quest for identity* by the Negro minority. Eminent Negroes participating for the first time in racial demonstrations have discovered that they can be proud to be Negroes. Through the civil rights movement the Negro announces to others, and thus to himself, his identity and worth. Without the struggle, the Negro would be left alone in an agony of isolation, in despair over his insignificance—an entity without identity.

The Negro's anguish does not rise only from brutalities of past oppression; in a system of exploitation the most humble can lay claim to an identity. The Southern Negro knew himself because he "kept his place" as required. Now there is no place to keep. The vast social changes in our society expose him to new experiences. The Negro, acutely aware of his unworthiness *to himself*, rebounds in frustration, extremely conscious of his insignificance as never before. As he becomes irrelevant to the white, he fears his relevance to himself. Martin Luther King writes in his letter from a Birmingham jail that Negroes "are forever fighting a degenerating sense of 'nobodiness'." Ralph Ellison writes of the "Invisible Man." James Baldwin declared during a television interview:

> I know how my nephew feels, I know how I feel, I know how the cats in the barbershop feel. A boy last week, he was sixteen, in San Francisco told me on TV . . . He said, "I got no country. I got no flag." Now, he's only 16 years old, and I couldn't say, "You do." I don't have any evidence to prove he does.

Baldwin notes that in the rural South the whites think of the Negro constantly; but in the great Northern urban areas they seldom think of him. Of these two conditions the second may be the more terrible.

THE OVERGROUND RAILWAY

Even the flight from the South is a manifestation of irrelevance rather than exploitation or rejection. The Southern Negro was once a powerless cog in an established system of exploitation; he flees his birthplace for Northern cities with thoughts of freedom. The South responds to this exodus not as a loss but as a beneficial "drainage" of the discontented. And the Northern white reacts to the Negro's arrival by fleeing to the suburb. Black and white both share the endeavor to avoid one another rather than make attempts to resolve differences. The Southern white is mistaken in thinking that the "Negro problem" has departed with the Negro; and the Northern white is now learning his error in fleeing the city. In this geographical relocation, the Negro becomes an orphan—forsaken, ignored, denied.

There is no possibility of resubjugating the Negro or of jailing 20,000,000 Americans of varying shades of "black." Thus the real frustration of the "total society" comes from the difficulty of discarding 20,000,000 people made superfluous through automation.

Out of the anonymity of our automating society the Negro will be attracted to organizations which can endow him with identity. It is doubtful that existing moderate organizations—NAACP, CORE, Southern Christian Leadership Council, and the rest—will meet his need for identification. Moderates strive for equality in the civil rights struggle so that the Negro might assimilate into the dominant white society. Equality, however, means the loss of identity through making all people into one homogeneous group. Actually, the moderate seeks to promote the Negro's escape from insubordination by eradicating the Negro—by making him a dark white man. But the Negro cannot establish his identity by erasing himself.

The organizations most capable of elevating him as an identifiable entity will in the long run have the greatest attraction. The extreme groups do not arise, as many writers claim, solely because the moderates fail. They arise because the moderate is likely to succeed—this success is not enough. The extremes persist because—untried—they still offer a hope, a dream, and identity.

Although an immigrant to the city, the Negro is not, as liberals hopefully assume, still another wave of the same sort that left Europe for America. The differences are too great for such analogy. The Negro's past is an American experience of subordination in a system of exploitation. It is no simple matter in our society for the Negro to shed his past as the European rid himself of his alien ways. Moreover, the Negro enters an urban setting at a time when the economy operates at a national rather than a local level. Corporations have replaced community-bound business interests and demand educated skills and knowledge. Negroes cannot become like early European immigrants, a large, unskilled, and poorly paid labor force. Urban growth today demands just the opposite. The Negro is as unprepared for today's cosmopolitan and automating society as he is unnecessary for the mechanizing Southern farms he flees.

Even Keynesian economics offers little hope. The consumption strategy for economic prosperity of the Keynesian school is already provided through our vast military expenditures. The "effective demand" is generated through the "institutionalized waste" of the arms race. Indeed, it was during World Wars I and II that the Negro made his greatest strides toward racial equality precisely because his labor was deemed essential to the war effort. But the military now needs missiles, not men; scientists, not soldiers. Our society prospers without a redistribution of income in favor of the lower brackets—despite liberal slogans. In the military system we have an impersonal, omnipotent consumer of tremendous proportions that, in effect, supplants a mass purchasing power that could have been placed in the Negro's hands.

Booms: Babies to Unemployed

There is a vital point that is seldom, if ever, noticed when scanning the unemployment figures along racial lines. It is quite correct that the unemployment rate for the Negro has been twice that of the white; but whites, too, are unemployed. If civil rights were the issue, why should a white displace a white? A common cause of unemployment, apart from race, apart from civil wrongs, exists. Harold Baron, Co-Director of the Research Department of the Chicago Urban League, writes:

> The decade 1960-1970 is witnessing a tremendous increase in the labor force as the progeny of the post-war baby boom enters the labor market. Twenty-six million new youths will hunt jobs, making a net addition of 15,000,000 to the total. If we make a projection based on recent rates of job increase (and even allow for a lesser loss in the number of agricultural jobs), we arrive at an increase of 3,500,000 jobs. *This leaves a staggering addition of 11,500,000 unemployed.* Add the 4,000,000 currently unemployed, and we will have 15,500,000 persons out of work. Even assuming a return to the higher rate of job increase of the 1947 to 1957 decade, there would still be an increase of 5,000,000. *(New University Thought, 1963).*

The civil rights myth actually perpetuates the economic status quo. As long as the issue is split along racial lines, divide and rule prevails, and we do not question the economic ideology that justifies prevailing production and consumption. If the contention can be presented as racial strife rather than economic dislocation, then the economic interests stand to gain a decided advantage: serious questioning of the merits and demerits of our production and distribution of wealth will not take place. The evil will be defined as Southern bigotry overflowing into the North rather than the economics of displacement.

In short and in summary, the historical transition for the Negro is not occurring in a civil rights context; it is instead a movement out of the Southern cotton fields into the Northern factories and then to the automated urbanity of "nobodiness." The issue becomes a question of human—not only civil—rights and involves white and Negro alike. For the Negro is merely a weathervane for the future. *His* experience will be a common one for many whites now deprived of some sort of usefulness; *his* frustrations will become those for many others the longer we hesitate to confront the meaning of human dignity in an automated society. As more of us become unnecessary—as human energy and thought themselves become increasingly unnecessary—the greater will be our social anxiety. Then perhaps we will become aware that racial strife today is not between black and white, but is instead a search for human rights in a world of machines that makes so many human beings utterly dispensable.

18. Whitewash Over Watts

ROBERT BLAUNER

On August 24, 1965, just one week after public order had been restored in the south-central area of Los Angeles known as Watts, Governor Pat Brown of California announced the appointment of an eight-man commission of leading citizens. In his charge to the group (which came to be known as the McCone Commission, after its Chairman, John A. McCone, former head of the CIA), Brown asked it to "prepare an accurate chronology and description of the riots"; to "probe deeply the immediate and underlying causes of the riots"; and finally to "develop recommendations for action designed to prevent a recurrence of these tragic disorders."

SOURCE: Reprinted from *TRANS-ACTION* Magazine, Washington University, St. Louis, Mo., 3 (March/April, 1966), pp. 3-9, 54.

For what appears to have been political considerations connected with possible repercussions of the Watts affair on the 1966 gubernatorial campaign, the Commission was given December 1, 1965, as the deadline for the completion of its report. Thus only 100 days were available for a "deep and probing" analysis of the most destructive incidents of racial violence in American history.

In an atmosphere of speed-up that made work on an automobile assembly-line appear leisurely by comparison, the Commission held a series of sixty formal hearings before which eighty sworn witnesses, including city and police officials, leaders and citizens of the white and Negro communities, eventually appeared. It also selected a full-time staff of thirty, primarily lawyers and legal-oriented investigators, to carry out the day-to-day work of assembling data and preparing to write the report. The staff called upon the services of twenty-six consultants (chiefly university professors in the social sciences) for advice and the sub-contracting of research; interviewed ninety persons from the 4,000 arrested; and opened an office in the riot area to receive testimony from Negro citizens. After a total expenditure of $250,000, Commissioner McCone presented the report to Governor Brown in the fanfare of television cameras on December 6.

In view of the conditions under which it was hurried into existence, it should be no surprise that *Violence in the City—An End or a Beginning?* is a slim volume with only eighty-six pages of blown-up type. But the report of the McCone Commission is not only brief, it is sketchy and superficial. Its tone and style are disturbing. There is much glib writing and the approach as well as the format is slick in the manner of our illustrated news weeklies before their recent upgrading. The depth analysis of this fateful outbreak can be read by an average reader in less than an hour—allowing ample time for contemplating the many photographs, both color and black-and-white.

A comparison with the careful and considered report of the Illinois' Governor's Commission which analyzed the 1919 Chicago race riots in a 672-page book *(The Negro in Chicago)* that required three years of planning, research, and writing to produce may well be unfair. But with the considerable budget and the academic sophistication available today, more was to be expected than the public relations statement presently in our hands.

It is not only the size and style of the McCone document that are disturbing. Its content is disappointing both in its omissions and in underlying political and philosophical perspectives. There is almost nothing in the report that is new or that gives consideration to the unique conditions of Los Angeles life and politics. As Los Angeles councilman Bill Mills commented, most of the material in the report documents conditions in the Negro ghetto that have been common knowledge to sociologists and the informed public for a generation.

More appalling are the report's deeper failures. With a narrow legalistic perspective that approached the riots in terms of the sanctity of law and order, the commissioners were unable (or unwilling) to read any social or political meaning into the August terror. There was no attempt to view the outbreak from the point of view of the Negro poor. The commissioners also play a dangerous game with the thorny problem of responsibility. The Negro community as a whole is absolved from responsibility for the rioting while local and national leaders (civil-rights moderates and extremists alike) are taken to task for inflaming mass discontent and undermining attachments to law and authority. (In his two-page dissenting comment appended to the main report, the Reverend James E. Jones, a Negro commissioner, criticizes the report for attempting "to put a lid on protest.")

In a crude attempt at "horse-trading" in the responsibility market, the positions of the Los Angeles police department and city administrators are consistently protected. In discounting the relevance of police provocation and city policies to the revolt without presenting any facts or evidence, the Commission not only protects powerful interests; it abdicates its mandate to seek out facts and establish as best as it could the objective reality. My most general and serious criticism of the report is this violation of its responsibility to seek truth and its frequent hiding behind opinion and hearsay.

Causes of the Watts "Revolt"

Lurking behind the Watts violence are three basic problems, according to the McCone Commission:

- the widespread unemployment and "idleness" in the Negro ghetto;
- the cultural and educational backwardness of black children that prevents the schools from preparing them for the labor market and integrating them into society;
- the troubled state of police-community relations in the Negro neighborhoods.

Employment

The chapter on employment is forthright in its emphasis on jobs as a central problem and correct in its understanding that male dignity and family responsibility can hardly be expected when men are unable to find steady work. For example: "The most serious immediate problem that faces the Negro in our community is employment—securing and holding a job that provides him an opportunity for livelihood, a chance to earn the means to support himself, and his family, a dignity, and a reason to feel that he is a member of our community in a true and a very real sense." The Commission calls upon federal, state, and city government to create jobs for the Negro and Mexican-American poor. Corporations and labor unions are asked to end discrimination once and for all and to police their progress by keeping careful records on minority employment. Because the Commissioners are convinced that the majority of jobless Los Angeles Negroes are presently unemployable, they call for an expanded and better-coordinated program of job training; they wisely recommend that control of this effort be placed inside the Negro community.

These proposals on employment are worthwhile and necessary but they encourage a deceptive complacency. The report does not probe sufficiently into the depth and seriousness of the problem. There is no consideration of the impact of population trends and technological developments on the availability of jobs, especially for the unskilled, and no willingness to face the escalating employment needs in the rapid expansion of Los Angeles' Negro population. The report is irresponsible because its style and tone convey the impression that its relatively mild and moderate recommendations provide real solutions.

EDUCATION

The treatment of education is the one section of the McCone report that is based on a careful and first-hand study. Kenneth A. Martyn, professor of education at Los Angeles State College, investigated five areas within the Los Angeles City Unified School District as a Commission consultant. Student achievement was compared for four "disadvantaged areas" (of which two were primarily Negro and close to the riot centers) and one "advantaged" area (predominantly white upper-middle class). Average student reading performances in the fifth, eighth, and eleventh grades reveal a consistent backwardness in the lower-class Negro and Mexican districts. The gap is most dramatic at the eighth grade, since by the eleventh many of the poorest "achievers" are already drop-outs. The average student in the white middle class area is in the 79th percentile in reading vocabulary based on national norms; the average students in "Negro" Watts and Avalon are in the 13th and 14th percentiles; the averages in the primarily Mexican areas of Boyle Heights and East Los Angeles are 16 and 17.

Martyn investigated the possibility of discrimination in educational facilities. Some inequalities were found, but hardly enough to explain the systematic backwardness of minority students. The Commission thus locates the problem of Negro school performance in what today is fashionably called "a culturally impoverished environment." Parents have little education and their own background does not foster an orientation toward achievement and learning. Crowded housing conditions are not favorable for disciplined study. And the precariousness of employment and the lack of models of achievement may further dull incentive. In order to break this pattern and "raise the scholastic achievement of the average Negro child up to or perhaps above the present average achievement level in the city," the Commission calls for an intensive infusion of educational resources into the Negro community focusing on three programs: pre-school learning on the model of "Headstart"; the reduction of class size; and the improvement of academic and behavioral counseling.

The McCone report accepts the conventional position that it is the "vicious circular" connection between education and employment that is the crux of the dilemma of the Negro poor. And it places its main bet on education and the future, rather than creating jobs to solve the problems of the present. If the achievement levels of present and future generations of Negro children can be sufficiently raised, they will be motivated to remain in the school system and assimilate the skills and training that will begin reversing this cyclical process. Unfortunately, the middle-class ethos which underlies the Commission's emphasis on future-orientation and achievement is irrelevant to the needs and outlook of the lower-class adult group whose problems of work and training are likely to intensify.

But even with a crash program in education, can the average poor Negro youth be motivated toward achievement and excellence when the condition of his people and community place him in a position of alienation and powerlessness *vis-a-vis* the larger society? What is missing in the report's analysis is a total picture of the Watts community as consistently deprived and disadvantaged in relation to Los Angeles as a whole. Fragmented hints of this picture abound in the report, particularly in the excellent discussion of the woefully inadequate transportation system, but the fragments are never pieced together. If they were, municipal officials would then have to bear some responsibility for permitting this systematic deprivation to persist. By singling out education as the strategic sphere for ameliorative efforts, the Commission aims its biggest guns on the target-area in which the city's hands are relatively "clean" and in which it is relatively easy to suggest that the cultural backgrounds and individual performances of *Negroes themselves* account for a good part of the problem.

THE POLICE ISSUE

> If we don't get no good out of this, it will happen again. By good I mean an end to police harassment, and we need jobs. I got eight kids, and I've only worked 10 days this year. I ain't ever been a crook, but if they don't do something, I'm gonna have to *take* something. I don't know how they expect us to live. (Young man in "a striped shirt" quoted by Louise Meriwether, "What the People of Watts Say," *Frontier,* Oct. 1965.)

When a deprived segment of the population breaks out in a violent attack on society and its representatives, the *underlying* causes refer to those long-term elements in its situation that have produced its alienation and despair. *Immediate* causes refer to those more short-run irritants and grievances that have intensified feelings of anger and hatred and focussed them on specific targets. The immediate grievances and conditions that spark illegal violence must have the effect of weakening the oppressed group's normal disposition to accept, at least overtly, the authority structure and legal norms of the society—otherwise mass violence could not erupt. The young Watts Negro quoted above seems to be saying that from his standpoint "jobs" are the underlying cause, "police harassment" the immediate issue. The governor's commission disagrees with his analysis and has its own explanation for the ghetto's sudden loss of attachment to the legal order.

It answers its own question, "Why Los Angeles?" in a way that almost totally relieves the city and county of implication. The rapid migration of Southern Negroes to the city's ghetto serves as their starting point, for these Negroes are unrealistic in expecting that California living will solve all their life-problems. In the context of this "crisis of expectations" Negro frustration and despair were fanned by three "aggravating events in the twelve months prior to the riots":

- "Publicity given to the glowing promise of the federal poverty program was paralleled by reports of controversy and bickering over the mechanism to handle the program here in Los Angeles, and when the projects did arrive, they did not live up to expectation."
- "Throughout the nation, unpunished violence and disobedience to law were widely reported, and almost daily there were exhortations, here and elsewhere, to take the most extreme and even illegal remedies to right a wide variety of wrongs, *real and supposed.*"
- "In addition, many Negroes here felt and *were encouraged to feel* that they had been affronted by the passage of Proposition 14—

an initiative measure passed by two-thirds of the voters in November 1964 which repealed the Rumford Fair Housing Act and unless modified by the voters or invalidated by the courts will bar any attempt by state or local governments to enact similar laws." (Italics mine.)

The argument is clear. Aside from some blunderings over the anti-poverty war, it was Negro leadership that undermined the commitment of law-abiding black citizens to authority and legal methods of redressing their grievances. What is important is the assumption that the Negro poor's attachment to law and political authority was not weakened by its own experience with police and other official representatives of society, but was instead subverted by an extremist and opportunist leadership. Such an analysis gives the Commission a free field to discount the role of the Los Angeles police and their presence in the ghetto as immediate precipitants of the violence. In short, the Commission has "bought" the line of Chief of Police William Parker who has consistently argued that the riot was a revolt of the criminal and lawless element, prodded on by a Negro leadership which inflamed the Los Angeles black community with the "bugaboo" of "police brutality."

The report devotes a chapter to law enforcement and police-community relations. It takes note of the severe criticism of the police department by many Negro witnesses and frankly admits "the deep and longstanding schism between a substantial portion of the Negro community and the police department." Considering the virtual unanimity in the Negro community concerning police practices as the foremost immediate cause of the outbreak, why did not the Commission seriously investigate the role of law enforcement in the ghetto? The Commission acknowledges that Negro *feelings* of oppressive police action were significant conditions of the rioting. However, it violates its responsibility to truth and impartiality by refusing to examine the factual basis of Negro opinion while stating the beliefs and hearsay of white officers in an aura of established truth:

> . . . the police have explained to us the extent to which the conduct of some Negroes when apprehended has required the use of force in making arrests. Example after example has been recited of arrestees, both men and women, becoming violent, struggling to resist arrest, and thus requiring removal by physical force. Other actions, each provocative to the police and each requiring more than normal action by the police in order to make an arrest or to perform other duties, have been described to us.

Precisely the same line is taken with respect to Chief Parker. The

Commission duly notes that the outspoken chief is a focal point of criticism and is distrusted by most Negroes. They feel he hates them. Yet the report conveniently omits all rational and objective evidence for such Negro "belief" based on a whole series of public statements made long before the riots. The inference is that Negro belief rests on misinterpretation of fact and paranoid reactions.

However, not only embittered Negro attitudes, but *facts* exist about the police presence in the ghetto—if the Commission would have only looked for them. There was a Youth Opportunities Board study available to the Commission based on intensive interviews with 220 people in the Watts, Willowbrook, and Avalon districts undertaken only two years before the outbreak in this very area. The sample included 70 delinquent and nondelinquent children, 26 parents, and 124 high administrators and lesser personnel of the major agencies in the community (schools, welfare and probation, recreation and youth groups). Attitudes toward the critical agencies of the community were probed, and it was found that of all the "serving institutions" of the larger society greatest hostility was directed toward the police department. A majority of adults as well as children felt that *the behavior of police aggravated the problems of growing up in the Negro community rather than contributed to their solution;* this was in direct contrast to their attitudes toward the schools, the parks, the health services, and the probation officers.

The real issue has perhaps been muddied by the outcry against "police brutality," the term that Negroes use to sum up their felt sense of grievance against law-enforcement agents. The police liberalization policy of recent years may well have reduced the number of cases of "classic" brutality—beatings, cruel methods of questioning, etc. What the Negro community is presently complaining about when it cries "police brutality" is the more subtle attack on personal dignity that manifests itself in unexplainable questionings and searches, in hostile and insolent attitudes toward groups of young Negroes on the street, or in cars, and in the use of disrespectful and sometimes racist language—in short, what the Watts man quoted above called "police harassment." There is no evidence that this assault on individual self-esteem and dignity has ceased.

Another facet of police brutality is the use of excessive force to control criminal and illegal behavior. Characteristically the Commission passed on its opportunity (and obligation) to assess the use of force by the various law enforcement agencies that put down the August violence, despite its considerable attention to their logistical and coordination problems and the concern of Negroes and liberal groups like the ACLU with what appeared to be unnecessary shootings of looters, including young children.

The police chapter is primarily devoted to the adequacy of procedures presently available for processing complaints against officer misconduct and to recommendations for improving both them and the general relation between law enforcement and the Negro community. Yet, the demand of Negro leaders and white liberals for an independent civilian review board is described as "clamor"; the proposal is rejected because this device would "endanger the effectiveness of law enforcement." Experience with its use in two cities "has not demonstrated" its "advantages," but characteristically no evidence is given and the cities are not even named. Instead the report advocates the strengthening of the authority of the present Board of Police Commissioners, the civilian heads of the department, and establishment of the new position of Inspector General under the authority of the Chief of Police. The latter "would be responsible for making investigations and recommendations on all citizen complaints." In addition, the police should improve its community relations programs in the ghetto areas and strive to attract more Negroes and Mexicans to careers in law-enforcement.

The Commissioners are aware that "police brutality" has been an issue in all of the Northern Negro riots in recent years and that each began with a police incident. But instead of asking why poor Negroes come to believe that law and authority are not *their* law and their authority, they go on to sermonize:

> Our society is held together by respect for law. A group of officers who represent a tiny fraction of one percent of the population is the thin thread that enforces observance of law by those few who would do otherwise. If police authority is destroyed, if their effectiveness is impaired, and if their determination to use the authority vested in them to preserve a law abiding community is frustrated, all of society will suffer because groups would feel free to disobey the law and inevitably their number would increase. Chaos might easily result.

Character of the Watts Outbreak

There is very little explicit consideration of the character and meaning of the outburst in the McCone Report, in spite of its great concern with causes. The Commission missed an important point of departure by not viewing the Watts violence as a problematic phenomenon, the essence of which needed to be determined through a careful weighing of evidence and through social and political analysis. For this reason the report's implicit assumptions must be inferred because they are introduced in passing and never clearly spelled out.

The analytical perspective is overwhelmingly *riot control* rather than collective or crowd behavior. The attempt of responsible Negro leaders to cool off the mobs is discussed, but the major emphasis is on the tactics used by the various law enforcement agencies. After a fairly thorough discussion of the arrest which set off the events, the Negroes who participated in violence are almost excluded from the story.

The very language of the Commission suggests that it has prejudged "the meaning of Watts," even though the debate that has been going on in Negro circles as to the appropriate term of reference suggests that determining the character of these events is a real and difficult question.

On page one of the report, the outbreak is called a "spasm" and "an insensate rage of destruction." Later it is called "an explosion—a *formless, quite senseless,* all but hopeless violent protest" (Italics mine). Only in its discussion of the business targets which were looted and burned does the Commission attempt to locate a meaning or pattern in what the rioters did, and here they conclude—unlike most informed observers—that there was no "significant correlation between alleged consumer exploitation and the destruction."

The legalistic perspective of the Commission and its staff seems to have blocked its sensitivity to the sociological meaning of the riots. When viewed simply as an uprising of the criminal element against law and order (aggravated of course by the more social, economic, and political causes of frustration already discussed), the Commissioners need not look seriously at its human meaning nor need they understand what messages may have been communicated by the rocks, gunfire, and Molotov cocktails. Let us not romanticize the Watts violence. I don't claim that everyone involved and everything done had rational motives. But it is a more humble and scientific attitude to leave the question open and to examine the limited evidence that is available. For the assumption of meaninglessness, the emptying out of content and communication from any set of human actions—*even nonrational violence*—reduces the dignity of the actors involved. In the present context it is a subtle insult to Los Angeles' Negroes. The report ostensibly avoids such an insulting stance by minimizing Negro participation and exculpating the bulk of the community from responsibility from the anti-social outbreak—except of course its leaders who aggravated the underlying tension:

> In the ugliest interval which lasted from Thursday through Saturday, perhaps as many as 10,000 Negroes took to the streets in marauding bands. . . . The entire Negro population of Los Angeles County, about two-thirds of whom live in this area (that of the riots), numbers

> more than 650,000. Observers estimate that only about two percent were involved in the disorder. Nevertheless, this violent fraction, however minor, has given the face of community relations in Los Angeles a sinister cast.

No evidence is presented for the 2 percent estimate, nor for the total of 10,000 participants on which it is based. We are not told how the Commission defines being "involved in the disorder." A number of distortions are apparently obvious, however. Even if 10,000 were the upper limit, this figure would indicate much more than 2 percent participation. For the Negro curfew area of some 500,000 residents contains many neighborhoods of comfortable middle-class people who were far from the riot center; they should be eliminated from a calculation of the extent of participation in an outbreak of the Negro poor and dispossessed. Second, the total population figures include women, children, and the aged. A more appropriate (and still difficult) question would be the extent of participation of young and mature Negro males in the low-income districts that were the centers of the action.

The Spirit of Revolt

Unfortunately, I cannot answer this question precisely, but in view of the Commission's unscientific methodology and dubious deductions there is no reason to accept their view of the participation issue. Consider on this matter Bayard Rustin, who visited Watts with Martin Luther King a few days after the outbreak:

> I could not count heads but reports I have received and my experience with the people leads me to believe that a large percentage of the people living in the Watts area participated. But most of them did not themselves loot and burn but they were on the streets at one time or other. *(New America,* September 17, 1965)

As Rustin suggests, the question is not simply how many engaged in lawless acts. Essential to the meaning of the revolt is the attitude of the "non-participants" toward those who erupted in hate and violence. In the most popular revolutions it is only a small minority that storms the Bastille or dumps tea in Boston Harbor. Only through considering the viewpoints of the "silent mass" is it possible to know whether the Watts riots represented an action of a large segment of Los Angeles Negro poor rather than a cutting loose of a small "violent fraction." Had the McCone Commission done its job, it would have conducted a systematic survey of community opinion to determine the distribution of sentiment in Negro Los Angeles.

My informants reported widespread support within the ghetto for the violent outbreak. Moral approval (as well as active participation) was stronger among youth and among the poor and working-class. Old people and middle-class Negroes were more likely to feel ambivalent and hold back. But there seems to have been at least some participation from all segments of the black community. In the countless interviews and feature stories that appeared in the press and on television, Watts Negroes were more likely to explain and justify the riots rather than to condemn them—certainly the mass media would have little interest in censoring accounts of Negro disapproval. In a statewide public opinion survey conducted in November only 16 percent of the Negroes interviewed attributed the riots to "lack of respect for law and order" in contrast to 36 percent of the whites; "outside agitators" were seen as a most important cause by a scant 7 percent of the Negroes compared to 28 percent of the whites. Seventy-nine percent of the Negro respondents fixed upon "widespread unemployment" and "bad living conditions" as prime causes, compared with only 37 percent of the whites. And months after the rioting a poll conducted by ABC Television found that the proportion of Watts residents who felt that the summer's events had helped the Negroes' cause was twice as much as those who felt it had hurt them.

If the Los Angeles revolt was not simply a "spasm" of lawlessness reflecting the violent inclinations of a minor criminal group, but represented instead the mood and spirit of the low-income Negro community—then we must look more closely at what the crowds were attempting to communicate in their assault upon society.

As the Governor's report correctly notes, the uprising was not organized in advance. Yet it was neither formless nor meaningless. The Negro crowds were expressing more than the blind rage and the anti-white hate epitomized in the "Burn, baby, burn" slogan. They seem to have been announcing an unwillingness to continue to accept indignity and frustration without fighting back. They were particularly communicating their hatred of policemen, firemen, and other representatives of white society who operate in the Negro community "like an army of occupation." They were asserting a claim to territoriality, an unorganized and rather inchoate attempt to gain control over their community, their "turf." Most of the actions of the rioters appear to have been informed by the desire to clear out an alien presence, white men, rather than to kill them. (People have remarked how few whites were shot considering the degree of sniping and the marksmanship evidenced in accurate hits on automobile lights and other targets.) It was primarily an attack on property, particularly white-owned businesses, and not persons. Why not listen to what people in the crowds were saying as did Charles Hillinger of the *Los Angeles Times* on the night of August 13:

- "White devils, what are you doing in here?"
- "It's too late, white man. You had your chance. Now it's our turn."
- "You created this monster and it's going to consume you. White man, you got a tiger by the tail. You can't hold it. You can't let it go."
- "White man, you started all this the day you brought the first slave to this country."
- "That's the hate that hate produced, white man. This ain't hurting us now. We have nothing to lose. Negroes don't own the buildings. You never did a decent thing in your life for us, white man."

A "Native" Uprising

Any appraisal of the Watts uprising must be tentative. All the facts are not yet known, and it always takes time to assimilate the full significance of historic and traumatic events. I suggest, however, that it was not primarily a rising of the lawless, despite the high participation of the *lumpenproletariat* and the clearcut attack on law and authority. Neither was it a "conventional race riot" for the Los Angeles terror arose from the initiative of the Negro community and did not fit the simple pattern of whites and blacks engaging in purely racial aggression. And it was not a Los Angeles version of a mass civil rights protest. Its organization was too loose. More important, the guiding impulse was not integration with American society but an attempt to stake out a sphere of control by moving against that society.

Instead my interpretation turns on two points. On the *collective* level the revolt seems to represent the crystallization of community identity through a nationalistic outburst against a society felt as dominating and oppressive. The spirit of the Watts rioters appears similar to that of anticolonial crowds demonstrating against foreign masters, though in America of course the objective situation and potential power relations are very different. On the *individual* level, participation would seem to have had a special appeal for those young Negroes whose aspirations to be men of dignity are systematically negated by the unavailability of work and the humiliations experienced in contacts with whites. For these young men (and reports indicate that males between the ages of 14 and 30 predominated in the streets), violence permitted expressing their manhood in the American way of fighting back and "getting even"—rather than the passive withdrawal which has been a more characteristic response of the Negro poor.

The gulf between Watts and affluent Los Angeles is disturbingly similar to the cleavage between the lives and interests of "natives" and their colonial masters. The poor Negro's alienation from the institutions and values of the larger society was made clear during the revolt. The sacredness of private property, that unconsciously accepted bulwark of our social arrangements, was rejected; Negroes who looted, apparently without guilt, generally remarked that they were taking things that "really belong" to them anyway. The society's bases of legitimacy and its loci of authority were attacked.

Thus Watts was not simply a racial uprising. Negro police and "responsible" moderate leaders were also the objects of the crowd's anger. Black businessmen who were seen as close to the Negro community were spared damage. From the standpoint of the poor, there was thus an implicit division of the Negro middle-class into those two segments that are found in the colonial situation: a "national bourgeoisie" on the side of liberation and a "native" middle-class that serves as agents for the dominant power arrangements.

Sartre has argued that colonialism reduced the manhood of the peoples it subjected in violating the integrity of indigenous ways of life and in creating the social status of "natives." The condition of slavery in the U.S. and the subsequent history of economic exploitation and second-class citizenship have constituted a similar attack on the manhood of Negro males. The chief contemporary manifestation of this crisis, according to the controversial "Moynihan report," is the precarious position of the man in the lower-class Negro family. The active dominance of the Negro woman and the male's relative passivity and instability are in part a residue of this historical process of manhood reduction; it is of course intimately reinforced by the unavailability of employment and the crisis of authority this brings about in the family. Unable to validate a sense of manly worth in terms of the larger cultural standards of economic responsibility, the lower-class youth orients himself toward the all-male street society whose manhood centers around other values and styles—hip, cool, and soul.

A new generation of Negro militants have created in the civil rights movement a vehicle for the affirmation of their manhood in the political struggle against its systematic negation. But the nonviolent movement which grew up in the South (with its more religiously oriented population, cohesive communities, and clear-cut segregation problems) is not well-adapted to the social condition and psychological temper of the Northern Negro. Unless new possibilities for the expression of initiative, assertiveness, and control are opened, we can expect that violent revolt will become increasingly frequent.

The Watts revolt was also a groping toward community identity. South-central Los Angeles has been a vast Negro ghetto with very amorphous neighborhood and district boundaries, with a glaring lack of leadership and organization. Most of the major civil rights groups were nonexistent in the ghetto; the gap between official Negro spokesman and the poor was even greater than is typical. The word "Watts" itself as a locational reference for the ambiguously-defined district around 103rd and Central had become a stigmatized term among Negroes as well as whites and was rarely used by residents. During the August uprising a reversal in all these tendencies became apparent. The mass action strengthened feeble communal loyalties. The term "Watts" appeared painted on walls and windows as an expression of pride and identity. Youth gangs representing the adjacent neighborhoods of Watts, Willowbrook, and Compton ceased their long standing wars and united to provide a core of organization during the rioting and the subsequent rehabilitation work. Many middle-class blacks saw that their interests could not be severed from those of the ghetto's poor, particularly when their streets and residences were placed within the curfew boundaries drawn by the militia—thus dramatizing the fact of common fate. And since August, a proliferation of community organizing, political action, and civil rights groups have risen up in the Watts area. All these processes—intensified communal bonds, ethnic identity, the hesitant return of the middle-class, and a new sense of pride in place—are graphically summed up in the experience of Stan Saunders, a Watts boy who had moved out of the ghetto to All-American football honors at Whittier College and two years abroad as a Rhodes scholar. His return to Watts two weeks before the revolt may be prototypical:

> At the height of the violence, he found himself joyously speaking the nitty-gritty Negro argot he hadn't used since junior high school, and despite the horrors of the night, this morning he felt a strange pride in Watts. As a riot, he told me, "It was a masterful performance. I sense a change there now, a buzz, and it tickles. For the first time people in Watts feel a pride in being black. I remember, when I first went to Whittier, I worried that if I didn't make it there, if I was rejected, I wouldn't have a place to go back to. Now I can say "I'm from Watts." (*LIFE,* August 27, 1965)

The McCone Commission missed the meaning of the Watts revolt due to the limitations inherent in its perspective. The surface radicalism of its language (in calling for "a new and, we believe, revolutionary attitude toward the problems of the city") cannot belie its basic status-quo orientation. The report advocates "costly and extreme recommendations," and while many of their excellent proposals are indeed costly, they are by no means extreme.

Truly effective proposals would hurt those established institutions and interests that gain from the deprivation of Watts and similar communities—the Commission does not fish in troubled waters. Possibly because they do not want Negroes to control their ethnic neighborhoods, they do not see the relation between community powerlessness and the generalized frustration and alienation which alarms them.

In their approach to the integration of the alienated Negro poor into American society, the Commission is guided by values and assumptions of the white middle-class ethos which are of dubious relevance to the majority of lower-class blacks. Their chief hope for the future is the instillation of achievement motivation in the ghetto poor so that they might embark upon the educational and occupational careers that exemplify the American success story. I am not against middle-class values—but in the immediate critical period ahead "middle classification" will be effective only with a minority of today's poor.

What is needed—in addition to jobs—is an experimental program for finding innovations that might link the values and social patterns of the Negro lower class with the social and productive needs of the greater society, thus reversing the trend toward alienation. Before the meaningful recommendations can be made that are in line with the enormity of the problem, the sociological and cultural character of the Negro low-income community must be understood. The legalistically-oriented Commission—with its primary commitments to control, law and order, a white-dominated *status quo,* and a middle-class ethic—has not been able to do this.

B. HOUSING

19. Housing Problems and Housing Policies

NATHAN GLAZER

The question of what is "good housing" is never as simple as it appears. Primitive dwellings on Greek isles delight architects and city planners who are horrified by the housing and planning of Levitt and Sons. In Japan, the sixth most powerful industrial nation in the world, and in its wealthiest city, Tokyo, we find that at least three-quarters of the dwellings *must* be substandard by American census standards, simply because they do not have flush toilets. Or if we consider a country that has, in common opinion, a most enlightened governmental housing policy and a very high living standard, Sweden, we find that the number of persons per room is one-third higher than in the United States.

So what is well housed? American housing experts apply three principal measures to the voluminous information provided by the housing census in order to determine adequacy of housing: (a) whether a housing unit is dilapidated or not, (b) whether it has hot running water and private toilet and bath, and (c) whether it is overcrowded (that is, more than one person per room). Using these measures—and we have indicated by reference to plumbing in Japan and crowding in Sweden how specifically they are the measures of this country, of this culture, and at this time—we find that 21 percent of the non-farm American families are ill-housed; and among specific groups, much larger numbers: 37 percent of those earning under $4,000, 53 percent of those with non-white heads of families, 65 percent of those with non-white heads and incomes under $4,000.

Thus, American housing, which from one perspective can be seen as the most spacious and best-equipped in the world, is, from another perspective, grossly inadequate. Since this last perspective happens to be our own, any discussion of American housing policy had better operate from within it.

On the Effects of Poor Housing

What is the effect of substandard and crowded housing on the families that live in it? Here we reach into the murkiest of sociological depths. I have indicated how culture-bound are our definitions of "the standard" and "the crowded." We can find examples of entire societies living in housing that by our measures are substandard and crowded, and yet these conditions seem not to create a serious problem for family living. That is understandable and obvious: we are all aware of how the prism of culture transforms the same physical reality into symbolically different settings. Less understandable and less obvious is the fact that defective conditions in housing within a single society, as defined by that society, seem to have such an irregular relationship to other social phenomena. Thus, we may observe that in preserves of technically excellent and uncrowded housing which are limited to low-income groups—that is, in public housing projects—there is no clear and specific relationship between the improvement in housing that the families have experienced and other social indicators. Families in low-rent-housing projects are neither stronger nor weaker, better nor worse off—except for having better housing.

Consider, for example, the most careful study—that of Daniel M. Wilner and his associates—of the effects of good housing, of the public housing project variety, on family relations. This study concludes: "It is not clear . . . that the change from bad to good housing has brought with it distinguishable alterations in relations among persons within the family." Equally inconclusive results are found in changes in attitudes and behavior toward neighborhood and community, and in a variety of recreational activities. On the other hand, in relations with neighbors and on various rather elusive (to this reader) psychological measures, housing seems to have made some small difference. And there is a clear, if also surprisingly small, improvement in health.

If we were dependent on Wilner's study alone to argue for the generally beneficial effects of better housing, our argument would not have much force. But we must also point out that Wilner studies the impact of housing *per se* in isolation from all other factors. And he is also studying the impact of what is, in one perspective (in the light of housing possibilities available to most American families), only a small improvement. Alvin Schorr, in a scholarly and insightful summary of the literature on this problem, has come to a balanced conclusion that indicates a somewhat more pessimistic view of the effect of inadequate housing, thus a more optimistic view of what better housing can do. But even if one accepts Schorr's estimate, there are still three points to be made:

First, the clearest bad effects come from "desperately inadequate" housing, as against mere "substandard" housing.

Second, many of these ill effects come from *overcrowding* rather than any of the structural characteristics of housing that we often think of when we speak of poor housing.

Third, it is arguable that some of the effects of poor housing ("pleasure in company but not in solitude," "relationships that spread out in the neighborhood rather than deeply in the family") are not entirely negative.

Negro Housing

On the whole, desperately inadequate housing is infrequent in this country outside the rural areas. In 1950, 96.4 percent had a bath; 96.6 percent had electricity. Among specific groups, and in particular for the Negro, it is true the situation is much worse, and the inadequate is more common. Thus, of housing units occupied by urban non-whites in 1960, 80 percent had inside hot and cold running water, but 15 percent had only cold water; 85 percent had private use of a flush toilet, but 8 percent shared a flush toilet and 7 percent had none; 78 percent had exclusive use of a bathtub or shower, but 7 percent shared it and 15 percent had none.

It is clear that the urban Negro—even more so, of course, the rural Negro—suffers from some of the worst housing conditions in the country. Unquestionably, for this group there is an important relationship between housing quality and the quality of family life. And yet, one must go on to point out that other factors are easily capable of overwhelming any positive efforts of an improvement in housing.

Some striking improvements have taken place in Negro housing with no impact on significant aspects of Negro family life (e.g., family break-up, illegitimacy, dependency, etc.). The proportion of non-white couples without their own household (that is, doubled up) dropped from 14 to 5 percent between 1950 and 1960 (white, from 6 percent to 2); the percentage of non-whites in substandard units dropped from 72 percent to 44 percent (white, from 32 percent to 13); and the percentage of non-whites in overcrowded housing (nonfarm only) was reduced more moderately from 32 percent to 27 (white, from 12 percent to 8). Meanwhile, various measures of Negro family disorganization actually increased.

Or we may note that there is no obvious correlation between the quality of housing in low-income Negro areas and the degree of social disorganization. Thus, the housing of Negroes in more newly-built Western cities is clearly superior to that in older Eastern and Northwestern cities (Watts versus Harlem, or Oakland versus Chicago's south side, to give the picture; in 1950, only 19 percent of dwelling units occupied by non-whites in the Los Angeles metropolitan area was substandard.) And in addition to newer, less substandard, less crowded housing, there is also in the West, in many respects, a better neighborhood ambiance (more recreational facilities, newer schools, etc.). But other conditions seem to destroy any positive relationship that might otherwise be expected to exist between housing conditions and family life.

The Effects of Crowded Rooms

Past the threshold of the most inadequate housing, it would appear that it is crowding that has the most serious effects. Thus, the excessive sexual stimulation, the attitudes toward privacy and self, the irritation of intra-family relations, the intrusive presence of non-family members—all these are consequences of crowding, of the simple shortage of space. Oscar Lewis's *Children of Sanchez* describes the incredible crowding of present-day lower-class urban living in Mexico City, where a dozen or more people, in three or four families, must use the same room for sleeping. Crowding conditions similar to these are described in the literature on the immigrant quarters of New York at the turn of the century. One would think the terrible effects of such crowding can scarcely be overestimated.

But even under such conditions of room crowding, cultural factors may come into play to mitigate the evil effects. Robert C. Schmitt has studied the effect of room crowding in Hong Kong, which reaches levels as high as any we know. In 1957, three-quarters of Hong Kong's households had less than a full room—and the average size of the household was 4.7! ("The Hong Kong average of 32 square feet is probably less than one-tenth of the metropolitan U.S. norm.") Despite this, health conditions do not seem to suffer much in comparison with the United States, and indices of social disorganization are lower.

But presumably even Chinese families, whose capacity, at least in the past, to cope with frightfully crowded urban conditions has been legendary, would do better with more space. And *certainly* families without long urban experience, and in a society in which the norms of space are much more lavish than in Hong Kong, may be expected to suffer from room crowding. Yet in contemporary America, the threshold we now consider "crowded" is so low that it is questionable whether transgressing it has significant effects on the family. This threshold, as we have pointed out, is now one person per room. Two persons per room is considered excessive crowding, and is so uncommon that census summary statistics do not even give figures for this degree of crowding. Can we say that densities of more than one person per room are factors in creating social problems and family disorganization? Perhaps they contribute (everything contributes); it is hard to see them as major factors. Consider for example the statistics in Table I—which show the proportion of households crowded (more than one person per room) by family income in 1960:

TABLE I

	% of households crowded	
Income $	*Owners*	*Renters*
under 2,000	6	16
2,000-2,999	9	20.5
3,000-3,999	11	19
4,000-4,999	11.5	17.5
5,000-5,999	11	16
6,000-6,999	10	14.5
7,000-7,999	9	13
8,000-9,999	8	11.5
10,000-15,000	7	11
above 15,000	4.5	8.5

(Source: *U.S. Census of Housing:* 1960, *Metropolitan Housing,* Final Report HC(2)-1, Table A-3.)

Crowding does decline with increase in income (the low crowding of the lowest income levels is accounted for by the high proportion of the elderly in this group). But what is striking is how *slowly* it decreases, and how substantial a proportion of the highest income groups still live under "crowded" conditions. They do this, one must assume, by choice, for they have the ability to allocate their income so as to eliminate crowding.

Under these circumstances, one wonders whether it should be a major aim of public policy to eliminate all crowding of more than one person per room. Still, it would seem to be an entirely proper aim of public policy to eliminate certain *extremes* of excessive crowding when these result, not from choice, in which privacy is a lesser value than some alternative good that may be purchased, but from economic incapacity to purchase space. In 1960, 1,690,000 families of five persons or more had incomes under $3,000. Most of these large, poor families must live under conditions that are truly crowded, and not merely statistically "crowded." This group forms a not insubstantial fraction of the American people.

Crowded Neighborhoods

We have spoken up to now of room crowding alone. Conceivably, room crowding, when measured by the current lavish American standard of one person per room, may have a less serious effect on the family than area crowding, that is, the concentration of too many households in an area, with the consequent crowding of streets with children and adolescents and young adults. Once again, Schmitt has carried through an interesting analysis, correlating various measures of crowding with various measures of ill-health and of family and social disorganization, for the census tracts of Honolulu. "Population per net residential acre"—a measure of area crowding—does correlate best with nine measures of ill-health and social disorganization, much better than does "dwelling units with more than one person per room." And yet I hesitate to conclude that crowding, whether area or room, in contemporary American cities, leads to family disorganization. What, after all, is the range of area crowding we are discussing? When we think of the conditions of the urban poor, we too often think of Harlem, which is far less typical of the country as a whole than Watts. Schmitt points out:

"Statistical subdivisions of American cities seldom exceed 150 inhabitants per gross acre. Analysis of recent census tract statistics indicates the highest densities to be about 450 persons per acre in both Boston and New York, 163 in Chicago, 150 in Philadelphia, 132 in Honolulu, and 62 in Seattle. Several blocks in Manhattan had as many as 1,300 persons per acre of ground space." In contrast, the highest densities in Hong Kong census divisions (equivalent to our census tracts) reach 2,800 per gross acre.

At 150 persons to the acre, assuming four to a household, and reserving one-third of the space for streets and open and public use, it would theoretically be possible to give each household a plot of 20 by 40, which does not seem excessively crowded for the most crowded urban housing—and these are the most densely settled tracts in American cities, leaving aside the exceptional cases of New York and Boston.

Rising Expectations and Standards

Indeed, the issue may not be whether housing, in terms of any world or absolute standard, is adequate or crowded. It may be: where does one's housing stand in terms of the standards of the system, and what does falling behind that standard mean? In a society in which quarter-acre lots become the norm, anything less will be correlated with a whole range of measures of poor health, family instability, and social disorganization. We may then say that housing has had such and such an influence upon the family, and in some sense it has. But it is not housing as such that has an effect, but housing as mediated through a complex culture and the expectations it variously distributes among its people. Thus, it is common to read—even in the writing of sociologists—that the housing of the urban Negro is now worse than it was, when it is by all measures better. But it may be—by some measures—further *behind* the housing of the urban white than it was; even more seriously, the expectations of the urban Negro are no longer—nor should they be expected to be—the expectation of the European immigrant of 1910, or the Negro migrant of 1930. But if this is so, we must expect to find paradoxes and ambiguities if we seek clear and determinate effects of poor housing and crowded housing, by our current standards, on family life; it will only have such effects if the housing reality is symbolically interpreted to mean degradation.

And we can be sure that even the measure of one person per room, lavish as it is by world standards, will soon be inadequate, too. If our society begins to define it as the right of every unmarried 21-year-old to have a separate household—and at least in the upper middle classes, this definition is spreading—and if our society defines it as the right of every older couple or older single individual to live alone, and not with his children, then the proportion of American households "overcrowded" is much, much more than the 12 percent listed as such by the one-person-per-room measure in the housing census of 1960.

It is to meet the demands of those with grossly inadequate housing, and of those with housing that compares too unfavorably with the American average, that we have evolved a national housing policy. The evolution is, of course, still incomplete. But there are already a flock of cautionary lessons to be learned from our experience.

The Constraints on American Housing Policy

Housing policy in any society, including ours, operates within a larger economic policy which limits, directly or indirectly, the resources that can be placed into housing. In societies in which central planning plays a larger role, a housing goal, in terms of amount of living space or numbers of houses or apartments to be built, is directly set, in the light of competing demands on economic resources. In this country, we do not set a grand goal for housing; but central economic policies affect directly or indirectly the flow of credit for housing, and the cost of labor and materials, and thus various government measures can control the number of housing units built almost as effectively as a central plan. At present, there is a crisis in the housing industry: credit is not easily available at interest rates that permit houses to be profitably built and sold. The maneuvers of the Treasury are dictated primarily by the need to avoid inflation and a heavier outflow of gold. The effect on the building industry is only one of the factors that are taken into account when making such central economic decisions. From the point of view of grand economic policy, the impact of decisions on the scale of *building* and *construction* operations may be important; but the impact on amount and types of *housing* available plays no role at all.

Aside from these general economic considerations, there are some special problems in establishing a governmental housing policy in a free society. When a public housing project operates with 20 percent vacancy rates, or when 20 percent of the buyers in a government-insured development default on their mortgages, the policy makers and administrators are subjected to great embarrassment. Yet in a free and relatively affluent society, such consequences may well occur. For where people have more choices before them, and more freedom to make such choices, it is certain that some of their choices will not correspond with the range that government policy has made available. Twenty percent of the American population moves every year—the opportunities for policy disasters in that simple figure are tremendous. Since World War II, we have consistently in this country built more housing than we have formed new households. There was of course, during the early postwar period, an enormous backlog of need, built up in the preceding fifteen years of war and depression. During the decade of the 1950's, 10,000,000 new households were formed and 13,400,000 additional housing units were added to housing inventory. In the first quarter of 1966, 7.5 percent of all rental units, and 1.4 percent of homeowner units, were vacant. The available for-rent vacancy rates (that is, units not deteriorated, available for year-round occupancy) was lower, but still substantial—2.7 percent and .8 percent. From the point of view of providing a desirable level of choice in the search for housing, these rates are still too low for many groups and in many areas. But from the point of view of builders and housers, the vacancy levels are too high; they are certainly higher than in any other major industrial nation.

Under these circumstances, just as the private builder of rental units or the developer of units for sale knows he may be courting disaster when he builds, and is therefore cautious, so too are the shapers and administrators of government policy cautious. In effect, choices are already so wide that a new choice, a new approach, must compete with many existing alternative possibilities. This is perhaps one of the chief constraints on American housing policy. In contrast, where shortages are or have been severe, and where more of the elements of investment policy are in the hands of the government (as is true of Western Europe, Eastern Europe, Japan, the developing world), one can operate with some assurance that almost any policy one decides upon will produce houses that are occupied, even if they come in a shape and style and are in a location that is less attractive than some conceivable alternative.

Thus, paradoxically, scarcity may permit greater freedom and experimentalism in policy, affluence—the presence of surplus—may impose greater caution.

A Home Is a House

There is also another constraint, perhaps the most distinctive constraint on American housing policies. This is the consistent bias in this country in favor of the owner-occupied, single-family, free-standing house, with a bit of land around it. When we speak of housing problems in this country, we tend to think of the city tenement, crowded with the poor, and of how to rehabilitate it or replace it with a more spacious and better planned multiple-family dwelling. But in the range of American housing problems, and of American housing policies, this situation is not central. Both the crowded slum and the type of multi-family housing that can replace it have received the chief attention of reformers, writers, analysts. On the other hand, it is the single-family, owner-occupied home—getting it built, getting it financed, saving it from the banks, reducing its cost, increasing its amenities—that has received the chief attention of elected officials, administrators, and the majority of the American people, perhaps even the poor among them.

The overwhelming preference of the American family in housing is the single-family home, preferably owned, preferably detached. Our housing policy, at local and federal levels, has been designed to facilitate the building of such a home, to protect its environment, to make it accessible to more and more people at lower economic levels. We have to keep this fundamental orientation in mind. If public housing fails—as it does in so many ways and so many cases—then we must realize this is a program to which our best attention as a nation has never been addressed. If our slums are uglier than those of any of the major industrial nations of Northwestern Europe—and they are—then we must realize this is in part because our interest in, and organization for, maintaining and policing the quality of rented dwellings for low-income people has never been fully developed—the low-income family is expected to get into a home of its own, somehow.

Thus, if we look at American housing policy, we will see that it consists of two large segments, and both are overwhelmingly directed toward facilitating the building, financing, and protection of the single-family home. On the local level, we find zoning regulations, building codes, and health codes. All of these, in their origins in the early 20th century, were designed to protect the low-income population, immigrant and working class, from frightful housing conditions. And to protect, too, the middle and upper-income population from the evil consequences, in health and amenities, that flowed from these conditions. Paradoxically, all these mechanisms of housing policy soon outgrew their origins, and they became adapted to the housing conditions and housing desires of the greater part of the population—that is they became policies for protecting the single-family home.

On the Federal level, we may trace a similar emphasis in policy. The first Federal action in the field of housing was a survey of slums in 1892. During World War I, the Federal government, directly and through loans to private builders, put up war housing. These initial forays into policy had no lasting consequences. But beginning in the early thirties, with the "President's Conference on Homebuilding and Home Ownership," Federal policy was set on the path of the encouragement of home-ownership, through the development of the amortized long-range mortgage, Federal insurance of home mortgages, encouragement of large-scale development of single-family homes, guidance of the supply of long-term housing credit. The Federal Home Loan Bank system in 1932, the Home Owner's Loan Corporation and Federal Farm Mortgage Corporation of 1933, and the National Housing Act of 1934, setting up the Federal Housing Administration, were all steps to the creation of a Federal policy which facilitated home ownership.

As against these two major forms of government policy—zoning, building and health codes at the local level, the encouragement of home-building and home ownership at the federal level—other major thrusts of policy have been relatively minor. Federally financed public housing (the United States Housing Act of 1937) was, in its origins, designed to combat the depression by encouraging building, as well as to clear slums and provide housing for the poor. It has always been operated on such a small scale that its achievement in all these areas has been minor. Today, a little more than one percent of the population is in public housing. (For certain parts of the population, of course, public housing is more important. In New York City, where public housing is most prominent, about 7 percent of the population, and a quarter of the Negro population, live in public housing.) Urban renewal, which began in 1949, even with the large areas that have been cleared in some American cities, is small potatoes compared to the central policy of encouraging single-family home building and ownership. In contrast to some 600,000 units of public that have been built during the history of the public housing program, and 80,000 that have been built under urban renewal, over 5,000,000 units have been built under FHA home mortgage programs.

What the People Want

This overwhelming central tendency in American housing policy undoubtedly reflects certain characteristics of the actual American family, and of the models, conscious or unconscious, that are held as to the ideal family life. Thus, the emphasis on a room for every individual and on space between the houses reflects an emphasis on familial privacy, and individual privacy within the family. There is no question this is what the American family—for the most part—wants. William Slayton and Richard Dewey, summarizing eleven opinion studies in 1953, assert simply that, "whenever given the opportunity, most American families express their desire to own their own homes." National surveys in 1935, 1940, and 1945 showed remarkably similar proportions—70 percent preferred to own (almost all the home-owners, and half or more of the renters, too). Since 1945, the jaundiced depression view of home ownership has receded in the face of FHA and VA-insured housing, and the percentages of those preferring to own, if we had recent surveys, might well be higher.

If this has been the taste of the American family, it can hardly be argued with, since the choice has a certain amount of face validity—it means more space for children, inside and out; it means the opportunity to invest one's resources, if they are available, in newer equipment and better upkeep; it means a generally rising investment; it means freedom to alter one's living accommodations at will and to keep pets and animals; and one may proceed from there to various more subtle gains, all of which quite overwhelmed the demonstrations of housing experts twenty years ago that ownership was often financially unwise. Together with the housing policies we have outlined, it has resulted in a home ownership rate of 62 percent of all housing units in 1962.

Even this understates the prevalence of the single-family house, for many are rented. In 1960, no less than 70 percent of all housing units in this country were one-family houses, detached; another 6 percent were one-family, attached; 13 percent were in structures with two to four units; a mere 11 percent were in structures with more than five units. Even in metropolitan areas, the apartment house was—statistically—a relatively rare phenomenon. Sixty percent of all *metropolitan* housing units were single-family, detached; another 8 percent were single-family, attached. New York is the unique city which, for reasons of culture, or crowding, or land value, breaks with this pattern. It contains the bulk of the apartment houses of the country—in 1950, 51 percent of all apartment units in structures of more than 20 units were in New York City!

Presumably, home-ownership and the single family detached dwelling have now reached most of the family units that might find it desirable. Of our fifty-three million households, 41 percent hold two persons or less, and many of these, we must assume, would not be interested in homeownership. Of our forty-five million families, only 52 percent contain children under eighteen, and many of the remainder, too, might find homeownership less attractive than renting. And indeed, after dominating the housing markets of the 1960's overwhelmingly (92 percent of all private housing units started in 1956 were single-family homes), the proportion of single family homes has been dropping, steadily, and in 1964 only 62 percent of all new units begun were single-family homes.

The Criticisms of American Housing Policy

The policy of the encouragement of homeownership has been subjected to three major criticisms. The first is that it has favored the better-off. (We cannot say simply the wealthier, for the homes of the wealthy do not need, and do not generally get, FHA insurance and VA guarantees—though even the wealthy have benefitted from the stabilization of the mortgage market and the availability of long-term amortized mortgages.) Policies for the poor, this criticism asserts, have been non-existent or paltry and demeaning (e.g., public housing). Thus, the slums endure and spread, in the face of a housing policy that serves only the top half or less of the income distribution.

The second major criticism of this policy is that it has destroyed urbanism. By urbanism, critics mean many things. They mean some appropriate level of *density,* so people can meet on a face-to-face basis, engage in casual encounter, be stimulated by new experience. They further mean heterogeneity of income group and of race and ethnic group, which may be expected to have the same "urbanizing," "urbane-izing," "civ-ilizing" effect. They also mean *mixing of uses*—of different kinds of residential uses (apartment and single-family houses), and of residential, commercial, amusement, and even some industrial uses.

This criticism comes in a variety of forms. We can trace a spectrum from those who emphasize most strongly the aesthetic (Lewis Mumford), to those who emphasize the aesthetic and the social with almost equal weight (Jane Jacobs), to those who emphasize the social (Charles Abrams)—and when we get to the latter end of the spectrum, one of the chief indictments made by this criticism is that Federal and local housing policy has created, indeed enforced, the growing division between the white suburbs and the increasingly Negro central cities.

Just as public housing is an unsatisfying answer to those who make the first criticism (i.e., that our housing policy has aided the better-off), so is urban renewal an unsatisfying answer to those who make our second criticism, that federal housing policy destroys urbanism. And once again, the criticism of urban renewal ranges from the aesthetic to the social, but here social criticism has been most intense—urban renewal is said to favor an even wealthier class than does FHA, with subsidies for the building of expensive apartments and houses, and to do nothing for the poor who are ejected from the central city.

The third major criticism of Federal housing policy is that it does not create a valid form of community expansion and community building. Here critics point to the experience of England, Sweden, Finland, Holland, where new communities are planned, where open space, "countryside," is maintained within easy access of new urban areas, where planned public transportation relates the residential to the work areas, where a non-wasteful and aesthetically and socially satisfying form of community building provides not only a house but an environment for families.

Obviously all three major criticisms, if true, would amount to a devastating indictment of Federal housing policy. But are they true, in whole or in part?

Criticism I: Does Policy Neglect the Poor?

The first criticism is to my mind the most serious. How have the poor fared under Federal housing policy?

In 1950, Charles Abrams argued that only 30 percent of American nonfarm families could afford private builders' houses—and this was at a time when FHA and VA together permitted no cash down payments for many home purchasers. At the same time, and on the other hand, another leading housing expert (Sherman Maisel) argued: "The generalization that houses can be and are being built only for the upper income groups is incorrect. It is more accurate to state that if existing veteran terms of no or low down payments, 4 percent interest rates, and thirty-year-amortization were made available to all, nearly every family receiving a minimum full-time income could afford to purchase a house if so desired."

Paul Wendt, who reports these contrasting judgments of the early 1950's, tries to bring them into harmony, and points out that Abrams was referring to *all* families, and that Maisel was describing generous terms that did not hold for all purchasers and in any case did not hold for long. Twenty percent of all families, too, he points out, were in 1957 "not in the labor force, unemployed, or in the Armed forces"—thus did not have "minimum full-time incomes." On the other hand many of the poor families who could not qualify for the FHA or VA housing were farm or rural families, with special housing problems which have, in any case, always been difficult for major government programs to overcome, while many others were older couples who might not be interested in purchasing new homes. So the question remains open: how far down in the income distribution has the government-insured and guaranteed new home reached—only the top 30 percent, as according to Abrams, or 80 percent, as according to Maisel?

Someone who is not an expert on the economics of housing might well strike a median. And indeed, it seems that the median income of families purchasing FHA houses hovers only about $1,000 above the median income of all urban families. Thus, in 1958, the median income of buyers of new FHA houses was $7,733, the median income of buyers of existing homes on FHA mortgages was $7,447. In 1959, urban husband-wife families had a median income of $6,454. (In the early postwar period, the median income of FHA purchasers was about the same as the median income of all families, for in those years it was possible to get mortgages at lower interest rates, and the FHA or VA house was cheaper, owing to smaller size, less equipment, and smaller lots.) This suggests that the FHA house is indeed pretty much within the means of the median American family, if we have in mind the urban, husband-wife family at which this policy aims. What it leaves out are the substantial numbers of families that fall below the median—for example, the non-white family, whose median income (again, urban and husband-wife families) was in 1959 only $4,329. It certainly leaves out the family headed by a woman, the elderly couple without resources, and other poor families. And yet we should avoid a position which often becomes polemical and exaggerated. For in 1963, 13 percent of new single-family homes were priced under $12,500, and in 1964, 11 percent; and this substantial part of the new home market *was* within the means of families earning well below the median that year.

Of course, for the bottom half of the distribution there were other programs. There was, in the post-war period, a great deal of rental housing (under an FHA program which created a scandal, and which was abandoned). After the revival of multi-family housing in the late fifties, however, new rental housing was too expensive for poor families. In New York City, where the apartment is still the norm, state and city funds made possible various kinds of subsidized apartment houses for middle-income and lower middle-income populations, and these have included enormous developments of cooperative apartments, sponsored by trade unions and other non-profit organizations. But these were not popular elsewhere. The federal government moved into this field of subsidizing lower middle income (or upper lower income) apartment units with its 221 (d)3 program, offering federally-insured mortgages to non-profit or limited profit builders at lower than market interest rates; but this program, which has a good deal of promise for the future, numbered only 15,000 units at the end of 1964.

THE "FAILURE" OF PUBLIC HOUSING

The major Federal program for the poor has been public housing. We have indicated above its relatively small scale. It has been starved by Congress; and low cost units have been built in recent years at a rate of only 20,000 annually, less than 2 percent of all housing starts. But if Congress has been unsympathetic, so too have a substantial part of the group for which it was ostensibly designed—the poor family. Thus, while poor families on urban renewal sites have priority in entering public housing projects, only a minority do so. Public housing has been much discussed, but as yet is little studied. Some of the best studies have been of public housing in Puerto Rico—where the program operates under the same federal laws as on the mainland, but where the prevailing conditions of poverty and the prevailing influence of rural patterns of living make the whole business something quite different. The best studies of public housing on the mainland are yet to come—and yet it seems clear they will come after the country as a whole, both Congress and a large percentage of those for whom it was designed, have indicated their sharp rejection of the program. Admittedly, the middle class liberal and the radical ally of the poor (along, of course, with older critics on the right) seem to be more sharply opposed to public housing than those who live in it and for whom it is designed. As we can see from the long waiting lists in most cities, many families are delighted to get into public housing. But this acceptance of public housing is based on the fact that it is a bargain (about $500 a year subsidy for an apartment) and that for many people it is the best buy available. Even though we do not have the evidence that could give us complete assurance in making our assessment, it seems clear than many who live in public housing also have sharp criticisms, and find it easy to think of something better.

Public housing has survived to the extent that it has only because it is beginning to serve a number of special elements in the population who either find it unobjectionable or who have no alternatives available. Thus, after 1956—and owing to its unpopularity with Congress and local communities—public housing began to accept single elderly persons, and began to build for the elderly. After World War II, the proportion of non-whites in public housing began to increase, and in some cities public housing is now largely Negro—which makes it more difficult to attract white families. And public housing has increasingly provided dwelling places for families without fathers. Thus, in 1964, 53 percent of families in public housing were non-white; 28 percent were elderly. In individual projects, such as that under study by Lee Rainwater in St. Louis, as much as 50 percent of the families may consist of women and children without husbands or fathers. There are, of course, complete families with children in public housing, and perhaps half or more of the units are occupied by them; but white families are a declining proportion, and in most cities they are concentrated in a few projects that are known as "good" projects.

If public housing has "failed"—and we mean that it is unpopular among those who pay for it, and those who are supposed to benefit by it—what explains its failure? The following seem to be the most important:

(1) It has been limited to the poorest. Thus, in 1964, the median income of public housing families was under $2,500. Inevitably, these families must include large proportions of families on relief, large proportions of broken families, large proportions of families without wage-earners, large proportions of families with problems that prevent earning. This is not true of all projects—but when the concentration of the unfortunate and the miserable becomes too large, other families shun the project and then, despite the attractiveness of good housing (physically speaking) at low rents, a too-high vacancy level may develop. And the income limits checked annually have also meant that the more productive and ambitious are required to leave.

(2) Administration has been rather more restrictive and intrusive than in alternative housing, and this has both limited the number of those who would enter, and perhaps created a restrictive and unpleasant atmosphere among those who have remained. Studies as to the reasons why people don't like public housing often refer to these restrictions—the inability to keep animals in the apartment and conduct businesses in them (in Puerto Rico), the restrictions on painting and alterations and even on pounding nails into walls (sometimes these restrictions do not actually exist—but the fact that tenants believe they do is itself evidence of the restrictive atmosphere), the prohibition on overnight guests (again, this may be an illusion), the fact that rents rise with income (which again makes administration—by law, and necessarily—intrusive). Under these circumstances, it is the helpless, fatherless families on welfare who flock to the projects.

(3) Public housing architecture and siting, as well as its regulations and its clientele, have often marked it off from other housing, stamping it as separate, institutional, deviant. One can find little evidence that the architecture as such has had unpleasant consequences—the same buildings, more or less, that house low-income families in New York seem to provide what is considered reasonable family housing for that city when inhabited by middle-income families. Unquestionably, those public housing projects that approximate in their design most closely single-family housing are most attractive to the public housing resident.

And yet "the jungle" is not created by the twenty-story apartment house. It is created by the social circumstances of the families who live in them. The physical setting only contributes to some undetermined extent—and largely as it becomes symbolic of a life set apart, of placement in a ghetto. Thus, it would be difficult to argue that curtains instead of doors over clothing closets, or toilet seats without covers, or elevators that stop on every other floor, by themselves lead to an unhappy life—but they become symbols of an unhappy life, and develop an exaggerated importance. Ironically, any form of physical deviance can be used to symbolize the social deviance. Thus, Marin City, north of San Francisco, which represents the efforts of the Public Housing Administration to break away from institutional architecture, and which is a daring creative solution to the problem of building apartment houses on a hill, has had more problems than more architecturally conventional public housing projects. Deviant architecture, even when it is deviant in a progressive direction, is taken to symbolize the deviant social condition of the population, and becomes a target of their aggression.

(4) Critics have also pointed to the fact that public housing

projects are set in old and dilapidated neighborhoods (originally, it was hoped the new building might help *improve* the neighborhoods), and are cut off from contact with middle-class areas, which might serve to encourage social mobility among the project population.

Much of this criticism is unfortunately undocumented with research, and the last point is perhaps least well supported. In New York, in Washington, and elsewhere, there *have* been efforts to place public housing adjacent to middle-income housing developments. It is not clear what effect, if any, this has had on the low-income population, as compared with projects that are placed squarely in low-income neighborhoods. One may feel confident that the poor prefer to live in a less poor neighborhood—there are more facilities, better stores, less crime. One must be less confident when one asserts that proximity to middle-class residential areas will have some specific social and psychological effects on the projects' dwellers.

A GRAVEYARD OF GOOD INTENTIONS

Are there solutions to these problems of public housing? Many earnest efforts have failed and others have been only partially successful. Thus, consider the efforts to create balanced communities within the projects. The New York City Housing authority has tried to limit the number of families on welfare—and this leads to the ironic necessity of the Welfare department paying inflated rents for slum dwellings for its clients, because it cannot place them in public housing. The objective of balanced communities means, too, that the Housing Authority may favor a family that financially is in lesser need over one that is in greater need because the first family will make a larger contribution to creating a balanced community. The Housing Authority has tried to create racially and ethnically mixed projects—and this, too, has led to the ironic conclusion that it will favor an elderly white couple (because whites are in short supply in public housing), over a Negro family with children (because Negroes are all too plentiful in public housing). It has tried to protect its families from potential and actual criminals and drug addicts, and has therefore set up a check-list for applicants—and this has meant that it has had to exclude those whose need is greatest. It has rehabilitated brownstones and older apartment houses so that its dwellings would blend into the New York scene—but the costs of rehabilitating to government standards have been frighteningly high in administrative time and money. It has tried to break up its projects and spread them in middle-class communities—and has roused the protests of these middle-class communities, who are convinced that public housing will make their neighborhoods less attractive, less safe, less desirable.

Public housing is a graveyard of good intentions. Some projects succeed, partially. Some projects are maintained as good communities, some are racially balanced, some rehabilitated dwellings are added to the public housing supply, some small projects are sited in middle-class areas. But to turn public housing into sound, low-cost family housing seems enormously difficult. And indeed, the government has put its hopes for low-income family housing into rent supplements—perhaps this will overcome the major problems I have outlined. But while Congress has accepted the principle, it has resisted the appropriation of the funds required to put a large rent-supplement program into effect. And rent supplements themselves raise a host of intriguing problems for the sociologist of the future. For if the homeowner and the middle-income renter have resisted the low-income housing project coming into their neighborhoods, how will they feel about the subsidized low-income family? What stigma will it bear? How will its relations with unsubsidized (or less subsidized) neighbors be affected?

My own conclusion is that while both traditional public housing and the new rent subsidy program have a place in providing housing for the poor, they are not the final or the best answers to the problem. In an egalitarian society, where the single family home, under home-ownership, is the *norm*, it must also become (as Charles Abrams has argued) the *objective* of public policy for the poor family—and less than that will generally become a sign of discrimination and degradation. This will not be true in situations where a substantial number of middle-income families live in apartments (as in New York), but it will be true in most of the country. And indeed, certain experiments now being conducted under the aegis of the Low Income Housing Demonstration Program of the Department of Housing and Urban Development are testing whether home ownership—with special government aids and subsidies—can be extended to very low-income families.

THE DANGERS OF BEING DIFFERENT

I would argue that one must avoid the danger of building for the poor under regulations or in a style very different from that to which the middle class is accustomed. The housing for the poor of the nations of Northwestern Europe, whether the council housing of England or the apartments of Scandinavia, are, in effect, the housing that most people in those countries have—and it is not marked by any stigma of deviance. In New York City, public housing is not all that different from the housing of other New Yorkers—and there public housing is politically acceptable, and various types of public housing are built with city and state funds, as well as with Federal funds.

Sam B. Warner, describing the history of two philanthropic projects to provide workingmen's homes in late 19th-century Boston, provides a cautionary tale for us in considering what kind of housing to provide for the poor. The first project, put up through the efforts of Robert Treat Paine, provided two-story brick row houses. Warner writes:

> "Though Paine's houses and narrow streets may have been suitable in Philadelphia, where there was a long and continuous tradition of row housing, in Boston these buildings had a strong philanthropic air. They were brick and fireproof and had a full set of plumbing facilities, but for all their safety and sanitation they remained mean, cramped row houses built a full decade after the main body of the middle class had ceased building row houses for itself. Like the wooden barracks and tenements of the neighborhood, these houses were suited to the momentary needs and capabilities of their inhabitants—all too suited to them, and not at all suited to their aspirations. . . . Because Paine had built minimal structures, and built without regard to some of the important middle class aspirations of the day, his houses suffered the fate of all the other homes in the area. For the last forty years they have served as slum dwellings, and, despite Paine's careful construction, they are falling to the ground."
>
> Paine's second undertaking was a "cheap project . . . but the streets do follow the contours of the land and are designed to make a traffic cul de sac. . . . such site planning was just then coming into vogue for expensive subdivisions in Brookline and other parts of greater Boston. . . .
>
> "The houses themselves came in several styles of detached frame single and two-family structures. A variety of contemporary ornament was also offered. . . . The houses were more than twice as big as the little row houses of the 1880's and sold for twice as much. . . . The whole suburban 'cottagey' effect of this hundred-house subdivision was underlined with street names of 'Round Hill' and 'Sunnyside.' . . .
>
> "Paine's houses are still kept up because for sixty years they have been the best choice of the neighborhood. They have been the best choice because they were more in keeping with the housing aspirations of Bostonians than any of the other cheap alternatives of the 1890's.
>
> "The success of Paine's experiment suggests that slum housing is one of the prices that a society pays for allowing any major amount of its building to proceed at a level below its common understanding among the middle class as to what constitutes a satisfactory home environment."*

An intriguing conclusion: but is this not what we have allowed to

*Sam B. Warner, *Streetcar Suburbs* (Cambridge, Mass., 1962).

happen with public housing? And is this not part of the reason why we are faced with the contradiction of social slums in what are some of the best built structures in our housing stock?

Criticism II: Does It Destroy Urbanism?

The second major criticism of American housing policy—that it is destructive of urbanism—has, as I have outlined it, a number of parts. Part of the criticism is of the design of the communities that have been built with federal subsidy and support, both new suburban communities and new developments within the city. This design criticism links up with social criticism of insufficient density and variety. And finally, we have placed under this criticism the charge that federal policy has encouraged the separation of the races.

Certainly there have been few creative achievements in the field of urban design, except for the shopping center—and that has been built without federal aid. But it is equally true that the demand for the kinds of design that urban designers have most favored has not been very great. Thus, urban designers have been attracted to the row house. The row house combines an economy in the use of space with a relatively high degree of privacy for the family. It offers the possibility of a common use of some of the saved space. It gives a larger opportunity to the architect to create a space than does the single-family detached house, and links up current building with the great tradition of urban architecture.

And yet there tends to be a conflict between the interest of the designer and the interest of the family. Regardless of its great historical associations for the architect, for the family seeking space and good living it generally means more cramped conditions than the detached house. Where land is expensive—e.g., the land of urban renewal developments in central cities, of near-in older areas of New York—the row house will be widely used; but it is clearly a second best. And for most of this country, land costs are still so reasonable as to permit most families to realize their first choice in the amount of space they consider desirable.

The variety that is so attractive to the architectural critic or urban designer is also less attractive to the homeowner. If the variety means only varied ornamentation on houses of the same basic style or price, that is fine with the homeowner. If it means the introduction of apartment houses, homeowners will object; if it means non-residential uses, they will object again. They do not want the convenience of corner shopping. They often do not even want the presence of a too-nearby church, regardless of the mildness of its activities. The use of the automobile is so widespread that the family prefers to put all these things at a distance, and approach shopping, work, worshipping, and most other activities by automobile. Only for the elementary school is an exception made, because children don't drive.

The variety arising from the heterogeneity of mixed income groups is fought even more vigorously. An as yet unpublished study of new communities in California by Werthman, Mandel, and Dienstfrey demonstrates the strength of the resistance to the nearby presence of cheaper residential developments. The homeowner is also an investor, and cheaper housing nearby (and any mixing of economic levels means that some of the housing will be cheaper) will be resisted. Thus, even the homeowner at the $21,000 level will resist the intrusion of development, if he can, at the $17,000 level. Ironically, one of the meanings—and indeed the chief meaning—of planning to the homeowner, according to this study, is that the homeowner will be protected from the intrusion of cheaper housing and from nearby non-residential uses. To the planner and new community developer, on the other hand, what planning means is just the opposite—that instead of the enormous tract in one style for one income group, he will be able to introduce a variety of groups, and a variety of uses.

WHAT ABOUT INTEGRATION?

The charge that Federal housing policy has contributed to the separation of the races is certainly the most serious part of this criticism. That residential segregation of Negro and white in the American city is extensive, and spreading is undeniable. On the other hand, it is difficult to trace this segregation to Federal policy. Charles Abrams has sharply criticized the FHA for encouraging segregation. (From 1935 to 1950 its official handbooks warned against the stability of areas that held both Negroes and whites, and discouraged guaranteeing mortgages in such areas.) Certainly Abrams has demonstrated that the Federal government did nothing for many years to encourage integration. But could it have used its powers to do so? Technically, yes. But politically this was most unpopular. And practical measures to overcome segregation are difficult to implement. Since President Kennedy's executive order of 1962, all Federal aid to housing and community development has been on the condition that discrimination will not be practiced. In 1964, the Civil Rights Act prohibited discrimination and segregation in any program that uses Federal funds. Many states and cities have had laws against discrimination in rental and sales of housing for some years. And yet the total effect of these measures in creating integrated neighborhoods has been hardly visible.

To produce integration in residential areas requires the most persistent and sophisticated measures of administration and enforcement before any major effect is produced, and even in New York City, where such laws have been in existence for the longest period, and with the widest support, one cannot be optimistic about the results. Neither Federal, state, nor local action can create integration by fiat. Segregation is an outcome that is shaped by complex forces on many levels: ignorance and prejudice; the differing economic levels of whites and Negroes; economic fears as to the loss of property values by homeowners and other property holders; social fears as to the decline of the neighborhood—which seem to refer to such elements as the quality of schools, level of public safety, degree of littering, and social patterns in the use of open space, the institutionalization of discriminatory practices and procedures in all the agents of the housing market—renters and buyers, builders and lenders, banks and appraisers, local government officials and employees; and personal choice by Negroes and white. On the whole, in this area, Federal policy has followed local practice, and on the whole, local practice has been discriminatory.

The executive order of 1962, the Civil Rights Act of 1964, and many local and state laws, now call on government to do more. But in this area—as in so many areas of social policy—it is not easy to find the Gordian knot to be cut at one stroke. One can find principles, policies, approaches. Perhaps the single most important principle that emerges from the literature on this question is that it is perhaps too much at this time to try to integrate *both* different economic levels and Negro and white in the same areas. When one keeps these two forms of integration separate, and tries to integrate middle-income Negro and white groups, and lower-income Negro and white groups, the problems may be manageable, even if difficult and delicate.

It is clear that the builder who is willing to accept a few losses and a somewhat lower rate of sale can successfully sell to both groups. But as we know from experience in other areas—such as higher education and the higher civil service—in which there has been no discrimination for some time, it requires active measures of recruitment to proceed from non-discrimination to integration. And as against the cases of the civil service and some universities and corporations, builders and developers who have gone out of their way in an attempt to create an integrated community are rare indeed. A few experiments have been conducted on a small scale. With a rising Negro middle-income housing market, it should be possible to extend the scale of these undertakings.

The period when active discrimination and segregation could occur in projects and developments that used Federal funds or services is coming to an end; but we have not as yet, except in a few areas and a few cases, moved to the next stage, of an active encouragement of integration. Until the summer of 1966, one would have said, on the basis of the experience of a few non-discriminatory builders and of a scattering of integrated neighborhoods, that a policy of active encouragement of integration—if it took into account the powerful feeling against mixing groups of different economic levels, regardless of race—could be implemented in many areas without massive resistance. This was the experience of many voluntary groups of suburban white home-owners who tried to encourage integration by getting neighbors to list their houses as available for rental or purchase to Negroes. One could not speak with any such assurance now. The marches led by Martin Luther King into white lower-middle class and middle-class areas of Chicago in the summer of 1966, and the furious resistance they encountered, helped to make the subject of residential integration one of the most inflammatory of civil rights issues, and led to the defeat of the Civil Rights Bill of 1966. And yet, the violent attacks on the Negro marchers in Chicago were not only or even primarily in defense of right to segregation: they were also reactions to the symbolism of marching and demanding Negroes in white areas, and reactions in defense of ethnic communities which it was believed were threatened by Negro demands. This belief was certainly encouraged by the inept form that was chosen by the King campaign. Had the integration campaign of Martin Luther King chosen to operate by encouraging Negroes to move into white areas and encouraging white areas to accept Negro homeowners and renters, it is hard to believe such massive resistance would have been encountered. Violence against the occasional Negro renter and homeowner is less and less frequent in the North and West—though it occurs, as in Philadelphia in the autumn of 1966.

It will take political "muscle" on the federal level to make residential integration a reality, more now than before the summer of 1966. And for some time, it would appear, that muscle, if it is available, will be directed to the objectives of reducing unemployment, raising welfare and social insurance levels, desegregating and improving urban education, and increasing Negro political representation. And, indeed, one may question the overall importance of the residential integration aim. Unquestionably, housing must be available; discrimination should be illegal (though when the discrimination is that of the individual home-owner, we have a serious clash of principles). But the task of creating a fully integrated residential pattern raises such overwhelming difficulties, and the gains to be achieved by it are so questionable—in light of the persistent tendencies of ethnic and racial groups in the past to prefer some degree of concentration, though nowhere the degree that is imposed by discrimination on Negroes—that I would question how far governmental power in this area should try to extend itself.

"BALANCED" COMMUNITIES

If we were to move ahead to a major policy of home-building for the poor, then we would have a different kind of problem. We would be faced with the same difficulty of achieving residential racial integration for low income Negroes that we now find in public housing. The concentration of Negro families in the low-income population in the worst housing is so great that any program designed to accommodate poor families in new housing would be a program largely for Negro families. The difficulties of distributing such housing in higher-priced neighborhoods would be immense. The tendency of any program that wanted to make an impact on this problem rapidly would be to by-pass the subtle and time-consuming political and administrative procedures required to distribute such housing among an upper-income white population, and build large tracts designed specifically for those whose housing needs were greatest, that is, poor Negro families. Thus, once again we would have the specter of racially segregated areas built with Federal funds.

Any proposal to eliminate the worst family housing along the lines I earlier suggested—single-family housing—would come into conflict with the aim of integration. One American New Town project, interested in achieving a balanced community of middle-income and low-income, white and black, has attempted to analyze with the help of social scientists how heterogeneity of this type could be introduced, and has concluded that some minimal degree of separation of income levels and races would, in effect, take place. Those who bought the more expensive housing would want the neighborhood benefits that came from more prosperous neighbors; and the poor neighborhoods would inevitably be largely Negro.

I would conclude that, while it is possible to integrate the races of the same economic level, to carry through such an integration when the whites are (mostly) prosperous and the Negroes are (mostly) poor would be enormously difficult, and no measures that we can project give hope that such integration on a major scale can take place in the near future. Under these circumstances, we must expect for some time to come that poor areas will be largely Negro, that more prosperous areas will be largely white, with some small degree of integration. This further raises the prospect that cities will become inhabited by majorities of Negroes, suburbs will remain overwhelmingly white, with slowly rising proportions of Negroes. At one time this prospect appeared disastrous; now that we know that we must undergo it, further analysis and reflection and experience suggest that it need not be. Growing Negro economic capacity will destroy this pattern—and if this develops rapidly enough, conceivably this pattern of Negro-central-city and white-suburbs will be limited to only a few metropolitan areas.

In considering this question of racial integration, as in our consideration earlier of the complex problems of creating a "balanced community" in a housing project, the question must come up: who wants balanced and integrated communities, and what are their virtues? Obviously this question would not arise if such a community developed as a result of the unguided play of economic and technological forces. Thus, the Middletown of the 1920's had workers and businessmen, community leaders and casual laborers, Negroes and whites. It had grown as a service and industrial city; and, in contrast to a Levittown of the same size thirty years later, seemed to have clear and obvious virtues. The classes could learn from each other by direct observation and contact something of the whole complex structure of society. Children growing up could see men at work, the aged, the houses of the rich and the poor.

On the other hand, Levittown and the housing project also came into existence for clear and sufficient reasons: one, to house rapidly great numbers of relatively low-income young families; the other, to house great numbers of truly poor people. And we have seen why it has been difficult to introduce a great range of social variation in such communities. The homeowners of Levittown would not want cheaper houses, and buyers of more expensive houses would not want to live there. The poor in the housing projects would be deprived of their right to subsidized housing if some substantial portion of this housing went to those who economically did not need it, whatever their presumed social virtues for the community.

The question remains, what efforts of social policy are justified in introducing a greater social variety into these communities? If this social variety is maintained by the exclusion of racial groups, it is in large measure illegal and it is certainly immoral. Beyond this, however, should we introduce a greater social variety through insisting on a wide range of economic levels and through a positive effort to recruit families of minority groups? One is cognizant of the fact that even where such variety exists (in the crowded central city), the mere fact of geographical proximity may lead to very little social contact. *Dead End*, in which the slum kids interact with the swells, is still fiction; most such interaction occurs through the intermediary of the police. Puerto Ricans and Negroes in the shadows of expensive apartment houses of New York scarcely have any interaction with the wealthy—they generally use different stores, schools, churches, and open spaces.

Geographical proximity may lead to little of that social interaction we want, and which we try to achieve when we press for communities with representatives of different economic levels and racial groups. On the other hand, the new monumental scale of our metropolitan areas and sub-areas does not necessarily isolate economic and racial groups more. Interaction between our larger ghettoes and larger suburban communities may be in some ways more intense than when low-income and middle-income groups share the same small community. This interaction today occurs through politics, the press and the mass media, through riots and demonstrations. It may be an interaction appropriate to our new urban scale.

Nor have we truly examined the gains of the one-class or one-race community. Herbert Gans has unemotionally and unideologically pointed out that middle-class families like to have people like them as their neighbors, and has questioned what gains would follow from imposing on them a random selection of un-likeminded neighbors. Certain ethnic groups, even forty years after the end of mass immigration, still seem to want to cluster together—consider the Italians of Boston's late West End, or the East European communities of Chicago that are resisting Martin Luther King's integration campaign.

I think we have good social grounds for imposing a certain amount of discomfort on people who would prefer to live in communities of like and like-minded people. We can impose this discomfort when this common desire restricts other's rights to housing; we may impose this discomfort when some larger social end dictates a new and different use for the land of the community in which they live. But I would stop at imposing this discomfort out of a theory that "progress" is the result of being uprooted from the familial and tribal wombs.

SEGREGATION BY AGE

Aside from racial and economic segregation, our new communities show another form of segregation—by family life-cycle. Young families with children live in new suburban single-family home areas;

older families will live in the older sections of the city. When children are grown and gone, elderly couples or single survivors will occupy a variety of specialized buildings or communities for the aged. Young couples without children occupy the new suburban apartment houses and—with more money, and a different style of life—the new inner-city apartment houses. Certainly we find a degree of segregation by family life-cycle that is more extreme than in the past, and that must have certain consequences for children and family life. It encourages the peer-group society, reduces the role of the generation of grandparents in the rearing of children, encourages a more rapid geographic mobility—for some neighborhoods are appropriate to one section of the family cycle, others to another part.

Has housing policy encouraged this segregation? In some degree it has. It has encouraged it simply because programs are defined in terms of certain specific needs—we have the standard FHA and VA programs, which are designed for the family with children, special programs for senior citizens, special programs for apartment building. Theoretically, a developer could mix together all these and other building types in the same development. Practically, he does not have the overhead resources for planning and negotiating with various federal agencies that this requires. It is hard to think of any good reason why the segregation should be as pronounced as it is. Perhaps senior citizens are annoyed by children's noise and prefer the company of others like them. Does this mean we should build communities of thousands of units for senior citizens alone? We cannot refer to any definitive studies—indeed, there are hardly any studies at all. But it does seem that, just as we have decided it was inhuman and murderous to segregate the mentally ill in vast institutions of many thousands, we may in time decide that the scale of some of our communities and developments for the aged is far too large. And we may find there are drawbacks in communities that recruit all their residents from the young family stage in the life cycle. One can only speculate as to the social and psychological effects, but we can point to inefficiencies in such communities—enormous pressures on schools followed by underutilization, for example. On the other hand, the drawbacks are not yet so obvious as to lead to any clear or strong demand that our policies be reviewed.

URBAN RENEWAL UNDER ATTACK

Urban renewal is one means by which urbanity is returned to the city—stronger commercial centers, cultural centers, new open space, new styles of center city living, a new mix in central city, in which upper-income groups are favored through government action. Its supporters have been central city mayors, trying to maintain the tax bases of their cities; central city economic interests—department store owners, banks; planners and architects, seeing the possibility of new urban forms. It has been resisted by the low-income people who inhabit the older buildings that have been cleared away; by sociologists, anthropologists, and psychologists defending the ways of life of the low-income population, or defending their rights, and concerned with the impact upon them of forced relocation; and by advocates of the free market, who see no reason for the government to subsidize certain types of development, and distort what may be a natural sound adaptation of people to the new technology of the metropolitan area. Herbert Gans's *The Urban Villagers* has been the most powerful criticism of urban renewal from the point of view of the low-income population; Martin Anderson's *The Federal Bulldozer* has been the most powerful from the point of view of the advocates of the free market. The defenders of urban renewal have not yet emerged with equally powerful defenses; one may say, cynically, that in view of the interests arrayed in its favor, literary and scholarly defense has been unnecessary.

Nevertheless, under the impact of political unpopularity and intellectual critique and resistance, the urban renewal program has changed. More—if not enough—is now done for the population to be relocated, the stores and businesses that will be uprooted; the role of rehabilitation is now greater in urban renewal, and with new government aids one does not have to be well-to-do to afford the rehabilitation of one's own home; and some projects—in part through the impact of the poverty program—now show a larger participation of the population on the site. Under the Demonstration Cities Program, urban renewal will be transformed into the direction urged by its opponents and critics—all the branches of government, all the forms of aid, for physical and social and psychological ends, will be brought together to improve the central city. The practical difficulties of actually bringing into effect, under American political conditions, an integrated program to improve the living conditions of the people of a neighborhood and prevent loss of property values, change in occupancy to poorer groups, and physical deterioration, are enormous. It remains a question whether this type of city-building and city-renewal can develop the powerful dynamic drive that only one American housing policy has developed—that is, support of new, single-family, home building.

Meanwhile, the score on Mark I urban renewal is still being totted up. Urban renewal has unquestionably reduced the quantity of low-cost housing and raised rents for the poor. On the other hand, in our cities the overall housing stock has been rising faster than the number of households; the average quality of the housing stock has been rising; the number of vacancies is slowly increasing. Thus, this increase in housing costs is matched, overall, by an increase in housing quality. Is this increase in housing quality essential, when there were so many poor who would have preferred their poorer housing at lower rents? One may take this side of the argument—but those who take it do not always realize that one necessary implication is that, in doing so, one accepts the legitimacy of a range of freedom of choice in housing by people that a wealthy and socially conscious society tends to restrict at the lower end. Thus, we do not allow people in cities to live in shacks without plumbing. But if we want to give them the freedom to spend only a small proportion of their income on housing, then we must give them this freedom. One cannot have both sides of the argument—insist that we should not undertake housing policies that improve housing and increase housing costs, and insist at the same time that we should not tolerate slums.

The increase in housing costs for the poorest as a result of urban renewal's destruction of cheap housing (which plays only a small role actually in eliminating cheap housing—other public and private investment policies have a much larger effect) has been to some extent matched by a general increase in income; but urban renewal raises sharply the need either to establish minimum incomes so that people can afford the minimum housing that society insists they occupy, or to subsidize the housing costs directly.

Criticism III: Are We Building Good Communities?

We come now to the last major criticism of American housing policies—that they have not created good communities. We have in part already considered this criticism in our discussion of the problems of balanced communities. Once again, this criticism has both an aesthetic and social side, and ranges from the attack on urban sprawl to the critique of a dreary suburbia. Once again, Herbert Gans has had some of the wisest things to say about this. In his huge study, *The Levittowners*, he argues that those who accepted the relatively unplanned community of the developer, built on the basis of Federal policies that stabilized a flow of cheap mortgage credit for minimum single-family homes, on the whole got what they wanted. They did not suffer when they moved out of the central city. They gained space, a new house well-equipped with modern machinery, new schools for the children, bright new shopping facilities. The sufferers were the young housewives, who could not get out and away easily, and the adolescents, for whom there were too few facilities. (Gans indicates how better planning might have accommodated the needs of these deprived groups; some good public transportation, a few corner drug-and-candy stores, some recreational facilities.) The community was certainly not attractive to intellectuals, incipient intellectuals, and the culturally avant-garde. But few of them actually lived there.

Was this a "community"? The community was being made by those who came to live there, and those who had lived there previously. The developer had supplied only the housing, the inner roads, and the shopping. Perhaps, Gans argues, some of the necessary communal organizations could have been prepared in advance. But the strain of creating them was also fun, and there were national organizations to help.

Socially, the gains of the more fully planned community are as yet still tenuous. Lord Taylor and Sidney Chave show a clear improvement in mental health and health for the planned New Town as against the less planned London County Council Estate. The latter, however, has older people, and more people with medical problems to begin with; the former has attractive clinics as centers for group practice—the evidence is less for planning overall than for planning good health facilities.

Aesthetically, the gains of the planned community are clear. Reston and Columbia will have better looking neighborhoods, admirable town centers, more open land usable for recreation. They will be in competition with less planned developers' communities. If their advantages seem clear to the buyers, then one suspects the developer's community will become as uncommon as the new corner grocery in competition with the super market—another area of enterprise for the small businessman will fall by the way, to the benefit of the consumer, or at least the majority of the consumers.

One of the chief benefits of the planned community is to be found in the saving of open land and recreational land. We can easily contrast the English preservation of "greenbelts" with the despoiling of the American countryside. The advantage for the planned community is clear—and yet once again, the analysis is not generally carried far enough. The English commitment to countryside is based on the power of generally accepted values, in particular the belief that park-like countryside is one of the glories of England and must be maintained. Our countryside is less park-like, more subject to commercial exploitation by farmers which reduces park-likeness. Our population is more motorized and seems to demand more recreational facilities at a distance, and less at home. Our normal home has more space about it, so that some of the virtues of the preserved countryside are enjoyed at home.

The commitment to the maintenance of open land also means that land values rise, because much of it cannot be built on. H. E. Bracey, who has written an interesting book comparing new suburban development in the United States and England, points out that while Bristol, England, and Columbus, Ohio, have about the same population, land for building on the outskirts of Bristol costs $11,200 an acre, while similar building land near Columbus, and closer to the city, costs $1,000 an acre. Part of the difference is caused by the planned withdrawal, in Britain, of land for maintenance as countryside.

The benefits of planning have to be balanced against the costs of planning. To calculate all the costs and all the benefits is difficult. But our approaches to this problem are still too crude to be politically effective. We are quick to calculate the benefits of open land to the exurbanite driving through it to work in the city; we do not calculate the cost to the working men or low-income white collar workers who might, if it were available for building, be able to put up cheap houses on it.

Conclusion

I would conclude that housing policy in this country has permitted the majority of American families to improve their living conditions, and to gain family settings for themselves that were superior to those they left. It has done little for a substantial minority of poor families who have not had the resources to achieve what the society considers (and they do, too) minimally desirable housing; for them, we must devise income maintenance policies that permit them to achieve such housing, or housing subsidies that work to the same effect. Nor has this policy been attractive to urban designers, architects, and all those sensitive to the value of maintaining or achieving subtle unities in the relationships between home, community facilities, work-places, transportation, and natural setting. Just as we are rich enough to provide decent minimal family settings for the economically deprived in our population, so I believe we are rich enough to provide some resources to the aesthetically deprived so as to maintain our more successful urban settings, and to devise new ones. But both new directions of policy must be fed, of course, through the complex procedures of a democratic society; and their proponents must convince the majority that they, too, will benefit from these extensions of our major policy commitments.

C. POVERTY

20. Our Invisible Poor

DWIGHT MACDONALD

In his significantly titled "The Affluent Society" (1958) Professor J. K. Galbraith states that poverty in this country is no longer "a massive affliction [but] more nearly an afterthought." Dr. Galbraith is a humane critic of the American capitalist system, and he is generously indignant about the continued existence of even this nonmassive and afterthoughtish poverty. But the interesting thing about his pronouncement, aside from the fact that it is inaccurate, is that it was generally accepted as obvious. For a long time now, almost everybody has assumed that, because of the New Deal's social legislation and—more important—the prosperity we have enjoyed since 1940, mass poverty no longer exists in this country.

Dr. Galbraith states that our poor have dwindled to two hard-core categories. One is the "insular poverty" of those who live in the rural South or in depressed areas like West Virginia. The other category is "case poverty," which he says is "commonly and properly related to [such] characteristics of the individuals so afflicted [as] mental deficiency, bad health, inability to adapt to the discipline of modern economic life, excessive procreation, alcohol, insufficient education." He reasons that such poverty must be due to individual defects, since "nearly everyone else has mastered his environment; this proves that it is not intractable." Without pressing the similarity of this concept to the "Social Darwinism" whose fallacies Dr. Galbraith easily disposes of elsewhere in his book, one may observe that most of these characteristics are as much the result of poverty as its cause.

Dr. Galbraith's error is understandable, and common. Last April the newspapers reported some exhilarating statistics in a Department of Commerce study: the average family income increased from $2,340 in 1929 to $7,020 in 1961. (These figures are calculated in current dollars, as are all the others I shall cite.) But the papers did not report the fine type, so to speak, which showed that almost all the recent gain was made by families with incomes of over $7,500, and that the rate at which poverty is being eliminated has slowed down alarmingly since 1953. Only the specialists and the statisticians read the fine type, which is why illusions continue to exist about American poverty.

Now Michael Harrington, an alumnus of the *Catholic Worker* and the Fund for the Republic who is at present a contributing editor of *Dissent* and the chief editor of the Socialist Party biweekly, *New America*, has written "The Other America: Poverty in the United States" (Macmillan). In the admirably short space of under two hundred pages, he outlines the problem, describes in imaginative detail what it means to be poor in this country today, summarizes the findings of recent studies by economists and sociologists, and analyzes the reasons for the persistence of mass poverty in the midst of general prosperity.

In the last year we seem to have suddenly awakened, rubbing our eyes like Rip van Winkle, to the fact that mass poverty persists, and that it is one of our two gravest social problems. (The other is related: While only eleven per cent of our population is non-white, twenty-five per cent of our poor are.) What is "poverty"? It is a historically relative concept, first of all. "There are new definitions [in America] of what man can achieve, of what a human standard of life should be," Mr. Harrington writes. "Those who suffer levels of life well below those that are possible, even though they live better than medieval knights or Asian peasants, are poor. . . . Poverty should be defined in terms of those who are denied the minimal levels of health, housing, food, and education that our present stage of scientific knowledge specifies for life as it it is now lived in the United States." His dividing line follows that proposed in recent studies by the United States Bureau of Labor Statistics: $4,000 a year for a family of four and $2,000 for an individual living alone. (All kinds of income are included, such as food grown and consumed on farms.) This is the cutoff line generally drawn today.

Mr. Harrington estimates that between forty and fifty million Americans, or about a fourth of the population, are now living in poverty. Not just below the level of comfortable living, but real poverty, in the old-fashioned sense of the word—that they are hard put to it to get the mere necessities, beginning with enough to eat. This is difficult to believe in the United States of 1963, but one has to make the effort, and it is now being made. The extent of our poverty has suddenly become visible. The same thing has happened in England, where working-class gains as a result of the Labour Party's post-1945 welfare state blinded almost everybody to the continued existence of mass poverty. It was not until Professor Richard M. Titmuss, of the London School of Economics, published a series of articles in the *New Statesman* last fall, based on his new book, "Income Distribution and Social Change" (Allen & Unwin), that even the liberal public in England became aware that the problem still persists on a scale that is "statistically significant," as the economists put it.

The Limits of Statistics

Statistics on poverty are even trickier than most. For example, age and geography make a difference. There is a distinction, which cannot be rendered arithmetically, between poverty and low income. A childless young couple with $3,000 a year is not poor in the way an elderly couple might be with the same income. The young couple's statistical poverty may be temporary inconvenience; if the husband is a graduate student or a skilled worker, there are prospects of later affluence or at least comfort. But the old couple can look forward only to diminishing earnings and increasing medical expenses. So also geographically: A family of four in a small town with $4,000 a year may be better off than a like family in a city—lower rent, no bus fares to get to work, fewer occasions (or temptations) to spend money. Even more so with a rural family. Although allowance is made for the value of the vegetables they may raise to feed themselves, it is impossible to calculate how much money they *don't* spend on clothes, say, or furniture, because they don't have to keep up with the Joneses. Lurking in the crevices of a city, like piranha fish in a Brazilian stream, are numerous tempting opportunities for expenditure, small but voracious, which can strip a budget to its bones in a surprisingly short time.

How Many Poor?

It is not, therefore, surprising to find that there is some disagreement about just how many millions of Americans are poor. The point is that all recent studies* agree that American poverty is still a mass phenomenon.

Thus the Commerce Department's April report estimates there are

17,500,000 families *and* "unattached individuals" with incomes of less than $4,000. How many of the latter are there? "Poverty and Deprivation" (see note below) puts the number of single persons with under $2,000 at 4,000,000. Let us say that in the 17,500,000 under $4,000 there are 6,500,000 single persons—the proportion of unattached individuals tends to go down as income rises. This home-made estimate gives us 11,000,000 families with incomes of under $4,000. Figuring the average American family at three and a half persons—which it is—this makes 38,500,000 individuals in families, or a grand total, if we add in the 4,000,000 "unattached individuals" with under $2,000 a year, of 42,500,000 Americans now living in poverty, which is close to a fourth of the total population.

The reason Dr. Galbraith was able to see poverty as no longer "a massive affliction" is that he used a cutoff of $1,000, which even in 1949, when it was adopted in a Congressional study, was probably too low (the C.I.O. argued for $2,000) and in 1958, when "The Affluent Society" appeared, was simply fantastic.

The model postwar budgets drawn up in 1951 by the Bureau of Labor Statistics to "maintain a level of adequate living" give a concrete idea of what poverty means in this country—or would mean if poor families lived within their income and spent it wisely, which they don't. Dr. Kolko summarizes the kind of living these budgets provide:

> Three members of the family see a movie once every three weeks, and one member sees a movie once every two weeks. There is no telephone in the house, but the family makes three pay calls a week. They buy one book a year and write one letter a week.
>
> The father buys one heavy wool suit every two years and a light wool suit every three years; the wife, one suit every ten years or one skirt every five years. Every three or four years, depending on the distance and time involved, the family takes a vacation outside their own city. In 1950, the family spent a total of $80 to $90 on all types of home furnishings, electrical appliances, and laundry equipment. . . . The family eats cheaper cuts of meat several times a week, but has more expensive cuts on holidays. The entire family consumes a total of two five-cent ice cream cones, one five-cent candy bar, two bottles of soda, and one bottle of beer a week. The family owes no money, but has no savings except for a small insurance policy.

One other item is included in the B.L.S. "maintenance" budget: a new car every twelve to eighteen years.

This is an ideal picture, drawn up by social workers, of how a poor family *should* spend its money. But the poor are much less provident—installment debts take up a lot of their cash, and only a statistician could expect an actual live woman, however poor, to buy new clothes at intervals of five or ten years. Also, one suspects that a lot more movies are seen and ice-cream cones and bottles of beer are consumed than in the Spartan ideal. But these necessary luxuries are had only at the cost of displacing other items—necessary, so to speak —in the B.L.S. budget.

The Conference on Economic Progress's "Poverty and Deprivation" deals not only with the poor but also with another large section of the "underprivileged," which is an American euphemism almost as good as "senior citizen"; namely, the 37,000,000 persons whose family income is between $4,000 and $5,999 and the 2,000,000 singles who have from $2,000 to $2,999. The authors define "deprivation" as "above poverty but short of minimum requirements for a modestly comfortable level of living." They claim that 77,000,000 Americans, or *almost half the population*, live in poverty or deprivation. One recalls the furor Roosevelt aroused with his "one-third of a nation—ill housed, ill-clad, ill-nourished." But the political climate was different then.

The distinction between a family income of $3,500 ("poverty") and $4,500 ("deprivation") is not vivid to those who run things—the 31 per cent whose incomes are between $7,500 and $14,999 and the 7 per cent of the top-most top dogs, who get $15,000 or more. These two minorities, sizable enough to feel they *are* the nation, have been as unaware of the continued existence of mass poverty as this reviewer was until he read Mr. Harrington's book. They are businessmen, congressmen, judges, government officials, politicians, lawyers, doctors, engineers, scientists, editors, journalists, and administrators in colleges, churches, and foundations. Since their education, income, and social status are superior, they, if anybody, might be expected to accept responsibility for what the Constitution calls "the general welfare." They have not done so in the case of the poor. And they have a good excuse. It is becoming harder and harder simply to *see* the one-fourth of our fellow-citizens who live below the poverty line.

> The poor are increasingly slipping out of the very experience and consciousness of the nation [Mr. Harrington writes]. If the middle class never did like ugliness and poverty, it was at least aware of them. "Across the tracks" was not a very long way to go. . . . Now the American city has been transformed. The poor still inhabit the miserable housing in the central area, but they are increasingly isolated from contact with, or sight of, anybody else. . . . Living out in the suburbs, it is easy to assume that ours is, indeed, an affluent society. . . .
>
> Clothes make the poor invisible too: America has the best-dressed poverty the world has ever known. . . . It is much easier in the

United States to be decently dressed than it is to be decently housed, fed, or doctored. . . .

Many of the poor are the wrong age to be seen. A good number of them are sixty-five years of age or better; an even larger number are under eighteen. . . .

And finally, the poor are politically invisible. . . . They are without lobbies of their own; they put forward no legislative program. As a group, they are atomized. They have no face; they have no voice. . . . Only the social agencies have a really direct involvement with the other America, and they are without any great political power. . . .

Forty to fifty million people are becoming increasingly invisible.

These invisible people fall mostly into the following categories, some of them overlapping: poor farmers, who operate 40 per cent of the farms and get 7 per cent of the farm cash income; migratory farm workers; unskilled, unorganized workers in offices, hotels, restaurants, hospitals, laundries, and other service jobs; inhabitants of areas where poverty is either endemic ("peculiar to a people or district"), as in the rural South, or epidemic ("prevalent among a community at a special time and produced by some special causes"), as in West Virginia, where the special cause was the closing of coal mines and steel plants; Negroes and Puerto Ricans, who are a fourth of the total poor; the alcoholic derelicts in the big-city skid rows; the hillbillies from Kentucky, Tennessee, and Oklahoma who have migrated to Midwestern cities in search of better jobs. And, finally, almost half our "senior citizens."

THE WRONG COLOR

The most obvious citizens of the Other America are those whose skins are the wrong color. The folk slogans are realistic: "Last to be hired, first to be fired" and "If you're black, stay back." There has been some progress. In 1939, the non-white worker's wage averaged 41.4 per cent of the white worker's; by 1958 it had climbed to 58 per cent. A famous victory, but the non-whites still average only slightly more than half as much as the whites. Even this modest gain was due not to any Rooseveltian or Trumanian social reform but merely to the fact that for some years there was a war on and workers were in demand, whether black, white, or violet. By 1947, the non-whites had achieved most of their advance—to 54 per cent of white earnings, which means they have gained, in the last fifteen years, just 4 per cent.

The least obvious poverty affects our "senior citizens"—those over sixty-five. Mr. Harrington estimates that half of them—8,000,000—live in poverty, and he thinks they are even more atomized and politically helpless than the rest of the Other America. He estimates that one-fourth of the "unrelated individuals" among them, or a million persons, have less than $580 a year, which is about what is allotted *for food alone* in the Department of Agriculture's minimum-subsistence budget. (The average American family now spends only 20 per cent of its income for food—an indication of the remarkable prosperity we are all enjoying, except for one-quarter of us.) One can imagine, or perhaps one can't, what it would be like to live on $580 a year, or $11 a week. It is only fair to note that most of our senior citizens do better: The average per capita income of those over sixty-five is now estimated to be slightly over $20 a week. That is, $1,000 a year.

The aged poor have two sources of income besides their earnings or savings. One is contributions by relatives. A 1961 White House Conference Report put this at 10 per cent of income, which works out to $8 a week for an income of $4,000—and the 8,000,000 aged poor all have less than that. The other is Social Security, whose benefits in 1959 averaged $18 a week. Even this modest sum is more than any of the under-$4,000 got, since payments are proportionate to earnings and the poor, of course, earned less than the rest. A quarter of them, and those in general the neediest, are not covered by Social Security. The last resort is relief, and Mr. Harrington describes most vividly the humiliations the poor often have to put up with to get that.

The whole problem of poverty and the aged is especially serious today because Americans are living longer. In the first half of this century, life expectancy increased 17.6 years for men and 20.3 years for woman. And between 1950 and 1960 the over-sixty-five group increased twice as fast as the population as a whole.

The worst part of being old and poor in this country is the loneliness. Mr. Harrington notes that we have not only racial ghettos but geriatric ones, in the cheap rooming-house districts of large cities. He gives one peculiarly disturbing statistic: "One-third of the aged in the United States, some 5,000,000 or more human beings, have no phone in their place of residence. They are literally cut off from the rest of America."

Ernest Hemingway's celebrated deflation of Scott Fitzgerald's romantic notion that the rich are "different" somehow—"Yes, they have money"—doesn't apply to the poor. They are different in more important ways than their lack of money, as Mr. Harrington demonstrates:

> Emotional upset is one of the main forms of the vicious circle of impoverishment. The structure of the society is hostile to these people.

> The poor tend to become pessimistic and depressed; they seek immediate gratification instead of saving; they act out.
>
> Once this mood, this unarticulated philosophy becomes a fact, society can change, the recession can end, and yet there is no motive for movement. The depression has become internalized. The middle class looks upon this process and sees "lazy" people who "just don't want to get ahead." People who are much too sensitive to demand of cripples that they run races ask of the poor that they get up and act just like everyone else in the society.
>
> The poor are not like everyone else. . . . They think and feel differently; they look upon a different America than the middle class looks upon.

The poor are also different in a physical sense: they are much less healthy. According to "Poverty and Deprivation," the proportion of those "disabled or limited in their major activity by chronic ill health" rises sharply as income sinks. In reasonably well-off families ($7,000 and up), 4.3 per cent are so disabled; in reasonably poor families ($2,000 to $3,999), the proportion doubles, to 8 per cent; and in unreasonably poor families (under $2,000), it doubles again, to 16.5 per cent. An obvious cause, among others, for the very poor being four times as much disabled by "chronic ill health" as the well-to-do is that they have much less money to spend for medical care—in fact, almost nothing. This weighs with special heaviness on the aged poor. During the fifties, Mr. Harrington notes, "all costs on the Consumer Price Index went up by 12 per cent. But medical costs, that terrible staple of the aged, went up by 36 per cent, hospitalization rose by 65 per cent, and group hospitalization costs (Blue Cross premiums) were up by 83 per cent."

The Defeat of Medicare

This last figure is particularly interesting, since Blue Cross and such plans are the A.M.A.'s alternative to socialized medicine, or, rather, to the timid fumblings toward it that even our most liberal politicians have dared to propose. Such figures throw an unpleasant light on the Senate's rejection of Medicare. The defeat was all the more bitter because, in the usual effort to appease the conservatives (with the usual lack of success—only five Republicans and only four Southern Democrats voted pro), the bill was watered down in advance. Not until he had spent $90 of his own money—which is 10 per cent of the annual income of some 3,000,000 aged poor—would a patient have been eligible. And the original program included only people already covered by Social Security or Railroad Retirement pensions and excluded the neediest of all—the 2,500,000 aged poor who are left out of both these systems.

Mental as well as physical illness is much greater among the poor, even though our complacent cliché is that nervous breakdowns are a prerogative of the rich because the poor "can't afford them." (They can't, but they have them anyway.) This bit of middle-class folklore should be laid to rest by a study made in New Haven: "Social Class and Mental Illness," by August B. Hollingshead and Frederick C. Redlich (Wiley). They found that the rate of "treated psychiatric illness" is about the same from the rich down through decently paid workers—an average of 573 per 100,000. But in the bottom fifth it shoots up to 1,659 per 100,000. There is an even more striking difference in the *kind* of mental illness. Of those in the four top income groups who had undergone psychiatric treatment, 65 per cent had been treated for neurotic problems and 35 per cent for psychotic disturbances. In the bottom fifth, the treated illnesses were almost all psychotic (90 per cent). This shows there is something to the notion that the poor "can't afford" nervous breakdowns—the milder kind, that is—since the reason the proportion of *treated* neuroses among the poor is only 10 per cent is that a neurotic can keep going, after a fashion. But the argument cuts deeper the other way. The poor go to a psychiatrist (or, more commonly, are committed to a mental institution) only when they are completely unable to function because of psychotic symptoms. Therefore, even that nearly threefold increase in mental disorders among the poor is probably an underestimate.

The main reason the American poor have become invisible is that since 1936 their numbers have been reduced by two-thirds. Astounding as it may seem, the fact is that President Roosevelt's "one-third of a nation" was a considerable understatement; over two-thirds of us then lived below the poverty line, as is shown by the tables that follow. But today the poor are a minority, and minorities can be ignored if they are so heterogeneous that they cannot be organized. When the poor were a majority, they simply could not be overlooked. Poverty is also hard to see today because the middle class ($6,000 to $14,999) has vastly increased—from 13 per cent of all families in 1936 to a near-majority (47 per cent) today. That mass poverty can persist despite this rise to affluence is hard to believe, or see, especially if one is among those who have risen.

Two tables in "Poverty and Deprivation" summarize what has been happening in the last thirty years. They cover only multiple-person families; all figures are converted to 1960 dollars; and the income is before taxes. I have omitted, for clarity, all fractions.

The first table is the percentage of families with a given income.

	1935-36	1947	1953	1960
Under $ 4,000	68%	37%	28%	23%
$4,000 to $ 5,999	17	29	28	23
$6,000 to $ 7,499	6	12	17	16
$7,500 to $14,999	7	17	23	31
Over $15,000	2	4	5	7

The second table is the share each group had in the family income of the nation:

	1935-36	1947	1953	1960
Under $ 4,000	35%	16%	11%	7%
$4,000 to $ 5,999	21	24	21	15
$6,000 to $ 7,499	10	14	17	14
$7,500 to $14,999	16	28	33	40
Over $15,000	18	18	19	24

Several interesting conclusions can be drawn from these tables:

(1) The New Deal didn't do anything about poverty: The under-$4,000 families in 1936 were 68 per cent of the total population, which was slightly *more* than the 1929 figure of 65 per cent.

(2) The war economy (hot and cold) did do something about poverty: Between 1936 and 1960 the proportion of all families who were poor was reduced from 68 per cent to 23 per cent.

(3) If the percentage of under-$4,000 families decreased by two-thirds between 1936 and 1960, their share of the national income dropped a great deal more—from 35 per cent to 7 per cent.

(4) The well-to-do ($7,500 to $14,999) have enormously increased, from 7 per cent of all families in 1936 to 31 per cent today. The rich ($15,000 and over) have also multiplied—from 2 to 7 per cent. But it should be noted that the very rich, according to another new study, "The Share of Top Wealth-Holders in National Wealth, 1822-1956," by Robert J. Lampman (Princeton), have experienced a decline. He finds that the top 1 per cent of wealth-holders owned 38 per cent of the national wealth in 1929 and own only 28 per cent today.

(5) The reduction of poverty has slowed down. In the six years 1947-53, the number of poor families declined 9 per cent, but in the following seven years only 5 per cent. The economic stasis that set in with Eisenhower and that still persists under Kennedy was responsible. (This stagnation, however, did not affect the over-$7,500 families, who increased from 28 per cent to 38 per cent between 1953 and 1960.) In the New York *Times Magazine* for last November 11th, Herman P. Miller, of the Bureau of the Census, wrote, "During the

forties, the lower-paid occupations made the greatest relative gains in average income. Laborers and service workers . . . had increases of about 180% . . . and professional and managerial workers, the highest paid workers of all, had the lowest relative gains—96%." But in the last decade the trend has been reversed; laborers and service workers have gained 39% while professional-managerial workers have gained 68%. This is because in the wartime forties the unskilled were in great demand, while now they are being replaced by machines. Automation is today the same kind of menace to the unskilled—that is, the poor—that the enclosure movement was to the British agricultural population centuries ago. "The facts show that our 'social revolution' ended nearly twenty years ago," Mr. Miller concludes, "yet important segments of the American public, many of them highly placed Government officials and prominent educators, think and act as though it were a continuing process."

The post-1940 decrease in poverty was not due to the policies or actions of those who are not poor, those in positions of power and responsibility. The war economy needed workers, wages went up, and the poor became less poor. When economic stasis set in, the rate of decrease in poverty slowed down proportionately, and it is still slow. Kennedy's efforts to "get the country moving again" have been unsuccessful, possibly because he has, despite the suggestions of many of his economic advisers, not yet advocated the one big step that might push the economy off dead center: a massive increase in government spending. This would be politically courageous, perhaps even dangerous, because of the superstitious fear of "deficit spending" and an "unbalanced" federal budget. American folklore insists that a government's budget must be arranged like a private family's. Walter Lippmann wrote, after the collapse of the stock market last spring:

> There is mounting evidence that those economists were right who told the Administration last winter that it was making the mistake of trying to balance the budget too soon. It will be said that the budget is not balanced: it shows a deficit in fiscal 1962 of $7 billion. . . . But . . . the budget that matters is the Department of Commerce's income and product accounts budget. Nobody looks at it except the economists [but] while the Administrative budget is necessary for administration and is like a man's checkbook, the income budget tells the real story. . . .
>
> [It] shows that at the end of 1962 the outgo and ingo accounts will be virtually in balance, with a deficit of only about half a billion dollars. Thus, in reality, the Kennedy administration is no longer stimulating the economy, and the economy is stagnating for lack of stimulation. We have one of the lowest rates of growth among the advanced industrial nations of the world.

One shouldn't be hard on the President. Franklin Roosevelt, a more daring and experimental politician, at least in his domestic policy, listened to the American disciples of J. M. Keynes in the early New Deal years and unbalanced his budgets, with splendid results. But by 1936 he had lost his nerve. He cut back government spending and there ensued the 1937 recession, from which the economy recovered only when war orders began to make up for the deficiency in domestic buying power. "Poverty and Deprivation" estimates that between 1953 and 1961 the annual growth rate of our economy was "only 2.5 per cent per annum contrasted with an estimated 4.2 per cent required to maintain utilization of manpower and other productive resources." The poor, who always experience the worst the first, understand quite personally the meaning of that dry statistic, as they understand Kipling's "The toad beneath the harrow knows/Exactly where each toothpoint goes." They are also most intimately acquainted with another set of statistics: the steady postwar rise in the unemployment rate, from 3.1 per cent in 1949 to 4.3 per cent in 1954 to 5.1 per cent in 1958 to over 7 per cent in 1961. (The Tory Government is worried because British unemployment is now at its highest point for the last three years. This point is 2.1 per cent, which is less than our lowest rate in the last fifteen years.)

It's not that Public Opinion doesn't become Aroused every now and then. But the arousement never leads to much. It was aroused twenty-four years ago when John Steinbeck published "The Grapes of Wrath," but Mr. Harrington reports that things in the Imperial Valley are still much the same: low wages, bad housing, no effective union. Public Opinion is too public—that is, too general; of its very nature, it can have no sustained interest in California agriculture. The only groups with such a continuing interest are the workers and the farmers who hire them. Once Public Opinion ceased to be Aroused, the battle was again between the two antagonists with a real, personal stake in the outcome, and there was no question about which was stronger. So with the rural poor in general. In the late fifties, the average annual wage for white male American farm workers was slightly over $1,000; women, children, Negroes, and Mexicans got less. One recalls Edward R. Murrow's celebrated television program about these people, "Harvest of Shame." Once more everybody was shocked, but the harvest is still shameful. One also recalls that Mr. Murrow, after President Kennedy had appointed him head of the United States Information Agency, tried to persuade the B.B.C. not to show "Harvest of Shame." His argument was that it would give an undesirable "image" of America to foreign audiences.

There is a monotony about the injustices suffered by the poor that perhaps accounts for the lack of interest the rest of society shows in them. Everything seems to go wrong with them. They never win. It's just boring.

"ADDRESS UNKNOWN"

Public housing turns out not to be for them. The 1949 Housing Act authorized 810,000 new units of low-cost housing in the following four years. Twelve years later, in 1961, the AFL-CIO proposed 400,000 units to complete the lagging 1949 program. The Kennedy administration ventured to recommend 100,000 to Congress. Thus, instead of 810,000 low-cost units by 1953, the poor will get, if they are lucky, 500,000 by 1963. And they are more likely to be injured than helped by slum clearance, since the new projects usually have higher rents than the displaced slum-dwellers can afford. (There has been no dearth of government-financed *middle*-income housing since 1949.) These refugees from the bulldozers for the most part simply emigrate to other slums. They also become invisible; Mr. Harrington notes that half of them are recorded as "address unknown." Several years ago, Charles Abrams, who was New York State Rent Administrator under Harriman and who is now president of the National Committee Against Discrimination in Housing, summed up what he had learned in two decades in public housing: "Once social reforms have won tonal appeal in the public mind, their slogans and goal-symbols may degenerate into tools of the dominant class for beleaguering the minority and often for defeating the very aims which the original sponsors had intended for their reforms."

And this is not the end of tribulation. The poor, who can least afford to lose pay because of ill health, lose the most. A National Health Survey, made a few years ago, found that workers earning under $2,000 a year had twice as many "restricted-activity days" as those earning over $4,000.

Although they are the most in need of hospital insurance, the poor have the least, since they can't afford the premiums; only 40 per cent of poor families have it, as against 63 per cent of all families. (It should be noted, however, that the poor who are war veterans can get free treatment, at government expense, in Veterans Administration Hospitals.)

The poor actually pay more taxes, in proportion to their income, than the rich. A recent study by the Tax Foundation estimates that 28 per cent of incomes under $2,000 goes for taxes, as against 24 per cent of the incomes of families earning five to seven times as much. Sales and other excise taxes are largely responsible for this curious statistic. It is true that such taxes fall impartially on all, like the blessed rain from heaven, but it is a form of egalitarianism that perhaps only Senator Goldwater can fully appreciate.

The final irony is that the Welfare State, which Roosevelt erected and which Eisenhower, no matter how strongly he felt about it, didn't attempt to pull down, is not for the poor, either. Agricultural workers are not covered by Social Security, nor are many of the desperately poor among the aged, such as "unrelated individuals" with incomes of less than $1,000, of whom only 37 per cent are covered, which is just half the percentage of coverage among the aged in general. Of the Welfare State, Mr. Harrington says, "Its creation had been stimulated by mass impoverishment and misery, yet it helped the poor least of all. Laws like unemployment compensation, the Wagner Act, the various farm programs, all these were designed for the middle third in the cities, for organized workers, and for the . . . big market farmers. . . . [It] benefits those least who need help most." The industrial workers, led by John L. Lewis, mobilized enough political force to put through Section 7(a) of the National Industrial Recovery Act, which, with the Wagner Act, made the CIO possible. The big farmers put enough pressure on Henry Wallace, Roosevelt's first Secretary of Agriculture—who talked a good fight for liberal principles but was a Hamlet when it came to action—to establish the two basic propositions of Welfare State agriculture: subsidies that now cost $3 billion a year and that chiefly benefit the big farmers; and the exclusion of sharecroppers, tenant farmers, and migratory workers from the protection of minimum-wage and Social Security laws.

No doubt the Kennedy administration would like to do more for the poor than it has, but it is hampered by the cabal of Republicans and Southern Democrats in Congress. The 1961 revision of the Fair Labor Standards Act, which raised the national minimum wage to the not exorbitant figure of $1.15 an hour, was a slight improvement over the previous act. For instance, it increased coverage of retail-trade workers from 3 per cent to 33 per cent. (But one-fourth of the retail workers still excluded earn less than $1 an hour.) There was also a considerable amount of shadow-boxing involved: Of the 3,600,000 workers newly covered, only 663,000 were making less than $1 an hour. And there was the exclusion of a particularly ill-paid group of workers. Nobody had anything against the laundry workers *personally*. It was just that they were weak, unorganized, and politically expendable. To appease the conservatives in Congress, whose votes were needed to get the revision through, they were therefore expended. The result is that of the 500,000 workers in the laundry,

dry-cleaning, and dyeing industries, just 17,000 are now protected by the Fair Labor Standards Act.

PERPETUATING POVERTY

It seems likely that mass poverty will continue in this country for a long time. The more it is reduced, the harder it is to keep on reducing it. The poor, having dwindled from two-thirds of the population in 1936 to one-quarter today, no longer are a significant political force, as is shown by the Senate's rejection of Medicare and by the Democrats' dropping it as an issue in the elections last year. Also, as poverty decreases, those left behind tend more and more to be the ones who have for so long accepted poverty as their destiny that they need outside help to climb out of it. This new minority mass poverty, so much more isolated and hopeless than the old majority poverty, shows signs of becoming chronic. "The permanence of low incomes is inferred from a variety of findings," write the authors of the Morgan survey. "In many poor families the head has never earned enough to cover the family's present needs."

> For most families, however, the problem of chronic poverty is serious. One such family is headed by a thirty-two-year-old man who is employed as a dishwasher. Though he worked steadily and more than full time, he earned over $2,000 in 1959. His wife earned $300 more, but their combined incomes are not enough to support themselves and their three children. Although the head of the family is only thirty-two, he feels that he has no chance of advancement partly because he finished only seven grades of school. . . . The possibility of such families leaving the ranks of the poor is not high.

Children born into poor families today have less chance of "improving themselves" than the children of the pre-1940 poor. Rags to riches is now more likely to be rags to rags. "Indeed," the Morgan book concludes, "it appears that a number of the heads of poor families have moved into less skilled jobs than their fathers had." Over a third of the children of the poor, according to the survey, don't go beyond the eighth grade and "will probably perpetuate the poverty of their parents." There are a great many of these children. In an important study of poverty, made for a Congressional committee in 1959, Dr. Robert J. Lampman estimated that eleven million of the poor were under eighteen. "A considerable number of younger persons are starting life in a condition of 'inherited poverty,' " he observed. To which Mr. Harrington adds, "The character of poverty has changed, and it has become more deadly for the young. It is no longer associated with immigrant groups with high aspirations; it is now identified with those whose social existence makes it more and more difficult to break out into the larger society." Even when children from poor families show intellectual promise, there is nothing in the values of their friends or families to encourage them to make use of it. Of the top 16 per cent of high-school students—those scoring 120 and over in I.Q. tests—only half go on to college. The explanation for this amazing—and alarming—situation is as much cultural as economic. The children of the poor now tend to lack what the sociologists call "motivation." At least one foundation is working on the problem of why so many bright children from poor families don't ever try to go beyond high school.

Mr. Raymond M. Hilliard, at present director of the Cook County (i.e., Chicago) Department of Public Aid and formerly Commissioner of Welfare for New York City, recently directed a "representative-sample" investigation, which showed that more than half of the 225,000 able-bodied Cook County residents who were on relief were "functionally illiterate." One reason Cook County has to spend $16,500,000 a month on relief is "the lack of basic educational skills of relief recipients which are essential to compete in our modern society." An interesting footnote, apropos of recent happenings at "Ole Miss," is that the illiteracy rate of the relief recipients who were educated in Chicago is 33 per cent, while among those who were educated in Mississippi and later moved to Chicago it is 77 per cent.

Slums and Schools

The problem of educating the poor has changed since 1900. Then it was the language and cultural difficulties of immigrants from foreign countries; now it is the subtler but more intractable problems of internal migration from backward regions, mostly in the South. The old immigrants wanted to Better Themselves and to Get Ahead. The new migrants are less ambitious, and they come into a less ambitious atmosphere. "When they arrive in the city," wrote Christopher Jencks in an excellent two-part survey, "Slums and Schools," in the *New Republic* last fall, "they join others equally unprepared for urban life in the slums—a milieu which is in many ways utterly dissociated from the rest of America. Often this milieu is self-perpetuating. I have been unable to find any statistics on how many of these migrants' children and grandchildren have become middle-class, but it is probably not too inaccurate to estimate that about 30,000,000 people live in urban slums, and that about half are second-generation residents." The immigrants of 1890-1910 also arrived in a milieu that was "in many ways utterly dissociated from the rest of America," yet they had a vision—a rather materialistic one, but still a vision—of what life in America could be if they worked hard enough; and they did work, and they did aspire to something more than they had; and they did get out of the slums. The disturbing thing about the poor today is that so many of them seem to lack any such vision. Mr. Jencks remarks:

> While the economy is changing in a way which makes the eventual liquidation of the slums at least conceivable, young people are not seizing the opportunities this change presents. Too many are dropping out of school before graduation (more than half in many slums); too few are going to college. . . . As a result there are serious shortages of teachers, nurses, doctors, technicians, and scientifically trained executives, but 4,500,000 unemployables.

The federal government is the only purposeful force—I assume wars are not purposeful—that can reduce the numbers of the poor and make their lives more bearable. The effect of government policy on poverty has two quite distinct aspects. One is the indirect effect of the stimulation of the economy by federal spending. Such stimulation—though by war-time demands rather than government policy—has in the past produced a prosperity that did cut down American poverty by almost two-thirds. But I am inclined to agree with Dr. Galbraith that it would not have a comparable effect on present-day poverty:

> It is assumed that with increasing output poverty must disappear [he writes]. Increased output eliminated the general poverty of all who worked. Accordingly it must, sooner or later, eliminate the special poverty that still remains. . . . Yet just as the arithmetic of modern politics makes it tempting to overlook the very poor, so the supposition that increasing output will remedy their case has made it easy to do so too.

He underestimates the massiveness of American poverty, but he is right when he says there is now a hard core of the specially disadvantaged—because of age, race, environment, physical or mental defects, etc.—that would not be significantly reduced by general prosperity. (Although I think the majority of our present poor *would* benefit, if only by a reduction in the present high rate of unemployment.)

To do something about this hard core, a second line of government policy would be required; namely, direct intervention to help the poor. We have had this since the New Deal, but it has always been grudging and miserly, and we have never accepted the principle that every citizen should be provided, at state expense, with a reasonable minimum standard of living regardless of any other considerations. It should not depend on earnings, as does Social Security, which continues the inequalities and inequities and so tends to keep the poor forever poor. Nor should it exclude millions of our poorest citizens because they lack the political pressure to force their way into the Welfare State. The governmental obligation to provide, out of taxes, such a minimum living standard for all who need it should be taken as much for granted as free public schools have always been in our history.

"NOBODY STARVES"

It may be objected that the economy cannot bear the cost, and certainly costs must be calculated. But the point is not the calculation but the principle. Statistics—and especially statistical forecasts—can be pushed one way or the other. Who can determine in advance to what extent the extra expense of giving our 40,000,000 poor enough income to rise above the poverty line would be offset by the lift to the economy from their increased purchasing power? We really don't know. Nor did we know what the budgetary effects would be when we established the principle of free public education. The rationale then was that all citizens should have an equal chance of competing for a better status. The rationale now is different: that every citizen has a right to become or remain part of our society because if this right is denied, as it is in the case of at least one-fourth of our citizens, it impoverishes us all. Since 1932, "the government"—local, state, and federal—has recognized a responsibility to provide its citizens with a subsistence living. Apples will never again be sold on the street by jobless accountants, it seems safe to predict, nor will any serious political leader ever again suggest that share-the-work and local charity can solve the problem of unemployment. "Nobody starves" in this country any more, but, like every social statistic, this is a tricky business. Nobody starves, but who can measure the starvation, not to be calculated by daily intake of proteins and calories, that reduces life for many of our poor to a long vestibule to death? Nobody starves, but every fourth citizen rubs along on a standard of living that is below what Mr. Harrington defines as "the minimal levels of health, housing, food, and education that our present stage of scientific knowledge specifies as necessary for life as it is now lived in the United States." Nobody starves, but a fourth of us are excluded from the common social existence. Not to be able to afford a movie or a glass of beer is a kind of starvation—if everybody else can.

The problem is obvious: the persistence of mass poverty in a prosperous country. The solution is also obvious: to provide, out of taxes, the kind of subsidies that have always been given to the public schools (not to mention the police and fire departments and the post office) —subsidies that would raise incomes above the poverty level, so that every citizen could feel he is indeed such. *"Civis Romanus sum!"* cried St. Paul when he was threatened with flogging—and he was not flogged. Until our poor can be proud to say *"Civis Americanus sum!,"* until the act of justice that would make this possible has been performed by the three-quarters of Americans who are not poor—until then the shame of the Other America will continue.

*The studies, all of which are referred to by the author, include, Dr. Gabriel Kolko, *Wealth & Poverty in America* (Praeger); Dr. James N. Morgan, et al, *Income and Welfare in the United States* (McGraw-Hill); "Poverty and Deprivation" (pamphlet), Conference on Economic Progress, Leon H. Keyserling and others.

21. The Poor Pay More

ESTHER PETERSON

"All we want is some time off from work during the day, so we can shop at the supermarkets near where we work."

The speaker represented a small group of Negro domestic workers who had unexpectedly come to my office shortly after I had been appointed chairman of the Committee on Consumer Interests by President Johnson. She went on to explain that they noticed that the middle-class supermarkets not only seemed to have better values, but were cleaner, and the food was fresher.

Thus, one of the first consumer questions the Committee was asked to examine was if it is true that the low-income consumer is penalized in the modern marketplace. We established a panel of experts from the government, business, universities, and social agencies, who reported in June of last year that the poor *do* pay more. " . . . because of lack of education, skill, and bargain stores in low income neighborhoods," the panel said, "the poor are apt to pay more for comparable merchandise than people in middle income areas."

The panel also asserted that food prices are a grievance in poor, big-city neighborhoods, for residents of low-income neighborhoods often believe they pay more, whether in fact they do or not.

SOURCE: *The Progressive* (January, 1967), pp. 27-29.

In searching for further information, the President's Committee then asked the National Commission on Food Marketing for more authoritative figures. The Commission was making a detailed study of the nation's food distribution system, including reasons for the increasing cost of food to all consumers, without a corresponding increase in return to the farmer. It agreed to our request and contracted with the Bureau of Labor Statistics, the fact-finding arm of the Department of Labor, for a study.

A BLS special report last June 12 revealed that food *did* cost more in low-income neighborhoods of the six major cities surveyed—New York City, Los Angeles, Chicago, Washington, Atlanta, and Houston. In most instances, the higher cost is not the result of deliberate and discriminatory practice. The major fault, rather, lies in the type of food distribution system which serves many low-income neighborhoods. For example, prices on staple items such as bread, milk, eggs, and sugar differed significantly, not so much between chain store branches in low-income and higher-income areas, but between chain stores and smaller independent stores; the latter did tend to charge more.

In all stores in low-income areas there was a lack of orderliness and cleanliness, with prices not marked as clearly, and with meats and produce not as fresh as in the middle-class neighborhoods.

Since the BLS study, corroborating evidence has arrived from other sources. *The New York Times* reported later in the summer that the low-income consumer in Harlem paid a significantly higher price for certain items: up to eighty-nine cents for a dozen eggs, which could have been purchased elsewhere for sixty-nine cents; as high as $1.05 for a pound of butter, or seventeen cents above the city average at the time.

But prices are only part of the story.

The poor also tend to buy in small, uneconomical quantities. As one housewife in a low-income family told me, "If I did have the money and I bought a week's worth of food it would be eaten in a day—and what would we do the rest of the week?" So she left the cupboard as bare as possible, buying only that which would be immediately eaten.

Just as there is a lack of supermarkets in low-income areas, so too, for items other than food, there is a lack of stores which offer the buyer a wide variety of choice, price, and quality. The dearth of large-scale shopping outlets, coupled with the fact that the poor prefer the "friendly," neighborly smiles of the door-to-door peddler or the personal service of the high-rate credit store, brings a definite price penalty.

This penalty is paid because many of the poor never learned the basic shopping skill of value comparison, and hence would rather buy from a man they know than to venture into a different and sometimes alien world.

A recent shopping tour made by low-income consumers in Boston and Providence revealed that the cash price for one type of television set varied from $99 to $189—with the higher prices charged by merchants dealing almost exclusively with welfare recipients. Added to the higher prices are often even more exorbitant credit charges.

Credit is, perhaps, the worst problem. A couple who signed a paper to buy a "custom made" orthopedic mattress and box spring for $22 each did not know, until too late, that taxes, carrying charges, delivery charges, and other fees brought the total cost to $247.

Hidden finance charges are common. Interest rates which are, at times, disguised to exceed the legal maximum, may not be divulged to the buyer. Frequently the buyer does not even know how many payments are due, and when he falls behind he may find his wages garnisheed and in some cases—if the employer is irritated enough by this procedure—lose his job.

In one case, a janitor who was persuaded by a glib salesman to buy two pairs of eyeglasses for $118 and could not maintain his payments, found that part of his meager $22.50 weekly paycheck was garnisheed. Legislative and judicial means can be used to insure that the poor are treated equitably when they use credit. Garnishment laws, all too harsh in many states, need amending and liberalizing.

An upgrading of laws in the states relating to frauds can also be of inestimable help. At present, the poor are often the prey of door-to-door peddlers and sharpster merchants who sell over-priced merchandise on exorbitant credit terms, misrepresenting the product or sale conditions. The perpetrators of such schemes frequently continue their activities for a considerable time after charges have been preferred, because court dockets are crowded and the delaying tactics many. A few states have now adopted injunctive protection, which can be granted when there is a likelihood that a seller "is about to engage in" an illegal practice. Injunctive procedure would halt the practice—a step far more important than other types of court action which permit the shady business to be conducted profitably by new operators.

State consumer fraud bureaus now exist in nineteen states—and their number is on the increase. Here, too, is another significant development that will help to chase out the racketeers—provided that all the fraud bureaus operate under laws that meet present-day needs.

But new laws and better law enforcement are only one part of the answer to correcting the abuses. Laws may provide scaffolding for corrective measures, but they cannot replace the need for a national commitment from all segments of society—from businesses, labor unions, voluntary organizations, and private individuals, as well as the Federal, state, and local governments—to assist in protecting the consumer.

I hope that the private sector assumes its responsibilities. We must, for example, rebuild our inner city marketplace as we are rebuilding our cities, for only an improved food distribution and retail system can lead the attack on the basic causes for the fact that the poor pay more for their food. To be sure, there are many factors which militate against building supermarkets in high-density areas. High land costs and often the unavailability of land; high (and sometimes unobtainable) insurance rates; and higher pilferage rates are among the obstacles.

In discussing this problem with a leading supermarket executive recently, to my gratification I heard him say, "If the will to find the answer is strong enough, the answers will be found."

And answers *can* be found. Perhaps, as I suggested on July 7 before the NAACP convention in Los Angeles, the Federal government could provide below-market interest rate terms on loans to stimulate construction of food markets in low-income neighborhoods, just as it is doing to spur private housing in slum areas.

I do not think that the supermarket executive was referring wholly to Federal aid, for lately such large-scale food markets have been profitably opened by private operators in at least two major cities. In Washington, D.C., a large chain opened a store on August 10 which now is busy serving an area where previously there had been no large market. The store is more than just a store, for it also provides a small park-like area and green space to help beautify the neighborhood. Among its services to consumers is a home economist, available on the premises, to advise customers. In New York City, two new stores in Spanish-speaking neighborhoods stress clean, orderly surroundings. They offer unadvertised specials and other advantages to customers. As one manager said: "They want the store they shop in not to remind them of the circumstances in which they're living." These stores, incidentally, have only minor pilferage problems.

One of the immediate needs of the poor is to obtain credit at a reasonable rate. There must be sources available in addition to the small loan agency or the store where low income families buy their goods. Not only do they need sources of credit badly—for obviously their financial reserves are far thinner than those of the middle class—but they need more flexible credit, perhaps a plan which will provide relief for the sudden emergencies and costs of illness, or loss of income. They may also need a more personalized type of service, one which includes financial counseling together with legal services. The Office of Economic Opportunity has been encouraging the development of credit unions in low-income areas, and this is a welcome step forward.

Another need of the poor is to buy insurance at a rate they can afford. At present, not only are automobile and liability rates extremely high in the inner-city poverty areas, but some casualty companies, fearing future losses, have resorted to large-scale cancellation of policies—whether or not an individual has a good risk record. I hope that the insurance companies can find the will and resources to provide adequate coverage.

The formation of cooperatives—for both buying and selling—also can be of great help. In the South, cooperatives are now being formed to make and market handcrafts and to operate service industries. Their success can help Southern Negroes break a pattern which has kept them dominated.

If the poor, with little cash to spend, are to achieve a net increase in purchasing power, much more than a net increase in income is required.

To help them, the OEO, under its nation-wide Community Action Programs, had approved 139 consumer education projects by August 10. The projects center around homemaker services, credit unions, cooperatives, legal services, consumer counseling, and consumer information.

These activities show good promise of success for they stress not book problems, but the daily task of eliminating wasteful expenditures and inefficient and costly ways of doing things. Their purpose is not to change values, nor to provide a panacea for poverty, but simply to help the poor become better consumers within the restricting limits of the poverty income. By stressing immediate, short-term goals, the program hopes to achieve long-range success.

The experience of social workers bears out the fact that all such programs must focus on counseling—legal, financial, health, nutritional—and that the needs are so many that cooperative action is necessary by business and private organizations as well as local, state, and Federal governments.

One community leader in Baltimore found that his discussions on "family life" were turning to questions on consumer problems. These informal sessions later became the nucleus of two consumer conferences which attracted more than 1,000 low-income people.

A Chicago family agency offered free sewing and millinery lessons to newcomers from the rural South. To find out about sewing and materials, the class took trips to the stores, where they also were advised on other related problems.

In Milwaukee, store-front ministers asked a speaker at a church conference to give them a course in financial management. The ultimate result was a credit union for low-paid factory workers.

No poverty program can succeed unless an educational program is an integral part. But to start these programs requires local initiative, and it requires that the people who are interested in helping others be more than do-gooders.

Our social philosophy now recognizes that the consciences of the upper four-fifths of the nation cannot be salved by good intentions. To help the lower fifth is a primary task of our national domestic policy and individual morality. We must, as President Johnson said when he established the Committee on Consumer Interests, "develop as promptly as possible effective ways and means of reaching more homes and more families—particularly low-income families—with information to help them to get the most for their money."

D. EDUCATION

22. Equal Schools or Equal Students?

JAMES S. COLEMAN

The Civil Rights Act of 1964 contains a section numbered 402, which went largely unnoticed at the time. This section instructs the Commissioner of Education to carry out a survey of "concerning the lack of availability of equal educational opportunities" by reason of race, religion or national origin, and to report to Congress and the President within two years. The Congressional intent in this section is somewhat unclear. But if, as is probable, the survey was initially intended as a means of finding areas of continued intentional discrimination, the intent later became less punitive-oriented and more future-oriented: *i.e.,* to provide a basis for public policy, at the local, state, and national levels, which might overcome inequalities of educational opportunity.

In the two years that have intervened (but mostly in the second), a remarkably vast and comprehensive survey was conducted, focussing principally on the inequalities of educational opportunity experienced by five racial and ethnic minorities: Negroes, Puerto Ricans, Mexican Americans, American Indians, and Oriental Americans. In the central and largest portion of the survey, nearly 600,000 children at grades 1, 3, 6, 9, and 12, in 4000 schools in all 50 states and the District of Columbia, were tested and questioned; 60,000 teachers in these schools were questioned and self-tested; and principals of these schools were also questioned about their schools. The tests and questionnaires (administered in the fall of 1965 by Educational Testing Service) raised a considerable controversy in public school circles and among some parents, with concern ranging from Federal encroachment

SOURCE: © 1966 by National Affairs, Inc. From *The Public Interest* (Summer, 1966), pp. 70-75.

on the local education system to the spectre of invasion of privacy. Nevertheless, with a participation rate of about 70% of all the schools sampled, the survey was conducted; and on July 1, 1966, Commissioner Howe presented a summary report of this survey. On July 31, the total report, *Equality of Educational Opportunity,* 737 pages, was made available (Government Printing Office, $4.25).

The summary of the report has appeared to many who have read it to be curiously "flat," lacking in emphases and policy implications. Much of the same flatness can be found in the larger report. The seeming flatness probably derives from three sources: the research analyst's uneasiness in moving from description to implications; the government agency's uneasiness with survey findings that may have political repercussions; and, perhaps more important than either of these, the fact that the survey results do not lend themselves to the provision of simple answers. Nevertheless, the report is not so uncontroversial as it appears. And some of its findings, though cautiously presented, have sharp implications.

Perhaps the greatest virtue of this survey—though it has many faults—is that it did not take a simple or politically expedient view of educational opportunity. To have done so would have meant to measure (a) the objective characteristics of schools—number of books in the library, age of buildings, educational level of teachers, accreditation of the schools, and so on; and (b) the actual extent of racial segregation in the schools. The survey did look into these matters (and found less inequity in school facilities and resources, more in the extent of segregation, than is commonly supposed); but its principal focus of attention was not on what resources go into education, but on what product comes out. It did this in a relatively uncomplicated way, which is probably adequate for the task at hand: by tests which measured those areas of achievement most necessary for further progress in school, in higher education, and in successful competition in the labor market—that is, verbal and reading skills, and analytical and mathematical skills. Such a criterion does not allow statements about absolute levels of inequality or equality of education provided by the schools, because obviously there are more influences than the school's on a child's level of achievement in school, and there are more effects of schools than in these areas of achievement. What it does do is to broaden the question beyond the school to all those educational influences that have their results in the level of verbal and mathematical skill a young person is equipped with when he or she enters the adult world. In effect, it takes the perspective of this young adult, and says that what matters to him is, not how "equal" his school is, but rather whether he is equipped at the end of school to compete on an equal basis with others, whatever his social origins. From the perspective of society, it assumes that what is important is not to "equalize the schools" in some formal sense, but to insure that children from all groups come into adult society so equipped as to insure their full participation in this society.

Another way of putting this is to say that the schools are successful only insofar as they reduce the dependence of a child's opportunities upon his social origins. We can think of a set of conditional probabilities: the probability of being prepared for a given occupation or for a given college at the end of high school, conditional upon the child's social origins. The effectiveness of the schools consists, in part, of making the conditional probabilities less conditional—that is, less dependent upon social origins. Thus, equality of educational opportunity implies, not merely "equal" schools, but equally effective schools, whose influences will overcome the differences in starting point of children from different social groups.

The Widening Educational Gap

This approach to educational opportunity, using as it does achievement on standardized tests, treads on sensitive ground. Differences in average achievement between racial groups can lend themselves to racist arguments of genetic differences in intelligence; even apart from this, they can lead to invidious comparisons between groups which show different average levels of achievement. But it is precisely the avoidance of such sensitive areas that can perpetuate the educational deficiences with which some minorities are equipped at the end of schooling.

What, then, does the survey find with regard to effects of schooling on test achievement? Children were tested at the beginning of grades 1, 3, 6, 9, and 12. Achievement of the average American Indian, Mexican American, Puerto Rican, and Negro (in this descending order) was much lower than the average white or Oriental American, at all grade levels. The amount of difference ranges from about half a standard deviation to one standard deviation at early grade levels. At the 12th grade, it increases to beyond one standard deviation. (One standard deviation difference means that about 85% of the minority group children score below the average of the whites, while if the groups were equal only about 50% would score below this average.) The grade levels of difference range up to 5 years of deficiency (in math achievement) or 4 years (in reading skills) at the 12th grade. In short, the differences are large to begin with, and they are even larger at higher grades.

Two points, then, are clear: (1) *these minority children have a serious educational deficiency at the start of school, which is obviously not a result of school;* and (2) *they have an even more serious deficiency at the end of school, which is obviously in part a result of school.*

Thus, by the criterion stated earlier—that the effectiveness of schools in creating equality of educational opportunity lies in making the conditional probabilities of success less conditional—the schools appear to fail. At the end of school, the conditional probabilities of high achievement are even *more* conditional upon racial or ethnic background than they are at the beginning of school.

There are a number of results from the survey which give further evidence on this matter. First, within each racial group, the strong relation of family economic and educational background to achievement does not diminish over the period of school, and may even increase over the elementary years. Second, most of the variation in student achievement lies within the same school, very little of it is between schools. The implication of these last two results is clear: family background differences account for much more variation in achievement than do school differences.

Even the school-to-school variation in achievement, though relatively small, is itself almost wholly due to the *social* environment provided by the school: the educational backgrounds and aspirations of other students in the school, and the educational backgrounds and attainments of the teachers in the school. *Per pupil expenditure, books in the library, and a host of other facilities and curricular measures show virtually no relation to achievement if the "social" environment of the school—the educational backgrounds of other students and teachers—is held constant.*

The importance of this last result lies, of course, in the fact that schools, as currently organized, are quite culturally homogeneous as well as quite racially segregated: teachers tend to come from the same cultural groups (and especially from the same race) as their students, and the student bodies are themselves relatively homogeneous. Given this homogeneity, the principal agents of effectiveness in the schools—teachers and other students—act to maintain or reinforce the initial differences imposed by social origins.

One element illustrates well the way in which the current organization of schools maintains the differences over generations: a Negro prospective teacher leaves a Negro teacher's college with a much lower level of academic competence (as measured by the National Teacher's Examination) than does his white counterpart leaving his largely white college; then he teaches Negro children (in school with other Negro children, ordinarily from educationally deficient backgrounds), who learn at a lower level, in part because of his lesser competence; some of these students, in turn, go into teacher training institutions to become poorly-trained teachers of the next generation.

Altogether, *the sources of inequality of educational opportunity appear to lie first in the home itself and the cultural influences immediately surrounding the home; then they lie in the schools' ineffectiveness to free achievement from the impact of the home, and in the schools' cultural homogeneity which perpetuates the social influences of the home and its environs.*

A Modest, Yet Radical Proposal

Given these results, what do they suggest as to avenues to equality of educational opportunity? Several elements seem clear:

a) For those children whose family and neighborhood are educationally disadvantaged, it is important to replace this family environment as much as possible with an educational environment—by starting school at an earlier age, and by having a school which begins very early in the day and ends very late.

b) It is important to reduce the social and racial homogeneity of the school environment, so that those agents of education that do show some effectiveness—teachers and other students—are not mere replicas of the student himself. In the present organization of schools, it is the neighborhood school that most insures such homogeneity.

c) The educational program of the school should be made more effective than it is at present. The weakness of this program is apparent in its inability to overcome initial differences. It is hard to believe that we are so inept in educating our young that we can do no more than leave young adults in the same relative competitive positions we found them in as children.

Several points are obvious: It is not a solution simply to pour money into improvement of the physical plants, books, teaching aids, of schools attended by educationally disadvantaged children. For other reasons, it will not suffice merely to bus children or otherwise achieve pro forma integration. (One incidental effect of this would be to increase the segregation within schools, through an increase in tracking.)

The only kinds of policies that appear in any way viable are those which do not seek to improve the education of Negroes and other educationally disadvantaged at the expense of those who are educationally advantaged. This implies new kinds of educational institutions, with a vast increase in expenditures for education—not merely for the disadvantaged, but for all children. The solutions might be in the form of educational parks, or in the form of private schools paid by tuition grants (with Federal regulations to insure racial heterogeneity), public (or publicly-subsidized) boarding schools (like the North Carolina Advancement School), or still other innovations. This approach also implies reorganization of the curriculum within schools. One of the major reasons for "tracking" is the narrowness of our teaching methods—they can tolerate only a narrow range of skill in the same classroom. Methods which greatly widen the range are necessary to make possible racial and cultural integration within a school—and thus to make possible the informal learning that other students of higher educational levels can provide. Such curricular innovations are possible—but, again, only through the investment of vastly greater sums in education than currently occurs.

It should be recognized, of course, that the goal described here—of equality of educational opportunity through the schools—is far more ambitious than has ever been posed in our society before. The schools were once seen as a supplement to the family in bringing a child into his place in adult society, and they still function largely as such a supplement, merely perpetuating the inequalities of birth. Yet the conditions imposed by technological change, and by our post-industrial society, quite apart from any ideals of equal opportunity, require a far more primary role for the school, if society's children are to be equipped for adulthood.

Self-Confidence and Performance

One final result of the survey gives an indication of still another —and perhaps the most important—element necessary for equality of educational opportunity for Negroes. One attitude of students was measured at grades 9 and 12—an attitude which indicated the degree to which the student felt in control of his own fate. For example, one question was: "Agree or disagree: good luck is more important than hard work for success." Another was: "Agree or disagree: every time I try to get ahead someone or something stops me." Negroes much less often than whites had such a sense of control of their fate—a difference which corresponds directly to reality, and which corresponds even more markedly to the Negro's historical position in American society. However, despite the very large achievement differences between whites and Negroes at the 9th and 12th grades, *those Negroes who gave responses indicating a sense of control of their own fate achieved higher on the tests than those whites who gave the opposite responses. This attitude was more highly related to achievement than any other factor in the student's background or school.*

This result suggests that internal changes in the Negro, changes in his conception of himself in relation to his environment, may have more effect on Negro achievement than any other single factor. The determination to overcome relevant obstacles, and the belief that he will overcome them—attitudes that have appeared in an organized way among Negroes only in recent years in some civil rights groups—may be the most crucial elements in achieving equality of opportunity—not because of changes they will create in the white community, but principally because of the changes they create in the Negro himself.

23. School Desegregation North and South: It Will Take Time

HENRY H. HILL

A prominent Negro minister of Nashville, Tennessee, accepted the invitation of a large congregation in Cleveland, Ohio, to be their pastor but returned to his former pastorate in Nashville after four months. His four young children had always attended desegregated schools in Nashville but they were compelled to attend segregated schools in Cleveland unless he moved his family to an area far away from his congregation. "In Nashville at least they know what desegregation is all about," he commented on his return. That the minister's children had always attended desegregated schools in Nashville is atypical, but the instance highlights the present divergent patterns in school desegregation in the South and the North.

Surely and not too slowly the big city systems of the North are becoming more and more segregated, with more Negroes attending all-Negro schools and fewer Negroes attending white schools. It is safe to say that more school desegregation is presently taking place in the South than in the big Northern and Western cities. True, the South moves from no desegregation to some desegregation, but it is also true that the big Northern cities are moving from some segregation to more segregation.

SOURCE: *Saturday Review* (July 16, 1966), pp. 54-56, 71.

During the past year, 217,000 Negro children in the eleven states of the former Confederacy were enrolled in schools with white children—a number three times greater than that of the previous year. In terms of percentage, the increase in enrollment was from 9.7 per cent to 15.2 per cent in the two-year period. Whether this progress toward greater desegregation is fast or slow depends somewhat on the point of view of the commentator. But all knowledgeable observers agree that the trend is toward segregation or resegregation in the big urban areas of the North and West, where more than 90 per cent of the Negroes outside the South live.

Washington, Louisville, St. Louis, Pittsburgh, and Chicago are illustrative of the desegregation status in the big cities. Shortly after the Supreme Court decision of 1954, the public school system of Washington, D.C., moved vigorously into desegregation. In 1950, prior to the Supreme Court Decision, 50.7 per cent of the pupils enrolled in Washington were Negroes. But the vigorous push for desegregation increased the number of white residents who moved to suburban areas, and, today, Negroes constitute 90 per cent of the school enrollment. Dr. Boise Bristor, statistician of the Washington School Board, estimated a year ago that by 1969 Negroes would constitute 95 per cent of the school enrollment in the District of Columbia. He stated further, "We are right back in the same situation we were in in 1954, practically all-Negro schools again. I don't know what the answer is. It wouldn't do us any good to bus the students, because we don't have enough whites to balance the races."

Louisville is a border city that desegregated in one year. The percentage of Negroes in all-Negro schools declined rather sharply from 1956 to 1960; however, during the past five years, the percentage of Negroes attending all-Negro schools has increased steadily, partly because of the increase in Negro population in Louisville.

St. Louis also took positive steps soon after 1954 to eliminate segregation. Each year during the past eleven years St. Louis has gained 3,300 Negro pupils and lost 1,000 white pupils. The elementary school population today is more than two-thirds Negro, and more than half the elementary school teachers are Negroes. Here, too, the story is the same as in Louisville—more Negroes attending substantially Negro schools each year.

These three large cities assumed some leadership in the desegregation process, apparently on the assumption that "integration" should take place rapidly and that sweeping changes were better than slow changes. The point emphasized here is that wholesale desegregation, as practiced by these three cities—and as has been and is now being urged in many big Northern cities—produced more, not less, segregation.

Pittsburgh was the location of one of the underground railroad stations during the days of slavery when benevolent abolitionists aided the escape of slaves to the safer realms of Canada, and it has remained substantially free of legal segregation. Here, where opinion is rather friendly toward Negroes, the story is much the same as in other big cities.

The number of Negro children enrolled in the Pittsburgh public schools rose from 18,000 in 1955 to 28,000 in 1965; in terms of percentage, from 26 to 37 per cent. Negro enrollment in the public schools increased disproportionately to the white increase in scholastic population because most Negro children attend public schools and one-third of the white children attend parochial schools. The number of substantially segregated schools increased almost 50 per cent from 1960 to 1965.

During the past year, 1965-66, for the first time, the majority of those enrolled in the Chicago public schools were non-white. According to a Chicago Urban League research report on *de facto* segregation submitted to the Committee on Education and Labor of the House of Representatives in July 1965, 188,000 of the 211,000 Negro pupils in the Chicago elementary schools were in substantially Negro segregated schools (schools with 90 per cent or more Negroes). That substantially all-Negro schools in Chicago are destined to continue—and probably increase—is the conclusion drawn from these hearings.

The new Bond School in Chicago may be cited as evidence of the difficulties of planning for desegregation in large cities. When this school was first planned, it was expected that 200 white children from the nearby completely white school would attend the new school, thus providing in the enrollment about 15 per cent non-Negro children. But two years later, when Bond School opened with an enrollment of 1,300, only forty white children, or about 3 per cent of the school population, enrolled. Most of the white families had moved out during the two years of planning and construction.

The continued migration of white parents from the old central cities and the immigration of additional non-whites to take their place is the single most persistent cause of greater segregation in the five cities described, and, for that matter, in all big Northern cities. Since there is no reason to believe that a Supreme Court interpretation of the law will prevent change of residence by either race, no immediate solution to this problem can be seen. The best long-term resolution of the situation appears to lie in the provision of better schools for *all* children and in the assurance that the real purpose of any school desegregation is not solely racial balance but quality education.

Efforts have been made by states and cities to achieve better "racial balance." Massachusetts is the first state to attempt by state law to eliminate racially imbalanced schools and to fix penalties for noncompliance. The report of the Advisory Committee on Racial Balance in Education to the Massachusetts State Board of Education in the spring of 1965 served as an impetus for the Massachusetts state law. This document defined racial imbalance as "a ratio between Negro and other students in public schools which is sharply out of balance with the racial composition in which Negro children study, serve, and work." The General Court of Massachusetts clarified this ambiguous definition, and added arbitrariness, by defining a racially imbalanced school as one with more than 50 per cent Negro enrollment.

Since Negroes comprise only 2 per cent of the population of Massachusetts, and only 4 per cent of the enrollment, the new law is generally innocuous—except in Boston, where forty-five of the fifty-five schools with more than 50 per cent Negroes are located. Boston nonwhites constitute only 26 per cent of the public school enrollment but are concentrated in a few areas.

Some questions arise concerning Boston. Will white parents agree to transfer their children from their present home neighborhood school to a school in another neighborhood? Under the law, they cannot be compelled to do so. If they do not agree in sufficient numbers to produce the required racial balance of 50 per cent nonwhite, then the Boston public schools must arbitrarily redistrict and transfer a large number of Negroes to substantially white schools. If this happens, will white parents move out? What happens when Negro children, many of whom are already behind in school achievement, are placed in a school where they immediately become farther behind? Will there be a better school—but not disturbingly better—to which disadvantaged Negro children can be transferred?

It remains to be seen whether the vigorous efforts of Massachusetts to promote desegregation will succeed where similar efforts have failed in Washington, Louisville, and St. Louis. To expect children in Boston or elsewhere, who are often one or two years behind in grade achievement, to advance solely because of desegregation is nonsense and a disservice to children and parents.

In an effort to obtain a better racial balance, the New York City public school system transports annually about 10,000 pupils at a cost of $3,000,000. This effort to provide both open-enrollment transportation for whole groups and free-choice transportation by public transit to Negroes and Puerto Ricans whose parents elect to have them attend certain designated schools outside of their neighborhood involves somewhat less than 1 per cent of the 1,100,000 pupils enrolled and a minor fraction of 1 per cent of the school budget.

New York is working on a proposal to reorganize its school system into a 4-4-4 pattern. This proposed pattern of organization has as one of its purposes that of obtaining better racially balanced schools. Whether these new middle schools will promote more desegregation will still depend largely upon residential patterns.

Not long ago I visited an East Harlem junior high school which enrolled only Negroes and Puerto Ricans. The building was modern, the teachers satisfactory, and my general impression was that the school was doing what it could for the slum children enrolled. But the eighth grade, as an example, was divided into twenty-seven sections, according to ability and school achievement. Only the top three of these sections could be classed as average. It would be unfair to expect this school to equal the achievement of another junior high school where children come from culturally advantaged homes. Likewise, it would be unfair to blame the schools of New York City, or of any city, for the problems involved in residential segregation, or to expect the schools by themselves to succeed in resolving exacerbating emotional issues.

Outside the South greater desegregation occurs only in the smaller school systems where the new Negro pupils constitute a small percentage of the total enrollment. The Princeton, New Jersey, plan of desegregation has been acclaimed, and with some justice. The Princeton "neighborhood school" stops with Grade Five, beyond which all children attend the same school, but the Negro enrollment there is only 6 per cent of the total enrollment of 4,000.

The most helpful and positive treatment of the difficulties of desegregation in large cities is found in the recent report prepared under the direction of the Pittsburgh Board of Education entitled "The Quest for Racial Equality in the Pittsburgh Public Schools." The report takes a firm stand on some matters treated gingerly by other school systems. The Pittsburgh Board of Education will not reassign or bus children from one school to another to achieve racial balance. The Board states it this way: "Forced, unnatural or irrational relocation of children shall not be imposed. Whether by busing or by other means, it is not the intent of the Board of Education to dislocate any children from their neighborhood, except for reasons of overcrowding, underpopulation of schools, or other reason acceptable to the Board." The Board also rejected the recommendation of civil rights organizations to appoint a "director of human relations."

Sydney B. Marland, superintendent of the Pittsburgh schools, favors the construction of massive new high schools, serving from 3,000 to 5,000 from large areas of the city, as a means of promoting desegregation. One of the two Negro board members considers it desirable to mix the races at an early age, preferably in the elementary school, rather than to wait until high school.

Beginning desegregation in the elementary schools is the procedure which has been used rather successfully by the Metropolitan school system of Nashville and Davidson County, Tennessee. In the Northern cities, however, apparently no large school system has been successful in following this procedure, chiefly because of the rapidly increasing Negro population and the continued exodus of white families.

I am arguing for less hurried and more careful desegregation of school children, chiefly on the grounds that this method will promote better education and provide increased opportunities for mutual racial respect. So-called integration comes only under favorable circumstances. Let us look at a case in point where desegregation has been slow but the results good.

In 1956 the Board of Education of Nashville, Tennessee, was ordered by the federal court to submit a plan of desegregation under the then prevailing dictum, "with all deliberate speed." In compliance with the order, the Board proposed desegregation of the first grade the following year and of one additional grade each year thereafter so that in 1968, twelve years later, the entire public school system would be desegregated. This plan was approved by the courts. When the Nashville and Davidson County school systems were merged in 1962, the new Metropolitan Board of Education followed the desegregation plan originated by Nashville. In 1965 the Metropolitan Board, without further compulsion, determined that, beginning with the 1966-67 school year, desegregation would be completed for Grades 10, 11, and 12, thus shortening the period of segregation from twelve to ten years. Let us see what has happened.

The metropolitan school system currently enrolls 90,000 children. The Negro enrollment has increased from 18,496 a year ago to 19,442 during the current year, and the number of public schools with both races represented has increased from forty to seventy-three. The number of Negroes attending school with white children rose from 1,801, or 9.7 per cent of the Negro scholastics, in 1964-65 to 3,405, or 17.5 per cent of the Negro enrollment, in 1965-66. In addition, nineteen white children are currently attending Negro schools, compared with three whites last year.

Although the slowness of this process has been at times an aggravation to civil rights leaders who feel that desegregation should be completed in "barracudalike bites," it apparently has retarded somewhat the movement of whites to the suburbs, and has allowed the transfer of Negro children to white schools to be made with greater regard to educational qualifications and, thus, with a better chance of success.

Such, in brief, is the story of school desegregation in a Southern metropolitan area of 450,000 people: The fact that this metropolitan area is now under a single government has made possible the amelioration of some of the problems of metropolitanism which are most difficult in walled-in cities, such as Boston and Pittsburgh. To ascribe wisdom and benevolence to the originators of the Nashville plan is hardly accurate. In retrospect, however, they seem to have been wiser than they knew.

For many years in the future—perhaps for all time—there will be thousands of public schools substantially all-Negro or all-white. It is inaccurate, unfair, and unhelpful to dub these schools *unequal* because their racial balance does not coincide with theoretical concepts or arbitrary legal fiats. Are Catholic schools *unequal* because they are substantially all-Catholic? Should we expect them to import Protestants and Jews in order to achieve religious balance? Are Choate, Exeter, and Groton *unequal* because they are substantially all-white and all-bright? Should we expect them to admit more nonwhites and more of the intellectually average to achieve both color and intellectual balance?

The Supreme Court of the United States declared compulsory separation of races in public schools "inherently unequal," but too many interpreters of this decision have drawn the unwarranted conclusion that to be equal a school must be racially balanced. Otherwise, at least by implication, it is, *ipso facto*, a bad school. Once compulsory racial segregation with its stigma of inferiority and absence of acceptable ethic is abandoned, the paramount consideration is good education, and not the exact degree of desegregation immediately obtained, whether the desegregation be in terms of color, religion, or intellect.

After all, what is a good school? A good school has good teachers, suitable facilities for learning, and a curriculum which fills the needs of the boys and girls attending. Some early appreciation and understanding of persons of other races, religions, and backgrounds is, as most people will agree, helpful for a young person who is going to live in the America of the future. But school associations must have some element of agreeableness and successful learning, or intercultural relations may be worsened, both for the present and the future.

It is not complimentary to our able Negro teachers and principals to imply that it is not possible to have good education in a substantially all-Negro school. Presently, outstanding Negro schools are exceptional, but the exceptions themselves offer promise for the thousands of Negro children who will continue to go to school during the next decade, or longer, in substantially Negro segregated schools. I cite only two examples of superior Negro schools.

The Moses McKissack Elementary School of Nashville, Tennessee, is the only one of 107 elementary schools in the metropolitan school system to be accredited by the Southern Association of Colleges and Schools. This Association has specific and general requirements. Quantitative standards include lower than average teacher-pupil ratios, libraries with full-time librarians, attractive buildings, and teachers with the best qualifications. More demanding in this case was the visit by sixteen individuals from colleges and school systems in the Southern Association. Over a three-day period they visited classrooms, talked with teachers and the principal, examined the philosophy and outlook of the school, and judged the spirit, success, and quality of the teachers. Since this was to be the first individual elementary school to be accredited in the South, the visiting team was unusually careful to do a good job. Metropolitan school supervisors and other competent visitors testify that the Moses McKissack Elementary School is the equal of any segregated or non-segregated elementary school in this community.

My second example of a superior Negro school is the Dunbar Vocational High School in Chicago. I visited this school briefly last fall and found it even better than I had anticipated. The modern $8,000,000 building with its spacious halls, attractively planted interior courts, and well-ordered school life is only one pleasing facet of the school. The real excellence is evidenced in the serious-minded students, competent instructors, and the fact that its graduates have obtained a well-rounded high school education which will be of value as long as they live. The school enrolls approximately 2,300 students, all Negroes except two. The faculty is approximately one-third white and two-thirds Negro; but it is the kind of school in which any first-class vocational instructor would feel at home.

Such schools, of course, do not happen overnight, and they must have the support, backing, and understanding of the board of education and the school administration. I am not advocating all-Negro schools. Quite the contrary. I do seek to offset somewhat the current obsession that desegregation is the "be-all" of good schools, even if attained sometimes by what seem to be arbitrary, unnatural, and unenforcible methods.

Moderates should be as militant as the extremists on both sides. And just what is a militant moderate? A militant moderate accepts school desegregation in spirit, as well as in law, and is willing to help school desegregation succeed. On the other hand, he resists those advocates of desegregation who would define good education only in terms of school desegregation, and he refuses to endorse or support shortsighted quick programs of the militant desegregationists. In my judgment, only the persistently rational position of school board members, superintendents of schools, and lay citizens can halt the present trend in many big cities toward *common* schools in the worst sense, schools which might conceivably sometime in the future attract only those who cannot afford to send their children to private schools. If anyone thinks this is an idle remark, he should note that the majority of white pupils in Philadelphia attend private and parochial schools, and the majority of non-whites attend public schools.

During the twelve years since 1954, the segregationists have lost every battle and finally, with the passage of federal civil rights legislation, their war. During the same period, the quick and wholesale school desegregation advocated by many civil rights leaders in the big cities has produced increased segregation and resegregation—*not* desegregation. In the long and eventful history of the United States, the balance and reasonableness of moderation has prevailed—but for one exception. In that case the extremists of North and South defeated the moderates on both sides, and helped bring on the tragic Civil War. Perhaps now, after a season of immoderation in many quarters and on many sides, the voice of the moderate may prevail.

E. CRIME

24. Crime in the Streets

JAMES Q. WILSON

Each year the FBI publishes its *Uniform Crime Reports;* each year the reports show crime rates increasing; each year the alert is sounded to warn Americans of our growing lawlessness.

Occasionally, an article appears in a scholarly journal suggesting that the data on which the *Uniform Crime Reports* are based are inaccurate, incomplete, or misleading; that the real crime rate is not known and may never be known (the FBI, after all, must rely on local police and sheriffs for its information); that the FBI sensationalizes what data do exist; and that there are reasons to believe that the crime rate is not really increasing at all.

The scholarly critics, on the whole, have the better of the argument—even if the public and the news media seem unaware of this fact. This superiority of the scholars is not surprising—it is the function of the FBI to help protect Americans and to encourage and support local law enforcement agencies; it is the function of scholars to doubt, to demand proofs, and to examine evidence critically. But this division of labor has also meant that our law enforcement agencies and our scholars have tended to talk past one another. And many of the scholars, having satisfied themselves that they are right and the FBI is wrong, have mistakenly concluded that nothing more need be said on the matter—if there is no massively rising "crime wave," then nothing need be done about crime.

It is only in the past year or so that there is some sign of a meeting of minds—if not an agreement—between the law enforcement alarmists and the academic skeptics. The President's Commission on Law Enforcement and the Administration of Justice has worked with scholars and FBI officials in studying how to improve crime reporting methods. More importantly, it is carrying out a nationwide household survey to ascertain how much crime of what kind is really occurring.

Due to appear soon after the first of the year, the Commission's report will contain a vast amount of new information, including an estimate of the amount of unreported crime, the probability of becoming a victim of crime (or of becoming a criminal!), and the relationship between crime and age, race, income, and the like. But we need not wait for the report to find some facts about American crime on which most people, in and out of the FBI, substantially agree.

Some Facts About Crime

"Crime" is mostly theft, and petty theft at that. The serious crimes that people think of when they fear to walk big-city streets at night—murder, rape, aggravated assault—make up only a tiny fraction (perhaps ten percent) of all "serious" crimes (the other crimes defined by law enforcement agencies as "serious" are robbery, burglary, auto theft, and larceny of items valued over $50).

The rates of some of these serious crimes—for example, murder and rape—have been fairly constant over the last few decades, and may even have declined. This may surprise some avid newspaper readers, but it is unquestionably so: at least with respect to murder, our statistics are fairly reliable—murders are reported, counted, and (in 90 percent of the cases) solved.

The crime rates which do appear to have gone up are theft (burglary, larceny, auto theft, and robbery) and assault. I say "appear," for it is here that the argument begins. Burglary rates may increase statistically, not because more things from homes and stores are stolen, but because more things in homes and stores are insured. The spread of theft insurance, and the willingness of insurance companies to pay off (at least on minor claims) with little or no proof of actual burgling, creates temptations to collect for missing items (or even items that are not missing, but that the owner wishes were). Larceny—which is defined as stealing things that do not require one to enter private premises surreptitiously, and includes the snatching of purses, the picking of pockets, rifling coin telephones and parking meters, and shoplifting—may also reflect not so much the presence of more criminals as more opportunities for "criminal" activity. Sometimes it really is criminal; other times it is more accurately described as merely illegal. A prosperous society multiplies public telephones and parking meters; until the belated advent of theft-proof devices, the more such instruments installed, the more chances for picking up loose change. Our department stores and supermarkets, packed to the rafters with the products of the world's richest society, offer tempting targets for people who want (and think they are entitled to pick up) more things than they can afford. This, incidentally, seems to be one main reason why big-city theft rates are higher than those in small towns and rural areas—it is not that the city dweller is less virtuous, it is only that he is more prosperous; thieves go to cities for the same reason businessmen and shoppers do—that's where the loot is.

Prosperity affects theft rates in other ways. The more bicycles we can afford to buy our kids, the more bicycles there are lying about in front yards, waiting to be "borrowed." The more fancy accessories—stereo tape players, built-in-bars, bucket seats—we can afford to pack into our cars, the more such things there are to pilfer from unlocked (or insecurely locked) autos. Moreover, the FBI counts as larceny—a "serious" crime—the theft of anything valued over $50. This definition has remained unchanged for several years. This means that as inflation, or improvements in quality, push up the price of common possessions past the $50 mark, thefts that were not counted at all, or which used to be counted in another category, are suddenly counted as "Part 1 larceny"—and the "serious crime" rate shoots up. As Albert Biderman has pointed out in a recent paper, soaring crime rates—as defined by the FBI—may in fact be nothing more than a slightly different way of measuring a soaring gross national product.

Some Questions About Crime

But when the average American thinks of crime, he is likely to think, not of a stolen bicycle or shoplifting, but of "crime in the streets"—muggings, purse-snatchings, strong-arm robberies, and other felonious assaults. Even the social scientists who write articles demonstrating that the alleged "crime wave" is a statistical illusion or simple myth are likely to tell their wives (or even themselves) that, if they live near such big-city universities as Chicago, Columbia, or Pennsylvania, they should not walk the streets alone after dark.

No one knows what reality lies behind the official statistics on violent assaults. The rates are going up—but different interpretations can be put on these figures.

In part, it may be that we are more shocked by violence than we used to be—we are richer, better educated, and less comfortable in the presence of the lower classes, the foreign, or the rowdy—and are therefore quicker to call the cops. A barroom fight that once was settled in the alley is now reported, by the saloon keeper or his nervous patrons, to the police, and thus becomes an "assault."

Another possibility is that we are indeed in greater jeopardy, because we have made it easier for lower class persons (common crime is, as the sociologists would have it, strongly and inversely correlated with socio-economic status) to move freely about the city. Crime-prone groups—especially recent immigrants to the city, not yet assimilated to the mores of urban life—were once confined to high-density ghettoes by ethnic segregation, by the fact that manual workers had to live within walking distance of their places of work, and by police employed by the respectable people to keep the undesirables cordoned off in one section of town. Now the flight to the suburbs has made it easier for the lower classes to find housing in many parts of the city; the automobile has made it possible for them to live some distance from where they work (and, of course, to flee more swiftly from the scene of a crime); and the police have been under strong pressure to treat everyone equally—which means, in this case, not to arrest a suspicious looking character until *after* he has committed a crime. As lower class people have spread out through the city, crime has spread out through the city. Those members of the middle class—professors, elderly couples, artists, certain businessmen and public officials—who have elected to stay behind in the city have suddenly found themselves the victims or witnesses of criminal acts which once the lower class perpetrated in lower-class privacy, amongst themselves.

There is another common—though in my opinion, erroneous—explanation for the urban crime wave. Some well-intentioned people believe that crime figures are inflated by the propensity of the police to arrest Negroes for every little infraction—and often for no infraction at all. If the police didn't discriminate against the Negro in this way, the argument goes, the crime figures would be lower and, in addition, the Negro would lose his undeserved reputation for having a higher crime rate than whites.

Nobody who has spent much time with the police in Negro sections of our big cities could accept this argument. Far from discriminating against the Negro by arresting him for every infraction, however minor, the police, if anything, discriminate against him by *not* arresting him for many crimes, including some serious ones. Partly this is the result of the situation within the Negro community itself—there is indisputably more unreported crime in Harlem, or Watts, or Roxbury, or the South Side of Chicago than there is in a white, middle-class neighborhood. Residents of lower-class Negro neighborhoods tolerate more disorder, are less trusting of the police, and are less willing to inform on their neighbors than are residents of higher-status neighborhoods, Negro or white. (The vast majority of Negro murders and assaults are inflicted on other Negroes.) And, partly, this lower arrest rate is the result of the view, common in at least some big-city police departments, that Negro crime is "less serious" than white crime—what in a white neighborhood would be booked by the police as a felonious assault may be booked in a Negro neighborhood as a simple assault ("a cutting") or merely as disorderly conduct. This results in an understatement of the extent of criminality. But since this kind of understatement has doubtless persisted for decades now, it is not likely to have any effect on reported crime rates.

Some Further Facts About Crime

In sum, we have crime statistics which we know are misleading; but we cannot say how much they mislead us or how important this misleading is. We do know that there is an official tendency to exaggerate the prevalence of crime. We also know—for what consolation it is worth—that street crime follows some regular patterns. Aggravated assaults, for example, are rarely practiced by unknown, cold-blooded assailants on innocent victims. On the contrary, two-thirds of such assaults involve hot-blooded assailants venting their fury on family or friends who themselves ought probably to share in the blame for the event. Such assaults tend to happen in the summer months and in private or semi-private places—homes, hotel rooms, and bars. The private nature of most such assaults is shown by the difficulty the police have in making a charge of felonious assault stick—although three-fourths of reported assaults result in an arrest, and four-fifths of the arrests result in formal charges being preferred, only a third of those charged are convicted of the same charge. Friends and relatives tend to drop charges, or change their stories once tempers have cooled.

Robberies tend to be more common in the winter months, especially just before Christmas. In November and December, women go out at night carrying purses filled with cash with which to buy presents. Robbers go right out after them. Most persons charged with robbery carry a weapon; the rest rely on strong-arm tactics. There were over a hundred thousand robberies last year, and though this accounts for less than five per cent of all serious crimes, a hundred thousand robberies is no laughing matter. (Unlike crimes against the person, most robberies and most thefts generally are not solved.) On the other hand, if one takes into account the growth in population, it is not certain that the situation is any worse than it used to be, say, fifty years ago. Our statistics for past periods are just too unreliable to enable us to make neat *per capita* estimates of crime rates.

A person is twice as likely to be robbed as he is to be killed in an automobile accident. Again, one doesn't know whether this is better or worse than things used to be—though one is aware that the number of fatalities in auto accidents has come to be widely regarded as a national scandal. Unlike burglary, robbery rates are probably not inflated by claims made purely for insurance purposes (why go to the trouble of having to make up a story about an assailant, and his description, when it is so much easier to report that your watch was "stolen" from your house while you were at the grocery store). Unlike larceny, robbery rates do not depend on the value of the article stolen, nor is robbery motivated by irresistible temptation—while a perfectly normal teenager might grab a transistor radio lying unattended on the front seat of an open convertible, there is nothing normal about a man who grabs a radio at the point of a knife from the hands of an innocent wayfarer.

Of those arrested for robbery (an arrest occurs in only about a third of the cases), two-thirds are under the age of twenty-five. Better than half are Negro. Young people account, in fact, for two-thirds or more of all theft crimes (indeed, they account for almost ninety percent of all auto thefts). These figures must be used with caution, since we don't know—and can't know—whether those arrested are typical of all criminals. Two-thirds of those arrested for crimes against the person, by contrast, are over twenty-five. Stealing is something that kids do; murder, manslaughter, and felonious assault appear to be things that adults do.

More Youth, More Crime

This last fact is far more important than would appear at first sight. Recognizing and developing its significance is one of the major contributions of the 1965 report, entitled *Prevention and Control of Crime and Delinquency,* submitted by the Space-General Corporation to the California Youth and Adult Correction Agency. Their analysis is based on the ages of persons arrested for various offenses. As such, it is of course biased somewhat by whatever biases exist in determining what kinds of persons will be arrested, but on the whole the bias does not seem to be serious, particularly if one examines separately arrest trends for adults and juveniles.

What Space-General did was quite simple—instead of calculating crime rates by dividing the number of crimes by the total population, they divided the number of crimes by the number of people within the age group (14-29) which produces most serious crime, at least according to arrest records. (In 1965, the FBI reported that over 72 percent of those arrested for a "serious" crime were between the ages of 13 and 29. If you add in those under the age of 13, the proportion rises to nearly 82 percent.) Figured the first way, the crime rate in California appears to be increasing, just as it is in the nation as a whole. But figured the second way, there is hardly any increase in the rate at all over the period 1960-1965. And if we consider only violent crimes (murder, rape, robbery, and aggravated assault) instead of all "serious" crimes, the increase all but disappears.

Why, then, are there more serious and violent crimes every year? *Simply because there are more young people every year, and because young people have always had a higher crime rate than adults.* Because the size of the younger age group is increasing twice as fast as that of the older age group, over the next ten years California can expect an increase in the number of serious crimes of 55 percent. (The "crime-susceptible" age group will at the same time increase in size by 110 percent.) *What appears to be a crime explosion may in fact be a population explosion.* Eventually, if birth rates decline (as they have been doing recently), the number of people in the crime-susceptible age group will no longer be so disproportionally larger than the number of people in other, older age groups. At that time, the crime rate figured on the conventional basis—number of crimes divided by the total population—will come down. For the present, the only sure way we know of fighting crime is birth control.

The Space-General Report is a rough first approximation to a sophisticated study of this problem, and its findings are not altogether well-supported. The President's Crime Commission will undoubtedly offer fresh information on this matter, but there is a limit to what it can say with confidence. We can never know for sure what age groups *commit* certain crimes; we can only know what age groups are *arrested* for them. The police today may be arresting young people that they once handled informally with "curbstone justice," thus producing higher arrest rates—and more records of "teenage crime" than previously. It may also be that a more thorough study will show that crime rates, *even after* adjustment for age differences, are increasing—though some preliminary studies by Marvin Wolfgang, of the University of Pennsylvania, suggest that, if there is any such increase, it is not nearly so dramatic as is often suggested.

But the significant point is that we must be cautious about what inferences we draw from the number of crimes being reported. Despite the indisputable increase in the *number* of crimes and the apparent, though probably exaggerated, increase in the overall *rate* of crimes, there is as yet no good evidence to justify the assertion that American society is becoming more criminal or less moral. Man for man—even young man for young man—we are, I suspect, *less* likely to commit a truly serious crime today than twenty or thirty years ago. This should not be so surprising—after all, we are a richer, better educated, more homogeneous society than ever before. People who complain about "crime in the streets" are prone to draw from crude crime statistics the conclusion that America is, morally, going to hell in a handbasket. It is important, therefore, to demonstrate that, statistically, we are a long way from hell, and in fact may not even be in that particular handbasket.

Crime Producers and Crime Consumers

This does not, however, close the subject, as some academics seem to think. Of what comfort is it to a man who [has] been hit over the head and has had his wallet stolen to be told that, statistically, crime rates are not really increasing, that the reason he is lying there in the gutter with a bloody head and an empty pocket is simply that there are now more teenagers in New York, Chicago, or wherever—and that, individually, even those teenagers are probably now more law-abiding? As a noted criminologist, Stanton Wheeler of the Russell Sage Foundation, has recently written: "Personally, it concerns me more whether my wife or children are assaulted at all, than it does whether they are assaulted by a Caucasian, a Puerto Rican, or a Negro . . . The important question would seem to be whether or not the rate has gone up for victims in *my* category." (My italics.) Dr. Wheeler calls for "consumer-oriented" crime statistics that will tell, say, a middle-income white resident of mid-town Manhattan what his chances are of being hit over the head, in place of "producer-oriented" crime statistics that simply tell the theoretician how many heads our society is hitting per capita in any particular year.

Dr. Wheeler's formulation has the virtue of assuming that, as individual citizens, we naturally take the victim's point of view. It has the additional virtue of causing us to wonder whether some of us, at any rate, are now *consuming* more crime, even though our society, as a whole, may be said to be *producing* less. The anomaly would be explained by the fact that consumer and producer used to be one and the same person—i.e., the lower classes. Now, it is suggested, the middle classes are consuming more of the declining crime production of the lower classes.

The Space-General report has some guesses as to what victim-related crime statistics would look like, at least for Los Angeles. On the basis of crime and arrest data, the report calculates the odds of being the victim of a serious crime in various parts of the city and gives the income levels of those neighborhoods. Unsurprisingly, the odds in favor of being the victim of a violent crime decline very quickly with increases in neighborhood income—the chances are nearly six per thousand population of being a victim of violent crime in an area with a median family income of under $5,500 a year, but less than one in a thousand in areas with incomes over $8,000 a year. In order to make sense of these statistics, we should need comparable figures for twenty or thirty years ago. Unfortunately, such figures do not exist and it will require a major research project to assemble a meaningful sample. Until this research is done, we shall not be able to say whether the present anxiety in the middle classes about crime is related to an increase in their victimization or simply to an increasing middle-class intolerance of crime.

What Is To Be Done?

Meanwhile, what can be done about the increase in crime, short of locking up everyone under 30 years of age? On present evidence, the social scientist's answer would have to be: not much. Walter Miller has reviewed most of the literature on the control and prevention of delinquency, including that on the glamorous programs involving detached workers, and has concluded that there is at present little or no evidence that any of the efforts have reduced delinquent behavior (which is mostly stealing) very much or for very long. (At breaking up and pacifying juvenile *gangs*, such programs are often quite useful; but kids don't need gangs in order to steal—indeed, they seem to prefer to steal alone, or in twos and threes.) This may change—there are delinquency-prevention programs underway which have not yet been fully evaluated; but it would be foolish to be too sanguine about this prospect. As far as violent crime goes, even the police despair, since so much of it takes place in private or semi-private places which police patrols cannot reach until it is too late. A murder or an assault can—and does—take place inside an apartment no matter whether there are one, two, or ten policemen outside on the sidewalk.

On the whole, more can probably be accomplished by making more secure the scene of the prospective crime than by operating farther back in the causal chain and reaching toward the criminal (or would-be criminal) himself. It is hard to identify criminals until it is too late; and unless they are identified, a lot of resources and effort will be wasted on the wrong people. Making cars harder to steal (with jump-proof ignitions), making doors and windows harder to open from the outside, putting merchandise displays under better and more continuous surveillance, making it easier for pedestrians to summon aid through warning signals of various sorts, rendering coin boxes and parking meters tamper-proof, improving street and doorway lighting—all of these measures, while hardly panaceas, might be very useful, and they certainly ought to be appealing to a gimmick-conscious society.

In the long run, only broad social changes will have substantial effects. Belton Fleisher, in a recently-published book, *The Economics of Delinquency,* concludes, after a careful econometric analysis, that economic factors—especially family income, and, to a lesser extent, unemployment—have strong effects on delinquency rates. Hollywood movies to the contrary notwithstanding, higher incomes reduce—though they do not eliminate—delinquency. Reducing unemployment also tends, with certain important exceptions and qualifications, to reduce delinquency. Fleisher estimates that a $500 increase in annual income for families in high delinquency areas would cut juvenile arrests by about five per one thousand population. Stated another way, "a 10 percent rise in incomes might well result in a 20 percent decline in delinquency." Interestingly, in the equations used to estimate the value of the various potential predictors of delinquency, race was statistically insignificant once income had been taken into account. *It is being in a low income group, not being a Negro, that seems most important in disposing persons toward the kinds of crimes committed by juveniles.* No comparable data exist for violent crimes, nor can we say with confidence how much crime is caused by narcotics addicts seeking money with which to feed their habit.

So it is possible that continued (and enhanced) prosperity, coupled with levelled-off birth rates, may gradually bring the crime rates down. But this is only in the very long run. The forecast for the next twenty years is that the crime problem will become worse: in absolute numbers, there will be more crimes; the rate for the population as a whole will go up (though not necessarily for specific age groups within that population); and, at least in the big cities, the "victim rate" in middle-class neighborhoods will remain high or get higher.

How will the American people react to this? One suspects that they are not going to be pacified by statistics, even accurate ones. It is not uncommon, after all, for a situation to become less tolerable—even intolerable—though it is not, in fact, getting worse. Nor are they likely to rest content with the long view of the social scientist. The American people have just decided that they will not "put up" with so many automobile deaths and injuries. What if they make a similar decision about crimes against the person?

It is possible that the issue of "crime in the streets" can become the major domestic issue of the far right, replacing "communist subversion" and even "socialism." Of its potential appeal, there can be little doubt—just as there can be little question of its potential danger. A less implausible or rigid candidate than Barry Goldwater could make such an issue—with its obvious implications for a Supreme Court that has allegedly "shackled" the police, for a federal government that "encourages" disobedience and even violence, and for intellectuals who want to "mollycoddle" or "explain away" immorality—a major element in a serious bid for power. This is not a problem about which American liberalism has hitherto had much to say—except to demand "citizen review boards" and to criticize the FBI. But unless liberalism can show an eagerness to cope with this problem—even if it only means spending more money on larger police forces—it will become a notable victim of crime in the streets.

25. Summary of President's Commission on Crime

This report is about crime in America—about those who commit it, about those who are its victims, and about what can be done to reduce it.

The report is the work of 19 commissioners, 63 staff members, 175 consultants, and hundreds of advisers. The commissioners, staff, consultants, and advisers come from every part of America and represent a broad range of opinion and profession.

In the process of developing the findings and recommendations of the report the Commission called three national conferences, conducted five national surveys, held hundreds of meetings, and interviewed tens of thousands of persons.

The report makes more than 200 specific recommendations—concrete steps the Commission believes can lead to a safer and more just society. These recommendations call for a greatly increased effort on the part of the Federal Government, the States, the counties, the cities,

SOURCE: *The Challenge of Crime in a Free Society* (Washington, D. C.: Government Printing Office, 1967), pp. v-xi.

civic organizations, religious institutions, business groups, and individual citizens. They call for basic changes in the operations of police, schools, prosecutors, employment agencies, defenders, social workers, prisons, housing authorities, and probation and parole officers.

But the recommendations are more than just a list of new procedures, new tactics, and new techniques. They are a call for a revolution in the way America thinks about crime.

Many Americans take comfort in the view that crime is the vice of a handful of people. This view is inaccurate. In the United States today, one boy in six is referred to the juvenile court. A Commission survey shows that in 1965 more than two million Americans were received in prisons or juvenile training schools, or placed on probation. Another Commission study suggests that about 40 percent of all male children now living in the United States will be arrested for a nontraffic offense during their lives. An independent survey of 1,700 persons found that 91 percent of the sample admitted they had committed acts for which they might have received jail or prison sentences.

Many Americans also think of crime as a very narrow range of behavior. It is not. An enormous variety of acts make up the "crime problem." Crime is not just a tough teenager snatching a lady's purse. It is a professional thief stealing cars "on order." It is a well-heeled loan shark taking over a previously legitimate business for organized crime. It is a polite young man who suddenly and inexplicably murders his family. It is a corporation executive conspiring with competitors to keep prices high. No single formula, no single theory, no single generalization can explain the vast range of behavior called crime.

Many Americans think controlling crime is solely the task of the police, the courts, and correction agencies. In fact, as the Commission's report makes clear, crime cannot be controlled without the interest and participation of schools, businesses, social agencies, private groups, and individual citizens.

What, then, is America's experience with crime and how has this experience shaped the Nation's way of living? A new insight into these two questions is furnished by the Commission's National Survey of Criminal Victims. In this survey, the first of its kind conducted on such a scope, 10,000 representative American households were asked about their experiences with crime, whether they reported those experiences to the police, and how those experiences affected their lives.

An important finding of the survey is that for the Nation as a whole there is far more crime than ever is reported. Burglaries occur about three times more often than they are reported to police. Aggravated assaults and larcenies over $50 occur twice as often as they are reported. There are 50 percent more robberies than are reported. In some areas, only one-tenth of the total number of certain kinds of crimes are reported to the police. Seventy-four percent of the neighborhood commercial establishments surveyed do not report to police the thefts committed by their employees.

The existence of crime, the talk about crime, the reports of crime, and the fear of crime have eroded the basic quality of life of many Americans. A Commission study conducted in high crime areas of two large cities found that:

- 43 percent of the respondents say they stay off the streets at night because of their fear of crime.
- 35 percent say they do not speak to strangers any more because of their fear of crime.
- 21 percent say they use cars and cabs at night because of their fear of crime.
- 20 percent say they would like to move to another neighborhood because of their fear of crime.

The findings of the Commission's national survey generally support those of the local surveys. One-third of a representative sample of all Americans say it is unsafe to walk alone at night in their neighborhoods. Slightly more than one-third say they keep firearms in the house for protection against criminals. Twenty-eight percent say they keep watchdogs for the same reason.

Under any circumstance, developing an effective response to the problem of crime in America is exceedingly difficult. And because of the changes expected in the population in the next decade, in years to come it will be more difficult. Young people commit a disproportionate share of crime and the number of young people in our society is growing at a much faster rate than the total population. Although the 15- to 17-year-old age group represents only 5.4 percent of the population, it accounts for 12.8 percent of all arrests. Fifteen and sixteen year olds have the highest arrest rate in the United States. The problem in the years ahead is dramatically foretold by the fact that 23 percent of the population is 10 or under.

Despite the seriousness of the problem today and the increasing challenge in the years ahead, the central conclusion of the Commission is that a significant reduction in crime is possible if the following objectives are vigorously pursued:

First, society must seek to prevent crime before it happens by assuring all Americans a stake in the benefits and responsibilities of American life, by strengthening law enforcement, and by reducing criminal opportunities.

Second, society's aim of reducing crime would be better served if the system of criminal justice developed a far broader range of techniques with which to deal with individual offenders.

Third, the system of criminal justice must eliminate existing injustices if it is to achieve its ideals and win the respect and cooperation of all citizens.

Fourth, the system of criminal justice must attract more people and better people—police, prosecutors, judges, defense attorneys, probation and parole officers, and corrections officials with more knowledge, expertise, initiative, and integrity.

Fifth, there must be much more operational and basic research into the problems of crime and criminal administration, by those both within and without the system of criminal justice.

Sixth, the police, courts, and correctional agencies must be given substantially greater amounts of money if they are to improve their ability to control crime.

Seventh, individual citizens, civic and business organizations, religious institutions, and all levels of government must take responsibility for planning and implementing the changes that must be made in the criminal justice system if crime is to be reduced.

In terms of specific recommendations, what do these seven objectives mean?

1. Preventing Crime

The prevention of crime covers a wide range of activities: Eliminating social conditions closely associated with crime; improving the ability of the criminal justice system to detect, apprehend, judge, and reintegrate into their communities those who commit crimes; and reducing the situations in which crimes are most likely to be committed.

Every effort must be made to strengthen the family, now often shattered by the grinding pressures of urban slums.

Slum schools must be given enough resources to make them as good as schools elsewhere and to enable them to compensate for the various handicaps suffered by the slum child—to rescue him from his environment.

Present efforts to combat school segregation, and the housing segregation that underlies it, must be continued and expanded.

Employment opportunities must be enlarged and young people provided with more effective vocational training and individual job counseling. Programs to create new kinds of jobs—such as probation aides, medical assistants, and teacher helpers—seem particularly promising and should be expanded.

The problem of increasing the ability of the police to detect and apprehend criminals is complicated. In one effort to find out how this objective could be achieved, the Commission conducted an analysis of 1,905 crimes reported to the Los Angeles Police Department during a recent month. The study showed the importance of identifying the perpetrator at the scene of the crime. Eighty-six percent of the crimes with named suspects were solved, but only 12 percent of the unnamed suspect crimes were solved. Another finding of the study was that there is a relationship between the speed of response and certainty of apprehension. On the average, response to emergency calls resulting in arrests was 50 percent faster than response to emergency calls not resulting in arrest. On the basis of this finding, and a cost effectiveness study to discover the best means to reduce response time, the Commission recommends an experimental program to develop computer-aided command-and-control systems for large police departments.

To insure the maximum use of such a system, headquarters must have a direct link with every onduty police officer. Because large scale production would result in a substantial reduction of the cost of miniature two-way radios, the Commission recommends that the Federal Government assume leadership in initiating a development program for such equipment and that it consider guaranteeing the sale of the first production lot of perhaps 20,000 units.

Two other steps to reduce police response time are recommended:

- Police callboxes, which are locked and inconspicuous in most cities, should be left open, brightly marked, and designated "public emergency callboxes."
- The telephone company should develop a single police number for each metropolitan area, and eventually for the entire United States.

Improving the effectiveness of law enforcement, however, is much more than just improving police response time. For example a study in Washington, D.C., found that courtroom time for a felony defendant who pleads guilty probably totals less than 1 hour, while the median time from his initial appearance to his disposition is 4 months.

In an effort to discover how courts can best speed the process of criminal justice, the known facts about felony cases in Washington were placed in a computer and the operation of the system was simulated. After a number of possible solutions to the problem of delay were tested, it appeared that the addition of a second grand jury—which, with supporting personnel, would cost less than $50,000 a year—would result in a 25-percent reduction in the time required for the typical felony case to move from initial appearance to trial.

The application of such analysis—when combined with the Commission's recommended timetable laying out timespans for each step in the criminal process—should help court systems to ascertain their procedural bottlenecks and develop ways to eliminate them.

Another way to prevent crime is to reduce the opportunity to commit it. Many crimes would not be committed, indeed many criminal careers would not begin, if there were fewer opportunities for crime.

Auto theft is a good example. According to FBI statistics, the key had been left in the ignition or the ignition had been left unlocked in 42 percent of all stolen cars. Even in those cars taken when the ignition was locked, at least 20 percent were stolen simply by shorting the ignition with such simple devices as paper clips or tinfoil. In one city, the elimination of the unlocked "off" position on the 1965 Chevrolet resulted in 50 percent fewer of those models being stolen in 1965 than were stolen in 1964.

On the basis of these findings, it appears that an important reduction in auto theft could be achieved simply by installing an ignition system that automatically ejects the key when the engine is turned off.

A major reason that it is important to reduce auto theft is that stealing a car is very often the criminal act that starts a boy on a course of lawbreaking.

Stricter gun controls also would reduce some kinds of crime. Here, the Commission recommends a strengthening of the Federal law governing the interstate shipment of firearms and enactment of State laws requiring the registration of all handguns, rifles, and shotguns, and prohibiting the sale or ownership of firearms by certain categories of persons—dangerous criminals, habitual drunkards, and drug addicts. After 5 years, the Commission recommends that Congress pass a Federal registration law applying to those States that have not passed their own registration laws.

2. New Ways of Dealing with Offenders

The Commission's second objective—the development of a far broader range of alternatives for dealing with offenders—is based on the belief that, while there are some who must be completely segregated from society, there are many instances in which segregation does more harm than good. Furthermore, by concentrating the resources of the police, the courts, and correctional agencies on the smaller number of offenders who really need them, it should be possible to give all offenders more effective treatment.

A specific and important example of this principle is the Commission's recommendation that every community consider establishing a Youth Services Bureau, a community-based center to which juveniles could be referred by the police, the courts, parents, schools, and social agencies for counseling, education, work, or recreation programs and job placement.

The Youth Services Bureau—an agency to handle many troubled and troublesome young people outside the criminal system—is needed in part because society has failed to give the juvenile court the resources that would allow it to function as its founders hoped it would. In a recent survey of juvenile court judges, for example, 83 percent said no psychologist or psychiatrist was available to their courts on a regular basis and one-third said they did not have probation officers or social workers. Even where there are probation officers, the Commission found, the average officer supervises 76 probationers, more than double the recommended caseload.

The California Youth Authority for the last 5 years has been conducting a controlled experiment to determine the effectiveness of another kind of alternative treatment program for juveniles. There, after initial screening, convicted juvenile delinquents are assigned on a random basis to either an experimental group or a control group. Those in the experimental group are returned to the community and receive intensive individual counseling, group counseling, group therapy, and family counseling. Those in the control group are assigned to California's regular institutional treatment program. The findings so far: 28 percent of the experimental group have had their paroles revoked, compared with 52 percent in the control group. Furthermore, the community treatment program is less expensive than institutional treatment.

To make community-based treatment possible for both adults and juveniles, the Commission recommends the development of an entirely new kind of correctional institution: located close to population centers; maintaining close relations with schools, employers, and universities; housing as few as 50 inmates; serving as a classification center, as the center for various kinds of community programs and as a port of reentry to the community for those difficult and dangerous offenders who have required treatment in facilities with tighter custody.

Such institutions would be useful in the operation of programs—strongly recommended by the Commission—that permit selected inmates to work or study in the community during the day and return to control at night, and programs that permit long-term inmates to become adjusted to society gradually rather than being discharged directly from maximum security institutions to the streets.

Another aspect of the Commission's conviction that different offenders with different problems should be treated in different ways, is its recommendation about the handling of public drunkenness, which, in 1965, accounted for one out of every three arrests in America. The great number of these arrests—some 2 million—burdens the police, clogs the lower courts and crowds the penal institutions. The Commission therefore recommends that communities develop civil detoxification units and comprehensive aftercare programs, and that with the development of such programs, drunkenness, not accompanied by other unlawful conduct, should not be a criminal offense.

Similarly, the Commission recommends the expanded use of civil commitment for drug addicts.

3. Eliminating Unfairness

The third objective is to eliminate injustices so that the system of criminal justice can win the respect and cooperation of all citizens. Our society must give the police, the courts, and correctional agencies the resources and the mandate to provide fair and dignified treatment for all.

The Commission found overwhelming evidence of institutional shortcomings in almost every part of the United States.

A survey of the lower court operations in a number of large American cities found cramped and noisy courtrooms, undignified and perfunctory procedures, badly trained personnel overwhelmed by enormous caseloads. In short, the Commission found assembly line justice.

The Commission found that in at least three States, justices of the peace are paid only if they convict and collect a fee from the defendant, a practice held unconstitutional by the Supreme Court 40 years ago.

The Commission found that approximately one-fourth of the 400,000 children detained in 1965—for a variety of causes but including truancy, smoking, and running away from home—were held in adult jails and lockups, often with hardened criminals.

In addition to the creation of new kinds of institutions—such as the Youth Services Bureau and the small, community-based correctional centers—the Commission recommends several important procedural changes. It recommends counsel at various points in the criminal process.

For juveniles, the Commission recommends providing counsel whenever coercive action is a possibility.

For adults, the Commission recommends providing counsel to any criminal defendant who faces a significant penalty—excluding traffic and similar petty charges—if he cannot afford to provide counsel for himself.

In connection with this recommendation, the Commission asks each State to finance regular, statewide assigned counsel and defender systems for the indigent.

Counsel also should be provided in parole and probation revocation hearings.

Another kind of broad procedural change that the Commission recommends is that every State, county, and local jurisdiction provide judicial officers with sufficient information about individual defendants to permit the release without money bail of those who can be safely released.

In addition to eliminating the injustice of holding persons charged with a crime merely because they cannot afford bail, this recommendation also would save a good deal of money. New York City alone, for example, spends approximately $10 million a year holding persons who have not yet been found guilty of any crime.

Besides institutional injustices, the Commission found that while the great majority of criminal justice and law enforcement personnel perform their duties with fairness and understanding, even under the most trying circumstances, some take advantage of their official positions and act in a callous, corrupt, or brutal manner.

Injustice will not yield to simple solutions. Overcoming it requires a wide variety of remedies including improved methods of selecting personnel, the massive infusion of additional funds, the revamping of existing procedures and the adoption of more effective internal and external controls.

The relations between the police and urban poor deserve special mention. Here the Commission recommends that every large department—especially in communities with substantial minority populations—should have community-relations machinery consisting of a headquarters planning and supervising unit and precinct units to carry out recommended programs. Effective citizen advisory committees should be established in minority group neighborhoods. All departments with substantial minority populations should make special efforts to recruit minority group officers and to deploy and promote them fairly. They should have rigorous internal investigation units to examine complaints of misconduct. The Commission believes it is of the utmost importance to insure that complaints of unfair treatment are fairly dealt with.

Fair treatment of every individual—fair in fact and also perceived to be fair by those affected—is an essential element of justice and a principal objective of the American criminal justice system.

4. Personnel

The fourth objective is that higher levels of knowledge, expertise, initiative, and integrity be achieved by police, judges, prosecutors, defense attorneys, and correctional authorities so that the system of criminal justice can improve its ability to control crime.

The Commission found one obstacle to recruiting better police officers was the standard requirement that all candidates—regardless of qualifications—begin their careers at the lowest level and normally remain at this level from 2 to 5 years before being eligible for promotion. Thus, a college graduate must enter a department at the same rank and pay and perform the same tasks as a person who enters with only a high school diploma or less.

The Commission recommends that police departments give up single entry and establish three levels at which candidates may begin their police careers. The Commission calls these three levels the "community service officer," the "police officer," and the "police agent."

This division, in addition to providing an entry place for the better educated, also would permit police departments to tap the special knowledge, skills, and understanding of those brought up in the slums.

The community service officer would be a uniformed but unarmed member of the police department. Two of his major responsibilities would be to maintain close relations with juveniles in the area where he works and to be especially alert to crime-breeding conditions that other city agencies had not dealt with. Typically, the CSO might be under 21, might not be required to meet conventional education requirements, and might work out of a store-front office. Serving as an apprentice policeman—a substitute for the police cadet—the CSO would work as a member of a team with the police officer and police agent.

The police officer would respond to calls for service, perform routine patrol, render emergency services, make preliminary investigations, and enforce traffic regulations. In order to qualify as a police officer at the present time, a candidate should possess a high school diploma and should demonstrate a capacity for college work.

The police agent would do whatever police jobs were most complicated, most sensitive, and most demanding. He might be a specialist in police-community relations or juvenile delinquency. He might be in uniform patrolling a high-crime neighborhood. He might have staff duties. To become a police agent would require at least 2 years of college work and preferably a baccalaureate degree in the liberal arts or social sciences.

As an ultimate goal, the Commission recommends that all police personnel with general enforcement powers have baccalaureate degrees.

While candidates could enter the police service at any one of the three levels, they also could work their way up through the different categories as they met the basic education and other requirements.

In many jurisdictions there is a critical need for additional police personnel. Studies by the Commission indicate a recruiting need of 50,000 policemen in 1967 just to fill positions already authorized. In order to increase police effectiveness, additional staff specialists will be required, and when the community service officers are added manpower needs will be even greater.

The Commission also recommends that every State establish a commission on police standards to set minimum recruiting and training standards and to provide financial and technical assistance for local police departments.

In order to improve the quality of judges, prosecutors, and defense attorneys, the Commission recommends a variety of steps: Taking the selection of judges out of partisan politics; the more regular use of seminars, conferences, and institutes to train sitting judges; the establishment of judicial commissions to excuse physically or mentally incapacitated judges from their duties without public humiliation; the general abolition of part-time district attorneys and assistant district attorneys; and a broad range of measures to develop a greatly enlarged and better trained pool of defense attorneys.

In the correctional system there is a critical shortage of probation and parole officers, teachers, caseworkers, vocational instructors, and group workers. The need for major manpower increases in this area was made clear by the findings from the Commission's national corrections survey:

- Less than 3 percent of all personnel working in local jails and institutions devote their time to treatment and training.
- Eleven States do not offer any kind of probation services for adult misdemeanants, six offer only the barest fragments of such services, and most States offer them on a spotty basis.
- Two-thirds of all State adult felony probationers are in caseloads of over 100 persons.

To meet the requirements of both the correctional agencies and the courts, the Commission has found an immediate need to double the Nation's pool of juvenile probation officers, triple the number of probation officers working with adult felons, and increase sevenfold the number of officers working with misdemeanants.

Another area with a critical need for large numbers of expert criminal justice officers is the complex one of controlling organized crime. Here, the Commission recommends that prosecutors and police in every State and city where organized crime is known to, or may, exist develop special organized crime units.

5. Research

The fifth objective is that every segment of the system of criminal justice devote a significant part of its resources for research to insure the development of new and effective methods of controlling crime.

The Commission found that little research is being conducted into such matters as the economic impact of crime; the effects on crime of increasing or decreasing criminal sanctions; possible methods for improving the effectiveness of various procedures of the police, courts, and correctional agencies.

Organized crime is another area in which almost no research has been conducted. The Commission found that the only group with any significant knowledge about this problem was law enforcement officials. Those in other disciplines—social scientists, economists and lawyers, for example—have not until recently considered the possibility of research projects on organized crime.

A small fraction of 1 percent of the criminal justice system's total budget is spent on research. This figure could be multiplied many times without approaching the 3 percent industry spends on research, much less the 15 percent the Defense Department spends. The Commission believes it should be multiplied many times.

That research is a powerful force for change in the field of criminal justice perhaps can best be documented by the history of the Vera Institute in New York City. Here the research of a small, nongovernment agency has in a very short time led to major changes in the bail procedures of approximately 100 cities, several States, and the Federal Government.

Because of the importance of research, the Commission recommends that major criminal justice agencies—such as State court and correctional systems and big-city police departments—organize operational research units as integral parts of their structures.

In addition, the criminal justice agencies should welcome the efforts of scholars and other independent experts to understand their problems and operations. These agencies cannot undertake needed research on their own; they urgently need the help of outsiders.

The Commission also recommends the establishment of several regional research institutes designed to concentrate a number of different disciplines on the problem of crime. It further recommends the establishment of an independent National Criminal Research Foundation to stimulate and coordinate research and disseminate its results.

One essential requirement for research is more complete information about the operation of the criminal process. To meet this requirement, the Commission recommends the creation of a National Criminal Justice Statistics Center. The Center's first responsibility would be to work with the FBI, the Children's Bureau, the Federal Bureau of Prisons, and other agencies to develop an integrated picture of the number of crimes reported to police, the number of persons arrested, the number of accused persons prosecuted, the number of offenders placed on probation, in prison, and subsequently on parole.

Another major responsibility of the Center would be to continue the Commission's initial effort to develop a new yardstick to measure the extent of crime in our society as a supplement to the FBI's Uniform Crime Reports. The Commission believes that the Government should be able to plot the levels of different kinds of crime in a city or a State as precisely as the Labor Department and the Census Bureau now plot the rate of unemployment. Just as unemployment information is essential to sound economic planning, so some day may criminal information help official planning in the system of criminal justice.

6. Money

Sixth, the police, the courts, and correctional agencies will require substantially more money if they are to control crime better.

Almost all of the specific recommendations made by the Commission will involve increased budgets. Substantially higher salaries must be offered to attract top-flight candidates to the system of criminal justice. For example, the median annual salary for a patrolman in a large city today is $5,300. Typically, the maximum salary is something less than $1,000 above the starting salary. The Commission believes the most important change that can be made in police salary scales is to increase maximums sharply. An FBI agent, for example, starts at $8,421 a year and if he serves long and well enough can reach $16,905 a year without being promoted to a supervisory position. The Commission is aware that reaching such figures immediately is not possible in many cities, but it believes that there should be a large range from minimum to maximum everywhere.

The Commission also recommends new kinds of programs that will require additional funds: Youth Services Bureaus, greatly enlarged misdemeanant probation services and increased levels of research, for example.

The Commission believes some of the additional resources—especially those devoted to innovative programs and to training, education, and research—should be contributed by the Federal Government.

The Federal Government already is conducting a broad range of programs—aid to elementary and secondary schools, the Neighborhood Youth Corps, Project Head Start, and others—designed to attack directly the social problems often associated with crime.

Through such agencies as the Federal Bureau of Investigation, the Office of Law Enforcement Assistance, the Bureau of Prisons, and the Office of Manpower Development and Training, the Federal Government also offers comparatively limited financial and technical assistance to the police, the courts, and corrections authorities.

While the Commission is convinced State and local governments must continue to carry the major burden of criminal administration, it recommends a vastly enlarged program of Federal assistance to strengthen law enforcement, crime prevention, and the administration of justice.

The program of Federal support recommended by the Commission would be directed to eight major needs:

(1) State and local planning.

(2) Education and training of criminal justice personnel.

(3) Surveys and advisory services concerning the organization and operation of police departments, courts, prosecuting offices, and corrections agencies.

(4) Development of a coordinated national information system for operational and research purposes.

(5) Funding of limited numbers of demonstration programs in agencies of justice.

(6) Scientific and technological research and development.

(7) Development of national and regional research centers.

(8) Grants-in-aid for operational innovations.

The Commission is not in a position to recommend the exact amount of money that will be needed to carry out its proposed program. It believes, however, that a Federal program totaling hundreds of millions of dollars a year during the next decade could be effectively utilized. The Commission also believes the major responsibility for administering this program should lie within the Department of Justice.

The States, the cities, and the counties also will have to make substantial increases in their contributions to the system of criminal justice.

7. Responsibility for Change

Seventh, individual citizens, social-service agencies, universities, religious institutions, civic and business groups, and all kinds of governmental agencies at all levels must become involved in planning and executing changes in the criminal justice system.

The Commission is convinced that the financial and technical assistance program it proposes can and should be only a small part of the national effort to develop a more effective and fair response to crime.

In March of 1966, President Johnson asked the Attorney General to invite each Governor to form a State committee on criminal administration. The response to this request has been encouraging; more than two-thirds of the States already have such committees or have indicated they intend to form them.

The Commission recommends that in every State and city there should be an agency, or one or more officials, with specific responsibility for planning improvements in criminal administration and encouraging their implementation.

Planning agencies, among other functions, play a key role in helping State legislatures and city councils decide where additional funds and manpower are most needed, what new programs should be adopted, and where and how existing agencies might pool their resources on either a metropolitan or regional basis.

The planning agencies should include both officials from the system of criminal justice and citizens from other professions. Plans to improve criminal administration will be impossible to put into effect unless those responsible for criminal administration help make them. On the other hand, crime prevention must be the task of the community as a whole.

While this report has concentrated on recommendations for action by governments, the Commission is convinced that governmental actions will not be enough. Crime is a social problem that is interwoven with almost every aspect of American life. Controlling it involves improving the quality of family life, the way schools are run, the way cities are planned, the way workers are hired. Controlling crime is the business of every American institution. Controlling crime is the business of every American.

Universities should increase their research on the problems of crime; private social welfare organizations and religious institutions should continue to experiment with advanced techniques of helping slum children overcome their environment; labor unions and businesses can enlarge their programs to provide prisoners with vocational training; professional and community organizations can help probation and parole workers with their work.

The responsibility of the individual citizen runs far deeper than cooperating with the police or accepting jury duty or insuring the safety of his family by installing adequate locks—important as they are. He must respect the law, refuse to cut corners, reject the cynical argument that "anything goes as long as you don't get caught."

Most important of all, he must, on his own and through the organizations he belongs to, interest himself in the problems of crime and criminal justice, seek information, express his views, use his vote wisely, get involved.

In sum, the Commission is sure that the Nation can control crime if it will.

F. TRANSPORTATION

26. The Urban-Transportation Problem

LYLE C. FITCH AND ASSOCIATES

Although most of America's national symbols glorify its rural heritage, more than half the nation's population has been classified as urban since the 1910 census, and today more than 70 percent is urban. Greatest urban growth has been concentrated in the metropolitan areas, which are centered around cities of 50,000 and over; metropolitan areas today encompass 63 percent of the nation's population.

The convenience, the productivity, and the incomes of the urban majority are dependent on systems for movement in and around cities, and so, indirectly, are those of the rural minority. Yet large cities, not only in America but throughout the world, are frustrated by the inadequacies of their internal transportation systems.

That some men cannot complete their journeys-to-work in our larger urban areas in the time in which other men can orbit the globe is today a cliché. The problem of movement through millions of people, buildings, activities, and topological obstructions is as complex in its own way as that of engineering travel in space, but financial and scientific resources have not been applied to the first in any magnitude comparable to the resources applied to the second. The technologies which have produced urban growth have not been fully exploited to reduce the friction of bringing together people and goods, which is the central economic function of urban settlement.

SOURCE: *Urban Transportation and Public Policy* by Lyle C. Fitch and Associates, published by Chandler Publishing Company, San Francisco.

Deficiencies of Urban Transportation

The most troublesome urban-transportation problem is meeting the peak demand of the journey-to-work in the largest metropolitan areas. About 50 percent of all daily travel by rapid rail transit occurs in the four peak hours. On many motor-vehicle arteries congestion is the main deterrent to the use of autos and buses during peak hours. Peak-hour demand on commuter railroads requires a concentration of labor and equipment which are idle during other hours.

Second only to the journey-to-work problem is that of the recreation peak, particularly on summer weekends. In New York, Philadelphia, Los Angeles, and other metropolitan areas certain highways, particularly those leading to the shore, carry the bulk of their weekly traffic during 10 or 12 hours on weekends. The recreation peak demand largely concerns private automobiles, rather than other transportation modes. Significantly, both types of peak demand for urban transportation involve movement of people rather than movement of goods, which is generally not as concentrated and therefore is a less obtrusive problem. The difficulties encountered in movement related to these two important human functions—work and recreation—have significant implications for the future development of urban areas.

The urgency of these problems has stimulated public action in various cities. But too many urban-traffic and urban-transportation programs designed to meet crises have failed in their purpose. The failure of these costly and frustrating ventures is rooted in lack of understanding of the nature of urban-transportation problems and inadequate organization of resources to meet them, with the result that symptoms rather than fundamental causes are treated. Underlying the continuing physical deficiencies of transportation facilities are institutional and conceptual deficiencies which handicap the approach to them.

The Physical Deficiencies

In many large cities the facilities for transportation are inadequate for fast, comfortable, and convenient travel at times and places of major demand. Present transportation systems have a variety of adverse effects on the urban environment.

TRAFFIC CONGESTION

Traffic snarls and costly delays are among the most severe and obvious problems of large urban areas. While snarls do occur elsewhere, particularly near shopping centers and at major highway interchanges, there they are less frequent and intense and more readily avoidable through skilled planning and engineering. Within urban centers the problem is one of too many vehicles competing for scarce road space which can be increased only at enormous cost. An increase in effective capacity resulting from traffic improvements often attracts more traffic so that congestion quickly closes in again to slow the pace.

Systematic measures of trends in traffic congestion in the United States are still inadequate to confirm with accuracy the widely held belief that urban traffic congestion is increasing. Measurement of congestion along particular routes by rate of flow or volume handled is likely to give a misleading impression of the efficiency of a total transportation system. The only effective way to evaluate the impact of increases or decreases in the number of vehicles operating in a system of roadways is to analyze the over-all system. The techniques of systems analysis as applied to this type of problem are in an embryonic state and there are not yet available any analyses covering significant periods of time.[1]

More direct evidence of congestion is found in the increasing difficulties of meeting schedules cited by bus companies and delivery services. Trucking associations report substantial increases in average time required for deliveries. Cary Transportation, Inc., of New York, reports that the time allowance between departure from New York's East Side terminal and flight time at La Guardia and Idlewild airports has approximately doubled in the past several years. A substantial part of this increase is attributed to traffic conditions.

Congestion may also reflect laxity in the enforcement of regulations concerning street parking and loading, inadequate techniques of traffic control, weather conditions, and other factors.

The costs of congestion are the time lost in travel and functions related to travel such as deliveries, the additional expenses of vehicle operation, and, of course, the inconvenience and frustration experienced by travelers. Wilfred Owen has pointed out that the time consumed in commuting has for many canceled the time freed by shortened working hours. The impact of these costs appears in the volume of complaints which reach the desks of mayors and traffic officials. One of the main reasons for the increasing interest of city officials in mass transportation, expressed in appearances before congressional committees and by the U.S. Conference of Mayors and the American Municipal Association, is the high cost of attempting to relieve congestion by providing more road space. An American Municipal Association policy statement says that: "Traffic congestion has slowed transit operations and the reduction in transit service in turn has increased traffic congestion. . . . In those large metropolitan areas now served by rail rapid transit and commuter railroads, the cost of diverting riders to the automobile is prohibitive."

DEFICIENCIES OF MASS TRANSPORTATION

Discomfort, inconvenience, low average speed, and obsolescence of equipment are the primary manifestations of the deficiencies of mass-transportation (particularly transit) operations in and around our large cities. The most serious cause of discomfort is overcrowding of buses and subways, particularly during the journey-to-work peak periods. Loads carried by many New York subway cars in rush hours exceed seating capacity by 200 percent and comfortable seating and standing capacity by 50 percent; the often-used simile of the sardine can is not an exaggeration at these times. In addition, noise, heat, unprotected or unattractive way stations and terminals, together with long periods of standing and waiting, are common disadvantages of transit travel. The transit industry has made little technological progress in increasing comfort standards, although significant improvements have been made on some long-distance buses and through-train equipment. For example, air conditioning, one of the major improvements on long-distance buses and trains, is seldom used on rapid rail transit.

A high proportion of obsolete and depreciated equipment is in use in urban mass transportation. Bad location and undersupply of stops and stations, the necessity for transfers, and infrequency of service contribute to the inconvenience of many mass-transportation systems.

Low average speed is a problem particularly within and near central cities and their central business districts. A survey of average rates of speed for rush-hour travel, starting from the busiest corner in town on the busiest outbound thoroughfare (for autos) and using the city's most heavily traveled transit or commuter rail route (for mass transportation), showed the over-all average for 25 cities to be 13 miles per hour for mass transportation as compared with 20 miles per hour for automobiles.[2] The only mode competitive in speed with automobiles is rail. The largest speed differentials are between automobiles and buses moving on city streets.

IMPACT ON CITY CONFIGURATION

Among the sources of dissatisfaction with urban transportation is its impact on the patterns of urban land use and on the aesthetic qualities of the city. Many parking lots; service stations, used-car lots, and other enterprises lining highways; railroad stations, tracks, and yards; and elevateds are notable for their unattractiveness, which is often reflected in the values of adjacent residential land.

The large space requirements of present transportation systems, moreover, have drastic effects on urban land-use patterns. The greater the space requirements of the transportation system, the less the proportion of space which can be used for other productive purposes, including space for relaxation and economic enterprise. The pattern of postwar urban development and the growing dominance of automobile travel, however, have tremendously increased the space requirements of urban transportation.

It appears that the proportion of urban ground space required for movement increases with the size—particularly daytime population—of the urban center. In other words, the larger the center, the greater the proportion of its land that must be devoted to transportation, assuming no change in the mix of transportation modes. A study by R. J. Smeed (using a theoretical model of a town with concentric circles of which the inner contains jobs and the outer homes) comes to the same conclusion and the related conclusion that the proportion of urban ground space required for travel increases with the number of persons traveling by surface transportation in a central area.[3]

Depending on assumptions concerning the average number of passengers per vehicle, the average journey-to-work at about 20 miles per hour requires by automobile roughly 6 to 45 times as much road space per person as by transit bus and 10 to 90 times as much road space as travel by a multiple-unit rail car. The differentials are even greater at higher speeds.[4] Moreover, the differential between space requirements of the automobile and those of other modes of transport increases with the size of the urban center. In other words, the larger the urban center, the greater the relative disadvantage of the automobile with respect to space requirements. Smeed's study concludes that the proportion of urban ground space required for travel (both movement and parking) by private auto increased more, relative to increase in city size, than that of surface transit.

It is these factors which have led some planners and urban specialists to despair of the unplanned effects of recent transportation developments on community structure and master plans. Wilfred Owen maintains that the effort to be urbanized and motorized at the same time is destroying both the benefits of cities and the advantages of the private car.[5] Senator Harrison Williams maintains that:

> Even if we were to try [to solve urban transportation problems by highways alone] with an urban highway program averaging $10 to

> $20 million a mile in high density urban areas, there is every possibility that the remedy would only succeed in killing the patient—by replacing valuable tax ratable property with nontaxable concrete and asphalt, by creating huge downtown parking demands which would further remove land for commercial and cultural purposes, and by slowly carving away the very activities that created the demand for access in the first place.[6]

Popular response to the conflict of values is generally raised over specific cases. Thus an editorial deplores the proposed destruction of historical buildings in Sacramento to make way for a new freeway[7] and widespread furor was raised over a proposal to route a 6-lane freeway through the campus of a small college, interfering with its expansion program. Merchants and residents in lower Manhattan have to date successfully opposed the construction of a crosstown expressway in the area.

HEALTH HAZARDS

Air pollution is increasingly recognized as a health hazard. It is one to which the urban-transportation system presently contributes in certain large cities. Rough estimates indicate that the proportion of existing air pollution attributable to motor-vehicle exhausts reaches 40 percent in New York City and 65 to 70 percent in Los Angeles (which has a high proportion of days in which atmospheric conditions are conducive to high pollution).[8] There is a growing conviction on the part of the public-health experts that air pollution in urban centers is a factor in the incidence of primary cancer of the trachea, bronchi, lungs, and esophagus and possibly of emphysema, nonoccupational tuberculosis and arteriosclerotic heart disease, and in the development of chronic degenerative diseases.[9]

Action on this problem is of very recent vintage. Crankcase ventilation systems and afterburner devices have been developed which reduce the emission of pollutants from motor vehicles. California requires certain of these devices for installation on new and used motor vehicles. New York State has required all motor vehicles registered in the state and manufactured after June 1963 to have crankcase ventilating systems. The U.S. Public Health Service and the state of California are sponsoring major research and experimentation to increase the efficiency of control systems.

The Institutional Deficiencies

The institutional arrangements for dealing with urban-transportation problems such as those described leave much to be desired as to both organization and financing. Institutional weaknesses underlie the failure of most public programs to date to produce large and lasting improvements in urban-transportation systems.

FRAGMENTED ORGANIZATION

Urban transportation probably suffers more from the fragmentation of the American administrative system than any other urban service. As Henry Fagin has put it:

> Metropolitan transportation is indivisible. It will be recognized as a problem in systems design. In future metropolitan networks, the several modes of transportation will be used in combination—rail *and* rubber, not rail *or* rubber; mass transport *and* individual transport, not transit *or* private vehicles; rail freight *and* trucks *and* air cargo *and* pipe lines *and* ships—all of them.[10]

Present fragmentation of planning and administration of urban transportation along modal and jurisdictional lines precludes consideration of metropolitan transportation as an integral and open system.

Metropolitan areas have leapfrogged jurisdictional boundaries. And even within jurisdictions, responsibilities for transportation are divided among manifold functional units. For example, transportation in New York City is the administrative responsibility of three great authorities, at least four major city agencies, three state agencies, seven commuter railroads, and numerous private and municipal bus lines. Until recently there has been a minimum of communication even among the New York City agencies and no institutional channels for resolving disputes on such vital policy matters as reserved lanes for transit buses which transcend the authority of a single agency. The city has developed no estimates of over-all future transportation needs, methods of meeting them, or financial requirements.

The 22-county New York metropolitan region involves three states, several major cities, several authorities including those referred to above, and over 500 local and county governments (excluding special districts), all with some degree of responsibility for transportation. Under these circumstances it is understandable that the region has never completed a comprehensive survey of transportation needs, nor even regional origin-and-destination studies. Only recently recognition of the regional aspects of transportation problems has resulted in the creation of two interstate organizations—the New York–New Jersey Transportation Agency and the Tri-State Transportation Committee. The latter, which may be established on a permanent basis by legislation recently passed in New York and Connecticut and pending in New Jersey, has responsibility for devising proposals for coordinated long-range transportation development in the region as well as solutions to immediate problems, particularly those of the commuter railroads.

Metropolitan Dade County, including Miami, is at the other end of the scale. There a single county government and a single planning commission have authority for planning and administering the over-all urban-transportation system, including arterial highways and streets and, as of 1961, transit. There is still some overlap of functions between the county and the state highway commission.

Metropolitan Cleveland is somewhere on the middle of the scale. Transportation is provided by the Cleveland Transit System, the Shaker Heights Rapid Transit Line, three other municipal transit systems, two commuter railroads, and some eight private suburban bus lines, in addition to state agencies. The Cleveland County Engineer, the Cleveland Port Department, the state highway department, and the municipalities are represented by law on the Regional Planning Commission. In actuality, however, highway and rail-transit systems are the respective provinces of the transit-system engineers and the county engineer's office, with the Planning Commission's comprehensive approach being as yet a voice crying in the wilderness. Thus the Cleveland County Engineer has successfully opposed extension of rapid-transit lines, including a downtown distribution loop for which a bond issue had been approved by the county's voters.

In only a few instances have states taken any action (other than promotion of studies) on development of intra-urban transportation facilities other than highways. Some state highway departments have developed cooperative relationships with local communities in highway and land-use planning, but others, including some concerned with large urban areas, have evidenced little respect for local-government policies and desires.

Although interagency cooperation at the federal level is increasing, at least eight separate units have a hand in making decisions, issuing regulations, financing, and otherwise shaping transportation services, all having direct or indirect bearing on urban transportation. No one agency has responsibility for considering transportation as such.

Such fragmentations and specialization of administration at all levels of government are historical and fortuitous in origin. Any effective program of transportation improvement, however, must recognize, first, that the job of moving goods and people is essentially one function the elements of which are closely interdependent; and second, that transportation in an urban area cannot be successfully controlled by a myriad of unrelated agencies, whether private or public, whether organized by geographic boundary lines or transportation mode. Efficient transportation requires consideration of patterns of development desired by the community, acceptance of plans which include transportation programs consonant with those goals, and administrative machinery to carry out the plans. This necessitates machinery at the regional level for planning, policy-making, and coordination of policy implementation, and organization at the state and federal levels to encourage and support effective regional action.

PERSONNEL

There is a shortage of personnel skilled in the numerous disciplines required for transportation planning and policy-making. It is now difficult to staff even one major transportation study, to say nothing of the considerable number which will be needed over the next few years. Transit and suburban rail service also suffer from lack of top-quality staff and management personnel.

FINANCIAL SHORTCOMINGS

Mass-transportation operations throughout the country have yielded declining returns or losses and in some cases have disappeared entirely. The weakest elements of urban transportation today are the commuter railroads. Some 30 cities in the last 10 years have lost all commuter rail service. The financial condition of most other commuter services is tenuous.

The implications of losing commuter service are portrayed in an American Municipal Association report which estimates that $17.4 billion would be required for highways alone if rail-transportation service in five cities were replaced by motor-vehicle facilities.[11] It is highly improbable that the entire adjustment to loss of suburban rail service in the great metropolitan centers would in fact take the form of increased motor-vehicle travel, particularly as parking space as well as highway space would be totally inadequate. Over a period of time there would doubtless be drastic changes (at tremendous social and economic costs) in the role and functioning of central business districts and certain suburban areas formerly served by suburban rail.

The five major urban rail rapid-transit systems in the United States[12] have suffered in varying degrees from financial difficulties. The systems of New York, Boston, and Philadelphia depend on public assistance from the cities they serve for capital improvements and replacement of rolling stock which are sorely needed. All the existing rail rapid-transit systems of the United States see a need for expansion of lines; none has secured financing for major expansion to date. Toronto is extending its system, with the assistance of Metropolitan Toronto and the Provincial Government. Proposals for construction of new rail rapid-transit systems are being promoted in four urban regions—Atlanta, Los Angeles, San Francisco, and Washington, D.C.—and are being considered in a number of others. Only in San Francisco have resources been committed to go ahead for a major expansion.

The financial picture is also gloomy with respect to nongrade-separated transit—primarily bus systems. Over the nation traffic-volume trends have been steadily downward although a number of individual systems have steady or increasing traffic volumes.[13] Many small cities have lost their transit service entirely. Local government in a number of other cities has taken over private transit systems, including the Fifth Avenue Coach Line in New York City. Metropolitan Dade County in Florida, for example, took over transit services from a private operator who reported that he saw "the handwriting on the wall." A number of private operators are hanging on but anticipate having to give up in the near future.

RESEARCH AND DEVELOPMENT

Compared to the hundreds of millions of dollars flowing into research and development related to private motor vehicles every year, expenditures on mass-transportation improvement have been almost negligible, although since 1961, federal aid for demonstration purposes has provided an important stimulus. Among numerous topics needing further study are the possibilities of automation, application of new power systems, body design, weight saving on vehicles, most appropriate functions of various transportation modes, improvements in comfort, cost-reduction factors, and factors (including price factors) affecting transportation demand.

CONCEPTUAL DEFICIENCIES

Many of the areas of dispute with respect to urban-transportation policy today reflect inadequate understanding of the functioning of urban-transportation systems and failure to consider the alternatives of urban development. As such they cannot be resolved without further analysis and development of valid concepts and goals. Primary among the reasons for these conceptual deficiencies are the paucity of research-and-development studies in certain areas and the fragmentation of institutions engaged in the study of transportation and development of policy. The most important unsettled issues include objectives of urban design and land-use planning, comparative roles of various modes of transportation, optimum means of financing intra-urban transportation, and the objectives and techniques of transportation planning.

URBAN DESIGN AND LAND-USE PLANNING

Despite the growing knowledge of urban structure, there is little consensus as to the shape which the modern urban area is assuming or should assume. Certain factors point to increased decentralization if past trends continue. But should they continue? Do we want density or dispersion? Do we prefer urban areas with a single center or with many functional nuclei? Should suburbs be integrated into the urban region or be largely self-contained? How should they be related to each other and to the central city? Do we want even development of urban land or clusters leaving sections of open space? These are questions which are unanswered in most developing urban areas and which vitally concern transportation planning as well as urban design.

Defenders of the integrity and vitality of the central city maintain that any comprehensive program for urban development must be premised on a recognition of the indispensability of the central city to our culture and economy. The decentralists, on the other hand, emphasize the inevitability or desirability of dispersion of enterprises and population into smaller separated cities or towns throughout an urban region.[14] The conflict concerns values as well as interpretation of trends. Settlement of this dispute must await both further analyses of urban development and the emergence of consensus as to goals within our metropolitan communities.

ROLES OF VARIOUS TRANSPORTATION MODES

Inextricably tied to the issues of urban design are questions of the optimum roles of motor-vehicle travel and mass transportation in the total urban system. Highway proponents point to increasing automobile ownership and the long record of declining transit and commuter railroad patronage. They question the validity of traffic projections for the proposed new transit systems, such as those of Washington, Los Angeles, and San Francisco. Holding that planning should focus on the widely decentralized type of city, which is made possible and best served by the automobile, they question whether grade-separated mass transportation has an important role in the future urban complex.[15] Those with primary interests in the suburban centers may fear that improved transit linkages would build up the central city at the expense of suburban expansion.

On the other hand, transit proponents point to mass transportation's enormous advantages in capacity, and hence in space economies, and the high cost of attempting to alleviate traffic congestion by building additional highways. They question whether low densities can long continue in view of the enormous urban-population increases projected for the next few decades and the ever-increasing demand for urban land. They claim that the declines in mass transportation can be attributed in part to the disadvantages under which it has operated—rising costs and fares, poor service, obsolete equipment, fragmented planning and administration, and lack of systematic promotion.

The validity of the conflicting arguments cannot be assessed with certainty in light of present information. Comprehensive analysis of development and transportation requirements is needed in nearly every major urban area to allow the community to arrive at consensus as to desired trends and optimum mix of various transportation modes. Major decisions, such as allowing mass-transportation facilities to go out of business on a large scale, undertaken without valid conceptual foundations and planning, may prove extremely costly.

FINANCING URBAN TRANSPORTATION

Flexibility and speed of movement throughout an urban region is an important value, but it is also a costly one considering the proportion of the community's resources which are required for its realization. Investments in transportation in a metropolitan area run to enormous sums. One of the first issues of transportation planning, then, is the budget issue.

The familiar economic rule for obtaining the best use of facilities and avoiding waste of resources is to make each major element of the transportation system self-supporting through charges imposed as directly as possible upon the users. The amount and type of transportation facilities employed is thereby determined by the amount which users are willing to buy at full cost. There are, however, valid economic reasons . . . for departing from this principle under certain conditions.

In establishing price structures for various transportation facilities, there has been little attention given to such matters as comparative cost factors or the effect of changes in price on demand. The various transportation modes have developed largely independent of each other, at different times, under different institutions, and with different means of financing. The structure of charges and subsidies for present facilities is full of inconsistencies mainly because it developed fortuitously and is generally not based on any conscious conceptual framework at all.

Pricing of automobile travel in congested centers is particularly inefficient. Considered as a charge for the use of roads, the gasoline tax is a highly inefficient instrument in that the charge is the same under all conditions—for high-cost roads and low-cost roads; for peak-hour travel when the supply of road space is scarce and at slack periods when it is plentiful. Parking fees aside, it does not cost the motorist any more to drive in downtown traffic on high-value land than on empty suburban streets or on lower-value land. (Flat-rate transit fares are subject to the same limitations.) In crowded urban centers automobile use is held in check by congestion and competition for parking space.

Moreover, the price system fails to communicate adequately the cost difference between the automobile and transit travel. The transit rider pays with each fare his share of depreciation and insurance, as well as labor and other costs, including those for the right-of-way. The private-car owner seldom keeps any true accounts, ordinarily pays nothing extra for more expensive rights-of-way, does the driving himself, and thinks that his heavy bills for depreciation and insurance have no connection with the individual decision to take the car because his payment for these items is annual and not related to each trip. Neither does he take into account as a cost of the trip the cost to the community of road and parking spaces, policing and maintenance. He thus makes his decision on what for him may be a rational basis but which is for the total economy a fallacious comparison.

At the same time, most cities and states insist that mass transportation pay its own way and require private mass-transportation companies to pay taxes which in many cases were established when they had a monopoly of intra-city service. And until very recently the federal government has not considered urban transportation at all, apart from highways, which were the only intra-urban transportation facility to receive substantial federal aid. This fact itself has tended to distort urban-transportation investment decisions. It may be argued that federal aid for highway construction is not a subsidy because it is financed by highway-user taxes. But the argument is beside the point as applied to the state- or local-government policy-maker, who must decide between facilities for which he can get substantial aid and facilities for which he cannot get such aid. He cannot base decisions primarily on an evaluation of the costs and benefits of various modes.

He must rather pick the mode which in view of the availability of federal aid presents the fewest financial problems from his own standpoint.

TRANSPORTATION PLANNING

The size of the public investment in transportation facilities and their longevity and important effects on the urban complex demonstrate the importance of comprehensive and perceptive transportation planning. The planning process encompasses the other conceptual issues we have discussed. Questions of desired patterns of urban development, mix of modes in the transportation system, and financing of transportation facilities are central to the process of transportation planning, which should offer the community's decision-makers alternatives which relate different land-use patterns to transportation systems of varying design and cost. The science of transportation planning, however, is as yet young, although planning activity has expanded continually in this country over the past 40 years. Much of the urban-transportation planning of the postwar period has suffered from two major defects. First, most projects have concentrated on planning of one mode alone, rather than on over-all transportation planning. Second, transportation planning has in many cases not been coordinated with systematic land-use-and-development planning.

The generation of transportation demand by different types and densities of land use has received increasing attention in regional-transportation studies, but projection of transportation demand is still a highly inexact science, depending on numerous arguable assumptions and untested relationships. On the other hand, there has been little study to date of the ways in which alternative transportation systems may influence regional development. Information on these relationships is just beginning to be developed.

---

[1]Toronto consultants have developed a computer model of the main Toronto arterials, designed to permit analysis of the impact on various parts of the system of increasing or decreasing the number of vehicles in the system and of making improvements at any given point. This model might be adapted to a more general analysis of congestion.

[2]Frances Bello, "The City and the Car," in Editors of Fortune, *The Exploding Metropolis,* Doubleday & Company, 1958, pp. 53-80. The comparison is only of the two busiest routes—one auto route and one mass-transportation route in each city. Hence the survey does not give an accurate comparison of over-all average speeds of various modes. For example, the Long Island Railroad was found to be the fastest route tested but did not qualify as the busiest mass-transportation route in the New York area.

[3]R. J. Smeed, *The Traffic Problem in Towns,* Manchester Statistical Society, 1961; and "The Space Requirements for Traffic in Towns," in T. E. H. Williams, ed., *Urban Survival and Traffic,* London, 1962.

[4]See: F. Lehner, *Public Transport Within the Framework of Urban General Traffic Plans,* International Union of Public Transport, XXXIV International Congress (Brussels, 1961), p. 28.

[5]Wilfred Owen, *Cities in the Motor Age,* Viking Press, 1959.

[6]U.S. Congress, Senate *Hearings on Urban Mass Transportation,* Subcommittee of the Committee on Banking and Currency, 1961, p. 26.

[7]*New York Times,* October 21, 1960.

[8]Estimates supplied by the New York City Department of Air Pollution Control.

[9]See for example, John H. Ludwig, "Some Ramifications of Air Contamination," *Public Health Reports,* May 1960; U.S. Surgeon General, *Motor Vehicles, Air Pollution, and Health,* Division of Air Pollution, Public Health Service, Department of Health, Education, and Welfare, 1962.

[10]Henry Fagin, "Improving Mobility Within the Metropolis," *Proceedings* of the Academy of Political Science, May 1960.

[11]American Municipal Association, *The Collapse of Communter Service: A Survey of Mass Transportation in Five Major Cities,* 1960.

[12]New York, Chicago, Boston, Philadelphia, and Cleveland.

[13]Data supplied by the American Transit Association.

[14]For discussion of these issues, see, for example, James M. Fitch, "In Defense of the City," *Proceedings* of the Academy of Political Science, May 1960; Jane Jacobs, "Modern City Planning: Victory Over Vitality," *Columbia University Forum,* Fall, 1961, and *The Death and Life of Great American Cities,* Random House, 1961; A. F. Parrott, "The Flight to the Suburbs Slackens," *Proceedings,* Social Statistics Section, 1960, American Statistical Association, Washington, D.C.; Wilbur Smith and Associates, *Future Highways and Urban Growth,* New Haven, 1961; *Cities in the Motor Age, op. cit.;* Lewis Mumford, *The Highway and the City,* Harcourt, Brace and World, 1963 edition.

[15]See John R. Meyer, John F. Kain, and Martin Wohl, *Technology and Urban Transportation,* Office and Science and Technology, Executive Office of the President, 1962.

G. AIR POLLUTION

27. The Struggle for Clean Air

GLADWIN HILL

In a large city in the Middle West a few weeks back, a nationally respected air pollution official concluded a disquisition on the nation's mounting smog problem by abruptly sweeping aside his sliderule, charts and tabulations and exclaiming:

"That's the official story. Now do you want to hear the truth?

"The truth is that the critical ingredient in smog simply is politics. By that I mean people and their instruments of government, and their attitudes about a community problem.

"We know how to cure smog. It's not unduly difficult or expensive. The problem is getting the people in the community to support a cleanup program.

"The most important part of a program is not technical expertise. It's having a wheeler-dealer who can put it across with the political establishment in a community. We've been long on engineering and short of wheeler-dealers. That's why our air is a mess."

The "mess" consists of a daily load of some 360,000 tons of gaseous wastes that pour into the nation's atmosphere and collect in palls of murk over some 7,300 communities. As population, urbanization, power generation and industry inexorably increase, so will the mess.

The official's observations are set forth here because they are authoritative in themselves, and because they reflect the virtually unanimous sentiments of the scores of Federal, state and local pollution officials who were interviewed in several months' research.

"Politically," the candid official continued, "air pollution is a far tougher can of worms than water pollution. With water pollution, the blame goes mainly to collective sources—municipalities and industries—and cleanup costs fall on them.

"A lot of air pollution goes back to individuals—their cars, their furnaces, their incinerators. When a cleanup program threatens to hit them directly, and change the way they're doing things, and cost a little bit, they back off.

"And if the pressure isn't there, the politician isn't going to do anything. He can think of 26 other ways of spending public money that will be more popular."

Consequently, of the 7,300 communities with air pollution, only 130 have control programs, and the Air Pollution Division of the United States Public Health Service appraises only about 90 of these as substantial.

Furthermore, in 1965 fewer than 20 came close to the per capita expenditure rate of 35 cents that Federal officials consider a minimum for an adequate community program. This reckoning is based on the fact that about 70 per cent of a budget goes for personnel, and the larger the population involved, the bigger the supervisory, engineering, inspection and enforcement staff that is needed.

The highest expenditure rate in the country in 1965 was the 83.3 cents that Cook County, Ill., spent on its 180,000 persons living outside Chicago. New York City's per capita rate was 15.7 cents.

"In cities under 200,000," the official continued, "it's very difficult to promote the money you need for an adequate staff.

"In cities under 100,000, you get into an industrial-power situation: one or two companies dominate the community and nobody is going to pass any laws to cause trouble for industry—unless you happen to run into an especially enlightened company."

The Public Health Service estimates that 133 million tons of contaminants pour into the atmosphere every year. Industry, inducing power generation, is the major source of the gross contaminants. (Automobiles produce more gases, but a lot of that is carbon monoxide, which is innocuous unless it becomes too concentrated.)

There are some 300,000 manufacturing plants in the country. If only two-thirds of them emit fumes, it still amounts to one plant for every 1,000 people. More than 500 communities have chemical plants. There are 300 oil refineries.

For generations, industry escaped regulation because its effluvia were considered an unavoidable concomitant of productivity and prosperity. Recent experience has proved this technically incorrect and ethically shaky.

The President's Science Advisory Committee, in its big report last November on "Restoring the Quality of Our Environment," set forth as a prime principle:

"The responsibility of each polluter for all forms of damage caused by his pollution should be effectively recognized and generally accepted. There should be no 'right' to pollute."

Such major segments of industry—and major sources of pollution—as the oil, chemical, power and steel industries are spending hundreds of millions of dollars on pollution controls.

The electric power industry says it has spent $750-million, and the oil industry says it has spent $250-million just in the last 10 years. The chemical industry reports it is spending $43-million a year to operate smog control equipment that has cost $250-million.

The steel companies in Chicago have joined in a program that will cost upward of $30-million in the next five years to reduce their discharge of soot. Every week industry buys more than $1-million of equipment to remove obnoxious chemicals from industrial waste gases.

But, pollution officials point out, such sums are not inordinately large in the economics of industry—the nation's newest oil refinery, for instance, will cost $100-million.

Neither, officials say, do the sums necessarily bear a relationship to the size of the ever-growing problem. Fifteen years hence, twice as much electricity will have to be generated as now; the burning of oil is expected to triple, and the burning of coal and natural gas to double.

Fume-belching plants can still be found in most cities, and fume abatement has tended to vary directly with the strictness of local enforcement. Contentions are sometimes made that pollution controls are technically or economically impossible—although Federal experts say that proper control equipment averages less than 5 per cent of the cost of an industrial facility.

Some industrial circles are expounding the "classification" system that they pushed for water pollution—the concept that different degrees of cleanliness, or dirtiness, are acceptable.

The latest idea along this line is that the skies can be used for industrial waste on a "push button" system. Under this, industries would discharge fumes when winds seemed likely to blow them away, but would stop on signal when weather conditions threatened to change.

Air pollution officials are skeptical about this. They say that, if an industry has proper pollution control equipment for periods of adverse weather, it might as well operate the equipment all the time.

They also say the plan would put control agencies in an impossible position, where they would be constantly accused of pushing the "stop" button unnecessarily.

There is a familiar pattern, when a community mounts a program to control air pollution, of industry representatives moving into a dominant role and slowing reforms.

"There are two main ways of doing this," the Middle West official said. "One is to go all out for an impressive technical program but give it no authority. The other is to give it impressive authority but no budget."

This kind of thing happens on the state level, too, the official said.

Industry is understandably touchy about air pollution control because it has, in one sense, been a whipping boy. Citizens like to think that their air pollution can be stopped by lambasting the factory on the other side of town.

But in most cases smog is a combination of industrial fumes, the effluvia of home heaters and incinerators, municipal refuse burning and automobiles. The public shares responsibility but is slow to face it.

"There are some remarkable fallacies that circulate as rationalizations for doing nothing about air pollution," says one Federal official. "I call them 'the six sophistries of smog.' They run like this:

"The air in any given area belongs to whoever got there first.

"Fumes strong enough to nauseate people and make their eyes water do not in any way adversely affect health.

"Until we can prove to everyone's satisfaction precisely how much of what pollutant is injuring which people to what degree, it is intelligent to do nothing at all about controlling air pollution.

"Air pollution is good because cigarette smoking is bad.

"Pollution control programs like Los Angeles' have been futile because smog has not completely disappeared.

"It's better for 2 million citizens to spend $10-million cleaning up the effects of air pollution than for 10 industries to spend $2-million to clean up the sources of pollution."

For years, clean-air campaigners have tried to overcome public inertia through the "scare" approach, stressing the presumable health hazards of atmospheric contaminants. It hasn't worked.

Despite strong statistical evidence that sieges of smog have hastened, if not caused, the deaths of thousands of persons in New York, London and elsewhere, the hazards seem as remote to the general public as those of cigarette smoking.

In a nationwide opinion survey commissioned last year by the chemical industry, more than eight out of 10 persons indicated they did not consider air pollution a community problem.

At this year's annual meeting of the Air Pollution Control Association, a joint industry-science-Government organization, there was pronounced sentiment that propaganda should emphasize smog's esthetic blight and economic drain, of at least $11-billion a year just in damage to crops and materials.

Unlike water pollution, in which a sample dipped from a river and analyzed in a laboratory may tell a good deal of the story, dealing with air pollution is a protracted and farflung operation.

It may take thousands of air samplings over many months to determine the dimensions of a community problem. Then comes a door-to-door inventory of pollution sources, followed by corrective recommendations.

Then there is the design, procurement and installation of equipment, and finally the enforcement of regulations through periodic inspections.

A classic joke in the pollution control profession is this aphorism from a seasoned engineer:

"A cleanup job takes 50 years—40 years to get the politicians out of the way and 10 years to do the work."

In the absence of extensive initiative by states and municipalities, the Federal Government has spearheaded anti-pollution activities.

. . . The Federal activities include public education, research, technical assistance to localities, subsidies to local control programs ($3.6-million in grants last year), and abatement actions for interstate pollution.

The division's annual budgets up to now have been under $30 million.

The law authorizes Federal abatement, intervention when one state's smog bothers another. The procedure is like that in water pollution cases: hearings, agreement on corrective programs, and supervised execution of the programs, with the possibility of Federal court action if there is no compliance.

Eight such interstate actions have been started so far, including one dealing with the "aerial garbage" that wafts back and forth between New York and New Jersey.

But most pollution is intrastate. And because each locality's smog problem is a unique combination of factors, responsibility for dealing with nonautomotive pollution is considered to rest, both legally and practically, with state and local governments.

If they will come to grips with air pollution, Federal officials think prospects are excellent for solving the problem. . . .

. . . On Dec. 12 the Department of Health, Education and Welfare will convoke a national conference on air pollution. There have been similar meetings before, but this one will be something of a milestone.

In essence, the gathering of public officials, scientists and engineers will tell the American people that they are inexorably involved in a long, arduous and complex campaign against creeping suffocation.

"The conference," says John W. Gardner, the Secretary of Health, Education and Welfare, "should help us insure that the air pollution problem, already serious, does not become critical in the decade ahead."

The federally prescribed equipment to curtail auto fumes, which will raise the price of all 1968 cars about $50, is only a dot in an endless vista of regulation and readjustments that confront the public.

Changes in Many Areas

Prospective changes range from those in such areas as trash disposal, home heating and automobiles to the field of local government and, ultimately, international relations.

Some 7,300 communities across the country are now confronted with air pollution problems, according to the Public Health Service. Few have done anything about it—although effective programs have been shown to be relatively inexpensive.

Where air pollution is not dealt with, it is axiomatic that it only gets worse, since it is the product of the everyday activities of an increasing number of people. Eventually, extensive and irrefutable evidence attests, there is insupportable damage to materials, crops, health and the general livability of communities.

Some air pollution officials expect a nationwide howl when the auto controls go into effect and the general public realizes that the days of only blinking at smog, literally and figuratively, are at an end. But howling seems unlikely to alter the facts of the situation.

"It's not a question of whether action has to be taken, once you've got atmospheric contamination," says Vernon MacKenzie, a recent director of the Air Pollution Division in the Public Health Service. "It's only a question of how quickly you get at it."

Acting on this premise, the Federal Government has quietly but emphatically committed the nation to a war on air pollution.

Up to now, Federal activities have consisted mainly of research, technical assistance to localities, and subsidies to local pollution control programs.

Under the Clean Air Acts of 1963 and 1965 the Federal Government has asserted control power in only two areas—interstate air pollution, in which abatement actions have been started in eight instances, and automobile fumes.

Air pollution from stationary sources, such as factories, homes and dumps, is considered primarily the responsibility of states and localities, because each place's problem is different.

Officials hope that the present Federal activities, along with the state-by-state enforcement of next year's automobile fume controls, will stimulate state and local action in the next few years.

But if public inertia persists, the Federal Government could press the war on smog through several channels.

Interstate Problem

Seventy-five major metropolitan areas, for instance, straddle state lines, making them subject to Federal abatement actions. The Air Pollution Division's guidelines for acceptable health standards and "recommended procedures" to minimize fumes in standard industrial processes could be made regulatory.

Finally, there has been some discussion of including pollution control provisions in Federal procurement contracts. These would affect industrial establishments in nearly every state.

Through one influence or another—Federal and local—the nation is moving into a new era of comprehensive air quality regulation.

This will not be a matter, which, like water pollution, the public can leave largely to experts.

The first decision confronting thousands of communities will be how to organize effective pollution control programs.

Because air currents ignore political boundaries, municipal pollution control often is a less effective answer than "airshed" programs covering several jurisdictions.

This poses the problem of creating the "metropolitan government" sort of agency that is anathema to many people. Yet a number of cities, including San Francisco, St. Louis, Cincinnati and Kansas City, are forging ahead with air pollution programs under several jurisdictions.

But some prominent authorities say the campaign for clean air requires a larger dimension than simple controls: namely, community and air-resource planning.

"Up to now," says J. J. Scheuneman, chief of the technical assistance branch of the Air Pollution Division, "control of air pollution has been based on correction of existing problems.

"Little consideration has been given to long-range planning—how proposed community or regional master plans might influence air quality.

"As long as this situation is allowed to exist, one can expect air pollution problems to be created faster than they can be resolved."

One phase of long-range planning is a coordinated approach to the disposal of the whole spectrum of wastes.

Solid wastes now are burned, aggravating the gaseous waste problem, or are allowed to contaminate waterways. Solid contaminants in water, in turn, often are extracted and burned—again simply exchanging one form of pollution for another.

To avert such lost motion, California has aerospace engineers studying the possibilities of an integrated handling of community and regional wastes of all types—solids, liquids and gases—through a device such as centralized byproduct plants. The Federal Government is starting similar research.

What Los Angeles Did

Meanwhile, citizens in countless communities will be confronted with decisions such as Los Angeles has already made—abolishing backyard incinerators, reorganizing rubbish and garbage collection, deactivating municipal incinerators that cost millions of dollars, abolishing burning dumps in favor of landfill disposal, replacing coal with oil, and partially replacing oil with natural gas and conventional fuels with atomic power.

The automobile is the national fixture most likely to be radically affected in the fight against smog.

Federal officials are planning a progressive tightening in the next few years of the emission limits being imposed next year on two constituents of exhaust fumes—nitrocarbons and carbon monoxide. Eventual control of other effluents, such as oxides of nitrogen, is contemplated.

But the best efforts against car fumes, authorities say, will hardly offset the constant increase in smog coming from the uncontrolled contaminants of an ever growing number of automobiles.

Neither changes in gasoline ingredients nor the experimental turbine engine, which burns less troublesome fuels, offers assurance of fully answering this problem.

"If the auto industry can't control car emissions down to 99 per cent, which at this point seems an unlikely achievement," says S. Smith Griswold, Federal pollution abatement chief, "the only answer for big cities is a different propulsion system."

Such alternatives as the liquid hydrogen or liquid oxygen fuel cells used in spaceships, superpower batteries and compact atomic-power units are being widely investigated. But they would be prohibitively expensive now for family cars; they are not an alternative in the smog war.

What will clear air cost? Federal experts say a typical community can operate an effective air pollution control program, exclusive of automobiles, for as little as 50 cents a person a year.

The current budget of Los Angeles County, which has had the nation's most aggravated pollution problem, is only $3,663,000.

Besides administrative expenses there are costs, such as industrial fume-suppressing equipment, for which the public ultimately pays. But even taking this into account, per capita costs in Los Angeles over a 10-year period average only about $3 a year.

Estimates Vary

Some businessmen have figured it would cost as much as $75-billion to clean up American industry. But in a detailed analysis last year, Fortune magazine estimated that two-thirds of the nation's air pollution from all sources could be eliminated for about $3-billion a year—$15 a person.

Deputy Assistant Secretary of Commerce James Collins said recently that industry and government together could cope with growing air pollution by spending $10-billion in the next eight years, or $1.25-billion a year.

These figures contrast sharply with the current annual outlay by industry and Federal, state and local governments of less than $550-million a year.

And it is in particular contrast with the $11-billion in damage, which, the Federal Government says, is done annually just to crops and materials.

The question of when the skies may be cleared, given a reasonable nationwide effort, involves many variables.

It will take at least 10 years to replace all the fume-belching cars on the nation's highways with the better post-1967 models.

Furthermore, in terms of controlling stationary pollution sources, five years is considered par for a community to organize a control effort, study the technical problems and install corrective equipment.

Vaguely, authorities believe that considerable improvement in the pollution situation may be registered in the nineteen-seventies, and that by the nineteen-eighties there may be restoration of fairly clean air.

Before then, air pollution may have become an international, rather than national, problem.

Dr. Morris Neiburger, professor of meteorology at the University of California at Los Angeles, is one of a growing number of scientists who are gravely concerned about man's casual use of the skies as a gaseous dump heap.

"Unless prompt, effective action to control pollution is taken," he said recently, "the atmosphere will grow progressively more polluted until, a century from now, it is too toxic to permit human life.

"To illustrate the consequences of unrestricted use of fossil fuels [coal and oil]," he continued, "just imagine the smog which would accumulate in the atmosphere if every one of the 800 million Chinese drove a gasoline-powered automobile, as every Los Angelino does."

While it will be a long time before all Chinese have automobiles, a comparable problem is posed by the collective technological advance of the underdeveloped nations.

A recent study by the Senate Public Works Committee said:

"While [natural] atmospheric purification processes may remove many pollutants before they can travel from one continent to another, it is quite evident, as demonstrated by nuclear testing in the atmosphere, that pollution can encircle the earth a number of times before reaching the ground.

"The present world population of 3 billion is expected to reach 4.5 billion by 1980. The increasing worldwide demands on, and pollution of, the common air resource, can reduce the quality of air which reaches the United States."

There is evidence that such apprehensions are more than conjectural.

One reason the earth is livable is that carbon dioxide in the atmosphere absorbs heat and helps to maintain a balance between incoming solar energy and the earth's heat radiation.

Carbon dioxide is a major product of combustion. Rising living standards around the world, involving heat, light, transportation and manufacturing, bring a proliferation of combustion processes.

These are now adding six billion tons of carbon dioxide to the atmosphere every year. Only 35 years hence, scientists figure, there will be 25 per cent more carbon dioxide in the atmosphere than there is now.

This, the President's Science Advisory Committee said last fall, "will modify the heat balance to such an extent that marked changes in climate could occur."

Although the effect of an increase in carbon dioxide can be determined in a laboratory, the exact climatic changes it would produce on a global scale are not known.

The panel had no ready solution for this problem, except the investigation of "possibilities of bringing about countervailing changes"—that is, reducing air pollution.

On the nation's prospects of accomplishing this, authorities are guardedly optimistic, if only because Los Angeles showed that, when air pollution got bad enough, people would institute drastic reforms.

But there is no guarantee that nature will grant other communities the years of grace that Los Angeles had to work on the problem. There was no reprieve for the 20 people who suffocated at Donora, Pa., in 1948.

"We cannot afford to make the same mistakes with regard to our limited air resources as we have in the past with regard to our other precious natural resources," Vernon MacKenzie says.

"The price of our neglect will be higher than any of us would be willing to pay."

28. Beware of the Air

MITCHELL GORDON

For four years, from 1952 to 1956, while he was Associate Professor of Pathology at the School of Medicine at the University of Southern California, Dr. Paul Kotin conducted an interesting series of experiments involving several hundred mice and some painstakingly collected particles of Los Angeles smog. His findings hold some frightening implications for urban humans.

Large blowers located next to Los Angeles County Hospital and on a portable rig parked near the city's four-level downtown freeway interchange drew in foul air. Tiny particles and gases in the air were caught in filter paper. Solutions were then made from the particles and painted on the skins of some 100 mice as often as 3 times a week over a period of 14 months.

By the end of that time, 75 percent of the mice had developed skin cancers.

Dr. Kotin admits his experiments do not prove smog causes cancer in humans. The cancers produced on the mice, he concedes, may have been due to an unusual concentration of regularly applied pollutants not necessarily dangerous to humans in the highly diluted, airy forms in which they make highly irregular appearances.

"Nevertheless," Dr. Kotin states, "the experiments do prove there

SOURCE: *Sick Cities* (Baltimore: Penguin Books, 1965) pp. 86-90. Reprinted with permission of The Macmillan Company from *Sick Cities* by Mitchell Gordon.

are chemical carcinogens (agents capable of producing cancer) in Los Angeles smog. Solutions made from washed and filtered air produced no cancers on test mice painted just as frequently over the same period of time. Furthermore, we know that what is capable of producing cancer in one mammal is generally capable of producing it in another.

"We know also," he said, "that the state in which these agents exist makes them capable of being breathed by humans and deposited on the lining of the lung where they can survive long enough to do damage."

Dr. Kotin and his colleagues at the University of Southern California are pushing their cancer studies further under long-term grants from the United States Public Health Service. In 1962 they placed some 3,000 rats, mice, hamsters, guinea pigs, and rabbits at four different sites in Los Angeles County, one of them in a broad open area between the inbound and outbound lanes of the heavily traveled Hollywood Freeway. Another 3,000 animals were kept in rooms supplied by filtered air. Their detailed studies were expected to shed further light on the relationship of air pollution to cancer.

In South Africa, Japan, and other lands being showered with an influx of automobiles and a surge of industry, concern over air pollution is likewise growing. In 1960 Dr. Geoffrey Dean, of the Union of South Africa's Eastern Cape Provincial Hospital, told a medical conference, "There seems to be very strong evidence that lung cancer results from environmental factors and that it has not been primarily genetically determined, that it results, in fact, from the air we breathe."

In Japan, where mortality rates from lung cancer quadrupled in the years from 1948 to 1960, belief is rising that some of the contributory causes, at least, may be found in polluted air, particularly from the rapid growth in vehicular traffic.

One of the most emphatic statements of all comes from former Surgeon General, Dr. LeRoy E. Burney. "There is a very definite association between community air pollution," says he, "and high mortality rates due to cancer of the respiratory tract, cancer of the stomach, esophagus and arteriosclerotic heart disease."

Consider some of the evidence.

Not long ago, Dr. David F. Eastcott, of New Zealand, found that lung cancer among Britons who emigrated to the down-under isles after they were thirty years old was 75 percent more common than among natives who had lived in New Zealand all their lives, though New Zealanders are known to be among the heaviest smokers in the world. New Zealand's air is nowhere near as badly polluted as Britain's, though it is getting fouler and fouler as additional autos and factories dot its scenic landscape. The theory, of course, is that polluted air breathed in Britain may have started a physiological sequence in the émigrés which the native-born, inhaling cleaner air, escaped.

Studies of cancer victims in England and Wales revealed a doubling of mortality from lung cancer in a ten-year period from 1944, but no increase at all in larynx cancer deaths. The lung, of course, is more exposed to air pollutants than the larynx.

South Africa's Dr. Dean notes that Durban, which suffers from a serious air-pollution problem not entirely dissimilar from that of Los Angeles, has twice as many cancer victims as Johannesburg or Capetown, cities with much less air pollution.

Medical authorities in recent years have also observed a notable increase in lung cancer among animals in zoos.

More than a score of studies in Britain and elsewhere have established the role of air pollution in chronic bronchitis. The ailment has taken more lives in Britain in some recent years than lung cancer and tuberculosis combined, and is one of the leading causes of death in that country.

In the decade when California's automotive population grew the fastest—from 1950 to 1960—mortality rate from emphysema, a chronic lung disease that many physicians contend is aggravated by foul air, quadrupled. The most notable increases, twice as many, in fact, were experienced by urban as compared with rural regions.

Dr. W. C. Hueper, chief of the Environmental Cancer Section of the National Institutes of Health in Bethesda, Maryland, describes modern man as "living in a sea of carcinogens." The cancer-causing agents, says he, include such ingredients of combustion exhaust as benzpyrene, arsenic, benzol, tar, asphalt, carbon black, creosote oil, paraffin oil, and a variety of metal particles.

According to some authorities, air pollution is already so bad in some cities, notably Birmingham, Alabama, that the mere process of breathing may cause the intake of as great a quantity of cancer-causing substances as the smoking of two packs of cigarettes a day. Medical authorities have measured the intake by inhalation of as much as 200 milligrams yearly of benzpyrene, which results from the incomplete combustion of fossil fuels, such as coal and oil. They figure this is a third more benzpyrene than one would take into his system if he smoked forty cigarettes a day throughout the year. . . .

A good many air-pollution experts believe some urban areas may be setting themselves up for air-pollution disasters in the not too distant future. At least three such disasters have occurred in modern times. In 1930, a heavy pall of industrial pollutants blanketed the Meuse Valley in Belgium for several days, leaving 63 dead in its wake. In 1948, aerial wastes snuffed out the lives of at least 18 persons in Donora, Pennsylvania, and brought illness to thousands of others, whose life spans were believed to have been shortened as a result.

In 1952, a fog steeped in smoke and soot that could actually be tasted squatted for a full week on London, England. Before it lifted, 4,000 deaths were attributed to its content. The mortality rate on certain days was higher than in any peacetime 24 hours in a century with two exceptions: during the influenza epidemic of 1918-1919 and during the cholera epidemic of 1854. The smoke content of London's air during the incident was as much as 9 times the normal amount.

The London week brought 10 times as many deaths from bronchitis, 7 times as many from influenza, nearly 5 times as many from pulmonary tuberculosis, and nearly 3 times as many from heart and circulatory failures as in a normal winter week. Some 90 percent of the victims were over 45 years of age, and a good many of the other 10 percent under 5—two groups especially susceptible to respiratory problems.

H. FINANCE

29. The Great Urban Tax Tangle

In view of the looming importance of local tax policy, FORTUNE *presents below the substance of a round-table discussion held last summer at Claremont Men's College, Claremont, California, and attended by many eminent tax and municipal experts. The conference was sponsored by the Lincoln School of Public Finance in cooperation with the National League of Cities, the Urban Land Institute, Action, and Time Inc. Time's Pierrepont I. Prentice acted as rapporteur and moderator of proceedings. This is a condensation of the consensus report Prentice submitted to participants.*

While federal tax policy has been recently subject to extensive debate, much less attention has been paid to the taxes that strike closer to home. Yet direct local government spending, including city, county, and school districts, has been going up much faster than federal spending—from some $9 billion in 1946 to a level of more than $50 billion currently. If it continues to grow at anything like this rate, it will reach the $100-billion mark in the 1970's.

How all this new money is raised can have an enormous and decisive effect on how cities grow, how cities redevelop, where industry locates. It can also have a major influence on what it costs people to live in cities and whether our cities are livable. The bigger the local tax take, the greater the need for wise policies and wise methods of collecting those taxes. Mistakes that did not make much difference at the $9-billion level of 1946 can be critical and destructive at present and future levels.

Almost all of us who participated in this round table would like to see local governments assume a bigger share of the responsibility for providing the standard of services their localities want, for we believe in keeping a maximum amount of decision making on spending close to the people who will have to pay. But the local governments cannot take on this bigger job unless and until they can find better ways to raise the revenues they will need. This raises such thorny questions as how much new money will have to be raised by property taxes, how property can be more justly assessed, and what the division of taxation should be between land and improvements.

None of us would dream of suggesting that local tax reform will cure all the ills of our cities. But most of us see a clear, close, and causal connection between what is wrong with our cities today and what is wrong with their tax systems. If slums are spreading in what should be fine close-in residential areas, how largely is this because old housing is so lightly taxed (compared with good new buildings) that it is more profitable to let it sink into slums? If our cities are disintegrating around their perimeters instead of expanding in an orderly way, how much of this sprawl is because underused land on the outskirts is so lightly taxed that its owners feel no tax pressure to let it be put to better use when it is needed? If mass transportation is half empty and downtown is choked with parked private cars, to what extent is this due to the fact that our cities subsidize those who ride in cars by letting them park on the downtown streets for a small fraction of what it costs? Are we abetting sprawl by subsidizing horizontal transportation while taxing vertical transportation?

Most of us agree that the purpose and function of cities is to overcome the handicaps and inefficiencies of distance and make it easy and economical for people to live and work close together. In doing so they find that their opportunities are multiplied and they enjoy cultural and recreational facilities that would otherwise be impossible. In addition, cities achieve the vast economies of a central market where industry can find a wide choice of suppliers and trade can find millions of customers close at hand. All these advantages are frustrated when cities lose their compactness and when their traffic arteries are jammed.

All of us agree that much better metropolitan planning is needed, but most of us think that planning can be pretty futile as long as our local tax system encourages land speculation and often makes it more profitable to misuse and underuse land than to improve it for its highest and best use. All of us agree that better zoning is needed, but zoning is only a negative power; it can prevent an unwanted land use but cannot assure a desired use; and today, alas, too much suburban zoning is snob motivated, speculation motivated, or tax motivated and does more harm than good. Too much suburban zoning seeks to block urban growth rather than to guide it; too much seeks to perpetuate a bucolic past; too much aims simply to keep lower-income families out and school costs down for the benefit of present property owners.

All of us recognize the urgent need for preserving plenty of open space in urban and metropolitan areas; but most of us think this urban open space should be open for everybody to use and enjoy. Very few of us think private owners and exclusive clubs should be given special tax consideration to let them hold large close-in areas off the market for their own exclusive enjoyment while waiting for the land price to multiply. Big estates, farms, and golf clubs belong out beyond the little plots where most people live, so they won't make so many families drive home past miles of "Keep Out" and "No Trespassing" signs.

Property the Key

We do not oppose the local governments' efforts to get more money from income taxes, sales taxes, and grants-in-aid, but we do think most cities would be wise to play safe and figure that most of the added money they will need will have to come from the property tax, which now provides nearly 90 percent of all local tax revenues. All other local taxes provide only a little more than 10 percent, and even that would be much smaller were it not for a very few large cities whose level of spending is close to the limit of what property taxes can provide.

Most of us think some cities might wisely collect more revenue—in some cases a substantial revenue—from more adequate service charges for what are in effect publicly owned utilities: water supply, sewage disposal, garbage collection, parking space on and off the streets, etc. Most of us think more cities might be wise to use neighborhood assessments rather than city-wide taxes to pay the first cost of parks, playgrounds, and other needed neighborhood facilities that will raise neighborhood property values. Many of us think more cities should be allowed to explore the local sales-tax potential to see how much added revenue it could safely produce. But when all these allowances have been made, it still looks as if local governments would have to rely on the property tax to meet an overwhelming part of their future needs.

So when we urge the need of local tax reform we mean mostly property-tax reform, and more specifically the taxation of real property, on which local government today enjoys an almost unchallenged monopoly. It is estimated that total tangible wealth of all kinds in the

U.S. has a value of close to $2 trillion. The market value of real property (land and improvements) runs to about $1 trillion. This enormous potential base today yields taxes of some $17 billion, or about 1.7 percent. This yield surely seems low.

We do not recommend raising effective rates on real property as high as 3 percent, but we do think it is important to note that millions of Americans now live in urban communities that collect 3 percent or more and find it something they can live with—and 3 percent is still far below the admittedly ruinous 6.64 percent peak reached in Boston in 1959. So except for a few big cities, it is just plain nonsense to say that our local governments' right to collect real-property taxes gives them an inadequate tax base.

On the contrary, the potential base is enormous and is constantly growing, and even without reforms revenues will be going up. The property tax as it is now conceived and administered may indeed be a bad tax as its critics charge, fraught with bad economic consequences and crying for reform. It may be an unpopular tax and a tax that makes voters unhappily conscious of what local government costs. But it is *not* inadequate as a source and it is very far from exhausted.

THE CRAZY QUILT

The first step in reforming and improving property taxes involves more equitable assessment of underlying values. The assessment pattern today is a crazy quilt. Some property is so underassessed that it carries almost no share of the load. Other property is assessed and taxed twenty or even forty times as heavily.

Assessments vary from place to place among the 4,142 municipalities, 2,575 townships, 6,004 school districts, and 5,411 special-tax districts included in 212 standard metropolitan areas. Assessments vary by age of property, with new improvements too often penalized by much higher percentage assessments than old buildings. They also vary with the competence, diligence, and motivation of the assessor, and often involve flagrant class favoritism. The 1962 Census of Governments showed vacant lots assessed an average of 20.5 percent of "true value" whereas the figure for nonfarm homes was 30.6 percent. Since then land prices have soared still higher, and today millions of acres needed for development are assessed at a small fraction of their asking price.

Local assessment inequalities are made worse by exemptions sponsored by the states. These include the limit of a few hundred dollars some states impose on assessment values of any land that is farmed (even when it may be held for development at many thousands of dollars per acre), and the homestead, veterans', and senior citizens' exemptions by which some state governments have sought to subsidize favored voters at the expense of local tax revenues. The limit on homestead exemptions is usually set at or below $5,000 of assessed value. But since assessments often run to only 25 percent of market value, this means that homes worth $20,000 may be completely tax exempt.

The importance of better assessments has been stressed by the Advisory Commission on Intergovernmental Relations, which in one of its reports indicates that substantive changes in the property tax will be largely meaningless without improved administration. "Over the past fifty years notable advances have been made in . . . State and local fiscal administration, but in very many areas assessment administration has not kept pace with this progress . . . few officials feel under obligation to enforce the tax law as written. In some States, in fact, compliance by the assessors with the constitution and statutes would be a cause for general consternation. The average assessor makes himself a sort of one-man legislature. He—not the State constitution and the State legislature—defines local taxing and borrowing power and determines the value of a veterans' or homestead tax exemption by the level at which he decides to assess property. He is likely, also, to administer his own version of the personal property tax . . . Such practices breed disrespect for the tax law . . ."

Since states make the laws that govern how local authorities can collect taxes, they must share the blame for most of what is wrong now with local taxation. Only the states can insist that all local tax districts should employ trained professional assessors; only the states can change the laws that make tax appeals so costly and often so futile; only the states can end the too common practice of making the cities pay for county services that the county performs only outside the limits of the great cities.

We urge that local governments should be given much wider control of their own taxing and borrowing powers than now prevails in most states. Most of us think all state limitations should be abolished, perhaps the reservation that any increase in the local limits must first be approved by a local referendum; and quite a few of us think the bond market can be trusted to keep local governments from exceeding their safe borrowing limits.

Not One Tax but Two

The second step in improving local property taxes is to realize clearly the difference between taxing land and taxing buildings and other improvements on the land. By and large, heavy taxes on improvements are bound to discourage, delay, or even deter their realization; the bigger the improvement tax the smaller the owner's incentive to spend good money to improve his property instead of investing it somewhere else or putting it to some other use. Contrariwise, taxes on land (or, more correctly, site values or, perhaps still more correctly, location values) tend to encourage, speed, or sometimes even compel improvements. The bigger the land tax the bigger the pressure on landowners whose property is underused to do something to increase its earning power—or sell it to someone who will. (These divergent effects can be pretty decisive when an owner is making up his mind whether to sell his property today or hold out for a higher price, or whether to invest more money in improvements, let well enough alone, or demolish an existing improvement to save taxes.)

Almost all economists agree that the social and economic consequences of increased taxes on land are much better (or much less bad) than the social and economic consequences of increased taxes on improvements. But today the policy of almost every state forbids local governments to recognize the fact that the property tax is really two different taxes. On the contrary, the law requires them to tax and assess land and improvements alike. Perhaps more important, the *practice* almost everywhere is to assess improvements much more heavily than land, perhaps because many assessors seem to confuse the property tax with an income tax and hesitate to assess underused land at anything like its market value. The 1957 Census of Governments showed that, even before land prices started soaring, the assessments on homes were about a third heavier, in terms of true value, than those on vacant lots. Today the differential is even bigger.

We agree with the Joint Economic Committee of Congress, which found that "State and local governments have failed to make maximum use of the enormous potential inherent in the property tax for either the prevention or the cure of poor housing and other blight conditions. In fact, since the tax is based on the value of land and improvements, those who permit their property to deteriorate, reducing area property values, are rewarded with lower property taxes. Landlords who enhance the value of their property have their assessments raised."

We urge that the present discrimination in assessment practice, which tends to penalize improvements, should be stopped. Beyond that there is no clear-cut consensus among us on what further tax steps should be taken to correct what is now pretty obviously wrong. A few of us would favor a local capital-gains tax on land values alone to recapture some of the unearned increment that has made close-in land such a rich speculation; but others say a local capital-gains tax on top of the federal capital-gains tax would just make more landowners hold their land off the market even longer, while other landowners would just evade the tax by leasing their land instead of selling it. Some of us feel that taxing idle and underused land as if it were put to its most profitable use violates the principle of ability to pay; others reply that *potential* ability to pay is a better basis for taxation than what exists today. A few of us are afraid separate assessment of land would be too difficult; most of us think it would be easier.

Some of us favor lightening the tax on improvements without increasing the tax on land. Others favor increasing the tax on land without changing the tax on improvements. Some of us favor penalty taxation on obsolete, dilapidated, or inadequate buildings occupying strategic land; others think the same purpose could be achieved more simply by taxing land at rates that would make its underuse unprofitable. Many of us favor the so-called Pittsburgh Plan of taxing land at twice as high a rate as improvements. Quite a few of us would go all the way and shift the whole burden of local property taxation to the site value alone, as in the majority of communities in Australia and New Zealand, and a number of cities of South Africa.

But whatever our disagreement on how to correct today's practice of taxing improvements more heavily than land, we are almost unanimous in our agreement on the divergent impact of the two components of the property tax, and that this divergence must be taken into account in any sensible program of reform.

Sowing Disincentives

The effects of taxing improvements can be far reaching and are not just theoretical. A tax of only 1½ percent per year, for instance, may seem small but when it's projected over the sixty-year life of a building it becomes a big item, and would be seen as such if it had to be paid in a lump sum. The results of having taxes go up the moment that improvements are made are all too visible today in the slow pace of replacement of millions of obsolete buildings that are still being used because it is not yet profitable to replace them. One big city, for example, found that one-fifth of all its housing violated its housing code. But the building department is helpless to close down these 40,000 units until enough good new units are constructed to give the tenants a better place to go. The proliferation of slums is to no little degree due to the fact that dilapidated and antiquated structures are assessed and taxed much less heavily than good new housing.

Ventures that promise a big profit yield will, of course, go ahead despite the present taxation system. But thousands of marginal ventures are held up. For example, on new shopping centers the taxes can run close to 40 percent of gross rents; on new office buildings close to 30 percent. The prospect of such a tax is bound to influence the investor's decision on what to build, how well to build, and whether to build at all.

Some highly pertinent research in this field has been done in Milwaukee by Professor Mason Gaffney of the University of Wisconsin under the sponsorship of the Urban Land Institute. This research indicates how lightening taxes on improvements and shifting them to unimproved land values would change the profit arithmetic for new buildings in the central business district and the close-in blight ring. On many locations in Milwaukee tax reform would make twenty-story office buildings profitable on prime sites where twelve stories is now the point of diminishing returns; it would make six-story elevator apartments profitable in good locations where walk-ups now pay off best.

Professor Gaffney states: "Untaxing improvements would make a much higher intensity of use profitable in the heart of the central business district. . . . But we would not expect to get higher intensity of land use everywhere. On the contrary, the more intensive development and redevelopment of the central city area would drain the demand that is now proliferating the urban sprawl. This would deflate the speculative land prices that are driving home builders far out into the countryside to find land they can afford to build on. Concentrating high densities where high densities make economic and social sense should actually enable many families to enjoy low-density living much closer in to the city and so save the millions of hours wasted driving home past vacant or semi-vacant lots."

Professor Gaffney goes on to say: "More intense downtown land use could be further stimulated if more of the tax dollars that must now be spent keeping up with sprawl could be directed to the central business district to provide, for example, two-level sidewalks, escalator crossovers for pedestrians at busy intersections, quick and easy off-street parking, and other public improvements needed to make downtown more efficient and more attractive. . . . We also found that exempting buildings would not necessarily reduce the tax base, for the value of building exemptions would be capitalized into the value of the underlying land. Then increasing the tax rate on land could just bring the value of well-developed strategic land back to where it is now."

THE LAND-TAX "EFFECT"

It is essential to see that larger reliance on land taxes will have very different results from taxes on improvements and indeed from most other forms of taxation. Most taxes raise prices, which tends to discourage sales and so cuts production and eliminates jobs. But taxing the site value of land without taxing its improvements can't discourage production because, by definition, no production is involved. All the unimproved land in the world has been there since before time began and so supply is fixed. Almost by definition, the unimproved value of urban land derives, not from anything that past or present owners have done, but from what the community has built around it, and from an enormous investment of other people's tax dollars (often more than $10,000 a residential lot) to install the streets, schools, water supplies, sewer systems, police and fire protection, libraries, etc., without which the land would hardly be accessible or usable.

Few students now question the conclusion reached long ago by Turgot, Adam Smith, and most of the classical economists that taxes on unimproved-land values cannot be passed on except in very special circumstances. Landowners cannot raise prices just because taxes go up. The value of land, after all, reflects the capitalized margin between the anticipated ground rent it can earn and the only cost that land as land has to carry—the land tax. The bigger the land tax the smaller this margin will be, and hence the lower the price at which the land can be capitalized. The lower the land tax the easier it is for owners of underused land to hold it off the market to get a higher price. Outside Montreal, for instance, it was found that over 600,000 acres of land were being held for speculative purposes—eight times as much as the city's booming growth could absorb in a decade.

Inside our cities, as we have seen, it is the combination of low land taxes and the customary low assessment of decaying structures that helps make slums highly profitable real-estate investments. It also thwarts current government plans for urban renewal. New York, for example, has had to pay between $400,000 and $600,000 an acre for slum clearance. At land prices like that only subsidized housing can provide low rents. In 1960 a special committee on tax policies in New York noted that even the $2-billion public-housing program had made no appreciable dent in the number of slum dwellings. Most of us agree with the committee's conclusion that "No amount of code enforcement, or tenement rehabilitation . . . will be able to keep pace with slum formation until and unless the profit is taken out of slums by taxation."

Meanwhile, in the suburbs, underused land is taxed lightly and prices have more than doubled. The National Association of Home Builders believes that the high price of land is one of the builder's most urgent problems; it threatens to price good new single-family homes out of the market. It is an important cause of premature subdivision as builders leapfrog far out into the countryside to find land on which they can afford to build—often on land that should be left open for years to come. Not all of us agree that the undertaxation of underused close-in land is the *only* cause of sprawl, but almost all of us recognize that heavy taxes on underused land could take most of the profit out of suburban-land speculation and so bring millions of close-in acres onto the market at much lower prices.

While increasing the incidence of property taxation from improvements to land would bring important shifts in how land is held and used, it is not true that such reform would precipitate a general deflation in realty values. Some land prices would indeed go down, but others would go up. Specifically, higher taxes on land would make it less profitable to keep land off the market and this, in turn, would deflate those prices that are now inflated by speculation-created scarcity. But lower taxes on improvements would give owners an incentive to go to work. This in turn would tend to bid up the price of strategically located land, assuming, of course, that market demand is there. The biggest increase in land values would be in the central city. The decline would mostly be in the outlying areas.

The price shifts up and down might perhaps balance out with no change in total real-estate values. Indeed, the total might increase insofar as reducing taxes on improvements led to more modernization of old buildings and more building of new ones. The point is that shifting the tax incidence would stimulate rather than stifle enterprise. The British economist Colin Clark has said: "Any good economist can demonstrate that the land tax is perhaps the only tax that doesn't discourage enterprise."

Reducing City Costs

It should be recognized that as we reduce the urban sprawl and put land to better use within cities we shall gain important side effects. Sprawl on the outskirts of our cities denies their basic purpose, which, as noted, is to maximize the ease of business and social contacts. It also multiplies the cost of all those municipal services whose economy depends on density.

Consider, for example, water distribution. If demand for water doubles in a fixed area, all we need is to expand pipe diameters. But if demand doubles by the doubling of the service area, we must *(a)* double our pipe mileage; *(b)* increase the cross section of our old system as its base to transmit the extra load to the new extension; *(c)* increase pressure at the load center to maintain pressure at the fringes; and *(d)* increase the allowance for peaking.

Or consider the far more urgent problem of streets and highways, which now cost local taxpayers more than any other item except schools. The greater the sprawl the more miles of streets that are needed to get from A to B, and the more cars that will have to travel more miles along those streets. Fewer people can get to where they want to go on foot, and fewer people can get to and from where they want to be by mass transit. Sprawl does not take cars out of the traffic centers; on the contrary, it brings in more. Sprawl is not a flight from traffic congestion but its principal cause. And in greater or less degree, today's tax-encouraged sprawl inflates every municipal cost, from sewage disposal to subsidized mass transit, from police and fire protection to education.

These costs are also inflated by the common practice of taxing city property for county services that stop outside the city line, a practice that should be stopped. Until recent steps were taken to correct the imbalance, Jefferson County, Kentucky, collected between 60 percent and 70 percent of its property taxes from Louisville, but spent more than 40 percent of its revenue for services it did not provide inside the city. As a result, the city was in effect paying a subsidy to its suburbs, and its tax rate was more than twice as high as the rate of nearly all other cities in the county. We urge the enactment of state legislation that would stop or at least discourage counties (or any other large tax district) from collecting taxes in any area to pay for services they do not offer equally throughout the area. Cities would not be the only beneficiaries of this legislation. It would also give some smaller tax relief to property owners in truly rural areas who may now be taxed to pay for the extension of certain urban services into the suburban fringe.

In addition, cities might greatly benefit by making direct charges for many municipal services. Just because a utility service like water supply, garbage collection, or sewage disposal is provided by the city instead of a private utility does not necessarily mean the service must be offered free or at a loss. Too few big cities seem to understand that they subsidize downtown traffic jams by charging much less than cost for downtown parking on and off the streets. It may or may not be good politics, but it is certainly crazy economics to let cars use metered parking space for 10 cents an hour (80 cents a working day, or some $200 a year) on land so valuable that stores just across the sidewalk pay from $1,000 to $10,000-a-year rent for the same frontage.

If parking charges equaled parking-space costs, many fewer people would drive their cars to work downtown. Many more people would use mass transportation, and downtown would be a lot pleasanter place to shop. The number of cars entering Manhattan's midtown and downtown business districts on a typical day soared from 382,000 in 1948 to 590,000 in 1960, though the total number of people entering the area actually fell from 3,691,000 to 3,349,000. Most of the falloff involved shoppers who probably decided to stay clear of the worsening traffic congestion caused by those who drive to work.

Simplifying The Structure

Obviously, there are many ways by which we can obtain better urban development and this report has touched only some of them. Central to the whole effort, however, is rethinking the subject of property taxation. Today many forms of personal property are taxed as well as realty. Many of these personal taxes have a very low yield and are little more than nuisances to the collector as well as to the taxpayer. There is a strong case, it seems to us, for dropping many of them. In addition to realty taxes (land and improvements), we shall probably continue to need personal-property taxes on producer durables (machinery and equipment). But consumer-property taxes should probably be limited to automobiles in order to help pay the multibillion cost of local streets paved for their use. Alternatively, it might be easier to drop the automobile tax and increase the state gasoline tax. In any case, the entire tax structure should be simplified.

In the process we should work to eliminate so-called "tax shelters" in the real-estate field. Tax shelters flourish in typically small and artificially designed jurisdictions that have large taxable resources and minimum tax obligations. In New Jersey, for instance, which has some 567 jurisdictions, the tax load of some is ten times higher than of others. Tax shelters of this kind contribute directly to the urban sprawl, giving industries an incentive to move into areas where they do not bear their fair share of municipal costs. The ideal solution to tax shelters is to abolish them. This can be done by insisting that all tax districts be made big enough to provide adequate service on the basis of adequate taxation without having islands of tax affluence and islands of tax property. An important start can be made by concentrating on the school tax, not only the biggest tax, but also the most variable. Most of us would favor putting the property tax for schools on a state-wide or at least a county-wide basis, with the state or county turning the tax take back on a per pupil basis to the local school districts. The latter would, of course, still be free to levy a supplementary school tax if the local voters wanted to pay for a higher local standard of education than the state-prescribed minimum.

The Vital 75 Percent

But the most urgent reform in the realty field, as already indicated, is to improve and change the principle of assessments. All property should be assessed at the same percentage of true value—a change one of our panelists says "would have earthshaking consequences." Today many states in theory require 100 percent assessments on all property, but in practice the majority of assessments range from 5 to 45 percent. Most of us think the level should be as close to 100 percent as is practical. Selling prices, of course, tend to be erratic and to fluctuate in the short term. Allowing for error, assessments should probably average about 75 percent of value.

All assessors should be trained professionals appointed under the merit system instead of elected. One full-time professional assessor can do a better job than six amateurs working part time, and assessment districts too small to employ full-time assessors should get together. State equalization boards should be given bigger budgets and should be required to reveal the local assessment ratios on basic classes of property, including vacant lots, farms, single-family houses, apartments, and commercial and industrial properties. Full publicity should then be given to the equalization board's findings as well as to the actual assessment of each parcel. Such publicity would tend to make assessments self-policing, since each property owner would know how his assessment compared with assessments on similar property in his own and other neighborhoods. Chicago is giving a fine lead toward full publicity by advertising all its assessments in paid space over a period of time, and so is Los Angeles County. In some other communities local newspapers are meeting the publicity need by publishing assessments free as news, which indeed they are.

Finally, and extremely important, assessments should distinguish between the value placed on land and the value placed on buildings and improvements. Once again, most states have laws to this end but they are often honored in the breach. As a result, the assessed value of underlying land sometimes tends to vary with the improvements erected upon it. In New York adjoining lots today may vary enormously in assessed value. Most of us think it is nonsense to say that land and buildings cannot in fact be assessed separately. Some Australian states have been assessing land separately for seventy years with less complaint than is common in the U.S. So has Denmark for almost as long.

THE JOB CAN BE DONE

Virtually all investors make separate appraisals of land and buildings before making mortgage commitments, and many states require banks and insurance companies to make these separate appraisals. All competent assessors know the standard methods for determining "the residual value" of land under a building, and presumably in many cases it would make just as much sense to set the land value first and assign the residual value, if any, to the building. Assessing land costs much less than assessing buildings because buildings have to be assessed one at a time, taking into consideration such diverse factors as age, obsolescence, maintenance, modernization, mechanization, etc. By contrast there is no need to place a separate value on each and every parcel of land. "Bench-mark" parcels are currently studied carefully in many assessment offices. And intervening parcels can be valued by interpolation. These bench-mark assessments could be greatly improved, and land assessments could be almost self-policing, for each landowner would know the assessments on nearby plots.

Thus, technically at least, it is feasible to improve our assessment system and to distinguish between the value of land and of improvements. How far the actual tax burden should be shifted toward land is, as already seen, a question on which experts differ. What is not open to question is that the *incidence* of property taxation, no less than its amount, is important in the development of our cities and outlying areas. And what is painfully true is that decisions made now will have larger and larger effects on the future. For, in one way or another, local communities will be raising more and more money, and, to repeat, mistakes that could be tolerated when local spending was at the $9-billion mark can be terribly burdensome now that it is heading for the $100-billion mark. Thus the case for reform of the local tax structure is every bit as pressing as and perhaps more pressing than the reform of the federal tax structure. It is time that it got more attention from all citizens.

PART V

Adaptation, Innovation, and Reform: Organizing for Urban Change

INTRODUCTION

The problems of social conflict, environmental control, human welfare, and public services presented in Section IV are compounded by another, more basic crisis in the metropolis—the inability to organize the necessary resources, power, and authority to deal with rapid urban change. The aggregate affluence of the wealthiest nation in the history of the world combined with the technological competence sufficient to send man to the moon and beyond would appear adequate to deal with the kinds of problems confronting the urban community. The real urban crisis is political and organizational. Whether or not the metropolis survives as a tolerable place to live and work at least, or an enjoyable one at best, depends on the ability of the urban community to respond to this challenge.

The political-organizational crisis can be defined as the inability of the metropolis to match resources to needs. The problem has several dimensions. One is the paucity of dynamic, imaginative leadership, both public and private, but especially from the big city mayors. A second dimension is structural: How adequate are the existing governmental arrangements of our cities and metropolitan areas? We expect too much of our leaders if we fail to give them the necessary authority to govern. And third, what kind of resources—intellectual, technological, and perhaps most significant, financial—can the nation bring to bear on what President Johnson has called our most critical domestic problem—the quality of urban life? In this, the last part of a book on the metropolis in crisis, we want to explore the problems and potentials of organizing for urban change through adaptation, innovation, and reform.

If the problems of the cities are going to be resolved, or even ameliorated, it will require bold, imaginative leadership on the part of those men who have legitimate political power—the city chief executives (mayors and city managers). But dynamic leadership and imaginative programs avail nothing if the mayor cannot gain the support of the community. The mayor's job is a formidable one because political power is not conveniently concentrated in the office of the mayor alone. He shares it with the city council, political party leaders (unless, as in the case of Richard Daley of Chicago, he is both party leader *and* mayor), the business community, labor organizations, racial and ethnic interest groups, the churches, the newspapers, and perhaps others.

The distribution of power and influence over programs and policies is a factor of no mean consequence in determining whether, when, and how urban problems get dealt with. No two communities will have the same constellation of political power. They range from those where power is concentrated in the hands of a few (a "power elite," which may or may not include the mayor; Dallas is a good example) to those where the power to govern is so widely scattered among contending forces that the situation closely approximates anarchy. (Cleveland, with its weak political parties, conservative mayors, crusading newspapers, diversified industrial-business base, and fragmented racial-ethnic fabric is perhaps the best example in the nation of the latter situation.) Where power is dispersed, the mayor's role becomes that of political broker, who must use all his acumen and skill to put together enough power to govern. This usually means bargaining and compromise to ensure that none of the contenders gets too much or too little. Such a situation is not calculated to produce bold, imaginative programs for serious problems, but it is usually sufficient to muddle through.

The selections in Section A of this part were chosen to give the reader an overview of the constraints placed on urban leadership by the distribution of power and influence in the community. Robert Presthus discusses the question of political power in theoretical and conceptual terms, differentiating between "elitism," where decision-making is characterized by limited mass participation in community issues and dominated by small groups of leaders, and "pluralism" where power and influence are widely shared and dispersed.

Scott Greer traces the shift in governance of the central city from the "exchange system" employed by political machines to what he calls "the machine of the incumbents." Greer argues that incumbency becomes a significant advantage in one-party central city politics. The mayor can control the party because he dispenses patronage and makes the key decisions, and he has the edge on the business community because it needs him more than he needs it. Greer's conclusion, however, is pessimistic; big city mayors are relegated to the role of municipal caretakers, without power to mount a major offensive against the problems of their cities.

Henry A. Maier is the mayor of a large American city (Milwaukee) and in his "Philosophy of Urban Leadership," he tends to confirm the conclusions reached by political observers, *viz.*, that big city mayors have to tip-toe around the major issues lest they upset the tenuous, loose coalitions they have been able to put together. Although Maier appears to be more optimistic than Greer, he gives little indication that the Mayor of Milwaukee can handle the really tough problems confronting the city.

The selection by Banfield and Wilson discusses the active participation of private individuals (civic leaders) and groups (civic associations) in the conduct of public business. The authors explain that civic leaders are encouraged to participate and use their influence by the decentralized urban authority structure and they do. The motivations for participating, which may be "business-serving" or "public-serving," are examined for each of several types of participation, and the authors attempt to evaluate the effectiveness of this kind of involvement in the urban political process.

The final selection in Section A is included to illustrate that it isn't only civic leaders and business elites who consider how political power might be used to influence public policy. In "A Strategy to End Poverty" Richard Cloward and Frances Fox Piven direct themselves to the problem of mobilizing the urban poor, in this case for the purpose of effecting reforms in the welfare system. Their goal is no less than an end to poverty through a program of guaranteed annual incomes. The strategy suggested in this article, after discounting the electoral process and economic leverage, is to disrupt the current urban political system by precipitating a public welfare crisis to which public officials must respond. Through a massive educational campaign, indigenous advocacy, and organized demonstrations, aimed at registering the eligible fifty percent of the poor not now on the welfare roles, Cloward and Piven would expect to generate a financial and political crisis in the cities. Once public attention is focused on the crisis, the poor would be in an advantageous position to bargain for a new welfare policy, if not with local officials, whose tenuous political coalition would be threatened, then with national leaders who increasingly rely on the ghetto vote.

The organizational crisis confronting the American metropolis is also structural. This dimension of the crisis is related to the problem of leadership discussed above because the ability to lead depends in part at least on matching authority with responsibility. But the structural problem has been complicated in the last few decades by the rapid growth of the suburbs.

All organizations face the problem at one time or another of how they should be structured in order to maximize goals which are often in conflict. The metropolis is no exception. Residents of the metropolis want efficient and economical government but they also want institutionalized checks and balances and the opportunity to "throw the rascals out" when they overstep their bounds. The result has been an emasculated local government with enough power to get by, but no more. Thus, we often find mayors who reign but do not rule because the authority to rule is too limited. The public demands effective government, but seems unwilling to give up the scepter.

This unwillingness to put power in the hands of public officials reflects a basic distrust of government which persists today despite the almost total demise of the corrupt political boss and his machine, which fostered it. Urban government today is practically antiseptic, but the public still subscribes to Lord Acton's dictum about power and corruption. The result has been mediocre management of our cities at best and mismanagement at worst.

The first selection in Section B deals with the efforts of the Progressives to overcome the evils of the political machines in the early years of this century. One of their strategies was to reform the electoral processes and change the governmental structure to deprive the machine and the special interests of the advantages the existing system gave them. The same strategy persists today, i.e., to tinker with formal structure in order to make urban government more honest, efficient, and economic. However, as Robert Merton points out in the second article, political machines, like other forms of social organization, were functional for a certain segment of the community; they fulfilled existing needs left unfulfilled by the official, legitimate structure of the community. Merton's thesis is worth emphasizing here: "To seek social change, without due recognition of the manifest and latent functions performed by the social organization undergoing change, is to indulge in social ritual rather than social engineering."

The short exerpt from William L. Riordon's delightful book on George Washington Plunkitt of Tammany Hall is intended to give the reader a "machine eye" view of reform and reformers around the turn of the century. The professional politicians' attitude toward reform has changed little to the present.

The last two selections in Section B focus on a more contemporary structural problem created by the growing patchwork of suburban governments and the mushrooming number of special district governments. Both are authorized to make policy and raise revenue outside the jurisdiction of the central city, which complicates the problem of making policy and designing programs for urban problems which overlap political boundaries. Metropolitan America is a socioeconomic community without a government, only governments. The selection from the Committee for Economic Development study of local government concludes that *drastic* changes must occur in the organization and structure of local government in the United States if it is to remain viable and capable of effective management. They urge, among other things, a radical reduction in the number of existing local governments, the curtailment of overlapping government jurisdictions, the strengthening of chief executives, and the professionalization of urban public administration. The last selection, by John C. Bollens and Henry J. Schmandt, analyzes the factors which account for the failure of modern reformers to achieve their goal of a rational reorganization of metropolitan area government.

The final dimension of the urban organization crisis is the question of resources—intellectual, technological, and financial. Urbanites have been excessively conservative and restrained when contemplating possible solutions to their problems. Proposals which suggest radical changes in the way problems are handled are dismissed as utopian and impractical even when they are technologically possible, economically sound, and the projected state of affairs which would result is acceptable, or even desirable. This conservatism tends to delay and denigrate new approaches to persistent problems although, to be sure, some radical proposals gradually become acceptable enough for serious consideration and some are eventually implemented. But too often, it is too little and too late to be effective. Recently, the new town concept, operational in European countries for some time, has been experimented with in several parts of the United States, but only *after* urban sprawl has decimated the countryside. Currently, serious debate is taking place about the feasibility of the guaranteed annual income, paid out of the public fisc, as a solution to the problem of urban poverty. Furthermore, new and radical approaches to such enduring problems as slum housing, urban education, and public transit are being encouraged. The best minds in the country, public and private, nation, state, and local, are being asked to think hard and dream big in a somewhat belated effort to match the size of the urban problems confronting the nation.

But imaginative new approaches to the urban crisis can prove fruitless unless the technological and financial resources are available to develop ideas into operational programs and put them into effect. Cities have not shown themselves to be strong in ideas, technological innovation and research, or tax base. But it must be remembered that the crisis of the cities is not theirs alone; it is also the crisis of the nation whose population is overwhelmingly urban, and the states of which the cities are a part. In Section C, real and potential contributions of the states and the nation toward improving the quality of urban life are examined.

The first two selections focus on the role of the states. Walker and Richter indicate that the states *could* do much more than they are presently to facilitate adaptation and change. They suggest that the states could provide, but haven't, considerable urban assistance and leadership, by offering technical assistance, greater financial aid, removing some of the outdated legal and administrative shackles which hamper the freedom to act, and authorizing and encouraging metropolitan area intergovernmental cooperation. Roscoe C. Martin sees the states caught in the middle between the calls for help from their cities and the ready and willing posture of the federal government to by-pass the state to assist the cities. Martin views the situation as a test of the federal system; how the state reacts to this dilemma will have consequences for future relations among city, state, and nation, not to mention the viability of the state as a participating partner.

This section concludes with three selections on the role of the federal government in urban affairs. The first is Senator Ribicoff's opening statement before his subcommittee's ongoing hearings on the subject, which began in 1966. He states, quite unequivocally, that the crisis of cities is a national concern and indicates that his committee and the entire Congress seek to understand the nature of urban problems so that an effective national policy on cities can be developed.

Michael Reagan makes a straightforward claim that the intellectual, technological, and financial resources of both states and local communities are too limited and parochial to provide adequately for the general welfare of the nation. He opts for federal-urban programs, using federal funds, which carry with them the requirement that national standards of excellence be met around the country.

In the final selection, Secretary of Housing and Urban Development Weaver details the relevance of "creative federalism" for the problems of the city. Creative federalism seeks to promote a strong partnership among all levels of government and between government and private enterprise. It is an effort to develop the best possible solutions to our urban problems within the framework of the federal system, while at the same time bringing to bear the valuable contributions of the private sector. This approach, patterned after the public-private coalition working on defense-space problems, stresses innovation, experimentation, and demonstration.

A. THE DISTRIBUTION AND EXERCISE OF POWER AND INFLUENCE

30. Theories of Community Power: Pluralism and Elitism

ROBERT PRESTHUS

. . . Max Weber defined power as the chances of "a man or group of men to realize their own will," even against opposition.[2] He did not, it should be noted, include the capacity to gain one's ends all the time on every issue. Instead, he speaks of the "chance," the probability of such, thus avoiding what seems to be an unduly stringent requirement that even the most arbitrary and powerful elite could not meet. Weber's emphasis upon *opposition* is also a critical factor; it not only sharpens the test of power, but postulates an essential condition of pluralism, namely that opposition to an elite is the best test of the existence of competing centers of power.

However, one shortcoming of Weber's definition is that in focusing upon the individual aspect of power, it neglects, to some extent, its more important *social* dimensions. This is a crucial omission, for even though the power of individuals *qua* individuals can be empirically determined, such an emphasis overlooks two vital characteristics of power. One is that individual power is always worked out within some larger framework of institutional power. Even Robinson Crusoe's relations with Friday faced this imperative. Men are powerful *in relation* to other men. The other fact is that the power of any given individual is in large measure a result of his ability to manipulate this larger system.

. . . We shall conceptualize power as a system of social relationships. This presupposes in every community a certain ongoing network of fairly stable subsystems, activated by social, economic, ethnic, religious, and friendship ties and claims. Such systems of interest, values, and power have desirable consequences for their members to the extent that they satisfy various human needs. In a sense, however, such subsystems are suprahuman, in that they tend to persist indefinitely and, more important, that their members may change but the underlying network of interrelated interests and power relations continues. The United States Senate provides an example of such an institutional system. It is a body with venerable customs, traditions, expectations, and rules that provide a given structure *within which* its members must learn to act. If they achieve and retain power as individuals, they do so within and through this larger social apparatus. Without the ability to form coalitions with like-minded colleagues, to avoid fracturing the prestige aspirations, seniority-based assignments and prerogatives, as well as the latent political commitments of their fellow members, no individual Senator can become powerful. In a word, his own power and effectiveness are inherently bound up in a social interpersonal system, with its own complex rules and expectations.

In community political life it seems that a similar conception of power may help us give order and meaning to our mass of empirical data. We will look for discrete, yet overlapping, constellations of power, each with a major *raison d'être,* comprising individuals who share common social interests and attributes institutionalized in a given subsystem. We shall not, of course, find that such a subsystem is composed of homogeneous members fully committed to its norms, but rather that individuals have several overlapping group memberships, each of which tends to meet one or another of their varied interests—political, economic, ethnic, cultural, and so on. Simply put, individuals of similar interests combine to achieve their ends, and such combinations of interlaced values and interests form subsystems of power. The community is composed of a congeries of such subsystems, now co-operating, now competing, now engaged, now moribund, in terms of the rise and fall of local issues. Some subsystems are more powerful than others; some are transitory; others persist, one supposes, because the interests which they institutionalize are persistent.

. . . The empirical implications of such a theory of community power include the need to redefine the meaning of the variables upon which research focuses. Thus the power disposed of by any given individual must be viewed less as an index of personal power than as an indicator of the existence of the social subsystems of power to which he belongs and from which, in some such manner as outlined above, he derives "his" power. As Hunter concludes, the "power of the individual must be structured into associational, cliques, or institutional patterns to be effective."[3] If individuals typically attribute great power to economic leaders in the community, we may assume that this is because such leaders personify an on-going system of power and interest relationships that are vital in the total apparatus of community life. Today the *primary* factor in assigning class status is typically occupational role. Class status is not mainly differentiated according to individual attributes of age, charm, political values, or any of a battery of other conceivable indexes; but instead one's role in the occupational arena is critical.

Obviously, power is attributed to individuals in any community on other bases than economic or occupational role, but it is interesting to note how often the bases for such attributions are honorific legitimations of economic status. A nice continuity often exists between an individual's official role in service, welfare, school board, and hospital board organizations and his economic role in the community. Such continuities emphasize the centrality and durability of power based upon this sector of community social systems.

. . . We will try to point up the relevance of this essentially social or institutional, as distinct from a purely individual, conception of community power. We shall probably find that individuals form coalitions with those of similar social and economic character and that the power of any given leader is in good part a function of the extent to which he is integrated into such coalitions. At the present time, the ability to command such resources often rests upon access and alliances that a local leader has with state and national systems of political and economic power. His "personal" resources, in this sense, become the commitments he can make of the economic, organizational, and prestige resources of one or another of such systems. His own power rests essentially upon his associations with various collective systems of power; without such alliances and reservoirs, he would not be deemed powerful.

In this context, we shall look for the social and economic bases upon which individual power rests. We will analyze community power through individuals, but we must go beyond this level of analysis to determine the larger, more permanent structure of *social* power within and outside the community. . . .

Community Power Structure and Pluralism

As noted earlier, community power structure research has been characterized by opposing assumptions and findings. Whereas sociologists have usually found an "elitist" leadership structure, political scientists have often found a "pluralistic" system in which power is shared among several competing groups. Where the former have assumed and found that economic resources provide the critical basis of community power, the latter have assumed and found that power has many bases, each of which tends to be decisive in a given substantive area. In both cases, it seems, ideology is at work, with sociologists finding that political behavior often fails to conform to traditional social and political values, and political scientists supporting the view that mobility, equality, and pluralism are characteristic of current political systems. Both believe in democratic values and procedure per se, but they often differ as to the extent to which contemporary institutions honor them.

. . . The community level provides the most favorable environment for the realization of democratic values of participation and pluralism. The opposing ideology of elitism with its pessimistic themes of mass powerlessness and alienation has usually been an urban phenomenon. For elitism connotes huge size, impersonal relationships and violent individualism, with every man seeking his own limited ends.

Democratic theory has always been concerned with these matters. From the time of the Greeks on, philosophers have set limits to the size of their ideal political communities. Aristotle insisted that "In order to do civic business properly, the citizens of a state should know one another personally."[6] Only then were a consensus and a constitution possible. Early critics of "mass democracy" rested their case in part upon the sheer size and numbers of modern society, and the consequent difficulty of achieving a feeling of community among its members. A similar concern persists in the United States today, symbolized by anti-trust legislation and the ambivalence with which huge organizations are regarded.

Viewed as independent systems, . . . the private groups that give meaning to pluralism are rarely pluralistic, in the sense of having competing power centers *within* them. Such groups no longer meet traditional pluralist assumptions, because of the great inequality of bargaining power that characterizes them. The pluralism that exists is too often restricted to the few powerful organizations that monopolize most social areas. Producer groups, linked fundamentally by an economic interest, dominate, and the less disciplined voluntary associations rarely compete successfully with them in the struggle for access and influence.

Such developments underlie the changed conditions and meaning of pluralism, which continues nevertheless to be defined and defended in traditional terms. An example of recent efforts to accommodate pluralism to its new environment is seen in the area of community power structure research. *Its advocates now argue that pluralism exists if no single elite dominates decision-making in every substantive area.* In effect, if bargaining and opposition among three or four elite groups (who usually make up something less than 1 per cent of the community) persist, pluralism remains viable. The existence of competition among elites, so to speak, has become the essential criterion. This is obviously a realistic theory in an age of superorganization, but whether by itself it provides a valid measure of "pluralism" remains questionable. Certainly this is a much more restricted definition than that traditionally associated with the concept.

SOME CONDITIONS OF PLURALISM

Such qualifications suggest that the concept of pluralism must be made more specific if it is to serve as a framework for systematic field research. Some necessary conditions of pluralism must be set down, against which research findings can be interpreted. Such conditions can provide empirically testable propositions which enable us to avoid a retreat into faith insofar as the documentation of the viability of pluralism is concerned. While the following propositions do not include every facet of pluralism, they do include several of the basic contemporary tenets:

1) *That competing centers and bases of power and influence exist within a political community.*

To meet the pluralist standard, lively competition among several individuals, elites, or groups is required. Moreover, in a pluralistic community, the *bases* upon which power rests will be variable, i.e. money power would be challenged by other bases of power, including class, expertise, access, and the control of the media of communication. To some extent, such power bases overlap; in a capitalistic society, for example, personal wealth and the control of the means of production often enable their possessors to co-opt several of the others. But viable competition among many elites possessing *different* bases of power is a critical factor in the pluralist equation, and it is related to the notion of "countervailing power," i.e. the assumption that a built-in stabilizer exists whereby the rise of highly organized centers of power inspires opposing centers which tend to bring the system into equilibrium.

2) *The opportunity for individual and organizational access into the political system.*

Access is vital because it provides an instrument by which support and opposition toward a proposed measure may be expressed. Penetration of the formal political system must be possible if decisions are to be rational and equitable, i.e. if they are to benefit from opposing points of view and to satisfy the demands of opposing interests. A panoply of constitutional and procedural guarantees makes such access possible. Yet, it remains necessary to determine empirically the extent of individual and group access by an analysis of specific decisions. It is important to note here that individual participation has been undercut by the complexity of issues and the growth of group representation as the typical means of political negotiation and influence. We shall, therefore, not expect to find very high levels of individual participation in the decisions analyzed here. Despite this, the amount of such participation provides a useful index of *comparative* levels of pluralism in the two communities analyzed in this study.

3) *That individuals actively participate in and make their will felt through organizations of many kinds.*

. . . The dichotomy between organizational leaders and their members is denied; unless groups are given some organic reality beyond that based upon their members, it seems that the group thesis must assume that individuals turn to collective action mainly to gain their individual desires. Certainly, voting, the most characteristic form of political participation, is in the last analysis an eminently individual behavior. Not that the individual's political values and electoral preferences are not influenced by his group associations, but rather that the political parties must evoke his participation on an individual basis.

4) *That elections are a viable instrument of mass participation in political decisions, including those on specific issues.*

Two facets of this proposition are important. Not only do elections presumably provide a meaningful method of generalized mass influence over political leaders, but the assumption is that most adult citizens do, in fact, *use* their electoral power when referenda are available on specific issues. This assumption is especially vital because the electoral instrument is more accessible than other media of influence and access, such as legislative hearings, officeholding, organizational leadership, etc. In this sense, it is the most practical weapon in the pluralist armory.

5) *That a consensus exists on what may be called the "democratic creed."*

The importance of this consensus lies in the motivation to participate inspired by the belief that the democratic creed of the community is, in fact, operational. That is, voting, organizational membership, and other political activity are activated by an acceptance of the validity of the normative propositions underlying the social system. To some extent, these values provide the cement that holds society together. The absence of this consensus, which may culminate in alienation, seems to result either in a withdrawal from active participation or in somewhat indiscriminate efforts to defeat all community proposals.

These five propositions encompass several of the basic premises of pluralism; an attempt will be made to test them in following chapters.

CONDITIONS OF ELITISM

We can now consider the nature of elitism. We shall use this term to define the condition that exists when the propositions above are not operational. Elitism is a pattern of decision-making characterized by limited mass participation in community issues, and their domination by small groups of specialized or general leaders. This term suits the main drift of the analysis in the sense that it seems to define the conditions sometimes found in community power structure research; for example, the tendency for decisions to be initiated and directed by one or a few leadership groups. "Elitism" also enables us to speak of change, "competition among the few," and differential bases of power according to the substantive character of a decision. Elitism, in sum, connotes rule by the few, and when it occurs, we may assume that the five conditions of pluralism outlined above are rarely met.[23]

In a community context, we assume that a decision-making continuum exists, ranging from a high degree of pluralism at one end to a low degree (i.e. elitism) at the other. Empirically, the position occupied by any given decision along this continuum will vary according to the combination of factors that characterize it, as well as according to the criteria used to define pluralism. This problem will be discussed below. For the moment, let us merely say that community decision-making is viewed here as occurring along a *continuum*, and is characterized by varying degrees of rank-and-file participation in major decisions and competition among the elites who play a direct, *initiating* role in them. Elitism connotes domination of the decisional process by a single group or a few men, limited rank-and-file access, little or no opposition, and a failure on the part of most of the adult community to use their political resources to influence important decisions. It refers to the tendency of power, defined as the chances of a group to achieve its ends despite opposition, to rest in relatively few hands.

It is not assumed here that those who have power can achieve their ends all the time, or that they constitute a single, impenetrable, monolithic entity, or that the locus of power does not change historically (formal political power passed from Democratic to Republican hands in the two communities we studied during the time of our research), or that community power rests entirely upon the possession or control of economic resources. Such requirements, it seems, are a caricature of power relations, if not a mere straw man.

We do assume that a power elite, if found, will constitute a very small proportion of the community, and that it will not be representative in social terms of the larger community. It will be made up largely of middle- and upper-class people, who possess more of the skills and qualities required for leadership, and who tend to share certain values about politics, mobility, and requirements of leadership that differentiate them to some extent from others. However, the most critical basis of differentiation will probably be found in class status and leadership resources, rather than in attitudinal differences.

A corollary of these assumptions is that such elites are subject to relatively little influence from the rest of the community. Their power may rest upon expertise, class, status, or wealth, but its distinguishing feature is a decisive control of such resources. Elitism connotes limited numbers, limited consultation with affected groups, disproportionate control of scarce resources of money, skill, and information, and a certain continuity and commonality of interest. While political elites in Western society will typically operate through nominally "democratic" forms, i.e. through public meetings, elections, referenda, and so on, these media are sometimes manipulated to achieve a democratic "consensus" that has little substance. For example, when presidential primary elections are made the target of vast and unequal expenditures of funds, organized like advertising campaigns, and carefully selected to ensure certain desired consequences, there is some doubt that the essentials of democratic participation have been met, even though technically its procedures have been followed. Elitism, as a political instrument, often rests upon similar highly differentiated and unequal access to valued resources.

A characteristic revealed in the community research of Hunter and the Lynds is the tendency for the power of a given elite to extend horizontally, as it were, across several decisional areas. That is, the elite's will may be decisive in economic, political, and social contexts;

it cuts across various substantive areas of health, education, housing, urban redevelopment, tax policy, and recreation. It is sometimes argued that specialization of interest and knowledge makes such "cutting across" unlikely, but one explanation for this pattern of influence is that specialists are available as consultants or hired-hands to those with economic and political power. Experts are aligned on either side of most technical issues, such as the effects of atomic radiation or the destructive capacity of 100-megaton bombs. The possibility of genuine disagreement among them, as well as the availability of some whose judgments nicely coincide with "official" policy, means that political leaders, allied with resourceful economic interests, may often make their will felt in several discrete and highly technical areas.

Empirical Analysis of Pluralism

Historically, much of political discourse has centered on the question of pluralism. The extent to which the political process in a given context meets pluralist expectations of participation and competition has been of continuing concern. In dealing with such questions, it has often been fashionable to categorize entire nations as being pluralistic or nonpluralistic on *all* issues, as when one speaks of "totalitarian" versus "democratic" political systems. At the community level, empirical research makes it possible to move toward more selective judgments, in part because the smaller universe permits more rigorous analysis.

If one is to verify the proposition that decision-making in a given community tends toward the "low" (elitist) end of the continuum, it is presumably necessary to demonstrate by some generally acceptable indexes of participation that a single elite group has exercised determinative influence across several policy areas.[24] Some such criterion has been set by pluralists who have either made such studies, or have made critical judgments about the research of others.

This criterion, however, seems unduly demanding, and to some extent unfair, because it puts the burden of proof squarely on the researcher to demonstrate that "elitism," so defined, exists. He must not only prove that a monolithic community power structure exists, but if he should find instead that, say, three or four distinct elite groups share power among different types of decisions, the case for pluralism presumably remains viable. I am not sure, however, that pluralism (any more than elitism) should be accepted as a given; it should be equally incumbent upon advocates of pluralism to demonstrate by equally careful research that the community political system is indeed pluralistic. Otherwise, the debate remains essentially normative, with the pluralist enjoying most of the advantages of tradition and normative preference. More important, there is little incentive for the pluralist to do additional field research, which might reinforce his claims.

Conclusions

In this chapter, a theoretical framework for an empirical study of power and pluralism has been suggested. Power has been conceptualized as a social phenomenon, as distinguished from the primarily individualistic view of power as an absolute quality possessing comparable utility regardless of the situational context in which it is invoked. Instead, the power attributions of individual leaders are conceptualized as *indicators* of their role and status in one or more social subsystems. These subsystems, in effect, provide the bases of individual power, and the substantive issues to which they direct themselves provide the boundaries within which such power is effective. It is hypothesized that the centrality and continuity of *economically* oriented subsystems give their members an inside track in community power relationships. By contrast, *politically* oriented systems tend to provide relatively less viable bases of power, subject as they are to the ebb and flow of political fortune and changing electoral loyalties. In sum, we will try to look beneath individual attributions of power to their underlying social contexts.

Pluralism has been broadly defined as a sociopolitical system in which power and influence are widely dispersed and shared. Pluralism honors the fear of government and of all forms of power—a fear which motivated the founding fathers, as well as the English and French philosophers whose values they reflected. They reasoned that if power could not be eradicated, at least its bad effects could be eased by spreading it about.

A belief of pluralism is that most citizens are wise enough to make judgments about public affair and to help manage them. Pluralism has meant more than the control of political affairs by organizational leaders. As Jackson maintained, the duties of public office are so simple that any man of ordinary intelligence can exercise them. This conception is important in the distinction made here between "pluralism" and "elitism." So defined, pluralism seems opposed to the belief that government works best when its leaders are selected from among the "elite," however this might be defined at a given time and place. It is opposed to this Burkian view in which parliaments are a necessary safeguard against the often ill-advised aims of the majority.

Nevertheless, sophisticated observers have concluded that some variant of elite rule by highly educated and interested groups is the essential requirement of our political system. Such assumptions are based upon research in public opinion and political behavior which indicates that apathy, ignorance of complex issues, and a certain alienation from "politics" are often characteristic of the "unpolitical man." The tension between "elitist" and "pluralist" conceptions of government has not been reduced. They remain as the visible manifestations of complex residual assumptions about man, society, and government.

Despite pluralist assumptions, the empirical question of the extent to which voluntary organizations participate in community decision-making remains. It is important to determine whether such organizations are active, if they are really among the principal means by which individuals gain access to the political system. The answer to this question becomes critical in making judgments about the position of any community along the pluralist continuum.

Clearly, many private organizations compete and co-operate with government in determining the allocation of governmental largesse. Pluralists maintain that bargaining among such organizations culminates roughly in the "public interest." However, this rationale has one rather pressing shortcoming, namely, that all interests are not equally represented in the bargaining arena.[25] Real competition on any specific issue is limited to relatively few powerful groups. The weakness of the *consumer* interest is one glaring example of existing inequities in bargaining power. The organizations that have most influence vis-à-vis government are producer groups, galvanized into action by a focused and compelling economic interest.

These structural facets of contemporary pluralism mean that bargaining often proceeds among a presidium of elites, which disadvantages unorganized segments of society. This condition is reinforced in turn by organizational imperatives such as the demand for leadership, power, and dispatch which makes for a tendency toward oligarchy *within* organizations.

Given the challenge to pluralism brought by technological change and organizational necessity, perhaps one must shift the argument away from expectations of widespread participation toward some less sanguine but more reasonable criterion, such as the opportunity for those who *disagree* with the decisions of the governing minority to make their voice heard. If this were done, Michels's proposition, "He who says organization says oligarchy," might prove less disenchanting. Perhaps democracy could be made more viable by a more candid recognition of the limitations upon pluralism brought about by economic realities, apathy, and disparities in power among different elements of the community.

In sum, field studies of the political process at the community level are needed to test pluralist assumptions, for it is here that widespread participation has the best chance to occur. One would expect to find the closest approximation between pluralist ideals and the realities of social and political organization. Barriers of size, distance, and organization are minimal. Access to the politician, the press, and economic leaders is relatively open. The issues are neither so complex nor so far-removed that one feels ineffectual. Politics, and, hopefully, power, is less a mystery.

---

[1]Review of *Power and Democracy in America,* eds. W. V. D'Antonio and H. J. Ehrlich, 28 *American Sociological Review* (February, 1963), pp. 144-5; for attempts to conceptualize power systematically, see R. A. Dahl, "A Critique of the Ruling Elite Model," 52 *American Political Science Review* (June, 1958), pp. 463-9; and F. Oppenheim, "Degrees of Power and Freedom," 54 *American Political Science Review* (June, 1960), pp. 437-46.

[2]*From Max Weber: Essays in Sociology,* eds. H. H. Gerth and C. W. Mills (New York: Oxford University Press, 1946), p. 180.

[3]Floyd Hunter, *Community Power Structure* (Chapel Hill: University of North Carolina Press, 1953), p. 6.

[23]Here, it should be noted, we are specifically rejecting the revisionist notion that pluralism is adequately defined when competition or specialization exists among the elites participating in community decisions. Our definition, which we believe is more in keeping with the historical spirit and meaning of the concept, requires as necessary conditions some measure of "rank and file" and organizational participation in such decisions.

[24]A problem of criteria arises here. Any researcher must establish cut-off points to differentiate categories that are not always intrinsically quantitative. Such categories include not only "elitism" and "pluralism," but the distinction between "decision-makers," "influentials," and those "rank-and-file" members of the community whose participation has often been found to be mainly limited to *referending* decisions made by others. In the next chapter, we will set down the criteria used in this study; they will provide an important basis for judgments about participation in the communities studied here. Obviously, if the criteria are regarded as invalid, it will be impossible to accept the conclusions.

[25]Among the few books by Americans which consider this unhappy theme are H. Kariel, *op. cit.;* C. Wright Mills, *The Power Elite* (New York: Oxford University Press, 1956); and K. Loewenstein, *Political Power and Governmental Process* (Chicago: University of Chicago Press, 1957).

31. The Governance of the Central City

SCOTT GREER

The aged central city, its structure reflecting the paleotechnic city of the nineteenth century, is the living past of the metropolitan area. Here we find the monuments to earlier technology, leaders, social circles, artistic achievement. Here the visitor feels that he has really discovered the essence of the metropolis. At Times Square in New York, the Loop in Chicago, Penn Center in Philadelphia, or Market Street in San Francisco the metropolis seems to come into focus. However, what was basic and definitive in an earlier city may be very misleading in a metropolis with half or two-thirds of its population living in the suburbs; the focus is far off center. Still there was a time not long ago when the central city did encompass the totality of the urban complex, and its downtown was the hub of the metropolis. Its governmental boundaries encircled the densely built-up urban area, and its polity was the public decision making process for the entire urban complex.

Before the automobile the central city included the entire array and variety of the urban worlds. It took the brunt of the rapid urbanization we have discussed; here was the process of increasing scale in concrete form. The soaring skyscrapers represented the "peak organizations" which were melding continental networks of activity. Railroads, banks, insurance companies, petroleum companies, all built their headquarters at the center. One saw also the other aspects of increasing scale—in the polyglot crowds of Sicilians, Poles, Hungarians, and Jews who crowded the streets of the lower East Side of Manhattan, the near North or near South Side of Chicago. Areas of cheap, dense housing lay close to the workplaces of the center and were the typical ports of entry for the immigrants and country boys drawn by economic opportunity and glamour to the city.

As we have noted, the government of the central city faced a congeries of tremendous tasks. Increasing scale produced new problems of intergroup relations. Expanding economic enterprises, based on new energy sources and machinery, were violent and radical departures from an older organization of work. Labor agitation and labor unions arose as a response to catastrophic change, from a workforce still oriented to small-scale family enterprises, shops and farms and crafts.[1] The relationships between organizing labor and manage-

SOURCE: *Governing the Metropolis* (New York: John Wiley & Sons, 1962), pp. 59-82.

ment were uneasy, unstable, and frequently bloody from the Civil War to the 1940's (and still are in regions of rapidly increasing scale, such as the South). The government of the city was usually the only agency responsible for maintaining public order among these forces. At the same time, the sheer mixture of populations produced endemic and violent conflict between ethnic enclaves. Negroes and Irish, Italians and Jews, Poles and Negroes competed for homes, neighborhoods, jobs—living space. Their competition frequently descended into overt conflict, and many of them did not understand the "rules of the road" in an urban place ordered by the inherited laws of the Anglo-Saxon people. Small nuances of expression and tone of voice could turn a policemen's friendly admonition to, for example, a newly arrived Pole into a brawl or a murder.

The variation in cultural background alone produced great areas of anarchy and danger in the organizational interstices. The cities of America have old histories of rioting, lynching, and pillaging. In the streets, alleys, parks, lobbies, terminals, and public transport there were always problems of policing. The need for police always outran the supply, for the consequences of increase in scale to the local community were typically disregarded or underestimated. Weakness of the law enforcement agencies led, in turn, to the organization of effective criminal gangs. The wide array of illegal behavior, the variety of cultural backgrounds, and the poor control system meant that fortunes could be made in gambling, prostitution, and the sale of narcotics. The organizations that carried on such illegal commerce were frequently of different ethnic origins; thus gang warfare was both pecuniary and ethnic in its nature.

The development of the physical plant also lagged behind demand. Only in the twentieth century did most American cities assure themselves of a safe water supply. Streets and streetlights, sidewalks and their maintenance, continually demanded new outputs of societal wealth. Sewage disposal was a continual problem. Only extreme failure of the system made most citizens aware of its importance, yet sewage disposal systems had to expand continually because of the mushrooming population. We have not mentioned schools, parks, museums, libraries: all were in short supply as the customers multiplied astronomically.

The solution of these problems had to be found, as we have observed, within the framework of a democratic dogma. Vast and difficult operations were to be commanded by any "common man" who could be elected by the votes of others; important operating decisions were to be made by the voters in referendum elections. The moral and technical control of the government depended in large part upon the judgment of the ordinary citizen. But these citizens were frequently unable to understand even the English language, much less the complex systems of American local government. Those who did understand were not competent to monitor the unprecedented process of city building and organization forced upon them by large-scale society in expansion.

Economics of Machine Government

The impasse was resolved by the development of powerful party machines at the local level. The party machine was an organization devoted to the control of the vote and, through the vote, power and the profits of power. Without a guiding ideology (or set of formulated ideals) it operated as an exchange system, a business enterprise. At the lowest level the precinct captains exchanged jobs, bonuses, turkeys on Thanksgiving, coal in winter time, for the votes of families, friendship cliques, ethnic enclaves. The machine was a vast retail system for trade in votes. Frequently, of course, the actual voting could be made irrelevant, for fraud was another means of affecting the tally (which in turn affected the supply of "Wholesale goods" or authority to be exchanged). Plunkitt describes the hardship of his early days, when his wife stayed up all night ironing out ballots so that they might be inserted through the crack in the bottom of the ballot box. Without extensive discussion of the technology of fraud, let us note that the exchange of favors for votes was the staple technique, with fraud a supplementary device. Together, these allowed the machine to count on a dependable plurality. Of course, there are usually two or more party machines in competition. This fact introduced the note of uncertainty which heated up the campaign and made politics a great spectator sport in the nineteenth century cities.

The dominant machine was related to the rest of the urban community through an exchange system. At the higher level, the political Boss treated with the financial and industrial interests of the city. His trading cards were franchises for the rapidly expanding transportation system, contracts for lucrative public works, permits to operate various businesses, as well as waivers of the public law for favored parties. His price was reciprocal favor or cash. Money, in turn, was reinvested in the machine, trickling down through district and ward to the precinct, where the precinct officers in turn distributed favors. (Of course, the Boss took substantial profits from the transaction.)

The importance of the cash nexus, and the relative public irresponsibility of the political Boss, meant that money could be translated into political power. Lincoln Steffens described, in some detail, the things that rich and respectable entrepreneurs bought from local government in the nineteenth century American city.[2] They were worth having. (A slightly fictionalized biography of Yerkes, the "Robber Baron" who bought the right to monopolize public transport in Chicago, is given in Theodore Dreiser's novel, *The Titan.*) Aside from using money, the upper class could also influence the local boss through the crusading daily newspapers (which might expose delicate and secret operations) and through power at the state or national governmental levels. In summary, there were many ways for business interests to determine policy in the city.

It was indeed a society oriented toward business. Businessmen were the first-class citizens, and the chief operations of government were delegated through contracts to business enterprise. The material tasks of local government, apart from such unprofitable enterprises as police and fire protection, were very small operations compared with the developing corporations of nineteenth century America. Though a majority of the citizens may have been ethnic and working class (in 1910 a majority of Americans were from minority groups), their interests were not paramount. Those of business were.

Such a system could be imagined as a pyramid, with a power elite at the top. The power elite was made up of the wealthy, whose control of men and money, whose ties with the national and state governments, whose influence with the newspapers, and whose "ownership" of the mayor and council (through the Boss) gave them tremendous leverage for the control of both the public and private aspects of the city's development. Such an interpretation was documented in dozens of novels; it was congruent with the stories of the muckrakers, as well as the ideology of the socialists, anarchists, and syndicalists. It was a conspiracy as local government, with politicians seen as merely tools of "the executive committee of the bourgeoisie."

The Power Elite of the City Today

This image of urban government has persisted into our own day. Floyd Hunter has spent a great deal of energy identifying the "thirty men who run Atlanta."[3] Other scholars have studied a number of American cities. In each case they move from expert informants, who know the situation, to a set of nominated power figures. These in turn nominate others until the circle is closed and new persons do not get mentioned; from those most frequently nominated they select the personnel for the power elite.

Their technique has recently been radically questioned. Some have noted that, if there is only a *myth* about a power elite and it is believed by the more informed citizens, then the scholar is only documenting that myth when he asks them how they think the city works. This would explain why we could find a power elite whether it exists or not. Others have more drastic criticisms. They note that when the "Big Mules" of Cleveland or St. Louis try to help reorganize the local government of the metropolis their projects go down in defeat at the polls. When the civic leaders of Chicago want to refurbish the near North Side, or locate a new campus for the University of Illinois, their efforts are frustrated and the final decision is made by the Mayor—or no decision at all results.[4] In short, the power elite image of control in the central city has lately been exposed to an extremely skeptical group of critics. This leads us to ask: Was the political image of the city equally fictitious in earlier days? Or do the critics of the power elite theory today simply misunderstand the nature of organization in the contemporary central city? It seems more likely that the discrepancy does not just reflect variation in opinion but instead indicates differences among cities and, more important, the continuing effects of increase in scale which change cities over time. The big city machine, a response to increase in scale, may also have become a victim of the continuing process. Let us look at urban government in this context.

Social Change and the Machine

Continual increase in scale has had four major consequences for the problems of urban government and their solution. It has produced an increasing bureaucratization of governmental and other functions: it has led to rapid organizational mergers in private enterprise; it has radically changed the general character of the urban population; and it has resulted in a massive multiplication of the population and therefore of the size of the organizational tools of urban government. Let us consider each of these in relation to its implications for the classic big city machine.

The bureaucratization of governmental services affected the machine in two separate ways. First, with the Great Depression of the 1930's it became apparent that all Americans were part of a nationwide economic system, and when that system failed the problem of unemployment and poverty was a nationwide problem. As a consequence, what had been charity became the work of the Department of Health, Education, and Welfare, and vast programs were administered through the nationwide bureaucracies of government. Second, the management of local governmental enterprises became increasingly professionalized; the reformers were successful in convincing the people (and later the politicians) that such services as the city provided were better handled by civil servants, selected and trained through nonpolitical methods to do their jobs without favoritism or political counsel. These two changes struck deep at the roots of politics as a simple exchange system. The goods which the precinct captain once traded for votes were disbursed by a federal agency staffed by civil servants. The decisions about street layouts, hospital construction, zoning, and planning, once so profitably controlled by politicians, were increasingly made by professional public personnel—planners, hospital administrators, traffic engineers. At the same time voting became better organized, and mechanized, with a bureaucracy (subject to review) in charge of the tallies. Quality control made fraud difficult and dangerous. Both at the lowest and highest levels the exchange system of the machine was mortally damaged.

CORPORATE MERGER AND LOCAL POLITICS

The rapid and continuous process of organizational merger had other effects upon the urban polity. The drawing of major enterprise into national organizations and the further bureaucratization of the corporation, as it separated ownership from management, resulted in a class of professional managers whose first duty was to the nationwide, or international, corporate network. The most powerful economic figure in town was no longer the owner of the major industry; he was a manager. Consequently, the economic dominants (as they are sometimes called in the literature on the power elite) became increasingly withdrawn from concern with the local community. Schulze has documented the steps by which Ypsilanti, Michigan, moved from a classical power elite structure to one in which the branch plant managers were interested in the local community only on rare occasions. Rather than wishing to run the show, they only wanted a veto on certain kinds of governmental act. Otherwise, they did not wish to be involved.[5]

The result of corporate merger has been the freeing of economic organizations from dependence upon, and hence interest in, particular cities. This has combined with the increasing geographical mobility of the managerial elite; as they move upward in the corporate hierarchy they move around the country. They become identified with one community only when they have ceased to be occupationally mobile. (One longitudinal study indicated that, even in Red Wing, Minnesota, a town of ten thousand, the personnel change among those nominated as civic leaders was more than 60 percent in the relatively short period of six years.)[6] Turnover of leadership makes effective organization (the compromising of interests, the assignment of tasks, the integrating of action) extremely difficult. Furthermore, we must remember that the business leadership in a city of any size is apt to be divisible on more issues than those on which it is unitable. (A recent study by Scoble, for example, shows a very low rate of consensus among the dominant leaders in a New England town of less than fifteen thousand persons.)[7] It requires more work to achieve coordination when there is high turnover, yet there are fewer people committed to achieving it. In short, the changing nature of exclusive membership organizations has greatly weakened their machinery for controlling the political decisions of the city. And such change is of particular importance in the metropolis, the headquarters city of the corporation.

POPULATION CHANGE AND THE MACHINE

Meanwhile, the population of the metropolis has been changing in the directions discussed earlier. Social rank has on the average moved upwards; the illiterate, unskilled workman of foreign birth is a vanishing breed. Even in the central city, education, occupation, and real income have risen to once-unimaginable levels in the past sixty years. At the same time, the children and grandchildren of the foreign born are socialized from the beginning to the American urban milieu. As a result of these changes in combination the definition of the vote has changed; it is no longer simply an expression of ethnic solidarity, but rather a more complex decision, based on a variety of interests. The children of the immigrants live in a different city from that of their parents and have different techniques for managing their urban environment. Their toleration for fraud shrinks as they become more informed and committed to American civic virtues. Their vote is not for sale.

An indirect effect of increasing size, but an important one, is the suburban central city dichotomy. With increasing population and static boundary lines, the population of the metropolis is almost equally divided between central city and suburbs. But we have also noted the difference between the population in the two areas: those who remain in the central city are predominantly ethnic and working class social types. In 1950, according to Philip Hauser, "Los Angeles was the only city among the five largest in the United States in which the native white population of native parentage was greater than half, and even there it was only 55 percent."[8] These populations are the ones most likely to prefer the Democratic party in national elections; when there is a partisan organization of local elections (and this is true of all but one of our very large cities) the working class and the ethnic voters go Democratic. A direct consequence is the collapse of the Republican Party in the political arena of the central city. One by one, Republican strongholds are giving way to Democratic majorities, as the Nordic white Protestant middle class makes its way to the suburbs. Today, in many of our great cities, two or three Republican councilmen represent the "two party system" among a host of Democratic officials. As the process of segregation by polity continues, the central city will become, in fact if not in theory, a one-party state.

GROWTH OF THE GIANT BUREAUCRACIES

Finally, we have to consider the increase in the size of urban concentrations. In 1900 two American metropolitan areas had a population of a million or more; in 1960, there were nineteen complexes this large. The sheer aggregation of population had two major effects upon the control system of the central city. First, and not to be overlooked, was the sheer increase in the size of the problems that had to be handled within the rounds of urban housekeeping, and the consequent size of the organizations which handled them. The City of New York, for example, employs 50,000 persons in its educational system, 26,000 in its police department, and 13,000 in its fire department.[9] The sheer aggregation of numbers and budget results in the proliferation of organizational centers with a degree of autonomy and, hence, power. The number and strength of leadership groups is multiplied with increasing population.

The total effect of these changes has been the destruction of the old-time political machine, and with it the power elite. Increase in scale has destroyed the basis for the political machine *as an exchange system;* in the urban wards of Stackton it is as hard to recruit precinct workers as in the small-town Republican strongholds of Illinois. Whyte reports the visible attrition of the Democratic machine in Boston during the 1930's, while Reichley discusses the steady weakening of Republican power in Philadelphia during the same period. The ability of the political boss to control his "Hessians" and through them the vote of the people, may have been over-rated in the past; it is very easy to over-rate it today.

The collapse of the exchange system has, in turn, destroyed the ability of the power elite to call the tune. Businessmen have never had a preponderant influence, at the polls, on the city population as a whole. They have relied upon the machine as a mechanism for translating money into political power. By bribing the politicians and by contributing to campaign chests, business interests assured themselves a strong voice in the political decisions of the central city. Even with the Republican Party's power fading away they could still exert leverage upon the Democratic machine, for the machine was primarily a nonideological exchange system. With its weakening, however, the business man had literally no way of reaching the voters.

The result is a drastic separation of numbers and wealth in the contemporary metropolis. Businessmen, resident in the suburbs, have great stakes in the central city polity. That polity, however, is controlled by a set of politicians who have a declining need for the businessman, and who are elected by the votes of the ethnic and working class constituencies of the center. Such a separation of numbers and wealth is not, of course, contrary to the democratic dogma. It is, however, an anomaly to those who still consider the businessman as the first class citizen and his interests as paramount for the community.

It is also anomalous to those who explain American government through the theory of the two-party system, with its assumptions of organized control and competition for power. The anomaly leads us to ask: How, then, does the government of today's central city operate? How is it that order is maintained and essential tasks are performed?

The Machine of the Incumbents

The disappearance of party competition in the general elections of the central city does not destroy party organization. Instead it changes the basis of organization: the old-style exchange system is replaced by a new order. Before discussing the new state of things, however, it is important to note the cause and consequences of one-party government for the dominant Democratic organization.

The central city electorate, with its predisposition to vote Democratic, is (like the Southern Democrats) basically a captive electorate. Whoever is designated Democrat on the ballot will usually get a majority of the votes. One might jump to the conclusion that such one-party government could mean only a sort of totalitarianism. Instead, it seems to result in a general loosening of the control mechanism; as V. O. Key demonstrates for the one-party system in the South, the very basis for much of the party's control is weakened by the disappearance of the opposition party.[11] The reduction of threat in the general election eliminates the need for party discipline and ferocious *esprit de corps* for, no matter what happens, the Democratic Party will take most of the elective offices.

Under these circumstances, however, the Republican minority is rapidly demoralized. Political organization is postulated upon occasional victory; moral victories are sustaining only when there is some eventual possibility of non-moral, tangible victory. In the central city, however, Republican votes continue to decline despite all efforts made by the Republican Parties. As this occurs, the Republican Party's leadership and its elected local officials in cities like St. Louis and Chicago begin to resemble Republicans of the South. They are either lonely idealists, whose words are purely symbolic since they lack power to implement them, or else a sort of auxiliary of the dominant Democrats. (Chicago's delegation to the State legislature in Springfield includes the "sanitary Republicans," Republican legislators whose chief source of income is office in the Democratic-controlled Chicago Sanitary District.) Such officials may even vote with the Democrats and against their fellow Republicans on crucial issues. Thus even if the Republicans had a powerful issue, it is doubtful that the existing leadership could mobilize a campaign to exploit it. They stand not so much for an alternative governance as for the existing distribution of electoral strength in the central city; in fact, they depend upon it for their working conditions.

THE DISASTER OF TOTAL VICTORY

The Democratic monopoly of victory in the general election, however, means that the primary election becomes the major arena for gaining office. And at the primary level the party organization is considerably weakened, for nomination to office (tantamount to election) becomes an apple of discord thrown among the Democratic ranks. In some cities the party cannot officially designate a slate in the primary; even when it can, its decisions are basically divisive. There are many deserving party men, and little to prevent one from running from his district. If he has been an effective leader at the block and precinct level, he may very well win, for the mobilization of friends and neighbors can easily produce strong opposition to the organization's designated candidate. Since the candidates do not need actual logistic support in the general election (the simple party designation will usually suffice), the field is clear for "mavericks" to compete.

Yet the party organization can usually control most of the offices in the primary election. The reason for this is clear enough; the ordinary voter usually does not know or care enough about the primary to vote. Thus the organization, though it may control only a small percentage of the potential vote, can nevertheless swing the margin of victory to its candidate. This organizational level is considerably augmented in many cities by the organization's control of the electoral machinery. Efforts range from differential requirements for certification as a candidate, to the ignoring of irregularities in the campaign and the voting (though the latter practices are becoming increasingly dangerous for reasons noted earlier). We may surmise also that much of the power of the organization results from a simple misapprehension of its effective force by potential dissidents. The machine *was* all powerful for many years in some of our cities; those interested in politics are differentially exposed to the organization. They may fear official disapproval, not just in the immediate election, but in the future. Even if the party machine's power is now a myth, myths may long outlive their factual base and have consequences.

Thus the organization maintains a continuing control, though not an ironclad one, over the distribution of offices. However, with the disappearance of effective opposition it no longer needs the money of the businessman to win its campaigns. Being able to win the general election in any event, the power relations between politician and business leader have shifted radically. The politician is clearly in the more advantageous position: he has the trading cards.

ONE-PARTY GOVERNMENT AND CONTROL OF THE MACHINE

There have also been radical changes within the dominant party's organization. With the weakening of the machine, the power relation between the nonelective party Boss and the elected officials reverses. First the elected mayor develops a considerable autonomy from the machine; standing above all other elected figures in the metropolis, his role is visible and his words are news. From the rostrum of office he tends to dominate the mass media, and through the media develops a powerful electoral attraction of his own. Then party ceases to be a differentiating label in the one-party central city; the major differentiator becomes incumbency. Those who are in office become *de facto* rulers of the party, for the party needs them more than they need its cohorts. They dispense the patronage and make the decisions.

Thus the central city mayor assumes a major if not dominating role in the *dramatis personae* of local politics. Other stellar roles include the head of the county government and perhaps the president of the council or board of aldermen. They also are familiar figures in the news, for they are elected officials with city-wide constituencies in image if not in fact. Along with them rise the managers of the great governmental bureaucracies, school superintendents, engineers, police commissioners, and the like. Such men, elected or appointed, stand for the expertise of their office, the legitimacy of the tasks which their bureaucracy performs, and the logistics of money and men. The dominant figures in central city politics tend to be the dominant officials of government; they constitute a "machine of the incumbents." No matter how they reached office in the first place, once there they are formidable forces.

The central city mayor can, indeed, become an enemy of his party's organization. Concerned with the entire city, he is sensitive to opinion in the middle class, familistic, outer wards of the city; his political score in the general elections depends upon his ability to carry these "good government" and "newspaper" wards. He responds to the criticism of the daily press and the statements of public leaders representing various interests: welfare, hospital, education, and the like. Though these interests cannot defeat him at the polls, he nevertheless engages in implicit bargaining with them, anticipating the effects of his words and actions on the newspapers, civic leaders, and hence, the outer wards. At the same time the central city mayor is the dominant public official for the entire metropolitan area. Insofar as there is a metropolitan community, he is its highest elected official. (In St. Louis, suburbanites and central city voters alike accorded the Mayor of the City more trust and confidence than all other leaders combined, and their reasons rested upon his office, his expertise, and his character as a civic notable.) As representative of more than the laundry list of special interests in the area, he stands for the general welfare. Businessmen, no longer his employers, return as influentials insofar as they are virtual representatives of many values and aspects of the metropolis.

In fact, the central city mayor tends to believe that good government is good politics. But in the process of pursuing good government he may destroy much of the effectiveness of the Democratic organization.[12] The separation of the offices of precinct captain for the party and precinct captain of police may be good governmental administration: it may also be very demoralizing for the political actors who had counted upon the promotion to police captain as a possible reward. Nevertheless, the metropolitan mayor is free to continue his swing towards good government, for the machine cannot control him. And he may look beyond the central city, to position in the state government, or the federal government in Washington, where his "good government" policies may count heavily. Furthermore, he is, ironically, strengthened at home by his symbolic separation from the machine. He can have his cake and eat it too. Meanwhile the old-style political machine is further weakened; the rewards of political work disappear right and left. As one consequence, the persons who can be recruited for the hard and tedious work at the block level change in character; the ranks of party workers become disproportionately composed of those who have few alternatives for social distinction and mobility. The over-all picture is one in which old-style machine politics fades away before the new order, the machine of the incumbents.

To repeat the argument: The continual segregation of population by governmental boundaries means an increasing domination of the central city vote by the poor, the ethnics, and therefore the Democratic party label. This, in turn, relaxes the tensions of conflict at a party level, leading to a one-party state. To be sure, the process has gone further in some cities than others; it is still possible for the Republicans to win a battle occasionally if their wards are numerous and the Democrats make a series of catastrophic mistakes.

This will become rarer as the proportion of working class ethnics increases. It is also true that, in West Coast cities like Los Angeles, Republicans may rule under the guise of nonpartisanship. It is likely, however, that such cities, never having known a machine, have simply skipped a stage and landed directly in the future—the one party or non-party polity ruled by the machine of the incumbents.

The Weakening of Positive Government

One-party government, in fact, approaches very closely the condition of non-partisan government. The weakening of the party organization's hold on the incumbents softens the impact of those who wish to translate wealth and social power garnered in other fields into pressure on the policy of the city. The incumbents are freed from many pressures; however, it is a "freedom from," rather a freedom to accomplish new and radical enterprises. This is because power becomes basically fractionated and dispersed. The elected officials, the heads of the great bureaucracies, state and federal levels of government, private capital, and the party organization, each hold certain resources necessary for massive action. To these must be added the governmental divisions of the metropolis. Multiple municipalities, counties, and special districts are vested with the legitimate power to perform certain tasks and to refuse to cooperate in others.

Banfield's description of Chicago emphasizes the continual deadlocking of these forces. In *Political Influence* he notes that the political head (usually the mayor) will ratify almost any proposal on which principal parties can agree. He thus escapes criticism from newspapers, civic leaders, and the like. However, he hesitates to force compromise because of the cost in goodwill, support, public image, or other intangibles of influence. He can usually afford to wait indefinitely for decisions to emerge: what usually emerges is stalemate. Of the six major issues Banfield studied (all of the major public issues for a two year period), two were resolved, one was abandoned by its protagonists, and the remainder were simply tabled. Thus half the major public issues remained in limbo. This is hardly evidence of a tightly knit ruling clique. Instead, Banfield sees the power elite as essentially part of "The Mythology of Influence."

> The notion that "top leaders" run the city is certainly not supported by the facts of the controversies described in this book. On the contrary, in these cases the richest men of Chicago are conspicuous by their absence. Lesser business figures appear, but they do not act concertedly; some of them are on every side of every issue. The most influential people are the managers of large organizations the maintenance of which is at stake, a few "civic leaders" whose judgment, negotiating skill, and disinterestedness are unusual and, above all, the chief elected officials. Businessmen exert influence (to the extent that they exercise it at all) not so much because they are rich, or in a position to make threats and promises as, in the words of one of them, "by main force of being right."[13]

To be sure, Banfield thinks that if all the wealth were organized in a permanent organization, it could exert great influence on the polity. This is not likely to come about, however, for three reasons: (1) There are fundamental conflicts of interest among private organizations, (2) the required communication would be great enough to cut seriously into the time necessary for private interest, and (3) any formal organization would rapidly become immobilized by its own commitments and organizational structure.

The overriding power of the mayor is also a logical possibility in Banfield's interpretation. He dismisses it in these words.

> To be sure, his power is great enough, thanks to the machine and to his ability to make the trades the planners deplore, so that he can exercise wide discretion in almost any mattter. But being able to exercise discretion in almost any matter does not mean that he can exercise it in *all* matters. With respect to any one or two, or any few, moves, he is free. But if he wishes to stay in the game and to win, most of his moves, like most of the moves of the "civic leaders" and the businessmen in *their* games, must be determined by the exigencies of the game itself. Like them, he must act as the game requires or else get out of it.[14]

Thus Banfield's picture of Chicago is one that underlines the stability of the order, its underlying resistance to change, and the recalcitrant nature of government as a tool for major control and planning.

Sayre and Kaufman come to similar conclusions with respect to the greatest city in the country, New York City. Much as they love it, they report that its government is essentially static and conservative. The council is hamstrung, the mayor has responsibilities far beyond his power, and the Board of Estimate (made up of borough presidents and some central city officials) has usurped effective power. The result is a city government which has no legislative process, no strong executive, no party division visible to the public: one which is, in short, neither democratically responsible nor capable of a strong polity. Neither innovation nor planning can come about except in piecemeal response to the maintenance needs of the great city bureaucracies whose managers are as important in New York as in Banfield's Chicago.[15] For the Mayor of New York to function as leader and responsible head of the government he must be a political genius. When any social role requires such a rare person to operate it, we can judge it poorly designed for a world dominated by the "fairly bright."

The mayors of our great cities, symbols and symbolic leaders of the metropolitan community, reign but do not rule. They are brokers, conciliators, who reconcile the people to what they get from their government. They legitimatize the *fait accompli* on the rare occasions when the necessary resources for action result from transitory coalitions among the major contending organizations. For the rest, they preside over routine caretaker governments. And from one point of view, this is what the situation may seem to demand. The pioneer work of building the plant and establishing an order for the central city is long since complete: the population explosion will not rock its foundations, for a vast apparatus is in existence, and new growth will largely settle outside the center, in suburbia. The great bureaucracies which provide necessary governmental goods and services are already in being: they pursue the organizational destiny of expansion, increasing professionalization and multiplying the career opportunities for civil servants. All this they can do within the precedents established in the past and legitimatized through use.

There is, however, no organization capable of mounting a major offensive for innovation. The central city's polity is passive and adaptive before the continuing results of increase in scale; only catastrophe seems capable of creating the opportunity for new development. Meanwhile, the trends continue; the suburban move of industry is added to the differentiation of central city and suburban populations, the increasingly obsolete neighborhoods, and the increasing proportion of colored populations who suffer most from economic depression and expect the most action from their city government. Taken all together these trends result in a rapid drift of the city away from its older status of centrality and totality. Faced with such changes, most people who consider the central city's destiny agree that massive counteraction, planning and construction, and governmental change are necessary. Such counteraction is difficult to imagine within the governmental structure of our great cities as they operate today.

---

[1]For an organizational analysis of the rise of the labor unions, see Scott Greer, *Social Organization,* New York: Random House, 1955.

[2]*The Autobiography of Lincoln Steffens,* New York: Harcourt, Brace and Company, 1931.

[3]*Community Power Structure,* Chapel Hill: University of North Carolina Press, 1953.

[4]For a careful study of the way major issues of Chicago were resolved (or, more often, tabled) see Edward C. Banfield, *Political Influence,* New York: The Free Press of Glencoe, Inc., 1961.

[5]Robert O. Schulze, "The Bifurcation of Power in a Satellite City," in Morris Janowitz, editor, *Community Political Systems,* Glencoe, Ill.: The Free Press of Glencoe, Inc., 1961.

[6]"Organizational Leadership and Social Structure in a Small City," Donald W. Olmsted, *American Sociological Review,* Vol. 19, pp. 273-281.

[7]"Leadership Hierarchies and Political Issues in a New England Town," by Harry Scoble, in *Community Political Systems,* Morris Janowitz, editor, Glencoe, Ill.: The Free Press of Glencoe, Inc., 1961.

[8]Philip Hauser, *Population Perspectives,* New Brunswick, N.J.: Rutgers University Press, 1960, p. 125.

[9]Wallace S. Sayre and Herbert Kaufman, *Governing New York,* New York: The Russell Sage Foundation, 1960.

[10]The political machine in Stackton is described and analyzed by Peter H. Rossi and Phillips Cutright in "The Impact of Party Organization in an Industrial Setting," in Morris Janowitz, editor, *Community Political Systems,* Glencoe, Ill.: The Free Press of Glencoe, Inc., 1961. For the Philadelphia case see James Reichley, *The Art of Government,* New York: The Fund for the Republic, 1959. William Foote Whyte presents a study, in depth, of the changing relations of the machine to the ethnic neighborhood he studied in Boston, in *Streetcorner Society,* Chicago: University of Chicago Press, 1943.

[11]V. O. Key, *Southern Politics,* New York: Alfred A. Knopf, 1949.

[12]Banfield discusses the destructive effect of the "good government mayor" at some length in *Political Influence,* New York: The Free Press of Glencoe, Inc., 1961.

[13]*Ibid.,* p. 288.

[14]*Ibid.,* pp. 302-303.

[15]Sayre and Kaufman, *op. cit.,* Chapter XVII.

32. A Philosophy of Urban Leadership

HENRY W. MAIER

A responsible institutional leader avoids both utopianism and opportunism. To avoid opportunism, he shuns the short-run advantage, or

---

SOURCE: Condensed from *Challenge to the Cities: An Approach to a Theory of Urban Leadership,* by Henry W. Maier. © Copyright 1966 by Random House, Inc. Reprinted by permission.

the quick disposition, in favor of the long-run benefit to the institution.[1]

For instance, he does not piously proclaim that there "should be better planning" and orderly programming of such matters as library priorities and then yield to a pressure group that will sabotage the whole premise of proper programming. He does not, opportunistically, gain the favor of the pressure group to the long-run disadvantage of his city. . . . He does not accept a safe, quick disposition . . . when the greater advantage to his city lies overwhelmingly in an alternative. Above all, he does not let the institutional character of his city suffer from a movement of his government based on sheer drift rationalized into a policy.

As he strives to exercise the creative aspects of institutional leadership, he must try to read the hopes of his city. He must try to relate these hopes to his programming; this is the basis of his strategy. Conversely, in his effort to communicate, he relates his programming to those happenings that affect the lives of people in their direct hopes, expectations, and frustrations; this is part of his effort toward enrollment.

He therefore develops a strategy related to the things people want and need. They have to make a living, to pay the grocery bill and the rent or mortgage payments. They want their city and its neighborhood kept in good condition—clean, bright, and attractive. If they are old, they want appreciation, companionship, and possibly help. If they are young, they want appreciation and opportunity. If they are members of the solid middle class—workingmen, tradesmen, or white collar employees—or if they are businessmen, professional men, or industrialists, they want a decent community where services are good. Whatever their station in life, they want a good educational and recreational climate for their children.

Their hopes in a big city embrace more than orthodox municipal service; they embrace the physical, the economic, and the social environment of the community. And these expectations have added new burdens to the office of mayor. The day of the simple municipal service government is gone. A new era has arrived, in which the big test of a mayor is whether he can cope with the demands and needs for economic, social, and physical development.

As he proceeds, he must have a most subtle understanding of his role in working to fill the needs of the people. He knows that he can never hope for perfect solutions to his city's problems—only satisfactory ones. He recognizes further that, in the overpowering tasks of his position, something will always go amiss. And because of the limitations on his position (limitations of time, of resources, of authority) some things must of necessity be neglected. But he can show the people that he is fighting for their needs. And the more they are convinced that he is trying to suit their wishes and needs, the more they tend to excuse or rationalize (or even misinterpret in his favor) his actions when he takes an opposing point of view.

Furthermore, there is one need that he can often fulfill—the need for recognition. (It seems an established condition of human behavior that people seek virtue through reason far less than they seek approval from the people around them and that generally man seeks community approval more than political power or economic riches).[2] Although the chief executive often can do little to change hard reality, he can bestow much nonmaterial gratification, which is more important to many people. By language, spoken or written, he can show respect, and thereby give honor or status.

INVOLVEMENT WITH STRATEGY

The mayor should think of leadership as a function. He must specialize in obtaining information, conveying ideas, and policing an information-processing system that solves problems. His main personal objective as a leader is to build a problem-solving organization. In this organization, he must encourage people to carry out specialized roles. Whatever his choices or decisions may be, he moves in a world of strategy and tactics deeply involved with gaining the consent of others.[3]

In a free city like Milwaukee, he must bear in mind at all times a fundamental of human behavior—that his citizens and the people with whom he deals are less concerned with their personal exercise of power than they are with the possibility that he may become too powerful, and they will always seek ways to limit his power. Therefore, the rule holds most forcefully for him that he must induce people to participate in his plans before he moves. He can almost never prevail simply by his own will in the freest of cities with its polylithic power structure; he must move with at least a squadron if he is to win an encounter. . . .

INVOLVEMENT WITH TACTICS: RELATIONSHIP WITH GROUPS

. . .[A] leader would do well to keep in mind and learn all he can about the conduct of groups, for the reservoir of his tactical strength consists in his understanding of the performance of groups.

In dealing with the Common Council, for example, one must remember that the group strongly influences the behavior of the members because the group supports or reinforces the cooperative members of the group or punishes members who rebel against its norms. So, in his approach to the council, he must seek to avoid antagonizing the council in such a way that attitudes will be conditioned permanently against him. He never attacks the council as a body; he seldom replies to attacks from its individual members. Further, he must seek ways to show his respect for the habits and persons of the group without lowering his own standards.

Whenever he strikes an issue, such as a pay raise for his staff, on which he can develop little outside assistance, the mayor is up against absolute control by the council, and he had better realize this. The group decides for itself what is correct, and there is unlikely to be any sort of significant external help for his position. On such an issue, he cannot even fight an effective public battle; few will support a pay raise for his people, no matter how good his case. Here he must often wait until a majority can be persuaded to support his request, or until other issues that may have created a situation which found frustrations expressed in complete opposition to his proposal have been resolved.

He must find ways, personally or through third parties, to ascertain the interaction among the members of the council, to judge the opinion of the council in order to have a reliable guide for his own behavior. Since there is constant interaction, this is a constant task.

There is a key to individual behavior in conjunction with groups that no local leader should ever forget: In maintaining man's morale, *the small group around the subject is often more important than the large issues involved in political affairs.* The individual votes with his friends as well as for the candidate. Often what is right is what one's peers agree is right.[4] The greatest single authority over the life of the individual would seem to be the authority of the group. (When an individual feels uncomfortable with this authority, he leaves the group.) *In testing sentiment of a formal group such as the Common Council, the mayor had best know the sentiment of the subgroups or informal groups.* For, as this sentiment jells, so will his program jell as they act upon it.

He must also recognize certain fundamentals about operating as the leader of a group. These are:

1. *He knows that the product of discussion by a group (five to seven for informality) is better than with individuals.* In a group, people are stimulated to produce, and many facets of an issue are revealed from different points of view. He recognizes that groups are likely to function best when the responsibility for action involves the

entire group. He also knows that he had better fix responsibility for coordinated action on an individual after the group meets.

2. *If he genuinely wants participation by the group, he had better keep his planning general and without predetermined conclusions.* Otherwise, his participants will anticipate the conclusions and tend to either resist, rubber-stamp, or withdraw without feeling that they are really participants.

3. *He must clarify objectives so that everyone knows where the project is headed and anyone can withdraw if he chooses.* He should poll the group, and as the group progresses, he should be alert for subtle goal displacement.

4. *He should realize that every meeting has a hidden agenda which consists of the motivations of the members, power, prestige, etc.* He should therefore look for opportunities to advance the personal goals of members, where these are compatible with group goals, to increase the effectiveness of the group.

5. *Occasionally, he ought to poll the group on how the members feel about the group's progress.* The group should be furnished the opportunity to relieve frustration so that change can come about (and change gets better support if it is discussed with the group rather than with individual members) and valid communication be maintained.

6. *Decisions should come only after everybody has had a chance to speak his piece; otherwise, vague feelings of hostility and eventual sabotage may follow.* Research shows that decisions are most likely to be carried into action if they are group-consensus decisions when the members by their own efforts can settle on a choice. Decisions imposed by a majority or by a leader are not likely to be effective. If total agreement cannot be reached, there must at least be agreement that action is needed. The minority may be more amenable after it has had a chance to express itself.

As Ordway Tead has put it: "There can be little question that partial consent is better than no consent or enforced consent, due to the absence of any prior sharing in discussion and decision. Also partial consent after deliberation is one of the ways toward eventually more complete agreement."[5]

Enrollments: The People a Mayor Depends On

The mayor should seek to enroll his institution in a high purpose. Such an effort has been made in the attempt to enroll Milwaukee in strategic and tactical planning; that is, analyzing the environment to determine how best to use the existing resources and capabilities through such means as the Community Renewal Program and the social development and economic development programs. Our effort is called the "Milwaukee Idea," a name that exemplifies a unified sense of mission. This is reinforced by a conception of leadership that has been most aptly expressed by the Municipal Manpower Commission in its report, *Governmental Manpower for Tomorrow's Cities*. In speaking of the public executive, the report states, "What distinguishes him most is his ability to achieve consensus at the highest possible level with the greatest benefit to the entire community and then to follow through with action . . . ."[6]

In order to do this, he must strain to the utmost to keep his program before those whose loyalty he would command, sharing the limelight with them, building their sense of participation, showing as clearly as possible that the project is more important than personal considerations. At the same time, he must realize that those he depends on have other loyalties that may override loyalty to his projects and that he must be willing to help them—perhaps do favors for them—to strengthen his position in competing with the other loyalties.[7] (At times, if he is sure that it will please them, he can ask them to do a particular thing for him that he knows they do well and enjoy doing.) He knows that his most effective pattern of leadership is evidenced by setting objectives and that at times he must make challenging demands to stimulate interest. He avoids close checking, however. In addition, although he should be a "person" (not detached or aloof), some social distance and independence from subordinates will probably make him more effective.[8]

He ought to get to know as much as he can about the people he depends on. Their factual history is not as important as their dominant likes and fears—the way they feel about things. This will enable him to estimate the meaningfulness of his potential actions to them.[9] If he wishes to change an individual he depends upon, he must use extreme caution in giving advice; it may violate the other person's defenses or be misunderstood and put into operation poorly, and he will be blamed.[10] If he wants a change, he must concentrate on helping the other fellow change himself. The other fellow must assume responsibility for the change, because of his superior knowledge of his situation. The mayor is just the helper.

Because he is surrounded by human reactions, by the reactions of individuals, groups, institutional leaders, the mass public, the most significant part of his philosophy of leadership must be his understanding of and approach to people. Basically, he might be guided by certain tested assumptions about people: that their feeling of insecurity must never be underestimated, that as a consequence of it they cling to old habits, familiar methods, and immediate security. In this knowledge, he must act to effect change only after involving the people who must effect the change.

People do not change (to act on anything new or to take initiative or give up a prejudice) unless there is a stimulus or until they feel uncomfortable. The mayor can contribute to this feeling by raising the level of aspiration so that the changee finds his old behavior inadequate and awkward. Another way is to enlist a third party to use his effectiveness to make the changee uncomfortable. (The "third party" as I mean it here may be references, statistics, and authority—presentations through written matter that stimulate thinking.)

Involvement with Power

The mayor learns that his formal authority may give him status, but that its most effective use is limited to situations calling for immediate action. He learns that command is not as effective a tool as is skill in human relations or mutual understanding. (However, his status sometimes bars him from such understanding, for some will tell him what they think he wants to hear and others will tell him things to alarm him in order to manipulate him.) He learns that even with his immediate staff his formal authority will "promote compliance with directives and discipline, but does not encourage employees to exert effort, to accept responsibilities, or to exercise initiative."[11] He faces the problems of all supervisors in finding ways to extend his influence beyond the narrow limits of formal authority.

To be sure, the leader cannot ignore the environment. His job is to test the environment to find out which pressures and demands can truly threaten him, to change the environment by finding allies and sources of external support, and to gird his organization by creating the means and the will to withstand attacks.[12] He had better know that he lives with a continuous degree of hostility and sometimes the cruelty of uncompromising opposition, with continuous threats to his authority as well as multiple demands upon his energy and his time.

There is a time for a mayor to fight and a time not to fight. He should not waste his ammunition on petty opposition or carping criticism about minor injustice. A responsible mayor should never dissipate his energy on matters that are not productive of progress. He *should* fight on important projects or programs and to combat serious attacks on his public prestige. He fights by attempting to win the cooperation of the necessary allies and by selecting his targets for opposition with great care (a carefully selected enemy can do his cause much good). And when he attacks he must "take the enemy at his weakest," as the proverb says.

But there are also other proverbs he should keep in mind. He must remember that on a particular issue argument seldom convinces anyone against his inclination and that during the battle and afterwards good language often cures great sores. More than anyone else in his city, the mayor should remember that man's evil comes from frustration, not from inherent nature—that this is often the basis of his opposition and that certainly it is the basis of antisocial action.

Conclusion

It would be relatively easy for the mayor to concentrate simply on the brush fires, on the issues of the day that are relevant to visible situations. Although he cannot ignore these, he must carry water on both shoulders if he is to be a responsible institutional leader.

The central city mayor survives only when he has the psychological capacity and the resourcefulness to handle at one time three man-eating gorillas of crises and two of the paper tigers that, it seems at times, are thrown upon his back just to test him. He must be Leavitt's "rare third man," who, in his reaction to frustration, "starts thinking about where to go from there . . . very few incidents in his lifetime would include insurmountable obstacles (because he would always have ways around them) . . . his self-esteem would be so solid that few things could threaten it. His egotistic needs instead would be needs for accomplishment of organizational goals."[13]

Whatever a mayor's choices or decisions may be, the desired results of his public leadership can be vetoed by others—by the Common Council (or its equivalent in his city), by department heads, by the channels of communication, or by the combined opposition of groups—unless he has carefully reckoned with the human element. For him the maxim most strongly applies, "For the burden and the benefit come from the same source; life, and reality, is other people."[14]

---

[1]Philip Selznick, *Leadership in Public Administration* (New York: Harper & Row, Publishers, 1957).

[2]Bernard Berelson and Gary A. Steiner, *Human Behavior* (New York: Harcourt, Brace and World, 1964), p. 666.

[3]Harold J. Leavitt, *Managerial Psychology* (Chicago: The University of Chicago Press, 1958), p. 229.

[4]Berelson and Steiner, *op. cit.*, p. 335.

[5]Ordway Tead, *Management in the Public Service* (New York: McGraw-Hill, Inc., 1951).

[6]Municipal Manpower Commission, *Governmental Manpower for Tomorrow's Cities* (New York: McGraw-Hill, Inc., 1962), p. 22.

[7]Peter M. Blau and W. Richard Scott, *Formal Organizations* (San Francisco: Chandler Publishing Co., 1962), p. 142.
[8]*Ibid.*, p. 153.
[9]Leavitt, *op. cit.*, p. 165.
[10]*Ibid.*, p. 164.
[11]Blau and Scott, *op. cit.*, p. 140.
[12]Selznick, op. cit.
[13]Leavitt, *op. cit.*, p. 44.
[14]Berelson and Steiner, *op. cit.*, p. 665.

33. Power Structure and Civic Leadership

EDWARD C. BANFIELD AND JAMES Q. WILSON

The American City is not run by its politicians and bureaucrats alone. They have the help—often the hindrance as well—of a vast array of formal and informal associations and of individuals who, although occupying no office and having no authority, nevertheless play important and sometimes leading parts in the making of public decisions. In this chapter we shall discuss the nature of this informal "power structure," offer some reasons why it is characteristic of American but not of other cities, and focus attention on such unofficial activities as are in some sense community-serving in intention ("civic leadership") and on the formal organizations ("civic associations") which are the vehicle of much of the activity. . . .

Power Structure

The term "power structure" was popularized by a sociologist, Floyd Hunter, who found in a study of "Regional City" (Atlanta, Georgia) that about forty "power leaders," most of them businessmen, "set the line on policy" in city affairs while an "understructure" of about several hundred persons, including the principal elected and appointed city officials, merely carried out the policies decided upon by the very few at the top of the power pyramid. "The structure," Hunter wrote, "is that of a dominant policy-making group using the machinery of government as a bureaucracy for the attainment of

Source: *City Politics* (Cambridge: Harvard University Press and M.I.T. Press, 1963), pp. 243-260.

certain goals coordinate with the interests of the policy-making group."[1]

Later investigators, using other research methods and studying cities that were doubtless very different from Atlanta, found power structures which, if they deserved to be called that at all, were entirely unlike that described by Hunter. In New Haven, for example, Robert A. Dahl found a highly pluralistic system, characterized by "stubborn and pervasive ambiguity," in which both leaders and led, drawn from many strata of the community and occupying diverse roles, both led and were led, and in which it was necessary to distinguish "direct" influence (possessed by relatively few) from "indirect" (possessed by a great many).[2] In Chicago, one of the present authors found that the heads of the Democratic party machine had ample power to decide almost any matter. For various reasons they preferred to "ratify" proposals put before them by affected interests, when the interests agreed among themselves, rather than to initiate proposals themselves. When the affected interests disagreed among themselves, the elected officials followed the strategy of delaying a decision as long as possible while at the same time encouraging those concerned to put pressure upon them. From the amount and nature—especially the "representativeness"—of this pressure they found cues by which to form an estimate of how the matter was viewed by the public at large. The elected official, according to this account, "feels that it is his duty to do what 'a broad cross-section of the community' wants"; efforts to influence him help him sense what the community wants.[3]

Despite such very important differences from city to city—differences that may be explainable largely but not entirely in terms of methodology[4]—one thing is common to all: persons not elected to office play very considerable parts in the making of many important decisions. The differences among cities in this regard (especially if Atlanta be left out of account) are more in degree than in kind. Public affairs in New Haven and Chicago, although not "run" by tiny, informal "power elites," are nevertheless much influenced by persons who occupy no official position.

Those who exercise power unofficially (we will call such people "influentials") do so for ends that range from self-serving or business-serving to group-serving or community-serving. A group of businessmen, for example, may urge an urban renewal project upon the city for no other purpose than to make money. Or again such a group may urge a project out of concern for the welfare of some part of the city's population ("the better class of people") or from concern for the welfare of the city as a whole ("restoring the central city will be good for everybody"). Almost always motives in such matters are extremely mixed. The Urban League may be supported by some contributors who do so for purely business reasons, by others who think "the community needs it," and by still others whose motives are of both sorts. Distinctions along these lines, despite the impossibility of applying them unambiguously in many concrete cases, are indispensable in a discussion of influence in the city. We shall distinguish exercises of influences that are "business-serving" from those that are "public-serving." Civic activity and civic leadership, as we shall use the terms, consist only of exercises of influence that are largely, or mainly, public-serving. Thus, insofar as a banker member of a housing improvement association seeks to serve the interests of his bank he is an "interest group representative" and insofar as he seeks to serve the interests (as he sees them) of the whole public, or of some considerable sector of it, he is a "civic leader."

American Political Culture and Private Influence

The active participation of private parties in the conduct of public business, whether as interest group representatives or as civic leaders, is a peculiarly American phenomenon. In many other free countries, it is taken for granted that public affairs are to be managed solely by those who have been elected or appointed to office; no others may participate in the management of them, although they may, of course, make their views known and, when an election is held, give or withhold consent. In London, for example, there is not even a chamber of commerce or a taxpayers' association, and no businessman would dream of "giving leadership" to a local council from behind the scenes. If he wanted to take part in local government he would stand for election, and if he won a seat he would regard himself as the representative of a public, not of the "business community."[5]

The presence of the influential on the American civic scene is to be accounted for on several grounds. The most important of these, perhaps, is the decentralization of authority that is so characteristic of the American political system. In Europe, the formally constituted authorities have ample power to carry out whatever schemes they may decide upon. In our country, by contrast, authority is almost always fragmented. Accordingly, the businessman (or anyone else) finds it easy to "get in on the act." Because he can check the public official, he can also bargain with him; as it is usually expressed, the official "needs his cooperation." Businessmen are active in American civic affairs, then, because the nature of the political system encourages them to get and use influence.

Another reason for the influential's presence in civic affairs is that the community (or at least some sections of it) often has more respect for his judgment and integrity than for those of the politician or bureaucrat. Rightly or wrongly, local politicians and bureaucrats are seldom held in very high regard; the politician is often considered an "opportunist" at best and the bureaucrat is usually thought to lack enterprise and imagination. As the mayor of Minneapolis recently explained,

> It is apparent that we have not yet evolved in America an understandable and acceptable role or status for the politician. The rewards of our economy and of our society are attached to other pursuits, notably to the professions and to business generally. "Success" is still identified with the amassing of wealth and the acquiring of economic "position." To some extent we now attach status to the leaders of the clergy and in higher education, but for the politician status is variable and uncertain. We do not have a tradition that regards the role of the civil servant or of the public official as involving a form of "calling" or dedicated service, such as religious or educational leadership.[6]

Since it is success in other than public service pursuits, especially business, that distinguishes the man of great capacity in our culture, it is not surprising that when a city wants assurance that its affairs are being managed efficiently it often turns to a businessman for "expert" opinion. In some cities politicians almost routinely exhibit to the electorate some "seal of approval" given by business and other civic leaders.[7] In others (Boston, for example) there are formal arrangements by which lay bodies are given powers to make continuing investigations of the conduct of city affairs.

The influential is often valued as much for his status attributes as for his judgment. One of the functions of much civic activity is to give some people an opportunity to "rub elbows" with others and by so doing to demonstrate that they and the institutions and causes they represent are worthy and statusful. Businessmen "keep score" on one another's prestige, and on the prestige of one another's firm, by noting who serves on the board of this or that civic association. For them and for others, sitting at the head table with "important" people may be a very rewarding experience.

The influential also serves a symbolic function in civic affairs. One who presides on public occasions must "represent" something to which the whole community aspires or gives allegiance. In England this is always the person closest to the throne. Lord So-and-So is the chairman of the committee to raise funds for the new hospital because in some mysterious way he partakes of the charisma attaching to royalty. Americans have to select their human symbols on a different basis, and often they select one who partakes of the charisma attaching to wealth. This need not mean that Americans are more materialistic than the British—only that it is much harder for Americans to symbolize what they have in common. According to Peter B. Clark, the businessman civic leader symbolizes a complex of widely held values, not only wealth but also achievement, efficiency, respectability, soundness, public-spiritedness, and the qualities that make for local growth and expansion.[8]

Still another reason for the influential's role is that he shares with the general public the view that he owes the community a debt of service. He may not make any payments on this debt; indeed, he may even serve himself at the expense of the public. Nevertheless, he agrees in principle that he is under a moral obligation to "serve." This is an idea which businessmen in many other cultures, even the British, would find quixotic and which is seldom entertained even by members of "old" and "noble" families.

Finally, businessmen and other influentials are encouraged to participate in civic affairs because they and their fellow citizens think that they ought to help promote the economic growth and prosperity of the city. For generations Americans have been making money from the rise in land values and the increase in commercial and industrial activity that have accompanied urban expansion; even those people who have not owned land or had other direct economic interest in growth have enjoyed a psychic income from living in cities that are "going somewhere." Americans, in short, are natural-born civic boosters, and the more influential they are the more powerfully they are expected to boost.

The Variety of Civic Authority

Peter B. Clark divided the universe of civic activity in Chicago into five subject matter fields which differ in personnel, style of operation, and significance for public policy.[9] Although based on one very large city, Clark's findings are, we think, reasonably representative of a pattern that exists in most large and (in abbreviated form) many small ones. His fields of civic activity are these:

1. *Race relations and inter-faith activities.* The welfare of the Negro, and to a lesser extent of the Jew and the Catholic as well, is the special concern of one set of civic leaders. The leaders in this field are not the most influential, wealthy, or prestigious ones. They tend to be

Jewish and Catholic businessmen or lawyers or else to be second-level corporation executives assigned to race-relations work by their companies. Much of their activity is behind the scenes. Civic associations in this field issue press releases on what are for them particularly important issues; for the most part, however, they work through private discussions with employers, politicians, and others whose cooperation is wanted. Big businessmen tend to steer clear of this field because they consider it controversial.

2. *Good-government activities.* In Chicago there are three principal associations in this field. One of them analyzes the records of local candidates for election and makes recommendations to the voters; another sponsors panel discussions of city and metropolitan problems and proposes new policies and changes in the structure of government; and the third keeps track of criminal activities and the operation of law enforcement agencies. Most of the civic leaders in this field are Protestants who have a religious, or quasi-religious, concern for "improving public morality"—a motive, incidentally, that is not conspicuous in the other fields of civic activity. Their tactic is to carry on "a constant but low-keyed harassment of politicians through the newspapers"; the effect of this, if any, is by its very nature hard to identify. Partly for this reason, perhaps, the most influential, wealthy, and prestigious civic leaders find the good-government field "uninteresting" when it is not "too controversial."

3. *Welfare and fund-raising activities.* Chicago raises about $250,000,000 a year by public subscription for charitable purposes. Organizing the various "drives" to collect money and giving general policy direction to the welfare professionals who spend it are what civic leaders in this field do. These leaders are of two general types: men of great wealth who contribute generously and representatives of the large corporations which put up most of the money in practically all "drives." Corporations take turns assigning their executives to service on civic fund-raising committees. Being on such a committee is, both for a wealthy family and for a corporation, a way of meeting a "civic responsibility" and of carrying on "good public relations." Civic leaders in this field do not, however, have much influence in public affairs by virtue of these activities.

4. *Cultural, university, and hospital work.* Those at the very pinnacle of civic prestige—people who have great inherited wealth or who are the heads of large corporations—are the trustees and officers of universities, hospitals, and art and other museums. These institutions have big real estate holdings in the city and are in many other ways sensitive to political and other changes; therefore their trustees are frequently called upon to exercise influence on their behalf.

5. *Business promotion, construction, and planning activities.* Decisions affecting the growth and prosperity of the central city, and above all of the downtown business section, particularly decisions about urban renewal, expressway routes, port development, airport improvement, and the location of major public buildings, are a field of civic activity in which bankers, real estate men and department store owners and other businessmen are prominent. There are, of course, always differences of interest and opinion among those who are concerned with these matters. To a large extent, therefore, civic activity in this field consists of efforts by civic leaders to reach agreement among themselves with regard to the recommendations that are to be made to the public authorities and, when agreement cannot be reached, of competitive efforts by the various factions of civic leaders to get their plans accepted and those of their opponents rejected or delayed.

Clark found that most Chicago civic leaders usually confine most of their civic activity to one or another of these fields, and that they are poorly informed about the fields in which they are not actually involved. The preoccupation of the wealthiest "old families" and of the heads of the largest corporations with cultural, university, and hospital work tends to make them unavailable for participation in the other fields of civic activity and therefore to leave civic leadership in these other fields to persons in the second rank of wealth and prestige.

The Civic Association

Much (but by no means all) civic activity takes place through the medium of voluntary associations—"the characteristic social unit of the modern city," as Oscar Handlin has called them.[10] Few cities are too small to have at least one or two associations devoted to the cause of civic welfare, and in the larger cities there are scores or even hundreds. Not many associations take the whole range of city affairs as their domain; most are highly specialized, confining themselves to some sector of one of the subject matter fields listed above. Some have long histories, large memberships, and big budgets, and others are no more than names on a letterhead. Some are ceaselessly active in governmental affairs; others are active only intermittently.[11]

A civic association is held together largely, or even entirely, by general, nonmaterial (intangible) inducements, especially the opportunity to enjoy mutual association and to serve the community.[12] Having no specific, material inducements to offer, the association cannot put its members under a strict discipline; it may entice or persuade them but it cannot order them, and it must always be on the lookout for "program material" that will attract their interest and create enthusiasm for the organization and its purposes. What Wallace Sayre and Herbert Kaufman say of New York City civic associations—that they are "run by relatively small inner cores of activists" —may be said also of the associations in other cities.[13] Even the activists, though they often spend much of their time on association drives, have no vital personal stake in them (no one entrusts his vital interests to an organization he cannot control). The nonactivists' connection is often entirely nominal.

The "voluntary" character of the civic association greatly influences its choice of activities—those it does not engage in as well as those it does. For one thing, it is constantly under the necessity of convincing its members that they are accomplishing something worthwhile through it. But it must do this without touching anything controversial; even though a large majority of its membership approves its stand in a controversial matter, it risks losing the support of the minority who do not. Usually it deals with this dilemma in one or both of two ways: it gives the members prestige, publicity, and other such satisfactions in lieu of a sense of accomplishment, and it substitutes evidence of accomplishment of means for evidence of accomplishment of ends. The Philadelphia Housing Association, for example, cannot show accomplishment in terms of its ultimate end, the improvement of housing, but it can show that it is doing many things that presumably further that end. Thus, according to a recent issuance:

> the Association undertakes research and data analysis in fields of concern; sponsors publications, public meetings, filmstrips, tours, and other educational and informational activities; regularly publishes ISSUES; provides counseling and assistance to individuals and groups; evaluates public programs and confers with public officials; operates two area committees; and organizes extensive committee activities. In all of its efforts, the Association works closely with other social agencies and with public agencies responsible for carrying out housing and renewal programs.

A civic association is in a particularly advantageous position if its activity is believed to be instrumental to the attainment of *several* ends. Even if the ends are mutually incompatible, it will be supported by those who entertain the ends, provided, of course, that it does not foolishly specify which of the incompatible ends it is trying to attain. The Community Service Organization in Los Angeles, for example, has had extraordinary success in registering Mexicans as voters: turnout among Mexicans, many of whom are low-income immigrants, is now among the highest of any group in the country. The organization's supporters (competing politicians, labor unions, and church groups) have different and in some cases opposed interests in getting out the Mexican vote; they support the organization *because* its goal is purely instrumental.

Selecting ends that are both very vague and very worthy makes it especially easy for a civic association to claim accomplishment. It can make its claims "without fear of contradiction" because the very vagueness of the end guarantees that the specific activities it engages in cannot be shown to be ineffective.

Civic associations often impress their members with their prestige, power, and accomplishment by establishing their right to be consulted by public officials. A politician who wants an association's "support" (not necessarily a declaration by it in favor of his candidacy; perhaps nothing more than a favorable reference to him in its newsletter or an invitation to sit at the head table at its annual dinner) may defer publicly to its views before making important appointments or policy proposals in the subject-matter field that is of particular concern to it. The consultative role of the civic association has in many places been given legal, or quasi-legal, standing. For example, the mayor of New York, in making appointments to the board of education, is required by state law to consider the recommendations of "representative associations, civil, educational, business, labor and professional groups active or interested in the field of education and child welfare." Whether formal or informal, such arrangements give an association something to point to with pride when the time comes to report some accomplishment to its members. To be sure, the politican may ignore the association's recommendation when he gets it and, even if he acts on the recommendation, the appointee does not necessarily take the policy positions that the association would like him to take. Nevertheless, it can claim—often with justice—that it has had some influence, albeit indirect, on events.

THE INFLUENCE OF THE PROFESSIONAL STAFF

A large and well-established civic association employs a professional staff to do research, maintain relations with government officials, the press, and other civic associations, put out press releases and publications, and prepare program material for the membership. Because the association represents a job to the professionals and only an avocation to the officers, and because the professionals are necessarily in much closer touch with the details of the association's affairs, *de facto* control is usually in the hands of the staff. By making recommendations as to who should be put on the board and "groomed for leadership," by "training" new board members to the organizational (i.e., staff) point of view, by selecting program material, by using "research" to influence policy, by writing speeches and press releases for uncritical and often uninterested officers and board members, the staff may—and indeed often must—play a principal part in deciding the association's character, style, and strategy. The civic leaders who are the nominal heads of the association can hardly prevent this if they try: they are too busy with more important (private-serving) activities to take charge and, moreover, they realize that the staff must have a considerable degree of freedom if it is to serve the association effectively.

The staff man, having a large personal stake in the maintenance and enhancement of the organization, is particularly sensitive to the dangers of controversy. He avoids doing anything that might split the association or impart to it an "unfavorable image." If a point is reached where some substantial achievement in terms of the association's ends can be made only at the cost of losing some membership support, he is likely to forego the achievement. Not to do so, he would say, would destroy the "effectiveness" of the organization in the long run.

The ideological bent of the staff man is often different from that of the civic leaders who comprise his board of directors. He is selected, usually on the recommendation of other staff people, for his ability to assemble facts, write memoranda on policy matters, get along with people (especially those in government, academic, and professional circles), and for his commitment to public-serving, as distinguished from private-serving, ends.[14] He is apt, therefore, to share the views —conventional wisdom, it may be—of the occupational groups in which he was trained, with which he works, and to which he looks for approval. Consciously or otherwise, he often "feeds" to the officers and members of the association a policy line which is different from the one they would choose for themselves and which may even run directly counter to their interests and views. In Boston, for example, an association of conservative Republican businessmen undertook to make recommendations with regard to local tax policy. The staff they employed—liberal Democrats, as it happened—submitted a report which recommended (among other things) a graduated income tax. The businessmen signed the report and published it as a matter of course, although none of them favored an income tax and although there were no grounds for supposing that the staff's view of what "the public interest" required was any more defensible than the businessmen's.

THE INEFFECTIVENESS OF ASSOCIATIONS

Civic associations are rarely effective in terms of their stated ends. Several reasons for this must be apparent from what has already been said. The civic leader has no vital personal interest at stake; the association cannot give him orders; its ends must be vague or instrumental to give him the illusion at least of accomplishment. These circumstances tend strongly to prevent any concrete accomplishment. Even more important is the association's deeply ingrained fear of controversy. The larger and more "powerful" (prestigious and well-financed) an association and—what often goes with this—the more completely it is controlled by its staff, the less likely it is to risk any loss of support by taking up a cause that its members consider controversial. In his study of civic activity in Chicago, Clark found that the large, permanent civic associations were generally ineffective because, even in the matters that concerned them most, they would not do anything that might alienate some of their support. In some instances, Clark found, they "took ambiguous positions; they could not influence politicians because the politicians did not know what the associations actually wanted. On other issues the associations took no stands at all; they withdrew. In still other issues, when they did take positions they used ineffective tactics."[15]

Associations which make their appeal to some highly homogeneous —and therefore relatively small—sector of the public are in a very different position in these respects from associations which make their appeal to the whole public or to some large—and consequently heterogeneous—sector of it. For example, the Parent-Teacher Association, which wants a large membership drawn from all walks of life, must avoid anything deeply controversial. On the other hand the National Association for the Advancement of Colored People, which wants a membership that will fight for racial justice, must have an uncompromising commitment to ends that (from the standpoint of the community, but not of its membership) are "extreme" and controversial. The controversy that is poison to the large, broadly based association is the staff of life to the small, narrowly based one. The very smallness of an association tends to become a cause of its remaining small; for in order to maintain itself it must appeal to extremists or deeply committed persons, and by doing this it condemns itself to remain small. And smallness usually means that it is relatively poor and ineffectual as well.

A circumstance which has further tended to make civic associations ineffective is the practice, now widespread, of financing many of them partly from the receipts of united community fund drives. Since this money is given by the public at large, organizations receiving it are required to refrain from "political" (i.e., controversial) activities. Although the rule is probably seldom enforced, its effect is undoubtedly to make the recipient associations even more wary of controversy than they would otherwise be.

Civic associations could often accomplish more in terms of their stated ends if they worked together harmoniously. In fact they very rarely do. What Sayre and Kaufman say about civic associations in New York can be said about them elsewhere as well, that "they are incurably pluralistic, competitive, specialized in their interests, jealous of their separate identities."[16] This is to be explained by their peculiar maintenance needs. Since they must compete for resources (money, prestigious names, volunteer effort) and for program material ("safe" issues, workable projects), they are usually more concerned with establishing and preserving their separate identities than with achieving something by joint action. Organizational rivalry is most intense among associations with similar objectives, clienteles, and memberships. Many large cities, for example, have four different Jewish "defense" agencies—the Anti-Defamation League, the American Jewish Congress, the American Jewish Committee, and the Jewish Labor Committee. With memberships and goals that overlap to a great extent, much effort is put forth to maintain the identity of each association and to resist efforts at consolidation or joint action. Uusually such agencies can make a good case for separateness. A merger, by reducing competition, would reduce the total amount of resources (members and funds) that they could raise without giving any assurance that the resulting unified association would be more influential than the several competing ones together.

More Effective Civic Activity

The civic leader, when he does not have to take account of the maintenance needs of an organization, that is, when he acts "as an individual," is less reluctant to take a stand on controversial matters. For this reason and others, he may exercise a considerable influence when "on his own" apart from a civic association. He is likely then to be in one or another of three quite distinct roles: (1) He may advise the mayor on some particular subject matter, such as downtown redevelopment, and act as a go-between for the mayor and some group or sector of the public, such as downtown businessmen. (2) He may negotiate the terms on which conflicting interests will agree to some specific undertaking (e.g., the main outline of an urban renewal program) that will then be presented to the public authorities for action.

(3) He may promote, publicize, or "sell" to the larger public some undertaking that has already been agreed upon by a small group of activists; he does this by arranging meetings, giving after-dinner speeches, and issuing statements to the press.[17] In order to be effective in any of these capacities a civic leader must have the respect of the leading politicians and businessmen, something which is fairly rare because of the differences in point of view and background between those two groups. Usually such a civic leader has little or no *partisan* political weight.

Civic leaders are also relatively effective when they act through *ad hoc* civic associations. Because it is brought into being for a particular purpose and is expected to pass out of existence when that purpose has been accomplished, the *ad hoc* association is not as preoccupied with its own maintenance as is the permanent association and therefore lacks the permanent association's motive to avoid controversy. Its membership and leadership, moreover, are recruited with its particular purpose in mind, and they are therefore relatively cohesive and highly motivated. Because it either has no staff or has one that has been recruited for temporary service, the *ad hoc* association is less likely than the permanent association to fall under staff control.

The limitations of the permanent association being what they are, it is not surprising that when "important" (and hence controversial) issues arise the almost invariable practice is to create *ad hoc* associations to do what the permanent ones cannot, or will not, do. There are scores of permanent associations concerned with housing in New York, but when some people wanted to persuade the City Housing and Redevelopment Board to build a middle-income cooperative apartment instead of a rental project in Brooklyn, they organized the Cadman Plaza Civic Association and required that each member deposit fifty dollars as evidence of his interest. With just one well-defined purpose to serve and with a membership that had a tangible stake in its affairs, the association was almost certain to be more effective than any of the big, well-staffed associations would be. The necessity of taking a stand in favor of cooperative and against rental housing would have paralyzed them.[18]

The Civic Participation Movement

Citizen participation, which as we have shown has always been characteristic of the highly decentralized governmental institutions of American cities, has in recent years come to be regarded in many quarters as a normative principle inseparable from the idea of democracy itself. Indeed, the spread of the doctrine that there *ought* to be "grass roots" participation in local affairs has largely coincided with a reduction in real opportunities for ordinary citizens to exercise influence in the matters of importance to them; for example, opportunity to "participate" in planning urban renewal projects has taken the place of opportunity to "fix" traffic tickets. Some efforts to stimulate "grass roots" community organization arise out of the need felt by elected officials to establish lines of communication with voters which will serve some of the functions formerly served by ward and precinct organizations. The decay or destruction of precinct organization has left the officeholder unable to mobilize neighborhood opinion in support of his program.[19]

Citizen participation has also been encouraged by certain national reform organizations. The National Municipal League and the American Council to Improve Our Neighborhoods (ACTION), for example, have published pamphlets telling how to start civic associations and how to lead them to success. Some advocates of citizen participation justify it on the theory, popularized by the TVA, that there ought to be "a democratic partnership" between government agencies and the people's institutions.[20] This view appeals at once to the popular opinion that government ought to be kept subject to constant citizen control and surveillance. It also appeals to the desire of the government agencies themselves to demonstrate the democratic character of their activities; the agencies, which are of course confident that they will be the senior members in any "partnership," like to have groups that will share with them, or take from them, responsibility for decisions that may be otherwise indefensible.

Thus, federal housing policy requires that before a city can receive federal funds for urban renewal projects, a local citizens' association must participate in and endorse the final plan. The law requires that this involvement include not only ready acceptance of the plans by the organized public but also the active participation by the public in the planning activity.

The one elaborate study that has been made of a civic association created to give citizens opportunities to participate in planning affords little basis for encouragement about such ventures. The study, by Peter Rossi and Robert Dentler, concerns the part played by the Hyde Park-Kenwood Community Conference in the development of a thirty-million-dollar renewal project in the neighborhood of the University of Chicago.[21] The Conference put the "democratic partnership" doctrine to the test under highly favorable circumstances. It had a public that was used to community-serving activities, for the neighborhood had a high proportion of university professors, professional workers, and other upper-middle-class people. It could draw almost without limit on the services of experts in planning, law, architecture, community organization, and other related fields. By every standard except one the Conference turned out to be a great success; it was ably led, it raised an adequate budget and employed a competent staff, and it had genuine "grass roots" support, for there was widespread support for the idea of improving the neighborhood and for the idea of keeping it genuinely interracial. Nevertheless, "citizen participation . . . played a relatively negligible role in determining the contents of the Final Plan," Rossi and Dentler concluded, although it played a considerable role in winning acceptance for the plan. If, as seemed likely to them, the Conference represented the upper limit of possible citizen participation in such an enterprise, then the "maximum role to be played by a citizen movement in urban renewal is primarily a passive one."[22]

One body was effective in determining the content of the plan. This, it is instructive to note, was a pseudo-civic association, the South East Chicago Commission, established, financed, and used as a kind of "secular arm" by the University of Chicago, which had a large, direct, material interest in the future of the neighborhood. The Commission did not have a mass membership, was not internally democratic, was not much interested in general principles; it was remarkably effective precisely because it was run by a man who knew exactly what he wanted and did not have to consult a membership. The Conference was in exactly the opposite position: its functions were mainly to bring about agreement by affording citizens opportunities to learn of the details of the proposed plan; to serve as a "lightning rod" to attract and ground dissent; and to impart to the plan a legitimacy which the Commission and the University, being "selfish" and "undemocratic" organizations, could not give it.

In New York, where Columbia University sought to rehabilitate its decaying neighborhood around Morningside Heights, no effective citizens' organization on behalf of the plan could be created at all. There a normal pattern was followed: The citizens organized on an *ad hoc* basis to *oppose* specific plans of the University as soon as these plans became known.

---

[1]Floyd Hunter, *Community Power Structure* (Chapel Hill: University of North Carolina Press, 1953), p. 102.

[2]Robert A. Dahl, *Who Governs?* (New Haven: Yale University Press, 1962). The quoted phrase is on p. 102.

[3]Edward C. Banfield, *Political Influence* (New York: Free Press of Glencoe, 1961), p. 287. For critical discussions of many other studies of influence and power, see Nelson W. Polsby, "Power in Middletown: Fact and Value in Community Research," *Canadian Journal of Economics and Political Science,* November 1960, pp. 592-603.

[4]The method of Hunter and others is to ask presumably well-informed people ("judges") to rank according to relative "power" the "top leaders" of the city. Those

nominated are then asked about their activities, associations, and friendships. The patterns thus revealed—"sociometric choices"—are assumed to describe "who really runs things" in the city. The method of Dahl, Banfield, and others is to discover who initiates, modifies, or blocks action on controversial matters. Attributions of power or influence, as distinguished from evidence of its exercise in concrete cases, are not relied upon. For discussion of the methodological question, see, in addition to the books already cited in this chapter, Herbert Kaufman and Victor A. Jones, "The Mystery of Power," *Public Administration Review,* Summer 1954, pp. 205-212; Nelson W. Polsby, "How to Study Community Power; the Pluralist Alternative," *Journal of Politics,* vol. XXII (1960), pp. 474-484; Polsby, "Three Problems in the Analysis of Community Power," *American Sociological Review,* December 1959, pp. 796-803: Raymond E. Wolfinger, "Reputation and Reality in the Study of Community Power," *American Sociological Review,* October 1960, pp. 636-644; Peter H. Rossi, "Community Decision-Making," *Administrative Science Quarterly,* June 1956, pp. 415-554; and Rossi, "Power and Community Structure," *Midwest Journal of Political Science,* November 1960, pp. 390-401; Howard J. Ehrlich, "The Reputational Approach to the Study of Community Power," *American Sociological Review,* December 1961, pp. 926-927; William V. D'Antonio and Eugene C. Erickson, "The Reputational Technique as a Measure of Community Power: An Evaluation Based on Comparative and Longitudinal Studies," *American Sociological Review,* June 1962, pp. 362-376.

[5]See Delbert C. Miller's two articles: "Industry and Community Power Structure: A Comparative Study of an American and an English City," *American Sociological Review,* February 1958, pp. 9-14, and "Decision-Making Cliques in Community Power Structure: A Comparative Study of an American and an English City," *American Journal of Sociology,* November 1958, pp. 299-310.

[6]Arthur Naftalin, in *The City,* a pamphlet published by the Center for the Study of Democratic Institutions (Santa Barbara, Calif., 1952), p. 34.

[7]See Banfield, *op. cit.,* p. 276 ff.

[8]Peter B. Clark, "Civic Leadership: The Symbols of Legitimacy," paper delivered before the annual meeting of the American Political Science Association, New York City, September 1960.

[9]Peter B. Clark, "The Chicago Big Businessman as a Civic Leader," unpublished dissertation, Department of Political Science, University of Chicago, 1959. See also Wallace S. Sayre and Herbert Kaufman, *Governing New York City* (New York: Russell Sage Foundation, 1960), pp. 76-80 and chap. xiii.

[10]In Lloyd Rodwin (ed.), *The Future Metropolis* (New York: George Braziller, 1961), p. 22.

[11]The variety of nongovernmental groups in New York is well described by Sayre and Kaufman, *op. cit.,* pp. 76-80.

[12]Peter B. Clark and James Q. Wilson, in their "Incentive Systems: A Theory of Organization," *Administrative Science Quarterly,* September 1961, pp. 129-166, distinguish three types of voluntary association: the *material,* which exists primarily to get tangible benefits for its members (e.g., a taxpayers' association); the *purposive,* which exists primarily to get intangible or ideological benefits (e.g., the National Association for the Advancement of Colored People); and the *solidary,* which exists primarily to afford the members the satisfactions of mutual association (e.g., B'nai B'rith). Their analysis of the significance of these differences in incentive systems for the role and strategy of associations in civic affairs is drawn upon in what follows.

[13]Sayre and Kaufman, *op. cit.,* p. 481.

[14]For example, in the fall of 1962 the Philadelphia Housing Association was seeking an assistant director for its professional staff of four (managing director, assistant director, research director, and community worker). The position paid $6,700 to $10,000, depending upon the experience of the person chosen. The qualifications were as follows:

Graduate study, preferably in government or public administration. At least three years of experience in a public or private agency involved in some aspect of urban renewal.

Commitment to the public interest and the objectives and program of the Housing Association.

General interest in urban problems and some knowledge of the literature.

Ability to gather information on specific topics quickly and accurately, and relate it to over-all policy considerations.

Ability to write easily and to speak with facility.

Ability to get along well with people of varying backgrounds and viewpoints.

[15]Clark, *op. cit.*, p. 119.

[16]Sayre and Kaufman, *op. cit.*, p. 80.

[17]See Banfield, *op cit.*, pp. 279-283.

[18]For other examples, see the cases described at length in Banfield, *op. cit.*

[19]See, for example, A. Theodore Brown's account of the efforts of the reform administration in Kansas City to establish neighborhood councils, in Banfield (ed.), *Urban Government* (New York: Free Press of Glencoe, 1961), pp. 543-553.

[20]For a discussion of TVA's doctrines and practice, see Philip Selznick, *TVA and the Grass Roots, A Study in the Sociology of Formal Organization* (Berkeley: University of California Press, 1949). For an application of the doctrines to urban affairs, see Coleman Woodbury (ed.), *The Future of Cities and Urban Redevelopment* (Chicago: University of Chicago Press, 1953), chap. iv. It is interesting that Woodbury refers specifically to the TVA experience.

[21]Peter H. Rossi and Robert A. Dentler, *The Politics of Urban Renewal* (New York: Free Press of Glencoe, 1961). See also Julia Abrahamson, *A Neighborhood Finds Itself* (New York: Harper, 1959).

[22]Rossi and Dentler, *ibid.*, pp. 5-12.

34. A Strategy to End Poverty

RICHARD A. CLOWARD AND FRANCES FOX PIVEN

How can the poor be organized to press for relief from poverty? How can a broad-based movement be developed and the current disarray of activist forces be halted? These questions confront, and confound, activists today. It is our purpose to advance a strategy which affords the basis for a convergence of civil rights organizations, militant anti-poverty groups and the poor. If this strategy were implemented, a political crisis would result that could lead to legislation for a guaranteed annual income and thus an end to poverty.

The strategy is based on the fact that a vast discrepancy exists between the benefits to which people are entitled under public welfare programs and the sums which they actually receive. This gulf is not recognized in a society that is wholly and self-righteously oriented

SOURCE: *The Nation* (May 2, 1966).

toward getting people *off* the welfare rolls. It is widely known, for example, that nearly 8 million persons (half of them white) now subsist on welfare, but it is not generally known that for every person on the rolls at least one more probably meets existing criteria of eligibility but is not obtaining assistance.

The discrepancy is not an accident stemming from bureaucratic inefficiency; rather, it is an integral feature of the welfare system which, if challenged, would precipitate a profound financial and political crisis. The force for that challenge, and the strategy we propose, is a massive drive to recruit the poor *onto* the welfare rolls.

The distribution of public assistance has been a local and state responsibility, and that accounts in large part for the abysmal character of welfare practices. Despite the growing involvement of federal agencies in supervisory and reimbursement arrangements, state and local community forces are still decisive. The poor are most visible and proximate in the local community; antagonism toward them (and toward the agencies which are implicated with them) has always, therefore, been more intense locally than at the federal level. In recent years, local communities have increasingly felt class and ethnic friction generated by competition for neighborhoods, schools, jobs and political power. Public welfare systems are under the constant stress of conflict and opposition, made only sharper by the rising costs to localities of public aid. And, to accommodate this pressure, welfare practice everywhere has become more restrictive than welfare statute; much of the time it verges on lawlessness. Thus, public welfare systems try to keep their budgets down and their rolls low by failing to inform people of the rights available to them; by intimidating and shaming them to the degree that they are reluctant either to apply or to press claims, and by arbitrarily denying benefits to those who are eligible.

A series of welfare drives in large cities would, we believe, impel action on a new federal program to distribute income, eliminating the present public welfare system and alleviating the abject poverty which it perpetrates. Widespread campaigns to register the eligible poor for welfare aid, and to help existing recipients obtain their full benefits, would produce bureaucratic disruption in welfare agencies and fiscal disruption in local and state governments. These disruptions would generate severe political strains, and deepen existing divisions among elements in the big-city Democratic coalition: the remaining white middle class, the white working-class ethnic groups and the growing minority poor. To avoid a further weakening of that historic coalition, a national Democratic administration would be constrained to advance a federal solution to poverty that would override local welfare failures, local class and racial conflicts and local revenue dilemmas. By the internal disruption of local bureaucratic practices, by the furor over public welfare poverty, and by the collapse of current financing arrangements, powerful forces can be generated for major economic reforms at the national level.

The ultimate objective of this strategy—to wipe out poverty by establishing a guaranteed annual income—will be questioned by some. Because the ideal of individual social and economic mobility has deep roots, even activists seem reluctant to call for national programs to eliminate poverty by the outright redistribution of income. Instead, programs are demanded to enable people to become economically competitive. But such programs are of no use to millions of today's poor. For example, one-third of the 35 million poor Americans are in families headed by females; these heads of family cannot be aided appreciably by job retraining, higher minimum wages, accelerated rates of economic growth, or employment in public works projects. Nor can the 5 million aged who are poor, nor those whose poverty results from the ill health of the wage earner. Programs to enhance individual mobility will chiefly benefit the very young, if not the as yet unborn. Individual mobility is no answer to the question of how to abolish the massive problem of poverty now.

It has never been the full answer. If many people in the past have found their way up from poverty by the path of individual mobility, many others have taken a different route. Organized labor stands out as a major example. Although many American workers never yielded their dreams of individual achievement, they accepted and practiced the principle that each can benefit only as the status of workers as a whole is elevated. They bargained for collective mobility, not for individual mobility; to promote their fortunes in the aggregate, not to promote the prospects of one worker over another. And if each finally found himself in the same relative economic relationship to his fellows as when he began, it was nevertheless clear that all were infinitely better off. That fact has sustained the labor movement in the face of a counter pull from the ideal of individual achievement.

But many of the contemporary poor will not rise from poverty by organizing to bargain collectively. They either are not in the labor force or are in such marginal and dispersed occupations (e.g., domestic servants) that it is extremely difficult to organize them. Compared with other groups, then, many of today's poor cannot secure a redistribution of income by organizing within the institution of private enterprise. A federal program of income redistribution has become necessary to elevate the poor en masse from poverty.

Several ways have been proposed for redistributing income through the federal government. It is not our purpose here to assess the relative merits of these plans, which are still undergoing debate and clarification. Whatever mechanism is eventually adopted, however, it must include certain features if it is not merely to perpetuate in a new guise the present evils of the public welfare system.

First, adequate levels of income must be assured. (Public welfare levels are astonishingly low; indeed, states typically define a "minimum" standard of living and then grant only a percentage of it, so that families are held well below what the government itself officially defines as the poverty level.) Furthermore, income should be distributed without requiring that recipients first divest themselves of their assets, as public welfare now does, thereby pauperizing families as a condition of sustenance.

Second, the right to income must be guaranteed, or the oppression of the welfare poor will not be eliminated. Because benefits are conditional under the present public welfare system, submission to arbitrary governmental power is regularly made the price of sustenance. People have been coerced into attending literacy classes or participating in medical or vocational rehabilitation regimes, on pain of having their benefits terminated. Men are forced into labor on virtually any terms lest they forfeit their welfare aid. One can prize literacy, health and work, while still vigorously opposing the right of government to compel compliance with these values.

Conditional benefits thus result in violations of civil liberties throughout the nation, and in a pervasive oppression of the poor. And these violations are not less real because the impulse leading to them is altruistic and the agency is professional. If new systems of income distribution continue to permit the professional bureaucracies to choose when to give and when to withhold financial relief, the poor will once again be surrendered to an arrangement in which their rights are diminished in the name of overcoming their vices. Those who lead an attack on the welfare system must therefore be alert to the pitfalls of inadequate but placating reforms which give the appearance of victory to what is in truth defeat.

How much economic force can be mobilized by this strategy? This question is not easy to answer because few studies have been conducted of people who are *not* receiving public assistance even though they may be eligible. For the purposes of this presentation, a few facts about New York City may be suggestive. Since practices elsewhere are generally acknowledged to be even more restrictive, the estimates of unused benefits which follow probably yield a conservative estimate of the potential force of the strategy set forth in this article.

Basic assistance for food and rents: The most striking characteristic of public welfare practice is that a great many people who appear to be eligible for assistance are not on the welfare rolls. The average monthly total of New York City residents receiving assistance in 1959 was 325,771, but according to the 1960 census, 716,000 persons (unrelated or in families) appeared to be subsisting on incomes at or below the prevailing welfare eligibility levels (e.g., $2,070 for a family of four). In that same year, 539,000 people subsisted on incomes *less than 80 per cent* of the welfare minimums, and 200,000 lived alone or in families on incomes reported to be *less than half* of eligibility levels. Thus it appears that for every person on welfare in 1959, at least one more was eligible.

The results of two surveys of selected areas in Manhattan support the contention that many people subsist on incomes below welfare eligibility levels. One of these, conducted by Greenleigh Associates in 1964 in an urban-renewal area on New York's upper West Side, found 9 per cent of those *not* on the rolls were in such acute need that they appeared to qualify for *emergency* assistance. The study showed, further, that a substantial number of families that were not in a "critical" condition would probably have qualified for supplemental assistance.

The other survey, conducted in 1961 by Mobilization for Youth, had similar findings. The area from which its sample was drawn, 67 square blocks on the lower East Side, is a poor one, but by no means the poorest in New York City. Yet 13 per cent of the total sample who were not on the welfare rolls reported incomes falling below the prevailing welfare schedules for food and rent.

There is no reason to suppose that the discrepancy between those eligible for and those receiving assistance has narrowed much in the past few years. The welfare rolls have gone up, to be sure, but so have eligibility levels. Since the economic circumstances of impoverished groups in New York have not improved appreciably in the past few years, each such rise increases the number of people who are potentially eligible for some degree of assistance.

Even if one allows for the possibility that family-income figures are grossly underestimated by the census, the financial implications of the proposed strategy are still very great. In 1965, the monthly average of persons receiving cash assistance in New York was 490,000, at a total cost of $440 million; the rolls have now risen above 500,000, so that costs will exceed $500 million in 1966. An increase in the rolls of a mere 20 per cent would cost an already overburdened municipality some $100 million.

Special grants: Public assistance recipients in New York are also entitled to receive "nonrecurring" grants for clothing, household equipment and furniture—including washing machines, refrigerators, beds and bedding, tables and chairs. It hardly needs to be noted that most impoverished families have grossly inadequate clothing and household furnishings. The Greenleigh study, for example, found that 52 per cent of the families on public assistance lacked anything approaching adequate furniture. This condition results because almost nothing is spent on special grants in New York. In October, 1965, a typical month, the Department of Welfare spent only $2.50 per recipient for heavy clothing and $1.30 for household furnishings. Taken together, grants of this kind amounted in 1965 to a mere $40 per person, or a total of $20 million for the entire year. Considering the real needs of families, the successful demand for full entitlements could multiply these expenditures tenfold or more—and that would involve the disbursement of many millions of dollars indeed.

One must be cautious in making generalizations about the prospects for this strategy in any jurisdiction unless the structure of welfare practices has been examined in some detail. We can, however, cite other studies conducted in other places to show that New York practices are not atypical. In Detroit, for example, Greenleigh Associates studied a large sample of households in a low-income district in 1965. Twenty per cent were already receiving assistance, but 35 per cent more were judged to need it. Although the authors made no strict determination of the eligibility of these families under the laws of Michigan, they believed that "larger numbers of persons were eligible than receiving." A good many of these families did not know that public assistance was available; others thought they would be deemed ineligible; not a few were ashamed or afraid to ask.

Similar deprivations have been shown in nation-wide studies. In 1963, the federal government carried out a survey based on a national sample of 5,500 families whose benefits under Aid to Dependent Children had been terminated. Thirty-four per cent of these cases were *officially in need of income at the point of closing:* this was true of 30 per cent of the white and 44 per cent of the Negro cases. The chief basis for termination given in local department records was "other reasons" (i.e., other than improvement in financial condition, which would make dependence on welfare unnecessary). Upon closer examination, these "other reasons" turned out to be "unsuitable home" (i.e., the presence of illegitimate children), "failure to comply with departmental regulations" or "refusal to take legal action against a putative father." (Negroes were especially singled out for punitive action on the ground that children were not being maintained in "suitable homes.") The amounts of money that people are deprived of by these injustices are very great.

In order to generate a crisis, the poor must obtain benefits which they have forfeited. Until now, they have been inhibited from asserting claims by self-protective devices within the welfare system: its capacity to limit information, to intimidate applicants, to demoralize recipients, and arbitrarily to deny lawful claims.

Ignorance of welfare rights can be attacked through a massive educational campaign. Brochures describing benefits in simple, clear language, and urging people to seek their full entitlements, should be distributed door to door in tenements and public housing projects, and deposited in stores, schools, churches and civic centers. Advertisements should be placed in newspapers; spot announcements should be made on radio. Leaders of social, religious, fraternal and political groups in the slums should also be enlisted to recruit the eligible to the rolls. The fact that the campaign is intended to inform people of their legal rights under a government program, that it is a civic education drive, will lend it legitimacy.

But information alone will not suffice. Organizers will have to become advocates in order to deal effectively with improper rejections and terminations. The advocate's task is to appraise the circumstances of each case, to argue its merits before welfare, to threaten legal action if satisfaction is not given. In some cases, it will be necessary to contest decisions by requesting a "fair hearing" before the appropriate state supervisory agency; it may occasionally be necessary to sue for redress in the courts. Hearings and court actions will require lawyers, many of whom, in cities like New York, can be recruited on a voluntary basis, especially under the banner of a movement to end poverty by a strategy of asserting legal rights. However, most cases will not require an expert knowledge of law, but only of welfare regulations; the rules can be learned by laymen, including welfare recipients themselves (who can help to man "information and advocacy" centers). To aid workers in these centers, handbooks should be prepared describing welfare rights and the tactics to employ in claiming them.

Advocacy must be supplemented by organized demonstrations to create a climate of militancy that will overcome the invidious and immobilizing attitudes which many potential recipients hold toward being "on welfare." In such a climate, many more poor people are likely to become their own advocates and will not need to rely on aid from organizers.

As the crisis develops, it will be important to use the mass media to inform the broader liberal community about the inefficiencies and injustices of welfare. For example, the system will not be able to process many new applicants because of cumbersome and often unconstitutional investigatory procedures (which cost 20c for every dollar disbursed). As delays mount, so should the public demand that a simplified affidavit supplant these procedures, so that the poor may certify to their condition. If the system reacts by making the proof of eligibility more difficult, the demand should be made that the Department of Health, Education and Welfare dispatch "eligibility registrars" to enforce federal statutes governing local programs. And throughout the crisis, the mass media should be used to advance arguments for a new federal income distribution program.[1]

Although new resources in organizers and funds would have to be developed to mount this campaign, a variety of conventional agencies in the large cities could also be drawn upon for help. The idea of "welfare rights" has begun to attract attention in many liberal circles. A number of organizations, partly under the aegis of the "war against poverty," are developing information and advocacy services for low-income people. It is not likely that these organizations will directly participate in the present strategy, for obvious political reasons. But whether they participate or not, they constitute a growing network of resources to which people can be referred for help in establishing and maintaining entitlements. In the final analysis, it does not matter who helps people to get on the rolls or to get additional entitlements, so long as the job is done.

Since this plan deals with problems of great immediacy in the lives of the poor, it should motivate some of them to involve themselves in regular organizational activities. Welfare recipients, chiefly ADC mothers, are already forming federations, committees and councils in cities across the nation; in Boston, New York, Newark, Cleveland, Chicago, Detroit and Los Angeles, to mention a few. Such groups typically focus on obtaining full entitlements for existing recipients rather than on recruiting new recipients, and they do not yet comprise a national movement. But their very existence attests to a growing readiness among ghetto residents to act against public welfare.

To generate an expressly political movement, cadres of aggressive organizers would have to come from the civil rights movement and the churches, from militant low-income organizations like those formed by the Industrial Areas Foundation (that is, by Saul Alinsky), and from other groups on the Left. These activists should be quick to see the difference between programs to redress individual grievances and a large-scale social-action campaign for national policy reform.

Movements that depend on involving masses of poor people have generally failed in America. Why would the proposed strategy to engage the poor succeed?

First, this plan promises immediate economic benefits. This is a point of some importance because, whereas America's poor have not been moved in any number by radical political ideologies, they have sometimes been moved by their economic interests. Since radical movements in America have rarely been able to provide visible economic incentives, they have usually failed to secure mass participation of any kind. The conservative "business unionism" of organized labor is explained by this fact, for membership enlarged only as unionism paid off in material benefits. Union leaders have understood that their strength derives almost entirely from their capacity to provide economic rewards to members. Although leaders have increasingly acted in political spheres, their influence has been directed chiefly to matters of governmental policy affecting the well-being of organized workers. The same point is made by the experience of rent strikes in Northern cities. Their organizers were often motivated by radical ideologies, but tenants have been attracted by the promise that housing improvements would quickly be made if they withheld their rent.

Second, for this strategy to succeed, one need not ask more of most of the poor than that they claim lawful benefits. Thus the plan has the extraordinary capability of yielding mass influence *without* mass participation, at least as the term "participation" is ordinarily understood. Mass influence in this case stems from the consumption of benefits and does not require that large groups of people be involved in regular organizational roles.

Moreover, this kind of mass influence is cumulative because benefits are continuous. Once eligibility for basic food and rent grants is established, the drain on local resources persists indefinitely. Other movements have failed precisely because they could not produce continuous and cumulative influence. In the Northern rent strikes, for example, tenant participation depended largely on immediate grievances; as soon as landlords made the most minimal repairs, participation fell away and with it the impact of the movement. Efforts to revive tenant participation by organizing demonstrations around broader housing issues (e.g., the expansion of public housing) did not succeed because the incentives were not immediate.

Third, the prospects for mass influence are enhanced because this plan provides a practical basis for coalition between poor whites and poor Negroes. Advocates of low-income movements have not been able to suggest how poor whites and poor Negroes can be united in an expressly lower-class movement. Despite pleas of some Negro leaders for joint action on programs requiring integration, poor whites have steadfastly resisted making common cause with poor Negroes. By contrast, the benefits of the present plan are as great for whites as for Negroes. In the big cities, at least, it does not seem likely that poor whites, whatever their prejudices against either Negroes or public welfare, will refuse to participate when Negroes aggressively claim benefits that are unlawfully denied to them as well. One salutary consequence of public information campaigns to acquaint Negroes with their rights is that many whites will be made aware of theirs. Even if whites prefer to work through their own organizations and leaders, the consequences will be equivalent to joining with Negroes. For if the object is to focus attention on the need for new ecomomic measures by producing a crisis over the dole, anyone who insists upon extracting maximum benefits from public welfare is in effect part of a coalition and is contributing to the cause.

The ultimate aim of this strategy is a new program for direct income distribution. What reason is there to expect that the federal government will enact such legislation in response to a crisis in the welfare system?

We ordinarily think of major legislation as taking form only through established electoral processes. We tend to overlook the force of crisis in precipitating legislative reform, partly because we lack a theoretical framework by which to understand the impact of major disruptions.

By crisis, we mean a *publicly visible* disruption in some institutional sphere. Crisis can occur spontaneously (e.g., riots) or as the intended result of tactics of demonstration and protest which either generate institutional disruption or bring unrecognized disruption to public attention. Public trouble is a political liability; it calls for action by political leaders to stabilize the situation. Because crisis usually creates or exposes conflict, it threatens to produce cleavages in a political consensus which politicians will ordinarily act to avert.

Although crisis impels political action, it does not itself determine the selection of specific solutions. Political leaders will try to respond with proposals which work to their advantage in the electoral process. Unless group cleavages form around issues and demands, the politician has great latitude and tends to proffer only the minimum action required to quell disturbances without risking existing electoral support. Spontaneous disruptions, such as riots, rarely produce leaders who articulate demands; thus no terms are imposed, and political leaders are permitted to respond in ways that merely restore a semblance of stability without offending other groups in a coalition.

When, however, a crisis is defined by its participants—or by other activated groups—as a matter of clear issues and preferred solutions, terms are imposed on the politicians' bid for their support. Whether political leaders then design solutions to reflect these terms depends on a two-fold calculation: first, the impact of the crisis and the issues it raises on existing alignments and, second, the gains or losses in support to be expected as a result of a proposed resolution.

As to the impact on existing alignments, issues exposed by a crisis may activate new groups, thus altering the balance of support and opposition on the issues; or it may polarize group sentiments, altering the terms which must be offered to insure the support of given constituent groups. In framing resolutions, politicians are more responsive to group shifts and are more likely to accommodate to the terms imposed when electoral coalitions threatened by crisis are already uncertain or weakening. In other words, the politician responds to group demands, not only by calculating the magnitude of electoral gains and losses, but by assessing the impact of the resolution on the stability of existing or potential coalitions. Political leaders are especially responsive to group shifts when the terms of settlement can be framed so as to shore up an existing coalition, or as a basis for the development of new and more stable alignments, *without* jeopardizing existing support. Then, indeed, the calculation of net gain is most secure.

The legislative reforms of the depression years, for example, were impelled not so much by organized interests exercised through regular electoral processes as by widespread economic crisis. That crisis precipitated the disruption of the regionally based coalitions underlying the old national parties. During the realignments of 1932, a new Democratic coalition was formed, based heavily on urban working-class groups. Once in power, the national Democratic leadership proposed and implemented the economic reforms of the New Deal. Although these measures were a response to the imperative of economic crisis, the types of measures enacted were designed to secure and stabilize the new Democratic coalition.

The civil rights movement, to take a recent case, also reveals the relationship of crisis and electoral conditions in producing legislative reform. The crisis in the South took place in the context of a weakening North-South Democratic coalition. The strains in that coalition were first evident in the Dixiecrat desertion of 1948, and continued through the Eisenhower years as the Republicans gained ground in the Southern states. Democratic party leaders at first tried to hold the dissident South by warding off the demands of enlarging Negro constituencies in Northern cities. Thus for two decades the national Democratic Party campaigned on strongly worded civil rights planks but enacted only token measures. The civil rights movement forced the Democrats' hand: a crumbling Southern partnership was forfeited, and major civil rights legislation was put forward, designed to insure the support of Northern Negroes and liberal elements in the Democratic coalition. That coalition emerged strong from the 1964 election, easily able to overcome the loss of Southern states to Goldwater. At the same time, the enacted legislation, particularly the Voting Rights Act, laid the ground for a new Southern Democratic coalition of moderate whites and the hitherto untapped reservoir of Southern Negro voters.

The electoral context which made crisis effective in the South is also to be found in the big cities of the nation today. Deep tensions have developed among groups comprising the political coalitions of the large cities—the historic stronghold of the Democratic Party. As a consequence, urban politicians no longer turn in the vote to national Democratic candidates with unfailing regularity. The marked defections revealed in the elections of the 1950s and which continued until the Johnson landslide of 1964 are a matter of great concern to the national party. Precisely because of this concern, a strategy to exacerbate still further the strains in the urban coalition can be expected to evoke a response from national leaders.

The weakening of the urban coalition is a result of many basic changes in the relationship of local party leadership to its constituents. First, the political machine, the distinctive and traditional mechanism for forging alliances among competing groups in the city, is now virtually defunct in most cities. Successive waves of municipal reform have deprived political leaders of control over the public resources—jobs, contracts, services and favors—which machine politicians formerly dispensed to voters in return for electoral support. Conflicts among elements in the urban Democratic coalition, once held together politically because each secured a share of these benefits, cannot now be so readily contained. And as the means of placating competing groups have diminished, tensions along ethnic and class lines have multiplied. These tensions are being intensified by the encroachments of an enlarging ghetto population on jobs, schools and residential areas. Big city mayors are thus caught between antagonistic working-class ethnic groups, the remaining middle class, and the rapidly enlarging minority poor.

Second, there are discontinuities in the relationship between the urban party apparatus and its ghetto constituents which have so far remained unexposed but which a welfare crisis would force into view. The ghetto vote has been growing rapidly and has so far returned overwhelming Democratic majorities. Nevertheless, this voting bloc is not fully integrated in the party apparatus, either through the representation of its leaders or the accommodation of its interests.

While the urban political apparatus includes members of new minority groups, these groups are by no means represented according to their increasing proportions in the population. More important, elected representation alone is not an adequate mechanism for the expression of group interests. Influence in urban politics is won not only at the polls but through the sustained activity of organized interests—such as labor unions, home-owner associations and business groups. These groups keep watch over the complex operations of municipal agencies, recognizing issues and regularly asserting their point of view through meetings with public officials, appearances at public hearings and the like, and by exploiting a whole array of channels of influence on government. Minority constituencies—at least the large proportion of them that are poor—are not regular participants in the various institutional spheres where organized interest groups typically develop. Thus the interests of the mass of minority poor are not protected by associations which make their own or other political leaders responsive by continuously calling them to account. Urban party organizations have become, in consequence, more an avenue for the personal advancement of minority political leaders than a channel for the expression of minority-group interests. And the big-city mayors, struggling to preserve an uneasy urban consensus, have thus been granted the slack to evade the conflict-generating interests of the ghetto. A crisis in public welfare would expose the tensions latent in this attenuated relationship between the ghetto vote and the urban party leadership, for it would thrust forward ghetto demands and back them with the threat of defections by voters who have so far remained both loyal and quiescent.

In the face of such a crisis, urban political leaders may well be paralyzed by a party apparatus which ties them to older constituent groups, even while the ranks of these groups are diminishing. The national Democratic leadership, however, is alert to the importance of the urban Negro vote, especially in national contests where the loyalty of other urban groups is weakening. Indeed, many of the legislative reforms of the Great Society can be understood as efforts, however feeble, to reinforce the allegiance of growing ghetto constituencies to the national Democratic Administration. In the thirties, Democrats began to put forward measures to circumvent the states in order to reach the big-city elements in the New Deal coalition; now it is becoming expedient to put forward measures to circumvent the weakened big-city mayors in order to reach the new minority poor.

Recent federal reforms have been impelled in part by widespread unrest in the ghetto, and instances of more aggressive Negro demands. But despite these signs that the ghetto vote may become less reliable in the future, there has been as yet no serious threat of massive defection. The national party has therefore not put much pressure on its urban branches to accommodate the minority poor. The resulting reforms have consequently been quite modest (e.g., the war against poverty, with its emphasis on the "involvement of the poor," is an effort to make the urban party apparatus somewhat more accommodating).

A welfare crisis would, of course, produce dramatic local political crisis, disrupting and exposing rifts among urban groups. Conservative Republicans are always ready to declaim the evils of public welfare, and they would probably be the first to raise a hue and cry. But deeper and politically more telling conflicts would take place within the Democratic coalition. Whites—both working-class ethnic groups and many in the middle class—would be aroused against the ghetto poor, while liberal groups, which until recently have been comforted by the notion that the poor are few and, in any event, receiving the beneficent assistance of public welfare, would probably support the movement. Group conflict, spelling political crisis for the local party apparatus, would thus become acute as welfare rolls mounted and the strains on local budgets became more severe. In New York City, where the Mayor is now facing desperate revenue shortages, welfare expenditures are already second only to those for public education.

It should also be noted that welfare costs are generally shared by local, state and federal governments, so that the crisis in the cities would intensify the struggle over revenues that is chronic in relations between cities and states. If the past is any predictor of the future, cities will fail to procure relief from this crisis by persuading states to increase their proportionate share of urban welfare costs, for state legislatures have been notoriously unsympathetic to the revenue needs of the city (especially where public welfare and minority groups are concerned).

If this strategy for crisis would intensify group cleavages, a federal income solution would not further exacerbate them. The demands put forward during recent civil rights drives in the Northern cities aroused the opposition of huge majorities. Indeed, such fierce resistance was evoked (e.g., school boycotts followed by counter-boycotts), that accessions by political leaders would have provoked greater political turmoil than the protests themselves, for profound class and ethnic interests are at stake in the employment, educational and residential institutions of our society. By contrast, legislative measures to provide direct income to the poor would permit national Democratic leaders to cultivate ghetto constituencies without unduly antagonizing other urban groups, as is the case when the battle lines are drawn over schools, housing or jobs. Furthermore, a federal income program would not only redeem local governments from the immediate crisis but would permanently relieve them of the financially and politically onerous burdens of public welfare[2]—a function which generates support from none and hostility from many, not least of all welfare recipients.

We suggest, in short, that if pervasive institutional reforms are not yet possible, requiring as they do expanded Negro political power and the development of new political alliances, crisis tactics can nevertheless be employed to secure particular reforms in the short run by exploiting weaknesses in current political alignments. Because the urban coalition stands weakened by group conflict today, disruption and threats of disaffection will count powerfully, provided that national leaders can respond with solutions which retain the support of ghetto constituencies while avoiding new group antagonisms and bolstering the urban party apparatus. These are the conditions, then, for an effective crisis strategy in the cities to secure an end to poverty.

No strategy, however confident its advocates may be, is foolproof. But if unforeseen contingencies thwart this plan to bring about new federal legislation in the field of poverty, it should also be noted that there would be gains even in defeat. For one thing, the plight of many poor people would be somewhat eased in the course of an assault upon public welfare. Existing recipients would come to know their rights and how to defend them, thus acquiring dignity where none now exists; and millions of dollars in withheld welfare benefits would become available to potential recipients now—not several generations from now. Such an attack should also be welcome to those currently concerned with programs designed to equip the young to rise out of poverty (e.g., Head Start), for surely children learn more readily when the oppressive burden of financial insecurity is lifted from the shoulders of their parents. And those seeking new ways to engage the Negro politically should remember that public resources have always been the fuel for low-income urban political organization. If organizers can deliver millions of dollars in cash benefits to the ghetto masses, it seems reasonable to expect that the masses will deliver their loyalties to their benefactors. At least, they have always done so in the past.

---

[1]In public statements, it would be important to distinguish between the income distributing function of public welfare, which should be replaced by new federal measures, and many other welfare functions, such as foster care and adoption services for children, which are not at issue in this strategy.

[2]It should also be noted that the federal government, unlike local jurisdictions, has taxing powers which yield substantially increased revenues as an automatic by-product of increases in national income.

B. THE REFORM AND REORGANIZATION OF GOVERNMENT

35. The Citizen and the Machine

RICHARD HOFSTADTER

If big business was the ultimate enemy of the Progressive, his proximate enemy was the political machine. The problem of political organization gave him somewhat the same sort of perplexity as that of economic organization; it similarly divided the Progressive community between those who proposed an aggressive and uncompromising struggle against organization as such and those who proposed to meet it by counterorganization, by increasing specialism and leadership, and by the assumption of new responsibilities. Unless the machine and its leader, the boss, could be broken, unless the corrupt alliance between special interests and the machine could be smashed, it seemed that no lasting reform could be accomplished. Hence this particular form of the struggle over organization was prominent in political discussions from the beginning to the end of the Progressive era. What the majority of the Progressives hoped to do in the political field was to restore popular government as they imagined it to have existed in an earlier and purer age. This could be done, it was widely believed, only by revivifying the morale of the citizen, and using his newly aroused zeal to push through a series of changes in the mechanics of political life—direct primaries, popular election of Senators, initiative, referendum, recall, the short ballot, commission government, and the like. Such measures, it was expected, would deprive machine government of the advantages it had in checkmating popular control, and make government accessible to the superior disinterestedness and honesty of the average citizen. Then, with the power of the bosses broken or crippled, it would be possible to check the incursions of the interests upon the welfare of the people and realize a cleaner, more efficient government.

The Progressives set about the task of political reform with great energy and resourcefulness. By 1910 they had had a considerable measure of success in getting their reforms incorporated into the electoral and governmental machinery, and this success engendered in some quarters a high optimism about the future of the movement for popular government. William Allen White's book *The Old Order Changeth,* published in that year, deserves analysis as a hearty expression of this optimism and as a statement of what was probably the dominant popular philosophy of politics. America, White believed, was in the midst of an inexorable "drift" toward democracy, which had produced gain after gain in the sphere of popular government—victories for the secret ballot and the direct primary, the widespread adoption of the recall of officials, the impending triumph of the popular referendum. Such changes would not have been dreamed of ten years before, "and to have told the campaign managers of '84 or '88 that within a quarter of a century the whole nation would be voting a secret ballot, the candidates nominated in two-thirds of the American states by a direct vote of the people, without the intervention of conventions or caucuses, and that . . . every dollar spent by a candidate or by a party committee would have to be publicly accounted for," would have aroused only a cackle of derision. Now in twenty-six states of the Union, Senators had to go directly to the people for their nomination, not to the railroads and utilities as before. "Capital is not eliminated from politics, but it is hampered and circumscribed, and is not the dominant force it was ten years ago." "It is safe to say that the decree of divorce between business and politics will be absolute within a few years." "Now the political machine is in a fair way to be reduced to mere political scrap iron by the rise of the people. . . . Under the primary system any clean, quick-witted man in these states can defeat the corporation senatorial candidate at the primary if the people desire to defeat him."[1]

White fully shared the dominant Progressive philosophy concerning organization. The business of reform in politics, he said, had to be done by taking the power to nominate and elect candidates and to get policies out of the hands of the old ruling caste of the machines. Such a thing "could always be done by breaking the machine of the moment or of any locality and establishing another machine." But such a remedy was no good—and here was the crux of the matter—because it was not "a permanent cure." The only permanent cure was in changing the system.[2] If theory was to be effective in practice, one would have no machines at all. White did not hesitate to emphasize the underlying individualism of the popular revolt: it was a change in "the public's moral average," the aggregate result of the transformation of a multitude of individual wills. Yet for all its need to bring property under control, it was far from socialistic: "the modern movement in American politics is bristling with rampant, militant, unhampered men crowding out of the mass for individual elbow-room."[3]

None of this movement for elbow-room was considered to be excessively self-regarding. White's book was full of references to the intelligence, the self-restraint, the morality, the breadth of view of the average man, the emergent New Citizen. The whole process of revolt was indeed so benign that he could only attribute it to the workings of "a divinely planted instinct." For it was essential that the individual be—as he was proving himself—disinterested. The New Citizen was the guilty and neglectful citizen of the muckraking literature after he had been reformed and aroused by all the exhortatory literature of the age. "The people are controlling themselves. Altruism is gaining strength for some future struggle with the atomic force of egoism in society."[4] It followed from this view of the citizen that his contribution to the public weal grew not out of his pursuit in politics of his own needs but, in the manner of the old Mugwump ideal, out of his disinterested reflection upon the needs of the community. Of course the struggle against the machines could not take place without the benefit of some form of counterorganization; but it was characteristic of this style of thought to conceive of these counterorganizations as private organizations based upon high principles rather than group interests—organizations like the National Civil Service Reform League, the Pure Food Association, the Child Labor Committee, the Consumers' League, the National Civic Federation, the Masons, and other fraternal groups. What all such things rested upon for their success was the civic virtue—White spoke rather of "righteousness" and "altruism"—of the individual, his willingness not to pursue his interests but to transcend them. "Democracy is, at base, altruism expressed in terms of self-government." "Practically all the large national organizations which jam the trains annually going to their conventions are fundamentally altruistic."[5]

We can now see in its broad outlines the persistent individualism of these Progressives. Although it was necessary for them to make some use of organization, they had a profound inherited distrust of it. At the core of their conception of politics was a figure quite as old-fashioned as the figure of the little competitive entrepreneur who represented the most commonly accepted economic ideal. This old-fashioned character was the Man of Good Will, the same innocent, bewildered, bespectacled, and mustached figure we see in the cartoons today labeled John Q. Public—a white collar or small business voter-taxpayer with perhaps a modest home in the suburbs. William Graham Sumner had depicted him a generation earlier as "the forgotten man," and Woodrow Wilson idealized him as "the man on the make" whose type, coming "out of the unknown homes," was the hope of America. In a great deal of Progressive thinking the Man of Good Will was abstracted from association with positive interests; his chief interests were negative. He needed to be protected from unjust taxation, spared the high cost of living, relieved of the exactions of the monopolies and the grafting of the bosses. In years past he had been careless about his civic responsibilities, but now he was rising in righteous wrath and asserting himself. He was at last ready to address himself seriously to the business of government. The problem was to devise such governmental machinery as would empower him to rule. Since he was dissociated from all special interests and biases and had nothing but the common weal at heart, he would rule well. He would act and think as a public-spirited individual, unlike all the groups of vested interests that were ready to prey on him. Bad people had pressure groups; the Man of Good Will had only his civic organizations. Far from joining organizations to advance his own interests, he would dissociate himself from such combinations and address himself directly and high-mindedly to the problems of government. His approach to politics was, in a sense, intellectualistic: he would study the issues and think them through, rather than learn about them through pursuing his needs. Furthermore, it was assumed that somehow he would really be capable of informing himself in ample detail about the many issues that he would have to pass on, and that he could master their intricacies sufficiently to pass intelligent judgment.

Without such assumptions the entire movement for such reforms as the initiative, the referendum, and recall is unintelligible. The movement for direct popular democracy was, in effect, an attempt to realize Yankee-Protestant ideals of personal responsibility; and the Progressive notion of good citizenship was the culmination of the Yankee-Mugwump ethos of political participation without self-interest. But while this ethos undoubtedly has its distinct points of superiority to the boss-machine ethos of hierarchy, discipline, personal loyalty, and personal favors, it was less adapted to the realities of the highly organized society of the late nineteenth and the twentieth century. It is not surprising, then, that so much of the political machinery designed to implement the aims of direct democracy should have been found of very limited use.

Of course, not all his Progressive contemporaries were quite so optimistic as William Allen White. There were a number of Progressive spokesmen who found fault with his assumptions, and there were a few outstanding Progressive leaders who surmounted them in their practical political dealings. Just as Progressive discussions of the business order were pervaded by an argument between two schools with contrasting schemes for dealing with the trusts, so the discussions of political reform took place between two sides that were divided by a difference in philosophy. On the left was a populistic school of thought that seemed to have hardly any reservations about the extent to which the management of affairs could and should be given into the hands of the populace. This school, which can be traced as far back as the time when Jackson argued for rotation in office on the ground that "the duties of all public offices are, or at least admit of being made, so plain and simple that men of intelligence may readily qualify themselves for their performance," found its contemporary expression in William Jennings Bryan's contention that the people were competent "to sit in judgment on every question which has arisen or which will arise, no matter how long our government will endure," and his argument that the great political questions were in the final analysis moral questions concerning which the intuitions of the people were as good as almost any degree of experience. Even a man like Woodrow Wilson, whose native impulses and earlier philosophy ran quite to the contrary, fell into this populistic conception of democracy when he asserted that the Democratic Party aimed "to set up a government in the world where the average man, the plain man, the common man, the ignorant man, the unaccomplished man, the poor man had a voice equal to the voice of anybody else in the settlement of the common affairs, an ideal never before realized in the history of the world."[6]

This faith in the lowest common denominator of political action was frequently coupled with an attack on political organization. The political evils that plagued the country, it was often argued, were not the consequences of deficient organization but of over-organization. The answer to these evils was to move as close as possible to a system of "direct government" by the people. It was considered not only that the people were capable of acting effectively as individuals, but that they were at their best when acting in this capacity because only then were they free of the corrupting and self-interested influence of parties and machines. Thus Albert Baird Cummins, when he ran for the governorship of Iowa in 1910, declared that his great object was "to bring the individual voter into more prominence, and to diminish the influence of permanent organization in the ranks of the party."[7]

Those who shared this style of thought tended to deny that the parties should be the property of the party organizations—that is, of the groups of persons who did the work of the party and held offices under its name—and to insist that the parties properly belonged to the voters at large. Indeed, the rhetoric of American party politics had encouraged this notion, and it was easy to conclude that in so far as the party was in fact not the property of the voters, democracy was being flouted. Democracy was considered to require not merely competition between party organizations that would afford the voters a choice, but rank-and-file control or dissolution of the organizations themselves. The movement for the direct primary was the chief embodiment of this conception of democracy.[8] Its historical inspiration presumably came from the town-meeting model, and from the widespread direct participation of the American citizen in civic affairs in the early and middle years of the nineteenth century.

Counterposed to this philosophy was a more conservative view, expressed by a good many men who recognized the value of the Progressive demands for reform and saw the importance of popular discontent, but who looked to new forms of political organization under responsible leadership as the most desirable and effective remedy for the evils against which the Progressives were working. The historical root of this point of view lay in the long-standing Mugwump concern with good government and in the implicit Mugwump belief in elite leadership. Brandeis, as we have seen, expressed its impulse when he called upon the lawyers to assume "a position of independence between the wealthy and the people, prepared to curb the excesses of either," and so did T. R. when he entitled one of his talks to businessmen "The Radical Movement under Conservative Direction."[9] Henry L. Stimson, writing to Roosevelt in 1910, gave vent to a somewhat partisan statement of this philosophy: "To me it seems vitally important that the Republican party, which contains, generally speaking, the richer and more intelligent citizens of the country, should take the lead in reform and not drift into a reactionary position. If, instead, the leadership should fall into the hands of either an independent party, or a party composed, like the Democrats, largely of foreign elements and the classes which will immediately benefit by the reform, and if the solid business Republicans should drift into new obstruction, I fear the necessary changes could hardly be accomplished without much excitement and possible violence."[1]

Somewhat more congenial to Mugwump traditions was the idea that the evils against which the Progressives were fighting could be remedied by a reorganization of government in which responsibility and authority could be clearly located in an executive, whose acts would be open to public view. The power of the boss, they argued, like the overweening power of great corporations, was a consequence of the weakness of the political executive and the more general division of authority and impotence in government. Spokesmen of this view scoffed at the inherited popular suspicion of executive power as an outmoded holdover from the days of the early Republic when executive power was still identified with royal government and the royal governors. "The true remedy for American misgovernment," said Stimson, "would lie, then, in exactly the opposite direction from that indicated by the advocates of direct democracy. The elected officials must have more power, not less. . . . "[2] The purpose of such devices would not be to flout public opinion, but to give expression to its demands in conformity with principles of organization that accepted the realities of a complex society.

The most ardent debate, however, did not take place between the two schools of reformers, but between the direct-government reforms and the ultraconservatives. To attend to the terms in which the various reforms intended to promote direct democracy were debated—and to these one should add the proposal for women's suffrage—one might think that the issue was utopia versus apocalypse. The conservatives moaned and admonished as though each new reform proposal portended the end of the nation, while many Progressives seemed to imagine and often, indeed, said that these reforms, once achieved, would open the way to a complete and permanent victory over the machines and corruption. Woodrow Wilson, for instance, once said of the short ballot that it was "the key to the whole problem of the restoration of popular government in this country"[3]—which was a heavy burden, sound reform though it was, for the short ballot to bear. There were of course more moderate men on both sides,[4] and in retrospect it is clearly these men who were right; for the popular reforms neither revolutionized nor restored anything; they had, indeed, only a marginal effect on the conduct of American government.

Here the more general Progressive uprising against bossism, corruption, and misgovernment must be distinguished from the attempt to realize mechanical changes that would guarantee permanent popular rule. Where the reform movements succeeded as they did in sufficient measure to bring a distinct improvement in American government, it was largely because they came in on a strong wave of popular enthusiasm or indignation or under the guidance of local leaders of exceptional magnetism. Such leaders and such public sentiments, I believe, would have had somewhat the same results within the framework of the older mechanism of government. In their search for mechanical guarantees of continued popular control the reformers were trying to do something altogether impossible—to institutionalize a mood. When the mood passed, some of the more concrete reforms remained; but the formal gains for popular government, while still on the books, lost meaning because the ability of the public to use them effectively lapsed with the political revival that brought them in, and the bosses and the interest promptly filtered back. Herbert Croly, while by no means unsympathetic to the "professional democrats," as he called them, argued cogently that their tendency "to conceive democracy as essentially a matter of popular political machinery" was one of their great weaknesses. Their dominant impulse was to protect the people against knavery, a negative goal, rather than "to give positive momentum and direction to popular rule." They sought, above all, "to prevent the people from being betrayed—from being imposed upon by unpopular policies and unrepresentative officials. But to indoctrinate and organize one's life chiefly for the purpose of avoiding betrayal is to invite sterility and disintegration." He concluded that the impulse toward popular rule was without meaning whenever it was divorced from a specific social program.[5]

The history of Progressive reform justified Croly's argument, for under the impact of the Progressive movement the people in many places won better public services, better parks, better schools, better tax policies, but they did not destroy narrowly partisan government, break up machines, or gain direct control of their affairs. With a few exceptions, the bosses found ways either to deflect or to use the new reforms that were meant to unseat them.[6] The direct primary, for instance, for all its wide adoption throughout the country, did not noticeably change the type of men nominated for office. It was expensive both to the government and to the candidates—for it introduced two campaigns in the place of one. It put a new premium on publicity and promotion in nominating campaigns, and thus introduced into the political process another entering wedge for the power of money. Without seriously impairing the machines, it weakened party government and party responsibility. The initiative and referendum were also disappointing as instruments of popular government. As critics like Herbert Croly pointed out, they were perfectly designed to facilitate minority rule in so far as the complex questions set before the voters in referendums could be passed with a distinct minority of the total registration.[7] Confronted by an array of technical questions, often phrased in legal language, the voters shrank from the responsibilities the new system attempted to put upon them. Small and highly organized groups with plenty of funds and skillful publicity could make use of these devices, but such were not the results the proponents of initiative and referendum sought; nor was the additional derationalization of politics that came with the propaganda campaigns demanded by referendums. Finally, the more ardent reformers who expected that the public will, once expressed directly, would bring a radical transformation of the old order were surprised to find the voters exercising their prerogative in the most conservative way, rejecting, for instance, proposals for municipal ownership, the single tax, and pensions for city employees.[8]

The reformers were, of course, entirely right in feeling that effective action against the old political machines and their bosses was both possible and desirable. Reform has been the balance wheel of the governmental system. The existing machines did their work at unnecessary cost and with gross inequities, and their humane care of their own constituents was matched by the outright brutality and the crass disregard of civil liberties with which they frequently dealt with opposition. Unopposed by the reform principle, the machine principle tended to deteriorate to the point at which good government and liberal politics both were threatened. But the characteristic mistake of the more dogmatic enthusiasts for direct government was their unwillingness to consider the possibility of a synthesis between the two principles, their faith in contrivances that would somehow do away with the machine process and even with party responsibility. Too many of these enthusiasts failed to see that the machine organizations they were trying to destroy did have a number of real functions, however badly they often performed them, and that any attempt to replace the existing machines had to provide not William Allen White's "permanent cure" for the whole machine system, but rather alternative machines. There are machines and machines. The real choice that lay before the reformers was not whether to have direct popular government or party organizations and machines, but whether, in destroying the existing organizations, they could create organizations of their own, with discipline enough to survive, that would be cleaner and more efficient than those they were trying to break up. It must be admitted at once that in this respect the practice of some skilled Progressive leaders was often superior to their theories and their rhetoric. La Follette was an excellent case in point. Although he expressed great faith in the efficacy of the direct-government reforms, he remained in power for a long time and exerted a strong and salutary influence on Wisconsin life because he was an extremely astute machine-master, who knew the techniques of the bosses and used some of them to build a militant and well-disciplined state organization.[9]

It is in our own times that the most notable decline in the strength and importance of the old-fashioned machines has taken place. This has occurred not because the machines have yielded to frontal assault but because some of their former functions have ceased to be necessary and others have been taken over by new agencies. There is no longer the great mass of immigrants to be patronized and introduced to American life. Federal centralization, especially since the New Deal, has nibbled away at the role of the local organizations, particularly in the sphere of social welfare. The growth of the mass trade unions has displaced the machines in some respects, while the development of stronger executives in state and local government has deprived them of some of their former patronage and power. Much of the work of political indoctrination and education that once belonged to them has been assumed by the mass media—radio, television, and the mass periodicals, while the work of sounding public sentiment has been taken over in some part by professional pollsters. These latter developments suggest that we are in a certain sense moving closer to the plebiscitarian ideals, the mass democracy, that the advocates of direct government had in mind. But they would not have been pleased with the prospect of having their goals approached in this way, for the means of influencing mass sentiment on a grand scale require the big money and the crass manipulative techniques that the Progressives were trying to eliminate from politics. This brings us back again to a central problem of the modern democrat: whether it is possible in modern society to find satisfactory ways of realizing the ideal of popular government without becoming dependent to an unhealthy degree upon those who have the means to influence the popular mind. Without taking an excessively indulgent view of the old machines or imagining that their failings were any less serious than they actually were, it is still possible to wonder whether the devices that are replacing them are superior as instruments of government.

---

[1]White: *The Old Order Changeth,* pp. 34, 36, 39, 47–53.

[2]*Ibid.,* p. 39.

[3]*Ibid.,* p. 121.

[4]*Ibid.,* pp. 57, 60–3, 66, 71, 120.

[5]*Ibid.,* pp. 132, 143; see chapter vi *passim.*

[6]Link: *Wilson: the Road to the White House,* p. 518.

[7]*Dictionary of American Biography,* Vol. IV (New York, 1930), p. 597. This point of view was expressed as late as 1923 by Senator George W. Norris in a defense of the direct primary: "One of the [most important] objections that is always made to the direct primary is that it takes away party responsibility and breaks down party control. . . . Politicians, political bosses, corporations and combinations seeking special privilege and exceptional favor at the hands of legislatures and executive officials, always urge this as the first reason why the direct primary should be abolished. But

this objection thus given against the direct primary I frankly offer as one of the best reasons for its retention. The direct primary will lower party responsibility. In its stead it establishes individual responsibility. It does lessen allegiance to party and increase individual independence, both as to the public official and as to the private citizen. It takes away the power of the party leader or boss and places the responsibility for control upon the individual. It lessens party spirit and decreases partisanship." "Why I Believe in the Direct Primary," *Annals* of the American Academy of Political and Social Science, Vol. CVI (March 1923), p. 23.

[8]See E. E. Schattschneider: *Party Government* (New York, 1942), pp. 53–61.

[9]Theodore Roosevelt: *Works,* National Edition (New York, 1926), Vol. XVI, pp. 86–99.

[1]Henry L. Stimson and McGeorge Bundy: *On Active Service in Peace and War* (New York, 1948), p. 22.

[2]*Ibid.,* p. 58; see the general argument of chapter iii, "Responsible Government," pp. 56–81.

[3]Quoted in Austin F. Macdonald: *American City Government and Administration,* 3rd ed. (New York, 1941), p. 279. Cf. Walter Lippmann in 1914: "I have just read a book by a college professor which announces that the short ballot will be as deep a revolution as the abolition of slavery. There are innumerable Americans who believe that a democratic constitution would create a democracy." *Drift and Mastery,* p. 187. Cf. La Follette's hopes for the direct primary, *Autobiography,* pp. 197–8.

[4]An excellent contemporary discussion of the whole problem of the public will and representative institutions was A. Lawrence Lowell's *Public Opinion and Popular Government* (New York, 1913); see also the critical reflections of Herbert Croly in *Progressive Democracy* (New York, 1914).

[5]Croly: *Ibid.,* pp. 213–14; see in general chapters x and xiii.

[6]Where the tone of a community was congenial to bossism it was impossible to find political mechanics that would prevent it. One of the signal illustrations of this comes from New Jersey, where the Walsh Act of 1911 permitted municipalities to change to the commission system of government. This was one of the reforms that worked to good effect in some places, but in New Jersey Frank Hague used his position as commissioner of public safety—i.e., the police and fire departments—as a stepping-stone toward that execrable regime for which he became notorious. Dayton D. McKean: *The Boss: the Hague Machine in Action* (Boston, 1940), pp. 37–45.

[7]Herbert Croly: *op. cit.,* p. 306.

[8]There is an extensive literature on such practices as direct primaries, the short ballot, initiative, referendum, recall, commission government, the city-manager plan, and other reforms of the age. For a brief general critique see William B. Munro: *The Government of American Cities,* 4th ed. (New York, 1933).

Some sober party estimates of the direct primary may be found in *Annals* of the American Academy of Political and Social Sciences, Vol. CVI (March 1933). The comments of working politicians on the direct primary in Ralph S. Boots: *The Direct Primary in New Jersey* (New York, 1917), pp. 262–76, are of unusual interest.

One of the more successful changes, useful chiefly in smaller municipalities, was the city-manager plan, which paid more deference to the need for concentration of power and *expertise* than the devices aimed to bring about direct popular government. The value even of this plan, however, has been impaired by the unwillingness of American voters to see their city managers (or their other administrators or political leaders) paid adequate salaries. On this see Thomas H. Reed: *Municipal Governments in the United States* (New York, 1934), chapter xiv.

[9]The whole subject of the types of political machines and the character of what might be called reform machines needs study by historians and political scientists. See, however, the suggestive article by Robert S. Maxwell: "La Follette and the Progressive Machine in Wisconsin," *Indiana Magazine of History,* Vol. XLVIII (March 1952), pp. 55–70, in which the author briefly analyzes the La Follette machine as a particular instance of the general proposition: "On those rare occasions when successful reform organizations have been welded together they have developed

techniques of political astuteness, leadership, and discipline not unlike the traditional machines." Cf. George Mowry's remarks on Hiram Johnson's California machine: *The California Progressives,* pp. 138–9, 292. The administration of Fiorello La Guardia in New York affords a municipal example of a reform movement that used machine methods.

36. Some Functions of the Political Machine

ROBERT MERTON

Without presuming to enter into the variations of detail marking different political machines—a Tweed, Vare, Crump, Flynn, Hague are by no means identical types of bosses—we can briefly examine the functions more or less common to the political machine, as a generic type of social organization. We neither attempt to itemize all the diverse functions of the political machine nor imply that all these functions are similarly fulfilled by each and every machine.

The key structural function of the Boss is to organize, centralize and maintain in good working condition "the scattered fragments of power" which are at present dispersed through our political organization. By this centralized organization of political power, the boss and his apparatus can satisfy the needs of diverse subgroups in the larger community which are not adequately satisfied by legally devised and culturally approved social structures.

To understand the role of bossism and the machine, therefore, we must look at two types of sociological variables: (1) the *structural context* which makes it difficult, if not impossible, for morally approved structures to fulfill essential social functions, thus leaving the door open for political machines (or their structural equivalents) to fulfill these functions and (2) the subgroups whose distinctive needs are left unsatisfied, except for the latent functions which the machine in fact fulfills.[92]

Structural Context: The constitutional framework of American political organization specifically precludes the legal possibility of highly centralized power and, it has been noted, thus "discourages the growth of effective and responsible leadership. The framers of the Constitution, as Woodrow Wilson observed, set up the check and

SOURCE: *Social Theory and Social Structure* (New York: The Free Press of Glencoe, 1957 [revised edition]), pp. 72-82.

balance system 'to keep government at a sort of mechanical equipoise by means of a standing amicable contest among its several organic parts.' They distrusted power as dangerous to liberty: and therefore they spread it thin and erected barriers against its concentration." This dispersion of power is found not only at the national level but in local areas as well. "As a consequence," Sait goes on to observe, "when *the people or particular groups* among them demanded positive action, no one had adequate authority to act. The machine provided an antidote."[93]

The constitutional dispersion of power not only makes for difficulty of effective decision and action but when action does occur it is defined and hemmed in by legalistic considerations. In consequence, there developed "a much *more human system* of partisan government, whose chief object soon became the circumvention of government by law. . . . The lawlessness of the extra-official democracy was merely the counterpoise of the legalism of the official democracy. The lawyer having been permitted to subordinate democracy to the Law, the Boss had to be called in to extricate the victim, which he did after a fashion and for a consideration."[94]

Officially, political power is dispersed. Various well-known expedients were devised for this manifest objective. Not only was there the familiar separation of powers among the several branches of the government but, in some measure, tenure in each office was limited, rotation in office approved. And the scope of power inherent in each office was severely circumscribed. Yet, observes Sait in rigorously functional terms, "Leadership is necessary; and *since* it does not develop readily within the constitutional framework, the Boss provides it in a crude and irresponsible form from the outside."[95]

Put in more generalized terms, *the functional deficiencies of the official structure generate an alternative (unofficial) structure to fulfill existing needs somewhat more effectively.* Whatever its specific historical origins, the political machine persists as an apparatus for satisfying otherwise unfulfilled needs of diverse groups in the population. By turning to a few of these subgroups and their characteristic needs, we shall be led at once to a range of latent functions of the political machine.

Functions of the Political Machine for Diverse Subgroups. It is well known that one source of strength of the political machine derives from its roots in the local community and the neighborhood. The political machine does not regard the electorate as an amorphous, undifferentiated mass of voters. With a keen sociological intuition, the machine recognizes that the voter is a person living in a specific neighborhood, with specific personal problems and personal wants.

Public issues are abstract and remote; private problems are extremely concrete and immediate. It is not through the generalized appeal to large public concerns that the machine operates, but through the direct, quasi-feudal relationships between local representatives of the machine and voters in their neighborhood. Elections are won in the precinct.

The machine welds its link with ordinary men and women by elaborate networks of personal relations. Politics is transformed into personal ties. The precinct captain "must be a friend to every man, assuming if he does not feel sympathy with the unfortunate, and utilizing in his good works the resources which the boss puts at his disposal."[96] The precinct captain is forever a friend in need. In our prevailingly impersonal society, the machine, through its local agents, fulfills the important social *function of humanizing and personalizing all manner of assistance* to those in need. Foodbaskets and jobs, legal and extra-legal advice, setting to rights minor scrapes with the law, helping the bright poor boy to a political scholarship in a local college, looking after the bereaved—the whole range of crises when a feller needs a friend, and, above all, a friend who knows the score and who can do something about it,—all these find the ever-helpful precinct captain available in the pinch.

To assess this function of the political machine adequately, it is important to note not only that aid *is* provided but *the manner in which it is provided.* After all, other agencies do exist for dispensing such assistance. Welfare agencies, settlement houses, legal aid clinics, medical aid in free hospitals, public relief departments, immigration authorities—these and a multitude of other organizations are available to provide the most varied types of assistance. But in contrast to the professional techniques of the welfare worker which may typically represent in the mind of the recipient the cold, bureaucratic dispensation of limited aid following upon detailed investigation of *legal* claims to aid of the "client" are the unprofessional techniques of the precinct captain who asks no questions, exacts no compliance with legal rules of eligibility and does not "snoop" into private affairs.[97]

For many, the loss of "self-respect" is too high a price for legalized assistance. In contrast to the gulf between the settlement house workers who so often come from a different social class, educational background and ethnic group, the precinct worker is "just one of us," who understands what it's all about. The condescending lady bountiful can hardly compete with the understanding friend in need. *In this struggle between alternative structures for fulfilling the nominally same function* of providing aid and support to those who need it, it is clearly the machine politician who is better integrated with the groups which he serves than the impersonal, professionalized, socially distant and legally constrained welfare worker. And since the politician can at times influence and manipulate the official organizations for the dispensation of assistance, whereas the welfare worker has practically no influence on the political machine, this only adds to his greater effectiveness. More colloquially and also, perhaps, more incisively, it was the Boston ward-leader, Martin Lomasny, who described this essential function to the curious Lincoln Steffens: "I think," said Lomasny, "that there's got to be in every ward somebody that any bloke can come to—no matter what he's done—and get help. *Help, you understand; none of your law and justice, but help.*"[98]

The "deprived classes," then, constitute one subgroup for whom the political machine satisfies wants not adequately satisfied in the same fashion by the legitimate social structure.

For a second subgroup, that of business (primarily "big" business but also "small"), the political boss serves the function of providing those political privileges which entail immediate economic gains. Business corporations, among which the public utilities (railroads, local transportation and electric light companies, communications corporations) are simply the most conspicuous in this regard, seek special political dispensations which will enable them to stabilize their situation and to near their objective of maximizing profits. Interestingly enough, corporations often want to avoid a chaos of uncontrolled competition. They want the greater security of an economic czar who controls, regulates and organizes competition, providing that this czar is not a public official with his decisions subject to public scrutiny and public control. (The latter would be "government control," and hence taboo.) The political boss fulfills these requirements admirably.

Examined for a moment apart from any moral considerations, the political apparatus operated by the Boss is effectively designed to perform these functions with a minimum of inefficiency. Holding the strings of diverse governmental divisions, bureaus and agencies in his competent hands, the Boss rationalizes the relations between public and private business. He serves as the business community's ambassador in the otherwise alien (and sometimes unfriendly) realm of government. And, in strict business-like terms, he is well paid for his economic services to his respectable business clients. In an article entitled, "An Apology to Graft," Lincoln Steffens suggested that "Our economic system, which held up riches, power and acclaim as prizes to men bold enough and able enough to buy corruptly timber, mines, oil fields and franchises and 'get away with it,' was at fault."[99] And, in a conference with a hundred or so of Los Angeles business leaders, he described a fact well known to all of them: the Boss and his machine were an *integral part* of the organization of the economy. "You cannot build or operate a railroad, or a street railway, gas, water, or power company, develop and operate a mine, or get forests and cut timber on a large scale, or run any privileged business, without corrupting or joining in the corruption of the government. You tell me privately that you must, and here I am telling you semi-publicly that you must. And that is so all over the country. And that means that we have an organization of society in which, *for some reason,* you and your kind, the ablest, most intelligent, most imaginative, daring, and resourceful leaders of society, are and must be against society and its laws and its all-around growth."[100]

Since the demand for the services of special privileges are built into the structure of the society, the Boss fulfills diverse functions for this second subgroup of business-seeking-privilege. These "needs" of business, as presently constituted, are not adequately provided for by conventional and culturally approved social structures; consequently, the extra-legal but more-or-less efficient organization of the political machine comes to provide these services. To adopt an *exclusively* moral attitude toward the "corrupt political machine" is to lose sight of the very structural conditions which generate the "evil" that is so bitterly attacked. To adopt a functional outlook is to provide not an apologia for the political machine but a more solid basis for modifying or eliminating the machine, *providing* specific structural arrangements are introduced either for eliminating these effective demands of the business community or, if that is the objective, of satisfying these demands through alternative means.

A third set of distinctive functions fulfilled by the political machine for a special subgroup is that of providing alternative channels of social mobility for those otherwise excluded from the more conventional avenues for personal "advancement." Both the sources of this special "need" (for social mobility) and the respect in which the political machine comes to help satisfy this need can be understood by examining the structure of the larger culture and society. As is well known, the American culture lays enormous emphasis on money and power as a "success" goal legitimate for all members of the society. By no means alone in our inventory of cultural goals, it still remains among the most heavily endowed with positive affect and value. However, certain subgroups and certain ecological areas are notable for the relative absence of opportunity for achieving these (monetary and power) types of success. They constitute, in short, sub-populations where "the cultural emphasis upon pecuniary success has been absorbed, but where there is *little access to conventional and legitimate* means for attaining such success. The conventional occupational opportunities of persons in (such areas) are almost completely limited to manual labor. Given our cultural stigmatization of manual labor,[101] and its correlate, the prestige of white-collar work, it is clear that the result is a tendency to achieve these culturally approved objectives *through whatever means are possible*. These people are on the one hand, "asked to orient their conduct toward the prospect of accumulating wealth [and power] and, on the other, they are largely denied effective opportunities to do so institutionally."

It is within this context of social structure that the political machine fulfills the basic function of providing avenues of social mobility for the otherwise disadvantaged. Within this context, even the corrupt political machine and the racket "represent the triumph of amoral intelligence over morally prescribed 'failure' when the channels of vertical mobility are closed or narrowed *in a society which places a high premium on economic affluence,* [*power*] *and social ascent for all its members.*"[102] As one sociologist has noted on the basis of several years of close observation in a slum area:

> The sociologist who dismisses racket and political organizations as deviations from desirable standards thereby neglects some of the major elements of slum life. . . . *He does not discover the functions they perform for the members* [of the groupings in the slum]. The Irish and later immigrant peoples have had the greatest difficulty in finding places for themselves in our urban social and economic structure. Does anyone believe that the immigrants and their children could have achieved their present degree of social mobility without gaining control of the political organization of some of our largest cities? The same is true of the racket organization. *Politics and the rackets have furnished an important means of social mobility for individuals, who, because of ethnic background and low class position,* are blocked from advancement in the "respectable" channels.[103]

This, then, represents a third type of function performed for a distinctive subgroup. This function, it may be noted in passing, is fulfilled by the *sheer* existence and operation of the political machine, for it is in the machine itself that these individuals and subgroups find their culturally induced needs more or less satisfied. It refers to the services which the political apparatus provides for its own personnel. But seen in the wider social context we have set forth, it no longer appears as *merely* a means of self-aggrandizement for profit-hungry and power-hungry *individuals,* but as an organized provision for *subgroups* otherwise excluded from or handicapped in the race for "getting ahead."

Just as the political machine performs services for "legitimate" business, so it operates to perform not dissimilar services for "illegitimate" business: vice, crime and rackets. Once again, the basic sociological role of the machine in this respect can be more fully appreciated only if one temporarily abandons attitudes of moral indignation, to examine in all moral innocence the actual workings of the organization. In this light, it at once appears that the subgroup of the professional criminal, racketeer or gambler has basic similarities of organization, demands and operation to the subgroup of the industrialist, man of business or speculator. If there is a Lumber King or an Oil King, there is also a Vice King or a Racket King. If expansive legitimate business organizes administrative and financial syndicates to "rationalize" and to "integrate" diverse areas of production and business enterprise, so expensive rackets and crime organize syndicates to bring order to the otherwise chaotic areas of production of illicit goods and services. If legitimate business regards the proliferation of small business enterprises as wasteful and inefficient, substituting, for example, the giant chain stores for hundreds of corner groceries, so illegitimate business adopts the same businesslike attitude and syndicates crime and vice.

Finally, and in many respects, most important, is the basic similarity, if not near-identity, of the economic role of "legitimate" business and of "illegitimate" business. *Both are in some degree concerned with the provision of goods and services for which there is an economic demand.* Morals aside, they are both business, industrial and professional enterprises, dispensing goods and services which some people want, for which there is a market in which goods and services are transformed into commodities. And, in a prevalently market society, we should expect appropriate enterprises to arise whenever there is a market demand for certain goods or services.

As is well known, vice, crime and the rackets *are* "big business." Consider only that there have been estimated to be about 500,000 professional prostitutes in the United States of 1950, and compare this with the approximately 200,000 physicians and 350,000 professional registered nurses. It is difficult to estimate which have the larger clientele: the professional men and women of medicine or the professional men and women of vice. It is, of course, difficult to estimate the economic assets, income, profits and dividends of illicit gambling in this country and to compare it with the economic assets, income, profits and dividends of, say, the shoe industry, but it is altogether possible that the two industries are about on a par. No precise figures exist on the annual expenditures on illicit narcotics, and it is probable that these are less than the expenditures on candy, but it is also probable that they are larger than the expenditure on books.

It takes but a moment's thought to recognize that, *in strictly eco-*

nomic terms, there is no relevant difference between the provision of licit and of illicit goods and services. The liquor traffic illustrates this perfectly. It would be peculiar to argue that prior to 1920 (when the 18th amendment became effective), the provision of liquor constituted an economic service, that from 1920 to 1933, its production and sale no longer constituted an economic service dispensed in a market, and that from 1934 to the present, it once again took on a serviceable aspect. Or, it would be *economically* (not morally) absurd to suggest that the sale of bootlegged liquor in the dry state of Kansas is less a response to a market demand than the sale of publicly manufactured liquor in the neighboring wet state of Missouri. Examples of this sort can of course be multiplied many times over. Can it be held that in European countries, with registered and legalized prostitution, the prostitute contributes an economic service, whereas in this country, lacking legal sanction, the prostitute provides no such service? Or that the professional abortionist is in the economic market where he has approved legal status and that he is out of the economic market where he is legally taboo? Or that gambling satisfies a specific demand for entertainment in Nevada, where it constitutes the largest business enterprise of the larger cities in the state, but that it differs essentially in this respect from motion pictures in the neighboring state of California?[104]

The failure to recognize that these businesses are only *morally* and not *economically* distinguishable from "legitimate" businesses has led to badly scrambled analysis. Once the economic identity of the two is recognized, we may anticipate that if the political machine performs functions for "legitimate big business" it will be all the more likely to perform not dissimilar functions for "illegitimate big business." And, of course, such is often the case.

The distinctive function of the political machine for their criminal, vice and racket clientele is to enable them to operate in satisfying the economic demands of a large market without due interference from the government. Just as big business may contribute funds to the political party war-chest to ensure a minimum of governmental interference, so with big rackets and big crime. In both instances, the political machine can, in varying degrees, provide "protection." In both instances, many features of the structural context are identical: (1) market demands for goods and services; (2) the operators' concern with maximizing gains from their enterprises; (3) the need for partial control of government which might otherwise interfere with these activities of businessmen; (4) the need for an efficient, powerful and centralized agency to provide an effective liaison of "business" with government.

Without assuming that the foregoing pages exhaust either the range of functions or the range of subgroups served by the political machine, we can at least see that *it presently fulfills some functions for these diverse subgroups which are not adequately fulfilled by culturally approved or more conventional structures.*

Several additional implications of the functional analysis of the political machine can be mentioned here only in passing, although they obviously require to be developed at length. First, the foregoing analysis has direct implications for *social engineering.* It helps explain why the periodic efforts at "political reform," "turning the rascals out" and "cleaning political house" are typically (though not necessarily) short-lived and ineffectual. It exemplifies a basic theorem: *any attempt to eliminate an existing social structure without providing adequate alternative structures for fulfilling the functions previously fulfilled by the abolished organization is doomed to failure.* (Needless to say, this theorem has much wider bearing than the one instance of the political machine.) When "political reform" confines itself to the manifest task of "turning the rascals out," it is engaging in little more than sociological magic. The reform may for a time bring new figures into the political limelight; it may serve the casual social function of reassuring the electorate that the moral virtues remain intact and will ultimately triumph; it may actually effect a turnover in the personnel of the political machine; it may even, for a time, so curb the activities of the machine as to leave unsatisfied the many needs it has previously fulfilled. But, inevitably, unless the reform also involves a "re-forming" of the social and political structure such that the existing needs are satisfied by alternative structures or unless it involves a change which eliminates these needs altogether, the political machine will return to its integral place in the social scheme of things. *To seek social change, without due recognition of the manifest and latent functions performed by the social organization undergoing change, is to indulge in social ritual rather than social engineering.* The concepts of manifest and latent functions (or their equivalents) are indispensable elements in the theoretic repertoire of the social engineer. In this crucial sense, these concepts are not "merely" theoretical (in the abusive sense of the term), but are eminently practical. In the deliberate enactment of social change, they can be ignored only at the price of considerably heightening the risk of failure.

A second implication of this analysis of the political machine also has a bearing upon areas wider than the one we have considered. The paradox has often been noted that the supporters of the political machine include both the "respectable" business class elements who are, of course, opposed to the criminal or racketeer and the distinctly "unrespectable" elements of the underworld. And, at first appearance, this is cited as an instance of very strange bedfellows. The learned judge is not infrequently called upon to sentence the very racketeer beside whom he sat the night before at an informal dinner of the political bigwigs. The district attorney jostles the exonerated convict on his way to the back room where the Boss has called a meeting. The big business man may complain almost as bitterly as the big racketeer about the "extortionate" contributions to the party fund demanded by the Boss. Social opposites meet—in the smoke-filled room of the successful politician.

In the light of a functional analysis all this of course no longer seems paradoxical. Since the machine serves both the businessman and the criminal man, the two seemingly antipodal groups intersect. This points to a more general theorem: *the social functions of an organization help determine the structure (including the recruitment of personnel involved in the structure), just as the structure helps determine the effectiveness with which the functions are fulfilled.* In terms of social status, the business group and the criminal group are indeed poles apart. But status does not fully determine behavior and the inter-relations between groups. Functions modify these relations. Given their distinctive needs, the several subgroups in the large society are "integrated," whatever their personal desires or intentions, by the centralizing structure which serves these several needs. In a phrase with many implications which require further study, *structure affects function and function affects structure.*

---

[92]I trust it is superfluous to add that this hypothesis is not "in support of the political machine." The question whether the dysfunctions of the machine outweigh its functions, the question whether alternative structures are not available which may fulfill its functions without necessarily entailing its social dysfunctions, still remain to be considered at an appropriate point. We are here concerned with documenting the statement that moral judgments based *entirely* on an appraisal of manifest functions of a social structure are "unrealistic" in the strict sense, *i.e.,* they do not take into account other actual consequences of that structure, consequences which may provide basic social support for the structure. As will be indicated later, "social reforms" or "social engineering" which ignore latent functions do so on pain of suffering acute disappointments and boomerang effects.

[93]Edward M. Sait, "Machine, Political," *Encyclopedia of the Social Sciences,* IX, 658 b [italics supplied]; *cf.* A. F. Bentley, *The Process of Government* (Chicago, 1908), Chap. 2.

[94]Herbert Croly, *Progressive Democracy,* (New York, 1914), p. 254, cited by Sait, op. cit., 658 b.

[95]Sait, op. cit., 659 a. [italics supplied].

[96]*Ibid.,* 659 a.

[97]Much the same contrast with official welfare policy is found in Harry Hopkins' open-handed and non-political distribution of unemployment relief in New York State under the governorship of Franklin Delano Roosevelt. As Sherwood reports: "Hopkins was harshly criticized for these irregular activities by the established welfare agencies, which claimed it was 'unprofessional conduct' to hand out work

tickets without thorough investigation of each applicant, his own or his family's financial resources and probably his religious affiliations. 'Harry told the agency to go to hell,' said [Hopkins' associate, Dr. Jacob A.] Goldberg." Robert E. Sherwood, *Roosevelt and Hopkins, An Intimate History,* (New York: Harper, 1948), 30.

[98]*The Autobiography of Lincoln Steffens,* (Chautauqua, New York: Chautauqua Press, 1931), 618. Deriving largely from Steffens, as he says, F. Stuart Chapin sets forth these functions of the political machine with great clarity. See his *Contemporary American Institutions,* (New York: Harper, 1934), 40-54.

[99]*Ibid.,* 570.

[100]*Ibid.,* 572-3 [italics supplied]. This helps explain, as Steffens noted after Police Commissioner Theodore Roosevelt, "the prominence and respectability of the men and women who intercede for crooks" when these have been apprehended in a periodic effort to "clean up the political machine." *Cf.* Steffens, 371, and *passim.*

[101]See the National Opinion Research Center survey of evaluation of occupations which firmly documents the general impression that the manual occupations rate very low indeed in the social scale of values, *even among those who are themselves engaged in manual labor.* Consider this latter point in its full implications. In effect, the cultural and social structure exacts the values of pecuniary and power success even among those who find themselves confined to the stigmatized manual occupations. Against this background, consider the powerful motivation for achieving this type of "success" by any means whatsoever. A garbage-collector who joins with other Americans in the view that the garbage-collector is "the lowest of the low" occupations can scarcely have a self-image which is pleasing to him; he is in a "pariah" occupation in the very society where he is assured that "all who have genuine merit can get ahead." Add to this, his occasional recognition that "he didn't have the same chance as others, no matter what they say," and one perceives the enormous psychological pressure upon him for "evening up the score" by finding some means, whether strictly legal or not, for moving ahead. All this provides the structural and derivatively psychological background for the "socially induced need" in *some* groups to find some accessible avenue for social mobility.

[102]Merton, "Social Structure and Anomie," chapter IV of this volume.

[103]William F. Whyte, "Social Organization in the Slums," *American Sociological Review,* Feb. 1943, 8, 34-39 [italics supplied]. Thus, the political machine and the racket represent a special case of the type of organizational adjustment to the conditions described in chapter IV. It represents, note, an *organizational* adjustment: definite structures arise and operate to reduce somewhat the acute tensions and problems of individuals caught up in the described conflict between the "cultural accent on success-for-all" and the "socially structured fact of unequal opportunities for success." As chapter IV indicates, other types of *individual* "adjustment" are possible: lone-wolf crime, psychopathological states, rebellion, retreat by abandoning the culturally approved goals, etc. Likewise, other types of *organizational adjustment* sometimes occur; the racket or the political machine are not *alone* available as organized means for meeting this socially induced problem. Participation in revolutionary organizations, for example, can be seen within this context, as an alternative mode of organizational adjustment. All this bears theoretic notice here, since we might otherwise overlook the basic functional concepts of functional substitutes and functional equivalents, which are to be discussed at length in a subsequent publication.

[104]Perhaps the most perceptive statement of this view has been made by Hawkins and Waller. "The prostitute, the pimp, the peddler of dope, the operator of the gambling hall, the vendor of obscene pictures, the bootlegger, the abortionist, all are productive, all produce services or goods which people desire and for which they are willing to pay. It happens that society has put these goods and services under the ban, but people go on producing them and people go on consuming them, and an act of the legislature does not make them any less a part of the economic system." "Critical Notes on the Cost of Crime," *Journal of Criminal Law and Criminology,* 1936, 26, 679-94, at 684.

37. Reformers Only Mornin' Glories

WILLIAM L. RIORDON

College professors and philosophers who go up in a balloon to think are always discussin' the question: "Why Reform Administrations Never Succeed Themselves!" The reason is plain to anybody who has learned the a, b, c of politics.

I can't tell just how many of these movements I've seen started in New York during my forty years in politics, but I can tell you how many have lasted more than a few years—none. There have been reform committees of fifty, of sixty, of seventy, of one hundred and all sorts of numbers that started out to do up the regular political organizations. They were mornin' glories—looked lovely in the mornin' and withered up in a short time, while the regular machines went on flourishin' forever, like fine old oaks. Say, that's the first poetry I ever worked off. Ain't it great?

Just look back a few years. You remember the People's Municipal League that nominated Frank Scott for mayor in 1890? Do you remember the reformers that got up that league? Have you ever heard of them since? I haven't. Scott himself survived because he had always been a first-rate politician, but you'd have to look in the newspaper almanacs of 1891 to find out who made up the People's Municipal League. Oh, yes! I remember one name: Ollie Teall; dear, pretty Ollie and his big dog. They're about all that's left of the League.

Now take the reform movement of 1894. A lot of good politicians joined in that—the Republicans, the State Democrats, the Stecklerites and the O'Brienites, and they gave us a lickin', but the real reform part of the affair, the Committee of Seventy that started the thing goin', what's become of those reformers? What's become of Charles Stewart Smith? Where's Bangs? Do you ever hear of Cornell, the iron man, in politics now? Could a search party find R. W. G. Welling? Have you seen the name of Fulton McMahon or McMahon Fulton—I ain't sure which—in the papers lately? Or Preble Tucker? Or—but it's no use to go through the list of the reformers who said they sounded in the death knell of Tammany in 1894. They're gone for good, and Tammany's pretty well, thank you. They did the talkin' and posin', and the politicians in the movement got all the plums. It's always the case.

The Citizens' Union has lasted a little bit longer than the reform

SOURCE: From the book *Plunkitt of Tammany Hall* by William L. Riordon. Dutton Paperback Edition (1963). Reprinted by permission of E. P. Dutton & Co., Inc.

crowd that went before them, but that's because they learned a thing or two from us. They learned how to put up a pretty good bluff—and bluff counts a lot in politics. With only a few thousand members, they had the nerve to run the whole Fusion movement, make the Republicans and other organizations come to their headquarters to select a ticket and dictate what every candidate must do or not do. I love nerve, and I've had a sort of respect for the Citizens' Union lately, but the Union can't last. Its people haven't been trained to politics, and whenever Tammany calls their bluff they lay right down. You'll never hear of the Union again after a year or two.

And, by the way, what's become of the good government clubs, the political nurseries of a few years ago? Do you ever hear of Good Government Club D and P and Q and Z any more? What's become of the infants who were to grow up and show us how to govern the city? I know what's become of the nursery that was started in my district. You can find pretty much the whole outfit over in my headquarters, Washington Hall.

The fact is that a reformer can't last in politics. He can make a show for a while, but he always comes down like a rocket. Politics is as much a regular business as the grocery or the dry-goods or the drug business. You've got to be trained up to it or you're sure to fail. Suppose a man who knew nothing about the grocery trade suddenly went into the business and tried to conduct it according to his own ideas. Wouldn't he make a mess of it? He might make a splurge for a while, as long as his money lasted, but his store would soon be empty. It's just the same with a reformer. He hasn't been brought up in the difficult business of politics and he makes a mess of it every time.

I've been studyin' the political game for forty-five years, and I don't know it all yet. I'm learnin' somethin' all the time. How, then, can you expect what they call "business men" to turn into politics all at once and make a success of it? It is just as if I went up to Columbia University and started to teach Greek. They usually last about as long in politics as I would last at Columbia.

You can't begin too early in politics if you want to succeed at the game. I began several years before I could vote, and so did every successful leader in Tammany Hall. When I was twelve years old I made myself useful around the district headquarters and did work at all the polls on election day. Later on, I hustled about gettin' out voters who had jags on or who were too lazy to come to the polls. There's a hundred ways that boys can help, and they get an experience that's the first real step in statesmanship. Show me a boy that hustles for the organization on election day, and I'll show you a comin' statesman.

That's the a, b, c of politics. It ain't easy work to get up to y and z. You have to give nearly all your time and attention to it. Of course, you may have some business or occupation on the side, but the great business of your life must be politics if you want to succeed in it. A few years ago Tammany tried to mix politics and business in equal quantities, by havin' two leaders for each district, a politician and a business man. They wouldn't mix. They were like oil and water. The politician looked after the politics of his district; the business man looked after his grocery store or his milk route, and whenever he appeared at an executive meeting, it was only to make trouble. The whole scheme turned out to be a farce and was abandoned mighty quick.

Do you understand now, why it is that a reformer goes down and out in the first or second round, while a politician answers to the gong every time? It is because the one has gone into the fight without trainin', while the other trains all the time and knows every fine point of the game.

38. The Politics of Reform

JOHN C. BOLLENS AND HENRY J. SCHMANDT

Civic leaders of recent decades have tended to view metropolitan governmental reform as comparable to the reorganization of a private business corporation. The issue to them has been less a political question than one of proper management methods and administrative tidiness. Unlike the city reformers of the early 1900s, who effectively utilized the battle cry of "throw the rascals out," the modern advocates of metropolitan restructuring have invoked the culturally respected symbols of efficiency and economy. In place of the charges of corruption and machine politics, they have aimed their fire at overlapping jurisdictions, governmental fragmentation, confusion of responsibility, and outmoded administrative structures. Disdaining the rhetoric of emotion and fear, they have appealed to the good sense and rationality of the citizenry. At times they have been shocked by

---

SOURCE: "The Politics of Reform" from *The Metropolis* by John C. Bollens and Henry J. Schmandt.

their opponents' tactics, but mostly they have been disillusioned and disheartened by the apathetic public response to their proposals.

The drive for metropolitan reform has rested on what appear to be sound premises. Supporters of the movement have consistently emphasized the theme that problems which are metropolitan in scope and impact demand treatment by an agency with area-wide authority, not by a fragmented local polity or governmental system. This position may be difficult to refute rationally; but reason, as we well know, does not always prevail in the world of reality. In basing their case on logic, the reformers have generally ignored, or at least minimized, the fact that governmental reorganization is a highly charged political question as well as an exercise in management efficiency. Although not unaware of the political obstacles, they have assumed that once the public was informed of the "convincing" facts, the resistance of "petty" interests and "small minds" would be swept aside in an inexorable march toward civic redemption.

The optimistic appraisal of the reformers has missed the mark by a wide margin. General public response to the "logic" of the situation has been lukewarm and disappointing, while political resistance to change has been strong and largely insurmountable. Why has this been so? When alterations are made in an existing system of government, the stakes of various individuals and groups are affected in one fashion or another. To some, the prospect of change may hold out inducements and promises of rewards; to others, it will appear as a threat to their interests. Metropolitan reform is no exception to the rule. Unfortunately for its success, however, the potential rewards of a reconstituted polity have seemed too remote in the eyes of most social and economic interests to call for deep involvement on their part. Hence, while many of them have been sympathetic to the objectives of metropolitan reorganization, few have been willing to commit more than token resources to the cause. The same cannot be said of the opposition. Reshaping the governmental structure of the metropolis directly impinges upon a variety of change-resistant interests and clusters of power, particularly on the established local public bureaucracy. These interests, as case after case has demonstrated, can be quickly mobilized into an effective opposition through the existing network of relationships among public officials and their allied cliques, such as political party organizations and leagues of municipalities.

No amount of wishful thinking can make metropolitan reform an apolitical issue. It is a question that must be resolved in the civic arena with the aid of political weapons and political techniques. It is not, as some would have us believe, a battle between the enlightened and unselfish on the one hand, and ignorant and self-seeking on the other. The tendency to view urban governmental reorganization in these simple and moralistic terms has handicapped the movement by divorcing it from reality. Neither side has a monopoly on virtue. Just as the most active opponents of reform are those who profit from retention of the status quo, so the most highly motivated supporters of reorganization are frequently those who stand to gain by the proposed alterations in the existing system. Actually, the weakness of the reform cause is that too few in its cadre have seen any real personal benefit in change. . . .

Barriers to Change

Scott Greer, in his brief but incisive analysis of metropolitan civic life, lists three groups of interrelated impediments to governmental restructuring: (1) the underlying cultural norms of Americans concerning local government; (2) the resulting legal-constitutional arrangements; and (3) the political-governmental system built upon them.[1] To these we would add (4) the indifference of the citizenry to structural change; and (5) the increasing scale of urban society. All of these relate, in one way or another, either to the ideology and theory that underlie the American urban polity or to the forces that are questioning the traditional concept of the metropolis and its governance.

The norms that have helped shape our system of local government are derivatives of Jeffersonian and Jacksonian ideologies. From Jefferson we inherited the "grass-roots" concept of government and the distrust of those who exercise the powers of office. His ideas on local government were always couched in terms of the small community of educated yeomen rather than the large city with its teeming populace. To him, the New England town with its meetings of all the citizenry was "the wisest invention ever devised by the wit of man for the perfect exercise of self-government and for its preservation." Jacksonians, too, stressed the "sacred right" of local self-rule, but unlike their aristocratic predecessors, they welcomed the urban masses to share in the function of government. Public office was opened to all on the premise that any citizen of normal intelligence could satisfactorily manage the affairs of his city or county. Rotation in office, popular election of numerous officials, and the spoils system became standard features of local government during the second half of the nineteenth century.

The municipal reform movement, at the turn of the present century, was a repudiation of Jacksonian practices but not of its grass-roots ideology. To combat the corruption of city politics, the reformers offered the short ballot, professional management, nonpartisan elections, and the initiative, referendum, and recall, which exposed the governmental system to the direct action or veto of the voter. The inherent right of the community to govern itself free from undue interference by the state legislature, a right implicit in both Jeffersonian and Jacksonian theory, was also institutionalized during this period by state constitutional and statutory provisions relating to municipal "home rule." These enactments supplemented the earlier guarantees of local self-determination, which included generous incorporation laws for the indiscriminate creation of municipalities. They were also accompanied by difficult annexation requirements permitting intransigent groups of fringe area dwellers to remain outside the corporate citadel and by legal conditions making it virtually impossible to consolidate or eliminate existing governmental units. So deeply entrenched in American folklore are the norms which these measures purport to safeguard that those who attempt to alter the system must be prepared to face charges of removing government from the people, infringing on basic human rights, and destroying local self-rule.

The political-governmental pattern that has evolved at the local level, grounded as it is on these norms and beliefs, stands as a formidable obstacle to change. Cloaked in the protective mantle of statutory and constitutional legitimacy and defended by the entrenched bureaucracy, the system has managed to maintain itself without submitting to major surgery. Any alteration of significance is viewed as a threat to the "establishment" and its retinue of followers. Few incumbent officeholders or others who benefit from existing arrangements are willing to gamble on possible gains that a reordered structure might bring them. Similarly, those who aspire to the rewards of local public office are willing to play the game within the existing system and according to its rules. The local "establishment," moreover, holds a strategic weapon for defending its stronghold against attack. Unlike the reformers who have no readymade machine for mobilizing support but must carry their message through the mass media and from the lecture podium, it has access to political cadres and mass-based organizations that serve as important reference points for voters. Add to this advantage the experience of local officeholders in the art of political in-fighting and the odds against major change become impressive.

The defense of the status quo is further favored by the apathetic attitude of the citizenry toward metropolitan reorganization. . . . An important reason for this indifference rests in the fact that urban dwellers are fairly well satisfied with their local governments and see no impelling reason for change. Both the St. Louis and Dayton surveys, for example, showed that residents in those areas had no strong criticism of any of their governments and few complaints about services.[2] In St. Louis, only one unit among the 149 was considered to be performing poorly by as many as 10 percent of the residents—and ironically, this was the sewer district, an area-wide agency. In Dayton, only about one of each ten persons felt that his local government was performing inefficiently or was unresponsive to the people. Less than one-half the residents had even registered a complaint or even felt like complaining about a local governmental service. Almost 60 percent could name no more than one service with which they were dissatisfied. Similar results were obtained in a group of Wisconsin communities. Only a relatively small number (less than 20 percent) of the citizens said that their local governments were inefficient or the performance of their public officials poor.[3] The story was the same in Cleveland, as Table 32 clearly demonstrates. To convince a relatively satisfied electorate of the need for major change is a substantial undertaking.

TABLE 32
CITIZEN EVALUATION OF LOCAL GOVERNMENTAL SERVICES, CLEVELAND METROPOLITAN AREA, 1958

Service	Percent Completely Satisfied	Percent Partly Satisfied	Percent Not At All Satisfied	Percent No Opinion
Water service	90	6	2	2
Fire protection	89	7	1	3
Public health	72	13	4	11
Police protection	70	22	7	1
School	67	22	6	5
Sewer services	64	17	13	6
Public welfare	61	15	5	19
Main thoroughfares	55	27	14	4
Bus and transit	40	24	28	8

SOURCE: James A. Norton, *The Metro Experience* (Cleveland: The Press of Western Reserve University, 1963), p. 61.

Urban life is characterized by increasing size: the concentration of large aggregations of people, growth in the size of business corporations and private associations, widespread expansion of the communications and transportation network. Made possible by technological progress and the resulting organizational transformation of society, the twentieth century metropolis finds itself in an ever-expanding web of activity and an ever-widening radius of interdependence. To work out a satisfactory and acceptable system of government for this complex entity is a challenging task. External as well as internal forces and factors impinge upon the local political process. Decisions made at the distant headquarters of a locally-based industrial plant or department store, in the Washington offices of a federal agency, or in the administrative bureaus at the state capital can often shape local policy. So also the cumulative effect of numerous land use decisions by private developers and financial institutions can do much to alter the face and even character of the metropolitan community.

It seems anomalous that the governmental organization of the metropolis should move in a direction opposite to that of other major segments of the society. While the local polity has become more fragmented, business, labor, and other associations have been able, by means of increasing organizational scale, to achieve a measure of control over their environment that is denied the metropolitan community. Some observers have speculated that the local governmental system represents for many the last stronghold against the growing societal scale, against "bigness."[4] They reason this feeling accounts for much of the lack of popular enthusiasm in reorganization matters and makes voters more receptive to "grass-roots" argument.

Whether this speculation is sound or not, the reformers are at a disadvantage in answering the rhetoric of the opposition. The intricate nature of the problems which the metropolis faces is not easily comprehensible. Because of this complexity, neither the problems nor the possible remedies can be articulated and expressed in clear-cut and readily understandable terms. The opponents of change may have little logic on their side, but they have the effective myths and symbols; the reformers may possess the logic but they lack myths and symbols with popular appeal. To the cry of "keep government close to the people," the reformers can only speak of the brighter future and better environment that reorganization will presumably assure. To the challenge, "show the people why the system which has served them for so long should be discarded," the proponents can only reply with generalized and vague statements about efficiency, orderly growth, and future dangers, or with arguments so complex that their importance escapes the average citizen. As one Cleveland official remarked in telling of the advantage he had in fighting the proposed comprehensive urban county charter, "I'd say to them, 'Say, what's wrong with the present situation? You've got a good government. What's wrong? Show me.' "[5]

Who Gets Involved

In a large-scale society, individuals acting alone are handicapped in affecting collective behaviour. It is primarily through organizational membership that they enlarge their opportunities and resources to influence social action. Hence, the question of who gets involved in metropolitan reform efforts pertains less to the individual actors than to the groups or associations of which they are a part. To answer the question, it is necessary to ascertain what organizations initiate change. Who provides the resources for carrying on the campaign? Where does the opposition arise? What stakes do the various participants have in the outcome?

We need not throw our net wide in this undertaking, since the active participants in metropolitan reform campaigns constitute a relatively minor segment of the organized populace. The issue has not generated deep community conflict or seriously involved a broad range of urban interest groups.

CIVIC ORGANIZATIONS

Much of the impetus for metropolitan governmental restructuring comes from two sources: civic organizations (sometimes referred to as the "good government" groups) and the central city daily newspapers. At times, a maverick politician or underemployed young lawyer seeking publicity may spark the revolt, but the flame will be short lived unless the fuel to keep it burning is supplied by the established groups. Most often, the initial push will come from organizations that are heirs of the municipal reform spirit and philosophy of the early 1900s: citizens' leagues, bureaus of municipal research, good government councils, and leagues of women voters. These groups began to turn their attention to the larger community as central cities became better governed and the critical urban problems outgrew individual corporate boundaries. Gradually, over the years, metropolitan reorganization came to occupy the place on the civic agenda that municipal reform held earlier.

The interests of the social and economic influentials were channeled into the metropolitan reform field largely by the professionals who staff the key civic organizations, by concerned political scientists, and by the promptings of the National Municipal League, the patriarch of the good government groups. Few of the notables who support such movements are motivated by prospects of personal gain. Some feel that reorganization will result in a better business and industrial climate, but most act out of a sense of *noblesse oblige*. As persons of civic reputation and stature, they have a feeling of responsibility for the well-being and governance of the area. Metropolitan reform provides them with a respected outlet for meeting this obligation. However, the role, as they see it, does not necessarily imply personal involvement; more often, it means legitimizing the issue as worthy of community support. The actual task of carrying the campaign forward is left to the professional staffs and younger aspirants in the group, to public relations hirelings, and to the workhorse civic organizations such as the League of Women Voters.

One element of the business community, the downtown interests, has a more personal stake in metropolitan reorganization. Concerned with the economic position of the central business district, many merchants and property owners feel that area-wide governmental change may in some way aid the center by giving it greater prominence in a reconstituted polity. In the Miami area, the downtown groups pushed vigorously for metropolitan government, seeing in it a means of relieving the tax pressure on property in the core city by spreading the base over a larger area. Central city or metropolitan chambers of commerce serve as the organizational mechanism for articulating and executing the support of these interests.

Aside from the nebulous prospect of direct economic gain for their members, chambers of commerce are ideologically disposed to regard such movements with favor. The "booster" spirit which permeates their operations finds expression in the gospel of "a bigger and better community." Most of the groups see metropolitan restructuring as a symbolic aid in promoting the image of a progressive community, one distinguished by civic vitality and modernized government. Typical was the plea in the Dade County charter campaign: "Give Miami a chance to be a big city." This view of metropolitan aggrandizement through governmental integration is not shared by the suburban chambers of commerce and the local merchants they represent. To them, reorganization means a loss or diminution of their influence over the public affairs of the suburbs in which they operate. As a consequence, they are usually found in the ranks of those actively opposing change.

THE PRESS

The daily newspapers in the central city are usually staunch advocates of metropolitan reform. In some areas, such as Miami, they have been prime instigators of reorganization movements. In others, such as St. Louis, they have editorially tried to prod the civic élite into action. As organs with an area-wide audience and outlook, they are attracted to metropolitan reorganization as an appropriate cause for their crusading zeal. And by championing the vision of the larger community, they can fulfill their role expectations as "integrative" symbols of the metropolis.

In contrast to the large dailies, the suburban community press is almost always opposed to major change in the existing system. Long characterized by bias against the central city and an equally strong anti-metropolitan press attitude, the suburban papers find area-wide reorganization measures useful targets. By picturing such proposals as the products of central city politicians or of "undesirable" elements seeking to invade suburbia, they can pose as protectors of small-community virtues. Metropolitan reorganization gives them an opportunity to launch a "safe" crusade of the type they can rarely afford on local issues for fear of alienating some of their readership. As locally based and locally oriented instrumentalities dependent on the business advertising of the village merchants and the subscriptions of residents in their limited area, they feel a personal stake in keeping the existing governmental system intact. The fiction of small community autonomy is a strong legitimizer for their existence. Any movement which threatens to undermine this fiction or lessen the importance of the suburban governments is a cause for battle.

THE LOCAL BUREAUCRACY

Wherever a "going system" of local government exists, we can expect it to react against radical transformation. If it did not, it could hardly be called a system. We can thus generalize that incumbent officeholders will usually be found in the camp of the opposition. There are, of course, many exceptions, some of them significant. The city manager of Miami, the county engineer of Cuyahoga County, the president of the St. Louis Board of Aldermen, the mayor of Nashville (in the 1959 campaign), all supported metropolitan reorganization efforts in their areas. In each instance, however, the incumbent could see in the proposed reform an opportunity to extend his sphere of control or obtain other rewards. Only on rare occasions will an individual support change that will abolish or reduce the powers of his office.

In the past, many central city officials strongly espoused plans for total merger. They viewed consolidation as an enlargement of the city's boundaries and hence an enhancement of its political power. On the other hand, they reacted negatively when lesser remedies were proposed—a federated system, for example—which would reduce the powers of the core city. Now the tendency is for central city officials to oppose even merger. This solution involves the risk that control may shift to the periphery where the suburban population in many metropolitan communities is rapidly approaching or exceeding that of the core. The risk is particularly great in areas where the politics of the central city is predominantly Democratic and that of the suburbs Republican. Central city officials have also become apprehensive that assuming responsibility for the suburbs might increase rather than diminish the city's fiscal difficulties. Mayor Raymond R. Tucker of St. Louis, for example, opposed a consolidation of the governments of that area in 1962, fearing the impact of such action on the redevelopment and other ongoing programs of the city and on its tax structure.

Suburban officialdom stands solidly against any major restructuring of the existing system. Only an occasional mayor of an upper socioeconomic community will support a metropolitan multipurpose district or other reform measure short of consolidation. Not uncommonly suburban officials express their willingness to have "true" metropolitan functions handled on a unified basis. Such a functon, as they conceive it, is one which they badly need but cannot perform for themselves because of cost. Water supply and sewage disposal are two common examples. In such cases, officials of the affected communities will usually acquiesce in the assumption of the service by the county government or the creation of a metropolitan single-purpose district to handle it. This kind of area-wide administration finds acceptance because it involves little or no loss of power for the local units and wards off the possible danger of more thorough changes by taking care of the most immediate and troublesome deficiencies.

OTHER PARTICIPANTS

In addition to the principal protagonists already mentioned, other groups such as political parties and labor unions are often found among the participants in the reform drama. The extent of their activity varies considerably, depending on the circumstances and the issues at stake. Occasionally, one or more of them may play a major role, but usually their participation is not great. The political parties provide the best illustration of this low degree of involvement. In few of the recent campaigns have they taken an official stand. Party regulars at the ward, township, and state legislative district levels in some instances have utilized the organizational machinery in their bailiwicks to mobilize support or opposition, usually the latter, but the extensiveness of these activities has varied from area to area. Individual political leaders have also taken public positions on the issue, but few have used their political "muscle" to influence the outcome. Neither the reorganization issue nor the potential rewards of an altered system seem to provide sufficient motivation for this kind of commitment. Moreover, the insignificant amount of patronage at the municipal level and the widespread use of nonpartisan elections contribute to this result by dampening party interest in local governmental affairs. Ironically, these two major accomplishments of municipal reformers now seriously impede the efforts of the metropolitan reformers.

Organized labor is another group frequently found among the participants in reorganization campaigns, but the degree of its involvement ranges only from token endorsement or opposition to moderate activity. Like the political parties, labor does not consider its stake in the outcome sufficiently great to warrant substantial expenditures of its resources. Its position and the extent of its activity in each case will be dictated largely by the possible effects of the proposed restructuring on existing political arrangements and coalitions. If the influence of those officials or political groups with which it has established working relationships will be expanded by the change, labor is likely to favor the movement; if the interests of these groups is threatened, it will probably join the opposition. In either case, however, is it likely to make large-scale commitments of energy and resources.

The Negroes are another group that has become of increasing importance in reorganization issues. For the most part, Negro political leaders look with disfavor on efforts to reorder the system. Their base of operation and strength lies in the central city. An area-wide government poses a threat to their hard-won and long-incoming major political influence by joining the predominantly white electorate of suburbia to that of the core municipality. It is not surprising, therefore, that both the comprehensive urban county proposal in Cleveland and the multipurpose district plan in St. Louis drew heavy opposition from the non-white wards. As a study of the vote on metropolitan reform issues in Cleveland over a period of years showed, the attitude of Negro voters toward area-wide reorganization became more negative as the political strength of the non-whites increased in the central city.[6] By 1957, their opposition had firmly crystallized, for by then they had acquired a considerable stake in the political status quo with seven Negroes on Cleveland's thirty-three member city council. There have been similar cases in other places like Miami, where Negro leaders opposed the metropolitan county charter. There, they had been able to establish a *modus vivendi* and an understanding with central city authorities in such matters as the allocation of city jobs; naturally, they have no desire to see these arrangements disturbed. . . .

Metropolitan Reform Factors

Until recent years, the work of researchers in the metropolitan field was focused on substantive problems and reorganization plans and little or no attention was given to examining reform campaigns systematically. The long persisting tendency was to consider the process of translating proposed structural changes into reality as a righteous crusade that somehow transcended politics. Only gradually has it become clear that reconstituting the governmental system is a political question to be treated as any other public policy issue. This realization has led to more realistic appraisals of reorganization movements and to a better understanding of the forces and factors that control the outcome.

Although the reform campaigns . . . took place in . . . metropolitan areas of widely varying characteristics, the pattern is strikingly similar. For the most part, the same classes of protagonists, the same evolutionary steps (from study commission through official charter-drafting board to public vote), the same demographic and political factors, and the same type of public response were present in each instance. The experiences in these four areas provide a basis for certain conclusions about metropolitan reform efforts.

1. The crusade for metropolitan governmental reorganization has not been the product of grass-roots dissatisfaction nor has it been initiated by public officials. It has been largely the creature of good government groups and civic notables who have been disturbed by the "irrationality" of the system.

2. The general public is indifferent to the reorganization issue. A sampling of residents in Cuyahoga County several weeks before the charter election in 1959 revealed that one of every three persons did not remember reading or hearing anything about the proposed new document despite the extensive publicity that had been given to it. More than three-fourths of the people could not name a single reason advanced for or against it. A survey in the St. Louis area after the district election also showed convincingly that the voters knew little about the issue and those who were involved in it. In 40 percent of the cases, leaders mentioned as supporters of the plan by the persons who had been interviewed were publicly on record as opposed to it.

Transmitting to the electorate the complex issues inherent in governmental reorganization of the metropolis is an extremely difficult, if not impossible, task. Change of this type does not ordinarily give rise to the use of effective and attention-capturing symbols. Thus, as Greer describes the recent campaigns, they proceeded behind a massive façade of logical argument:

> Seldom have so many thorny problems, involving theoretical and empirical unknowns, been aired on the front page of the daily papers. Seldom have so many businessmen, lawyers, elected officials, politicians, administrators, and League ladies taken public stands on ab-

> stract and difficult issues. Seldom have so few worked so hard and succeeded in confusing so many.[22]

Caught in a crossfire of conflicting and abstract arguments, and with the groups to which he normally looks for guidance on public issues silent or only slightly involved, the average voter is frequently confused and uncertain in reorganization elections.

3. Metropolitan reform movements involve only a small segment of the community's many organizations and of its "power structure." Seldom are the mass-based interest groups, such as the political parties and labor unions, seriously committed as either supporters or opponents. By concentrating on organizational efficiency, reformist activity has avoided the deeper and more controversial issues that can motivate such groups and enlist their active participation.

4. Except in loosely structured communities such as Metropolitan Miami, no major reorganization plan is likely to succeed without organized political support. Without such backing, civic groups cannot mount an effective campaign at the grass roots, an essential factor particularly when popular approval of proposed changes is required. The second Nashville consolidation attempt illustrates the importance of actively involving professional politicians in metropolitan reform movements. What in the earlier campaign had been simply a question of administrative reorganization fostered by the good government groups became a political issue in the later effort when two opposing factions, vying for the stakes of public office, seized upon it as a major point of disagreement. Voters who identified themselves with one or the other political faction had an "authoritative" referent to which to look for guidance in reaching a decision on the charter, even though they may have been completely ignorant of the plan it embodied or its effect on their own interests.

5. Voters who support metropolitan reform tend to be drawn from the better educated and high socioeconomic categories. In the Miami area, the precincts highest on the social scale favored the charter most sharply while those at the bottom voted against it most strongly. In Metropolitan Nashville, the findings were the same: the higher the level of an individual's income or education, the more likely he was to hold a pro-Metro attitude. These results are not surprising. We would expect the better educated voter to be more familiar with the issue and more likely to be persuaded by the logic and rationality of reformist arguments. Such an individual is also more likely to identify himself with the socially respected civic groups that customarily champion reorganization plans.

As an analysis of one of the Cleveland charter elections indicates, however, socioeconomic status is by no means the only variable in determining the direction of the vote. Using multiple correlation techniques, it was found that the combined effect of income, education, and occupation—the typical components of social rank—accounted statistically for only 48 percent of the variation in the voting.[23] This finding means that less than half the variations in the vote can be attributed to differences in socioeconomic status.

One factor or intervening variable that may help to explain the deviation in voting behavior within social categories was suggested by Booth in the Nashville study. He found that individuals who were members of formal organizations exposed to campaign propaganda tended to favor the side of the issue to which their group had been exposed at significantly greater rates than others of the same social rank.[24] The St. Louis area study suggested another variable, that of home ownership, thus indicating that property owners are more susceptible than renters to the usual opposition arguments.

Some observers have speculated that a small turnout is advantageous to reorganization elections since persons of higher social rank are more likely to participate and since they tend to favor change. This, however, is a dubious assumption. The Miami survey, for example, found no important difference between the high- and low-status precincts in voter turnout on the charter issue. A similar finding was made in St. Louis where the proportion of those who voted on the district plan did not differ significantly among the various social ranks. One explanation for this deviation from the general pattern of voting behavior is found in the more intensive organizational activity displayed by opponents at the grassroots level. This activity, coupled with lack of concern by many people in the higher socioeconomic categories, leads to a disproportionate turnout of lower-status voters in reorganization elections.

6. Because the strategies of support for change in metropolitan reform campaigns are usually determined by the good government groups and civic notables, effective communication is seldom established with the mass audience. Proponents have relied on the newspapers to perform this function, but the ability of the press to influence the public is limited by the interests and predispositions of its readers, their readiness to listen, and their capacity to understand the question. Thus far the strategists have been unable to translate comprehensive plans of reorganization into terms which are meaningful in the political vocabulary of local or neighborhood affairs. Change which must rely on the results of the ballot cannot move far beyond the understanding and interest of the voters. Political leadership, not civic exhortation, is required to foster this understanding and kindle this interest.

Regardless of the fate of major reform efforts, the governmental structure of the metropolis is certain to undergo modification with the passage of time. Only by so doing can it survive the great changes in the urban environment that the future will bring. This adjustment may be only a minimal accommodation to the emerging forces or it may involve a thorough alteration of the system. Whatever the change, it will probably take place through political channels, under the initiative of political actors, and through the process of political bargaining. Civic groups and civic leaders will remain important, but more as legitimizing symbols for the cause than as carriers of the movement.

[1]*Governing the Metropolis* (New York: Wiley, 1962), pp. 124-125.

[2]See John C. Bollens (ed.), *Exploring the Metropolitan Community* (Berkeley and Los Angeles: University of California Press, 1961), pp. 188-190; and *Metropolitan Challenge* (Dayton: Metropolitan Community Studies, 1959), pp. 241-251.

[3]Henry J. Schmandt and William Standing, *Citizen Images of the Fox River Valley* (Madison: University of Wisconsin Survey Research Laboratory, 1962), p. 13.

[4]See, for example, Robert Wood, *Suburbia* (Boston: Houghton Mifflin, 1959).

[5]Greer, *Governing the Metropolis,* p. 16.

[6]Richard A. Watson and John H. Romani, "Metropolitan Government for Metropolitan Cleveland: An Analysis of the Voting Record," *Midwest Journal of Political Science,* V (November, 1961), 365-390.

[22]*Metropolitics,* p. 193.

[23]Watson and Romani, "Metropolitan Government for Metropolitan Cleveland," pp. 382-385.

[24]*Metropolitics: The Nashville Consolidation,* pp. 45-54.

39. Modernizing Local Government

COMMITTEE FOR ECONOMIC DEVELOPMENT

American institutions of local government are under severe and increasing strain. Well designed, by and large, to meet the simpler needs of earlier times, they are poorly suited to cope with new burdens imposed on all governments by the complex conditions of modern life. Adaptation to change has been so slow, so limited, and so reluctant that the future role—even the continued viability—of these institutions is now in grave doubt.

The costs of local government are rising steeply. Direct expenditures by all municipalities, counties, New England towns, townships,

SOURCE: *Modernizing Local Government,* a statement on national policy by the Research and Policy Committee of the Committee for Economic Development (New York: July, 1966), Chapter I, pp. 8-11, 13-19.

independent school districts, and special districts rose from $20.1 billion in 1952 to $45.1 billion in 1962, or 124 per cent, and are likely to double again by 1972. While state and federal supporting aids are heavy and growing rapidly, local taxpayers bear the brunt of these increases. Partly because of this—and partly because of evidences of waste, injustice, and occasional corruption—popular discontent with both quantity and quality of services rendered by the nation's 80,000 separate local governments is greater today than it was ten, or twenty, or fifty years ago.

There are strong reasons for disenchantment. American crime rates in rural, urban, and suburban areas are high. Several countries with less per capita wealth have lower infant mortality rates and longer life expectancies. Public school deficiencies are more noticeable, as the necessity for higher skills and stronger educational qualifications becomes more obvious. The character of public welfare programs and the competence of their administration are under attack. Urban transportation problems outpace attempted solutions. Slum clearance and redevelopment lag behind the processes of decay. Economic development of most "communities"[1] is frustrated by want of government power. Local units depend too heavily on the property tax, administration of which is generally so inequitable as to be scandalous.

Most public problems have special local characteristics, even when needs are so serious and so widely prevalent that they arouse national concern. This is true in health, sanitation, protection to persons and property, transit and traffic systems, basic schooling, housing, public welfare, economic growth, and land-use planning, as obvious examples. Ideal solutions must be tailored to the conditions found in each community.

The nation's courthouses and city halls have often seemed to lack the vision and dedication—as well as the financial resources—to diagnose conditions, devise solutions, and make vigorous response. New functions needed to meet new situations are neglected by most local units, and old functions are conducted without benefit of new techniques. By default, initiatives have commonly been left to more resourceful federal forces. Cast in an archaic mold, unable to cope with new issues, many—if not most—local governments are centers of strenuous resistance to change of any kind.

The New Federalism

Sweeping initiatives by the national government, and to a lesser degree by a few state governments, have helped to fill the partial vacuum created by failures at the local level. Resulting changes have altered the basic character of the American federal system. Local governments tend to become administrative mechanisms for implementation of national policies, rather than dynamic centers of authority in their own individual right.

The pervasive presence of the national government is a twentieth century development in its realistic work-a-day aspects. This is clearly evident from financial data covering the past 60 years, and current tendencies reinforce the point. . . .

From 1952 to fiscal 1964 federal aids to local units quadrupled. Federal aids to the states also nearly quadrupled, permitting them in turn to increase their support to localities. State aids to local units have continued to exceed state receipts from the federal treasury, but the net difference has leveled out in recent years. The federal budget for fiscal 1967 proposed further increases in aids to states and local units of 50 per cent above fiscal 1964. There is no visible prospect of significant future deviation from established trends.

Fiscal realities have modified the legal concept that the states are the fountain source of all governmental powers. The states created the national government, assigning it certain functions and granting it essential powers. The powers of local units were also granted by the states. Realistically, however, capability of response to public desires and adequate financial resources take precedence over legal theory. The states seem less "sovereign" with 20 per cent of their total annual revenues drawn from the federal treasury.

There are scores of separate "categories" of federal aid to states and local units. These affect, directly or indirectly, every major function of local government. Resulting relationships have led to a new phenomenon that may be described as "functional government." Highway administration in this country now involves so many intricate intergovernmental relationships that responsible state, local, and federal officials concerned with it form hierarchies apart. They communicate directly with each other more often than they do with other agencies or with upper echelons in their own governments. This is also true in public welfare administration, public health, and public education.

Federal leadership in dealing with national problems at local levels has been beneficial in many fields. Stronger emphasis on professionalism has great merit in police administration and in every function where local units have been slow to develop competently trained staff. But federal aid—by helping to alleviate acute needs facing local governments—has concealed basic weaknesses. Some money grants tend to perpetuate obsolete machinery, even while serving useful functional ends.

It is time for the citizens of the 50 states to take stock of their systems of local government in relation to urgent present and prospective needs. This involves more than an assessment of current performance. It also demands a judgment of future capabilities in planning and executing activities essential to healthy community development. As we approach the twenty-first century, weaknesses in eighteenth and nineteenth century forms must be corrected—or new systems created—if local government is to survive as a vital force.

Inadequacies in Local Units

The weaknesses arousing concern are deep-rooted and extensive. While variety and diversity among local institutions make sweeping generalizations suspect, because there are almost always many exceptions to be found, we believe that available evidence fully sustains the following broad statements.

1. Very few local units are large enough—in population, area, or taxable resources—to apply modern methods in solving current and future problems. Less than half contain as many as 1,000 people; less than 10 per cent have more than 10,000 inhabitants; and less than 1 per cent have over 100,000. Even the largest cities find major problems insoluble because of limits on their geographic areas, their taxable resources, or their legal powers.

2. Overlapping layers of local government—municipalities and townships within counties, and independent school districts and special districts within them—are a source of weakness. These layers, in some cases numbering ten or more local units with power to tax the same parcel of land, compete in a struggle for revenue sources. The competition extends to the division—among layers—of "home rule powers" granted by the states, often leaving no local government with legal authority adequate to cope with urgent community needs. This impairs over-all local freedom to deal with vital public affairs; the whole thus becomes less than the sum of its parts.

3. Popular control over local governments is ineffective or sporadic, and public interest in local politics is not high. American voters collectively must select over 500,000 local elective officials—often obscure personalities with inconsequential duties. Less than 30 per cent of American adults vote in separately held city elections, while over 60 per cent vote in Presidential contests. County, school, township, and special district elections commonly attract even smaller fractions of voters. Confusion from the many-layered system, profusion of elective offices without policy significance, and increasing mobility of the population all contribute to disinterest.

4. Policy-making mechanisms in many units are notably weak. The

national government has strong executive leadership, supported by competent staff in formulating plans that are then subject to review and modification by a representative legislative body. Comparable arrangements are found in most cities, but seldom elsewhere among local governments. Multiple elective executives and malapportioned or gerrymandered legislative bodies abound. These factors—combined with lack of broad legal authority, financial resources, and geographic jurisdiction—inhibit the kind of long-range planning and decision-making essential to effective local government.

5. Antiquated administrative organizations hamper most local governments. Lack of a single executive authority, either elective or appointive, is a common fault. Functional fragmentation obscures lines of authority. Organizational concepts considered axiomatic in American business firms are unrecognized or disregarded in most local governments. The quality of administration suffers accordingly.

6. Positions requiring knowledge of modern technology are frequently occupied by unqualified personnel. Except in large cities, most department heads are amateurs. The spoils system still prevailing in parts of the nation has deep roots in many local governments, but is only one source of this difficulty. Pay scales are usually too low to attract competent professional applicants. Further, specialized skills in the public service are too often held in low esteem by influential citizens.

Choices Confronting the Nation

We are convinced that all American communities face urgent problems requiring competent governmental action. We expect these problems to grow, both in variety and intensity, in coming decades. The issues are not narrowly confined to matters concerning education, transportation, housing, health and safety, water supply, or air pollution—serious as they are. They extend to all the conditions of modern life, and to the social and material satisfactions that act as incentives for a constructive commitment of human resources.

We are also convinced that many local governments are unequal to the challenge. They are ineffective in coping with present problems, and inadequate in facing the escalation that surely lies ahead. But highly complex problems seldom have simple solutions; nor are acceptable solutions, once found, always easy to apply. There is obvious danger in oversimplification, but we visualize three alternative courses of action open to the nation.

FIRST, recent trends toward "functional government" might go on indefinitely, as in highway administration. This would imply an extension of federal standard-setting, decision-making, and administrative controls—with heavier transfusions of federal funds directly or through state channels. In theory, the present system of local governments could then endure without major structural change or modernization. Functional fragmentation under federal auspices discourages local planning and management on any unified, integral basis. In practice, federal efforts to use *existing* local governments as administrative agencies in executing national policy have already disclosed such serious faults that success cannot be expected within the present framework. Sole reliance on this approach would probably lead to (a) an increase in direct federal management of local affairs, (b) assumption by state governments of a larger share in administrative operations, (c) continued neglect of vital local issues, and (d) excessive costs for the services they render.

SECOND, the 50 states might expand their administrative mechanisms to supersede local authorities, gradually perhaps, in function after function. This might be done through regional or district centers, in order to relate state action more directly to local situations. Such an alternative would not be endorsed, however, by those who have found their state capitals consistently unresponsive to local needs, whether these are universal or vary from locality to locality.

THIRD, existing patterns of local government can be drastically revised, to encourage local policy decision-making and to permit effective management of local affairs. This will not be easy, for major structural adjustments are required if we are to preserve the fundamental values in local self-government. But competent local units, responsive to the requirements of an enlightened public, can serve two primary purposes. They can identify local problems and opportunities, and then plan and execute programs with optimum effect. They are also needed to serve in an effective partnership with state agencies, and with the federal government in its expanding fields of activity.

We strongly urge support of the third alternative. Granting the merits of professionalism in functional fields, conceding the importance of federal encouragement and support, and recognizing the need for action by the states consistent with their responsibilities, we still stress the fundamental values of local self-government. These values extend far beyond the efficiencies to be gained through consolidations and reorganizations. Citizen participation in community affairs is the central pillar sustaining a democratic society; it is an invaluable training school for service at other levels. Revitalized local governments will command greater public interest and popular support. Initiatives channeled through effective local units will foster creative experimentation in meeting the diversity of needs from region to region, from urban to rural areas, and from place to place within the same state.

We recognize the obstacles, including vested political interests and civic inertia, found in opposition to any modernization of local institutions of government. But reapportionments of state legislatures and of local governing bodies are creating wide new possibilities for reform. We are convinced that suitable local units can be designed to plan governmental operations fostering rapid community development, to administer programs effectively, and to contribute materially in their financing. The citizens can obtain the services they need at reasonable cost only through strong local governments, since neither federal nor state governments can be expected to deal competently with local situations.

Efforts to "tidy up" a chaotic situation will not cure the chief illness. Overemphasis on waste, inefficiency, and incompetence may obscure the main point: most American communities lack any instrumentality of government with legal powers, geographic jurisdiction, and independent revenue sources necessary to conduct local self-government in any valid sense. Our fundamental concern is that every community in the nation be capable of effective management of its local affairs. This is the *sine qua non* of a democratic society geared for entrance into the twenty-first century.

Before a local government can be expected to serve the purposes intended, it must meet four minimum qualifications:

- *Political unity.* Each population governed must have enough common interests, problems, and communications to qualify as a political entity able to produce political leadership responsive to active citizen concern.
- *Size.* Each local unit must be sufficiently large—in population, geographic jurisdiction, and financial resources—to make long-range plans, to attract professional staff, and to manage modern services.
- *Powers.* Each government must have legal authority adequate to cope with the problems for which it is responsible, and to enforce its decisions.
- *Rational structure.* Each government must have a representative governing body concerned with policy decisions, and a single chief executive to secure unity in administrative operations.

Summary of Recommendations

This statement on national policy calls for major changes consistent with these criteria: massive county consolidations to conform with logical geographic and economic boundaries; structural modernization and professional staffing for all local units; and severe reduction in the overlapping layers of local government. Changes of this character will require sweeping action by the states through comprehensive constitutional revisions. Only then—and the process may take a decade in some states—will it be possible to create modern systems of local government able to meet the challenge of the times.

Our proposals are nationwide in scope, and they apply to both urban and rural communities. Valid generalizations are usually subject to various exceptions, but the guidelines that follow have almost universal applicability. They define broad objectives, rather than forming a simple blueprint for any state or locality to adopt in detail. And they provide no pat solutions for problems unique to each giant metropolitan complex, or to contiguous urbanized areas forming "strip cities." While specific study of each "megalopolis" is required—supported by such assistance as federal, state, or private foundations may provide—prompt creation of the strong local governments here proposed would permit effective collaboration among them in the search for feasible solutions.

1. *The number of local governments in the United States, now about 80,000, should be reduced by at least 80 per cent.*

Reasonable minimum standards of size would disqualify most present units for continued existence, since average population for all local governments is less than 2,500. Failure to correct this situation, especially in those states where it is most acute, will further cloud the future of local self-government. Local units must be large enough to function effectively if power over local affairs is not to be centralized at higher levels.

2. *The number of overlapping layers of local government found in most states should be severely curtailed.*

Townships and most types of special districts are obvious targets for elimination as independent governments. Small municipalities unable to provide professional administration could continue to set levels of service desired by their citizens through contracts with larger units for their performance, or they could become special assessment "benefit districts" under general government management and without separate elective officials.

3. *Popular election should be confined to members of the policy-making body, and to the chief executive in those governments where the "strong mayor" form is preferred to the "council-manager" plan.*

Half-a-million local officials are elected by the people. Only about half of them are paid for their services, and five-sixths serve part-time. We believe local government would benefit greatly from severe reduction of this huge number. Public attention should focus more sharply on key elective positions and major issues, and citizen struggles with the "bed-sheet" ballot should be ended.

4. *Each local unit should have a single chief executive, either elected by the people or appointed by the local legislative body, with all administrative agencies and personnel fully responsible to him; election of department heads should be halted.*

Few Americans would deny the necessity for unitary executive authority in any serious group undertaking. Only in government—and especially in local governments—do we tolerate multiple independent uncoordinated executive authority, with its paralyzing effects. Review and control can be obtained through independent post audits of accounts and operations.

5. *Personnel practices based on merit and professional competence should replace the personal or partisan "spoils" systems found in most counties and many other local units.*

Specialized skills are increasingly essential to solution of most governmental problems, whether in highway engineering, public health and sanitation, police and fire protection, education, pollution control, slum clearance, public finance, or in management as such. Skills require training and experience, as well as innate ability. Persons with high skills must be recruited, developed, and utilized effectively. This is unlikely to occur in a climate of petty partisanship, low salaries, and confused authority.

6. *County modernization should be pressed with special vigor, since counties—everywhere except in New England—have high but undeveloped potential for solving the problems of rural, urban, and most metropolitan communities.*

Counties are less limited in area, population, and tax base than most local units, and consolidations could correct existing deficiencies in these respects. Their present legal powers are less adequate than those of municipalities, however. And county structural organizations and staffing patterns are obsolete. If the nation is seriously concerned about stronger and better local government, as it should be, these weaknesses must be remedied to permit counties to play a major role.

7. *Once modernized, local governments should be entrusted with broad legal powers permitting them to plan, finance, and execute programs suited to the special needs, interests, and desires of their citizens.*

The reluctance of the states to grant adequate discretion to even the largest city governments continues, although less evident than in the nineteenth century. Powers of other forms of local government are generally much more limited. State constitutions often prohibit legislatures from making effective grants of home rule. But broad grants of power should not be given to outmoded units incapable of using them properly.

8. *The 50 state constitutions should be revamped—either by legislative amendment or through constitutional conventions concentrating on local government modernization—to provide for boundary revisions, extensions of legal authority, and elimination of needless overlapping layers.*

The state legislatures must have authority to establish machinery to revise boundaries for all forms of local government. This function is wholly inappropriate to the local units themselves; they lack objectivity. The legislatures should also be entrusted with the extension of legal powers to the local units, subject to broad state policies.

9. *The terms and conditions of federal—and state—grants-in-aid should be revised to encourage the changes recommended in this statement.*

Presently, some aid programs favor small units over large. Prevailing patterns discourage coordination between governments and between departments of the same government performing different but related functions. Heavy financial aids to archaic structures tend to divert attention from the need to adapt to new conditions. They perpetuate obsolescence.

We are well aware of the sweeping scope of these proposals. Taken in combination they amount to a revolutionary readjustment of local forms designed to preserve the basic values in our federal system of government. Prevailing conditions and trends demand measures of such strength. But adoption of these recommendations—in whole or in major part—will, of course, face stern resistance. Concerted, persistent, and determined efforts must be made by dedicated community leadership before modern and efficient local government based upon the needs of today and the decades immediately ahead can be attained.

MEMORANDA OF COMMENT, RESERVATION, OR DISSENT

Page 12—By ALLAN SPROUL, with which EMILIO G. COLLADO has asked to be associated:

We are confronted not only with popular discontent with the quantity and quality of services rendered by the nation's separate local governments, but also with distrust of the competence of state and federal governments to render satisfactory local service. This admirable statement makes clear the need for modernizing our local governments if their weaknesses are not to invite further intrusion by federal and state authorities. The statement is less clear in its treatment of the means by which modernized local government is to acquire revenues equal to its needs. Federal and state governments have largely pre-empted the income tax, the source of government revenue which increases most nearly in step with economic growth. What is lacking and should be devised is a better method than we now have of returning some of this revenue to local governments which have been re-designed to meet the needs of the present and the future.

Page 13—By ALEXANDER L. STOTT:

I do not believe this Statement is ready for publication. While it suggests measures that seem persuasive, it does not offer sufficient guidance in solving the complex problems it presents. It is couched in generalizations, is overly long and does not provide practical means for implementing and applying the recommendations, with due regard for the needs and desires of the people concerned.

Page 14—By GEORGE RUSSELL:

While I am fully aware that there are many instances of lack of efficiency and overlapping jurisdiction of local governments, I am concerned about the sweeping character of the recommendations contained in the paper. Many units of local government are doing an outstanding job of meeting the needs of their communities. Consolidation of these units into a larger unit would not improve the quality of local government and could reduce it.

---

[1]The term "community" is used rather broadly in this statement, to apply to socio-economic groupings with some sense of common identity, channels of internal communication, and a degree of political cohesion. Examples include a small city with its surrounding trading area, a metropolitan area of medium size consisting of a central city and tributary urbanized territory, and a suburban segment with distinctive interests separating it from the remainder of a giant metropolitan complex. The boundaries of existing local governments seldom coincide with such "communities."

C. INTERGOVERNMENTAL RELATIONS: THE ROLE OF THE STATES AND THE NATION

40. The States' Role in Meeting the Urban Crisis: Positive or Negative

DAVID B. WALKER AND ALBERT J. RICHTER

Urban areas, we are reminded time and again, are where the action is. They are also where the problems are—enough problems to challenge all of our resources, and then some. State governments are an important part of these resources, but there is a general feeling that they have not been a very effective part.

What *should* the states do to play an effective part in attacking the pressing problems of our urban areas? How well will they fill that role in the future? These are critical questions for the American federal system as we begin the last third of the twentieth century.

WANTED: AN ACTIVE, POSITIVE ROLE

In its studies and deliberations since being established by Congress in 1959, the Advisory Commission on Intergovernmental Relations (ACIR) has expressed a firm belief that the states should play an active, positive role in meeting the problems of local communities. Two general reasons underlie this conviction: (1) the desirability of strong state government generally as an essential feature of effective federalism, as a vital instrument for helping to carry out at the state and local levels the increasing number of federal grant-in-aid programs, and as a way of continuing to insure diversity, innovation,

SOURCE: *Metropolitan Viewpoints,* Vol. 2 (May, 1967), published by the Graduate School of Public Affairs, State University of New York at Albany.

broad citizen involvement, and a broad-based political system; and (2) the need for harnessing maximum resources in attacking the tough problems of our urban areas—education, housing, employment, recreation, and culture.

The states have a number of unique qualifications for playing a leading role in urban affairs. By law they are the parents of local government, the source of localities' authority to tackle their problems —whether it is the authority to organize and reorganize, perform functions, or raise money.

The states have legal power to step in and direct local governments to act in certain ways if they feel such action is necessary.

In most cases, they have ample geographic spread to provide directly, or to set up machinery to render services and activities that cannot be administered or only inadequately administered by individual localities within the governmental mosaic of the average metropolitan area.

They have greater taxable resources upon which to draw, the capacity to equalize resources and services among their local units, and they do not have the same handicaps of tax competition that confront individual local governments.

Finally, states have the administrative structure and personnel to offer technical assistance to their local governments, especially the smaller ones, in many functional fields—welfare, engineering, education, and planning are examples.

Paths to Leadership

With this built-in capacity, states can and should move in a number of positive ways to provide urban assistance and leadership.

First, the states can unshackle their local governments to permit a maximum of local autonomy in meeting urban problems.

This means lifting tax and debt limits, authorizing optional forms of city and county government or granting local governments the power to determine their own internal organization, and permitting them to perform a wide variety of functions.

Second, the states can authorize the citizens and local governments of metropolitan areas to undertake certain collaborative actions to meet areawide problems not confined to municipal boundaries.

Annexation can be liberalized; counties can be reorganized and empowered to provide urban services, particularly where a single county embraces an entire metropolitan area. Where counties are not empowered to plan, zone, and regulate subdivisions in unincorporated areas, cities can be allowed to exercise such powers beyond their boundaries in order to control growth at their edges. Localities also can be empowered to form metropolitan planning commissions, and given authority to establish councils of governments for the purpose of developing areawide consensus and laying the basis for areawide action. Urban areas can be authorized to create metropolitan study commissions for reviewing local governmental structure and submitting modernization proposals to popular vote. All these measures can facilitate action toward more effective government in urban areas.

Third, recognizing that over-emphasis on local autonomy may lead to a stalemate among numerous and competing local units on areawide issues, the states must reserve to themselves the power to act on such issues.

They must not hesitate to use this power when needed. A state, for example, may need to establish a metropolitan planning commission or a multi-purpose authority to provide certain areawide services if localities have had the authority and time to act cooperatively, but have failed to do so. It may be that the function is such that localities cannot be expected to act cooperatively since redistribution of resources is involved and some localities refuse to act against their apparent self-interest. In the case of planning, construction, and administration of a metropolitan transportation system, sewage collection and treatment system, or air pollution control system, state action frequently is the only positive alternative. Similarly, in interstate metropolitan areas, state action in conjunction with the neighboring state government may be the only feasible alternative.

Fourth, states can and must provide expanded technical assistance to their local governments, especially their smaller ones.

The growing number of federal grant-in-aid programs has made such a program of technical assistance all the more critical. These aids for state and local governments now incline upwards of 175 programs and 400-odd separate authorizations. They are administered by more than 125 separate federal bureaus and divisions, vary as to their channeling through states, and frequently overlap in their scope. Further, requirements for application and administration of these grants vary widely.

In short, the complexity, variety, duplication, and fragmentation of the existing grant structure necessitate a vigorous state role. States can provide a valuable service to their local governments by offering accurate and up-to-date information on what grants are available for what purposes. They can clarify application requirements. They can assist their localities to organize and gear up for making applications and administering programs. They can help localities to file applications. In many fields, such as education and welfare, a state line agency has long-standing relationships with federal agencies administering new grant programs. These and other state agencies can be invaluable in bringing the new federal programs to the local communities, and in helping the latter to take advantage of them.

In addition, one of the critical needs in our federal system is the shortage of trained personnel. So serious is the need now that the Congress in 1967 is likely to consider legislation requiring extension of existing merit system requirements; making grants to assist state and local personnel administration; and providing financial aid for training state and local personnel. State governments can be of considerable assistance in helping recruit, select, and train local personnel as they already have done in the field of assessing.

Finally, and most important, states can increase the amount of financial assistance they provide for their localities.

Consistent with their responsibilities for achieving an equitable and balanced overall system of taxation and for husbanding their economic resources, the states should authorize their localities to levy new taxes, particularly as "piggy-backs" to state-wide sales or income taxes. They also should expand the amounts of grants-in-aid to their localities by increasing state aid and assisting localities in paying their share of federal programs. Only by "buying into" federal-local grant programs, picking up at least one-half the non-federal share, and establishing appropriate administrative machinery can the states fairly claim a right to participate in the direction and administration of federal grants to localities.

In administering their own programs of financial assistance, states must re-examine their aid formulas. They must be certain that adequate assistance is going to those municipalities that need it most. Specifically, the states should make sure that their aid formulas help offset the growing imbalance in resources between central cities and suburbs that plague metropolitan areas. They must take positive steps here to alleviate the mounting social and economic disparities, increased tensions, and specific urban problems such as poverty, housing, and race relations. As Professor Alan K. Campbell has pointed out, while state aid allocation formulas tend to favor rural over urban areas, within urban areas they tend to favor suburban as against central city areas. He warns: "(The) . . . figures demonstrate that, despite the increased fiscal efforts being made by state governments, they have not yet adjusted their aid systems to reflect the new metropolitan reality."

General Reputation—Negative

Clearly, the states have a broad and basic role to play in the urban affairs of the Nation. But ask most people if they are playing it, or if they are likely to. In most cases, you will get a skeptical, if not negative, response. Why? The reason stems from the generally critical view that many have of the states as effective members of our federal system. This, in turn, can be traced to one or more of the following: (1) the feeling that government in the United States is becoming more and more centralized in Washington; (2) the low visibility of state politics, caused by the shift of public attention to Washington during the depression and war, the country's preoccupation with foreign affairs, and complex state legislative procedures and administrative fragmentation; (3) the obstructionist role of some states in the Negro's struggle for equal rights in the past decade; and (4) the built-in standpat bias of many states.

This skepticism also stems in part from the fact that we have fifty state governments. For some, it is easy to judge all fifty on the basis of the behavior of two or three. The generally negative attitude of the reporting press toward state government tends to magnify the cases of failure and corruption and to underplay or ignore instances of outstanding and responsible performance.

A Look at Some Recent Indicators

But looking at state government as it is, rather than having hazy feeling about it, what can be said about whether the states actually will "deliver the goods" in the attack on urban problems? The record-to-date suggests a mixed response, first, because there are fifty different states and, second, because there are both hopeful and discouraging signs.

The ACIR's success in implementing its state legislative program provides one index of state effort in this field. The Commission keeps tab on the degree to which states adopt legislation similar in language or intent to "model" statutes which it has drafted to implement its recommendations. This complex task involves tracing developments in fifty states and defining and identifying legislation which meets the criteria of similarity to Commission proposals. Using a conservative approach, the Commission found that in the 1965-66 biennium, at least forty-three states adopted one to four pieces of legislation similar to its draft bills or consistent with Commission recommendations. These actions covered twenty-two of the sixty-three separate ACIR draft proposals and ranged from property tax reform and revision to financial and technical assistance to local governments. In addition, thirty-eight states enacted one or more statutes that are consistent with ACIR recommendations, but are either not yet framed in model bills or are framed along lines differing from the specific approach of ACIR bills.

These figures clearly highlight one basic finding: greater state legislative progress during the past two years compared to that of the preceding 1963-1964 biennium. This conclusion, however, tells us nothing about the distance still to be covered. Neither does it enable us to weigh the qualitative significance of different kinds of legislation in terms of developing a positive state role in urban affairs. Adoption of one program for state financial assistance to localities, for example, might well be much more crucial than adoption by five states of laws authorizing localities to contract with one another. To get this kind of appraisal, it is necessary to probe the substance of the legislation enacted.

Such a survey reveals some encouraging and some not so encouraging trends in state legislative activity on the urban frontier. Significant ones merit attention.

On the positive side, a growing number of states have established offices of local affairs or community development. These agencies generally advise the Governor and Legislature on matters of state-local relations, help coordinate state administrative agencies in their dealings with localities, and provide technical assistance to local governments, usually the smaller jurisdictions. At last count, eleven states had such agencies: Alaska, California, Colorado, Illinois, Missouri, New Jersey, New York, Pennsylvania, Rhode Island, Tennessee, and Washington. In some states, such as Maine, consideration is now being given to making a state office of local affairs responsible for passing on proposed annexations and municipal incorporations. The Department of Community Affairs in Pennsylvania and the Department of Community Affairs in New Jersey, created in 1965 and 1966 respectively, represent an expansion of the original concept by vesting certain operating functions in the department, mainly in the area of housing, urban development, planning, and financial supervision.

Additional states may move to establish offices of local affairs as a consequence of a provision of the Demonstration Cities and Metropolitan Development Act of 1966. Title IX of the Act authorizes grants to states to help them supply communities with a population under 100,000 with technical assistance and information on urban needs and assistance programs and activities.

Favorable signs also are found in various recently organized efforts to improve the image and performance of state legislatures and state government generally. A Citizens Conference on State Legislature, supported by the Ford Foundation and the Carnegie Corporation and headed by former Governor John Anderson of Kansas, is dedicated to stimulating "grass roots" activity to modernize the legislative articles of state constitutions. The Ford Foundation also is supporting a National Municipal League study of the constitutional and other barriers to legislative effectiveness. Finally, a Study of the States, under the direction of former Governor Terry Sanford of North Carolina, is conducting a two-year study of the administration of state services.

Stimulated indirectly by these efforts and directly by legislative reapportionment, states recently have shown renewed interest in constitutional overhauling after decades of inactivity. Constitutional revisions have been completed or are under way in California, Connecticut, Idaho, Kentucky, Maryland, New Mexico, New York, Rhode Island, and Wisconsin. The mixed results of the November 8, 1966 referenda on major constitutional revisions proposals, however, suggest the need for caution in predicting the final outcome of these efforts to modernize state governments.

In a similar vein, legislative reapportionment has been hailed as another positive force making for more enlightened state concern for cities since it will redress the long history of rural domination of state legislatures. Yet here again, the outcome is unclear, particularly as it affects metropolitan areas as a whole. Suburban areas, after all, are gaining representation while central cities are gaining relatively little, if at all, and suburbs frequently see things differently than central cities, especially when it comes to handling metropolitan problems. In the final analysis, reapportionment may heighten, rather than reduce, the urban tensions created by the growing economic and social cleavages in our urban areas.

Reapportionment and state constitutional reform thus present an uncertain picture. But clearly on the negative side is the lack of any great progress among the states in moving aggressively to regulate and provide funds in the major urban affairs areas that are now handled by the direct federal-local programs. Total state tax collections increased twelve and one-half per cent for the fiscal year ending in 1966 and were double the 1959 figure. Yet only a few states—large, populous ones—share in the non-federal portion of selected urban development programs.

Likewise, states are dragging their feet in taking strong fiscal and other action to overcome the growing economic and fiscal disparities between central cities and suburbs in metropolitan areas. Massive amounts of money must move from relatively affluent suburbs to help mount a real attack on the problems of central city ghettos and rural pockets of poverty. This transferring function can be performed by the federal government or the state. If it is left to the federal government, the states will have lost a really viable role in the federal system. In the final analysis, whichever level exercises financial control over the problem of our deteriorating cities will have de facto control over much of domestic government.

CONCLUSION

The states have ample potential to play a triple-threat role in urban affairs: as "unshacklers" of local governments; as leaders in encouraging and pointing the way to new forms of urban government and intergovernmental cooperation; and as coordinators and direct providers of funds with emphasis on mitigating economic and social disparities among local units in metropolitan areas. If the states are to retain their claim as positive partners in the federal system, they must fulfill this triple-threat potential.

Their record thus far is mixed, as we have seen. Some signs indicate positive commitment; others underline continuing passivity. But the urban challenge has not disappeared; the intergovernmental administrative crisis has not been overcome; and the pace of change in our federal system has not slowed down. . . .

41. The State: Reluctant Partner

ROSCOE C. MARTIN

. . .The subject may be discussed briefly at two levels. At the first, the states are confused because of the situation they are in. They find themselves suspended somewhere between total agrarianism and total urbanism. When agrarianism alone prevailed, the states could attend to the needs of their people through statewide service programs described in and supported by general legislation. Urbanism is not yet total, hence general legislation is not so neatly applicable as it was half a century ago. To the contrary, the states must identify special urban problems worthy of state action and programs deserving of support.

SOURCE: *The Cities and the Federal System* (New York: Atherton Press, 1965), pp. 80-82. Reprinted by permission of the publishers, Atherton Press.

This is a complex and delicate process, one that had only a rude precedent in the earlier and simpler days of an agrarian society. More and more, assistance to the cities, and more particularly the great cities, takes on the character of helping to meet specialized needs of individual places as identified by special groups. Such assistance is couched in the lofty terms of general legislation, but in truth it requires choices and action of a quite particular character. This is to say, in other words, that the vast new problems of urban America are unique in the experience of the states, which react to them in an impatient and sometimes a truculent manner. Nothing would please the states more than for the cities and their problems to dematerialize into thin air.

At another level the federal government has recognized the complex problems of urban America and has taken a hand in their solution. This confronts the states with the necessity of making decisions on matters they might otherwise ignore, and so adds further to their discomfort. Whose idea was public housing? Or urban renewal? Or pollution abatement? Surely not the states'. Yet the fact that problems exist and that programs have been devised to alleviate them poses a dilemma for the states: Shall they continue to pretend that the problems do not exist, or shall they join in a common attack on the ills of modern society? Answers by the states to this question have been equivocal, as has action spurred by its insistence. The dilemma is charged with consequence for the federal system, for the choices made will affect the balance among federal, state, and city governments in the practice of cooperative federalism.

Many observers believe that the states will prove equal to the challenges of the metropolitan age. The wish doubtless is father to the thought, and the thought perhaps to the hope; but one who allows hope to sire expectation ignores a considerable body of evidence. State readiness and capacity aside, many identify the states as necessary and proper actors in the war on urban ills because of their fundamental role as partners in the federal system. This is not a foregone conclusion, for there is an option to sole reliance on the states, especially on states approaching the issues of urbanism without conviction, enthusiasm, or adequate organization. The option emphasizes increased direct cooperation between the federal government and the cities. It is not an option that commends itself to state devotees, but it nonetheless offers the promise of positive action on metro-urban problems and reasonable support for programs aimed at their alleviation.

42. The Federal Role in Urban Affairs

SENATOR ABRAHAM RIBICOFF

. . .The crisis of our cities is the crisis of the modern United States. Seventy percent of all Americans now live in or close to cities. The number grows each year. So the fate of the city and the future of our country are one and the same thing.

As Richard Hofstadter put it: "America was born in the country and grew up in the city." As Americans have flocked to the cities, the tapestry of our national life has changed dramatically. Hope has been the magnet, a very American hope of bettering yourself, and improving the lot of your children. Into the cities have flocked the poor, the underskilled, the undereducated, the deprived. They have come for reasons of race or lack of opportunity—or both. Into the cities, too, have come those who simply wish to savor the full urban life. Too often too many do not find what they seek.

For as the central city grows, so do its problems. Out moves the middle class into the suburbs. Out, too, moves industry—source of jobs. Into the older houses move more people than they were built to hold; family and community patterns of social organization are lost. Up go costs—costs of schooling, crime control, and public welfare. Tax revenues decline; educated and concerned leaders move elsewhere; sometimes slums are razed but in their place rise shining buildings—with modern lobbies and swimming pools—which the poor cannot afford.

Our cities are in trouble. But we discovered long ago that our Nation is indivisible; that the interests of one are the interests of all. Omaha, Nebr., may be 1,200 miles from Harlem, but Harlem's riots affect the resident of Omaha as surely as the family in Scarsdale.

If the crisis is a national concern—and it is—then it is a concern to the Congress of the United States, and to this committee, whose duty it is to assure that the Federal Government is best organized to meet modern needs.

How much has our Federal Government been spending in our cities? $20 billion? $25 billion? . . . No one has the answer.

We hope during the next few weeks someone will know. We do know that through some 15 Federal agencies administering some 70 programs we have invested $96 billion over the past decade in city and State aid, and this does not include social security payments or FHA and VA mortgage insurance.

SOURCE: Hearings of the Subcommittee on Executive Reorganization (August 15, 1966), pp. 1-4.

Some programs have undoubtedly prevented starvation and brought new hope and opportunity to countless among the poor. And President Johnson has proposed other new programs to upgrade the quality of life in our cities. The President's demonstration cities program, especially, is a significant new departure deserving our unqualified support. . . .

But this program itself, and the larger job ahead, shows the awesome dilemmas of public choice that confront a nation about to embark on a meaningful urban policy. We must learn from past experience. We must ask ourselves some probing questions.

For example, have urban aid programs been too diffused and uncoordinated to guide the process of urban development?

Are the techniques of our city aid programs obsolete and limited? Do they reflect the needs and conditions of national life a generation ago, and not the needs of modern America?

Is the effectiveness of the programs that do exist hurt by division of authority among many agencies, and many levels of government?

Most serious of all, do the goals of major Federal programs conflict—some working to revitalize the central city, some encouraging new urban clusters, some causing regional sprawl?

In short, do we have a clear, constructive national strategy geared toward the improvement of our cities? If not, what steps must we take to obtain it?

History shows us that civilization has been based on cities. Some have vanished—some have flourished almost from antiquity. Now we cannot expect to find the answers to the problems of our cities in the United States in a month—or even a year. I expect that these hearings will continue a long time, as long as needed.

Since the problem of the cities is the problem of all Americans, we will hear from many besides responsible Federal officials. The Federal Government must assume the duties with which it is charged, but our system of government is not based on the concept that the Federal Government is the sole source of wisdom and skill.

We shall hear testimony from mayors—from men and women and young people working and living in the city slums—from sociologists and psychologists and other experts who have studied the problems of our cities, and gained insight and understanding.

We shall hear testimony from experts in many fields—for no one phrase—and no one area of concern can characterize the problems of our cities.

We shall explore the problems of police protection, health, justice, welfare, education, employment, economic development, finance, community organization, urban planning, housing, renewal and rehabilitation, transportation, environmental pollution, legal services, and more.

We shall explore and try to find the answers to the problems of the woman in Watts who has no hospital to go to; the mother holding her sick baby in the crowded clinic waiting room; the listless child, locked in a Harlem slum, in a crowded schoolroom with shattered windows; the high school dropout. Such problems illustrate the magnitude of the crisis facing our Nation. Building a constructive and realistic national urban policy will not be easy.

The questions are difficult—the answers will be complicated.

But there is nothing complicated about what we want. All of us want a society in which a woman is not afraid to stay home alone at night. All of us want a society where children are schooled to the uppermost limits of their ability, live in decent housing, and get three square meals a day. We want jobs and opportunity for all our citizens. No child in the United States should fear rat bites in his bed. All Americans should feel that justice and equal opportunity can be realized without resort to violence and looting.

We undertake these hearings thoughtfully and without preconceived solutions to all the problems. We will strive to get the pertinent facts, the sound ideas, and to look at people and their problems with understanding.

Our mission will be to come up with the understanding necessary to insure that our efforts are organized in the most efficient, effective, and coordinated manner. If what exists is good, we will recommend keeping it. But where we have failed, we must weed out our errors, and try new ways.

We must find how the huge complex of modern government can better develop help to our cities, and assure that our money and energies are wisely used. This effort must be made. Answers to the problems of the cities must be found.

The bell is tolling for all of us. The Nation is summoning this Congress and succeeding ones to action.

43. Uncle Sam Is Really Needed

MICHAEL REAGAN

Which areas of general welfare policy—housing and urban renewal, education, highways, hospitals and health, labor standards and unemployment compensation—are best left to the state and local governments? Which require national legislation, funds and standards, either in the form of Federal grants-in-aid or full national programs?

Those questions arise naturally and inevitably out of the constitutional principle of federalism, and are among the hardiest of American political perennials. They are also among the liveliest and most controversial. . . .

What are the financial and political capabilities of state and local governments for dealing with general welfare problems? What are the problems and obstacles? Is there a national interest in public welfare policies? What happens when attempts are made to return functions to the states? To answer these and related questions we need to examine the resources of state and local governments, the record of state-local action, and the meaning of the general welfare in a national community.

First, let us note that the states, cities and towns, the school and sewage districts, the highway authorities and the multitude of other special-function bodies that make up the maze of American subnational government have not, contrary to the impression in some quarters, atrophied in the face of the national Government's participation in general welfare problems. In fact, their activity has increased fantastically. As measured by expenditures, state-local government shows an increase from $13 billion in 1942 to $77 billion in 1961. Because it has been as difficult to increase revenues as it has been to hold down spending (although the Tax Foundation estimates a 326 per cent increase in state-local taxes since 1946), the result of heavy activity has been an extraordinary increase in state-local debt.

While the national debt rose 13 per cent in the years 1946-63—and did so to the accompaniment of much political wailing—the state-local rise was a whopping, though almost unnoticed, 448 per cent. If the national Government's budget should curl our hair, it should fairly frizzle as we contemplate state-local finances. And city fathers faced with demands for increased services may just pull their hair out

---

SOURCE: *New York Times Magazine* (September 13, 1964), pp. 31, 130, 132-133.

entirely as they run up against the debt-limits imposed upon municipalities by the governments of 34 states.

While the taxable resources of the nation are, distributively, the resources of the 50 states, it is much harder for the latter to tap those resources. Property and sales taxes are heavily used by state-local governments, compared to the Federal Government's greater reliance upon individual and corporate income taxes. If people's incomes rise, so does the national Government's tax share—and more than proportionately because of progressive rates. But if the value of a property increases, the city collector obtains no automatic increase; that awaits the slow process of revaluation.

Even greater are the political problems. Property and sales taxes are flat-rate taxes, and thus regressive. The man with a $4,000 income buying a $200 appliance may pay a 3 per cent sales tax ($6). The man with a $40,000 income pays the same amount of tax, but notices it less. Similarly with the property tax. It has therefore long been a basic tenet of the liberal creed that such taxes should be utilized as little as possible. The conservative, on the other hand, objects with equal vehemence to the notion of an income tax; it is progressive in rate structure and will hit him harder. The result is often a stalemate on tax increases while expenditures and debt go on rising.

Add to these difficulties the historic dominance of state legislatures by rural representatives not much impressed by the needs occasioned by urbanization and industrialization. This makes it understandable why the cities have in recent years run to the national Government for financial aid in the form of grants that bypass the state level. Urban renewal and airport construction are notable examples. In the words of Mayor Richard Lee of New Haven, "We have reached a point where the urban slum problem alone is greater than the farm problem. And with all these . . . things we have to do—providing police and fire protection, paying school teachers an adequate salary and offering a host of other services—the cities cannot solve these problems alone."

Finally, interstate competition for industry inhibits higher taxes to finance better general welfare programs. The fear is that if a state imposes an income tax, or raises its business receipts tax beyond that of a neighboring state, then national firms looking for new plant locations will not come in. The reasoning may be faulty (many other factors enter into such decisions), but the fear is there and it counts.

In short, although one can make a case in the abstract for state-local potential resources, the obstacles—as much political as economic, but just as real—are such as to make much of the potential unavailable.

Next, let us look at some parts of the state-local record. Education is probably the function most often assigned exclusively to local government by politicians and theorists of the localist persuasion. Although back-door aid to education (largely in the guise of defense or science) has become substantial, there is still no general national aid for classroom construction or teachers' salaries. What have the cities and states done on their own? (We can consider them together, for *state* aid is universally accepted even where Federal aid is anathema.)

In 1949-50, the average teacher salary was $4,200 in California, $3,700 in New York, $2,348 in Vermont and $1,416 in Mississippi. Ten years later (1959-60) the figures were: California, $6,600; New York, $6,537; Vermont, $4,466; and Mississippi, $3,314. A distinct improvement, yes; enough to attract a fair share of the best talent into public school teaching, no. In coping with the classroom space squeeze, state-local action has produced more than 400,000 classrooms, since 1955. Yet a need for 127,000 additional classrooms existed as of the fall of 1961, according to Office of Education figures. The state-local effort rates "A for effort," but it has not entirely solved the problem, and what has been accomplished in construction may have been partly at the expense of teachers' salaries.

One of the compromises between state and federal action is the unemployment compensation program. Through Federal inducement (forgiveness of a projected contribution to a federal system if the state enacted its own), every state has its own program. But in the recessions of 1958 and 1960-61 it was necessary for the federal government to supplement the benefits provided by the state systems with an additional period of benefit paid for by Congress. The state systems were proved inadequate to the challenge of long-term unemployment. Even apart from the special problem of recession, the period of benefit under the state systems varies from 39 weeks in Oklahoma to 22 weeks in South Carolina and Tennessee. The maximum dollar benefits range from $1,700 in Wisconsin down to $640 in Virginia.

Medical care for the aged again illustrates the absence of state action until Federal prodding. While those on welfare grants can obtain some kind of medical care in every state, the aged who were able to stay off relief had no public medical care program until the Kerr-Mills legislation of 1960. By 1964, 33 states had availed themselves of the Federal contribution—although the amounts and coverage remain inadequate even in the participating states.

In the nineteen-fifties a program of Federal grants for community sewage plants was started. After it had been in operation two years, President Eisenhower wanted to discontinue it and return this function to the towns and cities. He ran into an insuperable obstacle, however: the grant-in-aid program had worked and the rate of new sewage plant construction had jumped upward. The prodding effect of Congressional action was so pronounced that the legislators could not be persuaded to end the program and chance a sudden slackening in efforts to solve the worsening pollution problem.

The record suggests, the closer one looks at it, that the real issues have not been what to turn back to the states and cities, but what national programs to initiate and whether the national Government should administer them directly or bribe the state-local governments into participation through matching grants. Until Congress acted, too often nothing at all was done.

Instances of individual state leadership have been known—Wisconsin and New York were pioneers in labor standards legislation, for example, and in health and safety regulation—but the seeds have usually fallen on barren ground until the national Government took up the cause. After all, it is much easier to pass required legislation through one Congress than through 50 state legislatures or thousands of city councils. The pattern now is for Washington to initiate a response to a problem, then lead the localities into continuing participation.

Suppose—and it is a wild supposition—that we left the general welfare to the states and cities, what major obstacles would remain, what needs might be unfulfilled even if they set out enthusiastically to do the job?

One major problem is the lack of capable personnel. The national civil service not only outbids most states and all cities for professional talent (when associated with a university program of graduate training in public administration, I found that most students initially oriented toward local government careers nevertheless took jobs with such national agencies as Housing and Home Finance), but is a model of appointment and promotion by merit when compared to the states and cities.

One advantage of Federal grants-in-aid has been that they carry with them administrative standards that compel the receiving agencies to curtail the spoils system. Of course, the Federal Government has difficulty in recruiting a sufficient number of trained professionals itself, but the difficulty is compounded in most local jurisdictions.

A major need that would go unmet is that of equalization of standards. Compare the levels of unemployment benefits among the states, as given above, or unevenness of medical care availability, or discrepancies in teachers' salaries, or per pupil expenditures, which vary from $698 in New York to $268 in Alabama and $297 in Mississippi (1959-1960 figures). Granting some cost differentials, it is still beyond belief that education in the South can be as good as in New York or California in these circumstances. And it is not proportionate lack of will that makes the Southern record so poor; it is lack of resources: Mississippi, for example, spends a higher share of its revenues on education than does New York.

Why does the unequal education of Mississippians and Alabamians matter to the rest of us? There are two reasons, both resting on the premise of national citizenship in a national community.

First, I would argue the ethical claim to equality of opportunity for all Americans, wherever they live; and a good education is the key to equal opportunity. Practically, also, we are national as regards mobility of population: the Mississippi boy of today is likely to be the California, Ohio or Michigan citizen of tomorrow. Federal aid that makes equalization possible therefore benefits the giving as well as the receiving states.

While equalization may be a controversial goal, everyone desires curricular excellence. It is in the development of the best possible textbooks, teaching materials and conceptual approaches to subjects as diverse as mathematics, foreign languages, English and social studies that national efforts are most patently necessary.

No local school board could pull together leading university scholars and outstanding public school teachers to make such efforts. Yet they have been made, with outstanding success, by the School Mathematics Study Group and the Physical Science Study Committee, both underwritten by the National Science Foundation in cooperation with major universities. Many of us have already experienced the "new math" thus developed, by grappling with our children's homework. Now the Office of Education is sponsoring a similar project to improve instruction in English from kindergarten through college.

It is a national interest that is expressed in these projects, and also in the science and foreign language work done under the post-Sputnik National Defense Education Act. As a recent report of a special Presidential panel on educational research states, the model texts and materials "can indicate new paths in education without interfering with traditional local responsibilities." Whether to use the new materials is a choice still held by local officials; making them available is a legitimate national task.

Increasingly, the public welfare depends upon scientific and technological advance. Nuclear power and desalination, perhaps combined in single plants, exemplify the costly areas of research involved. Neither states nor cities are going to take on these tasks, for both cost and national benefit compel national expenditure. So far as basic research and graduate education centered in universities are concerned—and without these all advance ceases—a 1960 report of the President's Science Advisory Committee put the matter bluntly:

"Either it [the national Government] will find the policies—and the resources—which permit our universities to flourish and their duties to be adequately discharged—or no one will." As this committee pointed out, "There is not one physics for California and another for Texas."

The states and cities have already gone heavily into debt trying to meet the financial demands of the public welfare, yet the conditions of our educational system, of urban transit, of water pollution and of medical care and unemployment insurance all demonstrate the inadequacy of these valiant efforts. Of even greater importance, what is done with the money is better planned and better managed when the national Government underwrites the use of the best professionals and sets standards which call forth a stronger local effort (as with the Urban Renewal Administration's requirement that each community seeking Federal aid submit a workable program of community development).

The merits of national involvement and the genius of the grant-in-aid as a device to create a Federal-state-local partnership are, in my opinion, beyond dispute. Why do the cries of states' rights and localism continue almost unabated? I believe there are three primary reasons.

One is ignorance of what national action has accomplished and has stimulated throughout the nation. Another is the desire of local leaders, public and private, to maintain their familiar hold on the power structure of their communities, which they fear will undergo change and be opened up to a wider segment of interests if "outsiders" have to be permitted participation.

Finally, the cry of localism is often a "front" for those who do not really want many of the general welfare programs at any level of government—sometimes on financial grounds, sometimes because of a denial of need. Since it is demonstrably harder to obtain approval for public welfare expenditures in many states and cities than in Congress, anti-welfare strategy calls for leaving it to the local jurisdictions in the hope that nothing at all will be done.

But history does not easily reverse itself. The experience of the Eisenhower Administration, which ideologically wanted to cut away at Federal involvement, yet created one of the largest Federal grant programs (the $40 billion Interstate Highway System—90 per cent national, 10 per cent state funds), suggests that—despite the vehemence of campaign rhetoric—the national Government will continue to promote the general welfare and to recognize the limits of localism.

44. Creative Federalism and Great Cities

ROBERT C. WEAVER

[In 1964], President Johnson made an historic speech at Ann Arbor, Michigan, when he introduced two fresh concepts: creative federalism and the Great Society.

The first was cast as a path to the second, rather than an end in itself. And the President defined creative federalism as embodying "new concepts of cooperation between the National Capital and the leaders of local communities." And, as we have seen subsequently, he meant private leadership as well as public leadership.

Both concepts are, at once, a reflection of and guideposts for this nation. Both recognize the key characteristics of the nation at this point in time:

- It is urban.
- It is affluent.
- It is relentlessly innovative.

. . . The new Department of Housing and Urban Development, . . . both responds to and affects the many forces at work in this increasingly pluralistic culture. . . . The Department of Housing and Urban Development, . . . is charged with the basic responsibility for carrying out these programs and a major share of the responsibility for responding effectively to what the President has called our most critical domestic problem—improving the quality of urban life.

The forces of growth which are shaping our cities must be mastered, and the new Federal Department is only one instrument in the greater effort. Every level of government is faced by the urban challenge, and every unit of government must effect an appropriate response or face physical and economic anarchy.

The sum of these responses is what is meant by creative federalism. In the [1966] Budget Message . . . the President put it this way:

> "Many of our critical new programs involve the Federal Government in joint ventures with State and local governments in thousands of

SOURCE: Address to the National Press Club (February 16, 1966).

> communities throughout the Nation. The success or failure of those programs depends on timely and effective communication and on readiness for action on the part of both Federal agencies in the field and State and local governmental units."

The sort of "joint ventures" which the President has in mind represent a significant break with more traditional forms of governmental enterprise. Through the early years of our constitutional system, we operated under a concept of dual federalism—the conviction that Nation and State were divided by impenetrable walls of separate jurisdiction. The power struggle between those advocates of strong states' rights and those who favored more Federal centralism resulted in a peculiar sort of standoff. Problems which did not fall readily within one jurisdiction were swept under the rug.

But the nation developed and older antagonisms became subjugated to the need for solving new problems of economic and social growth. And so a new sort of federalism evolved—a cooperative federalism. This pattern brought together programs and activities of shared responsibility through the device of Federal grants-in-aid. These in turn meant a measure of collaboration on a number of fronts. But precincts of power were still staked out and jealously guarded as under dual federalism.

But the conviction remained that expansion of power in one level of government worked to lessen power in another, and the spheres of cooperation were largely restricted to policy execution and administration—not mutual development of new activities. Thus, the New Deal was essentially a national inspiration—a limited response to an emergency, not a fundamental change in the processes of government.

Today, and only very recently, a third interpretation of federalism has emerged, more suited to our times, more sensitive to the rapidly changing pressures and powers in an increasingly pluralistic society.

Creative federalism, unlike earlier brands, does not conceive of power as a static commodity, to be transferred from private to public sectors or State to National levels at the expense of the earlier possessor of power. Public policy, rather, arises in response to new needs and conditions and changes as pressures change. And the energies of the creative response from all levels and sectors in turn galvanizes the Federal sector into positive action.

Today, concern over issues has given way to concern for broad problems. As contemporary problems such as poverty, social disorganization, civil rights and rampant urbanization become readily identified, creative Federalism responds with solutions instead of ideologies.

This approach involves the initiation and shaping of new responses to urban or other domestic problems through a complicated interplay of many forces, public and private. In terms of urban problems, the major responsibility for such responses rests with government, as the public welfare is the focus.

Yet private enterprise and private institutions are increasingly being called upon, in this new form called Creative Federalism, to play key roles not only in program execution, whether as home-builders or campus developers, but in policy formulation as well.

This development, still in its early evolution, parallels what is happening in the defense and space industries. These are today vast complexes of private and public enterprise, contiguous in their operations at many different points but ordered systematically within the context of specific problems to be solved.

But let me first indicate the broader framework. Creative Federalism stresses local initiative, local solutions to local problems. The Federal role as a partner in creative federalism will continue to be one of support for locally initiated and locally administered activities. But this is not a passive role. Where the obvious needs for action to meet an urban problem are not being fulfilled, the Federal government has a responsibility at least to generate a thorough awareness of the problem.

The goals we have set for urban America are the most ambitious in our history. The times call for inventiveness and ingenuity to match the welter of change boiling in and around our great metropolitan areas. Indeed, none of our institutions is likely to be the same by the time this century draws to a close—by the time we have built another urban America.

Thomas Jefferson suspected and even feared the city. He was a gentleman farmer at heart, although certainly the most urbane farmer in this or perhaps any nation's history. But Jefferson understood change, and the necessity for adapting to it. And he once described change in a democratic society in terms which come strikingly close to defining what we now call creative federalism:

> "Laws and institutions must go hand in hand with the progress of the human mind. As that becomes more developed, more enlightened, as new discoveries are made, new truths disclosed, and manners and opinions change with the change of circumstances, institutions must advance, also, and keep pace with the times."

And so creative federalism and the approaches which evolve from its conceptual framework will, indeed, change our institutions. It must, if these institutions are to survive.

Our approach today stresses innovation and the breaking of customary ineffective patterns. We intend to do this through experiment and demonstration.

[In 1965], a striking innovation in providing housing for low and moderate income families was proposed. The President called the program, for rent supplementation, "the most crucial new instrument in our effort to improve the American city." It would bring the strength of the private building market to bear directly upon our greatest unsolved urban problem—the construction of decent housing for low-income families. This program involves mortgage insurance offered by FHA at market rates of interest of non-profit, limited dividend and cooperative sponsors. The housing is privately owned, managed and privately financed. . . .

Now we have pushed into the most dramatic form of experimentation this urban nation has ever seen—striving to demonstrate that whole chunks of cities, large and small, can be reborn in the image of this nation's promised urban greatness.

. . . I [have] outlined how this new Demonstration Cities program will work. . . . Its failure or success rides principally upon the . . . inventiveness and ability [of municipal leaders] for effecting the changes so badly needed to make their cities viable systems for human development. . . . While understanding that not all . . . cities can be in at the beginning of this experimental program, these officials realize that the solutions and approaches which will be developed, throughout the nation, will help them in their own problem solving. For while we have come to see that the city holds a myriad of facets to every major problem, there are solutions which can be developed and tailored to fit every individual situation. That is what we are looking for in this program.

This is, in a very real sense, where it all comes together. The President's message shows the way. It indicates that this new program has three major thrusts:

- To concentrate all available resources in planning tools, in housing construction, in job training, in health facilities, in recreation, in welfare programs, in education—to improve the conditions of life in urban areas.
- To coordinate all our available talent and skills.
- To mobilize local leadership and private initiative, so that local citizens will determine the shape of their new city freed from the constraints that have handicapped their past efforts and inflated their costs.

Solutions will be tailored by local officials, with a minimum of Federal direction but a maximum of Federal assistance and technical aid. Those cities developing the most imaginative solutions and energetic leadership will be the first aboard. This is, perhaps more than anything else, a time for the testing of the ingenuity and resiliency of the American urban intellect.

These demonstrations, and indeed all our programs, will be operated from a new context which in itself reflects the creative Federalism of which I have been speaking.

As most of you know, we have been in the midst of drastic reorganization, aimed at making all of our programs—including Demonstration Cities—most effective. At the same time, we are developing new management techniques, under the so-called Planning-Programming Budgeting-System, for getting the maximum impact from Federal expenditures, as well as the fullest measure of administrative efficiency.

The new organizational structure we are developing is facilitated by the legislation which created the new Department. That legislation places in the Secretary the authority to administer and effectively supervise all the programs now in, and to be assigned to, the Department. With such new powers, we are rearranging functions. In the organizational structure that will soon be announced responsibilities for supervision and direction of the major activities of the Department will be delegated to Assistant Secretaries. The grouping of activities, however, will be oriented to broad problem solving rather than on the basis of bureaucratic identification. For we are resolved that traditional agencies must be integrated to meet total objectives.

Consistent with principles of sound public administration and responsive to the needs of urban America, we shall place greater decision making authority closer to the problems and the people. For those programs which are established, the decision making authority will be in the regional offices. And in the new Demonstration Cities program, much of the decision authority will be at the local level centered in Federal coordinators.

These novel officials will be located at the local level. They will not, as has been affirmed, look over the shoulders of the mayors. Rather they will serve the local communities by coordinating HUD programs, assisting in the coordination of other Federal programs, aiding local officials in securing cooperation on the part of state agencies, and generally expediting Federal activities in the locality. Their usefulness has been recognized by many mayors in the nation. Speaking for a group of them, Mayor McKeldin of Baltimore recently said that they had been disabused of the fear that the Federal coordinator would be a czar dictating local policies.

Thus, in this new Department we are beginning to give form and substance to the new Federalism. Our efforts will be supported by a continuing program of research, demonstration, and experimentation. Not the least of our concerns will be to assert leadership for, and encourage, the development of techniques to solve the administrative problems which emanate from the long-existing proliferation and overlapping of local governments. We shall, with continuing careful evaluation of results, attempt to utilize and apply the newer tools of systems analysis to urban problems. . . .

This rebirth, this rebuilding of our great cities will start against the backdrop of the strongest economy in U. S. history. This year, the Gross National Product is expected to total over $722 billion, representing a rise of 5 percent in real growth, after accounting for possible price changes. Perhaps most important, this great and growing economic strength provides us with the opportunity to utilize as fully as possible our manpower and to direct a maximum effort at relieving those dislocations in our labor market which have particularly afflicted cities with pools of unemployed.

The economy is strong and the temper of the nation is, . . . for change and continued striving toward a better life. This might seem surprising because it has often been assumed that in times of prosperity, democratic peoples are content to sit and live off the fat of the land. This is hardly true today. Not only is there widespread support for a major campaign against poverty, both in cities and rural areas, but the nation is even . . . [excited] about beauty. And if you don't believe that, I refer you not only to the tremendous enthusiasm generated by last year's White House Conference on Natural Beauty, but also to what happened recently in the Kentucky Legislature, which just passed a pioneering law restricting strip mining in the state. This action opens the way for seven other nearby and adjacent states to enter into a compact which would halt the ravages of this wasteful practice, which has so brutalized the landscape.

So we move into the second half of this decade with a most fortunate combination of circumstances: a nationwide concern with the environment and the economic wherewithal to translate this concern to action programs.

[In 1965], the Congress provided great impetus to this situation, with both the Housing and Urban Development Act and the creation of the Department of Housing and Urban Development. The President also delivered a special message on developing goals for Natural Beauty. The latter pricked the conscience of almost every American community and has stimulated a growing preoccupation with the shape and condition of our total environment.

. . . There are a couple of important aspects of our whole approach which I want to emphasize. First, I cannot stress strongly enough that every effort will be made to see that what are perhaps the two most enduring characteristics of the city—diversity and opportunity—are greatly enhanced through all our programs.

Diversity is what makes the city exciting and vital. We recognize that it must be fortified and made to thrive. There must be room for all peoples, of many incomes and with many different notions about what constitutes the Good Community. Hopefully, these will continue to be aired, in democratic fashion, and out of the continuing consensus will come the sort of urban environment which can continue to make the democratic city the chief symbol of civilized men.

Diversity is a hollow virtue without opportunity, and the President has emphasized that the Demonstration Cities program will aim squarely at creating new opportunities not only for employment and training, but also in the choice of housing available and the use of community facilities. While we demonstrate new ways to achieve maximum opportunity, I trust we no longer need demonstrate that this is the essential element of the democratic city. That is what the rest is all about.

Another key aspect of this new program is an emphasis upon quality which will pervade every element of every project. This means not only the highest regard for architecture and design, but also for the critical interplay of building and spaces, for the strategic positioning of open green spaces and plantings, for the opening up of those areas long congested by rubble-filled alleys and junkyards, and for the development of community vistas which can make a lasting contribution to a spirit of pride and spiritual enrichment. . . .

. . . Our urban programs will be carried forward with a greater sense of purpose as our system evolves more effective solutions to problems plaguing our cities and metropolitan areas. In that process, our constant concern will be to lift the horizons of hope and expectation of urban America. For we are convinced that there can and must be a better America. We are dedicated to make a significant contribution to that objective. And we know that it can be achieved only through a partnership between government at all its levels and society. . . .